HAWAII GUIDE

BE A TRAVELER – NOT A TOURIST!

PRAISE FOR RACHEL CHRISTMAS DERRICK'S

HAWAII GUIDE

Recommended by *Conde Nast Traveler*, the first edition of *Hawaii Guide* was named one of the three best American and Canadian guide-books by the Lowell Thomas Travel Journalism Awards. The judges noted: "The author's conversational writing style and obvious knowledge of Hawaii lead the reader effortlessly and enjoyably from one island to the next.... [Her] willingness to express her personal reaction to restaurants, hotels, and sightseeing attractions enhances the book's readability and lifts it out of the sterility found in many others of this genre."

BE A TRAVELER – NOT A TOURIST!

Whether you're going abroad or planning a trip in the United States, take Open Road along on your journey. Our books have been praised by Travel & Leisure, The Los Angeles Times, Newsday, Booklist, US News & World Report, Endless Vacation, American Bookseller, Coast to Coast, and many other magazines and newspapers!

Don't just see the world – experience it with Open Road!

ABOUT THE AUTHOR

Rachel Christmas Derrick has spent many years poking around all the Hawaiian islands (even "forbidden" Niihau), evaluating everything from familiar attractions to lesser known wonders. By bringing the people, culture, and history of the islands to life, she provides a new perspective on vacationing in an old favorite.

Derrick's travel articles have been published in *The New York Times*, *The Washington Post*, *The Boston Globe*, *Los Angeles Times*, *Islands*, *Travel & Leisure*, *Essence*, *Travel Holiday*, *Diversion*, and *Newsweek*, among many others. In addition to Hawaii, assignments have taken her to Bora Bora, Moorea, Australia, England, Wales, Brazil, Costa Rica, Mexico, Bermuda, the Bahamas, and throughout the Caribbean.

BE A TRAVELER, NOT A TOURIST - WITH OPEN ROAD TRAVEL GUIDES!

Open Road Publishing has guide books to exciting, fun destinations on four continents. As veteran travelers, our goal is to bring you the best travel guides available anywhere!

No small task, but here's what we offer:

All Open Road travel guides are written by authors with a distinct, opinionated point of view – not some sterile committee or team of writers. Our authors are experts in the areas covered and are polished writers.

• Our guides are geared to people who want to make their own travel choices. We'll show you how to discover the real destination – not just see some place from a tour bus window.

• We're strong on the basics, but we also provide terrific choices for those looking to get off the beaten path and *experience* the country or city – not just *see* it or pass through it.

• We give you the best, but we also tell you about the worst and what to avoid. Nobody should waste their time and money on their hard-earned vacation because of bad or inadequate travel advice.

• Our guides assume nothing. We tell you everything you need to know to have the trip of a lifetime – presented in a fun, literate, no-nonsense style.

• And, above all, we welcome your input, ideas, and suggestions to help us put out the best travel guides possible.

HAWAII GUIDE

GUIDE

BE A TRAVELER - NOT A TOURIST!

RACHEL CHRISTMAS DERRICK

OPEN ROAD PUBLISHING

7th Revised Edition

Text©Copyright 1997 by Rachel Christmas Derrick
Maps©Copyright 1997 by Open Road Publishing

ISBN 1-883323-55-X
Library of Congress Catalog Card No. 96-72609

A multitude of thanks goes to my assistants, especially Mary Anne Howland, June Jackson Christmas, Walter Christmas, June Howland, Sonia Medina, Francisco Perez, Jr., William Shepard, and Paula Nixon Shepard.

Among the scores of other peple who made invaluable contributions to the book are Cathy Pescaia Sharpe, Aimee McIntyre, Leslie Dance, Donovan Dela Cruz, Connie Wright, Charlene Ka'uhane, Noelani Whittington, Ruth Limtiaco, Heidi Nelson, Lori Kennedy, Aubrey Hawk, Patricia Egan, Tereasa Calvert, Lynn Cook, Caroline Witherspoon, Gigi Valley, Babs Harrison, Lydee Ritchie, Nancy Daniels, Ann Williams, Mary Zazzaro, Donna Jung, Darlene Morikawa, Suzanne Erler, William F. Bigelow, Elyn Yao, Christine Stanton, Joyce Matsumoto, and Sonja Swenson.

TABLE OF CONTENTS

Contents

Contents

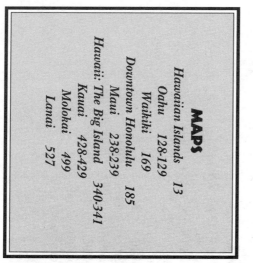

Contents

Contents

SIDEBARS

1. INTRODUCTION

I bet you're in the market for overwhelming beauty and exceptional outdoor action, plus a healthy dose of great restaurants, fabulous resorts, and memorable shopping. Hawaii is certainly all that and then some. But this group of Pacific islands isn't simply a place to be consumed. It's appreciated most when it's also examined beneath the surface, with more than a few glimpses of Hawaii beyond the tourist industry.

My emphasis is on the Hawaiiana that remains or has been revived, not on the things you can find in other American states. I steer readers away from the more commercial attractions and toward places where they can uncover true aspects of the indigenous culture. If you'd like to attend a luau, for example, it's best to check local newspapers for the more authentic, more intimate luaus hosted by civic groups and hula halau (schools) to raise money for various causes.

I spotlight cultural and social issues, sights, and activities concerning the islands' original inhabitants (such as traditional games, competitions, and the Hawaiian rights movement). Folklore, legends, and historical anecdotes are sprinkled liberally throughout the book. I introduce readers to life away from the resorts, including Hawaiian, Japanese, Chinese, and Filipino cultural festivals and practices.

Along with evaluations of sights, hotels, restaurants, shops, beaches, and sports, you'll find plenty of details about hiking, camping, and other activities and out-of-the-way places that put vacationers in touch with Hawaii at its most unspoiled. I've chosen the best of the most popular and the least known places and activities.

I include unusual tidbits, such as how to mail unboxed coconuts instead of postcards, which seats not to take during a helicopter ride, where to find redwood forests and volcanic swimming holes, when to pick various wild fruits, where to spot whales from shore. Readers are told when a hotel has some rooms not just without views but without windows, which sightseeing tours to avoid, and which roads and routes to steer clear of at certain hours or times of year.

Whatever your preference, this book will help you design a vacation that is tailor-made for you!

2. EXCITING HAWAII - OVERVIEW

The umbrella-like monkeypod trees, tubular African tulips and splashes of magenta bougainvillea thrilled my friend and me as we drove along one of Hawaii's winding roads. Just as our stomachs began to grumble, we came to a fruit stand piled high with papayas and bananas. But no vendor was in sight. Then, to our surprise, we noticed the sign that invited us simply to take some fruit and leave our money in a box.

This honor system was one of my earliest encounters with good old aloha, brought to this Pacific archipelago by the ancient Polynesians more than a millennium ago. Often replacing the words "hello" and "good-bye," aloha has come to mean many different things - from trust, tolerance, graciousness, and understanding to friendliness, caring and love. Above all, it encompasses the ideal of healthy interaction among human beings and between people and their environment.

Now existing in varying degrees, aloha has certainly faded in and out over the centuries. The selling of artificial leis and "handmade" plastic "wood carvings" speaks to the unfortunate commercialization of aloha here and there. But it has never disappeared completely, nor has it ever been distorted beyond recognition.

As you flip through the pages of this book, you'll find practical information about the most popular places, times, and ways to play, relax, and absorb nature's handiwork in Hawaii. You'll also learn about the islands' little-known treasures, the pulse of the people, and life beyond the resorts. Both despite and because of its geographic isolation, Hawaii has long been a powerful magnet for peoples from across the globe. Once you get a firsthand taste of the islands' physical beauty and the pervasive aloha spirit, you'll understand why.

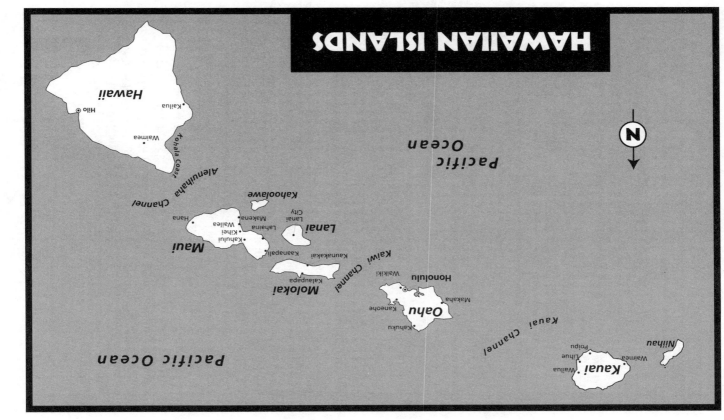

HAWAIIAN ISLANDS

THE MYSTIQUE OF ALOHA

Having survived encounters with exploitative European explorers, self-righteous, disapproving American missionaries, and, in some areas, overzealous real estate developers, the aloha spirit is clearly apparent in the welcoming faces of Hawaii's residents today. The cushiony aroma of fresh flowers hugs visitors the moment they step off the plane. Laden with fragrant leis, locals wait at airports to greet arriving travelers the traditional way: They brush their cheeks with kisses and place the thick floral garlands around their necks. Few other places rival the mostly harmonious racial and cultural blending that characterizes the diverse population of this 50th American state. This is one of the reasons that, in a world with countless other gorgeous, beach-fringed islands to choose from, about 3.5 million mainlanders vacation in Hawaii each year.

Some 130 islands, sandbars, and exposed reefs make up this Pacific state. The seven inhabited islands are certainly not devoid of problems - ethnic, economic, or otherwise. Yet somehow, the awe inspired by the drama of their stunning landscapes seems to spill over into a deep respect and appreciation for people's differences and commonalities. Negative thoughts about anything seem ridiculous once you've viewed the massive cliffs of Kauai's Na Pali Coast from a dwarfed rubber raft, watched the sun rise over the crater of Maui's Haleakala volcano, or stretched out under a palm tree on the coal-black sand of a beach on the Big Island of Hawaii. Throughout the islands, rich pumpkin-colored earth peeks through the flourishing greenery while waterfalls carve ridges into mountainsides.

BETWIXT & BETWEEN

With its closest neighbor the diminutive Christmas Island chain, about 2,000 miles to the south, Hawaii is the most isolated group of islands on earth. Some 2,400 miles of ocean lie between this US state and North America, the nearest continent. The islands of Hawaii began forming 25 to 40 million years ago when volcanoes gurgled, spouted, and belched their way up through cracks in the ocean floor. In a few short centuries, the spirit of aloha may spread to a new member of the archipelago. About 30 miles off the coast of the Big Island, another island, Loihi, is in gestation. Erupting as recently as the 1980s, this underwater volcanic cone is already nearly 16,000 feet tall, with only about 3,000 feet to go before it breaks the ocean's surface.

SOMETHING FOR EVERY LIFESTYLE

A vacation in Hawaii can mean very different things to very different people. Travelers with opposing tastes can easily find what they want here, often even within a single island. From quiet Molokai, which some claim is the most Hawaiian of the main islands, to action-oriented Oahu with its many T-shirt shops and fast food restaurants, each island has an atmosphere all its own.

If mobs of camera-toting visitors happily herded onto tour buses isn't the kind of scenery you have in mind, head for one of the quieter areas or one of the more tranquil islands. Those who turn up their noses at commercial luaus, crowded shopping malls, and high-rise resorts can camp out in a beachfront park or book a room in a bed & breakfast or a former plantation cottage. Independent travelers or families with children can check into a convenient home-like condominium. For a break from the tropical heat, rustic wooded cabins complete with well-used wood-burning stoves and fireplaces are nestled high in the cool mountains. Serving a variety of cuisines (including continental, Pacific Rim, regional American, Japanese, Italian, Chinese, Thai, Mexican, and Korean), restaurants range from candlelit to homestyle.

There are so many choices of settings in Hawaii that it doesn't matter that, for instance, what is elegant to one person may be overkill to another. I heard a couple talking at one of several mega-resorts that began cropping up in the late 1980s. The pair had just finished wandering around the grounds past horse-drawn carriages, life-size Far Eastern statues, marble columns almost as wide as redwood trees, canals with Venetian gondolas, and waterfall-fed swimming pools. Shaking his head, the man said to his companion, "After all this, the ocean seems superfluous, huh?" She replied with a frown, "After all this, *Hawaii* seems superfluous!" Mind you, this couple was surrounded by scores of other open-mouthed guests who were totally thrilled with the hotel.

SURPRISE, SURPRISE!

While the mere mention of Hawaii conjures up visions of a tropical paradise in many people's heads, the state is also full of surprises. As you might expect, Hawaii is just the place for surfing, snorkeling, scuba diving, deep-sea fishing, hiking, riding outrigger canoes or catamarans, watching volcanoes erupt or whales bound through the waves. It's the place for sightseeing from helicopters, sipping mai tais or Kona coffee, and munching macadamia nuts or fresh, juicy pineapple.

But you may not be aware that it's also a place where cowboys show their stuff in rodeos. On the Big Island, it's not unheard of to go water skiing one day and snow skiing the next. And beaches come with white, black, and even green sand. If you know which nooks and crannies deserve a peek, you can uncover hidden volcanic swimming pools or ancient *heiau* (stone temples) and rock carvings. You can explore deep, jungled valleys on horseback or on foot. On some islands, you can arrange to be picked up from the airport in a limousine complete with champagne or let a helicopter whisk you off to a secluded spot for an intimate picnic lunch.

Several of the things that have come to be associated with life in Hawaii actually originated elsewhere. For instance, the ukulele, which no luau worth its kalua pig is without, was first brought from Portugal. The requisite mound of rice in fast food "plate lunches" might not have become ever-present if the Chinese and Japanese had never arrived. And cockfighting, which goes on behind the scenes in some residential areas, came from the Philippines.

A CROSSROADS OF CULTURES

Some people proudly announce their multi-cultural heritage. Your chatty tour bus driver might mention that he's Hawaiian-Chinese-Portuguese or if you get into a conversation with your waitress, she might talk about her Filipino-Puerto Rican-Korean ancestry. There is a greater concentration of Asians in Hawaii than anywhere else in the country. This is the only US state where Caucasians are not the majority.

Many residents are quick to make the distinction between being Hawaiian (a descendant of the original brown-skinned inhabitants of the islands) and being from Hawaii (anyone of any race or ethnic group who was born here or has lived here a long time). Since 1778, when the first known Europeans set foot on these shores, indigenous Hawaiians have shrunk dramatically in number and much of their culture has disappeared or been diluted. According to recent estimates, Hawaiians now comprise only between 10 and 20 percent of the state's one million residents. Particularly since the early 1970s, Hawaiians have been pushing for reform of the social and economic system that has left them a disadvantaged minority in their own islands. They have also been attempting to revive pride in and respect for Hawaiian culture.

Indeed, visitors will certainly find plenty of elaborate luaus and sensuous hula performances. Some people still leave offerings of shells, rocks, and leaves at *heiau* (temples). Celebrating "Aloha Friday" is a popular custom among locals. On the last day of the work week, many residents deck themselves out in colorful, floral prints. People are simply saying "TGIF" by wearing sweet-smelling leis, muumuus, and aloha shirts to work that day, even to offices where the dress code generally dictates stockings and heels or business suits. Some families practically mortgage their homes to throw the traditional luaus celebrating their children's first birthday.

In general, however, Western and Asian influences have replaced the Hawaiian way of life. For instance, hamburgers are easy to come by, and the Japanese custom of removing shoes before entering a home has been adopted not only by residents throughout the state, but by many condominiums and bed & breakfasts as well.

EXPLORING YOUR SURROUNDINGS

By all means, get off the beaten path and explore. But before you head into remote areas (especially on Oahu), talk to locals about whether or not you'll feel comfortable there. With tourism and tourists such a dominant force in many parts of Hawaii, some residents aren't especially pleased with the idea of their secluded neighborhoods being open to outsiders too. In other cases, private property has been given over to marijuana fields and landowners may be less than friendly when it comes to protecting their income.

THE HAWAIIAN TONGUE

With few exceptions, the Hawaiian language is alive only on street signs, in place and hotel names, and in a sprinkling of words that pepper English and "pidgin," the local dialect. You'll hear common terms such as *kamaaina* (longtime island resident), *malihini* (visitor, newcomer, stranger), and *haole* (Caucasian and/or mainlander). As exotic as these islands may seem, resist the urge to refer to the rest of the country as "the United States" or "America." If you say "the mainland" or "the continental US," you'll avoid annoyed corrections.

CLIMATE

Generally speaking, weather in Hawaii can be divided into two seasons: summer and winter. Summer, which lasts from about May through mid-October, brings daytime temperatures in the 80s. This is the drier time of year; when it does rain, showers are usually brief. In the winter season, lasting from about mid-October through April, daytime temperatures hover in the high 60s to low 80s.

The high seasons, when some hotel prices are steeper and reservations are more difficult to come by, run from about late December to mid-April, then again during the summer.

ISLAND SNAPSHOTS

Hawaii's seven inhabited islands are at the southeastern end of the Hawaiian chain, along with Kahoolawe, which is unpopulated (unless you count the wild goats that roam its semiarid landscape). Oahu, Maui, Hawaii, and Kauai draw many more visitors and are much more developed than Molokai, Lanai, and Niihau. Islands other than Oahu are jointly referred to as the "Neighbor Islands."

To give you a glimpse of the distinct personalities of the main islands, some highlights follow. As with the chapters later in the book, the order of the islands is from the most developed to the least developed. Where more than one pronunciation of a name is given, the first is the most common and the last, with an abrupt pause before the final syllable, is the more correct.

Oahu (oh-*wah*-hoo)

The home of Honolulu, the capital of the state, Oahu is Hawaii's best-known island. It is only the third largest, after Hawaii and Maui, yet almost four-fifths of the state's total population resides here. Along with **Waikiki Beach, Pearl Harbor** and the **USS Arizona Memorial** are the most popular tourist attractions in the state. Two other stops that are high on most lists are the **Polynesian Cultural Center** (where you'll learn about ancient Hawaiians and others in the Pacific region) and **Sea Life Park** (where whales, dolphins, and other aquatic entertainers put on great shows).

The North Shore, across the island from Honolulu, is a world away from the highrises, shopping malls, and crowds of Waikiki. On this pastoral northern coast, waves curl at 30 feet during winter months. To the surprise of many who picture only Honolulu and Waikiki when they think of this island, most of mountainous Oahu is carpeted with country-side.

Maui (*mow*-ee)

The second most popular island among visitors, Maui is sometimes referred to as "Southern California" because of all of the Golden State residents transplanted from the mainland. Looking down on it from the air, you'll see what appears to be two islands joined by a valley. The West Maui Mountains dominate the smaller northern segment, while towering **Haleakala volcano** rises in the southeastern region. Quiet towns, eucalyptus forests, and wild rodeos are found along the cool "upcountry" slopes of Haleakala. Watching the sun rise over its crater, then horseback riding or hiking into it, or riding a mountain bike down the volcano, are favorite activities among visitors.

Some see **Kaanapali Beach**, a long, gentle crescent backed by highrise hotels and condominiums, as a younger, more low-key version of Waikiki. Other, smaller resort areas offer less congested choices. **Historic Lahaina**, the old whaling port, was once the capital of the whole Hawaiian kingdom. During the winter, Maui is Hawaii's **whalewatching** mecca. One of Maui's most spectacular drives is along the winding coastal "highway" that leads to isolated **Hana**, a lush, drowsy town tucked away in the southeast.

Hawaii (hah-*why*-ee, hah-*why*'ee' or hah-*vye*'ee)

Commonly referred to as the **Big Island**, Hawaii is so much larger than its siblings that the rest of the chain could fit inside it–with room to spare. Hawaii is the only island where you can see active volcanoes, which spout fireworks from time to time. With stark, ebony lava flows stretching for miles, it is also the most unusual-looking member of the family. The sand of beaches comes in white, black, salt and pepper, and even green!

In sharp contrast to its volcanic moonscape, the island boasts rain forests, flower nurseries, and lush valleys. Rodeos are held on one of the largest privately owned cattle ranches in the US. The beach-rimmed Kona Kohala Coast, in the west, is treated to the least amount of rainfall in all of inhabited Hawaii. When conditions are right, you can actually **ski down** the slopes of snowcapped Mauna Kea volcano.

Kauai (*cow-why*, *cow*-why, or *cow-wah*'ee)

By many accounts the most beautiful Hawaiian island, Kauai is a relative newcomer to tourism. Tiny rural towns are flanked by miles of sugarcane fields and flourishing foliage. The island's jagged mountains, plunging waterfalls, and isolated beaches have played supporting roles in films such as *Jurassic Park, Raiders of the Lost Ark, Body Heat,* and *The Thorn Birds* television miniseries.

Although Kauai receives more rain than other Hawaiian islands, a visit here is well worth risking a few soggy days. Besides, the lush landscape is almost as stunning when wet. The driest part of the island is around Poipu, in the south, where sandy crescents scallop the shore. Probably Kauai's most impressive natural attractions are massive, arid **Waimea Canyon** and the awesome cliffs of **Na Pali coast.**

Molokai (*mole*-oh-kye or mole-oh-*kah*'ee)

Mention Molokai to mainlanders, and the first thing many say is, "Oh, you mean where the leper colony is?" Molokai is certainly famous for the victims of Hansen's Disease, whose tragic story you can learn all about. But it is also known for its unspoiled landscape, slow pace, and delightfully small number of tourists. One of Molokai's most exciting activities is a ride down a 2,000-foot cliff on the back of a mule.

In the verdant eastern region, the road winds heavenward to striking cliff-edge views. In the parched west, photo safaris are conducted through a sprawling wildlife preserve inhabited by all kinds of animals from East Africa and Asia; you can even go on a "giraffe picnic." In January, hundreds of locals pack Kaunakakai Park for the annual **Makahiki Festival**, a revival of an old Hawaiian peacetime celebration marked with food, music, and competitions in Hawaiian games.

Lanai (lahn-*eye* or lah-*nah'ee*)

In 1922, Jim Dole bought most of Lanai to start the fields that gave "The Pineapple Island" its nickname. While neat rows of this sweet juicy fruit once blanketed the island, other types of agriculture are now being grown in its place. After slumbering happily with a single 10-room hotel since the 1940s, Lanai has been transformed in a major way by the birth of two luxury hotels, the first in 1990 and the second the following year.

Before then, most visitors were friends of residents, hunters, or hardy travelers looking for unadulterated peace and quiet way off the beaten path. True, the number of hotels has tripled. But since the grand total is only three, the island remains almost as undeveloped as before. Searching for ancient **petroglyphs** (rock carvings) and eerie rock formations continues to be a favorite pastime. Locals are still quick to strike up conversations with visitors over drinks on the wooden porch of the island's original accommodation, Hotel Lanai. Many residents of Lanai "City," the quiet inland plantation town nestled amid spikey Norfolk pines, welcome the advent of all the non-plantation jobs that larger-scale tourism has brought.

Niihau (*nee*-ee-how)

Known as "The Forbidden Island," Niihau has no tourist accommodations, nor plumbing, alcohol, or guns, for that matter. Only about 250 people live here, virtually all of them pure Hawaiians. While the rest of Hawaii has galloped toward the 21st century, the daily lives of residents of Niihau differ little from those of their 19th century ancestors.

This is the only island in the state where Hawaiian remains the dominant language. Most residents work on the cattle and sheep ranch run by the Robinsons, the *haole* family that has owned the island since 1864. Some outsiders applaud the Robinsons' success in preserving a culture that has nearly disappeared elsewhere in the state. Others call this family paternalistic and complain that they are simply maintaining indentured servitude.

With rare exceptions, until the late 1980s the island owners allowed only native Hawaiians to set foot on Niihau soil. Now helicopter flights from neighboring Kauai can introduce outsiders to this mystery island. However, some people who have taken the flights characterize the trips as "too much money to see too little." The whirlybirds land in dry, barren areas far from where people live.

Others are captivated by the island's dramatic, stark terrain and enjoy searching for tiny **Niihau shells** in the sand. If you've got (very) deep pockets, shop on other islands for the delicate necklaces made of these rare, colorful shells. (See Chapter 14, *Kauai*, for more information about this island.)

Kahoolawe (kah-ho-oh-*lah*-vay)

The smallest of the main islands, semi-arid Kahoolawe was controlled by the US Navy until May 7, 1994. It had been used for target practice from 1941 to 1990. The idea of bombs missing their mark had never sat well with residents of Maui, only six miles away. Peppered with sites of ancient Hawaiian settlements and *heiau* (temples), Kahoolawe has been put on the **National Register of Historic Places.**

It became a focal point for Hawaiian activists in the 1970s. In a series of demonstrations against the status quo, whereby most Hawaiians are at the bottom of the social and economic totem pole, they protested the island's military use. They felt that the return of Kahoolawe to state government jurisdiction, and allowing the public to have access to it, could help spark a newfound respect for, and pride in, Hawaiian culture and land.

The 45-square-mile island has finally been reclaimed by the state of Hawaii. Overlooking Kahoolawe from Palauea Beach on Maui, hundreds of people attended the moving transition ceremonies. The pounding of drums and the foghorn-like sound of a conch shell being blown over and over again signalled the island's new status. This sacred place is now a preserve for nature and Hawaiian cultural traditions. Luckily, the navy's bombs did not succeed in destroying all of the fishing shrines, thousand-year-old petroglyphs (rock carvings), and other historic and religious sites. But it will take a decade and some $400 million for the Navy to clear Kahoolawe of left-over explosives and to replant indigenous vegetation.

PRICES & TELEPHONE NUMBERS

All prices quoted are subject to change without notice. When no telephone area code appears, the number is local, using Hawaii's 808 area code.

3. SUGGESTED ITINERARIES

Many first-time visitors choose to sample two or three islands during their stay. Two are usually enough for people who truly want to get a feel for each place they visit. If you're one of those travelers who gets stir crazy if you stay in one place too long, don't worry. Hawaii is so diverse that, for dramatic changes in scenery, atmosphere, and even climate, you can move from one region to another on any single island.

When you're considering which two or three islands to visit, remember that Oahu, Maui, the Big Island of Hawaii, and Kauai are the most developed, while Molokai and Lanai are the most tranquil. You may want to arrange your island hopping before you embark, but it's also possible to take advantage of package deals or discount flights to other islands after you arrive in Hawaii. While there are flight-seeing tours that will take you to all the major islands in a single day, I don't recommend them since you get only a brief, superficial look at each destination. For aerial views, a helicopter tour of a single island is much more fun.

Don't plan many rigorous activities for your first couple of days, since you'll be recovering from the long flight and adjusting to the time difference. If you've traveled west to get to Hawaii, you'll feel perkiest early in the morning and start fading in the afternoon or evening. So wait a few days before going to any evening shows or night spots - unless, of course, you don't mind snoozing in public.

Folks who get hives at the thought of tall buildings and crowds should skip Honolulu. Most other vacationers will want to spend at least a couple of nights in this capital city, on Oahu, where most visitors enter Hawaii. Here are four suggested itineraries:

ITINERARY 1: 8 DAYS/7 NIGHTS

Spend four nights on **Oahu** and three nights on **Kauai**:

Day 1
When you finally get to **Oahu**, hit the beach!

Day 2
Hike to the summit of Diamond Head in the morning.

Day 3
Visit the Polynesian Cultural Center and the North Shore.

Day 4
Go to Pearl Harbor in the morning; then tour Iolani Palace and Bishop Museum or Mission Houses Museum.

Day 5
Fly to **Kauai**. Have a massage or a facial at the Hyatt or the Princeville resort; play some golf or tennis.

Day 6
Take a morning helicopter whirl, then a snorkeling cruise along Na Pali Coast.

Day 7
Drive to Waimea Canyon.

Day 8
Soak up your last rays on Poipu beach before you depart.

ITINERARY 2: 11 DAYS/10 NIGHTS

Spend five nights on Oahu and five nights on **Kauai**:

Day 1
Get your first taste of **Oahu** on the beach.

Day 2
Head to Sea Life Park.

Day 3
Visit the Polynesian Cultural Center and the North Shore.

Day 4
Go to Pearl Harbor in the morning; then tour Iolani Palace and Bishop Museum or Mission Houses Museum.

Day 5
Go mountain biking at Waimea Valley and visit Waimea Falls Park.

Day 6
Fly to **Kauai**. Have a massage or a facial at the Hyatt or the Princeville resort.

Day 7
Take a morning helicopter whirl, then a raft ride along Na Pali Coast.

Day 8
Have a picnic in Kokee State Park, overlooking Waimea Canyon.

Day 9
Go kayaking along the Hanalei River.

Day 10
Go scuba diving or snorkeling.

Day 11
Body surf at Poipu beach before you depart.

ITINERARY 3: 12 DAYS/11 NIGHTS

Spend four nights on **Oahu**, four nights on **Kauai** and three nights on **Molokai**.

Day 1
When you get to **Oahu**, try an outrigger canoe ride on Waikiki Beach.

Day 2
Sail on a catamaran.

Day 3
Visit the Polynesian Cultural Center and the North Shore.

Day 4
Go to Pearl Harbor in the morning; then tour Iolani Palace and Bishop Museum or Mission Houses Museum.

Day 5
Fly to **Kauai**. Play some golf or tennis.

Day 6

Take a morning helicopter whirl, then a leisurely drive along the scenic north shore.

Day 7

Hike through Kokee State Park and see Waimea Canyon.

Day 8

Soak up some rays on Poipu beach.

Day 9

Fly to **Mokokai** and go on the Giraffe Picnic at Molokai Ranch.

Day 10

Take the mule ride down the cliff.

Day 11

Drive east to the Halawa Valley Lookout.

Day 12

Relax on Papohaku Beach before you depart.

ITINERARY 4: 15 DAYS/14 NIGHTS

Spend six nights on **Maui**, six nights on **the Big Island**, and two nights on **Lanai**.

Day 1

After arriving on **Maui**, relax!

Day 2

Explore historic Lahaina.

Day 3

Go whale watching (in winter) or take a snorkeling cruise to Molokini Crater.

Day 4

Absorb the views along the road to Hana.

Day 5

Take a guided trek with Hike Maui.

Day 6

Watch the sun rise over Haleakala volcano, then ride a mountain bike down from the summit.

Day 7

Fly (or take the ferry) to **Lanai**.

Day 8

Look for dolphins on Lanai's Hulopoe Beach.

Day 9

Visit the Garden of the Gods. Fly to **the Big Island**. Float in the pool or splash in the ocean.

Day 10

Take a morning helicopter ride.

Day 11

Visit historic Puuhonua O Honaunau (Place or City of Refuge).

Day 12

Go horseback riding through Waipio Valley and visit the gorgeous Hamakua Coast.

Day 13

Tour Volcanoes National Park.

Day 14

Hike to Papakolea (Green Sand Beach).

Day 15

Cool out on Hapuna Beach before your long flight home!

4. LAND & PEOPLE

LAND

Hawaii's genesis lies in a hot spot deep inside the earth. Somewhere between 25 and 40 million years ago, a long cleft opened up in the ocean floor. Molten lava pulsed through, forming water-covered craters. Inch by inch and over millions of years, the part of the earth's crust called the Pacific Plate slowly shifted above the hot spot, resulting in a chain of undersea mountains. They grew taller with each eruption, but it wasn't until a few million years ago that, one by one, they finally broke the ocean's surface in their trek toward the sky.

The first of these mountain peaks to hit the air were the smallest islands, those at the northwestern end of the Hawaiian chain. Of these, the ones that survived the severe battering by natural elements remain deserted and mostly barren. Far to the southeast, the volcanic peaks that last appeared above the Pacific's surface became the inhabited group best known today. Wind, rain, and pounding waves carved jagged cliffs and scooped out wide valleys in the young islands. Plants began to sprout from spores that had traveled on the ocean breezes, and later from seeds brought by the tides and migrating birds.

Compared to most of the world's land masses, which came into their own about 300 million years ago, the Hawaiian Islands are geologic infants. **Kauai** is the oldest inhabited island in the chain, and the **Big Island of Hawaii** is the youngest. As you read these words, not only is a new island forming (the submerged **Loihi**, near the Big Island), but the Big Island itself is still growing. Here, the **Kilauea** and **Mauna Loa volcanoes** continue to put on periodic fiery displays that add land mass to the island. Although these are the state's only two active volcanoes, Hawaii also has a trio of dormant volcanoes: the Big Island's **Mauna Kea** and **Hualalai**, and Maui's **Haleakala**. Mauna Kea is now Hawaii's giant at nearly 14,000 feet above sea level. If measured from the ocean floor to their summits, Mauna Kea and Mauna Loa are the world's two highest mountains. Rising 30,000 feet from their aquatic bases, they beat Mt. Everest by a few hundred feet.

MOTHER & FATHER NATURE

According to ancient legend, Hawaii might never have existed had it not been for the chemistry between Papa, the earth mother, and Wakea, the father of the sky and the heavens. Their first offspring was the Big Island of Hawaii and their second, Maui. Worn out by the vigors of childbearing, Papa went to Tahiti to recuperate. While she was away, Wakea began an incestuous relationship with one of their daughters, producing Molokai and Lanai. Papa got wind of this affair and returned to Hawaii in a jealous rage. Wakea soon soothed away her fury, and they went on to produce Oahu, Kauai and Niihau. With their energy nearly spent, Kahoolawe was the last island they could manage.

HAWAII'S CRITTERS & GREEN THINGS

Even on Oahu, home of the skyscraper-studded capital of Honolulu, the wonders of nature are the main attraction. Vivid color is everywhere, from the neon blue of the ocean, the vibrant green of sugarcane fields and palm fronds, and the burnt-orange soil to the kaleidoscope of flowers, trees, birds, and fish. So whether you stay at a luxury beach resort or a mountainside campsite, you won't have to wander far to see Hawaii at its most natural.

Because of the direction in which the wind blows the clouds and air mass across the Pacific, the northeast sides of all of Hawaii's islands are wet and the southwest sides dry. As the clouds bump up against the mountains, rain falls on one side, leaving the other side more arid.

The seeds of Hawaii's first plants floated ashore or were carried by the wind and migrating birds. One new species appeared on Hawaii about

SKY HIGH

If you've ever wondered why leaves are flat, a Hawaiian legend explains: In the old days, the sky weighed heavily upon the earth, barely leaving breathing room between the ground and the heavens. Plants, with their bulbous leaves, were forced to push the clouds and the sky up into the stratosphere, inch by inch. The more they shoved, the flatter their leaves became. Eventually, the sky was raised far enough to allow human beings to crawl around from place to place. Then for the price of a drink from a woman's gourd, Maui, the demigod, hoisted the skies up even farther, past the tops of trees, beyond the summits of mountains. Thus, men could finally walk upright on earth.

every 40,000 years! When the ancient Polynesians began to settle the Islands, they brought a variety of fruits and vegetables, including bananas, coconuts, breadfruit, taro, and yams. At first, ancient Hawaiians lived in a world free from biting and stinging insects and poisonous snakes. They also had no communicable diseases. The arrival of European explorers in 1788 changed all that. Within a century after the first appearance of white people, the Hawaiian population had been devastated by new diseases they had no immunities to combat.

While Hawaii is certainly flourishing with all kinds of plant life, many of its more delicate native species have been crowded out by the more aggressive newcomers brought to Hawaii by outsiders. The introduction of cattle (for ranching) and other grazing animals has also killed off many of the Islands' original plants. For millions of years, these plants had lived in a world with no natural enemies; there had been no need to grow hardy. Thus, when a leaf or a branch was bitten off or trampled, the whole plant withered away.

Land & Sea Animals

Hawaii's only native land animal is a small **brown bat**. **Dolphins** are often spotted jumping playfully out of the water in pairs, and impressive **humpback whales** migrate to Hawaii during the winter. If you happen upon a **monk seal** lying on a beach, don't worry - it's not sick, so don't try to urge it back into the water. It's only resting while it digests its last meal. People who thought they were helping used to try to rouse these seals and ended up hurting the animals by disturbing their digestion. Now people are prohibited from going within 50 feet of a monk seal on a beach, and fines are stiff!

The early Polynesians, traders, and European explorers imported the small selection of animals that roam wild in Hawaii today: pigs, cattle (wild and domestic), deer, antelope, bighorn sheep, goats, jungle fowl, mice, rats, even a small group of wallabies (like small kangaroos) on Oahu. The long, low **mongooses** that often dart across roads in front of cars were brought to kill off the rats that wreaked havoc on sugarcane plantations. Unfortunately, people realized too late that rats are nocturnal while mongooses like to party during the day. Needless to say, their paths rarely crossed and both rats and mongooses were fruitful and multiplied.

Fish

Snorkeling and diving are wonderful in Hawaii. Darting in jerky unison around coral heads and sea plants, schools of fish surround human visitors in this underworld. Perhaps my favorite are the **parrotfish**, with their bright, iridescent colors. **Angelfish** could teach humans a thing or two about monogamy: They choose mates for life and forever swim in pairs. **Blowfish** are fun to watch when they feel threatened: They puff themselves up to more than twice their normal size; the thorns on their skin protrude, making predators think twice about attempting to swallow them.

Some of the other fish swimmers can see are **stripeys**, **Moorish idols** and **triggerfish** such as the **humuhumunukunukuapuaa**, Hawaii's tiny state fish. Also moving through the ocean are awesome but gentle **manta rays**, whose wingspan can be as great as 20 feet; **brown stingrays**, which can grow as long as four feet; and **eagle rays**. Big-game fishing enthusiasts find plenty of **sailfish, Pacific blue marlin, striped marlin and broadbill swordfish**.

Although there are **sharks** in some of Hawaii's waters, as there are in all oceans, they tend to leave humans alone. Watch out for the elaborate jellyfish called the **Portuguese man-of-war**, whose hump protrudes above the water like a fin while its stinging tentacles dangle below.

Birds

Frigate birds, called *iwa* (thief) in Hawaiian, could hardly be less neighborly. Instead of finding their own food, these seabirds glide through the air looking for other birds with fish clutched in their talons. They then attack these meal-carrying birds, forcing them to let go of the wriggling fish, which the frigate promptly snatches out of the sky. Other seabirds include the clumsy **Laysan gooney birds** and **tropic birds**, with their red or white tails.

Polynesian jungle fowl, which strut around Oahu's north shore, the path to Kauai's Fern Grotto, and other areas, are said to be descended from the chickens that arrived aboard canoes with Hawaii's Polynesian settlers. Their long, bright feathers resemble tresses of straight human hair.

The **nene goose**, Hawaii's state bird, lives at high altitudes on mountainsides on the Big Island and Maui. Also rarely seen is the **Hawaiian stilt**, which thrives in remote bodies of fresh water, mostly on the Big Island and Kauai. Hawaii is also home to a colorful variety of **cardinals, doves,** and **egrets** (some of which park themselves on the backs of cattle to enjoy a meal of insects).

Trees

The **koa**, Hawaii's tallest native tree, can pierce the air 60 to 80 feet above its base. It is also among the oldest species of trees in Hawaii. Its prized reddish wood with a striking grain, once cut into 15-foot royal surfboards and 70-foot royal canoes, is still used to make handsome bowls, furniture, wall paneling, ukuleles, necklaces, and earrings. Complex religious rites were performed whenever a koa tree was felled to be transformed into a canoe. Unfortunately, these trees are no longer as abundant as they once were.

Koa forests thrived long before human beings came to Hawaii. Botanists are stymied over how the koa originally reached Hawaiian shores, since its heavy seeds don't float. It seems to have come from Australia or Mauritius, off the coast of Africa, so it clearly had to travel across thousands of ocean miles.

Sacred to the Chinese, the **sandalwood** tree was probably brought to Hawaii by human beings. Like those of the koa, its seeds are too large to be eaten and excreted by birds, and too heavy to float in the ocean. Unlike more durable koa seeds, sandalwood seeds aren't viable for long. Within several decades after Westerners and Hawaiian chiefs began getting rich by selling fragrant sandalwood to China to be made into incense or carvings, sandalwood forests had been almost completely decimated.

LEAVE THOSE LEAVES

Ohia trees are noted for their fluffy blood-red blossoms, which are considered sacred to Pele, the volcano goddess. According to ancient Hawaiians, Madame Pele would send rainstorms, claps of thunder, or volcanic eruptions if mortals were fool enough to pick one of her flowers. This is Hawaii's most common native tree.

The **kukui** (or candlenut) is Hawaii's state tree. Roasted and shelled kukui nuts became candles for ancient Hawaiians. Strings of these lampnuts were tended by children, whose job it was to keep them burning. Lamp oil was made by grinding the meat of the nuts. But their usefulness did not end here. Dyes for *kapa* cloth were made from their husks, their oil became skin lotion (especially soothing after too much sun), and the nuts themselves were polished and made into gleaming necklaces. You can find kukui nut necklaces for sale in stores today.

Two of my favorite trees in Hawaii are the **African tulip**, with its blazing crimson flowers; and the striking smooth-barked **rainbow eucalyptus tree**, its trunk decorated with bright red, yellow, and brown vertical stripes, as if someone had spilled paint down its torso. Also called the gum tree, the eucalyptus gives off a wonderful aroma. The **jacaranda**, with its pear-shaped mauve flowers, and the monkeypod, with its dangling globular clusters of blossoms, are other beauties.

The **hapuu tree fern** of the Hawaiian rain forest always amazes me. As it grows up from the ground, the end of each branch is tightly coiled, like the top of a cello's neck. This plant takes more than half a century to reach its full height.

The yellow, buttercuplike blossoms of **hau** trees open yellow in the morning and turn red as the day goes by. The long, thin branches of this low-growing tree are like a mass of tangled, bony arms. Leaves of the **pandanus** are used for *lauhala* weaving ("lau" means leaves and "hala" is the Hawaiian name for the tree). Towering in rain forests and other areas, stands of **bamboo** serve as a musical instrument for the blowing wind.

Banyans, with those tentacles dripping from their branches, can sprawl as wide as a house. One of the most impressive is in Lahaina on Maui. Don't be put off by the dark fruit of the **baobab**; it only *looks* like rats dangling by their tails. **Norfolks** and **ironwoods** (also called casuarinas) are two distinctly different types of evergreens. The first is a perfectly triangular pine, while the second is a wispy, windswept, somewhat asymmetrical affair. The wood of **kiawes**, also known as mesquite, is used for cooking, to add a scrumptious flavor to grilled food.

Flowers & Plants

With thousands of varieties, the **hibiscus** is Hawaii's state flower. Each bright blossom can be anywhere from an inch and a half to ten inches across and have single, double, or ruffled petals. Some flowers are one color, while others are two- or three-tone. The most common, however, are a bright, solid red.

Tiny-petaled **bougainvillea** bushes sprinkle pink, yellow, orange, white, purple, and red throughout Hawaii. These flowers are especially dramatic on the Big Island, where they often grow in stark contrast to desolate charcoal lava flows.

As soon as most visitors step off the plane, they are surrounded by the mesmerizing fragrance of **plumeria** (known as frangipani elsewhere). These petals from flowering trees are most commonly strung into the leis that many travelers find placed around their necks as part of the traditional Hawaiian lei greeting. Parks and other open areas fortunate enough to have these trees are enveloped by their wonderful perfume.

Ginger plants come in many shapes, colors, and sizes, from a few inches tall to 15 or more feet high. Visitors can wander through one of the largest ginger gardens in the world at Waimea Falls Park on Oahu. Another extensive ginger garden is Nani Mau Gardens in Hilo on the Big Island. The edible type of ginger root is widely used to flavor Asian and Polynesian cooking. Small, aromatic ginger petals were once more widely fashioned into leis than the larger plumeria. But since ginger only blossoms from June to December (unlike plumeria, which blooms year-round), and since it took far more ginger petals to create a decent lei, plumeria eventually won out. Until the 1960s, it was common for young girls to hang ginger leis in their bedrooms, leaving them there to scent the air for months after they dried.

While white and yellow ginger were brought from the Himalayas, India, and the Caribbean in the 1880s, **shampoo ginger** probably came hundreds of years before, with the early Polynesian immigrants. It produces a bright-red, three-inch bulb. The thick juice of the ripe plant quenched thirst on long journeys. The clear no-suds liquid was, and still is, also used to wash hair, leaving it soft and silky.

One of Hawaii's rarest plants is the **silversword**. Growing on the lunarlike heights of Maui's Haleakala volcano, it resembles a cone-shaped, gray sea anemone. This delicate-to-the-human-touch-yet-hardy-to-the-elements plant thrives where few others can. There are extreme temperature fluctuations at these heights; after a 90-degree day, there might be a snowfall at night. It is against the law to remove or even touch a silversword plant.

Here are some more of Hawaii's impressive blossoms:

Pikake ("pee-*kah*-kay"), meaning peacock, is a sweet-smelling white jasmine that was named for Princess Kaiulani. Before her untimely death, she was known for her love of both peacocks and this flower.

Stiff, waxy **anthurium** has a pencil-like staff that sticks up in the center of the usually red (but sometimes green, white, pink, or orange) spade-shaped flower.

The most common type of **heliconia** is orangy-red and looks like a group of lobster claws stacked on top of each other.

The tall gold or orange **bird-of-paradise** looks like an abstract sculptor's version of its name. **Gardenias** emit a soft aroma and **oleander** comes in red, pink, or white.

I often wear leis when in Hawaii, but until the day a friend put a deep purple **orchid** lei around my neck, I had never received such a barrage of compliments. Everywhere I went, people fingered the moist, fleshy blossoms with admiration. The flowers come in many other colors as well.

Another plant to keep an eye out for is the **ti plant**. Hawaiians still use it for wrapping and cooking food. Since it is flame retardant, it also serves as the lining for *imu* (earthen ovens dug into the ground). Unlike grass skirts, which originated on other islands, ti-leaf hula skirts are authentically Hawaiian.

SACRED HIKES

You may come across hikers with ti leaves tied around their ankles or waists. Old-time Hawaiians will explain that a mischievous spirit hides behind bushes and rocks, waiting to trip up innocent passersby. However, since the ti plant is sacred to the god Lono, the spirit will not grab an ankle tied with its leaves.

PEOPLE

"Where are all the Asians?" a Japanese-American friend of mine from Hawaii asked during her first trip to the mainland. This is a question that occurs to many residents of the 50th state when they first visit the continental US.

Of Hawaii's one million Hawaiians, European-Americans, Chinese, Japanese, Portuguese, Koreans, Filipinos, Puerto Ricans, Samoans, and others, no single ethnic group is larger than the rest of the collective population. At about 30 percent each, Caucasians and Japanese make up the two biggest groups. Between only 10 percent and 20 percent of Island residents are Hawaiian or part-Hawaiian. Many people are products of a varied heritage. Nearly half of Hawaii's marriages each year are between people of different races and/or ethnic backgrounds. Here when people ask, "What are you?" they're not thinking doctor, electrician, or surfing instructor. They mean "What's your racial or ethnic background?"

Hawaii's economy has everything to do with its cultural diversity. Beginning in the mid-19th century, thousands of immigrants from many different countries were recruited to work in the Islands' sugarcane and pineapple fields. While Hawaii is certainly something of a cultural melting pot, many ethnic distinctions have remained sharp over the decades. This is in part due to the way the residential camps on the plantations were set up. Each housing area was reserved for a particular ethnic group. One village would be inhabited only by Hawaiians, another strictly by Japanese, another limited to Filipinos.

Living with people who shared a language, diet, and culture certainly made the transition to a foreign land a bit easier; in this way, immigrants maintained many aspects of their old religions, festivals, and culinary traditions and passed them on to their Hawaii-born children. However, the reason ethnic groups were separated was to discourage them from joining forces en masse against the *haole* plantation owners.

In most cases, living and working conditions were horrific. *Lunas* (akin to overseers) would sometimes whip or beat workers who did not move fast enough. It was common practice to pay Asians less money than Caucasian laborers doing the same work. Picking pineapples was especially arduous. Even in the sweltering heat, workers were forced to wear hats, scarves over their faces, and other heavy clothing to protect themselves from bugs and dust, and gloves to avoid cutting their hands on the serrated leaves.

For those lucky enough to escape the plantations, harsh treatment of Asians and other non-Caucasians did not end. Threatened by the success of many Chinese businesses, the *haole*-controlled Hawaiian government began to throw roadblocks at Asians who tried to open stores and restaurants. Laws were also passed that prevented people born in Japan or China from ever becoming Hawaiian citizens, a privilege that was available to other foreign residents.

After the arrival of the first **Europeans** in 1778, the Hawaiian population dwindled steadily. Many were killed or made sterile by newly encountered Western diseases that their immune systems were not equipped to handle. Those Hawaiians who survived disease and cultural genocide (which included the overthrow of their last monarch by a group of American businessmen) found themselves at the bottom level of society.

Today, ethnic and racial tensions, though certainly not pervasive, do exist in Hawaii. Some public schools had a difficult time ending the tradition known as "Kill a Haole Day," an excuse for tearing up and causing trouble. After suffering misdirected discrimination following the Japanese attack on Pearl Harbor in World War II, Japanese-Americans in Hawaii faced being painted with another broad stroke during the 1980s. Resentment was high against businessmen from Japan who bought up real estate in Hawaii with a vengeance, until the 1990s slump.

However, despite its problems, Hawaii remains one of the most intriguing cultural potpourris in the world. Here's a closer look at the main ethnic groups:

The Hawaiians

When **Polynesians** first arrived in the uninhabited Hawaiian Islands, somewhere between A.D. 300 and 750, they brought *aloha aina*. Inherent in this profound love for the land and the sea was a reverence for all life that the earth and ocean made possible. Therefore, preservation of the environment was of the utmost importance to ancient Hawaiians. Although in some parts of the state *aloha aina* has been overshadowed by real estate development, there are many places for visitors to see a Hawaii that has changed little since the early days.

Some modern families settle arguments with the *hooponopono* ritual, as ancient Hawaiians did: after everyone has gotten their concerns off their chests, they all eat the tender leaves of *limu kala*, a variety of seaweed (*kala* means to "forgive"). Herbal medicine is still practiced here and there. People who never went to doctors as children will tell you what they learned from their parents. For example, chewing baby guava leaves relieves motion sickness, guava juice can work better than Pepto Bismol, and tea made from eucalyptus leaves or ginger root sends colds and congestion packing.

There are Hawaiians who still leave offerings at *heiau*, the crumbling stone temples found around the Islands. Many, even those who practice Christianity, still worship old Hawaiian gods such as Pele, the powerful volcano goddess, who resides on the Big Island. To this day, people claim from time to time that they have seen Pele, with her fiery tresses, wandering about.

In the past, loved ones who had died were buried around their houses so that their *aumakua* (positive spirits) wouldn't have far to go when they returned to help living relatives. *Lapu* were the tormented spirits of the deceased who were unable to get out of the limbo between the worlds of the living and the dead. As late as the end of the 19th century, cases were reported in which people swore they had seen groups of *lapu* socializing on the corner of King and Nuuanu streets in Oahu's Chinatown. *Kupua* were the spirits that inhabited inanimate objects. Today, people tell stories of rocks at construction sites that could not be moved until after a Hawaiian *kahuna* (priest) arrived and had a tete-a-tete with the spirits inside the stones.

Most present-day Hawaiians are not ethnically pure, so they are not nearly as brown-skinned as their ancestors. However, they still tend to be large-in both height and weight. In Hawaiian culture, size was once equated with power, wealth, and social status - in other words, the bigger, the better. Rotund Kaahumanu, the favorite wife of King Kamehameha I, was said to be at least six feet tall and the monarch to have towered over her. A local joke about Hawaiian women in those loose-fitting dresses asks, "How is a Hawaiian woman in a muumuu like a bank?" Answer: "You know it's in there. You just don't know how much."

In the 1970s, Hawaiian activists began fighting for the interests of the indigenous population. Until the late 1960s, parents had not been permitted to give their children Hawaiian first names. The ban on speaking the Hawaiian language wasn't lifted until the late '70s, shortly after Hawaiians were allowed to resume practicing their own religion. People began joining *hula halau* (hula groups) and taking Hawaiian language classes. It's not unusual to meet older Hawaiians who speak little, if any, Hawaiian while their parents spoke little, if any, English. The parents communicated with their children through simple commands and by showing them what they wanted done. Although they had trouble learning English, they wanted their children to "be American" so they did not allow them to learn Hawaiian. They believed the government's message, that "being American" meant giving up their Hawaiian heritage.

During the '70s, activists also began pushing for land rights for Hawaiians and for restoration and preservation of ancient historic and religious sites. They have been vocal on the issue of digging up ancient Hawaiian burial sites. In the 1980s, they were successful in forcing the builders of the Ritz Carlton Hotel on Maui to move the resort inland, away from a sacred spot containing hundreds of antique skeletons. Periodically battles erupt among archaeologists, developers, and Hawaiians. They argue over whether the knowledge gained from dating and studying the bones or the economic surge that comes from building yet another hotel or shopping mall should outweigh the rights of present-day Hawaiians to respect their ancestors the way they see fit.

Some Hawaiians are succeeding very well in business, politics, and other areas today. Established in Honolulu for children of Hawaiian descent, the Kamehameha schools are a renowned academy. In 1986, John D. Waihee III became the state's first Hawaiian governor. However, too many Hawaiians are still struggling to gain a foothold, some even giving in to hopelessness or apathy. A disproportionate number of inmates in state and county jails are of Hawaiian descent. A large segment of the Hawaiian community receives state or federal welfare. Many young people drop out of school or become teenage and/or unmarried parents.

To help combat these problems, the Office of Hawaiian Affairs works with service organizations in the areas of health, economic development, education, legal services, and the promotion of an understanding of indigenous culture. Thanks to Prince Kuhio, the 1919 Hawaiian Homes Act set aside thousands of acres of land for farms and home lots for people who are at least half Hawaiian. Unfortunately, as well intentioned as this Congressional act was, most of the land is of poor quality. The cost of developing it has sometimes been astronomical, sending many Hawaiian families deeply into debt. Even so, the waiting list is decades long for these $1 a year, 99-year leases.

The Caucasians

No, haole ("how-lee") is not in itself a derogatory term (although it can be used as such). Most Caucasians in Hawaii refer to themselves that way. The word haole simply means foreigner, but has come to be synonymous with white people and/or mainlanders.

British Captain James Cook was the first known Westerner to arrive in Hawaii, in 1778. Many kamaaina ("kah-mah-eye-nah" - longtime Island resident) haoles are descendants of the New England missionaries who began showing up in 1820. These religious enthusiasts are credited with introducing Hawaiians to Bibles, muumuus, and quilts and with transforming the Islands into a literate society, among other achievements. They turned Hawaiian into a written language and taught the native population to read it. Descendants of missionaries moved on to agriculture and many were highly successful planters whose wealth became the foundation of present-day Hawaii. The Big Five, a powerful group of businesses, has its roots in missionary families.

Often called "Portagee" or "guavas" by locals, a few hundred **Portuguese** had settled in Hawaii before the arrival of Americans. They had reached these shores on whalers as sailors who had decided to jump ship.

But it wasn't until 1878, during the reign of King Kalakaua, that people from Portugal's Azores and Madeira islands began coming in large numbers. Unlike Asian immigrants, who had to start at the bottom, many Portuguese men found jobs as plantation *lunas* (foremen). Once out of the sugarcane and pineapple fields, some climbed the socio-economic ladder to high-level government or clerical positions.

The Portuguese are best known today for their sausage, red bean soup, *malasadas* (doughnuts without the holes), and the guitarlike instrument that came to be called the *ukulele*. Held in Hawaii during the spring, the **Seven Domingas** are weekly religious festivals and feasts that date back to 13th century Portugal.

The Chinese

The first known Chinese to set foot in Hawaii came as crew members on two ships sailing from South China and western Canada in 1789. But they didn't stay. In the 1790s, foreign traders started buying aromatic **sandalwood** from Hawaiian chiefs to be sold in China. The Chinese used this prized wood to make elaborate carvings and incense. The traders became wealthy and within four decades Hawaii's sandalwood forests had been completely denuded.

Groups of Chinese immigrants were first brought to Hawaii in 1852. They intermarried with Hawaiians and people of other races more readily than most other ethnic groups did. Many converted to Christianity. At the end of their terms, Chinese contract laborers, free at last, could not leave the plantations fast enough. Japanese immigrants had to be brought in to pick up the slack.

Contrary to popular belief, however, not all Chinese came as plantation laborers. Hundreds also migrated to these islands to work in restaurants and other businesses owned by relatives and friends or to serve as domestics for wealthy *haoles*. Many settled in Honolulu, creating the Chinatown that exists today.

Hawaii had a great deal to do with the early shaping of present-day China. In the late 19th century, **Sun Yat-sen** became one of the best-known members of Hawaii's Chinese community. He did so well at the school he attended in Honolulu from 1879 to 1883 that King David Kalakaua honored him for his accomplishments in English. After attending medical school in China, he returned to Hawaii where he formed a political organization that would eventually lead to the overthrow of China's Manchu Regime. In 1912, Sun Yat-sen became the first provisional president of the new Republic of China.

No matter how successful they became, Chinese residents of Hawaii had to contend with many obstacles, such as the Chinese Exclusion Acts of 1882-1884 that prevented them from becoming citizens of the US. In

1892, another act was passed (and not repealed by Congress until 1943), this time to restrict Chinese immigration. Then the US-controlled provisional government proposed prohibitions on any expansion or increase in Chinese businesses. The great number and prosperity of Chinese restaurants and stores threatened the economic monopoly that *haoles* wished to maintain in Hawaii.

In vain, the Chinese protested by the thousands, complaining that the government was all too happy to collect taxes from them, but when it came to treating them as the law-abiding, industrious people they were, that seemed to be another matter.

Today few travelers visit Honolulu without strolling through the picturesque streets of **Chinatown**. Celebrated here in full force with lion dances, long dragon costumes, and fireworks, the **Chinese New Year** is a major event on Oahu. The Chinese community also observes Buddhist, Confucian, and Taoist holidays.

Among the best known Hawaiian residents of Chinese descent are Republican Hiram L. Fong, the first Asian-American to be elected to the US Senate, in 1959; and nightclub entertainer Don Ho. When many people think of the Islands, Earl Derr Biggers' stereotypic Charlie Chan mysteries come to mind. These stories were based on the well-known Hawaiian-Chinese detective **Chang Apana**, who left the Honolulu Police Department in the 1930s.

The Japanese

From the ashes of indentured labor, racial discrimination, Pearl Harbor, and World War II internment camps, Japanese-Americans have risen to become probably the most politically and economically powerful ethnic group in Hawaii. They first came to Hawaii in significant numbers in 1868, followed by a second wave of immigration under King David Kalakaua in the 1880s. The king hoped that the Japanese would inter-marry with Hawaiians, creating a new "race" that would repopulate the Islands. When the first group stepped ashore in 1885, they were over-whelmed by masses of Hawaiians who welcomed them with gifts of fish, *poi*, and vegetables. By the time the Hawaiian Kingdom drew to a close in 1895, nearly 30,000 Japanese had migrated to Hawaii.

Unfortunately, however, Kalakaua's plan was a flop. The Japanese tended to stick to themselves. Not only did they rarely marry Hawaiians, or members of other ethnic groups, they failed to embrace Christianity, instead holding fast to their Buddhist beliefs. They set up Japanese Language Schools to teach their children how to become proper citizens of Japan and started Japanese-language newspapers.

During the 1880s, Japanese plantation workers began protesting the harsh conditions under which they toiled. Their marches, strikes, and walkouts inspired other ethnic groups to follow suit. During World War II, Japanese-Americans who attempted to prove their patriotism by volunteering for the army were rejected at first. Ever persistent, they kept trying to join the war effort. When they finally did, the 442nd Regiment and the 100th Battalion (made up of *nisei*, American-born children of Japanese immigrants) became the war's most successful and highly honored American military combat unit. **Daniel K. Inouye** (pronounced "in-*no*-way"), a veteran of the 442nd, led a labor movement that resulted in the demise of Hawaii's traditional Republican political control. In 1954, the labor-backed Democrats took over the territorial legislature. Inouye went on to become the first Japanese-American congressman, and later a US senator who gained national prominence as a member of the Senate Watergate Committee in the 1970s. In the 1980s, he served as chair of the Iran-Contra hearings.

Today, eating *soba* (buckwheat noodles) and *mochi* (stuffed rice dough) for good luck on New Year's Eve and removing shoes before entering homes are Japanese traditions shared by many non-Japanese residents of Hawaii. The springtime **Cherry Blossom Festival** is another way Hawaii honors Japanese culture.

The Koreans

Koreans, many of whom intermarried with people from other backgrounds, have succeeded in reaching a very high educational and economic level in Hawaii. There is a higher proportion of professionals among Koreans than in any other ethnic group. This is quite an accomplishment, considering their early years in the islands.

The sugar plantation laborers who began arriving in 1903 came without wives or girlfriends. In later years, the Korean men began sending for "picture brides" from home. Some Korean women worked as waitresses in a few of Honolulu's earliest and most popular "hostess bars," which were owned by Korean businessmen. Today, the term "Korean bar" is used to refer to any of the sex clubs scattered throughout Honolulu and parts of other islands, even though the owners and hostesses are now of many different races and nationalities.

Kim chee, vegetables pickled with garlic and chili peppers, is probably Korea's best-known culinary contribution in Hawaii.

The Filipinos

As field laborers began standing up for their rights, plantation owners decided to bring in Filipinos. Many were illiterate, and owners believed (in some cases, rightly so) that education meant activism. Filipinos, eager to get away from US colonial rule in their own country, fled to Hawaii. Those who were educated pretended that they couldn't tread or write and that they were too stupid to even consider joining a union. Plantation owners fell for it, and recruited thousands of workers from the Philippines, beginning in 1906. Much to their bosses' surprise, Filipinos pulled together some of Hawaii's earliest labor unions.

The first Filipinos to live in Hawaii arrived in 1888. They were musicians and acrobats who were members of an entertainment troupe on their way to San Francisco after performing in Japan and China. Four of the men who stayed ended up joining King Kalakaua's **Royal Hawaiian Band.**

In June, **Fiesta Filipina** erupts on Oahu and other islands. Though illegal, cockfighting matches (begun by Filipino plantation workers) draw smokey crowds. Men often bring their wives and children, making a family outing of this bloody sport. Heavy-duty betting is part of the action. On quiet country roads, you might see front yards studded with the raised, open-air, triangular shelters where fighting cocks reside.

In 1994, **Ben Cayetano**, a Democrat, became Hawaii's first governor of Filipino ancestry.

The Samoans

Hawaii's newest Pacific immigrants are Samoans, mostly from American Samoa. Many of them first arrived in 1952, the year after the control of their islands changed from the US Navy to the US Department of the Interior. Samoan men are renowned for their accomplishments in sports. Some have drawn national attention as football players. Many have also excelled in soccer, rugby, and cricket. Samoan parties and political meetings often feature traditional sarongs, chants, dances, songs, and the drinking of potent *kava* juice, made from the kava root. Many Samoans have settled in the Mormon community of Laie on Oahu, where the Polynesian Cultural Center is located.

The African-Americans

Although they may not know it, some residents, even those whose families have lived in Hawaii for generations, could include "African" when rattling off their multi-ethnic ancestry. In fact, some historians believe that ancient Hawaiians were the descendants of mariners from Asia and East Africa. While this theory is controversial, it certainly would explain why the dark brown-skinned, full-featured, pure Hawaiians in early drawings and photographs bear such a strong resemblance to African-Americans, except for their straight hair.

One of the first known foreigners in the Islands was **Black Jack**, a man of African ancestry who was living on Oahu when Kamehameha the Great seized control of the island in 1796. Black Jack helped build a stone house for Kaahumanu, Kamehameha's favorite and feisty wife, on Maui. **An-**

thony **Allen**, who arrived in 1810, is one of the best known of the 18th and 19th century African-American settlers who worked as seamen, traders, tailors, blacksmiths, merchants, farmers, and ranchers. Formerly enslaved in New York, Allen became a prosperous businessman and married a Hawaiian woman, with whom he had three children. He ran a boarding house and a popular tavern in Honolulu, where he built the first bowling alley on the island.

Only some three dozen others of African descent lived in Hawaii during Allen's years there, most of them men. When **Betsey Stockton** stopped by his store one day to buy milk, it was the first time he had seen a "colored female" in his two decades in the Islands. Freed from slavery, Stockton had come to Hawaii with an American missionary family. In 1823, she founded Hawaii's first school for commoners on Maui, so that people other than the *alii* could be educated.

Other black people escaping American slavery and racism migrated to Hawaii during the 1800s. African-Americans from Tennessee were later brought to labor on plantations. Merchants and civil servants followed to work at Pearl Harbor. Then came military men and women. Many bristled at the racism they faced from residents of Hawaii during World War II and were thrilled to go home. Others remained after the war, and some of those who were light-skinned enough "forgot" they were African-American. They married people of other ethnic groups and, passing for "Portuguese" or "part Hawaiian," they never divulged their true background to their children.

Many of the newest black residents are corporate workers relocated by their mainland-based companies, and, most recently, upper-middle-class entrepreneurs, who mirror their 18th and 19th century immigrant predecessors. Today most black people live on Oahu. The majority are business owners, other professionals, or in the military. Honolulu's Trinity Missionary Baptist Church has a predominantly black congregation. The Afro-American Association of Hawai'i, in Honolulu, is a social and political action organization that was instrumental in passing the bill that made Martin Luther King Jr.'s birthday an official holiday in 1988. (Trading Columbus Day for King Day, residents of Hawaii decided, "Columbus didn't discover us.")

It is heartening to see Asians, Caucasians, Hawaiians, and African-Americans marching down Kalakaua Avenue, Waikiki's main thoroughfare, during the King Day Parade.

Others in the Melting Pot

At the turn of the century, large numbers of **Puerto Ricans** (people of American Indian, Spanish, and African descent) came to Hawaii from the Caribbean. A Puerto Rican civic group periodically holds salsa dances in Honolulu, but for the most part, these Latinos have been absorbed into the broader Hawaiian culture.

Mexican cowboys went to the Big Island in the 1830s to teach Hawaiians about cattle ranching. The Hawaiian pronunciation of the word *Español* (Spanish for Spanish) resulted in *paniolo*, the term still used for "Hawaiian cowboy" today. Other groups of immigrants brought to work on Hawaiian plantations were Germans, Norwegians, Russians, and Spaniards.

ARTS & CULTURE

In the old days, the Hawaiian Islands themselves served as both a canvas for artistic expression and a playground for happy abandon. Stick-figure drawings were carved into the petrified lava flows that still blanket vast areas. Many of these **petroglyph** fields remain today, especially on the Big Island of Hawaii. Trees were whittled into totem poll-like **tiki**. The breasts of brightly plumed birds were plucked clean so that their feathers could be used to decorate cloaks and helmets worn by the *alii* (chiefs or aristocracy). Bowls and water containers made from gourds were often etched or painted with elaborate designs.

In the high art of **lauhala**, pandanus leaves were woven into baskets, and sleeping mats. Roots, vines, and other fronds used for weaving were frequently dyed black, red, and white to create intricate patterns when braided. Especially among the *alii*, **surfing** was a favorite sport. People also amused themselves with foot and canoe races, wrestling matches, sliding down hillsides on sleds, and many other games. Singing, dancing the hula, and strumming the **ukeke** (a Hawaiian stringed instrument not to be confused with the ukulele, a Portuguese import) were also popular pastimes.

When American missionaries began arriving in 1820, they swiftly put an end to all this frivolity. As far as they seemed to be concerned, Hawaiians were simply having too much fun. Where once there had been pride and enjoyment, the missionaries instilled guilt and a sense of shame for the scanty way Hawaiians dressed, their sexual freedom, their sensual dances, and their music (which sounded atonal to Western ears).

After decades of suppression by missionaries, the arts were briefly brought back to life in the late 1800s by King David Kalakaua, who earned himself the nickname "The Merrie Monarch" in the process. Then the overthrow of the monarchy and US annexation of the Islands sent this side of Hawaiian culture back underground. It was not until the 1970s that Hawaiian arts began to experience the renaissance that is still apparent today.

Some say that this renewed pride in things Hawaiian was sparked by the 1974 voyage of the *Hokulea*, a 60-foot reconstruction of an ancient

Polynesian sailing canoe. With several voyages back and forth to Tahiti and throughout the Pacific, this vessel proved once and for all that the stories told in ancient Hawaiian chants and dances had been historically correct: The ancient Hawaiians had indeed been master mariners who had set out for and arrived at the Hawaiian Islands on purpose, not by accident.

Ancient traditions that had been forbidden by the missionaries were once again embraced. Today, many hotels give free classes in *lei*-making, *lauhala* weaving, and *hula* dancing. Some hotels, especially those along the Kona-Kohala Coast on the Big Island, are virtual museums, packed with Hawaiian and other Pacific art and artifacts. A few Big Island hotels conduct tours of their art collections or petroglyph fields.

Bark Cloth, a.k.a. Kapa

Ancient Hawaiians created cloth, called *kapa* (or *tapa*), by pounding water-soaked bark. Unfortunately, few records remain of the specifics of this intricate, time-consuming process, so present-day artist have taught themselves by trial and error. *Kapa*-making seminars (sponsored by the Bishop Museum, the Honolulu Academy of Arts, Hawaiian civic groups, the University of Hawaii, and other institutions) are periodically conducted throughout the state.

For the most part, what is sold in Hawaii today (such as that at Oahu's Polynesian Cultural Center) is the kind of bark cloth called *tapa* that is still produced in Fiji and other Pacific Islands. (It makes gorgeous wall hangings, by the way.) Unlike bark cloth from elsewhere, Hawaiian *kapa* is often imprinted with a watermark design (the kind you see when you hold a sheet of bond paper up to the light).

In the old days, *kapa* was decorated with a wide variety of patterns and colors, from black, brown, and red to lavender, blue, and yellow. Men wore *kapa malo* (loin cloths) and women dressed in *kapa pa'u* (long skirts). Capes were used by both sexes, and sandals, blankets, house partitions, even wicks for stone lamps were also made from *kapa*.

Beating out a length of the cloth could take anywhere from several hours to a full day. Women were responsible for creating this cloth, no simple feat. First they had to soak the bark of mulberry trees in the sea for a week. Then they pounded it and soaked it for another seven days. After beating it again until it was thin enough, and allowing it to be dried and bleached by the sun, they painted or stamped designs onto it using woodcuts, ferns, or bamboo to apply dyes made from fruit, roots, leaves, or minerals. As if this weren't enough, they often scented the *kapa* by blending fragrances into the dyes.

Having the right anvil for pounding the *kapa* was very important. Women often judged the quality of their implements by the sound they made when struck, since different wood made different music. Women living a distance apart in the same village would sometimes communicate with each other through their percussive thumping.

Beginning in the late 18th century, when Westerners introduced Hawaiians to their own more durable woven fabric, the painstaking production of delicate *kapa* eventually came to an end.

DIVINE CLOTH

When ancient Hawaiians looked up into the sky and saw fluffy clouds, they knew that what they were really seeing was kapa spread out to dry by the goddess Hina, a renowned kapa maker. To hold the cloth down, she put large stones at the corners. When Hawaiians heard thunder, they were convinced that the weighty stones were being blown away by strong winds. When they saw lightning, they understood that Hina was rolling up her kapa and sunlight was glinting off the moving cloth.

Feathers, Quilts, & Whale Bone

Featherwork was another prized art in old Hawaii. Deep in the forests, birds were caught with poles or nets smeared with a gluelike paste. While their breast feathers may have been snatched off, the birds were not necessarily killed. Their brilliantly colored plumes, sewn so close together that they looked and felt like smooth velvet, were fashioned into royal leis, capes, and helmets. Helmets were often topped off with clumps of human hair from unfortunate enemies.

If ancient Hawaiians wanted to know what they looked like in all their feathered finery, they simply gazed into a mirror. They found their reflections in the smooth, flat slabs of lava rock they put in water or shined with oil. Combs carved from tortoise shell or bone were worn as decoration in women's hair. Necklaces were set off with pendants of whale's teeth, kukui nuts, shells, or wood strung on human hair. Bracelets were often made from the tusks of boars. During dance performances or other entertainment, some men wore necklaces and anklets made from row upon row of dogs' teeth.

With the demise of *kapa*, **quilts**, introduced by missionary women, began to replace Hawaiian blankets. These New England women stitched pieces of cloth together in geometric patterns. But since woven cloth was new in Hawaii and scraps were scarce, whole lengths of material were used instead. Known as *puiki* in Hawaiian, Island quilts developed their own distinctive style.

Remember those snowflakes you used to cut from folded paper as a child? Well, similar cutout patterns form the basis of designs for Hawaiian quilts. Nature is strongly reflected in Island patterns. Some say that the first Hawaiian-style quilt was inspired when a woman saw the shadow of the branches of a tree splashed across a sheet she had laid out to bleach in the sun. Hawaiian quilts are generally two colors: a bold, bright fabric appliqued onto a white background. Designs suggesting birds, fruit, flowers, and trees are common.

Considered real treasures, these comforters are very expensive today, whether new or antique. Since stitches are so intricate, they can take anywhere from several months to two years to produce. Finishing a quilt is such a major accomplishment that, in the old days, everyone honored the occasion by drinking *koele palau* (sweet potato wine) for a week. If you can't afford the few thousand dollars it could cost you to commission a quilt of your own, at least take a look at those on display in museums, hotels, and other public buildings.

Nineteenth-century whalers also made a major contribution to art in Hawaii, in the form of **scrimshaw**. Now Maui is one of the best places in the world to buy these bones, teeth, and tusks etched with nautical and other designs. The centuries-old Japanese art of **raku pottery** is another foreign form of creative expression that has found a place in Hawaii. Red-hot ceramics are removed from the kiln and put in a covered container filled with straw, dried leaves, paper, and other flammable materials that create irregular patterns on the surface of the pottery when they suddenly catch fire. This pottery is characterized by its cracked glaze, darkened non-glazed areas, and textured, matte finish. You can learn about this process at the **Hui Noeau**, an art institute in upcountry Maui.

Hula

With the beating of *ipu* drums in ancient evenings, everyone knew it was time for hula dances to begin. Surprisingly enough, hula was first performed exclusively by men. It was part of a religious ritual and was considered outside the realm of proper female activity. Much of Hawaii's history was passed on through the hand and hip movements of the meaning-laden dances and through the accompanying chants. Known as *kahiko* (kah-*hee*-ko), this often war-like old form of hula was serious business. If dancers lost their concentration and changed a single step or motion, there could be dreadful consequences, since in doing so they would be altering history. *Kahiko* is always accompanied by drums and chanting. In the more fanciful dances, performers would tell humorous tales of the soap opera love lives of the *alii*.

Modern hula, now danced almost exclusively by women, tends to be more graceful and sensual than the ancient style of dance. Called *auana* ("ow-*uah*-nah"), this newer version is accompanied by stringed instruments and songs. Smiling a lot (since they no longer have to worry about scrambling historical events by improvising a step), the dancers wear more revealing or form-fitting clothing. The bright green ti-leaf skirts worn by some dancers are authentically Hawaiian (if not somewhat skimpier than in the past), but the grass skirts you'll also see actually originated elsewhere in the Pacific.

Music

Whether or not people have visited Hawaii, most are familiar with its trademark (if sometimes sentimental) music. From 1935, when it was first broadcast from the Moana Hotel in Waikiki, until the 1970s, the popular "Hawaii Calls" radio program introduced many mainlanders to these Pacific sounds.

Contemporary Island music has been influenced by everything from ancient Hawaiian chants, Christian hymns, and European classical pieces to Portuguese ukuleles and Mexican cowboys playing Spanish guitars. **Ukulele**, by the way, is a Hawaiian word meaning "jumping flea." Hawaiians thought the fast-moving hands of Portuguese immigrants on this four-stringed instrument looked like they were busy scratching fleas. This is not to be confused with the three-stringed **ukeke**, a Hawaiian instrument that was around before Europeans arrived. Other early instruments were the shell trumpet, the nose flute, and gourd and ti leaf whistles.

Aloha Oe, probably the best-known Hawaiian melody, was written as a love song in 1878 by Liliuokalani, Hawaii's last queen. Also during the 1870s, King Kamehameha V hired a German composer to teach music to the royal family. The king wrote the words to *Hawaii Pono'i* (set to music by this composer), once Hawaii's national anthem and now the state song.

Its dulcet tones long associated with Hawaii, the **steel guitar** (*kila kila*) was developed by 15-year-old Joseph Kekuku in 1889. Also called a slack key guitar, it is played by sliding a steel bar against its loosened steel strings. With the renaissance of Hawaiian music in the 1970s, slack key guitar playing was revived. However, it remains music with a very local appeal. It is generally played at family gatherings or while sitting around "talking story" (shooting the breeze) with friends.

Fun & Games

The best-known and most popular ancient sport, **surfing** was once called "the sport of kings." This was because certain beaches and kinds of boards could only be used by the *alii*. Boards were once cut from koa or breadfruit trees, then lovingly carved, stained, and preserved with a rubbing down of glistening kukui oil. After missionaries succeeded in suppressing surfing, they were aghast that it was done in such scanty clothing, and sometimes even naked, the sport made its comeback in the early 1900's. Travelers from all over would come to learn at the expert hands of the "beachboys" who helped make Waikiki famous.

Canoes were often used for races, sometimes involving bets that caused the defeated to lose land or even wives. **Konane**, similar to checkers, was played with black and white stones. Children amused themselves by flying kites made from *kapa* or pandanus leaves, walking on stilts, swinging from vines, or throwing square balls made from woven pandanus leaves.

During the annual **Makahiki Festival**, bellicose pursuits were pushed aside in favor of pleasant diversions. This season of peace, lasting from October to February, was celebrated with wild feasting and heavy-duty competitions in games. Today, travelers can take part in annual revivals of this ancient event at Waimea Falls Park on Oahu in October or at the very local, very popular Makahiki Festival on Molokai in January. The games include *uhu maika* (lawn bowling), *'o'o ihe* (spear hurling), *kukini* (foot races), *pohaku ho'oikaika* (throwing a weighty rock or shotputting), *hukihuki* (tug of war), *uma* (handwrestling), *haka moa* (arm wrestling in a circle while standing on one leg), and *moa pahe'e* (sliding a wooden dart across the grass through two sticks).

Hawaiians didn't need snow to go **sledding** (although they could certainly find the white stuff at the summit of Mauna Kea on the Big Island). Children slid down hillsides on clusters of ti leaves. Adults played *holua*, the highlight of the Makahiki Festival. Competitors lay on narrow wooden sleds, called *papa*, and whizzed headfirst (sometimes faster than 40 miles an hour) down a runway made from piled, packed lava rocks cushioned with grass and doused with hundreds of gallons of water. You can see a remnant of one of these impressive runways on the Big Island.

THE HAWAIIAN LANGUAGE

Once, as I was passing through a parking lot outside a hotel in Kauai, I overheard a mainlander struggling to extract a piece of information from a tour bus driver. "Is this the bus to Wammy?" she asked. When he replied, "Where?" and she repeated her question, his face remained perplexed. Finally she snapped in indignant annoyance, "Wammy Canyon, I said!" She seemed to think that the driver should have known immediately that what she meant was "Waimea (why-*may*-ah) Canyon."

This woman was like the proverbial Ugly American who visits Italy and raises his voice-in English-when an Italian does not understand him. If she had paid any attention to the spelling of the word and taken a few moments to bone up on the pronunciation of Hawaiian, the woman would have been showing respect and staving off hassles at the same time. A local joke tells of a tourist on his way to a *luau* (feast) who ends up at a *lua* (toilet).

The credit for first putting Hawaiian on paper goes to the New England missionaries, who arrived in the Islands in 1820. As they created an alphabet, their Western ears had a tough time sorting through the language's dozens of different sounds. Unable to hear the distinction between *t* and *k*, or *l* and *r*, or *b* and *p*, for instance, the missionaries whittled the language down to a mere 12 letters. *Honoruru* turned into *Honolulu*; *Ranai* became *Lanai*; *Mauna Roa* was transformed into *Mauna Loa*; and *taboo* into *kapu*.

Although missionaries forever altered the way island tongues would move, Hawaiians learned to read with voracious speed. Within a little more than two decades, they were among the most literate people in the world. Today, one of the few arenas where the legacy of Hawaii's ancient Polynesians lives on in full force is in the state's street signs and place names, the vast majority of which are Hawaiian. Familiarizing yourself with the pronunciation of the language will make it easier for you to ask for directions, get around, and remember where you've been (or even the name of your hotel).

Since it's phonetic, Hawaiian is not nearly as difficult to pronounce as it appears to the uninitiated. It consists of only seven consonants (*h, k, l, m, n, p, w*), five vowels (*a, e, i, o, u*), and no letter is silent. Each syllable ends with a vowel. The accent is usually on the next to last syllable of a word.

Consonants sound just as they do in English, with the exception of *w*. This letter is pronounced like a *v* when it precedes the last vowel of a word (such as *ewa* or *Kahoolawe*). Vowels sound pretty much like those in Spanish: *a* as in *around*; *e* like the *a* in *day* (or sometimes like the *ee* in *bee*); *i* like the *ee* in *see*; *o* as in *so*; and *u* as in *sue*. When two or three vowels are together, they each get their own syllable (unless they are part of a diphthong). The double *o* in *Kahoolawe* sounds like "oh-oh" and the double *a* in *Kapaa* sounds like "ah-ah." The four diphthongs are *au*, pronounced *ow*; *ae* and *ai*, both pronounced like the *y* in *sky*; and *ei*, which rhymes with *hay*.

A mark like an apostrophe was once commonly used in many words to signal a sharp pause between syllables. This punctuation is rarely seen in writing anymore and pronunciations have changed accordingly. To purists, however, Hawaii (Hawai'i) will always be "Hah-*vy*'ee." You'll also hear some people correctly pronounce the names of Neighbor Islands: "cow-*wah*'ee" (Kaua'i), "mole-oh-*kah*'ee" (Moloka'i), and "lah-*nah*'ee" (Lana'i) instead of "cow-*why*," "*mole-oh*-kye," and "lah-*nye*." In this book, I've used this mark only when two letters might otherwise appear to be a diphthong, to indicate the difference between *pau* ("pow"-finished) and *pa'u* ("*pah*-ooo"-a long skirt), for instance.

You'll notice that even though quite a few names are long, in many cases syllables are simply repeated. Take, for example, one of the rainiest places in the world, Mt. Waialeale (why *ah-lay ah-lay*) on Kauai, or the historic valley on the Big Island of Hawaii called *Pohakuhaku* (poh *hah-koo hah-koo*). Wrapping your tongue around *humuhumunukunukuapuaa* (a small trigger fish with a shark-sized name) may appear an impossible feat at first. But if you look closely, you'll see that the trick is to sound redundant: *hoo-moo hoo-moo noo-koo noo-koo ah-poo ah-ah*.

Most residents today will greet you with "aloha" and say "mahalo" instead of "thank you." Knowing other common Hawaiian words can prevent you from going places you shouldn't, such as into a men's room (many of which are marked *kane*) if you're a *wahine* (woman). But when you don't understand what people are saying, the Hawaiian language will rarely be the reason. Among others, Japanese, Korean, Tagalog, Cantonese, and Pidgin, the local dialect, are far more widely spoken. Sometimes referred to as "lazy English," Pidgin is used with a real flourish among young Hawaiians and other locals. Originating with the laborers who came to work on Hawai'i's plantations, it is a colorful blend of Hawaiian, English, Cantonese, Portuguese and a chop suey of other tongues. Its vocabulary and pronunciation can vary from island to island and even region to region.

When Hawaiian residents speak English, their accent tends to be singsongy, elevating in pitch at the end of a sentence. Someone who answers your telephone call might ask you to "Hold on, yeh?" A person who gives you directions might end with, "Simple, yeh?" Be sure to spend some time "talking story" (chatting or gossiping) with locals.

Not all communication in Hawaii is either oral or written. When someone raises his palm with the three middle fingers down and the thumb and pinky extended and gives it a couple of quick shakes, this is a greeting or a good natured signal to "hang loose" ("relax" or "cool out").

Common Hawaiian & Pidgin Words & Expressions

aa (*ah-ah*): the rough kind of lava

ae (eye): yes

ahi (*ah*-hee): yellowfin tuna; or sometimes albacore or big-eye tuna

aikane (*eye-kah-nay*): friend

alii (ah-*lee-eee*): Hawaiian chief, royalty, person or people of high rank

aloha (ah-*low*-hah): welcome, hello, good-bye, love, friendship . . .

aole (ah-*oh*-lay): no

brah (bra) **bro'** (brother): friend

cockaroach: to steal something or take something in an underhanded manner

da kine (dah kyne): thingamajig; whatchamacallit

diamondhead: east toward Diamond Head on Oahu

ewa (*ay*-va-as in Eva Gabor): west toward Oahu's Ewa Plantation

hale (*hah*-lay): house

haole (*how*-lee): Caucasian, mainlander, foreigner

hapa (*hah*-pah): half

hapa-haole (*hah*-pah *how*-lee): part Caucasian and part Hawaiian; not authentically Hawaiian

hauoli la hanau (how-*oh*-lee lah hah-*now*): Happy Birthday

hauoli makahiki hou (how-*oh*-lee mah-kah-*hee*-key ho-oo): Happy New Year

heiau (*hey*-ee-ow): ancient Hawaiian temples

holo holo (*hoe*-low *hoe*-low): to cruise, bar hop, go from place to place, visit

hono (*hoe*-no): bay

hoolaulea (ho-oh-lau-*lay*-ah): gathering, celebration, street party

Howzit?: How goes it? What's happening?

hula (*who*-lah): traditional Hawaiian dance

imu (*ee*-moo): underground oven still used in luaus

kahuna (kah-*who*-nah): Hawaiian priest

kai (kye): ocean

kamaaina (kah-mah-*eye*-nah): longtime resident

kane (*kah*-nay): man

kapu (kah-*poo*): taboo, forbidden, off-limits, keep out

kau kau (cow cow): food

keiki (*kay*-kee): child

kiawe (key-*ah*-vay): mesquite tree or wood

koa (*ko*-ah): an increasingly scarce tree prized for its wood

kokua (ko-*koo*-ah): help

lanai (lah-*nye*): terrace, balcony, patio, porch

lauhala (lau-*hah*-lah): pandanus leaves (used for weaving)

lei (lay): long necklace made of flowers; garland

li' dat (lie dat): like that

li' dis (lie dis): like this

lilikoi (*leel*-lee-koi): passion fruit

lua (*loo*-ah): toilet

luau (*loo*-ow): feast, celebration

mahalo (mah-*hah*-low): thank you

mahi mahi (*mah*-hee *mah*-hee): dolphin fish (not the mammal)

makai (mah-*kye*): in the direction of the sea

malihini (*mah*-lee-*hee*-nee): visitor, newcomer

malo (*mah*-low): loincloth once worn by Hawaiian men

mauka (*mow*-kah): toward the mountains, inland

mauna (*mow*-nah): mountain

mele kalikimaka (*may*-lay keh-*lee*-key-*mah*-kah): Merry Christmas

muumuu (*moo*-moo or *moo*-oo-moo-oo): roomy, full-length dress

ohana (oh-*hah*-nah): clan, family

okole (oh-*ko*-lay): buttocks

onago (oh-*nah*-go): snapper

ono (*oh*-no): a fish similar to mackerel; also means that something tastes delicious

opakapaka (oh-*pah*-kah-*pah*-kah): pink snapper

pahoehoe (pah-*hoy*-hoy): smooth or ropy lava

pakalolo (pah-kah-*low*-low): marijuana

pali (*pah*-lee): cliff

paniolo (pah-nee-*oh*-low): cowboy in Hawaii

pau (pow): finished

pau hana time (pow *hah*-nah time): quitting time; when the work day is over

pa'u (*pah*-oo): a long skirt once worn by Hawaiian women

poi (poy): gooey, porridge-like food made from cooked and pounded taro root

puka (*poo*-kah): hole

pupu (*poo*-poo): hors d'oeuvres

shaka! (*shah*-kah): All right! Great! Excellent!

suck 'em up: go drinking

talk story: chew the fat, chat, gossip

tutu or **tutu wahine** (too-too wah-*hee*-nee): grandmother

ukulele (oo-koo-*lay*-lay): small, guitar-like instrument with four strings; literally "leaping flea"

wahine (wah-*hee*-nee): woman

wikiwiki (*wee*-kee-*wee*-kee): fast, quick

5. A SHORT HISTORY

STRANGERS IN A STRANGE LAND (A.D. 300-1778)

Hawaii-loa, the Polynesian sailor who legend says discovered these Pacific islands, gave them his name. The most recent archaeological research indicates that Hawaii's first inhabitants, thought to be from the Marquesas Islands (now part of French Polynesia), probably arrived around A.D. 750 (or as early as A.D. 300, according to some historians). About 3,000 years earlier, their ancestors had begun making their way west from Asia, traveling through Indonesia and other groups of islands. Following the stars, watching the paths of migrating birds, and interpreting the wind and the ocean currents, these early Polynesians were master navigators.

Landing first at **Ka Lae** on the Big Island (now the southernmost tip of the US), they traveled the 2,500 miles in double-hulled canoes connected by wide platforms on which they built shelters. Carrying whole families along with dogs, pigs, and fowl, some of these masted vessels were nearly 100 feet long. They also brought plants that would become staples in Hawaii, among them taro, breadfruit, yams, sugar cane, coconuts, and bananas. Around the year 1300, the first settlers were joined by Tahitians, most likely from the island of Raiatea (whose ancient name was Haiviki). Historians still puzzle over why, after sailing back and forth from Hawaii to Tahiti and its neighbor Raiatea for more than a century, these early settlers abruptly stopped leaving Hawaii somewhere in the 1500s.

In addition to plants and animals, the cargo transported by these hardy travelers included the intangible forces that were the glue of their lives. They not only brought *aloha,* but they also imported *mana,* the spiritual power that could give people unparalleled strength, skill, or courage. *Mana,* said to be found in varying degrees in human beings as well as in objects and in the land, was passed down from the gods. Contact between two people who had different amounts of this force could be gravely dangerous for the less powerful person.

To guard against such a situation and, above all, to follow the will of the gods, a system of strict *kapu* (taboos) evolved. Adhering to the *kapu* was considered crucial to the well-being of individuals and of the group. Some of these restrictions were dietary. For instance, women were not allowed to prepare or cook food, nor were they permitted to eat bananas, coconuts, or pork. Men were prohibited from eating dogmeat. Violating these or any other *kapu*, even unknowingly, would result in severe punishment, often swift death. The gods were also appeased with human sacrifices. When a *heiau* (temple) was being built, for instance, members of the enslaved class would be buried at each of the foundation's corners.

The **caste system** that controlled ancient Hawaiian society was extremely rigid. Each island had its own king. The *alii* (ah-*lee*-ee) - aristocracy or chiefs - were next in line, followed by the *kahuna* (high priests) and the *makaainana* (mah-kah-eye-*nah*-nah) or commoners. The *kauwa* were the enslaved people in the lowest class. The more directly a person was believed to be descended from the gods, the higher his or her rank. Marriages between brothers and sisters were celebrated, especially if the amorous siblings were of highborn bloodlines. On the other hand, if a *kauwa* and a member of the *alii* had the misfortune of producing a child, that infant was immediately killed. Polygamy, for both men and women, was also an accepted way of life. It was not uncommon for a couple with several children to give one to a childless couple to care for as their own. After all, since raising children was a group effort in many ways, the biological parents could still be involved in their children's lives.

Each island was divided into pie-slice sections; thus each wedge included inland and waterfront regions. The *alii* owned and governed these segments. For the privilege of farming the land, the *makaainana* paid them taxes, in a semi-feudal setup. Despite the spirit of aloha, ancient Hawaiians seemed to thrive on warfare. Chiefs continually battled each other for land and power.

However, while they may have shed a lot of blood, one thing Hawaiians painstakingly preserved was their environment. Conserving their natural resources, these **early ecologists** were careful not to exploit their plants or animals. They faithfully followed rules restricting the catching of certain kinds of fish during particular seasons. Not only was this balance with nature essential to their physical health, but they believed that it also maintained an important spiritual connection with their ancestors.

Hawaiians approached daily life with an **artistic flourish.** Their basketry and woven sleeping mats were intricately patterned. *Kapa* cloth (made from pounded bark) was not only decorated, but the dye used for the designs was often scented with flowers. Hangers for water containers looked as if they had been crocheted. Capes and helmets worn by chiefs were covered with a velvety layer of closely sewn feathers. When it was time to party, food and music were accompanied by foot races, wrestling matches, spear-hurling contests, surfing and diving competitions, and other games. Children flew kites, threw square balls, swung from vines, and slid down hillsides on a cushion of leaves.

Without a written language, Hawaiians preserved much of their history, as we know it today, in their lyrical legends, soothing songs, expressive hula dances, and detailed oral genealogies.

CAPTAIN COOK & HIS FLOATING ISLANDS (1778-1779)

Since warfare was so common, every year during the winter months, a "cease fire" festival called *makahiki* was held. Honoring the god Lono, this peaceful and sacred season was celebrated with unbridled feasting and dancing, wrestling and boxing matches, and other frivolity. It was at this time of year, in 1778, when British **Captain James Cook** and his men landed in Hawaii. Over the decades, occasional white foreigners had accidentally found their way to these shores, probably including the Spanish explorer Juan Gaetano in the mid-16th century. Thus the term *haole* was already part of the vocabulary.

On the night when Cook's two ships, the *Resolution* and the *Discovery*, reached the coast of Kauai, several Hawaiian men were fishing from their canoes in Waimea Bay. Suddenly, to their amazement, two hulking masses eased out of the darkness. Seeing the flickering lights on board, they decided that these must be floating islands, and they knew just who must be on one of them. The god Lono, whose festival was in full swing, had promised to arrive someday on moving islands. The tall masts must be the islands' bare trees. After all, weren't the sails just like the white *kapa* cloth banners that fluttered from the canoes of the chiefs who honored Lono at this time of year?

The awestruck fishermen rushed ashore to report the news, which washed over the island like a tidal wave. By the time the sun's first rays lightened the sky, the shore was jammed with people eager for a glimpse of Lono and his attendants. Torn between fear and wonder, some went out in their canoes to get a closer look. A priest and a chief even paddled out to the ships to present Lono with a red *kapa* cloth and to perform the sacred welcoming ceremony. Few paid any attention to the skeptics who, having heard stories of white-skinned strangers arriving in the past, said that these were nothing more than *haoles*.

Only one violent incident marred Cook's otherwise harmonious reception. Metal was extremely rare in the islands, found every once in a while in driftwood. A man who tried to take a piece of iron from one of the ships was fatally shot. Hawaiians were used to severe punishment for offending the gods and they had never seen a stick spout fire before. So they were more convinced than ever that this must be Lono himself.

Throngs of women swam out to the ships, scrambling onto the decks to offer their bodies to please Lono and his sacred attendants. In an attempt to prevent the spread of venereal disease from his men to Hawaiians, Cook had given strict orders against sexual relations. But after such a long time at sea, his crew members did not even attempt to resist the eager women. Thus began the decimation of the Hawaiian population.

Until the arrival of Captain Cook, Hawaii had been free from communicable diseases. Hawaiians' immune systems were therefore not equipped to combat them. The spread of gonorrhea and syphilis from Cook's crew to Hawaiian women, and from the women to Hawaiian men, had far-reaching effects. Not only did large segments of the population die from venereal disease, but sterility became a widespread problem, even for future generations. Measles and other Western ailments also began wiping out chunks of the population.

During the few days that Cook and his men spent anchored off Kauai, they traded iron and other popular items for fresh water and food. After leaving gifts of pigs, goats, and seeds for onions, melons, and pumpkins, they sailed away from Hawaii, journeying north, only to return during the following *makahiki* season. This time, when Cook and his crew reached Kealakekua Bay on the Big Island, they were welcomed in even greater numbers. The water around the boats churned with hundreds of people swimming or bobbing in canoes. When Cook came ashore, people gave him the highest respect by falling to the ground and covering their faces until he had passed.

A good-natured cultural exchange took place. Cook and his men were escorted into the mountains and thick forests, where they watched craftsmen making canoes and artisans collecting brightly colored feathers to be fashioned into elaborate cloaks and helmets for chiefs. In turn, the British entertained the islanders with a flute and violin concert and invited Hawaiians to tour the ships and see blacksmiths at work.

In the weeks that followed, Cook and his men began to strain the hospitality of the islanders by demanding large numbers of provisions, including the fence of a *heiau* (a temple) which was to be used for less-than-sacred purposes as firewood. Cook's men seemed to have an insatiable (and ungodlike) appetite for sex. When Hawaiian chief Kalaniopuu put a *kapu* on women visiting the ships, Cook's men simply mobbed the villages.

After virtually exhausting the resources of the Kona district, Cook and his crew finally left the Big Island. Then, to the distress of the residents, they returned a week later. A storm had damaged the ships and they had decided to come back to make repairs. Particularly since they had reappeared once the *makahiki* festival had ended, people began to share their doubts as to whether Cook and his crew were truly divine beings. Thefts of the ships' metal began to occur. Finally, after a longboat was stolen, a livid Cook went ashore with some of his men, determined to take **Chief Kalaniopuu** hostage until the boat was returned.

A scuffle broke out and one of the chief's protectors struck Cook. As the British captain screamed in pain, the Hawaiians realized that if he could be hurt, surely he must not be a god. Showered with more blows, he fell dead in the water at the rocky shore. Despite Cook's unmasking as the mortal he was, his body was given the sacred honors of an *alii* (a chief closely related to the gods), in a ceremony in which his bones were removed. His dismembered remains were turned over to his horrified and uncomprehending crew. They responded by burning a village, decapitating two Hawaiians, and, with the heads displayed on poles at the prows of their longboats, they returned to their ships. Surprisingly enough, by the time the British sailed away from Hawaii several weeks later, tensions had eased.

KAMEHAMEHA THE GREAT (1779-1819)

Kamehameha, the nephew of Chief Kalaniopuu, whom Captain Cook met his end trying to capture, was said to have been a towering six foot, six inches tall. Halley's Comet had marked the year of his birth, 1758, perhaps foreshadowing the unusual man he would become. According to some stories, as a teenager he moved the mammoth Naha Stone in Hilo, on the island of Hawaii. This awesome act not only exhibited superhuman strength but also heralded the fulfillment of the prophecy that the man who could do so would someday unify the Hawaiian Islands.

Cook's "discovery" of the Sandwich Islands, which he christened after his sponsor, the fourth Earl of Sandwich, sparked a great deal of interaction with foreign seamen. Hawaii became a regular port of call for reprovisioning trade ships. The late 18th century brought more British sailors, as well as French and American ships. Others came from China and Spain. Some sailors jumped ship and made new lives for themselves in Hawaii. Wanting to explore the world beyond their islands, some Hawaiians joined the crews of foreign vessels. Rapidly multiplying sheep, goats, cattle, and horses had been introduced. Hawaiians discovered that hooves could get them around faster than feet.

When Cook arrived, Kamehameha was an extremely curious young man in his early 20s. After meeting the British captain, he was invited to spend the night on the *Resolution*, where he became fascinated by the Western weaponry that in later years would play a major role in his consolidation of power. Making sure that foreigners dealt with him as an equal, Kamehameha learned as much as he could about Western technology. Once he became a chief, he began a large collection of muskets, cannons, and swords acquired from traders. To teach him how to use these weapons, he enlisted **John Young**, an Englishman who arrived on an American ship, and Isaac Davis, a Welsh seaman. In exchange, he gave these two *haole* men the status of chiefs. Settling in Hawaii, they acquired lands and married Hawaiian women. John Young's granddaughter, Emma Rooke, would wed Kamehameha IV in 1856.

Trade flourished as Chief Kamehameha exchanged land and export rights to natural resources for foreign-made goods. Unable to resist such a lucrative market, Kamehameha began the sandalwood trade that would eventually nearly deplete Hawaii's forests of their trees. To satisfy the voracious appetite in China for the beautiful wood, the strict adherence to conservation that had sustained Hawaiians for centuries was forgotten. More and more of Kamehameha's subjects were forced into this arduous work, which required their going increasingly deeper into the forests and higher into the mountains.

Legend has it that the demigod Maui tried to pull all the Hawaiian islands together by snaring them with a huge fishhook broken from a tremendous coral reef. When he failed, he decided that it simply couldn't be done. Nevertheless, Kamehameha decided to give it a shot. Using many of the weapons that had so intrigued him on Cook's ship, the ruthless chief had won the rule of Oahu, Maui, Lanai, Molokai, and Hawaii, his island of birth, by 1796. Kauai and Niihau were the only islands that remained beyond his grasp.

With a fleet of more than 600 war canoes, he set out from Oahu to capture Kauai, 90 miles across a treacherous channel. But he was forced to turn back after a vicious storm capsized the boats, killing many of his warriors. A few years later, he prepared to depart once again, this time with a fleet consisting of 800 canoes and 20 Western-style ships. The gods were still not with him. His men were hit with a plague that wiped out nearly half of them. Then finally, in 1810, by promising the chief of Kauai and Niihau nominal power, a tireless Kamehameha finally tricked him into agreeing to place these two islands under his domain.

In 1795, Chief Kamehameha had married high-born **Keopuolani**. Her royal breeding meant he could now father children of the supreme *alii* rank. Unfortunately, only three of his surviving sons lived to maturity. However, both of his surviving sons lived to succeed him on the throne: Prince Liholiho became Kamehameha II and Prince Kauikeaouli, Kamehameha III. For all her high status, Keopuolani was not Kamehameha's favorite wife. His heart belonged to six foot tall, 200 pound, strikingly beautiful **Kaahumanu**. Even though she was never able to bear him any children, he cherished this feisty and independent woman, whom he had married in 1785.

Kaahumanu was alone at her husband's bedside when he died in May of 1819. She claimed that with his last breath, he had named her *kuhina nui*, the person who would run his kingdom and take care of his heir, 20-year-old Liholiho. Although her words filled people with shock and disbelief, no one dared question the veracity of the imposing, intimidating favorite wife of Kamehameha the Great. So that the power that had driven the beloved king would never find its way into the wrong hands, Kamehameha's bones were hidden somewhere near Kailua-Kona on the Big Island.

BREAKING BREAD & TRADITION (1819)

By the time King Kamehameha died, the Hawaiian islands were much more than a stopover for vessels sailing across the Pacific. Choosing to seek their fortunes in this tropical paradise, many foreigners never reboarded their ships. A new community was rapidly growing, including Britons, Scots, Spaniards, French, Portuguese, Italians, European-Americans, and at least one African-American, a freedman from New York.

Alcohol, tobacco, and the sight of boisterous whalers and merchant sailors were now commonplace. These foreigners behaved with far fewer restraints than the *kapu* system allowed Hawaiians. Yet no gods flew down from the heavens to punish these disrespectful *haoles*. Many Hawaiians began to grumble about the choke hold their stifling *kapu* had on their lives.

Kaahumanu counseled Liholiho, who had become **Kamehameha II.** One of society's most vocal critics, she relentlessly prodded the young king to do away with the *kapu* system. Liholiho wavered, unable to turn his back on the ways of his ancestors, yet tempted by the idea of a less constricted life. One day Kaahumanu decided to force the issue by breaking two *kapu* at once: she boldly ate a banana (taboo for women) and she did so in the King's presence (men and women were not allowed to see each other dine). She went unpunished, but still Liholiho could not bring himself to make a decisive move.

Then came the night in late 1819 when Kaahumanu held an extravagant feast. The influences of foreign lands were clearly apparent in the absence of a screen to separate the men's and women's tables, and in the clothes the guests wore. Sitting at the head of the men's table, Liholiho had donned a British naval uniform, while several of the wives and mothers at the women's table were decked out in Chinese silks. On each table, Kaahumanu had placed both men's and women's foods.

Finally, Liholiho stood, walked to the women's table, and took a seat. As if this were not audacious enough, he then proceeded to eat dogmeat, along with other foods that were *kapu* to men. Everyone waited for the world to come to a cataclysmic end. When nothing happened, they decided that the king's symbolic actions must have done away with the supreme power of their gods forever. Most chiefs and commoners were ecstatic, gleefully smashing temple walls and setting fire to once sacred images.

BIBLES & MUUMUUS (1819-1824)

Perhaps the Hawaiian gods remained silent throughout the desecration of their temples because they knew this new-found freedom would be short-lived. Another brand of religious restraint was on its way to Hawaii. The first group of **American missionaries**, who would soon succeed in imposing their own strict code of behavior on Hawaiians, had already departed from Boston aboard the *Thaddeus*. **Henry Obookaiah**, one of the Hawaiians who had traveled overseas, had found his way to New England and had converted to Christianity. In many a sermon, he had requested that American missionaries go to the Sandwich Islands to spread the message that had brought him so much joy and peace of mind. His death from pneumonia had spurred the group of Protestant missionaries, led by the **Reverend Hiram Bingham**, to grant him his wish.

Along with three Hawaiian assistants, who had been in school with Obookaiah in Connecticut, the first company had set out on the six-month voyage to the Pacific. During their many weeks at sea, the 14 Americans diligently studied the Hawaiian language under the tutelage of the Hawaiian mission assistants. In April 1820, the *Thaddeus* finally arrived at Kealakekua Bay on the Big Island, where Captain Cook had met his end in early 1779.

Scandalized by all the bare-breasted women they found, and the practices of premarital sex, polygamy, and incest, the missionaries had their work cut out for them. Clad in long-sleeved dark-colored, scratchy woolens in the tropical heat, they seemed to believe the more uncomfortable they were, the more noble their challenge. First they set about convincing the women to cover up with the ankle-length, free-flowing dresses that would become today's muumuus. Then they began their campaign against such sinful pursuits as flying kites (long a beloved diversion), dancing the hula, and wearing flower leis. Boxing, wrestling, and starting fires on Sundays also had to go, along with the newly adopted vices of drinking alcohol and smoking.

With morals so alien to the people of the islands, the missionaries had no easy time foisting their religion on Hawaiians. However, having just lost their faith in their own gods, the highly spiritual Hawaiians were far more susceptible to the teachings of the missionaries than they might have been otherwise. Just as the break with the *kapu* system had come from the top down, so did the massive conversion of Hawaiians to Western religion.

Once Keopuolani, the mother of the king, was converted, others began following suit. But the greatest number of Hawaiians owed their conversion to the persuasive Kaahumanu, the *kuhina nui*. Before becoming gravely ill in 1823, she could hardly have been less interested in the message of the gospel. Then, as this powerful woman lay in an unaccustomed weakened state, she was cared for by **Sybil Bingham**, the wife of the mission leader. By the time of her miraculous recovery, Kaahumanu had become thoroughly convinced that her restored health was due to nothing other than Mrs. Bingham's prayers. Afterward, this born-again woman dedicated herself to converting as many other Hawaiians as she possibly could.

The American missionaries also prided themselves in presenting Hawaiians with the **first written version of their language.** The alphabet they developed would have been many times longer than its twelve letters if the Westerners had included all of the different sounds Hawaiian contained. But by using one letter to cover more than one sound, they felt they were simplifying the process of learning to read for Hawaiians. Having altered the pronunciation of the language considerably, they printed scores of primers and Bibles. By 1846, Hawaiians would become among the most literate people in the world.

Today, a common saying in Hawaii is, "The missionaries came to do good and they did very well indeed." Actually, for the most part, economic prosperity was reaped not so much by the first missionaries as it was by their descendants, whose wealth, concentrated in sugar plantations, created the famous Big Five family businesses. For the early New Englanders, life was pretty rough.

Just as the missionaries appeared to believe that the righteousness of their task was in direct proportion to their personal discomfort, they seemed to think that the greater the self-loathing of Hawaiians, the more deeply religious and virtuous they could become. Hawaiians were taught they were inferior to white people, that their culture and past were degenerate. Adopting Western religion could make them less inferior, but nothing could ever make them the equals of whites.

The more Protestantism spread through the islands, the more demoralized Hawaiians became. By 1823, epidemics of foreign diseases and widespread sterility resulting from imported venereal disease had taken a huge bite out of the Hawaiian population. It was in these troubled times that Liholiho, Kamehameha II, decided to take a trip to England to meet with King George IV. He planned to ask for advice on better ruling his islands and on improving his control of commerce and other interactions with foreigners in Hawaii. Accompanied by Queen Kamamalu, his sister and the favorite of his five wives, he set out on the seven-month voyage in November 1823. The merchant ship they traveled on carried

$25,000 in gold coins for spending money and a cargo of sperm oil. In 1824, less than two months after arrival, Kamehameha II and the queen both caught measles and died. The king was only 28 years old.

THE OTHER KAMEHAMEHAS (1824-1872)

When Liholiho's brother, Kauikeaouli, became **Kamehameha III** at the age of nine, Kaahumanu remained in power as *kuhina nui* and regent. In the care of Reverend Hiram Bingham, the child received a Christian education. However, although Bingham attempted to instill in him an unquestioning love for Western values, Kamehameha III would grow up to be steadfastly pro-Hawaiian in culture and beliefs. Locking horns with Bingham, the king would not agree to make the Ten Commandments the official law of his land.

Kaahumanu died in 1832 and was succeeded by the king's half sister, **Kinau**, who seemed to share more of Bingham's views than her brother's. In 1833, after an argument, Kamehameha III angrily stripped Kinau of her title. To further spite her, he declared all Western-influenced rules and regulations null and void.

For a brief period, Hawaiians happily reverted to their old customs and pastimes, enjoying a more guilt-free existence. Then in 1835, Kamehameha III had a change of heart and returned Kinau to power. To make sure that he was back in her good graces, he promised to declare her youngest son, Alexander Liholiho, his successor. With Kinau once again at the helm, Bingham's influence crept back in as well.

Together Bingham and Kinau established two exile colonies to keep the people in line. To Kahoolawe, they sent men convicted of theft, adultery, or murder. To Lanai, they banished women found guilty of these crimes. However, they underestimated both the strength and the sex drive of their captives: The men swam the six miles from Kahoolawe to Maui, liberated canoes and food, paddled to Lanai, freed the women, and took them back to Kahoolawe. When Kinau died in 1839, Bingham's political power was buried with her. Deciding there was another way to leave his mark on Hawaii, Bingham built Kawaiahao, the massive stone church that still stands today in Honolulu.

The love affair between Kamehameha III and his sister, Nahi'ena'ena, had the highest approval of traditional Hawaiians. They were thrilled at the meshing of the sacred *mana* of the last two living children of Kamehameha the Great and the high-born Queen Keopuolani. In 1836, Nahi'ena'ena died, at barely 20 years of age, not long after giving birth to a still-born baby. Even though both she and her brother had other lovers by this time, many people believed that the infant was his. A grief-stricken Kamehameha III moved the kingdom's capital from Honolulu to Lahaina, Maui, so that he could be close to the mausoleum of his beloved sister.

During the 1840s, the mortality rate among Hawaiians rose sharply, due only in part to foreign diseases. Hundreds of people weakened and wasted away, stricken with severe depression after having been told for so long by white people that their brown skin and their culture made them inferior human beings. A common saying at the time described the emotional malaise: "*Na kanaka okuu wale aku no i kau uhane*" ("The people simply dismissed their souls and died").

This decade was also a period when the independence of the Hawaiian kingdom was being threatened. France, a Catholic country, was convinced that its trade options in exporting wine and brandy were being limited. Liquor was not looked upon very kindly in these Protestant-controlled islands. France grumbled that it would annex Hawaii if trade conditions did not improve.

However, it was Britain, not France, that took over Hawaii for a few tense months in 1843. The British government charged that the property rights of Britons in Hawaii were not being honored. Kamehameha III regained power during a period when the whaling trade was about to peak, then slowly decline. It would finally fizzle out completely with the discovery of oil in the United States in 1859.

Maintaining autonomy for his kingdom was extremely important to Kamehameha III, so he attempted to surround himself with influential people he believed had Hawaii's best interests at heart. But it was the Scottish man who became his minister of foreign affairs, **Robert Crichton Wyllie**, who helped clear the way for the eventual downfall of the monarchy. Wyllie convinced the king to officially give all the rights native-born Hawaiians had to all foreigners who decided to reside in Hawaii. This meant that these "honorary Hawaiians" could serve in the highest governmental posts. When the king convened the first legislature in Honolulu in 1845, he had filled four out of five cabinet posts with foreigners, much to the displeasure of many Hawaiians.

As Hawaii's economy changed, Kamehameha III felt the need for foreign advisers. Land that had once been used for subsistence farming, during the heyday of the kingdom's semifeudal period, now sprouted crops for export. With the **Great Mahele of 1848**, a major reform ordered by King Kamehameha III, land once owned exclusively by chiefs and worked by commoners was turned into real estate to be bought and sold. The increase in export farming and the decrease in the Hawaiian population meant that **foreign labor** had to be recruited.

The first groups of indentured laborers arrived in Hawaii from China in 1852 and 1853. While most **Chinese** came to work on **sugar plantations**, some were brought to serve as domestics for wealthy *haole* families. In a sense, this move signaled a return to the semifeudalism of the past. It was also the beginning of the major change in Hawaii's population that would alter the racial makeup of the islands forever.

The kingdom's economy, government, and religious leanings were pulled in various directions by the often conflicting interests of foreign powers. Although the Protestants in Hawaii tried to prevent them from doing so, Catholics and Mormons established missions in the islands. When Kamehameha III died in 1854, he was content that the joint treaty that had just been signed by France, Britain, and the United States would continue to insure Hawaii's independence. But as the deceased monarch's nephew, Alexander Liholiho, became **Kamehameha IV**, the possibility of annexation by the US to secure American interests remained in the air.

Kamehameha IV had already had a first-hand taste of American hypocrisy and was adamantly opposed to US annexation. While riding a train during a visit to the US some five years earlier, he had been mistaken for an African-American by a Pullman conductor and ordered to leave the car. Never before, not in his travels to France, England, or anywhere else, had he faced such blatant racism. Insulted and infuriated, he found it ironic that a country that took such pride in its liberty could treat people with such a lack of respect.

Kamehameha IV married **Emma Rooke**, the granddaughter of the *haole* chief John Young whose advice on Western weapons had helped Kamehameha the Great unite the islands into a single kingdom. The king and queen were deeply disturbed by the decline in the native population and feared that Hawaiians might eventually die out altogether. In an attempt to stave off the highly contagious imported diseases that Hawaiian immune systems could not handle, they built Queen's Hospital in Honolulu, named in honor of Queen Emma. (Today called Queen's Medical Center, it is Hawaii's largest hospital and has received international recognition for its cardiovascular department.) Unfortunately, the efforts of the royal couple did little to improve the situation. Hawaiians continued to succumb to illnesses in large numbers. By the early 1860s, **leprosy** would pose a new problem, and victims of the disease would ultimately be shunted off to a remote peninsula on the island of Molokai.

In 1858, the good news was that the queen had given birth to a prince, the first heir to the throne born to a reigning monarch since the time of Hawaii's first king. Then four years later, the child died. Kamehameha IV was overwhelmed by guilt, since the little boy had fallen ill soon after he had held him under cold water to punish him for having a tantrum. Kamehameha IV carried another heavy burden as well. Two years earlier, in a jealous rage over murmurings that a close American friend had eyes for Queen Emma, he had shot the man. When the rumors were later proven false, a remorseful king spared no expense in caring for his wounded friend. But just before the death of the king's son, the man had finally expired from his wounds. In 1863, a 29-year-old Kamehameha IV, run down by grief, guilt, alcohol, and asthma, followed them to the grave.

By this time, missionaries and their families had begun to go into the sugar cane business. Two former spreaders of the gospel, **Samuel Northrup Castle** and **Amos Starr Cooke**, founded what became the multinational **Castle & Cooke** corporation, which bought the island of Lanai. *Haoles* were becoming increasingly entrenched in Hawaii's economy and politics. Hawaiian commoners and other landless citizens were restricted from voting or holding elective office. Alexander Liholiho's brother Lot, who became **Kamehameha V** in 1863, pressed for a greater degree of self-determination and a resurgence of the indigenous culture. Strengthening the power of the monarchy, he drafted a new constitution in 1864.

He built the luxurious **Hawaiian Hotel** in Honolulu, in an attempt to expand tourism as an alternative to the sugar-based, foreign-controlled agricultural economy. But agriculture continued to be the dominant business. At the end of their terms, Chinese contract laborers, free at last, could not leave the plantations fast enough. New Chinese workers were brought to Hawaii to replace them, as well as thousands of indentured laborers from other countries including Portugal, Norway, and Germany.

In 1872, Lot, the last of the Kamehamehas, died without having chosen a successor. For the first time in the history of the kingdom, a monarch would be elected.

THE TWILIGHT OF THE HAWAIIAN MONARCHY (1872–1893)

Fondly known as Prince Bill, **William Charles Lunalilo** had a reputation for heavy-duty drinking, womanizing, and spending. His father had to persuade him to appoint financial guardians so that he wouldn't squander his inheritance. Nevertheless, as the great-grandnephew of Kamehameha I, Lunalilo was the highest-ranking *alii* of his time and the legitimate heir to the throne.

Despite his royal blood, Lunalilo decided to prove his worth and popularity to anyone who thought him too irresponsible to be king. He would run in an election. His opponent, **David Kalakaua**, was outspoken in his pro-Hawaiian sentiments and did not take kindly to the trend of foreigners gaining increasing power and land in Hawaii. Lunalilo was more moderate in his expression of pro-Hawaiianism and more sympathetic to the interests of *haole* politicians and businessmen. In addition to being supported by foreigners, Lunalilo was also backed by the *alii*, who were making good money by leasing their lands to *haole* planters. In 1873, Lunalilo became Hawaii's first elected king.

To demonstrate his solidarity with his people, he walked barefoot to Kawaiahao Church to take the oath of office. During his brief reign, he restored the vote for Hawaiian commoners as well as their right to hold elective office. Run down from years of fast living and overindulgence in alcohol, Lunalilo caught tuberculosis and died in 1874. He had ruled for little more than a year. Again to illustrate his camaraderie with his subjects, he had asked to be buried at Kawaiahao Church, among commoners, instead of with the other kings and chiefs, who were traditionally laid to rest at the Royal Mausoleum in Oahu's Nuuanu Valley.

David Kalakaua decided to give the throne another shot, this time running against Queen Emma, the widow of Kamehameha IV. Despite her American grandfather, Emma Rooke was thoroughly anti-American, anti-missionary, and completely confident she would win. If Hawaii should be forced to lose its independence, she hoped it would be the British who took over. When Kalakaua won the election in 1874, Queen Emma and her supporters were both flabbergasted and furious. Her followers rushed wildly into the courthouse where the legislators had cast their ballots. The melee had to be quelled by British and American marines whose ships happened to be in Honolulu harbor.

Reviving the Hawaiian heritage was a high priority for Kalakaua. He resuscitated the hula, which had been banned by missionaries for many years, even contributing his own new dances. By playing his ukulele and composing songs, he ushered in a renewed appreciation for Hawaiian music. He wrote the words to "Hawaii Pono'i," the **national anthem** of the kingdom, which has since become Hawaii's state song.

Haoles complained that he was trying to return Hawaii to its heathen past. They dubbed him "The Merrie Monarch" because of his jolly style and his love of the performing arts. They were no less displeased when he built the new, opulent **Iolani Palace** in 1882 and held a lavish coronation ceremony for himself on the grounds. His supporters saw this as a welcome way to bolster national pride, but others said that the hefty expenditure would have been better spent elsewhere.

While Kalakaua viewed a strong cultural identity as essential to the wellbeing of Hawaiians, he realized the importance of ensuring friendly relations with foreign powers as well. In 1881, he had left for an around-the-world tour to find new sources for immigrant labor and to ensure that Hawaii's independence was recognized and respected across the globe. Kalakaua became the world's first reigning monarch to make such a trip and to visit the US, where he met with Ulysses S. Grant. During his rule, **Pearl Harbor** was granted to the US for use as a naval base, and the **Reciprocity Treaty** was passed, doing away with the tariff barrier, thereby giving a major boost to the American-controlled sugar industry.

PRINCESS KA'IULANI

The niece of Liliuokalani, Hawaii's last queen, **Victoria Kawekiu Ka'iulani Lunalilo Kalaninuiahilapalapa** (called Princess Ka'iulani for short) was next in line for the throne. She was only 15 when named the royal heir. Her mother, Miriam Likelike, King Kalakaua's sister, had died, and neither Kalakaua nor Liliuokalani had any children. Born in 1875, Princess Ka'iulani (the great-granddaughter of a first cousin of Kamehameha I) was one of few alii of her generation. Her father, Archibald Cleghorn, had come to Hawaii from Scotland in 1850.

Ka'iulani grew up in Ainahau, a 10-acre Victorian-style estate in Waikiki. It was in the colorful surrounding gardens, where her beloved peacocks roamed, that the princess met **Robert Louis Stevenson**, one of the many guests at the estate. He was so taken with the beautiful young woman that he immortalized her in his poetry. Today skyscrapers stand where these landscaped gardens once grew.

To groom the delicate princess for her role as worldly queen, Ka'iulani was sent off to study in England. Meanwhile, those who loved the Hawaiian monarchy and those who wanted the US to annex the islands battled it out in Hawaii. In 1893, when Ka'iulani was 17 and still away in England, Hawaii was taken over by a group of American businessmen based in Honolulu. Ka'iulani traveled to the US where she met with President Grover Cleveland and, in vain, begged him to restore the Hawaiian monarchy.

When the US Congress turned Hawaii into an American territory, the princess fell into a deep depression. In a letter to her aunt Liliuokalani, the deposed queen, she wrote, "They have taken away everything from us and it seems there is left but a little, and that little our very life itself. We live now in such a semi-retired way, that people wonder if we even exist any more."

Ka'iulani went to the Big Island for the wedding of a friend. After horseback riding in misty Waimea, she came down with a cold and fever. In 1899, at only 23 years old, Hawaii's almost-queen died of inflammatory rheumatism.

Although the 1870s had brought more **contract laborers** from China and the Portuguese islands of the Azores and Madeira, there were still not enough workers for the ever expanding sugarcane plantations. Kalakaua initiated a large-scale **Japanese** immigration, and the first group came in 1885. His greatest hope was that the Japanese would intermarry with Hawaiians and help "repopulate" the Islands. By 1886, with people from so many, different nations having settled in the islands, Hawaiians had become a minority.

Caucasians did not appreciate all the competition from the many **Chinese** businesses that were cropping up as these immigrants left the plantations. They blamed Kalakaua for allowing the Chinese so much economic freedom. Finally, in 1887, the king was pressured into giving in to the demands of the **Hawaiian League**, a group of influential *haoles*. Believing this was the only way to maintain peace in Hawaii, even though it meant that his power would now be nominal, he fired his cabinet and signed what came to be known as the "Bayonet Constitution." The new laws of the land stripped the Chinese of the vote and limited Hawaiian political power, basically turning the islands over to American and British residents.

In 1889, a coup attempt led by **Robert Wilcox**, a Hawaiian educated in Italy, was quickly squelched by the *haoles*. In 1891, having lost what he had worked so hard to build, Kalakaua, the last of Hawaii's kings, died in San Francisco, California. Upon his death, his sister **Liliuokalani** became the queen of an American-controlled nation. In 1893, she announced that she would draw up a new constitution, one that would return rule of the country to the monarchy and restore the right to vote and to run for office to all citizens of Hawaii. Declaring her intended actions revolutionary, a small, independent group of Americans (most of whom were Hawaiian-born sons of missionaries) promptly deposed her.

US ANNEXATION (1893-1941)

Hawaii's life as an autonomous kingdom had come to an end. For the next five years, the newly christened "Republic of Hawaii" would be ruled by a provisional government with **Sandford Ballard Dole** as president. In vain, nearly 40,000 people - practically every Hawaiian in the Islands - signed a petition of protest sent to the president of the United States. They wrote that they deeply resented the gall of the members of the provisional government, who had no right, legal or otherwise, to take control of them as if they were "a flock of sheep" or "a horde of savages." How dare this foreign minority presume to rule them? they asked. Not only had these independent Americans acted without the approval of the US government, but they could not even claim "conquest by fair-handed warfare."

In 1895, after a failed coup attempt was carried out by her supporters, Liliuokalani was taken from her Washington Place mansion and held captive in Iolani Palace. She spent the next eight months locked in a spartan room, permitted few comforts and allowed no visitors. The lonely queen passed her time by composing music and writing lyrics, including the words to the well-known *Aloha Oe*. She was told that if she did not sign the abdication papers presented to her, the 200 people who had been imprisoned for their loyalty to her would be killed. Believing she had no choice, she gave them her signature. Still bitter over her kingdom's loss of independence, Liliuokalani, Hawaii's last monarch, died in 1916.

With the onset of the Spanish-American War, which flared in the Philippines, the US Navy needed more control than it already had over Oahu's Pearl Harbor. In addition, the US wanted a larger chunk of the profits from Hawaii's thriving sugar business. President William McKinley gave annexation the green light.

The **changing of the flags** ceremony took place on August 12, 1898, at Iolani Palace in Honolulu. After the lowering of the Hawaiian flag, accompanied by a 21-gun salute from the American naval vessels in the harbor, the spectators heard a grief-laden collective moan seeping out of Kawaiahao church, a block away. While most of the people on the palace grounds were *haoles*, many Hawaiians had gathered in mourning at the nearby church. The doleful sound was soon replaced by cheers from the grounds of the palace as a specially designed version of the American flag was raised.

Although **Prince Kuhio** had been imprisoned as one of Liliuokalani's loyalists, he was chosen by the Republican-dominated Hawaiian government to be their Congressional delegate. His support by residents of the islands would come in handy. He would be instrumental in the design of the Hawaiian Homes Act, passed in 1919, which set aside 200,000 acres of land for farms or residential lots for people whose ancestry was at least half Hawaiian.

During the early years as an American territory, the population became more multiethnic than ever. A rainbow of foreign field laborers poured in at the turn of the century including thousands of Puerto Ricans, Koreans, Russians, Spanish, Filipinos, Okinawans, and African-Americans. The Big Five companies, **Castle & Cooke, Alexander & Baldwin, C. Brewer & Co., AmFac** (American Factors), and **Theo. H. Davies**, continued to flourish, and most remain strong today. Tourism picked up on Oahu. Guests still check into both the elegant **Moana Hotel**, built in 1901, and the lavish **Royal Hawaiian**, finished in 1927.

Hawaii could have done without the attention it received in 1931 when a highly controversial crime hit mainland headlines. **Thalia Massie,** the young white wife of a US Navy lieutenant, left a party alone late one night and went walking in Honolulu. When she was found, she was bruised and nearly incoherent, her jaw broken, her clothes ripped and bloodstained. Five Hawaiians and a Japanese-American were quickly arrested after she claimed she had been beaten and raped by a group of dark-skinned men. The public was never told that a drunken white naval lieutenant commander, with fingernail scratches on his face and a torn uniform, had been picked up that same night in the same area.

As the hysteria over the case rose, *haoles* howled that white women were no longer safe in Hawaii. When the defendants were acquitted due to lack of evidence, Thalia Massie's husband and mother were beside themselves with rage. They kidnapped one of the accused men and murdered him. Although Lieutenant Massie and his mother-in-law were found guilty, the sympathetic territorial governor commuted their sentence to one hour. They served out their 60-minute punishment sitting comfortably in the governor's office in Iolani Palace. Ironically, this office was right across the hall from the room that had held Queen Liliuokalani prisoner for eight long months.

PEARL HARBOR (1941-1954)

Thousands of US servicemen and many civilians died when the Japanese attacked Pearl Harbor on **December 7, 1941**. Along with many German, Austrian, and Italian aliens, scores of Japanese-Americans were rounded up and sent to internment camps on the mainland. But only on the island of Niihau was there a problem with patriotism, and it was an isolated incident at that.

Mr. Harada, a shopkeeper, was one of just two Japanese who lived among the 300 Hawaiians on *haole*-owned Niihau. A Japanese plane leaving Oahu after the attack was forced to land on Niihau. The desperate pilot convinced Harada to help him. The pilot and Harada took Mr. and Mrs. Benjamin Kanahele hostage, to prevent them from alerting others that the enemy plane had landed. Hours later, tormented by guilt, Harada killed himself. The pilot was so unnerved by this act that he shot **Benjamin Kanahele**. Enraged, the large Hawaiian man snatched the pilot into the air and ended his life by bashing him against a wall. Viewed as a local hero, Kanahele recovered from his wound.

The armed forces finally decided to accept *nisei* (American-born children of Japanese immigrants) volunteers in 1943, after realizing that Americans of Japanese descent could prove just as loyal as other citizens. Perhaps because they had so much at stake, the Japanese-American men of the 100th Battalion and the 442nd Regiment won the highest honors of any American army unit in combat.

The years following the war saw the spread of **unionization**. Laborers throughout the islands were attempting to improve the conditions imposed on them by large corporations. Because of the virus of McCarthyism sweeping across the US, many people began to believe that union activity was being backed by Communists. Turning to the Democratic party, the labor movement fought against the interests of Big Business, historically the Republican domain. Led by World War II veteran and future **Senator Daniel W. Inouye**, pro-union Japanese-

Americans were largely responsible for the 1954 shift of the territorial legislature from Republican to Democratic control.

THE FIFTIETH STATE (1959–PRESENT)

On August 21, 1959, Hawaii officially became the 50th state of the Union. Wild celebrations broke out on all the islands. Statehood brought a surge in development, with the greatest thrust on Oahu and then Maui. Hotels and condominiums sprouted up everywhere and new freeways cut across the countryside. As jets began to swoop down on Oahu, tourism became the major economic base. Many visiting mainlanders even turned themselves into residents. In 1972, Hawaii became the first state to ratify the **Equal Rights Amendment**. This was not surprising, since, at the time, Hawaii had the country's largest number of working mothers.

The 1970s were also a period of rebirth for Hawaiian cultural pride. Some say the **Hawaiian Renaissance** began with the 1975 launching of the *Hokulea*, a modern-day replica of a 60-foot Polynesian sailing canoe. Many *haole* historians believed that the Hawaiian Islands had been settled accidentally, after Polynesians lost in the stormy seas had stumbled upon them. The idea that ancient non-Europeans could have been expert navigators who knew exactly what they were doing and where they were going did not sit well with Westerners. Non-Hawaiian Americans were particularly uncomfortable with the notion that these Polynesian journeys of thousands of miles over open ocean could have taken place some 2,000 years before the Vikings did their thing.

The *Hokulea* was built to prove that the ancient Polynesians had indeed sailed from Tahiti to Hawaii in order to settle it. Hawaiian legends and petroglyphs (rock drawings) served as blueprints for the canoe. People from other, remote Polynesian islands who had preserved old traditions were brought in on the act. The vessel would be sailed using only ancient navigational techniques and equipment, so people familiar with these techniques had to be found. Women from other islands taught the people building the canoe the art of weaving sails from pandanus fronds and making rope from braided sennit. However, some adjustments had to be made. Trees in 20th century Hawaii did not grow as massive as they once had, so the hull could not be cut from a single log. Instead, the canoe was constructed of fiberglass.

The year following a 1975 voyage around the Hawaiian Islands, the *Hokulea* set sail from Maui for a month-long voyage to Tahiti. The 17-person crew was welcomed by a crowd of 15,000 Tahitians. When they sailed back to Hawaii, they were met with another uproarious greeting. During the 1980s, the *Hokulea* sailed throughout the Pacific, stopping at many islands, following the path of the ancestors of present-day Hawaiians. In 1987, when the canoe returned to Hawaii after its two-year

"Voyage of Discovery," distant cousins, including Tahitians, Samoan chiefs, Maoris from New Zealand, had come from all over the Pacific to join the celebration.

With the boom in tourism, Hawaii's economy continued to flourish, if not always in expected or respected ways. Nudging sugarcane and pineapple aside, marijuana had become the most profitable (though, of course, illegal) crop by 1979. In 1986, **John D. Waihee III** was elected Hawaii's first governor of Hawaiian descent. This made him the first Hawaiian to lead the Islands since the overthrow of the Hawaiian monarchy nearly a century earlier.

Today the cost of living in Hawaii is higher than that of almost any other state. However, residents also enjoy a high standard of living. Besides, how many other states can boast such a seductive blend of exotic surroundings, sophisticated creature comforts, and a warm, multiracial population?

6. PLANNING YOUR TRIP

BEFORE YOU GO

WEATHER & CLIMATE

Weather in Hawaii can be divided neatly into two seasons: winter and summer. During the **winter**, which runs from about mid-October through April, daytime temperatures are in the mid 60s to low 80s. At night, the mercury dips by about ten degrees so you may need a light jacket or heavy sweater. There is generally more rain at this time of year, especially in November and December. The driest places to be during the winter are Waikiki on Oahu (although crowds here are at their largest during these months); Makena, Wailea, and Kihei on Maui; Kona and Kohala on the Big Island of Hawaii; and Poipu on Kauai.

Summer lasts from about May through mid-80s. Daytime temperatures hover in the mid-80s. Evenings cool off by about five or ten degrees. Rain is less frequent, and when it does fall, it is usually in brief snatches.

Hawaii's busiest **tourist season** goes from Christmastime to mid-April, despite the possibility of wetter days. May through June and September through mid-October are actually the best times to go, since the islands are less crowded, the weather is driest, and the trade winds are at their most refreshing.

No matter what time of year, higher elevations are much colder than sea level. The northeast section of each island gets the brunt of inclement weather when wind and rain come. The southern and western areas of each island tend to be sunniest and driest. It's not unusual for people to be sprawled out on a beach in the blazing sun on one side of an island while the heavens have opened up on the other.

Hurricanes and earthquakes are few and far between. Volcanic eruptions are periodic on the Big Island. However, not only are they safe, but viewing them up close is a favorite pastime. Note that although a haze called "vog" hangs in the air after eruptions, the sun manages to shine through.

WHAT TO PACK

Keep your suitcase as light as you can. If at all possible, pack only what you can carry onto the plane. Then, while everyone else is waiting for their luggage in baggage claim, you'll be on your way to the beach!

By day, Hawaii is an extremely casual place. You'll spend most of your time in bathing suits, shorts and T-shirts, or sundresses, and sandals or rubber flip-flops (known as *zoris*, their Japanese name, or "slippers"). At night, dress can also be as casual as you want. However, if you're planning to splurge at any of Hawaii's excellent upscale restaurants, men should pack a sports jacket and women a few dressy outfits.

Be sure to bring plenty of sunblock and insect repellent, although you'll have no problem buying some once you arrive. If you'll be hiking, camping, or visiting high elevations (such as volcanoes), bring a heavy sweater and windbreaker, long pants, gloves, and sturdy walking shoes or sneakers. Strong shoes also come in handy if you're going to be walking across lava (for example, if you plan to search for petroglyphs or hunt for fallen coconuts on the Big Island).

GETTING TO HAWAII
By Air

Hawaii is served by a wide selection of major airlines, so you'll have a lot of flexibility in booking a non-stop or connecting flight. Heavy competition for your business means that while traveling to Hawaii is certainly not cheap, each airline has periodic economical deals and packages to convince you to fly with them instead of with another carrier. Most planes touch down in Honolulu, the capital, on Oahu, though you can also book flights on major carriers to Maui, the Big Island of Hawaii, and Kauai. Many travelers fly into Honolulu, then switch to a local inter-island carrier for flights to the Neighbor Islands.

The best time to select your seat is when you make your reservation. You can also reserve special meals at this time, such as vegetarian, kosher, low-salt, seafood, or fruit.

Many tour group or package deal travelers are met at the airport with the traditional **lei greeting**. This translates into a kiss on the cheek and a wreath of aromatic fresh flowers around the neck - pure heaven after all those hours in the air!

JET LAG

While most people suffer from jet lag after long flights, there are things you can do to take the edge off it. First, to help you adjust psychologically, set your watch to the time of your destination (Hawaii or home) as you board the plane. Dehydration is a major contributor to the groggy, sapped feeling after hours in the air; during your flight, drink at least a glass of water per hour and avoid alcohol. Eat meals at times that are as close as possible to meal times of your destination (try to nibble a little, even if you're not hungry when served). Doing stretching exercises in your seat and taking periodic walks up and down the aisle will improve circulation. Get as much sleep as possible before and during the flight.

National Airlines

American Airlines, *Tel. 800/433-7300,* flies to Honolulu from San Francisco, Los Angeles, Chicago, and Dallas/Ft. Worth. Flights from New York stop in California. Service is also available to Maui via Honolulu.

Canadian Airlines, *Tel. 800/426-7000,* flies from Vancouver or Toronto to Honolulu.

Continental, *Tel. 800/231-0856,* offers service to Honolulu from Los Angeles and San Francisco, and nonstop flights from Denver and Newark.

Delta, *Tel. 800/221-1212,* has many nonstop flights between Honolulu and Los Angeles, San Francisco, San Diego, Dallas, or Atlanta. Delta also flies nonstop from Los Angeles to Kahului, Maui.

Hawaiian, *Tel. 800/367-5320,* flies to Honolulu from San Francisco, Los Angeles, Las Vegas, Seattle, and Portland.

Northwest, *Tel. 800/225-2525,* flies to Honolulu from San Francisco, Los Angeles, Minneapolis, Seattle, and Portland.

TWA, *Tel. 800/221-2000,* serves Honolulu from St. Louis.

United, *Tel. 800/241-6522,* offers many nonstop flights to Honolulu from San Francisco, Los Angeles, Denver, Seattle, and Chicago. Nonstop service to Kahului, Maui, from San Francisco and Los Angeles is available as well. United also has direct service to Kona on the Big Island of Hawaii and Lihue on Kauai from San Francisco, Los Angeles, and Chicago.

Inter-island Airlines

Aloha, *Tel. 800/367-5250,* provides inter-island service to Honolulu; Kahului on Maui; Kona and Hilo on the Big Island of Hawaii; and Lihue on Kauai. Island Air, which flies to the other islands, is the sister carrier, so you can make reservations for all islands with one phone call.

FIRST FLIGHTS

It has been some fifty years since United and Pan Am started flying regularly from the mainland to Hawaii. United's first commercial flight, on May 1, 1947, was from San Francisco to Honolulu. The 44 passengers aboard the DC-6 were airborne for some ten hours! Today United will get you there in half the time and (if you're on a 747, which can carry 450 folks) with ten times as many fellow travelers. Quite a few contemporary vacationers won't use any other airline to get to the Aloha State. And passengers aren't the only people who stick with United. One of this carrier's first flight attendants, Ron Akana - who happens to be based in Hawaii - has been serving United's passengers for 48 of these 50 years!

Hawaiian, *Tel. 800/367-5320*, has inter-island flights to Honolulu; Kahului on Maui; Lihue on Kauai; Kona and Hilo on the Big Island; Hoolehua on Molokai; and Lanai.

Island Air, *Tel. 800/323-3345 or 800/367-5250*, offer flights to and from Honolulu; Kahului, Kapalua-West Maui, and Hana on Maui; Hoolehua and Kalaupapa on Molokai; and Lanai. Aloha Airlines, which flies to the other islands, is the sister carrier, so you can make reservations for all islands with one phone call.

Mahalo, *Tel. 800/4-MAHALO*, flies between Honolulu and Lihue, Kauai; Kahului and Kapalua-West Maui, Maui; Kona on the Big Island of Hawaii; Molokai; and Lanai.

By Cruise

These days, the only way you can sail to Hawaii is to board a cruise ship that calls briefly on Hawaii as one of its ports. For information on cruising the Hawaiian Islands, See the section on cruises and inter-island ferries in *Getting Around Hawaii* (in this chapter).

Getting from the Airport to Your Accommodation

Many air-hotel package deals include transportation to and from the airport. Taxis are expensive, and if you want to really see the islands, you'll probably be renting a car (see Getting Around Hawaii By Car in this chapter).

The drive from **Honolulu International Airport**, *Tel. 836-6413*, to Waikiki, where most Oahu hotels are, will take anywhere from 25 - 45 minutes, depending on traffic. Follow the signs to taxis, shuttle buses, public buses, and rental car desks.

From Maui's **Kahului Airport**, *Tel. 872-3893*, to Kaanapali, where hotels are concentrated, the drive is about an hour. Rental car agencies that aren't located at the airport provide shuttle service between their parking lots and the baggage claim area. Taxis and shuttle buses are also available at the airport.

If your first stop from the mainland is the Big Island of Hawaii, you'll swoop down at **Keahole-Kona Airport,** *Tel. 329-3423,* on the Kona Coast. Taxis and rental car stands are at the airport and some hotels will arrange shuttle service. The drive to Kona-Kohala Coast hotels is between 35 and 50 minutes, and to Kailua-Kona and Keauhou hotels, 10 to 20 minutes.

If you're flying directly to Kauai, you'll land at **Lihue Airport,** *Tel. 246-1440,* where you'll find rental car stands, shuttle buses and taxis. Poipu hotels are about 30 minutes away, while Wailua and Kapaa accommodations are about a 15 minute drive from the airport.

BOOKING YOUR TRIP
Using Travel Agents or Other Specialists

Before you talk to a travel agent, do some homework. Read through the descriptions of accommodations in this book. Scour newspaper travel sections for ads for money-saving deals. Travel agents should be able to advise you on flights that are discounted depending on the time of year, day of week, and time of day you want to travel. They should also provide inside information on getting the best rates for rental cars. Another source for the lowest available airfare is one of the discount companies such as *1-800-LOW-AIRFARE* or *1-800-FLY-4-LESS.*

GETTING AROUND HAWAII

On islands other than Oahu, it's best to drive or take a tour if you plan to see more than your hotel. Oahu is the only island with an extensive public bus system and taxis on the others islands can be quite expensive

By Bus

Oahu has a convenient public bus system, known as TheBus. It may take a little longer than driving for you to get where you're going, but why rush? - you're on vacation - and it's a lot cheaper. Bus and van tours to the most popular sights are available on all islands.

By Car

In comparing the charges of different car rental companies, make sure that you take into account factors such as the daily versus the weekly rate, the cost of insurance, whether you have to drop off/pick up the car at the airport, and whether you'll be charged a flat rate or have unlimited mileage. With unlimited mileage, compact rental cars with air conditioning begin at about $30 a day, plus insurance and a small daily surcharge. Two- or three-day or weekly rates are the most economical. If you're going to be island hopping, you can rent a car ahead of time for all islands through one company.

During the busiest seasons (winter and summer), you'll need to reserve a car well in advance, and you'll find that rates may be somewhat more expensive than during the rest of the year. Note that some hotels and condominiums include car rental in their rates.

WHEEL DEALS

If you haven't rented a car before arrival, avoid those "$5 a day" and other too-good-to-be-true deals offered by people handing out flyers on the street, especially in Waikiki. Hidden costs or ulterior motives (such as an attempt to rope you into a trip to a less than popular luau or a two-hour visit to a time-share resort with a mandatory tour) can often make these "incredible" deals more expensive than others. Once in Hawaii, it is best to rent a car either at the airport or through your hotel.

Rental companies prohibit drivers from taking cars, even 4-wheel-drive vehicles, onto unpaved or rugged roads. However, some of Hawaii's most dramatic sights can only be reached by less than smooth roads, so many travelers take the risk of violating their contracts.

National rental companies in Hawaii that usually offer the best deals are **Budget Rent-A-Car**, Tel. 800/777-0169, which gives a good selection of coupons that can save you money at restaurants, on cruises, and for other attractions, and **Dollar**, Tel. 800/367-7006, or, in Hawaii, Tel. 800/342-7398. Others to check out are **Avis**, Tel. 800/331-1212, **Hertz**, Tel. 800/654-3131, and **National**, Tel. 800/CAR-RENT. Through some firms (such as Budget), you can rent flashy sports cars or luxury sedans.

You'll get detailed driving maps at the rental company or from your hotel. Plan your route and note one-way streets, particularly in Honolulu. Avoid rush hours whenever possible. Find out locations of service stations, especially if you are beginning a long drive into a remote area. Also find out what the weather has been like in your destination and what Mother Nature has in store for the weather in the near future. A heavy rainfall one day can leave roads dangerously muddy the next, even if it's bright and sunny.

Since you never know when you might get snagged by an irresistible beach while driving, it's a good idea to take your beachwear, sunblock, hat or visor, sunglasses, and towel whenever you set out. So as not to cause accidents or annoy residents, pull over into designated overlooks to enjoy scenic spots instead of driving slowly to absorb your surroundings. Always allow extra time to get wherever you're going (especially the airport).

Never leave valuables in the car, even in a locked trunk. If you're one of the scores of vacationers driving a convertible, always put the top up when the car is parked so that an unexpected rainfall won't do any damage. The law requires that you always wear seatbelts and strap children under age three into car seats (which are available for rent).

By Cruise & Inter-Island Ferry

American Hawaii Cruises, *Tel. 800/474-9934,* offers three-, four-, and seven-day cruises through the Hawaiian Islands. Land-and-sea packages are available.

Built in 1951 and most recently refurbished in 1997, this line's *S.S. Independence* starts in Honolulu, Oahu. The 1,021 passenger, nine-deck cruise ship sails to Kauai, Maui, and the Big Island of Hawaii. It is decorated with Hawaiian art and artifacts and a *kumu* (teacher) is on board to help travelers learn about Hawaiian culture and history. And, of course, entertainment includes hula and Hawaiian music.

Like a floating hotel, the vessel comes complete with two dining rooms, three bars, a lounge, a showplace, two freshwater swimming pools, a fitness center, a beauty salon, a movie theater, a gift shop, and a recreation center for children. Shore excursions (at additional cost) allow vacationers to explore the islands by car, bus, or on foot, in submarines, catamarans, kayaks, sailboats, and rubber rafts, on horseback or a bicycle, or while parasailing.

The basic cost of your cruise will depend on your cabin's size (suites are available along with regular cabins), whether it's outside (with portholes) or inside, and what deck it's on. Note that even though cabins on the higher decks are usually the most expensive, you'll find smoother sailing if your seafaring bedroom is closer to the surface of the ocean. (But lower decks can be noiser, since they are closer to the engine.) Also, cabins closest to the center of the ship tend to afford the most comfortable rides, since the ship rolls and jerks less in the middle. Two cabins are accessible to people in wheelchairs.

Booking and paying for your cruise as far in advance as possible can save you a healthy chunk of change. On the other hand, if you don't mind taking a chance, you can sometimes find a bargain by booking at the last minute when the ship is eager to sell any unused cabins. Ask about round-trip, reduced-fare air supplements, and discounts for children traveling with full-fare adults. If you're traveling with younger editions during the summer, consider the Family Fun Package. Booking through a cruise-only travel agency, such as **Cruises, Inc.,** based in *Syracuse, New York, Tel. 315/*

463-9695 or 800/854-0500, can save you as much as 20%. You can save even more through cruise consolidators, companies that buy blocks of unsold cabins.

Some ferries are packed with local workers traveling between home and their jobs, while others are filled with tourists planning to spend a day or a night on Lanai or Maui.

Running between Maui and Molokai, the 118-foot *Maui Princess* used to carry bikes, mopeds, scuba tanks, kayaks and canoes, as well as people. However, this convenient and popular ferry has been discontinued and there are no plans to revive it.

The ferry *Expeditions'* ride between Maui and Lanai takes an hour. The trip is sometimes far from smooth. If you tend to get seasick, talk to your doctor about preventive measures before your vacation, or try acupressure wrist bands, sold in drug stores (they've worked for me!).

By Taxi

Taxis are plentiful in Honolulu. While cabs are available on other islands, distances can be great, so you could end up spending more than if you rented a car for a day or two. If you'd rather leave the driving to someone else, personalized taxi tours can be arranged.

ACCOMMODATIONS

There is a wonderfully varied array of places to stay in Hawaii, from rustic mountain cabins to opulent beach resorts. Choices in between these extremes are plentiful. Since competition for your presence is so stiff among accommodations in Hawaii, there are many comfortable, moderately priced hotels, condominiums, bed & breakfasts, and inns to choose from.

Note that a growing number of accommodations now have non-smoking rooms, so that guests need not be disturbed by stale odors from previous puffing vacationers. Most will lock your valuables at the front desk, and some have conveniences such as in-room safes, mini refrigerators, and coin-operated washers and dryers. Some accommodations lower their rates during the summer.

ROOM RATES

Note that all prices quoted for hotels, condos, inns, and bed & breakfasts in each island chapter are "rack rates," the published prices for two people sharing a double room for one night (unless otherwise indicated). However, especially at the larger properties, major discounts (often in the form of package deals) are usually available.

*When it's time to pay your hotel bill, you'll find that a 10.17% **hotel tax** has been added.*

Top Hotels

Several of the most luxurious of these are referred to as "megaresorts" or "Hawaiian Disneyland," since there is so much to do and see on the premises that guests need never leave the property. (I can't imagine, though, why anyone would want to come all the way to Hawaii and remain on the grounds of a hotel.) Especially outside of Oahu (where Waikiki hotels are close together), most top hotels are in sprawling, beautifully landscaped, oceanfront settings. Particularly on the Neighbor Islands, many have open-air lobbies with ponds and flourishing foliage. Some have extensive collections of Hawaiian, Polynesian, and Asian art.

While those in Waikiki may not be as spacious, all top hotels have features including swimming pools; air-conditioned rooms with remote-controlled color TV, stocked minibars, one or more telephones, clock-radios and *lanais* (balconies or patios); several restaurants (of far higher quality than you would expect to find in most mainland hotels); room service; daily and nightly entertainment; luaus; Hawaiian crafts demonstrations; a full menu of sports; a tour-booking desk; and a highly professional, attentive staff.

Extras often come in the form of fresh flowers; bathrobes and slippers (for use during your stay); bathrooms with double sinks, an array of toiletries, both tubs and shower stalls, and separate rooms for toilets; in-room safes (sometimes for a per-use fee); coffee-makers; refrigerators; and nightly turn-down service with chocolates on your pillows. Fax machines and other business-related services are often available.

Even if you can't afford to spend your whole vacation in a top hotel, consider booking a room in one for a night or two just for the fun of it.

Mid-range Hotels

Often on or near beaches, many of these have a wide array of facilities, activities, and services, including swimming pools, tennis courts, a choice of restaurants, and nightly entertainment. Quite a few of these hotels are frequently packed with tour groups.

Budget Hotels

Some are near beaches and many have swimming pools. Rooms tend to be basic, but comfortable, with no-frills decor. Fans often cool rooms instead of air conditioners. Some of the better budget hotels attract tour groups.

Condominiums

These are a pleasant alternative to luxury or mid-level hotels. Some are nearly indistinguishable from top hotels, except that each unit has a kitchen and most have one or more separate bedrooms. Condos tend to be quieter, offering more independence and privacy. Many are on or near beaches. Most have swimming pools, TVs, and laundry facilities. Some have tennis courts.

While you may receive plenty of personal attention from staff, services are likely to be fewer than at hotels. The front office may not be open at night and it may be closed or have limited hours on weekends. So be sure to make check-in arrangements in advance if you plan to arrive off-hours. There may not be an activities desk to help you arrange tours or helicopter rides. Although there are no restaurants in most condos, kitchens come complete with cooking and dining utensils. You probably won't be able to have meals brought to your room or your bags carried by porters. Maid service is generally available, but it is not always daily, and it sometimes requires a surcharge.

Some condominiums don't accept credit cards. Some units may not be air-conditioned, or may be partially air-conditioned, with just a ceiling fan in the bedroom or living room. Some have no telephones. During the most popular times of year (winter, summer, and holidays), a minimum stay of several nights may be required.

Bed & Breakfasts & Inns

Bed & Breakfast (B&B) rates include a bedroom and breakfast (often continental, sometimes to be prepared by you) in a home-like setting. Your hosts may be living on the premises. Guests are usually invited to use a common living room, often with a television. In some cases, you'll be put up in a separate cottage or apartment. Daily rates range from dirt cheap (under $50) to very expensive ($160 and up).

While small, inns often have more guest rooms than B&Bs, but no meals are served. Both inns and B&Bs are generally in residential areas.

Housekeeping Cabins

For a mere $10 to $45 per unit per night, rustic, spartan cabins in state and national parks are an inexpensive way to go. In some, basic kitchen facilities are on hand, and linens are provided.

THE BEST OF HAWAII

To help you decide where to go and when, here are some of Hawaii's bests:

BEST FESTIVALS & SPECIAL EVENTS

Hawaii's various cultures have contributed many annual festivals. In addition to these, sporting events may also help you determine when to travel. Check with the Hawaii Visitors and Convention Bureau (HVCB), *Tel. 808/923-1811 or 800/GO-HAWAII*, for the exact dates and locations.

January

Narcissus Festival: The Chinese New Year is celebrated in Honolulu's Chinatown with an eruption of fireworks, dances, a ball, a beauty contest, and other happenings. Beginning in January or February, the festival runs through March.

Cherry Blossom Festival: With roots in Japan, this Honolulu event features lessons in the skillful craft of arranging flowers and preparing food that looks like modern art. The festival, which runs through March or early April, also includes judo or aikido demonstrations, a golf tournament, a beauty contest, and a coronation ball.

Hula Bowl Game: College football teams slug it out for the championship at Aloha Stadium in Aiea, Oahu. Halftime is an elaborate production, with hula and Hawaiian music.

Annual Ala Wai Canoe Challenge: After an outrigger race on Honolulu's canal, paddlers compete in ancient Hawaiian games at Ala Wai Field.

Makahiki Festival: Far better known to locals than to visitors, this revival of an ancient celebration of peace includes competitions in Hawaiian games, free food, and music. Molokai's Kaunakakai Park is the locale, and events are open to both children and adults.

February

Narcissus Festival: See January. This festival continues through March.

Cherry Blossom Festival: See January. This festival continues through March or April.

Hawaii Opera Theatre: Opera season takes off at Neil Blaisdell Concert Hall on Oahu.

Great Aloha Run: Meet at Oahu's Aloha Tower Marketplace to run, walk, and even push a baby stroller through Honolulu.

The Waimea Town Celebration: Kauai residents throw a party and parade in Waimea to celebrate Hawaii's multi-ethnic heritage in the town where Captain Cook first came ashore. The fun includes food booths, games, 5K and 10K foot races, a canoe race, and a bike race.

March

Narcissus Festival: See January. This festival continues through March.

Cherry Blossom Festival: See January. This festival continues through March or April.

Molokai Celebrations: March is the month for a rodeo and a festival featuring Hawaiian dance and chanting.

Flying Kites: Honolulu's Kapiolani Park draws serious kite flyers to festivals that attract kite masters from around the world.

Art Maui: A major juried art show is on display at the Maui Arts & Cultural Center in Kahului.

Honolulu Festival: Japanese culture is the star of this Oahu celebration that includes street performers, sumo, o-bon dancing, and kite demonstrations.

Whalefest Week: Maui's Pacific Whale Foundation raises money for humpbacks through a 5K and a 10K race, music, crafts, a silent auction, and food booths.

Maui Marathon: Runners from across the globe jog from Kahului to Whalers Village in Kaanapali.

Kapalua Celebration of the Arts: Demonstrations and one-on-one instruction in featherwork, lauhala (palm frond) weaving, hula, and other traditional Hawaiian arts are part of this Maui festival, along with an elaborate luau.

April

Merrie Monarch Festival: Tickets are hard to come by for this premiere hula competition in Hilo on the Big Island of Hawaii. Hula halau (schools) come from all over the state to perform ancient and modern dance, chants, and music.

Maui Polo Season: Makawao, cowboy country, is the locale for polo matches.

International Pro Windsurfing: Master windsurfers from all over the world show their stuff in this competition at Hookipa Beach on Maui.

May

Filipino Parade in Honolulu: Revelers dressed in elaborate costumes dance down Kalakaua Avenue from Ala Moana Park to Kapiolani Park, where the Filipino Community Center hosts a big bash.

Big Island Bounty Festival: If you're into excellent food, don't miss this showcase of Hawaii's best regional cuisine prepared by the state's top chefs and held on the Big Island of Hawaii.

Annual Spring Arts Festival: This mixed media juried art show is open to all artists. It is held on the Big Island of Hawaii.

Molokai Ka Hula Piko: The birth of hula is celebrated at Papohaku Beach Park at Kaluakoi on Molokai with hula and musical performances as well as displays of crafts such as quilts, deer-horn scrimshaw, and featherwork.

Molokai to Oahu Kayak Challenge: Are you up for a 38-mile ocean paddle? If not, you can watch participants in this kayak race depart from Molokai or cheer them as they arrive at Oahu.

Memorial Day Yacht Race: Kauai's Nawiliwili Yacht club sponsors multi-hull and single-hull races from Lihue north to Hanalei Bay.

June

Annual Kapalua Wine & Food Symposium: Invented by the Kapalua Wine Society, this Maui program includes top food and drink.

King Kamehameha Day: A parade, music, crafts, and food stalls, along with a lei-draping ceremony at the statue of King Kamehameha in Kohala, are part of this Big Island of Hawaii celebration.

King Kamehameha Parade: A parade and ho'olaulea (street festival) take place in Kona on the Big Island of Hawaii.

Kapalua Music Festival: Chamber music is the main focus of this popular Maui event. Performers come from a variety of countries.

King Kamehameha Statue Decoration: On Oahu, the statue of King Kamehameha the Great that stands across from Iolani Palace in Honolulu is draped with ultra-long leis. Ceremonies are highlighted by music and hula.

Annual Oahu Ho'Olaulea: Hula, songs, handicrafts, and local food are among the entertainment during this Queen Kapiolani Park celebration.

July

Annual Mauna Kea Beach Hotel Pro-Am Golf Tournament: Serious golfers play 54 holes at this Big Island of Hawaii resort.

Parker Ranch 4th of July Rodeo: Head to paniolo (Hawaiian cowboy) country on the Big Island of Hawaii for a rip-roaring rodeo.

Makawao Rodeo: Held July 4th weekend, this Maui rodeo is Hawaii's largest. More than 350 cowboys come to upcountry Maui from around the world.

Annual Wailea Tennis Open: International players compete on Maui.

Floating Lantern Ceremony: During this beautiful traditional Japanese ceremony on Maui, floating lanterns honor the souls of the dead.

Prince Lot Hula Festival: On Honolulu, this Hawaiian dance festival was named for the prince who became King Kamehameha V and revived hula after it had been banned by missionaries.

Ukulele Festival: Kapiolani Bandstand in Honolulu is the site for this major performance by ukulele masters.

August

Maui Onion Festival: Sweet Maui onions are honored at Maui's Kaanapali Beach Resort with displays, music, and other entertainment.

Hawaii International Billfish Tournaments: The Big Island of Hawaii is the place for big game fishing, and this is one of the world's top fishing tournaments. Don't miss the daily weigh-in at Kona Pier.

Moikeha Hawaiian Sailing Canoe Race: The Big Island's Kohala Coast is where this canoe race takes place.

Queen Liliuokalani Long Distance Outrigger Race: In teams from the Pacific Basin, more than 2,500 paddlers participate in this open ocean canoe race that takes off from Kailua-Kona on the Big Island of Hawaii.

Hawaii State Windsurf Championships: Pro and amateur men and women enter boardsailing competitions at Kahana Beach Park in Kahului, Maui.

Molokai Music Festival: Considered by many to be the most Hawaiian of Hawaii's islands, Molokai is the perfect setting for this celebration of indigenous music, hula, crafts, and food.

Kauai Mokihana Festival: Various arts contests and demonstrations are held around Kauai.

Wilson Kapalua Open Tennis Tournament: Kapalua is a glorious setting for this tennis tournament that attracts top players.

Lanai To Maui Channel Relay Swim: This 9-mile, 6-person relay race takes swimmers from Lanai to Kaanapali on Maui.

Maui Music Festival of Jazz: Jazz and contemporary sounds brings music lovers to Kaanapali on Maui.

September

Aloha Festivals: Hawaiian music, hula, and visual arts are featured during various events on all islands throughout September and October.

Kauai Mokihana Festival: Lasting for more than a week, this series of cultural events on Kauai includes a composers' contest and concert, a hula competition, and folk arts workshops.

Parker Ranch Labor Day Rodeo and Horse Races: This one takes place at Paniolo Park in Waimea on the Big Island of Hawaii.

Wilson Kapalua Open Tennis Tournament: Local tennis stars compete in Kapalua, Maui.

Iolani Palace & Queen Liliuokalani: Honolulu's royal palace is the locale for entertainment in honor of the Queen's birthday.

Maui Triathalon: Supermen and -women swim, bike, and run around Maui.

Ironman Triathlon World Championship: On the Big Island of Hawaii, this triathlon takes international athletes through lava fields and across Kailua Bay. Crowds gather to party at the Kailua-Kona Pier start and finish lines.

Bankoh Na Wahine O Ke Kai: This women's long distance canoe race begins at Papohaku Beach at Kaluakoi Resort on Molokai and ends on Oahu, 34 miles across the rough channel.

October

Aloha Festivals: Hawaiian music, hula, and visual arts are featured during various events on various islands.

Maui County Fair: Rides, games, horticultural exhibits, a livestock tent, and other entertainment are part of the fun on Maui.

Ironman Triathlon: Athletes test their strength while swimming, biking, and running on the Kona Coast of the Big Island.

Spooky Stories Tour: Oahu's Mission Houses Museum sponsors a tour of historic downtown Honolulu complete with spine-tingling tales.

November

Kona Coffee Contests & Exhibits: Learn all about the growing and harvesting of this famous brew on the Big Island of Hawaii.

Mission Houses Holiday Craft Fair: Consider shopping here for the upcoming holidays.

December

Mission Houses Holiday Craft Fair: If you missed it last month, you have another chance to shop for the holidays.

A Candlelight Christmas at Mission Houses: The Oahu Mission Houses Museum shows visitors what a 19th century Christmas was like.

First Night Maui: Families enjoy this alcohol-free New Year's festival at the Maui Arts & Cultural Center in Kahului.

BEST HELICOPTER TOURS

As far as I'm concerned, birds gaze down on the most awesome scenery from the skies above Kauai (with Waimea Canyon, waterfall-bedecked Mount Waaialeale, jagged Na Pali Coast, and hidden sandy coves). Helicopter rides are also impressive on the alternately flourishing and desolate **Big Island of Hawaii**, especially if Kilauea volcano is erupting, and **Maui**, with its stark Haleakala crater and verdant Hana. While a helicopter tour of Oahu can have its thrilling moments, I recommend taking a whirl here only if you're not visiting any of the other islands.

Try to find a company with helicopters that have no middle seats. (Note that some ads say, "Every seat is a window seat.") Some copters are four-seaters while others seat six. By all means, take your camera and plenty of film, but don't spend so much time clicking the shutter that you miss the scope of your surroundings. Some people have a tendency to glue their eye to their camera's viewfinder instead of enjoying the breadth of the scenery. No photo can capture the panoramic vision that whirlybirds lay out before you, nor the feeling of the land suddenly dropping out from beneath you like a trap door as you fly over the edge of a cliff.

If you read local papers, you may see articles about some local residents fighting the profusion of helicopter tours. They may be exciting for those flying, but hikers and other nature lovers find them extremely disruptive.

BEST PLACES FOR ADVENTURE

You'll find plenty of adventures that will surround you with Hawaii at it's most natural. In a 23-foot-long rubber raft, for instance, you can cruise Kauai's northern shore, where the dramatic cliffs of Na Pali Coast rise from the electric-blue water. The raft is small enough to zip past waterfalls and into craggy caves at the bottom of the cliffs. This area is frequented by sea turtles, and dolphins jump out of the water as if their moves had been choreographed. Excursions run during the spring and summer when the rough water is at its calmest.

On Maui, the 38-mile bike ride down Haleakala volcano is spectacular. The road winds through magnificent scenery with frequent changes in sights and aroma. You can take the late-morning ride, but I highly recommend the sunrise excursion, even though you'll have to leave at around 3:00am to get to the summit on time. You'll ride down after watching the sun come up over the crater. If you'd like to become better acquainted with the stark crater, which is about the size of Manhattan Island, arrange to go horseback riding or hiking in it.

Another summit worth seeing is that of snowcapped Mauna Kea on the Big Island, where immense telescopes gaze at the heavens. Also visit the moonscape of Hawaii Volcanoes National Park on this island. Waipio Valley, a deep dip along the northern coast, hasn't changed a whole lot since the time of ancient Hawaiians. Take a shuttle tour in a four-wheel-drive jeep or go horseback riding here. The narrow "roads" are actually rocky riverbeds, and flowers and thick vegetation are everywhere. The black-sand beach is a great locale for a picnic, but swimming is best in the river that cuts across the sand, leading to the ocean.

On Molokai, a 3.2-mile trail snakes down a 1,600-foot-tall cliff on the north shore overlooking a huge peninsula that protrudes into the Pacific like the tongue of a giant. Hiking the trail is certainly possible, but many people go on the backs of sure-footed mules. Once below, they are given a tour of the area made famous by the victims of Hansen's Disease who were once forced to live here.

Biking is a good way to tour the islands. Among the companies that arrange two-wheel excursions, try **Backroads Bicycle Touring,** *Berkeley, California, Tel. 510/527-1555 or 800/533-2573,* for touring on Maui or the Big Island of Hawaii.

BEST PLACES TO FIND HAWAIIAN CULTURE & HISTORY

Many of the larger hotels have periodic demonstrations or classes in lei making, hula dancing and lauhala (palm frond) weaving. Some also have experts on hand to tell you all about poi making, canoe making, playing konane games, lomi lomi massage, making feather cloaks, and other old-time activities.

For a more in-depth look at Hawaiiana, Oahu's Polynesian Cultural Center is a good place to start. The historical exhibits and the authentic, recreated villages are fascinating, but the best part is lingering after the demonstrations to chat with the enthusiastic performers from Hawaii and other Pacific Islands. In beautiful Waimea Valley/Waimea Falls Park, you'll see old-fashioned hula demonstrations (a far cry from today's variety). You can also watch divers plunge into a pool from the top of a crashing waterfall.

Honolulu's Bishop Museum houses a wonderful display of Hawaiiana, from koa wood bowls and royal crowns to an authentic grass hut. Take an outrigger canoe ride at Waikiki Beach. Larger versions of this kind of boat carried the ancient Polynesians to Hawaii from Tahiti. Opulent, European-inspired Iolani Palace is the only former royal palace on American soil. Less elegant but just as intriguing is Queen Emma's Summer Palace.

Hiking along Kauai's Na Pali Coast, you may encounter ruins of agricultural terraces, *heiau* (temples), and other remnants of ancient Hawaiian communities that once thrived in the valleys here. According to many historians, this was the first region settled on the island.

For more history, explore the petroglyph fields on the Big Island, Lanai, or Molokai. These ancient rock carvings provide insight into early Hawaiian art. Half the adventure is finding the petroglyphs, many of which are hidden in remote areas. Some Big Island hotels offer guided walks to and through the petroglyph fields. Start with Anaehoomalu, on the grounds of the Waikoloa Beach Resort. In addition to petroglyphs, the Big Island's Kona-Kohala Coast has many other remnants of Hawaiian history: ancient royal fishponds, heiau, burial sites, canoe sheds, fishing shrines, and an old trail to the beach worn smooth by royal feet. The tastefully upscale hotels along this coast are packed with intriguing Pacific art.

South of here, totem pole-like *tikis* guard the waterfront at the Place of Refuge. This was where ancient Hawaiians went to avoid the severe punishment (often death) that resulted from breaking a *kapu* (taboo). In the Big Island's town of Kailua-Kona, oceanfront Hulihee Palace was a vacation retreat for *alii* (chiefs and kings). Puukohola Heiau and Mookini Heiau are two of the best preserved of the many ancient Hawaiian temples that once scattered the islands.

The picturesque town of Lahaina, on Maui, has been the capital of the Hawaiian kingdom and a whaling village. It's now a National Historic Landmark. Most of the people who live in remote Hana, a quiet town on Maui's east coast, are part Hawaiian. Hana is a good place to mingle and "talk story" with residents. Hawaiians also remain in Keanae, along the road to Hana.

Skip the commercialized luaus (most of those that take place at hotels or that you'll hear about through hotels) and check local newspapers for those sponsored by civic groups and other organizations. Fund-raising luaus are sometimes hosted by *halau* (hula groups) preparing to participate in the annual Merrie Monarch Festival (held on the Big Island in April) to cover the cost of costumes, airfare or ground transportation, and accommodations during this major hula happening. If you can get tickets, the Merrie Monarch Festival is the best place to watch live hula in all its splendor.

Molokai's annual Makahiki Festival, with food, Hawaiian games, music, and hula, is an exceptional event.

BEST PLACES TO GET MARRIED

There is no question that Hawaii is the stuff countless romantic dreams are made of. Not only do newlyweds from the mainland and Japan come to Hawaii by the planeload, but many couples kick off their honeymoons with a wedding here as well.

Among favorite places for tying the knot are the torchlit lagoon at Polynesian-style Kona Village Resort and the palm-shaded beachside spot at the Orchid Mauna Lani on the Big Island, the chapels at the lavish Grand Wailea and the scenic Ritz-Carlton Kapalua on Maui, and the lush, waterfall-and bird-filled grounds of the Hyatt Regency Maui. One of the most popular spots is Fern Grotto on Kauai, which bride and groom cruise to in a special wedding riverboat. At the mouth of this cave that is dripping with ferns, the acoustics for "The Hawaiian Wedding Song" could hardly be better. Beaches at sunset, botanical gardens, waterfalls and boats also make wonderful wedding settings.

Quite a few of the larger hotels and condominiums offer honeymoon and wedding packages including pampering, such as airport pickup in a limousine, champagne upon arrival, a honeymoon suite, a moonlight cruise, and a helicopter ride. Some resorts have wedding coordinators who will help you find the most appealing locale to say "I do." They make arrangements for flowers (such as bridal strands of *pikake*-fragrant Chinese jasmine - a sign of love), *maile* leis (symbolizing long life and prosperity), the cake, champagne, and a video or still photographer. They'll let the bride know that she should tuck a *ti* leaf inside one of her garters for good luck.

You'll need to obtain a marriage license from the State Department of Health in Honolulu or through agents on other islands. There is no waiting period, and the license is good for 30 days in Hawaii. Women are required to show a certificate confirming premarital screening for rubella. For a marriage information packet, contact the State Department of Health, *P.O. Box 3378, Honolulu, HI 96801, Tel. 808/586-4544*, Monday to Friday, 8am to 4pm Hawaii time, or *Tel. 808/586-4545* for an informational recording.

BEST NIGHTLIFE & DINING

For sheer variety, Waikiki on Oahu is the place to be. However, other islands also have a healthy choice of quality restaurants and after-dark action. Kaanapali and Lahaina on Maui have many restaurants and night spots. To a lesser degree, Kailua-Kona and Keauhou on the Big Island offer a good selection of restaurants and a sprinkling of evening hangouts. The resorts along the Big Island's Kona-Kohala Coast are also worth checking out.

Most hotels either host their own luaus or they can make arrangements for guests to attend one elsewhere. Many visitors enjoy these commercial affairs, but I prefer the more authentic, down-to-earth luaus hosted by civic groups and other local organizations. Keep an eye out for them in local newspapers or listen for radio announcements.

BEST SHOPPING

Even on some of the Neighbor Islands, Hawaii is a Nirvana for shopping mall addicts. Oahu, of course, is where you'll find the widest selection of stores, in and outside of malls. Chic boutiques and T-shirt shops line Kalakaua Avenue and other streets in Waikiki. The convenient

Royal Hawaiian Shopping Mall is centrally located in Waikiki. ABC discount stores, one of which seems to be on every corner, sell Kona coffee and macadamia nuts, usually at very appealing prices. Off the main tourist strip, the Ala Moana Shopping Center is among the world's largest malls. If you can't find it there, it probably doesn't exist. Also in Honolulu, the Ward Center is an attractive, upscale shopping and dining complex. Nearby is the older Ward Warehouse, with more stores to browse through.

For atmosphere, it is difficult to beat Kauai's Kilohana Plantation. Bedrooms, hallways, and even bathrooms in this handsome mansion and out buildings have been converted into eye-pleasing (if not always wallet-friendly) boutiques. Pottery, jewelry, antiques and paintings by local artists are plentiful. Other good areas for spending money are Lahaina and Kaanapali (Whalers Village) on Maui and Kailua-Kona on the Big Island. Many hotels, especially the larger ones, have shops, but you generally pay more for the convenience.

Now that I've dealt with where to buy it, here's what to buy:

If you absolutely must have an **aloha shirt**, I'd steer clear of the modern, most common (polyester) variety. Stop at thrift shops and other boutiques to sift through vintage shirts. Most are made of rayon (a natural fiber) or silk. They often have coconut shell buttons. Many of the best in quality date back to the 1930s and '40s and are silk-screened or stenciled with more subdued floral prints than the somewhat garish contemporary shirts. The only problem is, these older shirts run anywhere from $60 to well over $100. For **muumuus**, I would also suggest staying away from the more commercial outlets.

In shopping areas and malls, as well as hotels throughout the main islands, you'll find a wide variety of sportswear. Whenever I'm shopping in Hawaii, it seems as if I see more bathing suits or T-shirts in any single store than I've seen my entire life. With branches on the major islands, Crazy Shirts is one of the best places to go for quality T-shirts. **Pareaus** (also called pareos or sarongs) imported from Tahiti and other islands make wonderful beach cover-ups for women.

If you want something truly Hawaiian and are willing to dig deep into your pockets, consider a delicate **Niihau necklace**. Tiny, rare shells from the island of Niihau (where only Hawaiians are allowed to live) are painstakingly fashioned into intricate designs. Each a work of art in itself, these garlands can run hundreds of dollars.

Another worthwhile investment is a **Hawaiian quilt**, especially an antique one. Easily recognizable, these attractive comforters usually have a bold, one-color cut-out design appliquéd onto a white background. A new quilt can run well over a thousand dollars, and if it is commissioned, it call take up to two years to complete. However, your patience and money would be well spent, since you would then have an extremely durable heirloom to pass down in your family.

Many travelers return home laden with bowls, jewelry, and *tikis* (totem pole-like Hawaiian carvings) carved from glossy island wood, such as koa or monkeypod. **Necklaces** of chestnut-like *kukui* nuts (candlenuts), Maui's **scrimshaw** (intricate designs etched onto whale bone or teeth), and locally made paintings and ceramics are also popular. Imports from other Pacific island groups are plentiful, including *tapa* (or *kapa*) **cloth** (made from pounded bark), which can make striking wall hangings. There is also no scarcity of Asian imports, such as Chinese jade and Japanese vases.

At flower nurseries (especially on the Big Island) you can buy exotic blooming plants, either seedlings or mature, to he shipped (after being inspected) to the mainland. Particularly in Honolulu's Chinatown, **lei** stands are everywhere. Interested in taking one of these fresh floral garlands home? You can pick one up at most airports. Planning to keep a lei around your house as decoration after it dries? Orchids are among the blossoms that age nicely.

A burst of flavor has often transported me back to the place where I first experienced the taste. Hawaii certainly makes it easy to return over and over again, without having to get back onto a plane. Few people leave the Islands without **Kona coffee** (fresh beans, ground, or instant-caffeinated or de-caf). The rich volcanic soil of the Big Island, where it is grown, has a great deal to do with its trademark flavor. **Macadamia nuts** - plain, chocolate-covered, in cookies, or in many other incarnations - are another hot item.

You can arrange to have juicy, fresh **pineapples** inspected, boxed, and sent to your departure gate at the airport. Jams and jellies made from *lilikoi* (passion fruit), guava, papaya, and mangoes can be found in many stores. Once you taste thick, crunchy **Maui potato chips**, you'll probably want to take home a few bags. For your liquor cabinet, consider a bottle of **Okolehao** (Hawaiian whiskey, flavored with the native *ti* plant) or **wine** from Maui's vineyard, such as a sparkling white or a light pineapple wine.

Hawaii probably isn't the first place you think of going when you're in the market for quality **paintings**, **sculpture**, and **ceramics**. However, Oahu, Maui, Kauai, and the Big Island are peppered with thriving, tasteful art galleries. Maui weighs in with nearly 50 art showplaces, some featuring the work of locally known artists while others emphasize those with international reputations. Art expos and festivals are sprinkled throughout the year. A few Kaanapali Beach hotels, such as the Westin Maui and the Hyatt Regency Maui are virtual museums of enormous sculptures, basketball player-sized vases, and weathered artifacts from the Pacific, Asia, and Europe.

If hotels that look like spectacular museums are your thing, you'll get your fill along the Big Island's Kona-Kohala Coast, and on Kauai and Lanai.

BEST SPA VACATIONS

A number of hotels have excellent spas on the premises. The most extensive facilities for toning and pampering the body are at the Ihilani Resort & Spa on Oahu; the Ritz-Carlton Kapalua and the Grand Wailea on Maui; the Four Seasons Hualalai and the Orchid at Mauna Lani on the Big Island; and the Princeville resort and the Hyatt Regency on Kauai.

BEST UNUSUAL SIGHTS

For my money, the **Big Island of Hawaii** wins hands down in this category for its contrasting vistas. This island looks like few other places on earth. Not only does it have a pair of active volcanoes, but it also sports coal-black sand beaches, as well as a shore with green (yes, green) sand (olivine crystals). Smooth ebony lava flows form an eerie wasteland in sharp contrast to the lusher parts of the island.

Waipio Valley, with its own black sand beach, is a flourishing hideaway that is not to be missed. Black sand and an impressive volcano can also be found on Maui, and other islands are certainly not lacking in magnificent scenery.

7. BASIC INFORMATION

BUSINESS HOURS & HOLIDAYS

So that you can part with your money at your convenience, shopping malls and quite a few stores on main drags remain open in the evenings. Retail stores, especially those in hotels, rarely take Sundays off.

Banking hours are usually from 8:30am to 3 or 3:30pm, Monday through Friday. (However, some banks stay open until 6pm on Thursdays or Fridays.) ATMs are easy to come by. Businesses are generally open from 8am or earlier to 4 or 5pm.

Most post offices open at 8 or 8:30am and close at 4:30pm during the week; on Saturdays, hours are often 8am to noon. The main post office in Honolulu is open from 7:30am to 4:30pm Monday through Friday and 7:30am to noon on Saturdays.

Stores, banks, and most businesses are closed on the main US national holidays (New Year's Day, Easter Sunday, Thanksgiving, Christmas Day). Although banks and most businesses will be closed, a few stores stay open on Presidents' Day (third Monday in February), Prince Kuhio Day (March 26), Memorial Day (last Monday in May), King Kamehameha Day (June 11), the Fourth of July, Admission Day (third Friday in August), Labor Day (first Monday in September), Columbus Day (second Monday in October), and Veterans' Day (November 11).

COSTS OF TRAVEL

While package deals can be quite economical, they are only worth the saving if they take you where you want to go and if you can stay where you want to stay. In some cases, hotels that are part of packages are those that don't sell out easily because they aren't of the best quality, or aren't in the most desirable locations; or, while the hotel may be fabulous, the package rooms may be in the least expensive category (a.k.a. small or view-less). Be sure you are clear about exactly what is included in the price of the package (airport transfers, lei greeting, meals, tours, cruises, etc.).

Escorted and independent fly-drive-hotel packages are available through hotels themselves or through various airlines and tour companies. Honeymoon packages may not be much less expensive than other packages. But your VIP treatment might include a lei greeting, airport pick-up in a limo, chilled champagne and fresh fruit upon arrival, room upgrade, and a helicopter ride. Money-saving sports packages (such as for golfers) are also popular.

As far as attractions go, it's generally cheaper to shop around for good tour deals once you arrive in Hawaii than to prebook through a travel agent or your hotel activities desk. You can save 20 percent to 40 percent if you go directly to tour agents. Tax will usually be added to the quoted price for cruises, horseback riding, helicopter tours, and other excursions. **Budget Rent-A-Car** customers, by the way, receive money-saving coupons for restaurants, cruises, and other attractions.

FESTIVALS & SPECIAL EVENTS

See The Best of Hawaii in Chapter 6, *Planning Your Trip*.

HEALTH CONCERNS

Packing a small first-aid kit is a good idea. Also be sure to bring insect repellent, sunblock, and sunglasses. While it's perfectly fine to drink tap water in Hawaii, don't drink from streams or natural pools since they may contain parasites. Fresh vegetables, fruit, and dairy products are also safe.

No matter how dark the natural color of your skin is, be sure to use a good sunblock whenever you're outdoors. Sunglasses and a hat or visor will also come in handy. Don't spend your whole first day frying on the beach. Expose your skin to heavy doses of sun gradually, and avoid being in direct sunlight for long stretches between 10am and 2pm, when the rays are strongest. Don't forget that even on hazy days, the sun's powerful ultraviolet light comes through.

However, if you do end up with a burn, stay out of the sun. Take a cool bath and apply a first-aid spray or lotion. Aloe gel is especially soothing. Get medical help right away if your burn is so bad that you feel feverish, nauseated, dizzy, or have chills or a headache.

If you need a doctor, the staff at your accommodation can help you contact one. Hawaii's largest hospital, Queen's Medical Center in Oahu, is one of the country's best medical facilities.

In case of emergency, dial 911.

MAIL & FAXES

Most hotels in Hawaii sell stamps at the same price as in the post office. There doesn't seem to be a great deal of consistency in the length of time mail takes to travel between Hawaii and the mainland; allow anywhere from four days to ten days or more. Express Mail and courier companies, such as Federal Express, offer two-day service between the continental US and the main islands. However, be forewarned that weekend pick-ups and drop-offs may not be available on Neighbor Islands, so those two days can turn into three or four.

Most of the larger hotels have fax machines available for use by guests.

Some lei stands and many florists will send Hawaiian blossoms to you or your friends on the mainland.

Inspected, boxed pineapples can be purchased at the airport or at fruit stands that deliver them to the airport in time for your flight or mail them directly to the mainland. While in Hawaii, eat your fill of guava, passion fruit, mangoes, and avocados. The US Department of agriculture discourages people from bringing or mailing these fruits to the mainland since they can carry fruit flies and other destructive bugs. Visitors are urged to bake, can, dry, stew, or otherwise preserve fresh fruit before sending it to the mainland. Of course, this is only practical if you are staying in a private home or condominium with kitchen facilities.

If you're mailing boxes of macadamia nuts to the mainland, have them wrapped in plain brown paper instead of writing the addresses directly onto the boxes. Otherwise, those flashy, attractive packages may never reach their destinations!

MAILING COCONUTS

Everyone gets postcards from vacationing friends. But how many people receive un-boxed, unwrapped coconuts in their mail boxes? I've tried mailing coconuts to the mainland on several occasions, and it actually works. Friends have gotten such a kick out of it. Be sure to find fallen coconuts that are brown (not green), with smooth surfaces. There should be a little liquid sloshing around inside. Use a thick, indelible marker to write the name, address, and greeting directly onto the coconut. When you have it weighed at the post office, be sure that the stamps are firmly affixed. Some stores, in malls and elsewhere, sell coconuts for this purpose, but it is cheaper if you find and mail them yourself. One good place to look is under the coconut palms around the lava fields on the grounds of the Mauna Lani resort on the Big Island. (Be sure to wear sturdy shoes, since the lava can be very rough and sharp.)

MONEY & BANKING

While credit cards are widely used in Hawaii, not all establishments accept them and those that do don't necessarily honor all major cards. If you run out of money during your stay, ATMs are available in and outside of banks. You may also be able to cash a personal check, get a cash advance, or arrange for someone at home to wire you money through offices of American Express, Western Union, or your credit card company. Some of the larger hotels have American Express offices on the premises.

Traveler's checks are widely accepted. It is best to get at least a portion in small denominations ($10s or $20s) since some places have a limit on the amount they will cash. In case of loss or theft, be sure to keep your traveler's check receipt and a list of serial numbers separate from the checks themselves.

STAYING OUT OF TROUBLE

While Hawaii may have the look and feel of paradise, it is still a part of the real world and crime is no stranger. Whenever you can, take advantage of hotel in-room safes or front desk safety deposit boxes. Carry as few valuables as possible when you go out, and never leave your things unattended - not even in the locked trunk of a parked car. Especially when you're on the beach or in a park, always keep your eye on your possessions.

Do a little homework before you venture off the beaten path. Never hitch-hike. Ask locals if you'll be comfortable in the areas you plan to visit. Fields of marijuana sprinkle the countryside and are often heavily guarded, either by less-than-friendly people or by booby traps.

Speaking of marijuana (a.k.a. *pakalolo*), it's said by some to be the state's largest cash crop. As on the mainland, it's illegal. Anyone who possesses, smokes, sells, or grows it is subject to severe penalties. Possession of cocaine is far more serious. Enforcement of anti-drug laws in Hawaii is becoming increasingly strict. Narcotics officers don't differentiate between residents, and visitors who are "just having a little fun" on their vacation.

The legal drinking age is 21 in Hawaii. You can buy beer, wine, and hard liquor in many supermarkets and delis, even on Sundays. Be sure to follow safe drinking practices, just as you should at home. Particularly because you will be on unfamiliar territory, often on narrow, winding roads, it doesn't make sense to drink and drive. If you are planning to drink and drive anyway, allow an hour or more between your last alcoholic beverage and the time you hit the road. Call a cab if you or someone else thinks that you have had too much to drink. Your car won't mind being picked up the following day. Remember: The more alcohol you consume and the more quickly you consume it, the less you'll enjoy your vacation the next day. Note that no alcohol is permitted in Hawaii's state or national parks.

OCEAN SAFETY

As far as beaches in breathtaking settings are concerned, Hawaii has an abundance of riches. However, because the Pacific can be quite rough, some are better suited to sunbathing, picnicking and photographing than to swimming. Always use caution in the ocean and heed weather or sea condition warnings. Unless the water is calm, stick to a swimming pool. Be sure you know which of Hawaii's beaches are safe for swimming and which, because of rough waters or strong currents, are not. Note that water conditions change with the season, so that calm beach of summer may be treacherous in winter. Never turn your back on the ocean.

Many beaches have no lifeguards. Never swim alone. Don't overexert yourself by trying to swim great distances. Swim parallel to the shore if you get snagged by a rip current. Keep a close eye on children. Don't swim in the vicinity of surfers, since they can't always spot bathers.

Surfing and body surfing can be extremely dangerous. Try these sports only after you've had supervised instruction from someone who is highly skilled. When near coral reefs (which can give nasty cuts), wear protective shoes, such as reef slippers or diving booties. Avoid walking on partially exposed wet boulders, since a nearly invisible growth of algae can make them quite slippery.

When swimming in inland volcanic pools, be sure to note the locations of submerged rocks, which can be jagged. Even at pools where you see locals diving off ledges into the water, I don't recommend your trying this tricky feat.

Again, in case of emergency, dial 911.

TAKING THE KIDS

Hawaii is a great place for families with *keiki* (children). As far as activities go beyond the beach and pool, **Oahu** entertains with the greatest number of choices: Sea Life Park, the Honolulu Zoo, the Waikiki Aquarium, Waimea Valley/Waimea Falls Park, and the Polynesian Cultural Center (where some of the exhibits and demonstrations will leave kids wide-eyed), the al fresco Kodak Hula Show, the Pacific Aerospace Museum, Hawaii Maritime Center, and the USS *Bowfin* Submarine and Park. Then there are submarine and outrigger canoe rides, botanical gardens, kite flying in Kapiolani Park, and snorkeling cruises, to name a few of the many other activities the younger editions most enjoy.

On **Maui**, a winter whale watching excursion is a treat and kids get a kick out of riding the 1890s-style "Sugarcane Train." During the annual

Makahiki Festival on **Molokai** in January, visiting children will enjoy watching their Island peers compete in ancient Hawaiian games. On **Kauai** and **the Big Island,** as well as the other main islands, children love all the festivities, food, and entertainment at luaus.

Especially during Easter vacation, the summer, and Christmas season, many of the larger resorts and some of the middle-sized ones run supervised children's programs so parents can have a break. Some programs are free while others charge per day or per week, often including lunch. Among the activities offered are lei-making classes, basket-weaving workshops, hikes, athletic competitions, sightseeing excursions, and sand castle-building contests. Some resorts also offer movies and other entertainment at night.

When you're making flight reservations, consider requesting seats in the bulkhead of the plane, since this area is more spacious than other rows. Infants younger than two years of age fly free on most airlines, as long as they are held in someone's lap. The cost for children ages 2 through 11 is usually less than the adult fare.

TELEPHONES

Hawaii's area code is **808.** A local call is one that is made within an island. Calls to other islands or to the mainland are classified as long distance. To dial another island, you need to dial 1-808+number. Most hotels add a hefty surcharge to calls guests make from their rooms; note that a fee is often charged for access to a line even when a guest uses a telephone calling card or credit card.

In addition to toll free 800 numbers, the US now has toll free numbers that begin with 888. You'll see a few in this guide.

TIME ZONE

Hawaiian Standard Time is two hours earlier than the Pacific Standard Time of the continental West Coast and five hours earlier than Eastern Standard Time. So if it's 9am in Hawaii, it's 11am in California, noon in Colorado, 1pm in Illinois, and 2pm in New York. That is, unless Daylight Saving Time (from the last Sunday in April through the last Sunday in October) is in effect on the mainland. In this case, since Hawaii does not observe Daylight Saving Time, the difference in time is increased by an hour.

TIPPING

Tipping is 15 percent for waiters and, for tour guides, anywhere from a couple of dollars per visitor to 10% or 15%.

TRAVEL FOR THE PHYSICALLY CHALLENGED

Wheelchair accessibility is improving in Hawaii, as it is in many parts of the world. Oahu is probably the best island in for physically challenged travelers. To rent wheelchair-accessible vans or for transportation in one on Oahu, Maui, or the Big Island of Hawaii, call **Wheelers of Hawaii**, *Tel. 808/879-5521 or 800/303-3750.*

For help with planning your trip, contact an organization such as the **American Foundation for the Blind**, the **American Heart Association**, the **New York Diabetes Foundation**, the New York-based **Society for the Advancement of Travel for the Handicapped**, or **The Information Center for Individuals with Disabilities** in Boston. In addition, **Hawaii's Commission on Persons with Disabilities**, *919 Ala Moana Boulevard, Honolulu, HI 96814, Tel. 808/ 586-8121,* publishes the *Aloha Guide to Accessibility* series.

TRAVELING SOLO

Since "Hawaii" and "honeymoon" are practically synonymous, you'll see plenty of goo-goo-eyed couples everywhere. But travelers can certainly enjoy the Islands just as much alone. Many young singles head to Waikiki Beach and the North Shore on Oahu; Kaanapali, Lahaina, and Kihei on Maui; Poipu and Kapaa on Kauai, and Kailua-Kona on the Big Island.

You may want to avoid the larger, more luxurious resorts, which tend to be honeymoon havens. When I was single, I found that midsize hotels that sponsor group activities, small hotels, inns, and bed & breakfasts were most conducive to meeting people. Joining sightseeing tours and group sports (taking a snorkeling excursion or playing volleyball, for instance) is a good way to mingle. It's not uncommon to run into solitary visitors who are hiking and camping their way through Hawaii, making new friends at every stop. Whenever I travel alone around Hawaii, I find that residents and other visitors are much quicker to draw me into their social circles than when I'm with someone.

Unfortunately, "single supplements" cause what might be an economical hotel or tour package for two to be quite expensive for one. Especially at the larger hotels, the single traveler will often pay more than half of the cost of a double room. So this is another reason for solo travelers to seek out the least expensive ways to stay in Hawaii: Bed & Breakfasts, small hotels, a YMCA, a YWCA, or campsites. Another option is to join a travel club that specializes in matching compatible single travelers or a guided excursion geared to singles.

SINGULAR FUN

Backroads, 801 Cedar Street, Berkeley, CA 94710-1800, Tel. 510/ 527-1555 or 800/462-2848, hosts guided hiking or biking trips on the Big Island of Hawaii and hiking/biking/kayaking trips on Maui that are especially for single travelers.

Single women should feel perfectly comfortable traveling alone in Hawaii. However, Hawaii is not immune to crime, so women (and men) should take the same precautions they would in any other non-utopia. Don't hitchhike; never turn your back on your belongings; don't go into remote areas at night; etc.

Also see *Staying Out of Trouble* in this chapter.

WHERE TO FIND MORE INFORMATION ABOUT HAWAII

The main **Hawaii Visitors & Convention Bureau** (HVCB) office is on Oahu: *2270 Kalakaua Avenue, Suite 801, Honolulu, HI 96815, Tel. 808/923- 1811 or 800/GO-HAWAII, Fax 808/922-8991.*

8. SPORTS & RECREATION

Whether you want to hike through dense wilderness, camp out in a stark volcanic crater, fish, play golf or tennis, surf, dive, or windsurf, you'll have plenty of choices in Hawaii. Hiking, biking, camping, sailing, and kayaking excursions can be either guided or independent.

On Kauai, the rugged hiking trail along the cliffs of **Na Pali Coast** leads to wonderfully isolated beaches. Hiking the rim of Kauai's **Waimea Canyon** or the **Kalalau Trail** to **Kalalau Valley** could hardly be more exhilarating. **Iao Valley**, a thick rain forest on west Maui, is another good place to wander. Like a giant finger, 2,250-foot **Iao Needle** pierces the clouds. Maui's remote **Hana**, an area known for its profusion of flowers and series of volcanic pools, also draws many amblers. In the moonscape of **Volcanoes National Park** on the Big Island, you'll feel as though you're on another planet. Up north, you can hike through stunning **Waipio Valley**, and even follow the trail that connects it with the neighboring valley.

Campgrounds are just as varied, from mountainous settings where the air is thin and cool to sun-splashed beachfronts. Spartan but comfortable cabins in state and national parks are available on Maui, Kauai, and the Big Island for about $10 per person, per night. In many cases, beds and linens are provided, and some cabins contain hot showers, kitchens, and cooking utensils.

Hapuna Beach State Park, with one of the Big Island's prettiest sandy shores, has A-frame shelters for rent. You might consider hiking or horseback riding in Waipio Valley. Cabins are available in Kauai's elevated **Kokee State Park**. Pitch a tent in **Palaau State Park** in a thick forest in Molokai's mountains near the cliffside trail down to **Kalaupapa peninsula**. If you can brave the cold, try camping out in **Haleakala crater** on Maui.

CAMPING

You'll need to obtain a permit to camp in Hawaii. Call the Hawaii Visitors & Convention Bureau, *Tel. 808/923-1811 or 800/GO-HAWAII,* for details about permits and county, state, and national park sites.

The longest you may stay under each permit at any one park varies from two to five nights. While campgrounds are open every night on the Neighbor Islands, on Oahu they are open only from Friday through Tuesday nights. There are no fees for parking at, entering, or picnicking in state parks. However, you will be charged if you choose to stay in a cabin or A-frame shelter. Rates range from about $10 to $45 per cabin per night (for up to four people), plus $5 for each additional person.

Housekeeping cabins have kitchens, living areas, bathrooms, and one to three bedrooms. Linens, towels, dishes, and other cooking and dining utensils are provided. Group accommodations are also available in 8-person bunk-like units with toilet facilities, hot shower, linens, and a communal recreation/dining room. In cool mountain regions, you'll keep warm with wood-burning fireplaces or electric heaters.

Be sure to take insect repellent, sunscreen, a visor or hat, rain gear, warm clothing (if you're staying at high elevations or in Maui's volcanic crater), a waterproofed tent (if you're not staying in a shelter), plenty of drinking water, and if possible, a cellular telephone. The only place you'll need a hiking permit is Kahana Valley State Park on Oahu.

Not all campgrounds have drinking water, so be sure to bring your own, if necessary. Before settling into your hiking and/or camping adventure, note the location of the closest telephone if you're not carrying a cellular. No alcohol is allowed in parks.

FISHING

Because of its calm waters and abundance of blue and striped marlin, sailfish, swordfish and tuna, the Kona coast on the Big Island of Hawaii is a favorite for deep sea fishing. The annual Hawaiian International Billfish Tournament is held here each August. Other good fishing locations are Oahu's Waianae coast; Maui's southwest coast; and the northern coasts of Kauai and Molokai.

Kauai has an exceptional variety of fish and the bonefish are extra large and plentiful here.

If you follow the lead of locals, you'll find good fishing off beaches and rocky overlooks throughout the islands, such as at Hulopoe Beach on Lanai. It's not unusual to see residents fishing from outrigger canoes or even from surfboards in calm lagoons or near reefs.

You'll need a license for fresh water fishing. You'll also need one for deep sea fishing if you're not on a charter boat. Make arrangements to charter a boat as far in advance as possible. You can buy and rent fishing gear at tackle shops. "Head boats" generally have gear and live bait for rent, while the price for charters includes gear.

For fresh water fishing tips, stop in at local tackle shops. Ask about hooking up (pun intended) with local guides.

GOLF

Even nongolfers are drawn to Hawaii's golf courses, if only to absorb the striking colors: smooth greens contrasted with dark lava outcroppings, shimmering moss-colored ponds, and the vivid blue Pacific. Oahu boasts more than 30 places to tee off.

According to *Golf Digest*, Maui has some of the best courses in the state. The sixth tee at **The Village Course** in Kapalua affords a fabulous view. From this hilltop perch, you'll take in mountains that dip into pineapple fields, with the ocean in the distance. It will be difficult to resist feeding the ducks at the glistening lake here. If you're lucky, you'll catch a glimpse of humpback whales off the coast near the tee on the fifth hole of the **Bay Course**, also in Kapalua. Other good choices in Maui are the **Royal Kaanapali North Course**, designed by Robert Trent Jones Sr., and backed by the West Maui Mountains; and the **Blue Course** at the Wailea Golf Club.

At the **Frances I'i Brown Golf Course** at the Mauna Lani Resort on the Big Island, the rough, chocolate-colored lava sets off the electric green swards. Like everything else on the Big Island, Mauna Kea's course is in a very dramatic setting. One of the state's most difficult courses, it was designed by Robert Trent Jones, Sr. It winds through desolate-looking lava flows. The neighboring **Hapuna Golf Course**, with its stunning coastal views, was designed around all kinds of indigenous trees, plants, and grasses.

The **Makai Golf Course** at Princeville Resort on Kauai was designed by Robert Trent Jones, Jr. The 27 holes are surrounded by lush greenery.

Even though this part of the island receives a lot of rain, golfers still flock to this course.

Lanai is where you'll find two of Hawaii's newest and nicest courses, one, the **Challenge at Manele**, designed by Jack Nicklaus, and the other, **Experience at Koele**, by Greg Norman with Ted Robinson as the architect.

HIKING

Although some visitors ask "How can you get lost on an island?," many a hiker has found him- or herself seemingly walking in circles in Hawaii's dense mountainous regions for far more hours than planned. And even when stringent safety precautions are taken, accidents do happen. Searches for lost hikers, including one that resulted in the deaths of rescue workers in a helicopter crash, have prompted government officials and veteran hikers alike to reiterate hiking safety tips that every explorer should follow:

• Never hike alone.

• Before you go, let someone know where you're headed, what route you plan to take (leaving a marked map is a good idea), when you'll be back, who your companions are, and what you're taking with you.

• Before leaving, contact the National Weather Service to find out what the weather will be like in your target area. Be prepared for wide variations in temperature, even within a particular hiking area. The weather can be intensely hot during the day, then downright cold at night. If you're planning to hike in Haleakala (Maui), Mauna Kea or Mauna Loa (the Big Island) volcanoes, be prepared for very chilly temperatures. You might even see a dusting of snow during winter months.

• You may want to wear long pants, since thorny plants and jagged rocks aren't too kind to human skin. Wear sturdy closed shoes with a good tread. Pack rain gear as well as a long-sleeved shirt, extra socks, work gloves, and a piece of clothing that is brightly colored.

• Carry plenty of water. (I like to fill my water bottle halfway, put it in the freezer the night before, then fill it with H2O before I set out, insuring that it stays chilled for quite a while.) Snacks such as dried fruit and nuts or breakfast bars can come in handy.

• Take a first aid kit, a whistle, a pocketknife, paper and pencil for leaving notes and waterproof matches or a lighter. Carrying a cellular phone (protected in a thick plastic bag) can be a lifesaver. If you don't have one, note the location of the closest public phone before you set out.

• It's best to carry gear weighing no more than 35 percent of your body weight, especially when hiking in difficult areas such as Na Pali Coast on Kauai.

• For a complete selection of hiking maps, contact **Hawaii Geographic Maps & Books**, *49 South Hotel Street, Suite 215, Honolulu, HI 96813, Tel. 808/538-3952 or, in Hawaii, Tel. 800/538-3950, or the* **State Parks Outdoor Recreation Office**, *1151 Punchbowl Street, Honolulu, HI 96813, Tel. 808/587-0300.* Another good source of highly detailed information is the series of Hawaii hiking books by Craig Chisholm.

KAYAKING

It's difficult to find a more scenic and peaceful place to paddle than Kauai's Hanalei River, up north.

SAILING, DAY CRUISES, & SUBMARINES

All islands offer a good selection of sailing trips and cruises, whether on catamarans, trimarans, sailboats, Zodiac rubber rafts, or power boats. Some are highlighted by snorkeling, cocktails or dining, or sunset- or whale-watching.

On Oahu, Maui, and the Big Island of Hawaii, you can even take a plunge in a passenger submarine for underwater sightseeing.

SCUBA DIVING

Dramatic dropoffs, caves, hapless coral-encrusted ships, airplane wrecks, and, of course, a profusion of marine life - it's all wet in Hawaii. To participate in group dive excursions, rent gear, or fill tanks in Hawaii, divers must have taken a local resort course or be certified. Half-day resort courses are widely available through hotels or independent dive operators for those who don't have the time, money, or inclination to take the five-day certification course. Most islands offer dive packages and guided dives. If you are considering diving on your own, note that scuba can be dangerous along unprotected coasts during winter months. At this time of year, the water is much rougher, with strong rip tides and undertows.

Oahu has the greatest number of dive facilities in Hawaii. Scuba is year round on the protected leeward coast, where Waikiki is located. During the summer when the water is "flat," the diving is excellent along the beach-rimmed north shore. This is a good place for inexperienced divers.

With Molokini and Lanai nearby, Maui is a great home base for diving. Molokini, a partially submerged volcanic crater off Maui's southwestern coast, draws divers. The waters around isolated Hana are also excellent for diving. The Big Island's Kona Coast may have fewer sites, but some people say that this island has the best diving in the state, in part because of the clarity of the water. Kauai has a wide selection of exciting dive sites. Sea turtles and dolphins are often around the reef off the site of Nualolo Kai, an old fishing village in the north. The little-visited dive sites along the northern shore of the neighboring island of Niihau feature caves, walls, and arches.

SNORKELING

If you've never snorkeled before, don't worry- it's simple. Ask anyone who's done it to teach you tricks such as how to make sure your mask fits properly (without using the strap, place the mask against your face, breathe in, and bend your head down. If the mask doesn't fall off, the fit is fine, and no water should seep in while you're swimming); how to prevent the mask from fogging up (spit on the inside of the glass, rub your saliva around, then quickly dip the mask in the ocean - the secret ingredient is the enzymes in saliva); to be sure not to look back at your feet while swimming, lest you inhale a snorkel-full of salty water; and how to blow out any water that does get into your snorkel. You'll make fast aquatic friends if you bring along some bread or a bag of frozen peas to feed the fish.

Oahu's Hanauma Bay tops many lists for snorkeling. Scores of far-from-timid fish are used to receiving edible goodies from human fingers, and the curving, palm-shaded beach is backed by mountains. The only problem with the beauty of the setting and the kaleidoscope of fish is that you'll probably be appreciating this spot with a slew of other people.

From Maui, consider taking a snorkeling cruise to Molokini crater or Lanai. Playful dolphins often join snorkelers in Honolua Bay, north of Lahaina. The waters around isolated Hana, also on Maui, are excellent for snorkeling as well. On the Big Island, there is wonderful snorkeling in Kealakekua Bay, near the Captain Cook Monument, even though it can be crowded. Snorkeling is also great in Honaunau Bay near the Place of Refuge, an ancient religious site.

SURFING

Winter is serious surfing season in Hawaii and the state's premier surfing area is Oahu's North Shore. The waves here don't stop gathering steam until they reach heights of 30 feet or so. The relatively calm waters and the choice of good instructors draw many novice surfers to Waikiki. Quiet as it's kept, Kauai is also an excellent island for surfing. Here Poipu and Kapaa are the two leading surfing meccas. Even when waves are at their most enticing, beaches in these areas are far less crowded than on Oahu and Maui.

During the winter, Maui's Honolua Bay and Hookipa Beach Park are where most people ride the waves. In the summer, surfers head for Kaanapali Beach, Maalaea Bay, and Lahaina. On the Big Island, surfing conditions are often excellent near Hilo Bay and at south shore beaches. A major competition is held at Banyans Drive on Kailua Bay during the winter. Magic Sands Beach Park is popular with body surfers and boogie boarders.

TENNIS

Most of the larger hotels and condominiums have tennis courts. Since Maui has so many courts - mainly in Wailea, Kapalua, Kaanapali and Makena - you are likely to have a good deal of flexibility, playing when and where you want on this island.

UNUSUAL DIVERSIONS

From December to April, **skiers** can tackle the slopes of the Big Island's 13,796-foot Mauna Kea volcano - that is, if Mother Nature is cooperating. Unfortunately, it's not every winter she blesses the mountaintop with the necessary minimum of two feet of snow. The panoramic views from the summit can be fabulous when the weather is clear. The first people to glide down these slopes did so in 1937. But before they could go down, they had to climb the mountain with their wooden skis tied to their shoulders. Today, four-wheel-drive vehicles transport skiers to the top. Some people may suffer from altitude sickness; warning signals are fatigue, headache, and nausea.

Glider plane rides can be arranged on Oahu's North Shore. For the less adventurous, **parasailing** is also exhilarating. Try it on Oahu, Lahaina in Maui, and Kailua-Kona on the Big Island. On Waikiki Beach, visitors can ride the waves as the ancient Hawaiians did - in **outrigger canoes.** On Kauai and Oahu, go **kayaking** past beautiful scenery.

WHALE WATCHING

From about November through March or April, 40- to 50-foot long humpback whales migrate from Alaska to Hawaii. Maui is the best vantage point for getting close-up views of these majestic, graceful giants. Several whale-watching cruises depart from Lahaina and Maalaea harbors. But you don't have to leave the shore to get an eyeful (just remember: the higher your perch, the better). Actually, naturalists would prefer that whale-watching by boat be kept to a minimum or eliminated altogether. The noise from the motors interferes with mating. Spots on the Big Island, Molokai, and Lanai are also good for watching these giant mammals. You might want to bring a pair of binoculars. Early morning and late afternoon are the best times for spotting Moby Dick's brethren. You'll have the most luck when the ocean is calm.

WINDSURFING

While windsurfing is possible on all the major islands, Maui is heaven for this sport. Oahu also has some good spots for it.

9. FOOD & DRINK

The old saying "You are what you eat" couldn't be more true than in Hawaii. The food here is a melange of American, Hawaiian, Japanese, Chinese, Portuguese, Korean, Filipino, European - and so are the people.

A style of cooking known as Hawaiian regional or Pacific Rim cuisine has emerged throughout the Islands, particularly at the more upscale restaurants and resorts. Annual food and wine festivals are held at some of the hotels along the Kona coast on the Big Island of Hawaii and Kapalua on Maui. Incorporating Hawaii's freshest vegetables, fruits, macadamia nuts, seafood, and meat, these dishes are influenced by the Pacific, the East and the West. They are artistically presented, with special attention to texture, color, sauces, and seasonings. Gone is the heavy, old-fashioned "Polynesian" cuisine in which pineapple seemed to be the common demoninator.

THE GOOD OLD DAYS?

Some ancient Hawaiian culinary traditions have survived, but many have been lost, a few happily so. No one today seems to miss the old practices of eating dogmeat, having separate dining quarters for men and women, and banning women from consuming pork, bananas, coconuts and other "manly" foods.

Using planting, gathering, digging and cooking utensils made of wood, ancient Hawaiians lived off such staples as breadfruit, sweet potatoes, taro, bananas, and coconuts. They used shells to remove skins from cooked taro and breadfruit and fashioned knives from bamboo, rocks, and sharks' teeth.

Gourds, sometimes painted with intricate geometric designs, were transformed into bowls and drinking cups. Wooden plates were reserved for high ranking individuals. These *alii* also used special bowls to dispose of their leftovers and bones. It was the job of their servants to hide this uneaten food so that no one could use it to cast evil spells on the *alii*.

As in the old days, locals today throw **luaus** to celebrate births, birthdays, weddings, and simply being alive. These are quite different from the commercial affairs most tourists are herded off to. At these gatherings of family and friends, someone might spontaneously begin to sing, or play the slack key guitar.

LUAUS – THE REAL McCOY

If you scour local newspapers, listen to radio stations, and ask around, you might be lucky enough to find out about a luau sponsored by a civic organization or other group to raise money for one cause or another. Nothing feels packaged or rigidly programmed at these homestyle festive events.

Whether or not you attend a luau, you'll have plenty of chances to sample **pupus** (appetizers), usually a variety of tidbits served on a platter during happy hours. Also be sure to try the trademark dish of modern Hawaii: a **plate lunch** (also called mixed plate, a Bento lunch, or a box lunch). This blend of Japanese, Hawaiian, and Chinese food comes in the form of a meat or fish entree served with two scoops of white rice (which isn't considered rice unless it's moist and sticky), and a scoop of macaroni salad. It's often eaten with chopsticks and is sold in many mom-and-pop fast-food joints.

Also look out for Hawaiian-style curry, which is green and not very hot. Serving these and other local dishes, roadside "BBQ" stands and "drive-ins" border main roads, particularly on Oahu.

HAWAII'S MOST POPULAR FOODS
From the Sea

Ahi: Hawaiian big-game yellowfin tuna that often turns up grilled, as a "burger" sandwich, baked inside *ti* leaves, or served raw as sashimi or in sushi.

Aku: Skipjack tuna.

A'u: Marlin or broadbill swordfish.

Hapu: Hawaiian sea bass.

Lehi: Orange snapper.

Limu: One of the few ancient Hawaiian culinary traditions that thrives today is the prepared on and consumption of *limu*, commonly known as seaweed. This vegetable is extremely rich in vitamins and minerals.

It is served with raw fish as part of sashimi and sushi or cooked in soups and stews. Today, some Hawaiians still collect edible seaweed that has washed ashore, just as their ancestors did. Many varieties of this sea plant are also an important part of the diet in Asian cultures, such as Japan's. The Japanese presence in Hawaii has added to the wealth of traditional Hawaiian seaweed dishes. Most of the seaweed used for sushi in the state is imported from Japan.

Lomi lomi: Salmon diced with green leaf onions and tomatoes, served cold. Hawaiians created this dish with the salted and smoked salmon introduced by 19th century whalers.

Lomi o'io: With its bones soft enough to chew, raw bonefish is mashed and mixed with *limu*.

Mahi-mahi: A dolphin fish, not a mammal - so it's no relation to Flipper. The texture reminds me of moist pork chops. Perhaps Hawaii's best-known fish, it is especially delicious grilled.

Onaga: Red snapper.

Ono: A game fish also called wahoo. The very appropriate name is the Hawaiian word for "delicious."

Opakapaka: Pink snapper; popular for the first meal of the day.

Poke: Cubed or sliced raw *ahi*, mixed with pounded *limu*, tomatoes, onions, and *kukui* nuts.

Sashimi: A Japanese favorite; paper-thin slices of raw fish.

Sushi: Almost as common as tacos in some mainland cities, this dish is made by rolling vinegared rice, vegetables, and/or raw fish in seaweed or placing raw fish on a lump of sticky rice. It is even served in some McDonald's in Hawaii.

Uku: Gray snapper.

Ulua: Deep-sea pompano.

From the Land

Breadfruit: This large, round, starchy vegetable was brought to Hawaii by the early Polynesians. It is served baked, fried, roasted, or boiled. Its mild flavor makes it a good side dish with highly seasoned food.

Chicken luau: Cooked with coconut milk and *taro* leaves.

Kalua pig: The centerpiece of any luau; the entire (often deboned) porker is cooked in an *imu* (an earthen oven). The pig is stuffed with fiery hot lava rocks, wrapped in moistened burlap bags and *ti* leaves, surrounded by more hot rocks, and roasted in the pit for several hours, along with breadfruit, yams, fish, and other goodies. The crispy skin is considered the best part by many. At some luaus, guests are invited to observe the ceremony involving the removal of the pig from the ground.

Kim chee: Korean pickled and spiced cabbage or other vegetables.

Kula or Maui onions: Some of the sweetest onions around. You may be lucky enough to find them made into breaded rings and served with spicy mustard.

Lau lau: Ground pork and/or fish wrapped in *taro* or *ti* leaves and then steamed or baked.

Macadamia nuts: Perhaps macadamia nuts taste so good because they are so long in the making: It takes about seven years for a tree to grow its first nuts, then about eight more years before it is producing to capacity. They're also hard to get to: 300 pounds of pressure per square inch is needed to crack their shells. However, you won't have to worry about cracking them. They are sold in endless varieties, but shell-covered isn't one of them. You'll find them plain, salted, dipped in chocolate, or dressed in caramel or coconut glaze. You can also sample them in cookies, ice cream, pies, on fish and chicken, and on and on. They are rich and creamy in texture, and far from low in calories. Although they contain no cholesterol, they are usually roasted in coconut oil, a saturated fat.

Manapua: This steamed dough stuffed with pork or black beans originated in China.

Poi: Pounded, fermented *taro* root, cooked and mashed into a sticky paste. Sort of brownish-purple-gray in color, this side dish, served with meat or fish, has a mild, slightly sour or tangy taste. When mainlanders say *poi* tastes like wallpaper paste, Hawaiians remark that they don't know what that means since wallpaper paste isn't eaten in Hawaii. "You keep your sauerkraut and cottage cheese and we'll keep our *poi*," they joke. This dish is eaten with the fingers. Two-finger *poi* is thicker than the three-finger variety, because it takes fewer fingers to spoon up.

Portuguese sausage: Spicy; often eaten with rice for breakfast or used in Portuguese bean soup to add flavor.

Saimin: Noodle soup with dumplings and vegetables topped with sliced pork and/or seafood. Some say it originaced in Japan while others maintain it was inspired by a Chinese dish called *sae mein*.

SPAM: Remember that canned meat you haven't gone near since the days when your mother used to stick it in your lunch box? Well, in Hawaii people eat SPAM with a vengeance. This chopped pork shoulder and ham, in its blue Hormel tin, was introduced to Hawaii during the 1940s, mainly for use by the military. It thus has come to be referred to as **South Pacific Army Meat**, but its name is actually a contraction of "spiced ham." People in Hawaii eat it like a delicacy, putting it in soups, stews, on the side for breakfast, and as the main event for lunch and dinner. As a matter of fact, for several years, Maui hosted an annual summer SPAM cookoff where both professional and novice chefs competed for prizes for the tastiest, most creative recipes using the meat.

Teriyaki beef: A spicy Japanese dish made with soy sauce, sugar, vegetables and strips of meat. Teriyaki chicken and fish are also popular.

Taro: Starchy root from which *poi* is made; also served baked or roasted. When cooked, it looks and tastes something like a potato. Be sure to try highly addictive *taro* chips, sold in grocery stores bagged like potato chips. *Taro* leaves are used to wrap meat or seafood for steaming or boiling.

Ti leaves: Ancient Hawaiians believed that the *ti* plant held a godly power that warded off evil spirits. Food is often wrapped in these leaves for cooking or storage. The genuinely Hawaiian hula skirts are made from *ti* leaves (as opposed to the grass skirts you'll see a lot, which actually originated elsewhere in the Pacific).

FRUIT

Not only can you enjoy fresh, juicy fruit in restaurants or roadside stands, but, especially while hiking, you can pick quite a bit of it yourself. Coconuts, bananas, and pineapple are delicious in the 50th state. Here's a rundown on some of the other popular natural snacks:

Guavas are best for picking between June and October, when they are softest to the touch and unmarred. They contain five times more Vitamin C than oranges. The most common type of this thin-skinned fruit is the yellow, lemon-sized variety. Another, smaller kind is called the strawberry guava, because of its taste and red color. The yellow, oval **lilikoi** (passion fruit) is ripe during the summer and fall. It grows on vines that drape themselves on bushes and over tree limbs. The vines of the small, round purple passion fruit burst into color with their white and lavender flowers. The vines of the yellow, banana-shaped banana passion fruit bloom with pink blossoms. Lilikoi makes a wonderfully refreshing beverage.

Growing on bushy, towering trees, **mangoes** are a favorite tropical fruit. They are extremely juicy and their meat is slippery when ripe (during the spring and summer). Part of the fun - especially for children - is making a mess while eating them.

Summer is the best time to pluck **papayas** off their skinny trees. Pick them when they are just starting to turn yellow.

High up in lush, shady regions of Hawaii, **mountain apples** are waiting to be sampled. The trees bloom with fluffy red flowers. The small, pear-shaped fruit is red on the outside, with white meat inside. Mountain apples ripen between July and December.

Usually ripe in late May or early June, **Methley plums** (also called Kokee plums) are found throughout Kokee State Park on Kauai.

Be sure to try soft, sweet **lychee** and **poha** (Cape gooseberries). Peel the skin off the **red berries** that grow on coffee trees around November and suck on the two beans in each. The coating has a candylike flavor (but don't try to eat the beans!). Avocados, very popular in salads or pseudo-Japanese sushi, ripen from June to November in their towering trees.

SWEETS

To satisfy a sweet tooth in Hawaii, you can start with all kinds of juicy, fresh fruit, including papayas, guavas, mangos, bananas, pineapple, coconuts, mountain apples, plums and *poha* berries. Here are some other local favorites:

Haupia: Jiggly coconut pudding cut into squares. People often bring it to luaus the way mainlanders might carry a bottle of wine to a friend's house for dinner.

Lilikoi: Also known as passion fruit; it makes a tart pie or is sweetened and turned into a beverage, often mixed with other fruit juices.

Malasadas: From Portugal; sugary balls of fried dough often called "holeless doughnuts."

Manju: Sweet Japanese pastry with black bean paste inside.

Molokai sweet bread: Reflecting the "chop suey" heritage of many locals, this bread, based on a Portuguese recipe, is created in a Japanese bakery on Molokai.

Shave ice: Called a snow cone in some parts of the mainland, this refreshing cup of crushed ice is flavored with syrup made from *lilikoi*, pineapple, coconut or other fruit.

Hula pie: You'll find this for dessert at many restaurants, each serving its own variation. The basic ingredients are ice cream on a cookie crust, macadamia nuts, and whipped cream.

OTHER SNACKS

The Original Maui Kitch'n Cook'd Potato Chips, those thick and crunchy wonders, have played a large part in changing the face of potato chips across the mainland. There are other chips with "Maui" in their names, but this brand is the best. If you're on the Big Island, Hilo also produces a version.

Looking like potato chips with purple threads running through them, **taro chips** are also delicious. Other niblets eaten straight from the bag are **dried shrimp**, which can be very salty. They are also used in cooking.

BEVERAGES

Sure, you'll find plenty of rum-based **Mai Tais** and **Blue Hawaiis**, but for my money, nothing is more enjoyable than Hawaii's wonderful fruit juices, especially **guava nectar** (a pink beverage that has a thick, grainy texture something like pear nectar) and **lilikoi** (passion fruit juice).

If you want a potent kick, try some **okolehao**, a Hawaiian whiskey made from the root of the *ti* plant.

Kona coffee, originating on the Big Island, is renowned for its rich aroma and taste. It is sold in many flavors and blends, both regular and de-caf.

10. BEST PLACES TO STAY

Hawaii has some of the world's plushest and splashiest beach hotels. Each of the resorts that cropped up in the late 1980s seemed to be striving mightily to outdo the last. Some of Hawaii's most spectacular are along the Kona-Kohala Coast of the Big Island. But the good news is that you don't have to be Donald Trump to afford a fabulous place to stay in Hawaii. Many vacationers aren't aware that Hawaii also has some exceptional Bed & Breakfasts, several right on the water, along with some great moderately-priced hotels and condominiums.

Below are my picks for the places I like most. There are plenty of other wonderful accommodations in Hawaii, but I've chosen these because there is something extra special about each of them: Their decor, facilities, or location, their romantic setting, the friendliness and efficiency of their staff, their Hawaiian flavor, or all of the above.

Outside Waikiki, Oahu

KAHALA MANDARIN ORIENTAL, *5000 Kahala Avenue, Honolulu, HI 96816. Tel. 808/739-8888 or 800/367-2525. 370 rooms. Double room rates begin at $275. Major credit cards.*

First opened in 1964 and known as the celebrated Kahala Hilton for the next thirty years, this hotel became Kahala Mandarin Oriental in 1996 after a multi-million dollar transformation. During its first three decades, it built a reputation for attracting the rich and famous. On any given day, Lucille Ball, Frank Sinatra, Eva Gabor, William Shatner, or Julie Andrews might be seen lounging around the pool. Royalty and other world leaders have slept here as well, from Queen Elizabeth and King Juan Carlos to Indira Gandhi and the Dalai Lama. Once when I stayed here, Billy Joel and Christy Brinkley (in happier times, of course) were down the hall.

Located on the beach in a quiet, residential area with views of both Diamond Head and Koko Head craters, Kahala Mandarin Oriental is in a wonderfully tranquil, verdant setting. But it's also just ten minutes from Waikiki, the heart of Oahu's action. The renovation has made this hotel even better than before. Celebrities still beat a path to its doors. I recently saw Luther Vandross and his entourage wandering around the flowering grounds and the new Emperor and Empress of Japan were also among the first guests of the revitalized resort.

Vacationers still have a choice of excellent restaurants. Hoku's, offering a blend of French, German, and Asian cuisine, is open for lunch and dinner; Plumeria Beach Cafe, known for its bake shop, Japanese selections, and elaborate buffets, serves all three meals daily.

Mixing tropical and classic Asian and European decor, guest rooms (some with balconies) are decorated with handsome mahogany furniture and hand-loomed Tibetan rugs on teak parquet floors. Views take in the ocean, the Koolau Mountains and Waialae Golf Course, or the Dolphin Lagoon, where Flipper's cousins entertain spectators during the three daily feedings. When guests aren't on the beach or in the pool, they can hit the Fitness Center. There is a second, children's pool as well as a children's activities program.

MANOA VALLEY INN, *2001 Vancouver Drive (off University) Avenue, Manoa Valley), Honolulu, HI 96822. Tel. 808/947-6019 or 800/535-0085, Fax 808/946-6168. 8 rooms. Double rooms begin at $109. Major credit cards.*

Now, this is *my* kind of place! Two miles from Waikiki and down the street from the University of Hawaii, this former private home is a B & B. In a tranquil residential neighborhood in a flourishing, breezy valley, it has a mere seven guest rooms plus a private cottage that sleeps two. With a wooden swing and wicker chairs with thick cushions, the lanai overlooks the small lawn and the distant skyscrapers of Waikiki. Continental breakfast and an afternoon buffet of wine, fruit, and cheese are served.

The handsome main house, with its eaves and gables, was built in 1912. Now refurbished, it is listed in the **National Register of Historic Places**. The inn is decorated with oriental rugs, handcarved tables, beautiful aging tapestries, a grandfather clock, and other eye-catching antiques - even a nickelodeon that still works. Stained glass windows, lace curtains, and carved or brass headboards are features of guest rooms. The billiards room is a real knock out. Note that some rooms share baths.

Waikiki, Oahu

HALEKULANI, *2199 Kalia Road (at end of Leuvers Street), Honolulu, HI 96815. Tel. 808/923-2311 or 800/367-2343, Fax 808/926-8004. 456 rooms. Double rooms begin at $300. Major credit cards.*

For years I've been recommending this gracious hotel to newly married friends. My husband and I even chose it for our own honeymoon.

As tranquil as it is, it's difficult to believe that it's right in the heart of Waikiki, at the edge of the state's most crowded beach. Potted silver cup bromeliads and pink cactus blossoms decorate the white-columned porte cochere. A sweeping staircase fringed with waterfalls leads to the lobby and garden. Adjoining towers topped with high-pitched roofs enclose a grassy, palm-studded courtyard, a popular locale for weddings. The hotel's dazzling color scheme is white-in seven shades, that is-set off by the teak-stained wood of shopfronts and louvered doors. Best viewed from a balcony, one million tiles have been laid out to form a huge orchid on the floor of the oceanfront swimming pool.

Halekulani is full of personal touches. Guests are escorted to their rooms, where they are registered in plush privacy and shown around. You're greeted with complimentary fruit baskets and chocolates freshly made in the hotel's pastry shop. In the bathroom, floor-to-ceiling mirrors slide open to the closet, which contains a safe and is separated from the bedroom by sliding louvered wooden doors. Open these doors while in the tub, and you'll drink in a fabulous view through the room's windows. Although there's a stall shower, the deep tub also has a hand-held, snake-neck nozzle. Thick terry cloth robes are provided for guests during their stay. One of each room's three telephones is conveniently located in the bathroom. (Local telephone calls are free to guests, by the way.)

Lanais are very large and most look out to Diamond Head (the most impressive view) and/or the ocean. In addition to the expected color TV and minibar/refrigerator, there are marble vanities, and both fresh flowers and complimentary newspapers appear daily. When visitors order breakfast room service, don't be surprised if a toaster is brought to the room so you can have it your way.

Upstairs in the hotel's elegant original wing (built in 1931) is La Mer, for fine dining. Orchid's is a wonderful spot for an oceanfront breakfast, complete with fresh-squeezed guava juice and views of surfers and outrigger canoes. Head to the fitness center to work off any unwanted calories. All tours and sports activities are arranged by the concierge. For early arrivals or late departures, two hospitality suites provide changing rooms, showers, color TV, and complimentary refreshments. For December or January visits, make a reservation at least six months in advance and send your deposit in at least two months before your vacation.

Kapalua, Maui

THE RITZ-CARLTON KAPALUA, *1 Ritz-Carlton Drive, Kapalua, HI 96761. Tel. 808/669-6200 or 800/262-8440, Fax 808/665-0026. 548 rooms. Double rooms begin at $285. Major credit cards.*

Here at one of the newer additions to Hawaii's ever-growing group of luxury hotels, you'll find all kinds of extras - nightly turn down service;

bathrobes; a marble bath with a separate shower and a telephone; mini bar and refrigerator; an in-room safe. On these fifty sprawling acres, you'll have several bars and excellent restaurants to choose from, along with tennis courts, and a three-level swimming pool. Sports include snorkeling; scuba diving, windsurfing, sailing, and hiking. Be sure to spend some time - perhaps "A Day of Beauty" - in the health spa.

Picturesque trails have been designed for jogging and strolling. Set on a gentle slope above the white sand beach, the hotel borders one of Kapalua's three championship golf courses with views of the Pacific and the cloud-capped island of Molokai. For nightly entertainment, stop by the lounge. Transportation between the airport and the hotel can be arranged.

Wailea, Maui

FOUR SEASONS RESORT MAUI AT WAILEA, *3900 Wailea Alanui Drive, Wailea, HI 96753. Tel. 808/874-8000 or 800/334-MAUI, Fax 808/874-2222. 380 rooms. Double rooms begin at $340. Major credit cards.*

The elegant lobby, done in polished and unpolished marble and granite, sets the tone for this gracious beachfront hotel, which opened in the spring of 1990. The Four Seasons Resort Maui's reputation for exceptional cuisine has spread quickly, with Seasons restaurant its culinary showpiece. Save this dining room for a very special evening (if you can afford it). Even the smallest guest rooms are large, each complete with a TV and VCR. Comfortable teak furniture decorates lanais. The brightly lit bathrooms are fabulous, all with glass-enclosed, marble-tiled stall showers, bath tubs, double sinks, and endless counter space. Room service is available around the clock.

Talk about serious pampering! Sit by one of the swimming pools and attendants periodically bring you ice towels and glasses of ice water, and they might even spritz you with Evian. (It's easy to understand why celebrities such as Elton John and Arnold Schwartzenegger have chosen to stay here.) The two-level upper pool, complete with a waterfall, has a section for children designed so that parents can be in the deeper area while keeping an eye on the kids. With two Jacuzzis, the main pool has a fountain in the middle. At sunset, Hawaiian music wafts out from the poolside cafe.

Have morning coffee and tea in the library or browse through the wide selection of books and periodicals when you need a quiet moment. Live dance music draws people to the Lobby Lounge at night. A pool table, large screen TV, and full bar are found in the game room. Along with an exercise room, massage rooms (your body will love you after a lomi lomi massage), and a steam room, the health club has a centrifugal dryer so you can work out or take a swim on your last day without having to pack a wet bathing suit. Parents should ask about the complimentary children's program for those aged five to 12.

Kona-Kohala Coast, The Big Island of Hawaii

KONA VILLAGE RESORT, *P.O. Box 1299, Kailua Kona, HI 96745. In Ka'upulehu, six miles north of airport. Follow sign to Kona Village 1.5 miles to gate house. Tel. 808/325-5555 or 800/367-5290, Fax 808/ 325-5124. 125 rooms. Double room rates begin at $425, including three meals a day. Major credit cards.*

Popular among families with children, this has to be the most unusual resort in the state. As you drive along the chocolate-colored lava road that twists and turns through a wasteland strewn with dark crumbly boulders, your first thought is likely to be, "What have I gotten myself into!" Then you'll see the guest houses, built in the architectural styles of a variety of Polynesian peoples, from Hawaiians and Tahitians to Samoans and Fijians. Some with thatched roofs, these cottages stand on stilts above rugged lava flows, at the edges of beaches, or overlooking a lagoon. Just as when the resort was built in the 1960s, they contain no telephones, radios, TVs, or air conditioners. Tradewinds and ceiling fans keep visitors comfortable in rooms attractive with their Polynesian decor.

However, fresh Kona coffee, a coffee maker, and a mini bar are provided. Colorful batiks and other textiles decorate the walls and furnishings. When guests don't want to be disturbed, they simply place the room's coconut outside the door. (There are no room keys but in-room safes are provided). If you lock your door at night, be sure to press the button that unlocks it before leaving the next day, or you'll find yourself locked out as I once did.

Use of the fitness center and all sports, from tennis to snorkeling, are complimentary, as are children's programs, transportation to golf, and sports equipment. All meals, including weekly luaus and steak cookouts, are included in the rates. Pacific rim cuisine includes an emphasis on fish, accented by tropical fruits. A strong emphasis is placed on Hawaiiana and historical programs.

Sandy shores here come in black, salt and pepper, and white. There are also two swimming pools, two whirlpools, and three night-lit tennis courts. Sunsets are especially picturesque through the floor-to-ceiling windows of the main dining room.

Guests who dine at the Hale Samoa, the second restaurant, pay a surcharge. Tours can be arranged of the petroglyph fields and fish ponds, near where the hotel's famed luau is held. At night you may hear the wild donkeys that sometimes visit the resort.

Kaihua-Kona, The Big Island of Hawaii

KAILUA PLANTATION HOUSE, *75-5948 Alii Drive, Kailua-Kona.*
Tel. 808/329-3727, Fax 808/329-7323. Five rooms. Rates: $145 per room.
Major credit cards.

Built in 1990 in the style of an old plantation house, this beautifully designed Bed & Breakfast is among Hawaii's nicest accommodations. On two stories, the five spacious guest rooms are individually decorated. In yours, you might find a window seat, mosquito netting over the bed, a walk-in closet, a whirlpool tub, or a party-sized shower. Three rooms are oceanfront, one is ocean view, and the other looks out at the mountains. All have private lanais, refrigerators, ceiling fans, TV, books and magazines.

Some of the furniture is antique, such as the desk on the upstairs landing. Breakfast, featuring home-baked muffins, island fruit, and freshly ground Kona coffee, is served in the living/dining room, with its overstuffed couches. The plentiful windows and high ceilings give the house a bright, airy feeling. Water trickles over lava rocks into the tiny pool (large enough for a dip) and whirlpool at the edge of the rugged ebony coast. The surf crashes against the rocks. Sandy beaches are close at hand and the restaurants and shops in Kailua-Kona are within walking distance.

Poipu, Kauai

HYATT REGENCY KAUAI RESORT & SPA, *1571 Poipu Road,*
Koloa, HI 96756. Tel. 808/742-1234 or 800/233-1234, Fax 808/742-6229.
600 rooms. Double rooms begin at $300. Major credit cards.

Lavishly landscaped, this luxury resort is built into a hill. In memory of the sugar cane fields that once blanketed the land where the Hyatt now stands, a brass sugar-cane leaf motif is used in everything from wall decorations to railings and door handles. It's great that the hotel sprawls horizontally instead of vertically. However, you may have a very long walk between your beautifully appointed room and the elegant lobby, restaurants, pools, and beach. So make sure you haven't forgotten anything when you leave your room! (Note that some rooms face the parking lot, golf course, and mountains.)

The ocean here can be dangerous for swimming, but it remains a prime local surfing spot. Heated saltwater lagoons have been built at the edge of the Pacific, and elaborate swimming pools are terraced down the hillside. Complete with waterfalls, the main pool winds under bridges, past flourishing greenery and boulders draped with bougainvillea. Both children and adults climb the steps over and over again to the top of the 150-foot water slide for the splashy ride to the bottom.

At the extensive health spa, the lap pool is in a sunny courtyard, and whirlpools are open-air. Each massage or wrap room has a private courtyard. One special shower has twelve spouts positioned to massage different parts of the body simultaneously. Four tennis courts and an 18-hole Robert Trent Jones, Jr. golf course also keep guests occupied. Tennis racquets can be borrowed.

For many, Kuhio's night club is the place to be after dark. Authentic hula halau (schools) entertain guests as well, and Hawaiian old-timers have been enlisted to teach visitors traditional arts such as making leis, quilts, and Niihau necklaces. The Library contains many books on Hawaiiana. Ask about the children's program if you're traveling with little ones.

GLORIA'S SPOUTING HORN B&B, *4464 Lawai Beach Road, Koloa, HI 96756. Tel. 808/742-6995, Fax 808/742-6995. Three rooms. Rates: $160 per room. No children under age 14. No smoking inside the house.*

For those who would like to stay in a Bed & Breakfast and want to be on the ocean, this is the place. It's also a great spot for honeymooning (as my husband and I did) or even getting married, particularly because Bob Merkle (co-owner with and husband of Gloria) is a Congregational minister. Although the shore is rocky here, it's wonderfully scenic, with a small sandy beach and dramatic crashing surf. Look for the sea turtles that feed along the shore here. Vacationers enjoy absorbing the view from the hammock strung between two palms. Popular Poipu Beach is a mile away.

A romantic outdoor lava rock beach shower is shaded by a mango tree - but don't worry, it's enclosed and perfectly private! The Punana Aloha (love nest) room, overflowing with character, opens onto a terraced deck and Japanese rock garden at the water's edge, as well as a pond filled with koi. (In keeping with Japanese tradition, guests are asked to remove their shoes before entering the house.) Gloria's sports a striking willow-branch canopy bed in one room. Each of its three guest rooms has a Japanese-style soaking tub in its private bath.

All rooms have TVs, VCR's, microwaves, bar sinks, telephones, refrigerators and ceiling fans. The lobby/dining area is decorated in American farmhouse pine. Breakfast is served on the oceanfront lanai or at the dining table inside on linen and English china with crystal and silver. Guests (including my husband and me on our own honeymoon) have raved about the generous helpings of peach French toast with peach syrup, well-seasoned quiche, and fluffy pancakes that Gloria whips up. In addition to complimentary coffee, tea and cocoa, guests can choose from various liqueurs, wines and soft drinks, also complimentary. The Spouting Horn seawater geyser is a short stroll up the road.

Princeville, Kauai

PRINCEVILLE HOTEL, *P.O.Box 3069, Princeville, HI 96722. Tel. 808/826-9644 or 800/826-4400, Fax 808/826-1166. 252 rooms. Double rooms begin at $360. Major credit cards.*

This resort is terraced into a cliff above the beach. After being closed for two years for a $120-million renovation, the former Sheraton Mirage Princeville reopened in the spring of 1991 - only to be hit by Hurricane Iniki the following year. Damage has been fully repaired. As you drive into the porte cochere, you'll feel as though you're driving right into the huge lobby, which is behind a tall wall of glass sliding doors. Inside, the two- or three-story windows dazzle with fabulous views of Hanalei Bay and the jagged Bali Hai mountains. Sunshine pouring in through skylights in the ceiling glints off Italian marble. (The only problem is that the floors can be quite slippery when it rains.) Antiques catch the eye, such as the 18th-century Flemish tapestry of children playing. One fireplace is near the entrance and another is found in the living room, where the lobby bar is. Here travelers relax in hefty couches and chairs while absorbing the view or listening to nightly live music. The ambience is one of quiet elegance.

Four times its original size, the swimming pool area sports a swim-up bar, three half-moon-shaped Jacuzzis, a children's pool, and one of the hotel's three restaurants. A fitness center is nearby. Some guestrooms are graced with imported antiques, whirlpool bathtubs, VCRs and lanais. Rooms feature papered walls and overstuffed couches with throw pillows. The Hawaiian quilts that once covered beds have been framed and put on display outside the ballroom. Guests get a kick out of the magic windows in all rooms; a flip of a switch turns them from opaque to transparent, revealing the ocean and the Bali Hai mountains.

All rooms also have snazzy marble baths with double sinks accented with gold-plated fixtures. Movies shown in the 65-person cinema are complimentary to guests, as are daily scuba lessons in the pool. If you're on your honeymoon, or simply in love, ask about the romantic beachside dinners for two. The gourmet meal served by your private waiter isn't cheap, but some couples can't resist. Transportation to the Princeville golf courses, extensive health spa, tennis courts, and shops is complimentary.

Lanai

MANELE BAY HOTEL, *P.O. Box 310, Lanai City, HI 96763. Hulopoe Beach, south shore. Tel. 808/565-7000 or 800/321-4666, Fax 808/565-2483. 250 rooms. Double rooms begin at $265. Major credit cards.*

At Lanai's first luxury beach resort, the lobby (on the third floor of the terraced building) is for admiring, strolling, mingling - not for mundane activities such as checking in. Arriving guests are escorted to their elegant rooms. Along the way they pass murals depicting the plight of the son of the king of Maui who was banished to Lanai to rid it of evil spirits; Oriental rugs; antiques and reproductions; striking sculpture, statues and vases; and Chinese, Hawaiian, and Japanese gardens where lily pads float on ponds.

Some guest rooms overlook the ocean while others gaze out to the flower-filled courtyards and pool. All have lanais and can be cooled by either ceiling fans or air conditioning. The dazzling marble baths come with double sinks and glass-enclosed stall showers in addition to tubs. Videos for VCRs are complimentary.

Guests relax in the bar; game room; library, with its old globe, chess and backgammon sets; and the Hale Aheahe, where they can hear contemporary Hawaiian and European classical music. Two whirlpools sit at the edge of the swimming pool on the broad patio off the lower lobby lounge. Tennis courts, a spacious exercise room, steam room, Swedish shower (with many nozzles), and beauty center (for facials, manicures, and massages) keep vacationers in good shape. Jack Nicklaus has designed the island's third golf course for the resort, a challenging oceanfront 18-holer. Water sports include scuba diving, snorkeling, and sailing. Frequent shuttles link Manele Bay Hotel with its upland sister hotel, the Lodge at Koele.

HOTEL LANAI, *P.O. Box 120, Lanai City, HI 96763. Tel. 808/565-7211 or 800/795-7211, Fax 808/565-6450. 11 rooms. Doubles begin at $95. Major credit cards.*

Built in the 1920s for guests of the Dole Company, this wooden country lodge has lots of character. The small rooms are found in two wings connected by the glassed-in lanai. They have a real homey feel, with hardwood floors, ceiling fans, and quilts. Some of the twin, queen, and king-sized beds are four poster. Tiled baths come with pedestal sinks.

Many island residents gather on the front lanai after work for drinks and conversation. From there, there's a great view of the sun setting between the pine trees. Some guests at this hotel come to hunt deer while others simply want to get away. I've met several couples from Oahu who use this as a weekend haunt. A separate cottage is also available.

11. OAHU

To many outsiders who equate Oahu with Waikiki's highrises, crowds, and kitschy-to-sophisticated stores and restaurants, it comes as a surprise that most of the island is countryside. Breezes ripple sugarcane fields and hibiscus petals. Jagged red cliffs plunge to royal blue waters edged in frothy white foam. Plump clouds lounge on the tops of rugged, jade-colored mountains. Master surfers balance their boards on mammoth curls. In some parts of the island, peacocks and jungle fowl freely strut their stuff. Even a small group of shy, wild wallabies hops around in the area near Tantalus.

In the minds of some mainlanders, particularly those on the East Coast, Hawaii is something of a paradisiacal blur. They know it is the home of **Honolulu, Waikiki Beach**, the extinct **Diamond Head** volcano, and the **USS Arizona Memorial at Pearl Harbor**. But they're not exactly sure which island these attractions are on. The fact that they're all found an Oahu is one of the reasons this is the state's most visited island. It is also the most populous chunk of the archipelago. However, it's not the largest. That honor belongs to the island of Hawaii, commonly known as the Big Island (and thus often mistakenly thought to be the main island). Following Maui in size, Oahu is only the third largest.

This island has grown on me over the years. In part, it's because I've become better acquainted with the Oahu that sprawls beyond Honolulu. There's a small town feel to much of the island. Witness the Mom-and-pop "plate lunch" restaurants and shave ice (snow cone) stands that dot streets. But my feelings have also grown warmer toward the busy capital itself, which is among the dozen largest cities in the US. This change of heart has everything to do with the beautification program that swept across Waikiki during the late 1980s. Tile-paved sidewalks, newly planted trees, improved traffic conditions, and the lessening of the hawking of leaflets advertising discount car rental companies and tourist attractions have all added up to a much more pleasant resort area than in earlier years.

If you're looking for action, you'll find plenty on Oahu. It would take ages to sample all the excellent restaurants, nightclubs, discos, bars, and concerts. You can give your wallet a real workout in the stores and boutiques that hit you from all sides as you walk down **Kalakaua Avenue** and Waikiki's other streets or as you wander around your hotel. Oahu also has more than a few upscale **shopping malls.**

Riding the waves in an ancient Hawaiian-style outrigger canoe or learning to surf on Waikiki Beach are only the beginning of the many water and land sports available. For fabulous (though crowded) snorkeling, few people pass up a trip to picturesque **Hanauma Bay.** Across the island from Waikiki, the **North Shore,** famed for its lush foliage, rural atmosphere and beautiful beaches, seems to be in another world. During the winter, its excellent surfing conditions draw scores of sports enthusiasts, whether they come just for fun, to compete in one of the tournaments, or simply to watch the action (and all the bodies in skimpy bathing suits).

Oahu is a great place to bring children, since there are so many attractions to keep them occupied. In addition to the beach, there are a zoo, an aquarium, Sea Life Park, the Maritime Center with its Children's Touch and Feel Museum, Kapiolani Park where kite flying is all the rage, and even rodeos.

When you're ready to dig a bit below the surface of the island, visit the exhibits and recreated villages at the **Polynesian Cultural Center.** Explore unspoiled, flower-splashed **Waimea Falls Park,** on the site of an old Hawaiian settlement. **Iolani Palace,** the only royal palace in the United States, is well worth your time. In Honolulu's **Chinatown,** the aromatic herbal shops are intriguing, and inexpensive restaurants serve a variety of Asian cuisines. Browse through the **Bishop Museum,** filled with Hawaiian artifacts, or visit **Byodo-In Temple,** a recreation of an ancient Japanese place of worship, surrounded by artful gardens.

Hawaiian Roots

Modern examples of old Hawaii are here and there throughout the island of Oahu. After a storm, it is not unusual to see picnicking Hawaiian families walking stooped over along Ewa Beach, near Pearl Harbor. Nope, they're not looking for shells; they're actually collecting *limu* (edible seaweed) brought in by the tide after having been uprooted by rough weather. Cooking with seaweed is a Hawaiian tradition that has been passed down for countless generations.

Among the people who have made a noted difference on Oahu is acclaimed Hawaiian-Irish sculptor Rocky Kaiouliokahikoloehu Jensen. He has worked with Hale Naua III, the **Society of Hawaiian Artists,** to broaden the appeal and understanding of Hawaiian creativity and cul-

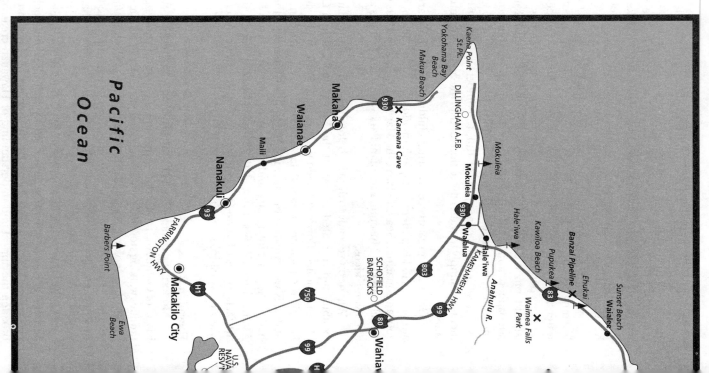

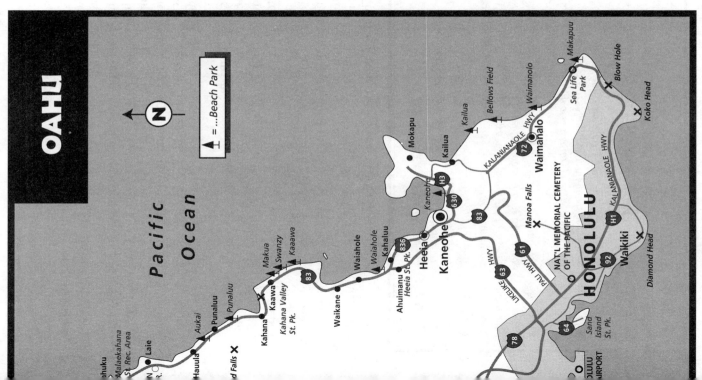

OAHU

N

⚑ = ...Beach Park

Pacific

Ocean

ture. One of his totem pole-like *tikis* has been displayed at the McDonald's in Waimanalo. Works done by Hale Naua artists — including feather creations, paintings, spears, and sculpture — have been displayed at Honolulu airport's inter-island terminal and Fort DeRussy's US Army Museum in Waikiki.

Na Hoa Hoala Kapa

(Friends of the Reawakening of Kapa) is a group that continues the ancient tradition of making cloth from bark. It oversees everything from growing the trees to picking the plants for the dyes that create the designs. To learn about this complicated yet rewarding art, check local newspapers for the group's periodic demonstrations and lectures at the Bishop Museum, schools, and cultural festivals.

Waikiki's Early Tourism

Some of the tall, modern buildings of Waikiki are built on top of old Hawaiian ruins and burial grounds. In the early 1800s, Waikiki was nothing to write home about. The beach was devoid of its coconut palms, the groves, which had grown thick, having been uprooted by a storm. Dilapidated grass huts were scattered here and there. The streams that ran through the swamps often overflowed, creating marshes that were homes to mosquitoes and rats. Hawaiians used these wetlands for planting rice paddies and taro patches and for building duck and fish ponds. The driest region was reserved for a banana grove.

THE WRITE STUFF

Despite its seeming lack of appeal, early Waikiki welcomed visitors, several of them noted writers. In 1848, **Herman Melville** *jumped ship and earned a little cash picking up pins at a Honolulu bowling alley.* **Mark Twain** *spent some time here in 1866, and* **Jack London** *learned to surf along Waikiki Beach. Captivated by the beautiful Princess Ka'iulani, who lived in Waikiki with her parents,* **Robert Louis Stevenson** *passed many days sitting in the shade of the hau tree that still stands at the New Otani Kaimana Beach Hotel.*

Along with Hawaiian alii, wealthy foreigners built themselves elegant waterfront homes in the driest areas. Small hotels began cropping up in the late 1880s. It wasn't until the 1920s that tons of coral were dumped into extensive marshlands, turning wet land into dry. Once Hawaii became a state in 1959, tourism began to boom. **James Michener's** *epic historical novel,* Hawaii, *was published that year, introducing the Islands to millions of mainlanders and whetting their appetites for first-hand looks.*

Mark Twain visited Hawaii in 1866, during the reign of Lot, better known as Kamehameha V, the last of the royal Kamehameha line. A few Americans had settled in Honolulu, and they were already pressuring the United States to annex Hawaii, to secure their personal economic well-being. New England missionaries were hard at work in their continual battle to convert any Hawaiians who had slipped through the cracks and to bolster the faith of those who had already turned to Christianity. Twain remarked jokingly that he never met anyone in Hawaii who wasn't either a missionary or a whaling captain.

Serving as a reporter for the *Sacramento Union*, Twain sent his sometimes poetic, often humorous articles about the islands to San Francisco by ship. While sightseeing on horseback, he discovered a Hawaii far different from that depicted by other members of the US press. Although King Kamehameha V had been called a drunken, ruthless pagan by some American writers, Twain found him diligent, gentlemanly, and dignified.

Extolling the islands' beauty, he said, "The good that die [in Hawaii] experience no change, for they fall asleep in one heaven and wake up in another." He was less kind to the Hawaiian staple called *poi*, however, saying, "An unseductive mixture it is, almost tasteless before it ferments and too sour for a luxury afterward. But nothing is more nutritious." Twain's *Letters from the Sandwich Islands* gives a fascinating glimpse into daily life in 19th century Hawaii.

HAWAII CALLS

Many outsiders got their first taste of Hawaiian music from the popular "Hawaii Calls" radio program, which began in 1935, during the Depression, in an attempt to revive the tourist industry. Broadcast to the US, Canada, and, Australia from the lanai of the Moana Hotel, it remained on the air until 1975.

In 1936, the first travelers reached Honolulu by air: seven passengers flown in from San Francisco. If you think flights are tedious these days, be thankful you weren't on this 22-hour Pan Am Clipper trip. By the end of World War II, flying time between San Francisco and Honolulu had been shaved to a mere nine hours.

After the war, developer Henry J. Kaiser decided to breathe new life into Waikiki by building the Hawaiian Village, now with Hilton in front of its name. Especially after undergoing an extensive renovation in the late 1980s, this hotel — with its tile-covered Rainbow Tower, lagoon, theater, and shops — is still one of Waikiki's most impressive accommodations. The 1970s saw a serious building frenzy, when most of Waikiki's present sky-scraping hotels and condominiums were born.

ARRIVALS & DEPARTURES

Honolulu International Airport, near Pearl Harbor, is *ewa* (west) of downtown Honolulu and Waikiki, where most hotels are located. The 20-minute drive can turn into 45 minutes during rush hours. Especially when rooms are booked as part of fly/stay package deals, complimentary airport shuttle service is often provided to hotels. The far-flung Turtle Bay Hilton picks guests up and drop them off at the airport for $30 per person each way. Ihilani Resort & Spa, also outside of Honolulu, can get you to and from the airport in a limousine for $70 for up to six adults each way.

The least expensive way to get to from the airport to Waikiki is by the **TheBus** (#19 or #20), the public buses that depart from the airport baggage claim exits every 20 minutes or so. Light packers can take advantage of this, as passengers may carry on only one bag each and they must ride with their luggage on their laps.

For about $7 per person each way (or $12 round trip), **Airport Express**, *Tel. 949-5249 or 941-4028*, and **Trans Hawaiian**, *Tel. 566-7333*, are among the shuttles that take vacationers to and from various hotels and condominiums. However, you can often get a better deal with coupons in tourist booklets such as *This Week Oahu*, which you can pick up at airport tourist information counters.

Car rental agencies located at or near the airport provide complimentary shuttle service from the baggage claim area to and from their offices. You'll see courtesy phones for contacting them. **Taxis** and **limousines** are also available, but most visitors opt for the less expensive shuttle buses.

THE NAME GAME

Some hotels in frenetic Waikiki have dizzyingly similar names, particularly those that are parts of chains. So be sure you know exactly which one is yours before you try to get a taxi or airport van driver to take you there. Oahu's main chains are Outrigger, Aston, Marc, Sheraton, and Hilton.

ORIENTATION

There is no question that Oahu is the most developed island in the chain. Yet most of the development is contained on the southern coast, where Honolulu, the capital of the state, is located. The vast majority of the island's hotels (most of which are highrises) are clustered in Waikiki.

But this tourist haven is only a small (albeit jam-packed) neighborhood within Honolulu, which in turn takes up only a small portion of the island's 608 square miles. Honolulu and its suburbs are along the leeward coast of Oahu. Tunnels pierce the Koolau Mountains between the city and the windward coast, the far side of the island.

If you're planning to drive in Hawaii, you'll have to get used to the local way of giving directions. If someone tells you to "Go diamondhead," that means to drive east, toward Oahu's Diamond Head volcano. If you are east of Diamond Head, they might send you "Koko Head," toward another easterly landmark. "Ewa" (*ay-vah*) means to go west on Oahu, toward Ewa Beach (the *w* should make you think "west," even though it's pronounced like *v*). On both Oahu and the Neighbor Islands, "mauka" (*mow-kah*) is Hawaiian for "toward the mountains" (remember that the first syllable sounds like that of "mountain"), while "makai" (mahk-*eye*) means to go toward the sea.

GETTING AROUND OAHU

By Bus

There is a convenient public bus system on Oahu, and often the most interesting and the least expensive way to see the island is by city bus, since you'll be riding with residents going about their business. In addition to traveling to many points in and around Honolulu, some of the best coastal views of the island are from the **Circle Island** transit bus (#52 or #58); in about four hours, you'll travel practically the entire perimeter of the island. Fares on these public buses are less than $1. *For route information, call Tel. 296-1818 and enter 8287.*

By Car

If you're based in Honolulu, driving a car can be far more trouble than it's worth. Who wants to spend their vacation fighting traffic or grumbling about how much they have to pay for parking?

However, for the greatest degree of freedom, you might consider renting wheels for part of your stay for explorations beyond the capital city. Many of the national and state wide car rental agencies have offices at the airport, as well as in Honolulu and other parts of Oahu. In addition to the major companies, a variety of smaller local agencies appeal to people who want a car for just a few days. Convertibles are very popular among visitors.

In the morning and afternoon, traffic is especially thick between Honolulu and its suburbs, such as Mililani and Hawaii Kai. Unless you don't mind moving at a crawl, avoid the Pali Highway going into the city from Kailua on Monday through Friday mornings and going toward

Kailua after the workday. During the winter when the North Shore waves are ready for individual surfers and annual surfing championships, the line of cars can become particularly lethargic between Hale'iwa and Laie. This problem has been alleviated quite a bit, however, since much of the traffic on the two-lane road through Hale'iwa has been diverted to the new bypass road outside town.

On smaller roads outside of the city, watch out for the long, low mongooses (no, not mongeese) that zip across the road near fields.

By Foot

Seeing the sights in Waikiki and downtown Honolulu is perfectly manageable on foot.

By Guided Tour

The next best choice to the public bus is to be guided by one of the tour companies that use minibuses or vans (as opposed to slightly less expensive trips in full-size buses), such as **E Noa Tours**, *Tel. 591-2561*. The cost is about $55 per person.

You can book a bus tour through a hotel activities desk or by contacting the company directly. Although there are many different companies, the various itineraries are relatively standard. The three types of **circle island tours** are the half-day trip around Oahu's southern shores; the all-day drive including the North Shore; and the all-day "grand circle," which takes in both. All half-day circle island trips cover Diamond Head; the ritzy neighborhood of Kahala; the Blowhole; Hanauma Bay, a beautiful powdery crescent lapped by fish-packed waters; other beaches; Waimanalo farmlands; rain forests; and lookout points with overwhelming views. Some of these tours also include admission to Sea Life Park, the marine playland, or stops at Iolani Palace, Queen Emma's Summer Palace, or Punchbowl National Cemetery.

Some circle island tours introduce visitors to the windward coast and North Shore, stopping at Japanese Byodo-In Temple, overlooked by the Koolau Mountains; the Mormon Temple in Laie; Sunset Beach (surfing heaven); beautiful Waimea Bay; and Waimea Falls Park, a botanical garden with Hawaiian cultural demonstrations, in Waimea Valley. Some tours also include brief visits to the Polynesian Cultural Center (which is actually best left for its own day), lunch at a casual restaurant, or a beach picnic with enough time for swimming.

Note that guided tours to the **Polynesian Cultural Center** are available for those who want to see the evening musical extravaganza, but don't want to have to drive themselves back to their hotel at night. You can also get to **Pearl Harbor** on the USS Arizona Memorial Shuttle Bus ($3 per person each way).

Departing from the Royal Hawaiian Shopping Center, the bright red San Francisco-style **Waikiki Trolley**, *Tel. 596-2199 or 591-2561*, makes the rounds of central Honolulu's highlights. For $17, you can listen to this narrated tour, and climb on and off the trolley as often as you like between 8am and 4:30pm, spending as much time (and money!) as you want at each site.

However, although Chinatown, Iolani Palace, the Kamehameha Statue, the Academy of the Arts, and the Maritime Center are among the stops, many tourist traps are also included (such as Dole Cannery, Hard Rock Cafe, TGI Friday's, and, for aloha wear, Hilo Hattie's—although the quality of the clothing here has improved over recent years).

Some Honolulu city tours stop at Pearl Harbor and the USS Arizona Memorial. Most include Punchbowl National Cemetery, Iolani Palace, the State Capitol, Washington Place (once the home of Hawaiian royalty and now the Governor's mansion), Mission Houses Museum, Kawaiaha'o Church (the first mission church), the judiciary buildings guarded by the statue of King Kamehameha the Great, and Chinatown. With the exception of Pearl Harbor and Punchbowl, these sites are all easily covered on foot in one or two (very leisurely) days, so I don't recommend a bus tour of the city. If you'd like a guide, a better bet is to take one of the walking tours sponsored by the Mission Houses Museum, Iolani Palace, Chinatown Chamber of Commerce, and the Hawaii Heritage Center (see sidebar on Walking Tours in this section).

Several companies sponsor tours with a twist: In its 17-passenger minibuses, **E Noa Tours**, *Tel. 591-2561*, offers one circle-island trip that takes visitors to plantations and introduces them to lei-making, hula, and Hawaiian music.

One **TransHawaiian**, *Tel. 566-7300 or 800/799-0685*, half-day city tour includes a walking tour of Chinatown and glass-bottom boat and helicopter rides; another guides hikers up Diamond Head and takes them to a garden club. Another good tour company is **Roberts Hawaii**, *Tel. 831-1575*, which conducts tours in both vans and buses.

Most companies pick visitors up either right at their hotels or at neighboring accommodations. Drivers expect tips (of at least $1 per passenger), and in the vast majority of cases, they well deserve them.

By Rickshaw

Rickshaws (some motorized) transport visitors around Waikiki and between the Diamond Head Crater trailhead and Waikiki.

By Taxi

Taxis are also convenient within Honolulu.

By Trolley

There is even a fire engine-red **trolley** that takes tourists from Waikiki to surrounding attractions.

WHERE TO STAY

Especially in Waikiki, Oahu's accommodations are so competitive that many are continually being renovated and refurbished in an attempt to convince travelers to choose them over others. Both on and off the beach, there is a broad range of types of hotels and condominiums.

The **Outrigger** chain has a slew of Waikiki hotels, most of which appeal to people with beer budgets and some of which also draw those with champagne taste. Sporting many reasonably priced rooms, the Outrigger Reef (not to be confused with the Outrigger Reef Towers or the Outrigger Waikiki) is on one of the best sections of the beach. Breakfast is included in the rates of some Outrigger hotels. The **Aston**, **Marc**, and **Sheraton** chains also have some good hotels for non-sheiks. If you stay at one of Oahu's five Sheratons, you'll be able to charge meals and entertainment to your room while you're visiting any of the others.

You'd rather sleep outside Waikiki, away from the crowds? You'll have a choice that ranges from plush, secluded beach resorts to a historic Bed & Breakfast in a lush valley.

OAHU'S BEST BEDROOMS

Cream of the Crop

Halekulani, Waikiki: This plush beach hotel manages to maintain its peacefulness, elegance, and dignity in the frenzy of Waikiki.

Kahala Mandarin Oriental, Kahala: Only ten minutes from Waikiki, this tranquil luxury resort draws the rich and famous.

Ihilani Resort & Spa, Kapolei: Get away from it all and let yourself be pampered head to toe here.

Hilton Hawaiian Village, Waikiki: More like a city than a village, this sprawling beach resort contains everything you'll need for a memorable vacation.

Less Expensive

Outrigger Reef on the Beach, Waikiki: For a moderately-priced beach hotel, this is an excellent choice.

Aston Waikiki Beachside, Waikiki: Actually across busy Kalakaua Avenue from the beach, this is a beautifully decorated oasis.

Manoa Valley Inn, Honolulu: A Bed & Breakfast graced with antiques, this one, in a flourishing valley near Waikiki, is listed in the National Register of Historic Places.

Hawaii Polo Inn, Ala Moana: Just outside Waikiki, this pleasant budget hotel is convenient to Oahu's action.

Outside Waikiki

KAHALA MANDARIN ORIENTAL, *5000 Kahala Avenue, Honolulu, HI 96816. Tel. 808/739-8888 or 800/367-2525. 370 rooms. Double room rates begin at $275. Major credit cards.*

Featured in Chapter 10, *Best Places to Stay.*

This hotel became Kahala Mandarin Oriental in 1996 after a multi-million dollar transformation. The renovation has made this hotel even better than before and celebrities still beat a path to its doors. Located on the beach in a quiet, residential area with views of both Diamond Head and Koko Head craters, Kahala Mandarin Oriental is in a wonderfully tranquil, verdant setting. But it's also just ten minutes from Waikiki, the heart of Oahu's action.

Vacationers still have a choice of excellent restaurants. Hoku's, offering a blend of French, German, and Asian cuisine, is open for lunch and dinner; Plumeria Beach Cafe, known for its bake shop, Japanese selections, and elaborate buffets, serves all three meals daily.

Guest rooms (some with balconies) are decorated with handsome mahogany furniture and hand-loomed Tibetan rugs on teak parquet floors. When guests aren't on the beach or in the pool, they can hit the Fitness Center. There is a second, children's pool as well as a children's activities program.

IHILANI RESORT & SPA, *92-1001 Olani Street, Kapolei, HI 96707. Tel. 808/679-0079 or 800/626-4446, Fax 808/679-0295. 387 rooms. Double rooms begin at $275. Major credit cards.*

About a half-hour drive from the airport, Ihilani ("Heavenly Splendor") overlooks a series of calm, C-shaped, sandy lagoons. A sea water fish pond wanders through the grounds, and three restaurants feature Japanese, continental, and Mediterranean cuisines. In the triangular lobby, a 15-story wall of glass brings the dramatic mountains inside. Overhead, greenery drips from railings along the open corridors outside guest rooms, most of which have views of the ocean. The quietest, all oceanfront, are in the shorter four-story wing. Here you can book a unit with a private whirlpool on the lanai. Other rooms gaze down on the busy circular swimming pool, the main lagoon, and the Pacific. (Note that although room #539, a minimum category room, is spacious, it has no view at all, unless you consider the roof of an adjoining building scenic.)

Upon check-in, vacationers are introduced to the state-of-the-art computerized telephone system. Each room has three phones (by the bed, in the living area, and in the bath). With a touch from your bedside, you can control the room temperature and the "Do Not Disturb" notice at your front door or turn your lights on and off, among other high-tech activities. And, mind you, this system communicates with the user in any of six languages! (By the way, Ihilani is one of Hawaii's few hotels that does not charge guests for making local calls.) You'll also find a minibar, personal safe, and both Western bathrobes and Japanese-style *yukatas* for use during your stay. You can even bring your favorite music for the room's CD player. The marble baths are large, with twin sinks.

Along with six tennis courts, Ihilani has **an excellent spa** for indulging in treatments such as thalassotherapy, herbal wraps, facials, and massages. Facilities are extensive for both men and women. The hotel's more peaceful second swimming pool is on a sunny deck at the spa, near the exercise room and studio where fitness classes are given. (Don't forget your sneakers if you want to work out; you aren't allowed in the exercise room without them.) Transportation to the golf course is provided.

TURTLE BAY HILTON GOLF & TENNIS RESORT, *57-091 Kamehameha Highway, Kahuku, HI 96731. Tel. 808/293-8811 or 800/ HILTONS, Fax 808/293-1286. 485 rooms. Double rooms begin at $160. Major credit cards.*

Far off the beaten path, near the famous surfing beaches of the North Shore (about a 60-minute drive from the airport), the Turtle Bay Hilton is a pleasant, self-contained resort. The beaches are beautiful here. Unlike many other North Shore beaches, which can be dangerous for swimming when the winter surf is high, Kuilima Cove is protected by a reef and always calm. Snorkeling is good and scuba certification courses are given through the hotel. Visitors also spend aquatic time in either of the resort's two pools.

An attractive wedding pavilion has been built on the waterfront. There are ten tennis courts and two golf courses. Horseback riding is also available on the lush, expansive grounds. The spacious lobby is home to shops and boutiques where Polynesian woven baskets and exotic flower leis are on sale. While not every room has a lanai, they all contain a color television, refrigerator, clock-radio and coffee makers. Moderate in size, rooms are comfortably furnished. Nonsmoking rooms are available upon request.

ALLIGATOR ROCK BEACH RENTAL, 61-285 *Kamehameha Highway (four miles from central Hale'iwa, one mile from Waimea Bay), Hale'iwa, HI 96712. Tel. 808/637-5783. 1 cottage. Rate: $,1000 per week.*

This three-bedroom/one-and-a-half-bath house sits smack on Kawailoa Beach on Oahu's serene North Shore, about a 40-minute drive from Honolulu airport. The living room, master bedroom, kitchen, and deck all gaze out to the water. Complete with cable TV, telephone, microwave, washer and dryer, garbage disposal, barbecue grill and its own parking area, this rental is pleasantly furnished with an attractively decorated patio. Shared among six people, it's a real steal.

Views of sunsets or the ocean in the moonlight, with offshore Alligator Rock on the horizon, can be fabulous from here. The nearby scenic town of Hale'iwa has an appealing collection of restaurants, health food stores, and boutiques. This cottage is also convenient to Waimea Valley/Waimea Falls Park and surfing beaches.

ALA MOANA HOTEL, 410 Atkinson Drive, Honolulu, HI 96814. Tel. 808/955-4811 or 800/367-6025, Fax 808/944-6839. 1,169 rooms. Double rooms begin at $115. Major credit cards.

At the edge of Waikiki, this attractive modern hotel is just a block from the 77-acre Ala Moana Beach Park. A ramp leads from the hotel to the popular Ala Moana Shopping Center next door. Rooms, most with private lanais, look out to the ocean, the Koolau Mountains, or Diamond Head. All have refrigerators and coffee makers, and most have private safes. A swimming pool is on the grounds and 24 Hour Fitness is a five-minute stroll away.

If you'd like to be pampered with extras such as a spa, and complimentary breakfast and turn-down service, ask about the concierge floors. In addition to **Rumours,** one of Honolulu's most popular night clubs, the hotel boasts a variety of restaurants and a pleasant lobby bar.

MANOA VALLEY INN, *2001 Vancouver Drive (off University Avenue, Manoa Valley), Honolulu, HI 96822. Tel. 808/947-6019 or 800/535-0085, Fax 808/946-6168. 8 rooms. Double rooms begin at $109. Major credit cards.*

Featured in Chapter 10, *Best Places to Stay.*

Now, this is *my* kind of place! Two miles from Waikiki and down the street from the University of Hawaii, this former private home is a Bed & Breakfast. Continental breakfast and an afternoon buffet of wine, fruit, and cheese are served here.

The handsome main house, with its eaves and gables, was built in 1912. The inn is decorated with oriental rugs, handcarved tables, beautiful aging tapestries, a grandfather clock, and other eye-catching antiques - even a nickelodeon that still works. Stained glass windows, lace curtains, and carved or brass headboards are features of guest rooms. Note that some rooms share baths.

RODEWAY INN HUKILAU RESORT, *55-109 Laniloa Street, Laie, HI 96762. Tel. 808/293-9282 or 800/526-4562, Fax 808/293-8115. 48 rooms. Double rooms begin at $80. Major credit cards.*

Near the Polynesian Cultural Center, this modest accommodation is the only game in town. Some people choose to stay here before or after the long drive from Honolulu to the Center or the North Shore, but don't expect anything special. The studio units are equipped with air conditioning and TV. Lanais have views of the swimming pool. There is no hotel restaurant, so it's convenient that a fast-food joint is next door. The owners arrange for fresh fish to be sold to their guests.

HAWAII POLO INN, *1696 Ala Moana Boulevard, Honolulu, HI 96815. Tel. 800/669-7719 or 808/949-0061, Fax 808/949-4906. 72 rooms. Double rooms begin at $75. Major credit cards.*

If where you sleep isn't as important to you as where your hotel is located, this budget property could be a good choice. After all, you'll be spending much more time out and about than in your room! Hawaii Polo Inn is conveniently located right at the edge of Waikiki, within easy walking distance of great restaurants and shops, the yacht harbor, and the beach. – Ala Moana, that is, which is much less crowded than Waikiki's sandy shore. An activities desk on the main level is where you can book sightseeing excursions, sailing trips, and other fun. The no-frills guest rooms are spacious, neat and clean, with lanais, refrigerators, and coffee makers. Baths have stall showers instead of tubs. Mini suites and suites come with kitchenettes. There is a swimming pool on the premises, along with laundry facilities and a garage.

Hawaii Polo Inn always offers special discounts, often significantly less than its lowest rack rates. For instance, with the Airport Special, your room could be as low as $55 a night if you make your reservation by calling from the airport upon your arrival to see if anything is available. This hotel attracts many Europeans, as well as backpackers, surfers, and young world travelers, quite a few from Australia and New Zealand.

PAPAYA PARADISE BED & BREAKFAST, *395 Auwinala Road, Kailua, HI 96734. Tel. or Fax 808/261-0316. 2 rooms. Rates: $70.*

Two of the bedrooms in this modern one-story home have been transformed into guest accommodations decorated in wicker and rattan. There are twin beds in one, and a queen and a trundle bed in the other as well as two comfortable lounge chairs. Each has a private entrance, air conditioning, ceiling fan and cable TV.

Guests are welcome to borrow from the collection of paperbacks, which even includes books in German. A large covered lanai faces the swimming pool, whirlpool, and the Koolau mountains. Attractive plantings surround the pool. Kailua Beach is a short walk away and a bus stop is right on the corner. Breakfast, though continental, is generous, featuring fresh fruit, homemade apple-cinnamon, orange-almond, or papaya muffins, and mango or banana-nut bread. A large refrigerator-ice maker and a microwave are available for guest use. Beach regalia is provided (mats, towels, swim goggles, hats, coolers and chairs).

Waikiki

Here's a run-down of the best of the bunch, beginning with water-front hotels and condos, then moving away from the beach:

On Ala Wai Yacht Harbor

HAWAII PRINCE HOTEL WAIKIKI & GOLF CLUB, *100 Holomoana Street, Honolulu, HI 96815. Tel. 808/956-1111 or 800/PRINCE-4. 521 rooms. Double rooms begin at $370. Major credit cards.*

This hotel stands at the edge of Ala Wai Yacht Harbor on the site of the old Kaiser Medical Center. In fact, footage of Ala Wai Yacht Harbor on the site of demolition made its way into an episode of the "Magnum P.I." television series. The hotel's two pinkish glass and stone towers poke 33 stories into the sky. Tall stone pillars stand in the lobby, which has glass doors and floor-to-ceiling windows that make the forest of masts in the harbor seem like part of the room. Marble, granite, polished slate and brass are everywhere. Walkways bordered by thriving greenery cut through the grounds.

More than 50 of the 500-plus guest rooms are one- and two-bedroom suites. Each room – accented with marble, wood, and natural fabrics – has an ocean view through floor-to-ceiling windows. Room service is available. Beds are turned down at night and complimentary newspapers are available each morning. Travelers who have been to the sister hotel, the Maui Prince, will be pleased to encounter the same high, unobtrusive quality of service. They'll also find two of the same gourmet restaurants:

the Prince Court (regional American food) and the Hakone (Japanese cuisine). Along with a fifth-floor pool deck with a striking waterfront view, a variety of lounges and shops also keep guests occupied. This luxury hotel is within walking distance of the Ala Moana Shopping Center. Complimentary shuttles take vacationers to and from the beach and nearby shopping centers.

THE ILIKAI HOTEL NIKKO WAIKIKI, *1777 Ala Moana Boulevard, Honolulu, HI 96815. Tel. 808/949-3811 or 800/NIKKO-US. 800 rooms. Double rooms begin at $200. Major credit cards.*

At the western edge of Waikiki, this huge hotel attracts many business travelers. Its "Value Plus Rates" provide good savings. Its two towers are located next door to Ala Moana Beach Park, which is popular for swimming and jogging, and it shares a beach with neighboring Hilton Hawaiian Village. Two pools, a fitness center and five tennis courts also lure the active set. Every evening, a torch-lighting ceremony takes place in the busy lobby.

The large rooms are complete with either full kitchens or extended dressing areas complete with safes, refrigerators, toasters and coffee machines. Those without kitchens have full bathrooms, while those with kitchens have showers instead of tubs. The color scheme includes shades of blues and grays. Little elephants form the bases of lamps, and white-washed rattan and marble-topped tables add to the attractive decor. The popular Coconuts provide Hawaiian musical entertainment at night. Canoes Restaurant features Hawaiian cuisine for breakfast, lunch, and dinner; Tanaka of Tokyo West offers *yaki*-style steak and seafood.

On the Beach

THE ROYAL HAWAIIAN, *2259 Kalakaua Avenue, Honolulu, HI 96815. Tel. 808/923-7311 or 800/325-3535, Fax 808/924-7098. 532 rooms. Double rooms begin at $365. Major credit cards.*

Affectionately known as the Pink Palace, this low-lying, Moorish hotel dates back to 1927, making it the second oldest in the Islands. Tall, flourishing trees and other vegetation obscure the flashy neighboring Royal Hawaiian Shopping Center, which adjoins the grounds of this subdued hotel. It was built on the site of King Kamehameha V's summer cottage, which stood here in the mid-19th century. In the early days, it catered to wealthy tourists who, with their servants in tow, sailed to Honolulu by steamship, often remaining for months at a time. The first registered guest was Princess Kawananakoa, who would have become queen of Hawaii had the monarchy survived.

The roomy lobby is decorated with marble, crystal chandeliers and sparkling mirrors. Picture windows draw shoppers into stores. Fresh banana bread welcomes guests upon check-in. Rooms contain colonial style furniture, including twin cherry wood beds, plus refrigerators, minibars, a sitting area, cut-glass light fixtures and plush baths with marble. Having cocktails at the beach front cafe is a popular pastime. The oval swimming pool also faces the water.

HALEKULANI, 2199 Kalia Road (at end of Lewers Street), Honolulu, HI 96815. Tel. 808/923-2311 or 800/367-2343, Fax 808/926-8004. 456 rooms. Double rooms begin at $300. Major credit cards.

Featured in Chapter 10, Best Places to Stay.

Halekulani is full of personal touches. Guests are escorted to their rooms, where they are registered in plush privacy and shown around. In the bathroom, floor-to-ceiling mirrors slide open to the closet, which contains a safe and is separated from the bedroom by sliding louvered wooden doors. Although there's a stall shower, the deep tub also has a hand-held, snake-neck nozzle. Lanais are very large and most look out to Diamond Head (the most impressive view) and/or the ocean. As tranquil as it is, it's difficult to believe that it's right in the heart of Waikiki, at the edge of the state's most crowded beach. The hotel's dazzling color scheme is white-in seven shades, that is-set off by the teak-stained wood of shopfronts and louvered doors.

Upstairs in the hotel's elegant original wing (built in 1931) is La Mer, for fine dining. Orchid's is a wonderful spot for an oceanfront breakfast, complete with fresh-squeezed guava juice and views of surfers and outrigger canoes. Head to the fitness center to work off any unwanted calories. All tours and sports activities are arranged by the concierge.

HILTON HAWAIIAN VILLAGE, 2005 Kalia Road, Honolulu, HI 96815. Tel. 808/949-4321 or 800/HILTONS, Fax 808/951-5458. 2,545 rooms. Double room rates begin at $300. Major credit cards.

This is one of those resorts that many guests don't leave until it's time to go home. It's actually more like a small city than a village. In the grandiose, open-air lobby, handsomely uniformed porters push gleaming gold luggage carts through the whirl of activity. More than 2,500 rooms and a slew of hard-to-resist shops and restaurants are located in and around its towers, the most distinctive of which (from the outside) is the mosaic-covered Rainbow Tower, a Waikiki landmark.

In the Rainbow Bazaar, many people photograph the Thai temple and the 400-year-old farmhouse that was brought from Japan in pieces and put back together here. The split-level swimming pool rambles over 10,000 square feet and is bordered by colorful blossoms and lava rock waterfalls. The grounds are also graced with fish ponds, a penguin pool, Japanese sculpture on marble and granite pedestals, palm trees, and a profusion of other tropical greenery. It's no wonder that Hilton Hawaiian Village is a popular locale for weddings.

Guest rooms, in varying degrees of luxury, come with and without ocean views. Some look out to gardens and mountains. Features of all rooms include lanais, mini-bars, refrigerators, and remote-control color cable television. The executive suites in the Alii Tower are individually decorated, with special touches such as vanities with retractable shaving mirrors and mini-TVs in the dressing area, silver ice buckets and cut crystal glasses. Guests here can have continental breakfast and complimentary pupus in the afternoon. Those staying in this tower have their own registration desk, swimming pool, sauna, whirlpool, exercise room, and fitness center with massage facilities. Nonsmoking rooms are available in every tower, and there are also rooms for guests with physical disabilities.

At the activities desk, guests set up their itineraries, from cruises and horseback rides to tours and car rentals. Pedi boats, snorkeling equipment, canoes, Hobie cats, surfboards and other water sports equipment are rented on the beach. A seven-day children's program is conducted throughout the year; special activities include a wildlife and ecology tour, a cooking session, and (for those aged eight to 15) a guided hike up Diamond Head crater.

SHERATON MOANA SURFRIDER, *2365 Kalakaua Avenue, Honolulu, HI 96815. Tel. 808/922-3111 or 800/325-3535, Fax 808/923-5984. 791 rooms. Double rooms begin at $290. Major credit cards.*

Of these two hotels that became the one, the Moana is the more intriguing. Built in 1901, it is Hawaii's oldest. Its first guests paid a whopping $1.50 a night. This four-story Italian Renaissance building, once one of Hawaii's tallest, has been on the National Register of Historic Places since 1972 and has also been named one of the Historic Hotels of America. "Hawaii Calls," the famous radio program, was broadcast from the 1930s to the '70s from the Banyan Court, near where the elaborate pool now sprawls. Don't miss the elaborate buffet breakfast at the water's edge with live harp music in the background. Nearly two years of painstaking restoration in the late 1980s, to the tune of $50 million, brought back much of the Moana's original elegance. Twenty 15-foot columns stand in the dazzling white and oak lobby. Front-desk attendants wear Victorian ivory and lace dresses. Copies of turn-of-the-century antiques were made from prized native koa wood. To see nearly a century of Moana memorabilia, stop by the hotel's Historical Room.

If you want to be surrounded by old-fashioned architecture, be sure to request a room in the Banyan Wing, which includes the Moana portion of the complex. In quiet pastels, rooms are decorated with wood and wicker. Each has an armoire with a television, refrigerator, mini bar and safe hidden inside. Baths are modern, with art deco touches. Cotton *yukatas* (Japanese robes) are provided for guests to use during their stay.

Room service is available all day and night. Rooms throughout vary greatly in size, decor, and view, so make sure you know what you're getting when you make your reservations.

SHERATON WAIKIKI, 2255 Kalakaua Avenue, Honolulu, HI 96815. Tel. 808/922-4422 or 800/325-3535, Fax 808/922-7708. 1,852 rooms. Double rooms begin at $230. Major credit cards.

Many guests return to this beach front hotel, with its two connected towers forming a V. In part because of its coveted location, it is the world's number-one revenue-producing Sheraton. It is especially popular among Japanese tour groups. Special rates are given for extended stays.

The lobby is dressed in oak, with blue and green accents, and it's constantly busy. Decorated exactly alike, the attractive rooms differ in price according to view. A glass elevator whisks diners up to the Hanohano Room, a rooftop restaurant with a stunning view of Waikiki Beach and Diamond Head. One of the two swimming pools is shaped like the head of a mushroom, while the other is round. Both nonsmoking floors and wheelchair access rooms are available. Hawaiian music entertains pool side each evening from 6pm to 8:30pm while the sun sets. The hotel's year-round children's program (for those aged five to 13) is free to guests. Honeymooners should ask about the limousine service to and from the airport.

DIAMOND HEAD BEACH HOTEL (A Colony Resort), 2947 Kalakaua Avenue, Honolulu, HI 96813. Tel. 808/922-1928 or 800/367-2317, Fax 808/924-8980. 52 rooms. Double rooms begin at $190. Major credit cards.

If you'd like to be on Waikiki Beach, but can do without the crowds, this small hotel is a good choice. The artificial beach here is petite, but good stretches of sand are on either side of the hotel. Guests don't pay anything to use the boogie boards and snorkeling gear. Rooms are comfortably furnished. Families often book the units with kitchenettes. A light breakfast is included in the rates. Really want to feel at home? Take advantage of the washer/dryer. Be sure to ask about special discounts, which can cut the room rate in half!

OUTRIGGER WAIKIKI ON THE BEACH, 2335 Kalakaua Avenue, Honolulu, HI 96815. Tel. 808/923-0711 or 800/688-7444, Fax 808/921-9749. 530 rooms. Double rooms begin at $165. Major credit cards.

Busy day and night, this large, modern hotel is the best known of the Outriggers. One side faces the beach while the other overlooks Kalakaua Avenue, Waikiki's main drag. The Society of Seven, a local group that blends song and humor and one of Oahu's most popular acts, performs here. Murals decorate the lobby walls. There is a whirlpool by the hotel pool, and guests are welcome to use the exercise room and fitness center. Guest rooms have private lanais with varying views, refrigerators, color TV with pay movies, and safes. Suites also come with minibars, wet bars, kitchenettes with microwave ovens, and two baths. For extra pampering, Voyagers Club offers a concierge level of rooms and services. Duke's Canoe Club, the hotel's popular beach side restaurant, features Hawaiian and contemporary music at night.

OUTRIGGER REEF ON THE BEACH, 2169 Kalia Road, Honolulu, HI 96815. Tel. 808/923-3111 or 800/688-7444, Fax 808/924-4957. 885 rooms. Double rooms begin at $150. Major credit cards.

I'd probably call this Waikiki's best choice for a moderately priced yet highly attractive beach front hotel. This accommodation is often referred to simply as The Reef so as not to be confused with the many other Outriggers. The dignified lobby — which was a cluttered tangle of garish souvenir stalls before a $50 million renovation — is graced with a rock and water sculpture, stone tile floors, and round columns. Hawaiian music is played nightly. The bordering stores have tasteful facades. When guests aren't shopping, swimming, or out sightseeing, they can hit the fitness center.

Furnished in ivory and pastels, guest rooms are contemporary, with private lanais and refrigerators. Suites feature honor bars, wet bars, kitchenettes, microwave ovens and two bathrooms each. The Voyagers Club offers a concierge level of rooms and services. Extensive water sports are the draw by day, and lounges and restaurants provide entertainment at night.

THE NEW OTANI KAIMANA BEACH HOTEL, 2863 Kalakaua Avenue, Honolulu, HI 96815. Tel. 808/923-1555 or 800/356-8264, Fax 808/922-9404. 124 rooms. Double rooms begin at $100. Major credit cards.

At the quieter eastern end of Waikiki Beach, this hotel sits at the foot of Diamond Head, on Sans Souci Reach, at the edge of Waikiki close to the 500-acre Kapiolani Park. When Robert Louis Stevenson visited in 1893, he spent five weeks at the Sans Souci Inn, which stood near where the New Otani Kaimana is found today. Prominent local *haole* families once built private homes in this area.

Kaimana is the Hawaiian word for "diamond." A convenient jumping off point for hiking to the crater's summit, the hotel provides free Diamond Head Climbers Club memberships and guide books. The New Otani Kaimana is refreshingly small. Guests particularly enjoy the open air dining at the beach side Hau Tree Lanai restaurant. The beach is alive with kayaking, sailing, and snorkeling. There is also a fitness center and shops on the premises.

OUTRIGGER ISLANDER WAIKIKI, 270 Lewers Street, Honolulu, HI 96815. Tel. 800/688-7444. 287 rooms. Double rooms begin at $90. Major credit cards.

Formerly the Pleasant Holiday Isle Hotel, this family-oriented accommodation is one of the newest and most affordable members of the

Outrigger chain. Its central location makes this a convenient choice. In early 1997, the entire hotel, from guest rooms to corridors, was renovated and cheerfully redecorated.

Across from the Beach

No buildings are between these hotels and the ocean.

ASTON WAIKIKI BEACHSIDE, *2452 Kalakaua Avenue, Honolulu, HI 96815. Tel. 808/931-2100 or 800/922-7866, Fax 808/931-2129. 79 rooms. Double rooms begin at $180. Major credit cards.*

With a staff that wins praise for service and courtesy, this compact elegant hotel is decked out with arresting antiques and reproductions in Japanese, French Provincial, Italian, Malaysian, and Chinese styles. Walking through the front door from busy Kalakaua Avenue, you'll feel instantly at peace. The small guest rooms, which vary greatly in views, have TVs with video cassette players, refrigerators and snazzy baths with black lacquer sinks with brass fixtures. Mirrors help the rooms seem larger. The deluxe oceanfront rooms are fabulous, with unobstructed views of Waikiki Beach and lanais tiled in Italian marble. But some rooms look out on to walls. Another not so pleasant surprise is that two lines of rooms have no windows at all!

Both Hawaiian-style and traditional English afternoon tea are served (you'll need to make an appointment). There is no restaurant on the premises, but a complimentary continental breakfast is served every morning in the Palm Court, the sitting room off the lobby. As you sip the day's first cup of coffee, your eyes will take in the Japanese lacquer desk, the overstuffed sofas, and the marble tables inside, along with the fountain and umbrella-shaded tables at the open end of the room. Guests can sign for meals at the nearby Hyatt Regency. Feel like splurging? Then consider having a private chef cater an elaborate gourmet dinner served in the Palm Court; prices begin at $95. Visitors are welcome to borrow beach towels and reading material, kept in the chest in the lobby, and video tapes are available at the front desk.

HAWAIIAN REGENT, *2552 Kalakaua Avenue, Honolulu, HI 96815. Tel. 808/922-6611 or 800/367-5370, Fax 808/921-5255. 1,346 rooms. Double rooms begin at $165. Major credit cards.*

Just across Kalakaua Avenue from the Waikiki Beach, this five-acre resort is a huge busy complex. Appealing mostly to young mainland and Japanese tourists, it encompasses a mall of shops and designer boutiques, a tennis court, two swimming pools, several restaurants and night spots, and a hospitality suite for guests who arrive early or depart late. The lobby, spacious and open-air, is decorated with a carefully crafted fresh water fountain. The walls serve as a gallery of salable fine art created by local artists. Hawaiian cultural events take place around the grounds. Aqua is the hotel's signature restaurant. Each with a private lanai, guest rooms are pleasantly enhanced with many extras, such as refrigerators, private safes, and marble basin tops.

HAWAIIAN WAIKIKI BEACH HOTEL, *2570 Kalakaua Avenue, Honolulu, HI 96815. Tel. 808/922-2511 or 800/877-7666, Fax 808/923-3656. 715 rooms. Double rooms begin at $140. Major credit cards.*

Right next door to the Honolulu Zoo, Kapiolani Park, Waikiki Aquarium, and a slew of fast-food restaurants, this is an especially good choice for families traveling with children. It is also the best Kalakaua Avenue location for viewing both the June 11 King Kamehameha Day Parade and the Aloha Week Parade in September. People fight to get seats on the terrace of the hotel's main dining room.

The beach across the street is the quieter end of Waikiki's sandy strip. A heated swimming pool is just off the lobby, which is one flight up from the ground floor. Since hotel towers keep most of the sun off the pool during the day anyway, many prefer to swim in the evening when other guests are out on the town. Some of the small, crowded guest rooms have no lanais at all, while others have either large balconies or standing lanais (just big enough for a couple of pairs of feet). The largest rooms are those that face Diamond Head. Oceanfront and junior suites come with refrigerators, and two rooms are set up for people in wheelchairs.

ASTON WAIKIKI CIRCLE HOTEL, *2464 Kalakaua Avenue, Honolulu, HI 96815. Tel. 808/923-1571 or 800/922-7866, Fax 808/926-8024. 104 rooms. Double rooms begin at $120. Major credit cards.*

You can't miss this tall, tubular hotel right across Kalakaua Avenue from the beach. It's a good choice if money is an object. The hallways are indeed circular and the oddly shaped rooms, though small, come with lanais (facing the beach). There are also TVs, mini-refrigerator, and baths have stall showers.

Near the Beach

ASTON WAIKIKI BEACH TOWER, *2470 Kalakaua Avenue, Honolulu, HI 96815. Tel. 808/926-6400 or 800/922-7866, Fax 808/926-7380. 140 units. Rates begin at $410 per condo. Major credit cards.*

The beach is just down the street from this all-suite resort, which is probably Waikiki's most upscale condo. Grounds include a swimming pool, whirlpool, sauna, and paddle tennis court. A spacious lanai runs on two sides of each one- and two-bedroom unit. The most expensive vistas are from floors twenty and above. Apartments sport full kitchens, wet bars, and washer/dryers. Housekeepers tidy your digs twice a day and concierge service is available. You can sign for meals at a choice of nearby restaurants. Valet parking is included in the rates.

HYATT REGENCY WAIKIKI, 2424 Kalakaua Avenue (off Ka'iulani), Honolulu, HI 96815. Tel. 808/923-1234 or 800/233-1234, Fax 808/923-7839. 1,230 rooms. Double rooms begin at $215. Major credit cards.

Across Kalakaua – which borders Queen's Beach, famous for its soft sand – this hotel takes up an entire block. Just look for the two connected towers. The three-story atrium has waterfalls, tropical foliage, and exotic birds. Yet with a labyrinth of 65 designer shops and boutiques on the property, the congested lobby, gleaming with rich koa wood, brings to mind the Galleria shopping mall in Dallas, Texas.

Guests who can afford it would probably do best booking rooms in the deluxe Regency Club. Its pampered members have exclusive use of its rooftop sun deck, with its wonderful panorama of the mountains and the Pacific. All the spacious hotel rooms are done in light colors with furniture of rattan, whitewashed oak or glass-topped wrought iron. Hawaiian and Asian influences are apparent in the decor. Rooms offer a variety of views, with Diamond Head/partial oceanfront being the most popular. The swimming pool provides an alternative to a stroll to the beach.

SHERATON PRINCESS KA'IULANI, 120 Ka'iulani Avenue (off Kalakaua), Honolulu, HI 96815. Tel. 808/922-5811 or 800/STAY-ITT, Fax 808/931-4577. 1,150 rooms. Double rooms begin at $185. Major credit cards.

Adjoining a lounge alive with greenery, the large pool patio of this Sheraton opens to Kalakaua Avenue, which borders the beach. Picturesque King's Village mall is across the street. Arrangements for golf, guided tours, rental cars, and other activities can be made at the Travel & Entertainment Desk in the lobby, which is decorated with plants and elaborate floral arrangements. Within walking distance are the Honolulu Zoo, Waikiki Aquarium, and Kapiolani Park (where night-lit tennis courts are open to the public at no charge). The hotel's year-round children's program is free to guests.

The cheery guest rooms vary greatly according to size and view. Some have twin beds and no lanais. Other rooms contain king-sized beds and writing desks. Rooms for nonsmokers and people in wheelchairs are available, and guests receive complimentary newspapers.

Dining choices include three restaurants, a food court, and a pool side lounge. Cuisines range from continental to Japanese and Chinese. For evening entertainment, the hotel's "Spectacular Polynesian Revue" pays tribute to Hawaii's monarchy (two dinner and cocktail shows are offered each night). Speaking of the monarchy, the namesake of this hotel died, heartbroken by the overthrow of Hawaii's kingdom, at the tender age of 23. Her handsome portrait is prominently displayed in the lobby. Be sure to ask about money-saving special hotel packages.

ASTON WAIKIKI SUNSET, *229 Paoakalani Avenue, Honolulu, HI 96815. Tel. 808/922-0511 or 800/922-7866, Fax 808/923-8580. 362 units. Rates begin at $180 per condo. Major credit cards.*

Three short blocks from the beach and near the zoo and Kapiolani Park, this all-suite condo caters mainly to families and students. Thus, it's not the quietest place in the world. The studios, one- and two-bedroom units, and penthouse suites are all comfortable. A swimming pool, tennis court and shuffleboard keep guests entertained. The restaurant serves inexpensive Japanese and American food, and the fifth-floor Mini Mart — which stocks everything from eggs and liquor to film and Nintendo for rent — is another welcome convenience. Many guests prefer rooms with more dramatic mountain views (spectacular at night with all the lights on the hillsides and in the valleys) to those with (usually partial) ocean views.

WAIKIKI PARC, *2233 Helumoa Road (at Lewers), Honolulu, HI 96815. Tel. 808/921-7272 or 800/422-0450, Fax 808/923-1336. 298 rooms. Double rooms begin at $170. Major credit cards.*

If this tasteful hotel appears to be an understated Halekulani (the ultra-luxury beach resort across the street), it's because it's owned and operated by the same corporation. Opened in 1987 with just under 300 rooms, it is considered small by Waikiki standards. The spare, modern lobby is done in pastels and various shades of white, greeting guests with uncrowded charm.

The bright, comfortable rooms are studies in blue, beige and eggshell. On one side, lanais and standing balconies look out to the ocean, while on the other three sides have views of parking lots, other tall buildings, and mountains. Each chicly decorated room has one telephone at bedside and another in the bathroom; a refrigerator/mini-bar; a 19" color remote control cable television; an AM/FM clock radio; and a safe. Feet tread on carpets and ceramic tiles. For those who like to sleep in, shutters keep the sun from pouring through the sliding glass balcony doors.

Room service is available from 6am to 10pm. Guests have the use of washers and dryers. Eight rooms are equipped for the physically challenged, and one is totally wheelchair-accessible, including the shower. When it's time to play, beach activities can be arranged through the hotel. Ask to be on the eighth floor if you don't want to have to take an elevator from your room to the pool. Two excellent restaurants, the Parc Cafe (continental and American regional) and Kacho (Japanese) serve three meals a day. The dinner buffet at the Parc invites diners to design (if they wish) their own seafood and pasta dishes for the chef to prepare.

Ask about economical packages that include breakfast, car, and parking.

WAIKIKI JOY HOTEL, *320 Lewers Street, Honolulu, HI 96815. Tel. 808/923-2300 or 800/922-7866, Fax 808/924-4010. 94 rooms. Double rooms begin at $160.*

One of the area's "boutique hotels," the Waikiki Joy opened in 1988. Most guests are business travelers. The suites and individual rooms here suit a wide range of wallets. Each unit comes with a lanai, a high-tech stereo system with a bedside control panel, and a Jacuzzi. Some also sport kitchens, while others have refrigerators or wet bars. The decor has an art deco feel. The only full ocean-view room in the hotel is #1109. For a mountain view, ask for #1115.

Complimentary coffee, fresh orange juice, and muffins are served in the small lobby from 7 to 10am each morning. There is also a restaurant on the premises. The small swimming pool and sauna are on a terrace off the lobby. Laundry facilities are available for guests.

WAIKIKI BEACHCOMBER, *2300 Kalakaua Avenue, Honolulu, HI 96815. Tel. 808/922-2646 or 800/622-2646, Fax 808/923-4889. Double rooms begin at $150. Major credit cards.*

This hotel may be called the Beachcomber, but it's not on the sand. Instead, you'll find it on busy Kalakaua Avenue, across from the Royal Hawaiian Shopping Center. To get to the beach, you'll have to walk across the street. Head to the pool terrace if you'd rather swim closer to home. On the street below the hotel, awnings shade the large display windows of glitzy Fifth Avenue-style stores. An escalator takes guests up from the ground floor to the shop-filled but pleasant looking lobby. Every night except Saturday and Monday, **Don Ho** performs at the Beachcomber.

All guest rooms come with private lanais, refrigerators, safes, TVs, either half or full bathtubs, and ironing boards. (You call for an iron.) Furniture is done in oak. Ocean view rooms look out to the water all the way across Kalakaua Avenue. Ask about the economical room/car or room/breakfast packages.

ASTON WAIKIKI TERRACE HOTEL, *2045 Kalakaua Avenue (near juncture with Kuhio), Honolulu, HI 96815. Tel. 808/955-6000 or 800/922-7866, Fax 808/943-8555. 242 rooms. Double rooms begin at $140. Major credit cards.*

Flowering potted plants are terraced up the front steps. The lobby and overlooking mezzanine are done in marble, glass, and brass. However, during a recent visit, I noticed that things have begun to look a bit worn around the edges. Leather seats were torn and the carpeting on the elevator walls was curling off. Also, twice the operator forgot to give me my messages and when she did, one of them wasn't for me. So, before you book here, check to see when the most recent renovations were done and what, exactly, has been spruced up or improved.

Most of the individual rooms and one-bedroom suites have two double beds. Some rooms have full or partial ocean views. All contain refrigerators, in-room safes (guests are charged for use), and television. The restaurant specializes in Chinese-style seafood. Guests mingle in the cocktail lounge. A swimming pool, fitness center, shops, and laundry facilities are on the premises, and room service is available.

MARC HAWAIIANA HOTEL, 260 Beachwalk, Honolulu, HI 96815. Tel. 808/923-3811 or 800/535-0085, Fax 808/926-5728. 95 rooms. Double rooms begin at $130. Major credit cards.

While this small hotel is rather simple in decor, it is a half block from Waikiki Beach. Its low-rise wings surround colorful gardens, which sit just outside guest room doors. Some of the air-conditioned studio and one-bedroom units have lanais, and all contain kitchenettes and safes. You'll be treated to fresh pineapple when you arrive and leis go to women guests on departure. In the mornings, juice and kona coffee are served on the pool side patio, and complimentary newspapers are available. A hula show is held twice a week. Guests are welcome to use the washers and dryers.

OUTRIGGER PRINCE KUHIO, 2500 Kuhio Avenue (off Ohua Avenue), Honolulu, HI 96815. Tel. 808/922-0811 or 800/688-7444, Fax 808/923-0330. 625 rooms. Double rooms begin at $130. Major credit cards.

While the Prince Kuhio, the top of the Outrigger line, is just a block from the beach, it's away from the most congested sections of Waikiki. Unlike other large hotels, each guest room has its own character. Special features include marble baths and wet bars. For the best view, request a room on a high floor on the Diamond Head side, or opt for special pampering in the Voyagers Club. Each night, Trellisses Restaurant serves a themed buffet. With just a few stores, the spacious, open lobby is a pleasant place to relax in the morning over complimentary coffee that flows from a silver urn. The Honolulu Zoo and Kapiolani Park are two blocks away.

THE ROYAL GARDEN AT WAIKIKI, 440 Olohana Street, Honolulu, HI 96815. Tel. 808/943-0202 or 800/367-5666, Fax 808/946-8777. 220 rooms. Double rooms begin at $130. Major credit cards.

Born in December 1993, this upscale hotel welcomes guests with a marble lobby, complete with soothing music from a player piano. Swim in the large or the small pool, relax in the whirlpool or sauna, or work out in the petite fitness room with a view of a slice of the canal. No-smoking floors, wheelchair access rooms, and a business center are available. All the rooms in this 25-story building have balconies, some with canal views. You'll also find wet bars and mini refrigerators. Rooms vary in size and decor. Some deluxe rooms are smaller than less-expensive units, but they have more marble and their baths have a separate shower and tub. Guests choose between two restaurants. A complimentary shuttle bus takes vacationers to Ala Moana Shopping Center, Waikiki shopping areas, and the beach. Continental breakfast is included in the rates.

WAIKIKI PARKSIDE, *1850 Ala Moana Boulevard, Honolulu, HI 96815. Tel. 808/955-1567 or 800/237-9666, Fax 808/955-6010. 250 rooms. Double rooms begin at $110. Major credit cards.*

Across from Hilton Hawaiian Village, this pleasant hotel is a brief walk from Waikiki Beach, Ala Moana Beach Park (which has tennis courts), a public golf course, and Ala Moana Shopping Center. The cheerful lobby is done in pink marble. Rooms, some of which have balconies, come with one queen-size bed, two doubles, or two queens. Views are of Waikiki and the mountains. While standard rooms are small, they are pleasantly furnished. All are equipped with refrigerators, TVs, and in-room safes. (There's a small charge for locking up your valuables.) If you want a bathtub instead of a stall shower, book a deluxe room. The swimming pool and pool bar are found on the second floor. Guests are welcome to use the laundry room.

OUTRIGGER REEF LANAIS, *255 Saratoga Road, Honolulu, HI 96815. Tel. 808/923-3881 or 800/688-7444, Fax 808/923-3823. 110 rooms. Double rooms begin at $110. Major credit cards.*

Some rooms in this economy hotel have kitchens, and at least one has a microwave. All simply decorated, they vary in size from cozy to spacious, some with stall showers and adjoining walk-in closets. Continental breakfast is included in the rates.

THE BREAKERS HOTEL, *250 Beach Walk, Honolulu, HI 96815. Tel. 808/923-3181 or 800/426-0494, Fax 808/923-7174. 66 rooms. Double rooms begin at $95.*

Stretching from Beach Walk to Saratoga Avenue, and halfway between Kalia Road and Kalakaua Avenue, this hotel is close to both the ocean and the main shopping thoroughfare. The Breakers is a pleasant surprise along a strip of low budget hotels. Shingled roofs cover a handful of buildings. Banana trees, palms, and other tropical greenery add color to the pool patio. Attractively furnished in rattan, bright guest rooms surround the pool. You'll find books for borrowing at the nearby open-air front desk. Each air-conditioned unit has a kitchenette, color TV and safe. Some are two-room suites that sleep four. Staff is happy to arrange tours around Oahu or sightseeing excursions to Neighbor Islands.

OUTRIGGER WAIKIKI TOWER, *200 Lewers Street (at Kalia Road), Honolulu, HI 96815. Tel. 808/922-6424 or 800/688-7444, Fax 808/923-7437. 439 rooms. Double rooms begin at $95. Major credit cards.*

Not to be confused with the countless other Outriggers, this one is across from the plush oceanfront Halekulani Hotel, in one of Waikiki's busiest areas. Bordered by stores, the lobby is pleasant enough, especially when compared to the cluttered public rooms of some of its neighbors. Guest rooms are comfortable and all kinds of street action is on view from the Waikiki Broiler Restaurant.

OUTRIGGER REEF TOWERS, 227 *Lewers Street, Honolulu, HI 96815. Tel. 808/924-8844 or 800/688-7444, Fax 808/924-6042. 480 rooms. Double rooms begin at $85. Major credit cards.*

The convenient location — on a palm-lined block near the beach and in the thick of Waikiki hurly-burly — makes this budget hotel a good choice. Here at the Polynesia Palace Showroom, regular performers include Charo, the coochie-coochie girl herself. There isn't much to see from the windows of the comfortable guest rooms, but who cares? Just step outside, and you can see (and do) as much as you'd like.

OUTRIGGER ROYAL ISLANDER. 2164 *Kalia Road (off Saratoga), Honolulu, HI 96815. Tel. 808/922-1961 or 800/688-7444, Fax 808/923-4632. 101 rooms. Double rooms begin at $80. Major credit cards.*

While you can't see the beach from the hotel grounds, a short path leads to it. The beach is actually located at the Outrigger Reef. This budget accommodation is just across the street from the beach front Waikiki Shore Apartments. Standard rooms are small but perfectly comfortable. All rooms are air-conditioned and have TVs, refrigerators, lanais, and baths with stall showers.

MALIHINI HOTEL, 217 *Saratoga Road (just off Kalia Road), Honolulu, HI 96815. Tel. 808/923-9644. 29 units. Double rooms begin at $50.*

In an unusual display of honesty in marketing, the postcard/brochure says it best: "Small, plain hotel with no extra frills. Just a place to stay in an excellent location." A (very) modest apartment hotel, this accommodation is a short stroll from the beach. The studios and one-bedroom units, all with kitchenettes and televisions, are cooled by either fans or air-conditioning.

WHERE TO EAT

Unlike in many other vacation spots, hotel restaurants in Hawaii are some of the best places to eat. Not only do they keep visitors pouring in, but locals make a habit of returning often to their favorites as well. Now, don't get me wrong: there is also an excellent selection of independent eateries. Competition in recent years has brought Oahu in particular and Hawaii in general a long way from the once-prevalent "Polynesian" menus that featured heavy dishes that were mainly sweet and sour.

Honolulu boasts Hawaii's widest choice of restaurants, both within and outside of hotels. They range from popular roadside "BBQs" and "Drive-Ins" to dining rooms bathed in top-drawer elegance. For the most part, Waikiki restaurants tend to be more expensive than elsewhere in the

OAHU'S BEST EATS

Cream of the Crop

La Mer, *Halekulani hotel, Waikiki: Get to this beach front spot before sunset and you'll have a fabulous view along with your gourmet continental-Pacific rim cuisine.*

Roy's, *Honolulu: On weekends, Hawaiian music accompanies the East meets West cuisine during dinner.*

3660 on the Rise, *Honolulu: The purple taro bread may be unexpected, but it's just as delicious as the rest of the imaginative melange of cuisines served here.*

The Golden Dragon, *Hilton Hawaiian Village, Waikiki: The signature dish at this gourmet Chinese restaurant is Imperial Beggar's Chicken, which you'll have to order a day in advance.*

Kacho, *Waikiki Parc hotel: This is the place for beautifully presented Japanese specialties.*

Less Expensive

Singha Thai, *Waikiki: This restaurant offers a good choice of delicious vegetarian dishes along with the wonderfully seasoned fish and meat on the Thai menu.*

Saigon Cafe, *Waikiki: The excellent Vietnamese food here keeps this small dining room filled.*

Cafe Hale'iwa, *Hale'iwa: Breakfast is hearty at this casual North Shore restaurant.*

state, particularly for dinner. While some visitors dress up at dinner time just for the fun of it, men are required to wear jackets at only a handful of restaurants. Casual chic is more commonly the way to go.

Several good (if somewhat trendy) dining spots are found along **Restaurant Row**, at 500 Ala Moana Boulevard in Honolulu, not far from Waikiki. During the week, you can get here from downtown Honolulu by city bus #19, 20 or 47 from Waikiki. Head to **Chinatown** in downtown Honolulu for Vietnamese, Filipino, and (what else?) Chinese cuisine in small, family-run eateries. A stroll through Chinatown can be a gustatory adventure. Bakeries and other small shops sell everything from peanut-rice squares, custard pies, and candied papaya, coconut, lotus root, and ginger to black sugar donuts and moon cakes. Selling goodies such as *manapua* (steamed Chinese rice-flour dough stuffed with pork or black beans), lunch wagons parked near beaches cause lines to form.

Hawaii's pervasive Japanese influence shows itself in the deli-like stores that do a brisk business in sushi, tempura, and plate lunches. A hybrid culinary institution of the Islands, a fast-food **plate lunch** generally includes a teriyaki or curried meat or fish entree, two scoops of rice, and macaroni salad. **Zippy's**, a fast-food chain restaurant popular among locals, serves saimin (noodle soup with meat or fish) and other Japanese and Chinese dishes, as well as burgers. **Denny's**, another chain, is a good bet for mahi mahi sandwiches, saimin, pancakes, waffles, and omelets. Thai and Korean food are also big on Oahu.

Few people pass through **Hale'iwa**, the little surfing town on the North Shore, without stopping at **Matsumoto's** for a **shave ice**. Known as snow cones in other parts of the world, the Hawaiian version comes doused with mango, passion fruit, coconut, and other tropical syrups.

Greater Honolulu

JOHN DOMINIS, *43 Ahui Street, at Keuaolo Basin, Honolulu. Tel. 523-0955. Reservations recommended. Dinner entrees: $27 to $39. Credit cards accepted.*

The excellent food is neck and neck with the wonderful ocean view. Surfers ride the waves in the distance while fishing boats pull up to shore. Seafood is the specialty here, and the location — right near the Honolulu Fish Market — could hardly be more convenient. A lobster-filled pond meanders through the restaurant. Treats from the sea are prepared in a variety of tasty ways, from broiled in butter to steamed with ginger. Tiger prawns — tempura, sautéed, broiled, with black bean sauce, as you wish — are a specialty. Save room for a slice of Bailey's mud pie.

This upscale restaurant borrows its name from John Owen Dominis, the son of an Italian ship captain. Dominis married Hawaii's last queen, Liliuokalani, in 1862 and later became governor of Oahu.

CLIQUO, *Niu Valley Shopping Center, 5730 Kalanianaole Highway. Tel. 377-8854. Reservations recommended. Closed Sunday. Dinner entrees: $25 to $40. Credit cards accepted.*

Excellent French cuisine highlights the menu. Although the a la carte entrees may be quite expensive, consider trying the rack of lamb with grilled eggplant or the veal chop. For a somewhat less costly meal, the prix fixe menu offers an appetizer, choice of one of two entrees, and a dessert. My favorite choice is between tournedos with Cabernet sauce and fresh opakapaka with a puree of organic pumpkin and balsamic vinegar. The food is delicious, beautifully presented and well worth the price.

IRIFUNE, *563 Kapahulu, Honolulu. Tel. 737-1141. Dinner entrees: $20 to $30.*

It's easy to understand why longtime residents love the delicate stir-fried entrees that combine crisp vegetables with tofu, chicken, or fish. The plain but homey atmosphere adds to the appeal. Try the New York steak with shiitake mushrooms.

SAM CHOY'S DIAMOND HEAD, *449 Kapahulu Avenue. Tel. 732-8645. Dinner entrees: $20 to $30. Credit cards accepted.*

Residents love Sam Choy's for Pacific Rim cuisine. Portions are huge, so come hungry or plan to split one dish between two people. The emphasis is on local-style seafood, such as seafood laulau, fish and veggies wrapped in ti leaves, and marinated fresh ahi salad. The menu might also include continental favorites, like bouillabaisse, with a regional twist, or roast duck with orange sauce. Expect surprises such as wontons filled with brie and served with pineapple marmalade.

KEO'S THAI CUISINE, *625 Kapahulu Avenue. Tel. 737-8240. Reservations recommended. Dinner entrees: $20 to $25. Credit cards accepted.*

Celebrities beat a path to the original Kapahulu Avenue Keo's, decked out with Asian antiques, Tiffany lamps, and fresh flowers. Keo Sananikone continues to build on his reputation with spicy Thai dishes such as crispy fried shrimp rolled in lettuce and cucumber with a delicious dipping sauce, and vegetarian spring rolls with mint leaves. Peanuts, basil, lemongrass and other flavors wake up the palate. Curries are also quite popular. For a fruity, coconut cocktail, try the Evil Princess.

THE PRINCE COURT, *100 Holomoana, Hawaii Prince Hotel, Ala Wai Yacht Harbor, just outside Waikiki. Tel. 956-1111. Reservations recommended. Dinner entrees: $18 to $32. Credit cards accepted.*

I am always pleased to find the same good food and service here that folks in Maui have come to know at the celebrated restaurant of the same name at the Maui Prince hotel. Tall windows afford views of the harbor. The inspired Hawaiian regional cuisine includes colorful, artful creations such as crab and lemongrass crusted opakapaka. Other selections I like are kiawe-grilled free range chicken and prawns and slipper lobster in coconut saffron sauce served with wild rice with pecans. The set menu, though expensive, is very attractive way to sample this excellent cuisine.

3660 ON THE RISE, *3660 Waialae Avenue, Kaimuki. Tel. 737-1177. Reservations recommended. Dinner only. Closed Mondays. Dinner entrees: $18 to 25. Credit cards accepted.*

I love the creative combinations at this popular restaurant, such as the Chinese steamed opakapaka with black bean sauce. Another favorite is ahi katsu, which is tuna wrapped in spinach and nori, dipped in bread crumbs, quickly deep fried so that the ahi is still raw; it's served with ginger wasabi sauce. No, it's not food coloring that makes the bread purple inside; it's taro root, a local staple. Wash it all down with mango ice tea or fresh lemonade.

For dessert, I highly recommend the Mile High Wailae ice cream pie, layered, with pralines and a macadamia nut crust, the Harlequin creme brulee with chocolate mousse, and banana Napoleon.

SUNSET GRILL, *Restaurant Row, 500 Ala Moana Boulevard, Honolulu. Tel. 521-4409. Reservations recommended. Dinner entrees: $18 to $25. Credit cards and personal checks accepted.*

New World Bistro is the term used to describe the way this restaurant prepares the fresh vegetables and other local products. Grilled sandwiches and grilled vegetables are featured. The fresh pastas, peppery warm spinach and calamari salad, and creme brulee are also delicious. If you're looking for a quiet place, this isn't it. The noise level in this see-and-be-seen dining spot is often on the high side. Patrons giggle over the drawings they have done on their place mats with the crayons provided on each table. The best creations are framed and hung around the room.

A PACIFIC CAFE OAHU, *Ward Centre, 1200 Ala Moana Boulevard, Honolulu. Tel. 593-0035. Dinner entrees: $16 to $26. Credit cards accepted. Closed for lunch on Saturday and Sunday.*

With restaurants also on Kauai and Maui, Chef Jean-Marie Josselin brings his popular cuisine to Oahu. A bamboo fountain and reflecting pool greet entering patrons. Dishes, which feature local ingredients and freshly harvested organic produce, are influenced by Mediterranean, French, Italian, and Indian culinary traditions. The menu changes seasonally. Vegetarians have a welcome choice of selections and the beef, lamb, and fish are prepared in unusual ways. The handmade plates used at the appetizer bar, which has an open kitchen, were designed by Sophie Josselin, the wife of the chef.

Pizza (served for lunch) is cooked in a wood-burning oven (try the smoked salmon pizza with herb cream cheese and arugula salad). For dinner, you might start with seared sea scallops with white truffle mashed potato, then move on to herb-crusted opakapaka (pink snapper) with couscous and sun-dried tomatoes, or lamb with pinenuts and barley risotto.

FISHERMAN'S WHARF RESTAURANT, *1009 Ala Moana Boulevard, on the harbor at Kewalo Basin, Honolulu. Tel. 538-3808. Reservations recommended. Dinner entrees: $16 to $18.50. Credit cards accepted.*

This seafood restaurant is so popular that many people call Kewalo Basin, the jumping-off point for many sightseeing and party cruises, Fisherman's Wharf. Fresh fish daily and live lobster are their signature.

RESTAURANT SADA, *1240 South King Street, Honolulu. Tel. 949-0646. Entrees: $16 to 18.*

Ask a Honolulu resident to direct you to her favorite sushi bar, and chances are you'll find yourself at this Japanese restaurant. Another recommended dish is kamameshi, steamed rice prepared with either crab, oyster, shrimp or chicken. Served with tempura or sushi, it's worth the 30 minute preparation time.

ROY'S, *6600 Kalanianaole Highway, Hawaii Kai, Honolulu. Tel. 396-7697. Reservations suggested. Dinner entrees: $13.95 to $21.95. Credit cards accepted.*

About eight miles east of Waikiki, in the ritzy suburb of Hawaii Kai, Roy Yamaguchi has made a culinary splash. Before coming to Hawaii, he began by thrilling diners in Los Angeles with his imaginative creations that married the East to the West. This duplex restaurant, high on my list of Oahu favorites, gazes out at the mountains and Maunalua Bay. The bar, with its outdoor tables, is downstairs. The upstairs dining room, with its tall picture windows, is always packed. In the center of the room, the gleaming white-tile and stainless-steel kitchen is open to full view of the diners at the surrounding tables. On Friday and Saturday nights, live Hawaiian music entertains patrons.

The ever-changing menu might include steamed pork dumplings served with a mustard and soy vinaigrette dressing; seafood-filled potstickers in a sauce made from sesame seeds and butter; beef stir-fried with roasted macadamias, fresh mint and Maui onions; scallops flavored with ginger and basil. Pizza here is for the adventurous, who enjoy it with such toppings as marinated Chinese chicken, Japanese sprouts or shiitake mushrooms.

KINCAID'S FISH CHOP AND STEAK HOUSE, *1050 Ala Moana Boulevard, Ward Warehouse, Honolulu. Tel. 591-2005. Credit cards: $13 to $19.*

Overlooking Kewalo Basin, this restaurant provides upscale atmosphere and good food for down scale prices. The attractive dining areas are spacious and ceiling fans circulate the air. The emphasis is on salads, soups, and seafood. Many guests love the Hunan lamb. Try the mahi-mahi (or another fish) stuffed with shrimp and crab, pasta, or bamboo steamed fish. Wine is served and there's a wide selection of beer. For dessert, try the delicious burnt cream (a custard). On Friday and Saturday nights, there's live music.

HARD ROCK CAFE, *1837 Kapiolani Boulevard, Honolulu. Tel. 955-7383. Reservations taken for lunch only. Dinner entrees: around $13. Credit Cards accepted.*

Like the other Hard Rock Cafes around the world, this casual restaurant is plastered with gold and platinum records, famous guitars, and other musical paraphernalia, with the addition of a few aloha shirts and surfboards once used by celebrities. Hamburgers, grilled fajitas, and watermelon barbecued ribs are on the menu. However, if you ask me, the food isn't special enough to choose this over so many other restaurants on Oahu that make you feel more like you're in Hawaii. Although all ages come, its appeal is to the young. Live bands play weekends.

CHAN'S CHINESE RESTAURANT, *Puck's Alley, 2600 South King Street, at University, Honolulu. Tel. 949-1188. Reservations recommended for large groups. Entrees: $9.95 to $11.95. Credit cards accepted.*

Famous for its dim sum, served only for lunch, this family-run restaurant is always busy. Sometimes one person's dish arrives well before those of fellow diners, but the food is plentiful and tasty. Popular dishes include seaweed soup, beef with black bean sauce, roast duck, and curried chicken. Sea bass in casserole, honey walnut shrimp, and tofu-stuffed shrimp are among the seafood dishes. The five spice tofu is a tasty appetizer.

COMPADRES MEXICAN BAR AND GRILL, *1200 Ala Moana Boulevard, Honolulu. Tel. 591-8307. Reservations required for parties of 10 or more. Dinner entrees: $9 to $19. Credit cards accepted.*

This large, attractive restaurant draws a young, lively crowd. Dine outside on the balcony or indoors. Grilled fajitas (chicken, beef, vegetable, and seafood) are delicious; the ingredients are marinated in wine and tequila and sautéed with vegetables. Along with the usual Mexican fare, you'll find hamburgers and great margaritas, as well as T-shirts and sweatshirts, emblazoned with the restaurant logo, for sale.

THE OLIVE TREE, *4614 Kilauea Avenue. Tel. 737-0303. Personal checks accepted. Entrees: around $9.*

Not to be confused with the Olive Garden chain, this very friendly place offers "not-so-fast" food. The taverna atmosphere is a good setting for souvlaki, avgolemono soup and baklava, well-done Greek staples, tastefully seasoned and presented. Except for the special of the day, everything is cooked to order. There is indoor and outdoor seating. Free parking is a bonus.

ALOHA POI BOWL, *2671 South King Street, Manoa area; Tel. 944-0798. Entrees: $8 to $11.*

This is another good choice for Hawaiian cuisine in a very informal setting. Lomi salmon (salted salmon in a sauce of tomatoes and onions), laulau, and kalua pig are well done. Poi and coconut dessert (haupia) are good ways to end the meal.

SEKIYA'S RESTAURANT & DELICATESSEN, *2746 Kaimuki Avenue (across from Kaimuki High), Honolulu. Tel. 732-1656. Entrees: $7.25 to $11. Closed Monday.*

Some residents say Sekiya's prepares the best plate lunch on Oahu. Corned beef is the specialty of this sixty year old family business; corned beef hash tempura may sound unusual, but it's very popular. Whether they eat it in or take it out, patrons also enjoy Japanese dishes such as beef teriyaki, sushi, and shrimp or vegetable tempura, as well as chow fun (warm noodles with vegetables), breaded butterfish, and fried Spam.

KEN FONG, 69 North Hotel Street, Chinatown, Honolulu. Tel. 537-6858. Entrees: $7 to $16.

This small plain restaurant is especially popular among Chinese residents. Family style service of Cantonese food provides steamed fish with ginger and green onion sauce, tofu with shrimp sauce, and steamed chicken with sausage and mushrooms

MOCHA JAVA, Ward Centre, across from Ala Moana Beach Park, Honolulu. Tel. 591-9023. Entrees: $7 to $8. Credit cards accepted.

This is a good place for a filling, inexpensive lunch — and, of course, coffee. Although the emphasis is on "health food," ham and chicken can also be found along with the vegetarian choices. You might try one of the curries or stir fries. Thick sandwiches come on cracked wheat bread. The variety of crepes is quite appealing.

ONO HAWAIIAN FOODS, 726 Kapahulu Avenue, Honolulu. Tel. 737-2275. Entrees: $6 to $10. Closed Sunday.

There are only ten tables at this unassuming local favorite. Entrees include kalua pig (cooked in a pit over hot rocks), laulau, poi, butterfish, and that Hawaiian staple, Spam. Other popular choices are chicken long rice and stir-fried sliced steak with vegetables. Portions are quite generous; after lunch here, you may feel like skipping dinner.

DAI-RYU HOUSE OF NOODLE, 1610 South King Street, Honolulu. Tel. 941-1939. Entrees: up to $7.50. Credit cards accepted.

This is the only place for gyoza (dumplings), hot sauce and shoyu yakisoba, fried and cold noodles, and almost any other noodle you can think of, as far as many residents are concerned.

WOODLANDS, 1289 South King Street, Honolulu. Tel. 596-8102. Entrees: up to $7. Credit cards accepted.

This no-frills storefront eatery serves good Chinese dumplings, soups, and homemade noodles. Its Northern Chinese cuisine includes many soups; pot stickers and boiled dumplings are popular choices.

YUM YUM TREE, Kahala Mall Shopping Center, Tel. 733-3544; Pali Palms Plaza, Tel. 254-5861; Mililai Town Center, Tel. 625-5555; and Westridge Shopping Center, Tel. 487-2487. Entrees: $5.25 to $14. Credit cards accepted.

Appealing to families, these home-style restaurants serve steak, seafood platters, pizza, burgers, and pasta salads. It may take forever to decide which of the twenty or so different pies to choose for dessert: macadamia nut cream, blueberry apple, English toffee, and pumpkin crunch are just a few. At brunch, people munch waffles, pancakes, French toast, and all kinds of eggs.

KIM CHEE No. 2, 3569 Waialae Avenue, Honolulu. Tel. 737-5512. Inexpensive.

Of the various Kim Chee restaurants, this is the closest to Waikiki. Served in a down-to-earth atmosphere, the highly seasoned Korean fare includes barbecue chicken, spare ribs, and, of course, kim chee (spicy cabbage or other vegetables). This makes a good lunch stop. Also try Kim Chee No. 3 (1040 South King Street, Tel. 597-8017).

CHIANG MAI NORTHERN THAI CUISINE, 2239 South King Street, Honolulu. Tel. 941-1151. Inexpensive.

Once low on atmosphere, this dining spot has been spruced up to give the better known Keo's some competition for lunch and dinner. The Thai specialties, including a good selection of vegetarian dishes, remain as delicious as ever.

RAINBOW DRIVE-IN, 3308 Kanaina Avenue, Honolulu. Tel. 737-0177. Entrees: around $5.

Locals drive-in here for some of the best plate lunches around. The popular mixed plate includes teriyaki beef, boneless chicken, and mahi mahi. Another choice is boneless chicken with brown gravy.

HA-BIEN VIETNAMESE RESTAURANT, 198 North King Street, Chinatown, Honolulu. Tel. 531-1185 or 524-5991. Inexpensive.

This large corner restaurant, located in what was once the red light district, pulls in a steady stream of diners, mainly Vietnamese immigrants.

Waikiki

LA MER, the Halekulani hotel, 2199 Kalia Road. Tel. 923-2311. Jackets required for men. Dinner entrees: $36 to $42. Credit cards accepted.

Tables in this elegant dining room — done in warm rusts, golds, and browns — are spaced so that everyone has a view of the ocean. At night, patrons can look out to the catamarans taking the partying crowd on dinner cruises. While the walls are decorated with Hawaiian carvings, the accent of the food is continental. Consider starting with the grilled lobster salad with sea scallops and hearts of palm. Then for an entree try the bouillabaisse, the rack of lamb, or the pan cooked duck with a corn cake. The macadamia vanilla coffee is also delicious.

ORCHID'S, the Halekulani hotel, 2199 Kalia Road. Tel. 923-2311. Dinner entrees: $28 to $42. Credit cards accepted.

Right at the edge of the beach, with a view that takes in Diamond Head, this restaurant serves three meals a day. Hardwood floors, white tablecloths, and a profusion of orchids and greenery make this a particularly pleasant locale. For dinner, consider the swordfish marinated in miso, the lemongrass and cashew chicken, or the beef rib roast coated with coriander. If you're in Waikiki on a Sunday, this is the place for brunch. The pastry department outdoes itself with its fresh oversized popovers and other baked goodies.

HANOHANO ROOM, Sheraton Hotel Waikiki, 2255 Kalakaua Avenue. Tel. 922-4422. Not open for lunch. Reservations required. Jackets and ties recommended for men at night. Dinner entrees: $25 to $35. Credit cards accepted.

A glass elevator glides from the lobby thirty floors up to this restaurant showcasing local fish and contemporary cuisine. From one of the best vantage points around, the sweeping view encompasses Diamond Head, especially dramatic at sunset, and famed Waikiki Beach. Crystal chandeliers sparkle while the mellow sounds of a combo pull diners onto the dance floor in the evening. For dinner, you might find breast of duck, prime rib, *onaga* in saffron sauce, banana flambe, and passion fruit sorbet. The Sunday brunch is popular, and breakfast is served daily. No shorts are allowed in the dining room.

KACHO, *Waikiki Parc Hotel, 2233 Helumoa Road. Tel. 921-7272 or 924-3535. Reservations recommended. Dinner entrees: $24 to $30. Credit cards accepted.*

An excellent Japanese restaurant, Kacho serves a traditional breakfast that includes seafood and vegetable appetizers, broiled fish, pickled vegetables, steamed rice, and miso soup or okayu (rice soup), plus natto (fermented beans). For lunch and dinner, the Kyoto-style cuisine consists of sushi and sashimi, a variety of soups, tempura, and seafood. No jeans, shorts, or flip-flops are allowed at dinner.

NICK'S FISHMARKET, *Waikiki Gateway Hotel, 2070 Kalakaua Avenue. Tel. 955-6333. Reservations required. Dinner entrees: $20 and up. Credit cards accepted.*

In a dark, candlelit setting, this restaurant serves some of the best seafood I've had in Waikiki, along with rack of lamb. Lobster, Monterey abalone, and the filling bouillabaisse are signature creations.

ACQUA, *Hawaiian Regent Hotel, toward Diamond Head end of Kalakaua Avenue. Tel. 924-0123. Dinner entrees: $18 to $22.*

This bistro features very well-prepared steak, seafood, and Pacific Rim cuisine. Pastas, rack of lamb, and crusted pepper steak, are also excellent. After the guava barbecued prawn appetizer won first place in the seafood category of the Taste of Honolulu People's Choice contest, the dish became so popular that it was added to the menu as an entree. Another winner was chocolate mousse cake that garnered the second prize in the Dessert Fantasy at the Pacific Beach Hotel.

THE HAU TREE LANAI, *New Otani Kaimana Beach Hotel, at the foot of Diamond Head, 2863 Kalakaua Avenue. Tel. 921-7066. Reservations required. Dinner entrees: $18 to $26. Credit cards accepted.*

Right on the beach, this appealing restaurant is built around the same hau tree that shaded the Victorian home that stood on this spot in the early 1900s. Breakfast may consist of a coconut smoothie, papaya muffins, and thick Belgian waffles topped with crunchy macadamia nuts. Fresh fish is its specialty. A good fitness choice for lunch is broiled *ahi* steak with tomato chili sauce. Dinner appetizers are unusual, including Cajun sashimi and smoked salmon lomi style. Opakapaka, ahi or mahi mahi can be prepared Chinese style, bamboo steamed with bok choy and other vegetables in a soy sauce. Another entree is opah, moonfish, seared, topped with a mixture of crab, spinach and shiitake mushrooms, and then baked. The sunsets complement the fine cuisine. At night, diners can eat under the dancing light of blazing torches.

KYO-YA, *2057 Kalakaua Avenue. Tel. 947-3911. Dinner entrees: $18 to $25. Credit cards accepted.*

One of the most elaborate Japanese restaurants I've ever seen, Kyo-Ya, with shoji screens and enamel, looks like the headquarters of a fancy Japanese corporation. The food is cooked right at your table. Try the sukiyaki or the shabu-shabu (thinly sliced beef in a noodle and vegetable broth). The food is equal to the decor.

CASTAGNOLA'S ITALIAN LANAI, *1920 Ala Moana Boulevard, 2nd floor. Tel. 949-6277. Dinner entrees: $18 to $20. Credit cards accepted.*

Oahu residents consider this one of Hawaii's best Italian restaurants. The osso bucco, shrimp scampi, and varied veal dishes are very tasty. You may have to wait a bit for your order because dishes are individually prepared, but it's worth it.

MOMOYAMA JAPANESE RESTAURANT, *Sheraton Princess Ka'iulani Hotel. Tel. 922-5811. Dinner only. Entrees: $17 to $61. Credit cards accepted.*

Among the selections at this traditional teppan-style restaurant is the special that includes a lobster tail, broiled New York steak, miso soup, salad, pickled vegetables, rice, ice cream and green tea.

PARC CAFE, *Waikiki Parc Hotel, 2233 Helumoa Road, at Lewers. Tel. 921-7272. Dinner buffets: $16.50 to $24.50. Credit cards accepted.*

This brightly lit hotel dining room serves delicious gourmet creations three meals a day. The breakfast buffet includes pancakes and French toast with coconut or maple syrup, fresh fruit, muffins, croissants, eggs, assorted breakfast meats, and other goodies. Sunday brunch is more elaborate, with rotisserie chicken, eggs Benedict, and fresh catch. Lunch or dinner buffets might begin with freshly made soup, followed by meats cooked on a rotisserie and carved to order, pasta, fish, chicken, freshly baked pastries and chocolate mousse. Salads are especially good, such as the deep-fried tofu salad. There's also a Hawaiian buffet at lunch time Wednesday and Friday.

THE GOLDEN DRAGON, *the Hilton Hawaiian Village. Tel. 946-5336. Dinner only. Entrees: $12.50 to $35. Credit cards accepted.*

A gourmet Chinese restaurant, the Golden Dragon is on the lagoon side of the hotel's landmark Rainbow Tower (with its colorful mosaic design). As you enter between golden Chinese horses, you'll see a large tropical fish tank. Decorative carts resemble Chinese chariots. Good selections might be smoked spare ribs, sharkfin soup, seafood egg rolls, and lobster with curry and haupia (Hawaiian coconut pudding). For the delicious Peking duck with plum sauce, you'll need to place your orders 24 hours in advance. Sinking your teeth into Imperial Beggar's Chicken also requires a day's notice. The bird is seasoned and stuffed, wrapped in leaves and then clay, and baked for several hours. The dish is brought to your table still encased in its shell and you're given a wooden mallet for making the first crack. This flavorful chicken is *so* tender.

SEAFOOD VILLAGE, *Hyatt Regency, 2424 Kalakaua Avenue. Tel. 971-1818. Dinner entrees: $10.95 and up.*

Avoid this tourist trap. Many visitors have been enticed by signs and flyers advertising great prices, only to discover that everything on the menu inside is more expensive! During a recent visit, we had to argue with a less-than-gracious waiter to get the "shrimp and Mongolian beef" for no more than the "special" price on the sign outside. Although the decor is fine and the food is palatable, this Chinese restaurant is annoyingly overpriced.

CALIFORNIA PIZZA KITCHEN, *1910 Ala Moana Boulevard, Tel. 955-5161; 4211 Waialae Avenue, Tel. 737-9446. Entrees: around $10. Credit cards accepted.*

This cafe serves lunch and dinner. Pastas and salads are on the menu along with pizzas topped with goodies such as Thai chicken and peanuts, barbecued chicken, shrimp scampi, and pineapple.

SINGHA THAI, *1910 Ala Moana Boulevard (across the street from Hilton Hawaiian Village), Honolulu, HI 96815. Tel. 941-2898. Reservations recommended for dinner. Dinner entrees: $9.95 to $19.95. Credit cards accepted.*

A Thai temple guards the entrance to this excellent Thai and Hawaiian regional restaurant, which is decorated with Thai masks and golden Buddhas. During your meal, you'll be treated to a performance by elaborately costumed dancers, whose sensual belly and hand movements are truly impressive.

Vegetarians are pleased to find a variety of well-seasoned selections along with the seafood and meat on the menu. Many people choose the multi-course family style meals, so they can sample the greatest number of dishes. For appetizers, you can't go wrong with the blackened ahi summer rolls or the chicken sate. Most dishes, such as the Tom Kah soup (lemongrass with coconut milk, chicken breast, mushrooms, and lime juice) come mild, medium, or hot.

Among the best entrees are the spicy long eggplant with tofu and shiitake mushrooms, the red curry shrimp, the pan-fried mahi mahi with chili sauce, and the seafood Pad Thai noodles. Good sides include the vegetarian fried rice and steamed sticky rice. There's an extensive wine list, with wines chosen specifically to complement the highly seasoned food.

TEXAS ROCK-N-ROLL SUSHI BAR, *Hyatt Regency Waikiki, 2424 Kalakaua Avenue. Tel. 923-7655. Dinner only. Entrees: $5.75 to $16.50. Credit cards accepted.*

Have a taste for Little Richard's Texas Pizza? A hankering for Buddy Holly's Cattleman Beef? Then be sure to hit this lively, western-style restaurant that mixes Japanese delicacies with hearty Southern fare. Most of the patrons will be young, loud, fellow vacationers. People have to shout to be heard over the music blasting from speakers. Leather banquettes, wooden plank tabletops, bandannas serving as napkins, and paneled walls adorned with motifs such as cacti, cowboy boots, and cattle head all fit the theme. Then, of course, there's line dancing on Tuesdays and Thursdays, and live music on Friday and Saturday nights.

Most folks come here for the entertainment and party atmosphere. But the eats aren't bad. You might start with the sushi sampler (with a Western Barbecue Roll and a Saddle Sore Beef Fajita Roll), then move on to Little Richard's pizza (crab, shrimp, and lobster atop a fajita), and end with the Fats Domino peach cobbler.

SAIGON CAFE, *1831 Ala Moana Boulevard, 2nd floor. Tel. 955-4009. Open 6:30am - 9:30pm. Inexpensive.*

I've always enjoyed this cheerful spot, which gets high marks from many Oahu residents. Among the tastiest dishes on the Vietnamese menu are five spices chicken, garlic shrimp, and spicy beef lemongrass. If you order spring rolls (and you should!), the waiter will show you how to wrap them in fresh mint and lettuce, then dip them in a delicious sauce. Some items are on the greasy side, but they are good nonetheless. Wall to wall windows afford views of busy Ala Moana Boulevard.

Elsewhere on Oahu

HAIKU GARDENS-CHART HOUSE, *46-336 Haiku Road, Kaneohe, southeastern windward coast. Tel. 531-5586. Dinner entrees: around $25.*

Grilled meats are the trademark of this restaurant in a glorious garden setting, complete with jungled greenery and lily ponds. Steaks, prime ribs, chicken and fish are featured. Dining in the open air, you'll see the Koolau Mountains before you.

JAMESON'S BY THE SEA, *62-540 Kamehameha Highway, Hale'iwa, North Shore. Tel. 637-4336. Dinner entrees: $18 to $20. Credit cards accepted.*

Along with well-prepared seafood, evening diners are treated to fabulous sunsets at this ocean view restaurant. (It's the only restaurant whose dining room actually overlooks the ocean.) Torches flame at the edge of the open-air dining area. Jameson's is packed for lunch, cocktails, and dinner. Good choices include Portuguese bean soup, Boston clam chowder, the grilled crab and shrimp sandwich, veggie burgers, Thai summer rolls, Caesar salad, and Cajun chicken wings.

Stop at the restaurant's **crafts shop,** where you'll find all kinds of ceramic sculpture and wall hangings, cards, and paintings, along with fudge that you can have mailed back to the mainland.

BUENO NALO, *41-865 Kalanianaole Highway, Waimanalo, southeastern windward coast. Tel. 259-7186. Inexpensive. Credit cards accepted.*

Despite the startlingly bright, somewhat gaudy decor of this modest joint, people often line up outside to sample the delicious Mexican food. You can order nearly any combination of tacos, tamales, chili rellenos and enchiladas.

KUA AINA SANDWICH, *66-214 Kamehameha Highway. Tel. 637-6067. Inexpensive.*

Residents say this place has the best hamburgers on Oahu (some claim it's the vermouth), and the fries get raves as well. Sandwiches and fish burgers are also on the menu. Packed at lunch time, this small eatery is very popular among surfers.

CAFE HALE'IWA, *66-460 Kamehameha Highway. Tel. 637-5516. Inexpensive.*

Breakfast, lunch, and dinner are served at this popular dining spot. In the morning, I can't get enough of the huge whole wheat or buttermilk pancakes, the omelets, or the mahi-mahi with rice. Mid-day, try the burritos, tostadas or a sandwich (such as veggies with avocado and melted cheese). If you order a tuna- stuffed tomato, no worries: the fish is "dolphin safe." Walls are decorated with original paintings and photographs for sale.

BARBECUE KAI, *85-973 Farrington Highway, Waianae. Tel. 696-7122. Inexpensive.*

Since this roadside stand is located right next to the Waianae Army Recreation Center Beach, one of the area's best spots for swimming, it's a good place to stop for a take-out lunch. Choose among *mahi mahi* sandwiches, *saimin, teriyaki* pork chops, sweet and sour ribs, and chicken *katsu* (deep fried, breaded chicken cutlet). Although the very low prices attract some down and out looking diners, the food is delicious.

WAIANAE BAKERY, *85-888 Farrington Highway, Waianae. Tel. 696-3959. Closed Monday. Open 4:30am - 1:30pm. Inexpensive.*

The cooks move quickly behind the counter at this cozy family-run restaurant. Breakfast is the signature meal, with French toast, pancakes, eggs, Spam, Portuguese or Vienna sausage, and all kinds of baked treats. Hash browns are served, but you might pass for a local if you eat your eggs with a mound of white rice. Corned beef hash is among the meats on the Kaamaina breakfast plate that also includes two eggs and potatoes. Burgers and sandwiches feed the lunch crowd.

SEEING THE SIGHTS

Waikiki Today

Waikiki may be a mere one and a half square miles in size, but its glitz and glitter get most of the attention given Oahu. By daybreak, the streets are filled with activity as pedestrians stroll by joggers, families munch early breakfasts, and men with metal detectors comb the beach for wayward coins. Hundreds of hotels, restaurants, shops, nightclubs, and bars are packed into Waikiki. ABC Drug Stores (which sell everything from groceries and liquor to clothing and gifts) are omnipresent — there are sometimes even two on a single block, anchoring it like bookends. The low profile of the rest of the island is fine with both residents and visitors who, leaving the hordes behind, escape to greater Honolulu and the rural regions. If you like mingling with locals, the only part of Waikiki to hang out in is **Kapiolani Park**. Otherwise, unless their employment brings them to this resort area, residents spend little time amid its forest of tourists.

Created by human hands (to rid the once swampy area of mosquitoes), the **Ala Wai Canal** forms Waikiki's north and west borders. Luxury condominiums with views of verdant hillsides stand along the shores of this glistening waterway. Canoe races take place on the canal in the evenings. In the east, Waikiki is bounded by Kapahulu Avenue, Kapiolani Park, and **Diamond Head**, the extinct volcano that has become an unforgettable landmark. Waikiki Beach and the Pacific Ocean command the southern coast.

During the 1980s, Waikiki underwent a multi-million dollar transformation. What had degenerated into seedy tackiness by the 1970s — with advertising fliers scattered on sidewalks and plastic leis and palm trees in abundance — has become downright respectable. Crosswalks on **Kalakaua Avenue**, the main thoroughfare, are decorated with Hawaiian *kapa* cloth designs. Visitors pour in and out of shops such as Tiffany, Gucci, Chanel, and Celine. Sidewalks were widened, lined with flowers, outfitted with new benches, and repaved with bricks in warm earth tones. More trees, including Madagascar olive, monkeypod, and autograph, provide a break from the sun. To lessen traffic congestion, the number of pedicabs decreased and street signs were made more legible. Sidewalk distribution of commercial handbills has been cut down. (Don't be caught jaywalking, by the way.)

However, a controversy rages over the recent bloom in street vendors selling T-shirts, Indonesian pareos (sarongs), and other items geared to visitors. Feeling that their prices are being undercut, many merchants who are paying for overhead are disturbed by this trend. They note that the goods are usually lower-quality than what you'd find in the stores.

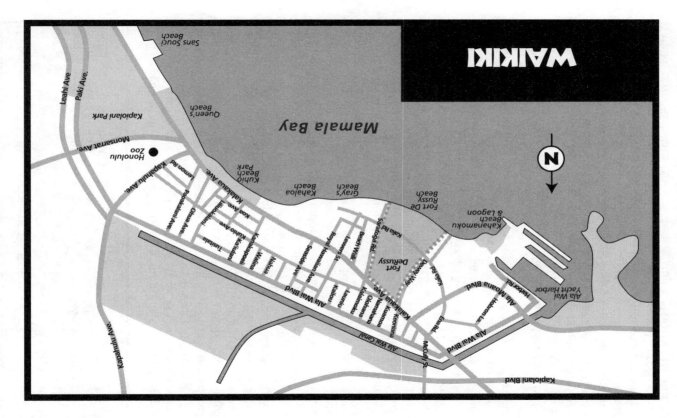

WAIKIKI

The centrally located **Royal Hawaiian Shopping Center** takes up a chunk of Kalakaua Avenue. Out front, the **Waikiki Old Town Trolley** departs for tours of Honolulu, but it concentrates an tourist traps.

Other shopping meccas include the crowded, open-air **International Marketplace** and **King's Village**, with its clock tower, both near Kalakaua and Kaiulani. King's Village is tucked behind the twin-towered Hyatt Regency Waikiki and across from the Sheraton Princess Kaiulani Hotel. The cobblestone alleys and the appealing old architecture make this a pleasant place to stop, if only to see a Burger King in a most unlikely building. In addition to the restaurants and shops here, you can watch hula or candle-carving demonstrations, among other activities. For a pleasant diversion, follow the royal path through King's Village to trace the history of Hawaii's royalty described on handcrafted plaques along the way.

If dignified, historic architecture is your thing, take a stroll through the Moana Hotel on Kalakaua. Built in 1901, it is Waikiki's oldest hotel. After undergoing a massive renovation, it has become part of the **Sheraton Moana Surfrider** complex. On the beach next to the Moana wing, colorful rows of surfboards stand on a rack, waiting to be taken out to play (for a rental fee). Look for the **Wizard Stones** on the beach here (near the showers), especially if you have an ailment. During the 16th century, these rocks were said to have been endowed with healing powers by four Tahitian prophets as a gesture of thanks after the stones were put there in their honor.

The queen of Waikiki is still the multi-tiered **Royal Hawaiian Hotel** (the second oldest), built in 1927 and known as the Pink Palace ever since. Stop for a drink at the hotel's outdoor beach-side bar and watch life go by while Diamond Head crouches like a lion in the background. Waikiki hotels are a welcome mix of luxury, moderate, and low-budget accommodations. Quite a few luxury and some moderate hotels are directly on the beach. Hotels in all three categories are also near the beach or several blocks away. On the second floor of the twin-towered **Hyatt Regency Waikiki**, across Kalakaua from the beach, stop by **Hyatt's Hawaii** museum, with its display of Hawaiian arts, including antique quilts and

A CHINESE CIRCLE

The Aston Waikiki Circle Hotel, the tall cylindrical building across Kalakaua Avenue from the beach has an intriguing history. It was founded by the first Asian woman to own a hotel in exclusive, central Waikiki. **Emma Kwock Chun,** *who transformed herself from an illiterate immigrant to a millionaire, was born in China in 1892. When she was only 12 years old, her parents sent her to Hawaii to work as a nanny and housekeeper for a Chinese family. At age 16, she was married off by a matchmaker to a 40-year-old shoe cobbler. She began buying property with the money she thriftily saved.*

Eventually, she managed to purchase a rooming house for World War II soldiers and she cooked and cleaned for these military men. In 1962, her Circle Hotel opened on the site of the rooming house. Still an inspiration to many, Emma Kwock Chun died in 1975.

artifacts. At the Waikiki branch of the **First Hawaiian Bank**, huge murals by Jean Charlot illustrate the history of the various ethnic groups that came to Hawaii.

The **US Army Museum**, *Battery Randolph, Kalia Road, Fort DeRussy, Waikiki*, housing artillery before World War I, has been transformed into a museum with military displays concerning the US Army's involvement in the Pacific.

Of course, grand **Waikiki Beach** is the focus of Waikiki. Different sections of this long sandy strip are known by various names. You'll note that some hotels that call themselves beach front (and even have brochure photographs to "prove" it) are actually across Kalakaua Avenue from the ocean.

Catamarans glide across the water, taking visitors on sailing, snorkeling, and sunset cruises. Sunsets on Waikiki Beach are among Hawaii's best, by the way. (For a fabulous vantage point, after 5:30pm take the glass elevator to the lounge at the top of the Ilikai Hotel.) Outrigger canoes bounce over the waves. But the main attraction is surfing. Everybody's into it. I first realized that age is no factor the moment I saw a slim, gray-haired, elderly woman in short shorts walk by with a surfboard tucked under her firm arm.

Waikiki Beach was one of the first areas in the Islands where Hawaiians began to surf: Certain beaches and kinds of surfboards were used only by the *alii* (aristocracy). This ancient sport was squelched by puritanical missionaries during the early 1800s. But it came back full force at the turn of the 20th century.

ON THE OPEN SEA

Most of Oahu's dinner and moonlight cruises, and glass-bottom boat trips leave from Kewalo Basin, just beyond the ewa (western) end of Waikiki. For booze cruises and dinner excursions, you can often arrange free transportation to and from the boat so you don't have to worry about drinking and driving.

Dinner cruises are quite popular on Oahu. Try Windjammer Cruises', Tel. 537-1122 or 531-0286, multi-deck Kulamanu. There is a sunset cruise daily from 5:15pm - 7:30pm. Choose from three dinner services. For a far more intimate experience, Tradewind Charters, Tel. 973-0311, sets sail with a maximum of six people on a private yacht. **Navatek I, Tel. 848-6360,** offers sightseeing, sunset, and dinner cruises aboard an exceptionally stable high-tech vessel. Watch the skyline or the Honolulu city lights, dance to a lively band, and have a cocktail or two. Rates range from $47 to $155 per adult; less for children.

Today, "beachboys" (also serving as lifeguards) still teach surfing on Waikiki Beach. Some of the older ones made names for themselves in Hollywood movies, such as Steamboat and Moon Doggie, who, when in their 80's, still guaranteed you'd be standing on your board in half an hour. Even if you're not up for testing your skill, spend some time talking story with some of these men. However, if you're a woman who decides to enjoy the company of one of these "beachboys" after hours, know that you probably aren't the first tourist to succumb to their charms and it isn't likely you'll be the last.

Another water ride to consider is a ride on a **submarine,** *Tel. 973-9811 or 800/548-6262.* While it is certainly exciting, a ride on one of Atlantis's 48- or 64-passenger touring subs is an expensive affair. Packages start at $60 for adults and $40 for children (minimum 3 foot height) for the 45-minute dip. I think your money would be better spent scuba diving or taking several snorkeling trips. But if you'd rather stay dry while you visit the depths, the Atlantis can help you out. First you'll board a catamaran, at the Hilton Hawaiian Village dock in Waikiki. When you climb into the sub, waiting a mile out in the ocean, you'll descend about 100 feet, seeing a sunken naval tanker amid the fish and coral around an artificially created reef. The submarine ride is less than an hour, but, including the catamaran shuttle, plan to spend two hours on this excursion. Ask about tours that combine the sub trip with a Waikiki cocktail musical show or dinner at Planet Hollywood.

Where oiled bodies now happily lie cheek by jowl, the land here was once rice paddies and swamps. After solidifying the ground with landfill,

SURF'S UP

In the early days of Hawaii's tourism, "beachboys" taught visitors to surf. One of the best known was **Duke Paoa Kahanamoku,** *a world championship surfer who maneuvered a 114-pound, 16-foot board made of koa wood. In 1915, he went to Australia to introduce the sport to hundreds of amazed onlookers. Waikiki's Kahanamoku Beach and Lagoon is named for this master athlete who was a champion Olympic swimmer as well. When you see the huge statue of Kahanamoku, by the "healing stones" along the beach, you'll wonder how the sign that says "Actual Size" could possibly be true. Whether these words refer to the man or the surfboard he's holding, he had to have been one powerful dude. The feet are as long as my forearms!*

the sand for Waikiki Beach was brought in from other Hawaiian islands, California, Hong Kong, and the far side of Oahu. The main section of Waikiki Beach is especially crowded during the summer and again between December and March. Sun worshippers can escape the bustle by going to nearby **Diamond Head Beach** or **Kahala Beach,** farther east.

In 1895, at the base of Diamond Head by **Sans Souci Beach,** a vicious four-day battle erupted between the businessmen who had pushed Liliuokalani off her throne and those who were loyal to the queen. The supporters of the Hawaiian monarchy lost, and more than a 100 of them ended up behind bars. Among those imprisoned on charges of treason was George Lycurgus, the flashy hotelier who had opened the Sans Souci Inn on this beach.

Beginning inside **Diamond Head crater,** a well-defined trail leads to the top of this extinct volcano. Sunrises and sunsets are especially breathtaking from these heights. Attractive **Kapiolani Park** spreads itself out at the base of Diamond Head. Especially on weekends, it churns with people jogging; playing soccer, softball, Frisbee, and tennis (on lighted courts); and flying kites (not just during the three-day kite-flying festival in March, either). Many Sunday afternoons at 2pm, the Royal Hawaiian Band gives free concerts at the bandstand.

David Kalakaua, who reigned as Hawaii's king from 1874 to 1891, was inspired to create this park by his visits to the mainland, where he saw large patches of green set aside for public pleasure. He dedicated this verdant spot in 1877, naming it after his queen. In those days, peacocks roamed freely and there were ponds stocked with goldfish. But these ponds were filled in during the 1920s. Horse racing thrived here for a while, until public distaste for the increasingly wild betting put an end to it.

WONDERFUL DRIVES

One of the most dramatic is from Diamond Head past Makapuu Lookout to Waimanalo, then through the Koolau Mountains along the Pali Highway, to Honolulu. Others are the mountainous Tantalus-Round Top Drive; and the beach-trimmed windward coast and North Shore.

Today locals gather in clusters to hear each other strum ukuleles or slack key guitars. On Lei Day (May 1), the park is given over to all kinds of Hawaiian entertainment, including displays of leis and other arts and crafts, a lei-making contest, and the coronation of the lei queen.

Even the **Honolulu Zoo**, *Kapiolani Park, 151 Kapahulu Avenue, Waikiki; Tel. 971-7171; Open 9am - 4:30pm daily; Admission: $6 adults, $1 children 6-12, free for children 5 and younger*, located in the park. Built in 1914, this zoo has added nearly 1,000 animals to its original half a dozen. Children enjoy the petting zoo, with more than 100 friendly animals. On Wednesdays and weekends, look for art by local painters displayed, for sale, on the Monsarrat Avenue fence. During the summer, free musical shows are performed here on Wednesday nights.

Three times a week, visitors stream into the park for the **Kodak Hula Show**, *Kapiolani Park, Waikiki; Showtimes: Tuesday, Wednesday, and Thursday at 10am; Free admission*, which has been running since the 1930s. The performances of modern **hula** (done by women, as opposed to the earlier version done by men) take place at the 8,000-seat **Waikiki Shell**, an open-air amphitheater. To begin the show, a man dressed as King Kamehameha I (a.k.a. Kamehameha the Great) calls out "Alo—*hah!*" and the audience responds in kind. Some of the ukulele-strumming, acoustic bass-plucking musicians are *tutus* (grandmothers) dressed in colorful mumus, leis, and straw hats. Wearing traditional skirts made of *ti* leaves (glossy, forest green) and plumeria leis and crowns, a younger generation of women performs the hula, shaking feathered gourds (and parts of their bodies). The bright reds, yellows, greens and other colors make snapping photos (with your Kodak film, of course) difficult to resist. Also included in the show are examples of Tahitian dances, which require much faster hip action than Hawaiian hula.

Concerts of Hawaiian, European classical, or popular music also take place here. If you follow the lead of locals, you'll buy lawn tickets and bring a picnic dinner and a blanket to spread on the grass, with Diamond Head looking down on you.

The **Waikiki Aquarium**, *Across from Kapiolani Park, Waikiki; Tel. 923-9741; Open 9am - 5pm daily (Admission desk closes at 4:30pm); Admission: $6, seniors (age 60+) $4, children (age 3-17) $2.50, free for children under age 3*, though petite, makes a worthwhile stop. It opened in 1904, making it one of the oldest in the country. Among the hundreds of species of Pacific marine life now residing here are seals, giant clams, sharks, sea turtles. lobsters, crocodiles, and a rainbow of fish.

Across the street from the park, right next to the Waikiki Aquarium, is the **Waikiki War Memorial Natatorium**. Built in 1927 in tribute to residents of Hawaii who had served in World War I, this stately oceanfront structure consists of a huge saltwater pool with a diving tower, and enough bleachers for 2,000 people. In the middle of the bleachers, a tall, elaborately carved arch provides entrance. In its glory days, the Natatorium played host to many swimming competitions. In one held during its first year, Hawaii's own Duke Kahanamoku, winner of four Olympic gold medals, trained in this pool. It also served as a social gathering spot for the general public. School children took swimming lessons here. Swimming and picnicking, families unwound at the end of the workday and on weekends. The two wading pools for children were eventually transformed into fish ponds, then later filled in and turned into volleyball and basketball courts.

Unfortunately, the Natatorium now stands neglected, crumbling, and strewn with trash, its bleachers sometimes serving as beds for homeless people and stray cats. The pipes through which the saltwater flowed into the pool became increasingly blocked and the pool water grew stagnant. The city and the territory could never agree on whose responsibility it was to maintain the memorial, so it fell deeper into disrepair. Finally, in 1980, it closed.

Just as the Natatorium was on the brink of being torn down, it was declared a landmark. For many, allowing it to continue to decay would not only be insulting to the people who fought and died in WWI, but it would be sacrilege since this is such an impressive piece of architecture. The city and the state locked horns over who should take the initiative for its renovation. Meanwhile, a nonprofit organization called the Friends of the Natatorium is vying to raise enough money for its total restoration.

IN THE YEAR 2026

Any chance you're planning to return to Hawaii in the year 2026? You'll be just in time to see what the City of Honolulu buried here in a 50-year time capsule in 1976, as part of the US bicentennial celebration.

The **Damien Museum and Archives**, *130 Ohua Avenue, Waikiki; Tel. 923-2690; Open Monday-Friday, 9am - 3pm; Free admission*, is a small museum dedicated to the man who helped Hawaii's ostracized victims of Hansen's Disease (leprosy). Near the Hawaiian Regent Hotel and Saint Augustine's Catholic Church, its two rooms are brimming with memorabilia in tribute to Father Damien, the selfless Belgian Catholic priest who joined the exiles on remote Makanalua Peninsula on Molokai. The display includes old photographs of Kalaupapa, which the peninsula is commonly called, and of the people who were forced to move there, never to return to their families; old letters handwritten by Damien; a photograph taken of the priest the day he died—of Hansen's Disease; and a 20-minute video that fills in the gaps in his story. Father Damien was beatified in June 1995.

IMAX Theater Waikiki, *325 Seaside Avenue, off Kalakaua, Waikiki; Tel. 923-4629; Open 11am - 10pm; Admission: $7.50 for adults, $5 children ages 3-11*, is a nice diversion. Watching the building-sized screen, you'll feel as if you've been sucked into the action. The 45-minute films generally feature Polynesian themes. Seats are steeply terraced, so everyone has an excellent view. (However, some people have been known to get slight motion sickness.) Spend some time in the upscale gift shop, which carries feather leis, carved gourds, jewelry, wooden replicas of petroglyphs (rock carvings), and other Hawaiian crafts, along with handsome T-shirts. You can save money by seeing a double feature.

Greater Honolulu

When you're ready for a break from Waikiki (or wherever else you're staying), spend some time in the rest of Honolulu. While you'll need to drive or take public transportation to get to some parts of the city, seeing the sights in the heart of downtown Honolulu (about a 10-minute bus, taxi, or car ride from Waikiki) is perfectly comfortable on foot. At the far northwestern end of the city are **Honolulu International Airport**, a 15-minute drive from downtown Honolulu and about 25 minutes from Waikiki, and **Pearl Harbor**.

At the airport, you'll find the Pacific Aerospace Museum, *Honolulu International Airport, central waiting lobby; Tel. 839-0777; Open daily 9am - 6pm; Suggested donation: $3 adults, $2.50 students 13 and older, $1 children 6-12*. Both children and adults will enjoy the short film on famous aviators, the "magic vision" display on the attack on Pearl Harbor, and the other sights at this small museum.

The **USS Arizona Memorial at Pearl Harbor**, *US Naval Reservation, Pearl Harbor, Honolulu; Tel. 422-2771*, is Hawaii's number-one visitor attraction. More than 2,000 Navy, Army, and Marine personnel and civilians died and some 1,000 were wounded in the December 7, 1941,

Japanese attack on Pearl Harbor that thrust the United States into WWII. Most of the American casualties occurred when the *USS Arizona* was bombed. Only about 150 of the 1,200 or so bodies on board could be recovered from the broken, twisted battleship, so the sunken vessel became an aquatic grave for the remaining dead.

The white concrete memorial above the ship was built in 1962. It does not touch any part of the sunken wreck. Even after so many decades, the oil still seeps from its tanks and creates a rainbow slick on the surface of the water. These shimmering bands of color, often scattered with leis tossed by visitors, look like abstract art. Across the harbor (which gets its name from the pearl oysters that were found in it), the **Visitor Center** houses a museum, bookstore, and a theater that shows a moving film about the attack.

Elvis Presley fans are proud to note that "The King" gave all of the money he made at his 1961 Pearl Harbor concert to the USS Arizona War Memorial building fund. This was the largest single donation.

Departing from the Visitor Center, you can take one of the free Navy shuttle boats across the harbor to stand on the Memorial (shuttles run from 7:45am to 3pm); excluding the time you'll spend waiting your turn, the tour lasts about an hour and 15 minutes.

If you're driving to Pearl harbor, it's best to set out as early as possible so you can arrive when the wait for the shuttle boat is shortest. (Even "short" waits can last more than an hour, but at least you can visit the museum and shop during this time.) Other options are to board one of the Pearl Harbor tour boats that depart daily from Kewalo Basin near Waikiki, or to take the Arizona Memorial shuttle bus from Waikiki for $3, *Tel. 839-0911,* or the public bus (under $1).

If you're pressed for time, consider a bus tour, such as the Pearl Harbor/Honolulu City Tour offered by **Roberts Hawaii,** *Tel. 539.9400.* Prices range from $14 to $23, depending on who makes your arrangements.

PEARL HARBOR PRICE WARS

If you book the tour directly through a major company like Roberts Hawaii, you may pay more than if you book the same trip through one of the many sub-contracting discount companies whose fliers you'll find at hotels and handed out in the street. When you find the lowest price, just remember to make sure there are no hidden costs.

The **USS Bowfin Submarine Museum and Park**, *Tel. 423-1341; Open daily 8am - 5pm; Admission: $8 ($6 for active or retired military personnel, with I.D), $3 children 4-12*, is next to the Pearl Harbor Arizona Memorial Visitor Center. Here you'll see the *USS Bowfin* submarine, now a memorial to the 52 subs and more than 3,000 men who died in them that were lost during WWII. Walk through the cramped vessel to see what life was like for the men.

In addition to hosting football and baseball games, 50,000-seat **Aloha Stadium**, nearby, also draws crowds for concerts.

Heading northwest from Waikiki, you'll pass **Kewalo Basin**, frequently called Fisherman's Wharf (which is really just the name of a restaurant there). Located at Ward Avenue, across Ala Moana Boulevard, this is the commercial harbor where many visitors board glass-bottom boats or catamarans for dinner and sightseeing cruises, set sail for Pearl Harbor, and charter deep-sea fishing boats. The upscale **Ward Center** shopping mall is nearby, along with the more ordinary **Ward Warehouse** mall. **Ala Moana Center** is noted for being one of the world's most humungous conglomerations of stores and restaurants and is a favorite among residents. Locals also flock to **Ala Moana Park**, a long beach bordered by grass and shaded by trees. The waves here are extremely gentle.

About a mile from Waikiki is **Ala Moana Farmers Market**. This makes a good stop for visitors who want a glimpse of traditional Hawaiian foods rarely seen at restaurants. Families shopping for luaus and everyday cooking mill around counters crowded with octopus, squid, piles of fresh fish, *lomi 'o'io* (chopped raw bonefish mixed with bits of seaweed), fish *poke* (bits of raw fish with seaweed), *kalua* pig, beef jerky, and containers of *poi* (mashed, fermented taro root).

A number of worthwhile sights sit just outside the heart of downtown Honolulu. You'll find the **Bishop Museum and Planetarium**, *1525 Bernice Street, Honolulu; Tel. 847-3511 or 848-4129 (visitor information recording); Open 9am - 5pm, daily; Admission: $7.95, children 6-17 $6.95, seniors $6.95,* with its fabulous collection of Hawaiiana.

Named in honor of **Bernice Pauahi Bishop**, the granddaughter of Kamehameha the Great, this museum is a must for anyone even remotely interested in Hawaii's heritage. When Charles Bishop met Princess Pauahi after he came to Hawaii from New York in 1846, she was engaged to Lot Kamehameha, who was next in line to take over Hawaii's throne. But her plans soon changed. The princess and her foreign husband went on to open Hawaii's first bank, and he became a noted politician and entrepreneur as well as a generous philanthropist.

Extremely proud of her culture, Bernice Bishop loved collecting Hawaiian arts and antiques. So it was only fitting that, as a memorial to her after her 1884 death, Charles Bishop founded this museum in 1889. As the years passed, the collection snowballed and now encompasses items from many Polynesian cultures. The museum also serves as a center for research in anthropology and the Islands' natural history.

The two main galleries, demonstration and performance hall, **Science Center**, and **planetarium** are set on ten acres. The fascinating show at the planetarium vividly and visually explains how the ancient Polynesians sailed to Hawaii in canoes about 1,000 years ago. Enter the old stone main building, and you'll step onto an intricately patterned tile floor leading to a beautifully carved central koa staircase. The lustrous native wood is a rich orange-brown. Portuguese laborers dug the volcanic rock used to construct this wing.

In the gallery to the right, two levels of wooden balconies overlook the **main hall**, with its glass-encased exhibits. A huge whale skeleton hangs from the ceiling. Displays include an old-fashioned grass *hale* (house); *kapa* (cloth made from pounded bark); a Hawaiian throne; elaborate royal feathered capes and headdresses; crowns worn by King Kalakaua and Queen Kapiolani; and paintings of members of the Hawaiian monarchy. Human teeth (of dead enemies) are artfully inlaid into wooden waste bowls. If you take a tour, you'll learn of old beliefs: For instance, human waste products had to be disposed of very carefully, lest they get into the hands of enemies, who could then pray for the death of the other person.

The museum also exhibits **whaling** implements, including a pot for boiling blubber; a sexy female figurehead from a whaling ship; a small insect zoo; and displays of Hawaii's volcanoes, plants, birds and other animals.

Bishop Museum is about three miles from Waikiki. Departing from Waikiki, the Waikiki Trolley makes several round trips a day. You can also take Honolulu city bus No. 2 (be sure to board the "School Street" bus, not the one to "Liliha"), and get off at the Kam Shopping Center. Walk *makai* (toward the ocean) one block. If you're driving, head *Ewa* (west) on H-1 and get off at the Houghtailing Exit. Make a right turn onto Houghtailing and then take the second left onto Bernice Street.

Near the Bishop Musuem is the **Punchbowl**, *2177 Puowaina Drive, Honolulu; Tel. 566-1430; Open daily 8am - 6:30pm,* with its commanding views of the city way below. The military and their families are buried at scenic Punchbowl, officially called the **National Memorial Cemetery of the Pacific**. Headstones lie flat on the manicured lawns and small clusters of flowers decorate graves. High up winding roads, this peaceful locale has a lookout with a wraparound view of the mountains; Diamond Head, which seems to rise out of Honolulu's tall buildings; the avant-garde State Capitol; the Ala Moana Shopping area; and the Pacific Ocean. As tranquil and attractive as the grounds are, don't get any ideas about picnicking here as I once did. When I tried, I was promptly informed that no food is allowed on the premises.

Foster Botanic Gardens, *180 North Vineyard Boulevard, Tel. 522-7066 (for reservations); Open daily 9am - 4pm; Admission: $1,* blossoming with thousands of species of tropical flowers, trees, and plants, is also nearby.

Paths wend their ways through nine acres and thousands of species of tropical vegetation, including ferns, orchids, multi-colored bromeliads, ginger, vanilla plants, pineapple, guava and banana trees. Birds call back and forth to each other throughout the grounds. Afternoon tours are conducted three times a week (be sure to make reservations). Other times, you're on your own to relax and wander as you please. Next to the garden, which is a five-minute walk from the Chinese Cultural Center, stands the **Kwan Yin Temple.** Here you can sit in the sun on the verandah or spend a few pensive moments inside.

Contact the Friends of Foster Botanic Gardens about the **hikes** they lead on Oahu and Neighbor Islands.

Graced with sunny courtyards and a variety of galleries, **Honolulu Academy of Arts,** *900 South Beretania Street, Honolulu; Tel. 532-8701; Open 10am - 4:30pm, Tuesday-Saturday, 1-5 pm on Sunday; Admission: $5,* is also on many sightseeing lists.

Especially if you're into Asian art (from furniture and bronzes to Japanese prints), don't miss this venerated museum. The collection also includes contemporary and traditional Western works. Spend some time relaxing in one of the courtyards with tiled fountains. In a sunny enclosed garden, you might come upon a class of art students busily sketching by a lily pond while birds provide background music.

Now bordered by condominiums and office buildings, **Thomas Square** sprouts sprawling banyan trees. In 1843, this was the site where Kamehameha III reclaimed the rule of his islands. For a few trying months, a British admiral had stolen power out from under the Hawaiian king. During the 1989 bicentennial of the arrival of the Chinese in Hawaii, this square erupted with wild celebrations. The highlight was the 600-foot-long Chinese dragon snaking from along King Street. This colorful, ferocious creature was 120 feet longer than the 1988 Singapore dragon that found its way into *The Guinness Book of World Records.*

Downtown Honolulu

Wearing your walking shoes, you'll be prepared to take a stroll around downtown Honolulu and Chinatown, where the captivating buildings, architecture, stores, and people tell a great deal about Hawaii's history. The **Mission Houses Museum,** *553 South King Street, Honolulu; Tel. 531-0481; Open 9am - 4pm, Tuesday - Saturday; Admission: $5 for adults, $1 for children age 4-18, free for those age 3 and younger,* can be an all day affair.

OAHU'S BEST ATTRACTIONS

The Polynesian Cultural Center
Falls Park
Hiking, Mountain Biking & Kayaking at Waimea Valley/Waunea
Iolani Palace
Mission Houses Museum
Pearl Harbor
Hiking to the Summit of Diamond Head Crater

You can spend a lot of time there, especially if a Living History Program or a crafts fair is in progress.

This museum is made up of three restored buildings that were once homes and headquarters of missionaries. In 1820, the one wooden house (the other two are of coral stone) was sent dismantled, all the way from Boston, and is the oldest home in Hawaii. It just didn't seem right to folks back home to have American missionaries living in grass houses while they did God's work. Adding local wood and old ship timbers to the pre-fab materials, the missionaries constructed a cozy four-bedroom house, now the Islands' oldest remaining wooden structure. As many as three or four families lived in this house at any given time!

Hawaiian chiefs came here, dressed in their new European clothes, to learn to read and write Hawaiian or take singing lessons in European music. Commoners also flocked to the house, for religious services and to get Western medicines to combat the new diseases foreigners had brought to Hawaii, which were devastating to the indigenous population. Missionary books, quilts, furniture and other household items are on display.

The second-oldest house, where the museum entrance is, was built in 1831. The third, dating back to 1841, is where the old hand-operated printing presses are exhibited and demonstrated. The shelves in this building are piled with worn books and illustrations printed in the early 1800s with engraved plates or wood blocks.

In addition to taking a guided tour of these houses, on Saturdays visitors may participate in the **Living History Program.** Playing 19th century missionaries and others, costumed actors are found cooking in the kitchen or in the parlor discussing social and political issues of the time. Visitors are invited to join in spirited conversations with people who've been dead for years — the driven, uncompromising Hiram Bingham, one of Hawaii's first and most influential missionaries; David Malo, the Hawaiian man of letters; Anthony Allen, the black Waikiki

WALKING TOURS

The best way to get to know Waikiki, downtown Honolulu and Chinatown is to put on some comfortable shoes and take a stroll. For a walking tour of historic downtown Honolulu, pick up a brochure at **Hawai'i Geographic Maps and Books**, 49 S. Hotel Street #218, Chinatown Gateway Plaza, Tel. 523-2900.

Various organizations also offer informative guided walks. Don't miss Glen Grant's tours, including his popular "haunted Hawaii" walking tour. Grant has his own company, **Honolulu Time Walks**, Tel. 943-0371, but still occasionally also leads tours for the **Historic Hawaii Foundation**, Tel. 593-9564.

The Mission Houses Museum, Tel. 531-0481, and **Kapiolani Community College**, Tel. 734-9425, lead tours of the nearby historic sections of downtown Honolulu, as well as tours of the museum itself. During the Kamehameha Dynasty in Old Honolulu Tour, amblers learn about 19th century Hawaii's struggle to maintain its independence despite powerful foreign outside influences. They even get a chance to discuss social, cultural, and political issues of the time with (costumed actors playing) the Reverend and Mrs. Hiram Bingham, missionaries who helped shape the Islands' history. A downtown walking tour is offered every Friday at 9:30am. Reservations required. This tour costs $8 per person and includes admission to the museum.

Among the other walks is the **Historic Crime Tour**, conducted at night, in which participants are told about Hawaii's eerie supernatural heritage, including the Night Marchers, Chinese ghosts, Japanese folk monsters, and documented hauntings involving places such as Iolani Palace, Kawaiaha'o Cemetery, Queen's Hospital, and the State Capitol. Beginning around 6pm, this tour departs from the State Library on King Street. Once a month, there's a tour called **A Musical Odyssey Into 19th Century Honolulu**, which culminates in a noon concert by the Royal Hawaiian Band on the grounds of Iolani Palace.

The Chinese Chamber of Commerce, Tel. 533-3181, sponsors a three-hour walking tour of **Chinatown**, every Tuesday morning 9:30am - noon. Cost: $5. Reservations recommended at least one day prior to tour.

The three-hour Chinatown tours conducted by the Hawaii Heritage Center, Tel. 521-2749, take place on Fridays beginning at 9:30am - noon, and the cost is $4, plus lunch, if you like. While you walk and talk with your guide, you might learn about herbal medicine, Asian arts, or the differences among Buddhism, Taoism, and Shinto. As you go from store to store, there is time for shopping if the mood hits.

farmer and businessman; or whaling captains and other seamen. During the Thanksgiving program, visitors may sample a 19th century meal.

In late November or early December, the annual **Holiday Fair** takes place on the grounds. Food and all kinds of quality crafts are for sale. Various walking tours are offered, both of the museum and of the surrounding downtown Honolulu neighborhood.

Ask about the historic downtown Honolulu walking tours hosted by the museum.

Just across the way is **Kawaiaha'o Church**, *King Street, Honolulu; Tel. 522-1333*, the original permanent Protestant church built by the missionaries of hand-cut coral stone in 1843. Fourteen thousand coral blocks were used to construct this church, across the way from the Mission Houses Museum and down the street from Iolani Palace. While the porous coral may appear light in weight, each block would tip a scale at about 1,000 pounds. Designed by famous missionary Hiram Bingham and built between 1837 and 1842, Kawaiaha'o Church has a prominent clock tower. Services are conducted in both English and Hawaiian. Many people wear leis with their muumuus or jackets. Japanese weddings frequently take place here during the week.

On July 31, 1843, Hawaiian rule was returned to Kamehameha III after a brief stint under British control. For many years afterward, this day was considered a holiday of thanks. During the first service after Kamehameha was back in control of his country, he coined the phrase that turned into the motto of the land and that is now the state motto: *Ua mau ke ea o ka aina i ka pono* ("The life of the land is preserved in righteousness").

Outside, you'll see the tomb of Lunalilo, who became Hawaii's first elected king in 1873. To show how close he felt to his people, he walked barefoot to this church for his swearing in. Although his reign was brief, he was able to restore the vote for Hawaiian commoners and return to them their right to hold elective office. Instead of being buried at the Royal Mausoleum in Nuuanu Valley with the other *alii*, Lunalilo chose to end up here, with the regular folks.

On the other side of King Street, **Honolulu Hale** (City Hall) was built in 1929 in Spanish/Moorish style. The beige adobe building is topped by a red tile roof and surrounded by thick palms. If you happen by around noon, consider listening to one of the frequently held free concerts at the Skygate sculpture. Continuing west along King Street, you'll come to the white-columned **Hawaii State Library**, on the right. Across the street, to the left, is **Kekuanoa**, a state government building whose exterior was featured as the Honolulu Police Department in the television series "Magnum PI." Nearby, the Kamehameha I Statue guards **Aliiolani Hale**, the Renaissance-style Judiciary Building that was built to serve as a royal palace in 1874. Ironically, the statue of the King who is heralded for having unified the Hawaiian Islands was based on an Italian model and made by an American. Not that most modern-day onlookers would notice, but the gold-leaf clothing he is wearing is not historically correct.

A short stroll back to the right, on King Street, is the opulent **Iolani Palace**, 364 South King Street (at Richards Street), Honolulu, Tel. 538-1471 (tour information) or 522-0832 (reservations); Open 9am - 2:15pm, Wednesday-Saturday; The 45- to 60-minute tours begin every 15 minutes; Admission: $8 adults, $2 for children 5-12; Note: children under 5 are not allowed in the palace, Purchase tickets at least 30 minutes prior to tour time.

Be sure to take a tour of this gracious building. Dignified Iolani, the United State's only royal palace, sits on a smooth patch of green in the midst of the capital's choking traffic and tall, modern buildings. A fence of gold-tipped spears encloses thriving pandanus, banyan, and flame trees, while a palm-lined promenade leads to the entrance. Its name meaning "bird of heaven," this four-story Victorian palace is Italian Renaissance in style.

Ironically, it was built in 1882 by King Kalakaua, who was revered by Hawaiians for reviving pride in Hawaiian culture. For example, he is credited with bringing back the hula, traditional music, and songs and poetry written in the Hawaiian tongue. All this had been sent underground by American missionaries. The first leader of any country to sail around the world, Kalakaua borrowed from the architecture that most impressed him during his visits with nearly a dozen heads of state, from Britain to Japan. Apart from its residents, the main Hawaiian presence in the palace was the ubiquitous prized native koa wood.

Moderation was a concept for which this king had little use. On at least one occasion, he threw a banquet for 5,000 guests. He antagonized Honolulu's business community (most of whom were *haole* descendants of missionaries) by his extravagant spending. Bent on designing a regal mansion Hawaiians could be proud of, he cut no corners when he had elaborate Iolani Palace built.

The high-ceilinged interior is graced with intricately carved balustrades, plaster cornices with detailed designs, chandeliers, candelabras, mirrors with gold leaf frames, and spacious bathtubs lined in copper. The furniture Kalakaua chose was custom made by a Boston firm that had built furniture for the American White House. Amid this splendor, King Kalakaua entertained many notable guests, including Robert Louis Stevenson.

After the king's sudden death in San Francisco in 1891, his sister, Liliuokalani, followed him to the throne. In 1893, she was deposed by a group of mostly foreign, Hawaii-based businessmen who turned Iolani Palace into the seat of their provisional government. In 1895, they

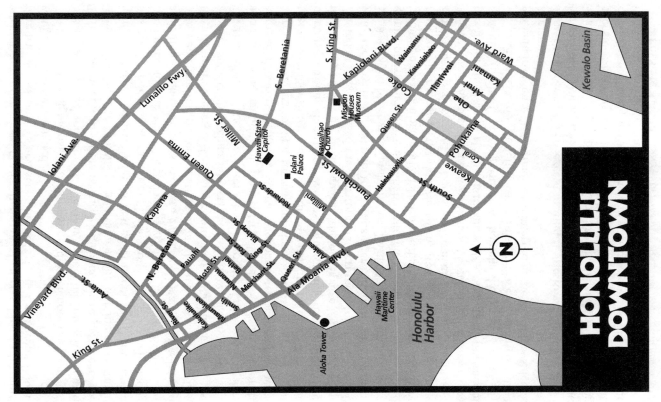

HONOLULU
DOWNTOWN

convicted Liliuokalani of treason for being part of a widely supported attempt to restore her to power. In a move that could hardly be more humiliating, the queen's accusers held her trial in the **Throne Room**, where she had once reigned.

Upon entering the palace today, visitors don felt booties so as not to mar the glossy hardwood floors. They may wander into the velvet-draped Throne Room and the upstairs guest bedroom where the queen was imprisoned for nine months as punishment for wanting to continue leading her own country. Under the new government, the Throne Room was used for legislative meetings. Today you'll see a seven-foot-long twisted narwhal tusk here topped with a gold ball. Given to Kalakaua by a whaling captain, the tusk served as a *puloulou* – a staff that was infused with *mana* (spiritual power) and thus ensured that the area surrounding the monarch was sacred. The Senate convened in the dining room, just across the hall. Silver, china, and crystal are now on display there.

During the 1930s, people on the mainland read newspaper articles about the eerie **haunting** of Iolani Palace. The state legislature actually suspended its work for a while, after a series of mysterious accidents were attributed to angry spirits in the mansion. Even today, some people swear that at night they sometimes see candlelight dancing in the window of the upstairs bedroom where the queen was imprisoned. Others say they hear the tinkling keys of the palace guards who once patrolled the mansion.

Iolani Palace housed the Territorial Government for more than 50 years and served as the capitol for a while after Hawaii became a state in 1959. Headed by Abigail Kawananakoa, Kalakaua's great-grandniece, a group of volunteers painstakingly restored the palace, locating and bringing back much of the original furniture that had been sold off. A rare early copy of *Legends and Myths of Hawaii*, written by Kalakaua, sits in the king's quarters along with his books in Hawaiian, English, German, and French. (You can pick up a new edition of *Legends* today in bookstores throughout the Islands.) In the entry hall, walls are hung with portraits of Hawaiian royalty, beginning with Kamehameha the Great.

A **grave site** on the left lawn of Iolani Palace is enclosed with a wrought-iron fence. The remains are interred at the Royal Mausoleum, Nuuanu.

At noon every Friday except in August, the **Royal Hawaiian Band** gives a free performance at the bandstand in front of the palace. This band was established in 1847 by King Kamehameha III and has been playing ever since. Bring a picnic lunch and a mat or towel, don your lei, muumuu, or Aloha shirt, and you'll blend right in with the crowd. (Aloha wear is the dress code on Fridays on Oahu.)

The State Capitol, *South Beretania Street, between Punchbowl and Richards Streets (near Iolani Palace), downtown Honolulu; Tel. 586-0178 tour* *office*, a modern building built in 1969 above Hawaiian ancestral graves, took over the role of Capitol after Iolani Palace. Its architecture is heavy with meaning: The 60-foot pillars around the building suggest the Islands' coconut palm trees; the ceilingless central court brings the sky, one of nature's wonders, into the building; and circling the Capitol, reflecting pools represent the ocean that surrounds Hawaii.

On the grounds, the statue of **Queen Liliuokalani** clutches the *Kumulipu*, Hawaii's oldest and the most cherished creation myth; the proposed constitution of 1893 that was designed to maintain Hawaii's monarchy; and the music for famed *Aloha Oe*, the melancholy song written by the queen. In front of the building stands a statue of **Father Damien**, clearly suffering from Hansen's Disease (leprosy), which he contracted while helping its shunned victims in Hawaii. Out of respect and admiration, people often decorate these statues with leis. The legislature is in session from the third week in January to the end of April.

While the nearby governor's mansion, **Washington Place,** also on South Beretania Street, is not generally open to the public, passersby can look through the gates to try to catch a glimpse of the head of state. Built in 1846, this Greek Revival mansion has been home to Hawaiian governors since 1921. Before that, Hawaiian royalty, including Queen Liliuokalani, resided here. On the same street is **St. Andrew's Cathedral,** with its stained glass windows illustrating notable events from Hawaii's past. Spend some time relaxing in the sunshine on nearby Richards Street at the **Armed Services YMCA,** formerly the Royal Hawaiian Hotel. Near Iolani Palace, it boasts bright, peaceful courtyards.

A couple of blocks west of the Cathedral, **Tamarind Park** is a welcome oasis in the heart of the city. This flourishing patch of green was born of compromise. Much to the distress of many residents, the historic Alexander Young Hotel was torn down in 1981 to allow an office complex to grow. However, more than an acre of the land was saved for this trim park, which is now filled with trees such as monkey pod, shower and, of course, tamarind. A stream flows through the foliage and a 12-foot Henry Moore sculpture is anchored in a reflecting pool. If you're lucky, you'll pass by during one of the periodic concerts, featuring big band music, or, every once in a while, slack key guitar.

Beginning just northwest of the statue of Kamehameha the Great, five-block-long **Merchant Street** was Honolulu's business district for nearly a century. The names behind these well-preserved 19th and early 20th century buildings are those of the *haole* families whose wealth was born in agriculture, blossomed with whaling, and later flourished through commerce. The melange of architectural styles ranges from Hawaiian Regional to European classical and contemporary.

Just off Merchant, on Bishop and near Queen, the 1929 **Alexander & Baldwin Building** is one of my favorites. Headquarters of one of Hawaii's Big Five companies and topped by an Island-style double-pitched roof, this is a dramatic example of Hawaiian art deco. At the entrance, columns are carved with fruit and flower designs; round Chinese symbols are cut out above the door; lanterns hang from the ceiling; and tiles turn walls into color-splashed murals of marine life. **Bishop Street** was once the most beautiful road in Honolulu. The mountains could be seen at one end and the water at the other. Now the harbor view is obscured by buildings.

Back on Merchant, the **Stangenwald Building**, constructed in 1901, has Hawaii's first electric elevator. A central staircase sets of the upscale lobby, with its eye-catching mural. At six stories, this was once Hawaii's tallest building. Near Bethel Street, the cannons protruding from the sidewalk in front of the old post office were once used as hitching posts. They came from the waterfront Fort of Honolulu, now replaced by **Irwin Park**. You can see some of the old fort's huge, dismantled coral stones in the water off the edge of the parking lot in front of where cruise ships dock at the harbor.

On the corner of Merchant and Bethel, the stone, Spanish Colonial-style **Honolulu Police Station Building** was built in 1930. Attractive tile work decorates the lobby, where photographs show the history of the building. One of Hawaii's most famous police cases was the 1930s Massie murder case. A group of Hawaiian and Japanese-American men was accused of beating and raping a white woman. When the defendants were acquitted, since there was not enough evidence to back up the claim, the woman's mother and naval lieutenant husband kidnapped and murdered one of the men. This dignified building now houses city services.

Across from here, on the same side of Bethel Street, the handsome brick and terra cotta **Honolulu Publishing Company** building began life in 1910 as the Yokohama Specie Bank. This Japanese financial institution opened in Hawaii to serve the influx of Japanese immigrants. The architecture of this stone and brick building, its facade decorated with intricate terra cotta work, reflects the period when admiration for things Western was strong in Japan.

At the end of Merchant, at Nuuanu, the impressive 1890 **Royal Saloon** has been transformed into a bar and grill. This brick and stucco building was once a popular waterfront hangout for many, even King David Kalakaua.

Our Lady of Peace Cathedral is planted at the Beretania Street (northeastern) end of Fort Street Mall, which cuts across Merchant Street. Here Father Damien, who helped those afflicted with Hansen's Disease, was ordained a priest. Walking southwest, through a somewhat rundown area, you'll pass the **Blaisdell Hotel**, dating back to 1912. A block over from this promenade, on Bethel and Pauahai, **Hawaii Theater** was the Islands' premier stage before it became a movie house. Built in 1922 and once threatened with demolition, it has been beautifully restored.

At the harbor end of Fort Street mall, 184-foot **Aloha Tower**, built in 1921, overlooks the water and **Aloha Tower Marketplace**, *Pier 9, Honolulu Harbor, Honolulu.* This 10-story tower, a short walk from the Maritime Center, was once the tallest building in Hawaii. Built in 1926, it was turned over to the military for use during WWII. From the top floor observation deck, you can take in the view of Honolulu Harbor, the city's forest of buildings, and the coast. The Marketplace offers a variety of outdoor vendors, shops, and restaurants.

During the 1820s, in the old whaling days, more than 50 ships a year anchored off Honolulu, bringing many foreigners who decided to settle in this Pacific city. A century later, great numbers of tourists began to pour off ships here, welcomed by crowds of people selling leis and the music of the Royal Hawaiian Band.

Now ten-story Aloha Tower is part of the **Hawaii Maritime Center,** *Pier 7, Honolulu Harbor, near the foot of Punchbowl Street; Tel. 536-6373; Open 8:30am-5pm daily; Admission: $7.50 adults, $4.50 children 6-17, including the use of a portable cassette for listening to the taped guided tour,* which has been established near where King Kalakaua's boathouse stood in the late 1800s. It was from here that the king, known as the Merrie Monarch, sponsored surfing meets and canoe races, reviving these Hawaiian pastimes. He also entertained friends at the boathouse with parties and performances that resuscitated hula and Hawaiian music. He and his friends spent so much time here that he installed Hawaii's first telephone line, between the boathouse and Iolani Palace.

The museum opened in 1988 on November 16, the king's birthday. The highlight of the center is the Kalakaua Boathouse Museum, which resembles the original two-story building. Displays and videos celebrate Polynesian and Western maritime contributions, as well as the monarch's love of the Hawaiian arts. Exhibits include everything from shark tooth tools and an intricately woven Hawaiian red and yellow feather cape to rotund iron caldrons first used to melt whale blubber, then later for boiling sugar or making *okolehao* (*ti* plant liquor).

Docked at pier 7, the *Hokulea* is a 60-foot replica of an **ancient double-hull sailing canoe.** Using only ancient navigational techniques, this vessel has traveled between Hawaii and Tahiti and throughout the Pacific, retracing the path of the ancient Polynesians. Also at this pier is the *Falls of Clyde,* a four-masted, square-rigged ship dating back to 1878. Board the ship and step into history.

Down Nimitz Highway, which now separates downtown buildings from the harbor, is the **Dole Cannery Square.** Today an industrial and commercial zone, this area was once a red-light district. Shops, restaurants and a video show on pineapples in Hawaii and on the role of the Dole Company draw many visitors, *Tel. 548-6600.*

Chinatown

Chinatown, just off Nimitz Highway, takes up about 16 blocks, bordered roughly by North Hotel, River, Beretania, and Nuuanu streets. Orange ducks hang in restaurant windows. Bakeries and stores selling homemade Chinese candy lure passersby inside. At herbal medicine shops, wooden drawers filled with natural ingredients line walls like library card catalogues. Dried lizard tails sit in jars, and the air is thick with incense, tiger balm, and ginseng. People go in and out of acupuncture offices. The streets are perfumed by fresh flowers from lei stands. Men gather at pool halls, while Chinese, Vietnamese, and Filipino restaurants do a brisk business. Many immigrants have also settled here from Cambodia and Laos.

Especially on Saturday mornings, serious shopping takes place. At sprawling **Oahu Market**, on King and Kekaulike streets, boxes are heaped with live crabs attempting to claw their way out in slow motion. Counters are covered with whole suckling pigs, glistening fresh fish, chicken feet (for soup), and all kinds of cabbage, seaweed, *ti* leaves, fruit and other vegetables. Built in 1904, the market was about to be sold to developers by its owners in 1984. Not only did the merchants get together to buy it, but they also raised thousands more dollars to renovate it. **Maunakea Market**, at Maunakea Street between Hotel and Pauahi, is geared more toward tourists.

One of Honolulu's first neighborhoods, Chinatown got its name during the late 19th century, when Chinese immigrants began moving in. They took jobs as laundry workers, tailors, bakers, and grocers. During the 1890s, hundreds of prostitutes frequented Nuuanu and Pauahi streets. Many were Japanese wives or picture brides who had been abandoned by their husbands or intended spouses.

Ironically, notorious Bill Lederer's Bar at Hotel Street is now a police station. King Kalakaua was known to have a drink or two at the old **Pantheon Bar**. In the 1880s, people could have a cocktail at this bar, take a horse-drawn trolley ride to Waikiki, get swimwear, a bath towel, and a cabana at the Longbranch Bath House – all for one price.

In 1900, the Board of Health ordered the fire department to burn down a block in Chinatown in an attempt to stem the spread of bubonic plague. While the plague may not have spread further here, the flames certainly did. The wind changed direction and suddenly nearly 40 acres of houses and businesses went up in smoke. More than 4,000 people were left homeless. People in the area had practice rebuilding their neighborhood. Back in 1886, another devastating fire, which started in a restaurant on the corner of Smith and Hotel streets, had left 7,000 Chinese and 350 Hawaiians without shelter.

Still somewhat scruffy today, Chinatown has been hit by a wave of gentrification. Architectural firms and a number of good art galleries have moved in. However, it remains best not to venture into the area alone at night. Through the Chinese Chamber of Commerce or the Hawaii Heritage Center, you can arrange to take a daytime walking tour of the neighborhood. The Chinatown Historical Society is also good place for information.

CHINATOWN FESTIVALS

In January or February, the Chinese New Year celebration erupts with a barrage of firecrackers. The dragon dance is often a highlight. It can take more than 70 people to bring the long, elaborate dragon costume undulating to life. For two nights, the cultural Plaza (at Mauna Kea and Beretania streets, bounded by Kukui and River streets) is packed with food booths selling Chinese and other ethnic foods. Chinese music and the machine-gun pops of firecrackers mingle in the air. Jewelry shops and other stores around the plaza remain open.

For the first couple of months of the year, the Narcissus Festival is in full swing in Chinatown. At the Queen Pageant, a talent and beauty competition, women take baby steps in their close-fitting cheong-sam gowns, embroidered with intricate Chinese designs. After the free cooking demonstration, the noted local and foreign chefs give their artful creations away as door prizes.

During the evening Chinatown Open House, the queen walks through the streets of Chinatown with her court of Chinese Chamber of Commerce officials. They visit stores, where the merchants give her lishee (gifts of money wrapped in red paper). Lion dancers accompany her: One dancer is at the head, the other at the tail.

Beyond Downtown Honolulu

Honolulu may be crowded with tall buildings, but there is a great deal of leafy green at its fringes. Manoa Valley, not far from Waikiki, is home to the **University of Hawaii**.

Hiking is very popular among students and other locals in this area, particularly the short trek to **Manoa Falls**, for swimming and picnicking. In the early 1800s, the coffee that was to become the famous Kona was first planted here, before being grown on the Big Island of Hawaii. Imported from Brazil, this coffee was a big hit with sailors, whalers, and traders in port. Consider stopping at the small **organic vegetable market** in the valley. With acoustic jazz playing in the background, it's a great place to shop for a picnic when you're on your way to the North Shore.

ROMANTIC HEIGHTS

Head for Makiki Heights, in the Manoa area, for the stunning seven-mile **Tantalus-Round Top Drive**, *in the Manoa area. City bus No. 15 takes this route. However, it goes along lower Makiki Drive, not to the top. If you're doing your own driving, be sure to get very specific directions from a local. And don't forget a sweater. The drive is named for the two hills the loop crosses. You'll cut through dense tropical forest, where wild passion fruit, guava, and other natural sweets are begging to be picked.*

Some vantage points seem designed for sunset watching. From petite **Ualakaa Park**, *you'll look down on the sprawling capital city and its harbor, as well as the Waianae Mountains, Diamond Head, and Koko Head. At night, when the city lights are twinkling, locals thinking romantic thoughts often make this winding drive.*

A popular picnic spot, the **Tantalus** area is speckled with white and yellow ginger blossoms from June to December. Hikers found that the more they walked toward the 2,013-foot peak of Tantalus Mountain, the farther away it seemed. So this region was named for the mythical Greek king. His royal punishment for displeasing the gods was to be forever submerged, thirsty and famished, in water up to his chin. Each time he bent his head in an attempt to drink, the water would suddenly drain away. And whenever he tried to pick the succulent fruit dangling from the overhanging trees, it would slip from his fingers as the wind shoved the branches aside. Today the marked trails make reaching the mountain's peak none too difficult. You might even spy some wild wallabies in this area.

Near the Tantalus Lookout, is the **The Contemporary Museum at Spalding House**, 2411 Makiki Heights Drive, Tel. 526-0232; *open 10am to 4pm Tuesday - Saturday, and on Sunday, open noon to 4pm; admission: $5 (except third Thursday of each month, when admission is free)*, where art created since the 1940s is on display in this hillside estate.

Taking the Pali Highway, one of the two roads that slice the Koolau Mountains, you'll come to **Queen Emma Summer Palace Museum**, 2913 Pali Highway, Nuuanu Valley, Honolulu; Tel. 595-3167; *Open 9am - 4pm daily; Admission: adults $5, children under age 18 $1*. Built in 1848, this restored mansion, with its Greek columns and broad front lanai, was the home of Queen Emma and King Kamehameha IV. Now a museum, it houses an impressive collection of family furniture and memorabilia, including quilts, *kapa* cloth, calabashes, feather fans, silverware, koa cabinets and the striking koa cradle of Prince Albert, the ill-fated heir to the Hawaiian throne. Lauhala mats cover the glossy wooden floors and mango trees shade the expansive grounds.

Queen Emma was much loved and is still revered for her compassion toward others. She built schools and hospitals, even caring for victims of a smallpox epidemic in her own home. Born Emma Rooke, she married Alexander Liholiho (Kamehameha IV) and inherited this home from her uncle, John Young II. Hanaikalamalama, as the palace was originally known, was built by John George Lewis (who was part Hawaiian, despite his Western name), after he bought the land from the government. He paid $800, then, a few years later, sold the estate to Young for $6,000.

Prominent people, such as the Duke of Edinburgh, came often for dinner, dancing, and croquet on the lawn. The house remained empty for five years after Queen Emma died in 1885, since she had already buried her husband and young son, prince Albert. In 1913, the mansion narrowly escaped being torn down and replaced by a baseball field. In stepped the Daughters of Hawaii, a historical preservation society, and the rest, as they say, is history.

In the Fall, the palace hosts an annual fundraising event, complete with food, arts and crafts demonstrations, and hula.

Keaiwa Heiau, *Aiea Heights Drive, Aiea,* located west of Honolulu, is a place of healing in old Hawaii. This crumbling temple is enclosed by low walls.

At the **Pali Lookout** (Nuuanu Pali) in 1795, Kamehameha I (of the Big Island) forced enemy soldiers (of Oahu) off the cliff in his successful (and bloody) drive to unify the Hawaiian Islands. Some say the 300 men were pushed, while others claim they hurled themselves over the edge instead of surrendering to the man who would be known as Kamehameha the Great. The **view** from the Lookout takes in nearly the entire windward coast.

The Royal Mausoleum, *2261 Nuuanu Avenue, Honolulu; Tel. 536-7602; open Monday-Friday from 8am to 4pm, closed Saturday and Sunday; free admission,* covering three acres, is where most members of the Kamehameha and Kalakaua royal families are buried. While the mausoleum was built in 1865, the chapel wasn't added until 1922.

Another way to cut across the mountains from Honolulu to the windward coast is to take Likelike Highway. When you emerge from Wilson Tunnel, a **spectacular vista** will be laid out before you: Peppered with houses, vibrantly green open spaces sweep to the foot of the mountains and to the water's edge. Banana trees and wild guava border the road. This side of the island is wetter and thus more lush than the leeward coast.

Eastern Oahu

You can get to windward Oahu by heading east from Waikiki, taking the coastal route. Even if you only spend a half day — going as far as Waimanalo and returning to Honolulu through the mountains on the Pali Highway — you will have seen some of Oahu's most impressive and varied scenery.

Passing the Honolulu Zoo, across from Waikiki Beach, you might catch a **windsurfing** championship in progress below Diamond Head Lookout. Frequently empty, Diamond Head Beach Park sits at the bottom of a cliff. While waves on the North Shore can build to more than 30 feet in height during the winter, five feet is considered high for this side of the island. In addition to a few scattered surfers, you might see people dragging in fishing nets. Molokai is anchored out in the ocean, with Lanai and Maui silhouetted in the distance.

Bougainvillea sprinkles color everywhere and plumeria sweetens the air. In the Diamond Head, Kahala, and Hawaii Kai suburbs, Rolls Royces, Jaguars, and Lamborghinis wait outside multi-million dollar homes shaded by mango, monkeypod, purple-blossomed jacaranda, and orange-blossomed African tulip trees. Millionaires tee off on the Waialae Country Club greens. Near the Hawaii Kai Golf Course, look for the rough dark stones of developer Henry J. Kaiser's **Rock Farm**. Many mainland celebrities live in these posh neighborhoods.

Makai (in the direction of the sea) of Hawaii Kai, gumdrop-shaped **Koko Head** (Blood Hill) serves as a prominent landmark in this area. Neighboring **Hanauma Bay** is Oahu's premier (and therefore crowded) snorkeling spot. Cupped by mountains, the palm-fringed beach forms an almost complete circle. From the overlook high above, coral and smooth sandy patches are visible through the glass-clear blue water.

Across Kalanianaole Highway, the mountains give way to orange and brown earth. The greenery is alternately dusty and bright. Striated, craggy cliffs border the road on one side while the white surf from the navy blue ocean thrashes the rocky coast below. **Blow Hole**, where the water sprouts up through the rocks, is most dramatic when the waves are rough.

Body surfing and boogie board championships are held at nearby **Sandy Beach**, which is also a popular locale for kite flying. The whole windward coast unfurls itself from **Makapuu Lookout**, across the highway from **Sea Life Park**, *41-202 Kalanianaole Highway, Makapuu Point, Waimanalo (windward coast, southeastern Oahu); Tel. 259-7933; Open 9:30am -5pm daily, except Friday, when Sea Life closes at 10pm; Admission: $20 adults, $10 children age 4-12, free for children age 3 and under.* Whether you're traveling with younger editions or not, animal lovers shouldn't miss this center of aquatic entertainment.

Backed by horizontally streaked cliffs and with views of the ocean and offshore islands, it claims a gorgeous setting. Mock killer whales, dolphins, penguins, sea lions, and even a wholphin (a cross between a whale and a dolphin) perform amazing feats to the delight of the audience, even when folks get splashed. Marine exhibits also include colorful local sea life as well as hammerhead sharks and other menacing creatures seen through glass in their natural habitats; and a display of license plates, hub caps and old bottles — all removed from the stomachs of sharks! Ask about the special behind-the-scenes tour.

Dolphin-lovers won't want to miss the program called Splash U. People get the chance to sit pool side and work with one of the trainers instructing the dolphins to perform various tricks. Participants are permitted to reward the animals with fishy treats. Only five to ten people are allowed into this program each day, depending on the moods of the dolphins. So be sure to arrive early to register (note that there's an additional charge).

If you visit on a hot day, be sure to bring hats or visors, sunglasses, and plenty of sun block since there is little shade in the park.

Below the lava rock cliffs of **Makapuu Point**, boogie boarders and body surfers congregate at the beach. Sharks now breed in a cave at the bottom of Makapuu Point. But some say that people once could swim into the cave and find the entrance to a dry lava tube that would lead them all the way to Molokai!

You might see a group of schoolchildren on a nature walk along the cliffs or daring hang gliders swooping down from the Koolau peaks. The **Makapuu Lighthouse**, more than 600 feet above sea level, is said to have the world's largest lighthouse lens (13 feet by 9 feet). Made in France back in 1887, it has a 50-mile range.

BURIED GUNS

*Although lush **Waimanalo** is an economically depressed area, it has an intriguing atmosphere and history. More than half the people who live here are Hawaiian. When the monarchy was overthrown by a mercenary group of American businessmen in 1893, Hawaiians in this area got busy. They rounded up as many rifles and guns as they could manage, intending to use them to restore Queen Liliuokalani to power. But before these loyal royalists had a chance to use their weapons, which they had hidden in the sand on Rabbit Island, their plans were exposed.*

Also called **Manama**, offshore **Rabbit Island** bears a mild resemblance to one of Bugs Bunny's relatives, with its ears pinned back. To me it looks much more like the head of a lioness. Some say it wasn't named for its appearance after all, but because rabbits were let loose on it by a Spanish friend of Kamehameha I. Ancient Hawaiians used the island to bury their dead, who were interred in the sand in standing position. Today it serves as a nesting spot for thousands of seabirds and it is *kapu* (off limits) to human beings.

Baby Norfolk pines and bushy ferns decorate mountainsides around **Waimanalo**. Bright red earth clings to cliffs, and flower nurseries thrive. Trucks park along the road selling fresh corn, which you shouldn't pass up if you're staying in an accommodation with cooking facilities.

This is *paniolo* (cowboy) country. Horses, cows, and wide-brimmed hats are everywhere. There is also a golf course, backed by the massive **Koolau Mountains**, Oahu's most extensive range. Whenever it rains, the deep ridges become healthy waterfalls.

BATHING IN GOLD

An old legend tells of a mysterious and disconcertingly beautiful woman, Kauhololakiki, who was only allowed to bathe in golden waters. A chief fell in love with her on sight, married her, then was devastated when she told him about the restrictions of her personal hygiene. He dreaded making the arduous journey to another island to search out yellow waters for his bride. If he failed to find them, he would have to give up the woman he loved. Then when she told him about the golden Waimanalo stream that flowed from the foot of the Koolau Mountains, he was beside himself with joy.

Oahu's longest nonstop strip of white sand, three-and-a-half-mile **Waimanalo Beach**, stretches across Hawaiian Homestead Land. In 1921, a congressional law was passed returning certain sections of the Islands to Hawaiians. The most popular sandy expanse in the area is at **Bellows Field Beach Park**, on a military reservation. However, the public is welcome only on holidays and during weekends from noon on Fridays to midnight on Sundays. **Kailua Beach**, just north of here, is high on the list of Oahu's nicest.

In this area, you'll also find **Ulu-Po Heiau**, *Off Kailua Road, Kailua (eastern windward coast)*. Time has reduced this *heiau* (temple) near a swamp to a rock pile. It's not easy to find, but you'll know you're on the right track when you see the YMCA, which is in front of it. If only one *heiau* is on your Oahu itinerary, make it Puu o Mahuka on the North Shore instead.

The quiet hometown of entertainer Don Ho, **Kaneohe** (Skinny Man) is where you emerge from the Koolau Mountains if you cut across the island from Honolulu on the Likelike Highway (Route 63). At low tide, a sandbar appears in **Kaneohe Bay**. This on-again-off-again island is a popular oasis among people on boats for picnics and relaxation. If you pass by on a weekend, you might see a few beach umbrellas on this tiny, treeless strip of sand far out in the deep.

Take Kahekili Highway (Route 83) to **Valley of the Temples**. Here you'll find **Byodo-In Temple,** *47-200 Kahekili Highway, Valley of the Temples, Kaneohe, off Route 83 (eastern windward coast); Tel. 239-8811; Open daily 8:30am - 4pm; Admission: $2 adults ($1 over age 65), $1 children up to age 12*, a reconstruction of an ancient temple in Kyoto, Japan. Backed by the vertical cliffs of the Koolau Mountains, it is set amid delicately landscaped Japanese gardens, which make the trip especially rewarding. There is even a two-ton statue of Buddha and a carp-filled pond on the grounds.

About a 40-minute drive from Honolulu and near the Byodo-In Temple is **Senator Fong's Plantation and Gardens,** *47-351 Pulama Road, Kahaluu (southern part of the windward coast); Tel. 239-6775; Open 10am - 4pm daily; Admission: $8.50 adults, $5 children ages 5-12*. These botanical gardens are also a working plantation, with many different types of fruit and nut trees. Trams amble through the 725-acre estate, taking visitors on tours. Run by Hiram Fong, the first Asian-American to be elected to the US Senate, the gardens have a visitor center with a gift shop and snack bar. Fong's father emigrated from China to Maui to work in the sugarcane fields. His family struggling to stay afloat, Hiram Fong began working (picking kiawe beans) when he was only four years old. His industriousness landed him at the University of Hawaii. From there he moved on to Harvard Law School, and finally to the US Senate, serving under five presidents, from Eisenhower to Ford.

Off Heeia State Park, **Coconut Island** is alive with flowers — from aromatic plumeria to ruffled hibiscus — which you can pick to your heart's content. From **Heeia Kai Boat Harbor,** arrange to take a glass bottom boat ride or to rent jet skis, go windsurfing, or canoeing.

A string of secluded beaches lie off Kamehameha Highway. Skip the **Coral Kingdom Market** in Waikane. This tangle of jewelry stalls is usually choked with passengers from tour buses.

If you don't mind the crowds, you can arrange to participate in a number of activities at **Kualoa Ranch and Activity Club,** *Kaaawa (central windward coast), Tel. 237-731, 237-8515, or 800/ 231-7322; Open 7am to 3pm daily; Reservations required*. At this working cattle ranch, you can horseback ride in Kaaawa Valley, go snorkeling, scuba diving, windsurfing, and jetsking, take a helicopter tour, an ATV ride, and have lunch. While activities are also available individually, the one-price-fits-all package includes round-trip transportation from a Waikiki hotel, a *paniolo* (cowboy) show, a buffet lunch, and a choice of diversions.

Note, however, that there's caste system here: The folks who've paid the all-inclusive "VIP" rates wear red bracelets and get first pick of activities (and healthier portions of dessert!). Everyone else dons blue bracelets; once the red-braceleted VIPs make their selections, the rest of the crowd is left to fight it out. Since space is limited, blues may literally have to run to a line to sign up for an activity. At times it's unclear whether this place is considered a ranch because of the cattle and horses or because of the way people are herded around!

The most popular activities, such as the jet ski and ATV rides are so packed that even though you're booked for 45 minutes, you actually only get about 15 minutes of action so that everyone gets a chance to participate. The pick up and transport to the snorkeling area is so lengthy that you really have only about 20 minutes in the water. Also, during my last visit, the horseback riding was too crowded and understaffed. When horses nudged, bit, and kicked at each other, riders had to deal with this themselves, since the staff was spread so thin.

Many octopuses hang out around offshore **Mokolii Island**, more commonly known as **Chinaman's Hat** because of its shape. At low tide, you can stroll out to the island, but be sure to walk back before the tide comes in! Fishing is good in this area, as well as on most of this side of the island.

LIONS & HAWAIIANS

Ancient Hawaiians once settled in Kahana Valley. To hear them tell it, the Crouching Lion, on the ridge along the shore, isn't a feline at all, but Kauhi, a god who was chained to the cliff to stand guard. For years he performed his duty faithfully, if less than happily, until one day Hii-aka, the younger sister of the volcano goddess Pele, happened by the sleeping Kauhi. Struck by her beauty, the awakened god struggled to stand. He tried to break free of his chains so that he could go away with the goddess and be finished with his boring job.

However, his joints rusty and his strength sapped from moving so little for so many years, he could only manage to rise to the crouching position he maintains to this day.

Kaaawa (yes, the word has a triplet of *a*'s, plus one more for good measure) is another sleepy town. After passing more pleasant beach parks, watch for the **Crouching Lion** rock formation, overlooking **Kahana Bay.** Canoe races take place at the beach here, and people relax in the shade of its pine trees. Inland from **Punaluu Beach Park** a slippery trail leads to **Sacred Falls Park.**

After passing a few more beaches you'll come to **Laie,** where the **Polynesian Cultural Center,** *55-370 Kamehameha Highway, Laie (on the windward coast); Tel. 293-3333 or 800/367-7060 from the mainland; Open 12:30pm - 9pm daily, except Sunday; The luau package (including all shows and demonstrations, dinner, and admission to the Hawaiimax Theater) costs $59 (adults), $39 (children age 5-11); For the buffet instead of the luau: $47 (adults), $30 (children) and less expensive tickets are available for the villages or the show only,* is located. Run by Mormons, this center features a variety of authentic Polynesian villages and many exhibits.

Wandering around authentic recreations of traditional villages from islands all over the Pacific, visitors get an intimate look at contrasting architectural styles and ways of life. The cultures of the indigenous peoples of Hawaii, Tahiti, the Marquesas, Tonga, New Zealand, Fiji and Samoa come alive through musical performances, crafts demonstrations, exhibits of artifacts, and historical mini-lectures.

You might watch a group of Hawaiian women pounding out bark to make *kapa* cloth, a young Tongan walking almost effortlessly up a giant palm to lop off a coconut, or a Maori warrior sticking out his "tattooed" tongue to let his enemies know he means business. The canoe ride down the "river" is pleasant, and at the end of the day, visitors are serenaded by each village they pass along the way

Wearing traditional dress, the people who work in the villages are actually from the islands they represent. Most of them are students at Brigham Young University whose Hawaii branch is run by the Mormons who run the Polynesian Cultural Center. (Note that no alcohol or caffeinated beverages are served here since it would be against the Mormon religion.)

For the most rewarding part of visiting the Center, spend some time chatting with the staff between demonstrations. Many of them plan to return to their countries, while others end up marrying Americans and staying in the United States, some moving to the mainland. Once I talked to a Fijian grandmother whose daughter had married an American and moved to Philadelphia. She told me about old Fijian songs and legends that explained how these Pacific islanders had originally come from Africa.

At the **Hawaiimax** theater – with a screen that is 65 feet tall and 96 feet wide – you will be able to see 40-minute, multimillion-dollar films.

The huge screen and the cinematography make you feel as if you're in the middle of the action. Seats are steeply terraced so that no views are obstructed by heads. One side effect: some people experience slight motion sickness. But if you close your eyes, it should pass.

After an afternoon of visiting villages, the buffet dinner or luau is followed by a musical extravaganza incorporating dances from all the islands. This colorful show is al fresco. Be sure to stop by the indoor-outdoor shopping complex, which sells crafts from all the islands.

Brigham Young University's Hawaii campus here is also run by the Mormons. Their eye-catching, white Mormon Temple stands at the end of a street lined with handsome Norfolk pines.

In the evenings, windsurfers can be seen in the bay at **Laie Point**. Out in the water, the surf crashes up against long, low-lying **Puka Rock**, which has a large, neat hole clear through it. Perhaps inspired by the hole in the rock, one of the many modern homes in the neighborhood is also round. Crabs scramble across the rocks at the edge of the churning water. If you're visiting during the winter, you might be lucky enough to spot migrating **whales** from here.

Near **Malaekahana State Park** beach, with its extensive strip of pines, the village of **Kahuku** is known for its sweet corn and watermelons, which are often sold at roadsides. At the **Mill at Kahuku**, visitors wander around a turn-of-the-century mill, then stop for lunch at the eclectic restaurant. Locals joke that almost everyone in this neck of the woods has at least one of the following: a skateboard, a surfboard, a boogie board, and a bike. Not far north of here is the **Turtle Bay Hilton**, practically the sole accommodation in the area, and certainly the only large one. The small **Rodeway Inn Hukilau** in Laie is not far.

The North Shore & Central Oahu

Surfers' paradise begins with **Sunset Beach**. During the winter, this two-mile sandy expanse draws crowds of master surfers with its 20- and 30-foot waves. In the summer, when the water is "flat" (with waves a mere 10 feet tall), only experienced windsurfers and bodysurfers should attempt these sports. Even strong swimmers should not venture far from shore and no one should ever enter the water alone. Right off the road, the beach is backed by a thick row of pines.

Along with the other surfing meccas along the north shore, **Ehukai Beach Park** and the famed **Banzai Pipeline** get their share of board-masters during the winter. During the championships, a festive atmosphere prevails. Blaring rock music sails past busy photographers, judges, and tables stacked with T-shirts. Lines form at food trucks parked along the road.

At **Pupukea Beach Park**, a marine reserve next to Sunset, snorkeling could hardly be more exciting. When you need a lift after all your aquatic action, take a drive along one of the nearby steep, narrow roads that go up into the hills. In this area, dotted with small ranches and orchards, the Pacific Army trained for jungle warfare during WWII. During the summer, roadside fruit stand vendors sell all kinds of fresh pickings.

Puu O Mahuka Heiau, *Off Route 83, 4 miles northeast of Hale'iwa,* is also on the north shore on a hill near Waimea Beach Park and Sunset Beach. Oahu's largest *heiau,* Puu o Mahuka is a rectangular collection of stones less than a mile up Pupukea Road (which should not be traveled during or immediately after wet weather). You'll notice that people still place offerings at this **ancient temple,** such as rocks wrapped with *ti* leaves. A stunning view is laid out from the bay side of this heiau. Declared a National Historic Landmark, it was once the site of human sacrifices. In 1794, several of Vancouver's crewmen had their lives snuffed out here.

Waimea Bay has a wide, especially attractive beach. Across from here, in the valley that was once one of Oahu's most sacred places, is **Waimea Valley/Waimea Falls Park,** *59-864 Kamehameha Highway, Hale'iwa (across from Waimea Beach Park, North Shore); Tel. 638-8511; Open 10am - 5:30pm daily; Admission: $19.95.*

Many weddings take place at the Waimea Falls Park botanical gardens in a historical setting. Parrots flutter and peacocks parade around the colorful tropical flora, including one of the world's largest ginger gardens. The platter-sized lily pads on a pond look large and sturdy enough for a person to walk on. In one meadow, the immaculate flower beds resemble multicolored confetti at the edge of a plush grass carpet.

Visitors ride a tram through the gardens, getting on and off as they please. Few people miss **the dive show**, in which men plunge from cliffs to the base of a waterfall. Visitors are welcome to swim, but diving is strictly for those daring professionals. In addition to old grass huts and ancient agricultural terraces, people can watch demonstrations of early hula — when dancing was restricted to men.

Near the main parking lot, an ancient *heiau* (temple) has been renovated and reconstructed. Historians believe that it was dedicated to the god Lono, the divinity of the heavens. It is probably at least eight centuries old, making it one of the earliest in Hawaii. In honor of Lono, ancient Hawaiians held the annual Makahiki festival at the end of each harvest. All fighting was suspended during this time, and wild feasting and fun and games broke out. Each October, Waimea Falls Park hosts a reenactment of this festival, including old religious rites and Hawaiian games. Be sure to stop by the *kauhale* (ancient living site), where, through demonstrations of tools and crafts, you'll learn about daily life in Waimea Valley during the 1700s.

Waimea Valley is also the place for guided **mountain bike** tours, nature **hikes, all-terrain-vehicle** (ATV) excursions, and **kayak** rides along Waimea River. The mountain bike trail rides last from 90 minutes to 2 hours, depending on the pace of the group. You'll receive helmets, water bottles, gloves, and long-sleeve shirts, which the guides suggest you don in addition to shorts and sneakers. Before you take off, you'll get the feel of your bike (becoming comfortable with its braking and gears) on the circular mini course. Everyone is encouraged to ride at his or her own pace and you'll have a choice of two routes, one with steeper climbs and descents.

If you're a half-decent bike rider, then I highly recommend the extra effort of the more difficult trail. The views of the park and Waimea Bay are fabulous with the higher elevation. During the winter surfing season, when North Shore waves are at their most impressive, you'll come to a great spot for viewing the hang-ten competitions. Unlike on the beach, where you can see maybe 100 feet from shore, up on the peaks you can follow each surfer's entire ride, from the time they first catch the wave until the end.

Along with historical and cultural tidbits about Hawaii, both hiking and biking guides share their knowledge of plants and fruit along the trails. You'll sample strawberry guava mango, and papaya (when in season) and assorted edible flowers.

The guided ATV rides are not for absorbing the beauty and tranquility of your surroundings. You'll be traveling so fast on these four-wheeled motorcycle cousins that the only things you'll be able to concentrate on are maneuvering the ATV (which, unlike mountain bikes, can roll over rocks, sand, gullies, and tree stumps) and the road ahead. The ATVs are so loud that any wildlife you might otherwise have seen will be long gone. The thrill is in the adrenaline rush you get from moving at such a high speed. But don't worry, just as with the mountain bikes, you'll have time to practice beforehand, to make sure that this is really something you want to do.

Hale'iwa, the plantation town about an hour drive northwest of Waikiki, is the main settlement on the North Shore. Handsome old buildings are set off by African tulip trees and palms. Turn up winding Paalaa Road, at the western end of the main road, for a scenic drive past banana plantations, private homes, and an old Buddhist temple with colorful gardens.

Looking at this small, remote town today, it is hard to believe that it ushered in tourism before Waikiki did. In 1899, Benjamin J. Dillingham, a wealthy businessman, put a stately hotel here, christening it Hale'iwa, meaning House of the Frigate Bird. This elegant Victorian lodging stood between the ocean and graceful **Anahulu River.** Fleeing Honolulu for seashore vacations, city residents climbed aboard the train that Dillingham had built for the surrounding sugar plantations and rode it here to the end of the line. Both the railroad and the hotel are long gone now. Hippies replaced the many of whom remain — began setting up studios and galleries. Today most newcomers arrive with surfboards tucked under their arms and head for the appealing beach park.

In 1984, Hale'iwa became a Historic, Cultural and Scenic District. However, this was just a few months too late for the rose-colored, art-deco Hale'iwa Theater, which protesters could not save from being torn down. Despite the demise of this theater, the old feeling of the frontier town has been preserved and, in some cases, manufactured. Weathered wooden buildings — both old and new — house some exceptional boutiques, health food stores, restaurants, and galleries.

In Hale'iwa, no new structures can look as though they were built after the 1920s. Dating back to 1926, **H. Miura** specializes in all kinds of fabrics from Japanese designs to Hawaiian *kapa* cloth patterns. The owners also run a shave ice stand next door. **Ishimoto Grocery** is in another old wooden building. **Liliuokalani Church,** erected in 1932, is one of the town's earliest buildings. Named for the queen who worshipped there, it contains a whimsical wall clock, a gift from the monarch herself in 1892. Instead of numbers on this timepiece, you'll see the 12 letters of the queen's royal name.

Spanning the river and dating back to 1921, the nearby concrete **Hale'iwa Bridge** serves as a stationary diving board for children in the summer. During the popular August Hale'iwa Lantern Festival, delicate paper lanterns are sent floating down the river by Japanese residents to honor their ancestors. To escape into the jungled interior, some people go **kayaking** along this serene waterway. Houses perch on stilts along its banks while chickens scurry around yards.

Few people pass through town without stopping at **Matsumoto's,** a mom-and-pop general store, for a shave ice. Lilikoi, coconut, banana, and rainbow are the most-licked flavors. Red *azuki* beans or scoops of ice cream are often added to these snow cones. Don't be surprised if you have to wait on a wrap-around line. At **Jameson's by the Sea,** near the island's narrowest bridge, diners can watch surfers navigate 20-foot waves. Sunsets give the restaurant a romantic glow.

Polo is all the rage at **Mokuleia Field,** beginning at about 3pm on Sundays from early April through August. Here the Hawaii Polo Club battles teams from the mainland, South America, Australia and Britain. If you don a big bonnet and a lei, you might blend in with the dignified ladies who make it their business to attend. People have picnics before the games. No one is bored between the two matches. They are too busy watching the sky divers, airplane stunts (provided by nearby Dillingham

Airfield), people in fancy Hawaiian clothing, riding horses, and other entertainment. If you'd like to take a ride in a **glider plane**, pay a visit to the gliderport at the airfield.

The road dries up just west of Mokuleia, and a rigorous, two-mile hike to narrow, rocky **Kaena Point**, the end of the island, begins. Here, the desolate land sits high above the pounding surf. The point, which no longer has a road around it, can also be approached from the leeward coast.

Turning inland at Hale'iwa toward acres of fields, you might pass a sugar cane truck piled high with cane brimming over its edges. Visitors have been stopping at **Dole Plantation** in Wahiawa since 1951. In addition to fresh pineapple for sale in the shops here, you'll find fudge, baked goods, and wooden bowls. Horseback riding is offered outside, where various types of pineapple are labeled for the edification of passersby.

Del Monte's Pineapple Triangle also has a garden growing pineapple in a wide variety of shapes, colors, and sizes. If you've ever wondered what the difference is between a Saigon Red and a Philippine Green, or how one from Samoa compares to one from Brazil, you'll find out here. If you're sorting through the neat rows of pineapple late in the afternoon, trucks packed with pickers might rumble by.

The Western Coast & Kaena Point

Here the Waianae Mountains slide into lush valleys that slip into the ocean. Peaceful beach parks are scattered along Oahu's western shore (the leeward coast). Overall, the swimming is pretty good during the summer when the water is calmest. Yet, since the **Sheraton Makaha Golf Club** and **Ihilani Resort and Spa** are the only resorts, and condos are few, this area draws far more locals than tourists.

While I've never had any problems in this area, residents warn visitors not to leave their rental cars out of sight for too long when they're away from their accommodation. Radios have been known to disappear. People will also tell you not to venture into deserted areas by yourself, but you should heed that advice in many other parts of Oahu and the rest of the state as well.

Farrington Highway (Route 93), the main drag along the Waianae Coast, is lined with small businesses, modest homes, and fast-food restaurants. Amid the familiar commercial dining spots are some worthwhile homegrown restaurants known as "Drive-Ins" and "BBQs." They serve inexpensive local food, blending Asian, American, and Hawaiian cuisines.

A good surfing spot, **Nanakuli Beach Park** hugs the coast just off the highway. Many Nanakuli dwellers are Hawaiians who are on the seemingly endless waiting list for Hawaiian Home Lands, which they can lease for $1 a year for 99 years. The delays are caused in part because, before homestead lots can be developed, they must undergo archaeological examination to make sure they contain no endangered animals, plants, or Hawaiian artifacts.

ON DEAF EARS

The name Nanakuli, meaning "to look deaf," originates from the time when people in the area were too poor to share their food with passersby, as was the custom. When they looked at strangers, they feigned deafness.

One of Oahu's most scenic drives is north of Makaha, where you'll find beaches frequented by surfing and barbecuing local families and, in a nearby valley, the **Sheraton Makaha Golf Club**. Mountains border one side of the main road while the ocean trims the other. The land is wonderfully undeveloped, with only a few houses here and there. On the *mauka* side of the road, **Kaneana Cave** has a very high, gaping entrance. When you see the graffiti scrawled way at the top of the mouth of the cave, you'll wonder how anyone could possibly have accomplished such a feat. You'll need a flashlight to explore much deeper than the spacious entry area and you'll probably have to crawl in some places. Of course, this is not something that should be done alone.

Near Makaha Golf Club, in Makaha on the leeward coast, is **Kaneaki Heiau**. Used for agricultural worship, this *heiau* is tucked away in a lush park. Watch your step as you climb the rocks up to the second level, where a thatched shelter has been built. The original platform was constructed between 1450 and 1640 AD. Archaeologists believe that this place of worship may have been converted into a temple for the god of war. However, the setting is wonderfully peaceful today. Wild peacocks strut past banana trees and the sound of chirping birds interrupts the thick quiet. The surrounding area is full of good **hiking** trails.

The paved road comes to an abrupt end at Yokohama Bay beach, where the rough waves draw boogie boarding kids. **Kaena Point** itself, the island's northwest corner, can no longer be traveled by vehicle, not even motorcycles or four-wheel-drives. The road that ran around the point until late 1988 had been built nearly a century earlier, in 1899, for a railroad line. The train chugged along here until the 1940s. Now the unrelenting surf has eroded about 30 feet of the old road. You can still circle the island, but you'll have to do this section on foot.

Oahu's leeward and windward coasts come together at Kaena Point, which can be reached from either the west or the North Shore. During the winter, some of the state's highest waves thrash the point, sometimes jumping 40 to 50 feet into the air. Both onshore and offshore fishing is good here. Ask the ancient Hawaiians, who built a fishing camp at the tip of the point near the graffiti-covered lighthouse. You can still see the rocky remnants of the camp.

Mynah birds and sea gulls putter about Kaena Point. Non-swimming frigates steal fish from other birds. Ancient Hawaiians believed that the soul of each dead person would come to Kaena, where a spirit would decide whether the time for death had truly arrived. If not, the soul would be sent back to the body. If ending life was appropriate, the spirit would guide the soul to the white boulder just east of Kaena Point, on the windward side. As the soul jumped off the rock into death, a god would decide whether it deserved to end up in *Kahiki* (heaven) or the place of never-ending night.

Kaena is also said to be where the demigod Maui attempted to bring all the Hawaiian islands together. By tossing a giant coral fishhook over to Kauai and tugging, he tried to join it with Oahu. But he fell backwards to the ground when only a chunk of Kauai popped off, leaving the rest of the island anchored where it was. This chunk of Kauai, a small island known as **Pohaku o Kauai** (Rock of Kauai), remains in the water just off the point. Using a far more violent strategy, Kamehameha I succeeded in unifying the Hawaiian Islands in 1810.

HALFWAY POINT

Along the shore around Kaena Point, multicolored marine life thrives in tide pools. Among the shells and volcanic rocks you'll find along the sand dunes, you'll also see naupaka plants, with their white flowers. Half of each blossom seems to have been neatly lopped off. Look, but don't touch, since destroying the plant also destroys the land: Naupakas help secure the sand dunes.

NIGHTLIFE & ENTERTAINMENT

In Waikiki and the rest of Honolulu (where Oahu's nightclubs, dance floors, and bars are concentrated), life after dark is frantic every night of the week. If you make some local friends, they might invite you to *holo-holo* (hop from nightspot to nightspot) and "suck 'em up" (toss down a few drinks). There are plenty of Polynesian revues, luaus, loud bars, rock and pop concerts, and video dance clubs with confetti sprinklers and laser lights. Many hotels have their own night clubs and lounges, featuring everything from throbbing dance music to romantic old-time big band combos and ukulele-strumming Hawaiian singers.

There is also no scarcity of good local theater companies. Even seasonal symphony concerts, chamber music, ballet and opera are in the mix. For details about sunset, dinner, and moonlight cruises (most of which leave from Kewalo Basin near Waikiki), see the section on *Sports & Recreation* in this chapter. Here are a few of the most popular places to be after dark:

Hawaiian Style

Many hotels and independent companies regularly host luaus, some in dramatic oceanfront settings. Although these feasts, with entertainment, will certainly give you a taste of Hawaiian food, music, dance, and traditions, these crowded, touristy affairs don't appeal to everyone. I prefer to steer clear of the larger feasts. Instead, I check the newspapers for fundraising luaus sponsored by local churches, civic groups, or hula schools.

JUBILATION, *1007 Dillingham Boulevard, Honolulu. Tel. 845-1568. Open from 8pm to 4am.*

When you're ready for some real live Hawaiian music, without the commercial trappings, try this very local night spot where the atmosphere could hardly be more laid back.

DON HO, *Hana Hou Showroom, Waikiki Beachcomber Hotel, 2300 Kalakaua Avenue. Tel. 931-3009 or 922-4646. There is one 7pm show nightly, except Mondays and Saturdays. Dinner seating: 5:15pm. seating for cocktails only: 6:30pm. With dinner: $52 for adults, $26 for children ages 6 to 12; with cocktails only: $32 for adults, $16 for those under age 21.*

Don Ho continues to charm some and make others shake their heads. He often tells his audiences how much he hates "Tiny Bubbles," the song he's best known for. But then, of course, he sings it anyway, to the delight of the crowd, along with all his other hits. What makes the show most enjoyable is Ho's sense of humor – and the fact that he doesn't seem to take himself seriously. He banters with the audience (with special attention to honeymooners and those celebrating anniversaries). Other performers also get a chance to show their stuff, including his teenage daughter and a pint-sized hula dancer. Music ranges from nostalgic Hawaiian to Latin and country.

The meal served during the show is surprisingly good. After a crisp salad with a tasty dressing, you'll have a choice of mahi-mahi, chicken, or prime rib, perhaps followed by rainbow sherbet and coffee or tea. One cocktail comes with dinner. When the show is over, you'll be invited to have your photo snapped (by a professional photographer or with your own camera) with Don Ho himself.

HAWAIIAN CROONER

A musical institution in Oahu, Don Ho, spent his early years in rustic Kaneohe, across the Koolau mountains from Honolulu, where he tended bar at his parents' restaurant. Graduating from the University of Hawaii with a degree in sociology, he became an Air Force pilot. Part Hawaiian, Chinese, and Portuguese, Ho has been a hot entertainer since the 1960s and his often-sentimental songs have become synonymous with Hawaii for many people.

Millions of mainlanders who never set foot on Hawaiian soil were introduced to the islands through his network television variety show that ran in the 1970s. He also toured the mainland continually, performing in glittery night clubs in Las Vegas, Los Angeles, and other cities. Some listeners may find his music a bit commercial or corny. But scores of other loyal fans never miss an opportunity to see and hear him in action.

THE POLYNESIAN CULTURAL CENTER, *Laie, windward coast. Tel. 293-3333 or 800/367-7060 from the mainland. The show follows dinner, which starts being served at 4:30pm. See Getting Around Oahu for details about guided transportation.*

This lavish production, performed by students from Brigham Young University's Hawaii campus, is an exciting way to close a day of visiting the Center's recreated villages. The show even includes a fiery volcano. In living color, you'll see the differences and similarities among the dances and music of various Polynesian islands.

THE AINAHAU SHOWROOM, *the Sheraton Princess Ka'iulani Hotel, 2342 Kalakaua Avenue, Waikiki. Tel. 922-5811.*

Some say this is one of Oahu's strongest Polynesian revues. The stage is brought to life by energetic dancers from Fiji, Samoa, New Zealand, and Tahiti.

PARADISE COVE LUAU PARK, *Ko Olina, Ewa (27 miles from Waikiki). Tel. 973-5828 or 800/ 775-2683 from the mainland. Held nightly. Cost: $50 for adults, and $28 for children aged 6-12 (including round trip transportation from Waikiki).*

As far as commercial luaus go, this is one of the most enjoyable. The food is nothing special, but the setting, the visitor participation in ancient Hawaiian activities, and the sometimes campy entertainment make the trip worthwhile.

Located on 12 acres in a beach park on Oahu's uncrowded Leeward Coast, Paradise Cove is a great spot for spectacular sunsets. Before the extensive buffet and performance, you'll be treated to live Hawaiian music and watch demonstrations such as palm frond weaving and coconut tree climbing. When it's time for the *hukilau* (net fishing), everyone watches the huge net being thrown out to sea, then helps pull it in.

Guests may try their hands at husking coconuts, pounding poi, and stringing leis. They are also invited to participate in games such as *ulu maika* (Hawaiian bowling), spear throwing, and Tongan shuffleboard. If you'd rather not make the 50-minute drive yourself, you can arrange to be picked up by bus in Waikiki (you'll leave around 4pm and be dropped off at about 10:30pm.

MAGIC OF POLYNESIA SHOW, *Hilton Dome Showroom, Hilton Hawaiian Village, 2005 Kalia Road, Honolulu. Tel. 941-0924 or 800/775-2683. Showtimes: 6:30pm and 8:45pm. Dinner seating: 5pm, Cocktail seating: 6pm and 8pm. Cost: $57 per adult, $40 per child age 12 or younger for the regular dinner show (steak and fish); $130 per adult, $90 for each child 12 or younger for the deluxe dinner show (filet mignon and lobster tail); for show and cocktails only, $30 per adult, $21 per child age 12 or younger.*

Reminiscent of a Las Vegas casino act, this entertaining show includes Hawaiian costumed singers and dancers, along with the sawing-people-in-half type of magic and a fabulous laser show. The spectacular setting — a geodesic dome — adds to the appeal. Both children and adults enjoy evenings here.

Local Hangouts & Happenings

GUSSIE L'AMOUR'S, *3251 Nimitz Highway, Honolulu. Tel. 836-7883 or 836-9180.*

Some name brand bands perform at this nightspot that attracts a young party crowd.

SCRUPLES, *Waikiki Marketplace, 2310 Kuhio Avenue, Waikiki. Tel. 923-9530.*

If you're in the mood to socialize with more locals than tourists, try this dance spot, which plays Top 40 songs, between 8pm and 4am.

RUMOURS, *Ala Moana Hotel, 410 Atkinson Drive, Waikiki. Tel. 955-4811. Open Tuesday-Wednesday from 5pm to 2am, and Thursday-Sunday until 4am. Closed Mondays.*

Residents flock here after work, some remaining until the wee hours. Flashing lights slice through the crowd on the dance floor, which is set off with videos. If you happen by on a Big Chill night, you'll shake it up to oldies from the 1960s and 1970s.

THE WAVE WAIKIKI, *1877 Kalakaua Avenue, Waikiki. Tel. 941-0424. Open 9pm - 4pm daily.*

The music at this disco ranges from hard rock to boogie, both live and recorded.

FAST EDDIE'S DISCOTHEQUE, 52 Oneawa Street, Kailua. Tel. 261-8561. *Club open Monday to Saturday 6pm to 4am, Sunday 8pm to 4am.* Let your hip bones slip to Top 40s tunes or pounding rock music played by live local bands or, occasionally, groups from the mainland. Some folks are turned on by the famous **Male Revue**; call for the schedule.

RYAN'S GRILL, Ward Center, 1200 Ala Moana Boulevard. Tel. 523-9132.

Luring Oahu residents after work, this is where singles mingle while sipping beer and munching *pupus* and other snacks.

ANNA BANNANA'S, 2440 South Beretania Street, Honolulu. Tel. 946-5190. *Open nightly until 2am (recorded music on Monday and Tuesday).*

Slightly on the raunchy side, this smoky, high-decibel club plays host to reggae bands, blues singers, and other quality live music (9pm to 2am, Wednesday to Sunday). Name-brand performers (such as Taj Mahal) show up from time to time to entertain enthusiastic crowds.

THE HAWAII INTERNATIONAL FILM FESTIVAL, Honolulu. Tel. 528-3456.

This week-long festival, one of the world's most extensive, is both a cultural and a social event. Important movies from the US, the Pacific, and Asia are shown during the day and evenings at various Oahu theaters. The free films, workshops, and lectures draw people from all over the state.

KUMU KAHUA THEATRE COMPANY, 46 Merchant Street, Honolulu. Tel. 536-4441. *Tickets: $12.*

If you're interested in what makes Hawaii tick, consider attending one of the productions by this theater company, which uses the ins and outs of the 50th state as a theme for its plays and shows.

DIAMOND HEAD THEATER, 520 Makapuu Avenue, Honolulu. Tel. 734-0274. *Tickets: $10 to $40.*

In the shadow of Diamond Head volcano, right in Waikiki, this company puts on very good musicals, dramas, comedies, and the classics throughout the year.

THE MANOA VALLEY THEATER, 2833 East Manoa Road, Honolulu. Tel. 988-6131. *Tickets: $23 to $40.*

These actors may not be professionals, but they certainly put on spirited productions, which run from September through June.

ROCK & POP CONCERTS

Especially when internationally acclaimed artists or groups are in town, young folks pack the stands at **Aloha Stadium**, Tel. 486-9300, and **Neal Blaisdell Center Arena**, Tel. 591-2211, in Honolulu.

HAWAII SYMPHONY, 444 Hobron Lane, Suite V-B, Honolulu. Tel. 946-1161.

On Tuesday evenings and Sunday afternoons from September to April, the Hawaii Symphony orchestra (sometimes joined by well-known international musicians) makes sweet music. Performance locations vary, so you'll need to call for the schedule. Also ask about the Symphony on the Light Side.

KAPIOLANI PARK CONCERTS, *below Diamond Head, Waikiki.*

During the summer, the Hawaii Symphony holds its Starlight Series in the park. Other performances, from slack key guitar to ukulele, take place here as well. Locals buy lawn tickets, pack picnic baskets and spread blankets on the grass.

THE HAWAII OPERA THEATRE, *the Blaisdell Concert Hall, Honolulu. Tel. 596-7858. Tickets: $22-$75; to charge them on MasterCard or Visa, call Tel. 596-7858.*

Local and mainland opera singers come together on stage in February and March, accompanied by the Honolulu Symphony and the Hawaii Opera Chorus.

CHAMBER MUSIC HAWAII, *Tel. 947-1975.*

Throughout the year, concerts take place at the Honolulu Lutheran Church at 1730 Punahou Street, Honolulu Academy of Arts on Beretania Street and Ward Avenue, among other Oahu locations.

EUROPEAN AMERICAN DANCE

Ballet Hawaii, *Tel. 988-7578,* and **Hawaii State Ballet,** *Tel. 947-2755,* appeal to dance lovers; both showcase "The Nutcracker." Ballet Hawaii, a home-grown troupe, performs it each year at Christmas time at the Blaisdell Concert Hall.

Other Nightclubs & Dance Spots

HANOHANO ROOM, *Sheraton Waikiki, 2255 Kalakaua Avenue, Waikiki. Tel. 922-4422. No minimum or cover charge.*

Complimentary appetizers accompany the spectacular view of Waikiki Beach each day from 4pm to 7pm. Beginning at 8:30pm, a jazz band brings couples onto the dance floor. With lights from all the hotels lining the shore, the view of the beach is breathtaking after dark as well.

SOCIETY OF SEVEN, *Outrigger Waikiki Hotel, 2335 Kalakaua Avenue, Waikiki Beach. Tel. 923-4450 or 922-6408 (reservations).*

The multi-talented members of this group know their way around songs, dances, musical instruments, and hilarious impersonations. Two shows are performed Wednesday, Friday, and Saturday nights, at 7pm and 9pm, with only one show on Monday, Tuesday, and Thursday at 9pm.

MAHARAJA HAWAII, *Waikiki Trade Center, 2255 Kuhio Avenue, off Seaside Avenue, Waikiki. Tel. 922-3030.*

Oodles of money was spent on this Japanese-owned dance club and, judging by the number of people always standing on line to get in, the investment has paid off. The sound system is so major that you can feel the music rumbling through your body. It's not uncommon for people to dance on the bar. Most patrons at this expensive hangout are Japanese tourists.

MOOSE McGILLYCUDDY'S PUB AND CAFE, *310 Leuers Street, Waikiki. Tel. 923-0751. Wednesday to Saturday, live bands from 9pm to 3:30am.*

Beer is the beverage of choice at this casual hangout where live bands play Sunday to Thursday from about 9pm to 1:30am.

NICK'S FISHMARKET, *Waikiki Gateway Hotel, 2070 Kalakaua Avenue, Waikiki. Tel. 955-6333.*

This restaurant and club is one of Waikiki's most popular. Every night, it is filled with music and dance. (Hours vary, so be sure to call ahead.)

NICHOLAS NICKOLAS, *Ala Moana Hotel, 410 Atkinson, Waikiki. Tel. 955-4466.*

Put on a snazzy outfit, take in the wonderful view, and shake a leg to some great music. The dance floor wakes up Sunday through Thursday from 9pm to 2am; and Friday and Saturday from 10pm to 3am.

Special Events

Oahu hosts many annual events in addition to the **winter surfing championships** on the North Shore. The state's largest cultural event is **Aloha Festivals**, which takes place on the major islands each fall. The highlight is the 27.5-mile **canoe race** from the island of Molokai to Oahu.

During half-time at the January **Hula Bowl** at Aloha Stadium, there's an elaborate performance of music and hula, as well as other entertainment. Tailgate parties crowd the parking lot with entire families barbecuing to a tangle of rock music from sundry stations.

Other happenings include **Chinese New Year** and the Chinese cultural **Narcissus Festival** in Honolulu's Chinatown from January through March; the Japanese **Cherry Blossom Festival** from January through March; and **ukulele** and **slack key guitar festivals, and kite flying competitions** in Kapiolani Park in Waikiki.

SPORTS & RECREATION

Water sports, the prime attraction for active travelers, can be arranged through most hotels and condominiums, even those not situated on the beach. Sports concessions and "beach boys" (life guards, surfing instructors, outrigger canoe paddlers, etc.) sprinkle Waikiki's sandy shore. You can also stop at the Waikiki Beach Center, adjacent to the Sheraton Moana Surfrider hotel. Some beaches or adjoining parks have volleyball courts. Details about water and land sports follow.

Beaches

Oahu is rimmed with more than 50 beach parks, some of which have lifeguards, bathrooms, changing facilities, showers and picnic tables. Only highly skilled surfers should enter **North Shore** waters during winter months, when the waves are massive. This shore is the site of winter surfing tournaments. At all beaches, heed warnings about surf conditions. Like any ocean, the extremely powerful Pacific must be handled with care.

Be sure to apply sunscreen before and immediately after leaving the water. Let the rays darken your skin slowly. Don't spend your whole first day stretched out on the beach. It may not be a good idea to find shade beneath a palm tree, since falling coconuts could klonk you on the head. Leave your valuables in your hotel or condominium safe. Unfortunately, theft is an all-too-common pastime at the shore, especially along the economically depressed Waianae Coast. While this western shore has some good beaches, it may not be a good idea to venture much beyond the coast near the Makaha Golf Club, unless you are accompanied by local friends. Note that no alcohol is allowed on Hawaii's beaches.

Waikiki, *southeastern shore (leeward coast)*

The best view of Waikiki Beach is from the Hanohano Room high at the top of the Sheraton Waikiki. By day, you'll look down on the many other hotels lining the curve of beach and boat-studded water, with Diamond Head volcano at the far end. By night, the scene is lit with glittering lights from all the hotels.

The busiest and best-known beach in the entire state is actually a two-and-a-half-mile series of beaches. Although it's often difficult to catch a glimpse of the sand between all the glistening bodies lying, walking, and playing on top of it, no one seems to mind the crush. At a string of concessions along the shore, "beachboys" make arrangements for people to sail on catamarans, ride outrigger canoes and aqua-bikes, go parasailing, and learn to surf, among other pursuits. Particularly in the waters in front of the Sheraton Waikiki, you're likely to spot endangered *honu* (Hawaiian green sea turtles) swimming and feeding on the *limu* (seaweed). Most of these harmless creatures weigh anywhere from 17 to 180 pounds.

Human swimmers looking for the calmest waves and the sandiest ocean floor gravitate toward **Kahaloa** and **Ulukou** beaches, facing the Royal Hawaiian ("the Pink Palace") and the Sheraton Moana Surfrider hotels. Many people consider this section the cream of Waikiki's crop. Even the police get to work from a station here.

The beach in front of the Hilton Hawaiian Village is known as **Kahanamoku Beach and Lagoon.** It is named after Duke Kahanamoku, Hawaii's beloved surfing champion and Olympic swimmer, and is a good spot for young children, since the waves are gentle. If you don't mind mixing with military personnel, try **Fort DeRussy Beach**, the broadest section of Waikiki Beach. You might want to join a volleyball game here.

The Halekulani hotel overlooks calm, narrow **Gray's Beach**, once a Hawaiian retreat for spiritual healing. Surfers find great waves out past the reef.

Kuhio Beach Park, by the Waikiki Beach Center, is an especially good spot for viewing the sunset. Although a sea wall that protrudes into the ocean keeps waters relatively calm at shore, swimmers must be very careful since the ocean floor is potholed with unexpected drops. Surfing and bodysurfing are good on the oceanside of the wall. The sand becomes particularly powdery at **Queen's Beach**, near the Honolulu Zoo. This is a popular picnic site with the gay community, as well as with families. Locals and visiting singles flock to **Sans Souci Beach**, near the New Otani Kaimana Beach Hotel, for sunning, picnicking and volleyball.

Ala Moana Beach Park, *just ewa (west) of Waikiki; across from the Ala Moana shopping center*

Although this beach teems with families, couples, and singles swimming, playing volleyball and tennis, jogging and just plain socializing, it is less crowded than Waikiki, which begins on the other side of the Ala Wai Yacht Harbor. Locals and visitors congregate here for picnics.

Diamond Head Beach Park, *near Waikiki, on the Koko Head side of Diamond Head crater*

Watched over by a lighthouse, this is not a good beach for swimming since the water is dangerously rough. But if you're into strolling and peering into tidal pools, consider stopping here.

Hanauma Bay, *near Oahu's southeastern tip*

You'll arrive here at the top of a hill, looking down on the palm-lined, mountain-backed C-shaped beach. This is one of Oahu's most beautiful settings. Even from above, you can see all kinds of coral through the transparent blue water. Walk down to the sand or take a jitney. Because snorkeling is so good here, the beach remains packed all day. If you don't own snorkeling gear, be sure to rent some before you come, or take a Hanauma Bay snorkeling excursion (see the section on *Sports & Recreation* in this chapter)

Sandy Beach, *at the southeastern tip of the island, near Sea Life Park*

Look at but don't touch the water here. Despite the many body surfers who pack the shore, this part of the Pacific is extremely dangerous, even for champion swimmers. Very strong currents and jagged, hidden rocks create hazards not worth risking. Rock music blares from radios while young people show off their cars. Kites flutter high in the sky. At one of the food wagons parked across the street, consider sampling a **plate lunch** (generally teriyaki steak, chicken, or fish; two scoops of rice; a mound of macaroni salad; and *kim chee* (Korean pickled vegetables), or try **manapua,** a Chinese rice flour bun filled with meat or beans. Sandy Beach is sometimes referred to as **Koko Head Beach Park.**

Makapuu Beach Park, southeastern tip of Oahu, across from Sea Life Park

Body surfing and **boogie boarding** are big here, but only attempt them if you're an expert. Riptides can be life-threatening for the novice. However, the locale – a small cove at the bottom of impressive cliffs that serve as a jumping-off point for **hang gliders** – makes this a wonderful spot for soaking up the sun. Petite **Rabbit Island** is just offshore.

Waimanalo Beach Park, southeastern end of the windward coast

Locals fill the lawn here with barbecue grills, coolers, lawn chairs and radios. They are sometimes less than pleased to see outsiders, so you might feel more comfortable if you come with a local friend or two. You'll feel less like an intruder on the beautiful beach, with its non-intimidating waves that draw **boogie boarders and body surfers.**

Bellows Field Park Beach, southeastern end of the windward coast

Because of the gentle waves, the swimming and **body surfing** are great here. Locals set up picnics in the shade of ironwood trees. Unfortunately, this US Air Force beach is only open to the public from Friday afternoon until Sunday night, and on federal holidays.

Lanikai Beach, southeastern windward coast

Known to few outsiders, this beach is great for **swimming.** The tranquil setting is enhanced by the view of two silhouetted offshore islands. To find this beach, you'll have to take one of the lanes between the houses on coastal Mokulua Drive.

Kailua Beach Park, windward coast, at Kailua

Excellent for **windsurfing** and **swimming,** this four-mile palm-shaded beach is frequented by local families in addition to board sailors. The curving shore and the mountains make this an especially scenic place. Windsurfing equipment is available for rent in Kailua. **Sailing** and **boating** are also fine here (see the *Sports & Recreation* section in this chapter).

Leanani & Waiahole Beach Parks, on Kaneohe Bay, windward coast

The bay here is **polluted**, so the only reason to visit these parks is to relax or picnic on dry land.

Kualoa Beach Park, north of Kaneohe Bay, windward coast

Consider absorbing this lovely setting. Views from the long, slim, often windy beach take in the bay and the Koolau Mountains. At low tide, you can walk out to Mokolii island, better known as **Chinaman's Hat.** Picnicking and camping are popular here

Kaaawa Beach Park, near Kaaawa, on the windward coast

The swimming and snorkeling are quite good here.

Swanzy Beach Park, near Kaaawa, on the windward coast

This spot is far better for sunning than for swimming, since sharp and lumpy coral interfere with being in the water.

Kahana Bay Beach Park, windward coast

The shallow waters here make for better wading than swimming, so this is a good place to introduce toddlers and other **children** to the Pacific. This shady, picturesque site is also fine for a picnic or simple relaxation. Pandanus and ironwood trees provide ample shade. **Boating and fishing** are popular here as well. Not far from here is an ancient Hawaiian fish pond, which was still being used as late as the 1920s. See if you can find some ripe mangoes or bananas in lush Kahana Valley, across the road.

Punaluu Beach Park, northern windward coast, near the Polynesian Cultural Center

The swimming is good here, but the beach is often crowded in the afternoon with tour bus groups that stop at an adjacent restaurant for lunch.

Malaekahana Beach Park, northern windward coast, between the Polynesian Cultural Center and the Turtle Bay Hilton

Even though the beach is narrow, it is quite long and the waves are perfect for **swimming** and **body surfing**. When the tide is low, you can slosh out toward offshore (and off-limits) Goat Island. This shady beach park is a popular **camp site** with local families.

Ehukai Beach Park, North Shore

Home of the famous **Banzai Pipeline,** this is one of the North Shore beaches packed with master **surfers** during the winter. Even walking close to the water can be dangerous during winter months since 20- and 30-foot waves may suddenly come barreling further in than expected. Mother Nature does a dramatic about-face in the summer, when waves here become manageable for swimmers and snorkelers.

Sunset Beach, *North Shore*

In the winter, you can join the festive atmosphere while **surfing contests** take place here and at nearby North Shore beaches. Another dangerous spot during the winter for all but expert surfers, Sunset calms down enough during the summer to allow strong swimmers and good body surfers some safe fun. Look for food trucks, parked across the street, where you can buy plate lunches, shave ice and beverages.

Waimea Bay

Swimming and snorkeling are good here during the summer, that is if you're a strong swimmer. Forget about entering the water during the winter. Don't even get close to the shore. Just watch the **expert surfers** doing their thing on 25-plus-foot waves. Right across the road from Waimea Falls Park, this beach is broad and has a shady picnic area.

Pupukea Beach Park, *North Shore*

Admire this beach from a safe distance during the winter. Strong swimmers can enjoy snorkeling here during the summer, when the water is kinder to humans.

Hale'iwa Beach Park, *North Shore*

At funky little Hale'iwa, the North Shore's only town, this beach is good for swimming and snorkeling during the spring and summer, but, like all North Shore beaches, should not be entered by anyone but accomplished surfers in the winter. Feel free to join a volleyball game or to toss a Frisbee around.

Hale'iwa Alii Beach Park, *North Shore*

Once known as Waialua Beach Park, this spot is good for swimming during the spring and summer only. Other times, surfing and watching (from a safe distance) should be the main activities.

Mokuleia Beach Park, *North Shore*

This long, wide, white strand is often nearly empty. The **windsurfing** is quite good here. But while the waters can be excellent for snorkeling, swimming is sometimes rough. During the winter, people often spot **whales** from here.

Yokohama Bay, just north of Makaha, on the Waianae Coast

Never crowded, this surfing beach lies at the northern end of the leeward coast road. (However, you won't be able to get to the North Shore from here unless you hike it, since this is where the road ends.) A prime fishing spot among locals, this broad beach also attracts young boys with boogie boards and, on weekends, picnicking families. During the summer when the water is calmest, small children splash in the waves.

Makaha Beach, Makaha, leeward coast

A lifeguard is sometimes on duty at this long curve of sand. The often rough waves make for challenging boogie boarding and body surfing.

Keaau Beach Park, Makaha area, leeward coast

Backed by a grassy expanse studded with picnic tables and palm trees, camping tents are pitched at the edge of a rocky shore. A sandy beach is adjacent, but the water is quite rough.

Waianae Rest Camp, just south of Waianae Small Boat Boat Harbor, leeward coast

Officially known as Waianae Army Recreational Center Beach, this is the best place for swimming near the Makaha Golf Course. A breakwater at each end of this stretch of sand keeps the water flat. Palm trees and views of the mountains make this an appealing locale for watching the sun go down.

Ewa Beach Park, leeward coast, near Pearl Harbor

This long, broad strand of white sand is bathed by calm waters. Diamond Head and the skyscrapers of Honolulu and Waikiki loom in the distance. On weekends, residents flock here to swim, socialize, and play basketball on the court in the expansive grassy park. Swings, a jungle gym and picnic tables attract families. After a storm, it is not unusual to see Hawaiians gathering uprooted *limu* (seaweed) to use in salads and other dishes. Hawaiians have been cooking with seaweed for generations. Asian immigrants have added their own seaweed recipes to Hawaii's culinary melange. Park facilities also include bathrooms, showers and changing areas. To get here, you'll drive past sugarcane fields and open farmland interspersed with sprawling housing developments backed by mountains.

Biking

Cycling on Oahu can be enjoyable, as long as you steer clear of Waikiki and the rest of Honolulu, where traffic is thick. Many airlines allow bikes on board for a small additional charge. If you haven't brought your own you can rent one; your accommodation can recommend a good bike shop.

The **Hawaii Bicycling League**, *Tel. 735-5756 or 785-6679. Organizes* rides every Saturday and Sunday that leave from the Kapiolani Park bandstand in Waikiki and wend their way to various parts of Oahu. Beginner rides cover less than 20 miles while the most experienced cyclists can participate in the 134-mile Oahu Perimeter Ride each fall.

Also see "Waimea Valley/Waimea Falls Park" in *Seeing the Sights.*

Camping

Most of Oahu's 18 campsites are in beach parks, each of which has a distinct look and feel. County beach parks have bathrooms, showers, drinking water, and garbage disposal areas. You won't be able to make campfires if you stay in one of these, but you can cook on a grill or portable stove, as long as you bring your own. Open year-round, the campgrounds are closed on Wednesdays and Thursdays. You'll need to get a free permit two weeks ahead of your arrival by applying *in person* to the **Department of Parks and Recreation**, *650 South King Street, Honolulu, Tel. 808/523-4525.*

State campgrounds - on the shore in Hale'iwa, Malaekahana Beach, Waimanalo Bay, and Sand Island, and inland at Aiea Heights - are also closed on Wednesdays and Thursdays. Facilities are similar to those at county sites. You'll need to make a reservation at least 30 days in advance and get your free permit a week in advance by writing or visiting the **Division of Parks**, *1151 Punchbowl Street, Honolulu, HI 96813, Tel. 808/587-0300.*

Canoeing

Along Waikiki Beach, "beach boys" compete for the chance to take tourists out in 30- to 40-foot outrigger canoes to ride the waves as the ancient Hawaiians once did. For about $6, paddlers will allow several good waves to push you toward shore. In this sport, sometimes called "canoe surfing," boats can travel faster than 25 miles an hour.

Fishing

Kewalo Basin, near Waikiki, is the place most visitors go to arrange full- and half-day excursions on charter fishing boats. Reliable companies include **Coreene-CII Sports Fishing Charters**, *Tel. 226-8421 mobile phone;* **Island Charters**, *Tel. 593-9455 or 596-2028;* **ELO Sport Fishing**, *Tel. 947-5208;* and **Tradewind Charters**, *Tel. 973-0311.*

To share a boat for a full day (usually 6:30am - 3pm), rates range from about $80 to $100 per person. For a half-day, plan to spend $55 to $70 per person. To charter a boat, rates run from $450 to $650 for a full day, and from $350 to $400 for a half-day. Rates include fishing gear, but you're expected to bring your own lunch. In most cases, the fish you catch go to

CANOES OF THE PAST

When Hawaiian kings, queens, and high chiefs used to ride their canoes or surfboards, commoners knew to stay away from the beach, lest they sully these royal sports. When a kapu (taboo) was placed on a site reserved for alii at play, a commoner foolish enough to trespass might even be put to death.

After the 1820 arrival of American missionaries, canoe surfing along with many other Hawaiian pastimes, was almost wiped out. The god-fearing haoles were appalled at all the glistening skin exposed – on both men and women – during water sports. By the end of the 19th century, aquatic games had begun making their comeback, thanks in large part to King David Kalakaua, who also revived the hula and other Hawaiian traditional arts. However, canoe surfing was never quite the same as it had been. In an attempt to preserve this disappearing segment of Hawaiian culture, Alexander Hume Ford started the Outrigger Canoe Club in Waikiki in 1908. A rival association, called the Hui Nalu Canoe Club, was put together in 1911 by a group consisting mainly of Hawaians.

the captain. Plan to tip the captain about $20. Ask about less expensive North Shore charters for tuna and marlin fishing.

Wahiawa Reservoir, not far from Schofield Barracks in central Oahu, is home to many big peacock and black bass. **Nuuanu Reservoir**, near the Pali Highway (Route 61), just outside Honolulu, is also good for small-boat freshwater fishing.

If you want to fish for sport, not for dinner, try some of the narrow streams and small ponds that drain and irrigate sugar cane and pineapple fields, such as those along Kunia Road going toward Waipahu, in southern central Oahu (near Pearl Harbor). The catch is (pun intended), you must ask the landowner for permission. Remember that agricultural chemicals render these fish inedible.

Plenty of petite saltwater fish reside along **Kaneohe Bay**, near Kaneohe Beach County Park on the windward coast, making wade-fishing enjoyable here. However, these fish are not to be eaten either. Also, you'll have to watch out for Portuguese Man-O-War and other jellyfish (apply meat tenderizer or urine if you do get stung) and be sure to wear good sunglasses, a hat or visor, sneakers, a long-sleeved shirt and long pants. Tide pools lie in waiting for those who slosh through the flats and climb over jagged reefs.

FISHING SAFETY TIP

You may see locals fishing from cliffs, such as at a spot near Hanauma Bay, but I don't recommend your trying this yourself since it can be very dangerous. The edges of precipices can be extremely slippery; and unexpectedly high waves can suddenly burst up from the ocean.

Glider Plane Rides

Through **Glider Rides/Honolulu Soaring Club**, *Tel. 677-3404,* the operation with the most experience, you can take an exhilarating 20- to 30-minute glider plane ride from Dillingham Airfield at Mokuleia, near the polo grounds on the North Shore. A tow plane pulls the glider into the sky, then releases it. Wrapped in silence (since there's no motor), you'll float over gentle hills, the rugged Waianae Mountains, deep valleys, sugarcane fields, and long broad Mokuleia Beach.

During the winter, you might even spot whales. You can generally see for more than 40 miles and sometimes as far as 80 miles, to the island of Kauai. The pilot will take you up by yourself (about $60) or with a (very good or very slim) friend (about $45 each) – quarters are extremely close for two passengers! Gliders fly seven days a week; there are only about 30 unflyable days a year. Be forewarned that occasionally people experience slight altitude sickness (drowsiness, headache, nausea). I got a slight case during my first glider flight, but the friend beside me was fine.

Golf

Oahu has more than 30 golf courses, the majority of which are open to the public. There are more courses here than on any of the Neighbor Islands. However, since Oahu receives more visitors, many tend to be crowded. **The Ko Olina Golf Club**, *Tel. 676-5300,* completed in early 1990, is an 18-hole championship links that sprawls on the leeward coast, near Ihilani Resort & Spa, about a half-hour drive from downtown Honolulu. The lakes and rock gardens make this green especially picturesque. Golfers have to drive their carts under a waterfall to get to the 12th hole! Because the municipal **Ala Wai Golf Course**, *Tel. 296-4653,* is right near Waikiki and offers a discount to seniors, it is quite popular and often packed. In fact, it made it into the *Guinness Book of World Records* as the busiest golf course in the world.

Vacationers will probably do better at the **Hawaii Kai** Executive Course or the Hawaii Kai Championship Course, *Tel. 395-2358 for both,* just east of Waikiki. Transportation from Waikiki is provided to and from the course at the **Sheraton Makaha Golf Club**, *Tel. 695-9511,* on the Waianae coast (40 minutes from the airport). This course is set in a picturesque valley where peacocks and other birds hang out. Also a distance from Waikiki, The Turtle Bay Hilton's **Links Kuilima**, *Tel. 293-8574*, is on the North Shore.

Waikiki's Hilton Hawaiian Village, *Tel. 949-4321*, offers golf packages in conjunction with Turtle Bay, including round-trip transportation, lunch, a cocktail, a T-shirt, and a chance to go swimming.

Helicopter

I recommend taking a helicopter ride on Oahu only if you're not going to Kauai, the Big Island, or Maui. Most flights are from 30 minutes (about $75) to an hour (about $150). You can make arrangements through your accommodation.

Hiking

Oahu is interlaced with many good hiking trails, several close to Waikiki. From the summit of **Diamond Head** crater, for instance, your eyes will take in Koko Head, Honolulu, the Waianae and Koolau mountains, and the ocean, among other sights. The trail to the top is clearly defined. A flashlight will come in handy when it's time to enter the tunnel used by the military during WWII. For a leisurely pace, allow about an hour going up and 45 minutes coming down. The interior of the crater is surprisingly lush.

Note that facilities, open from 6am to 6pm, include drinking water and bathrooms. Start out as early as possible, before the day gets too hot. The trailhead is about a 30-minute walk (or a quick public bus ride) from the heart of Waikiki. When you're finished with the hike to the summit, you may be as grateful as I was for a ride back to Waikiki in one of the motorized rickshaws waiting in the parking lot (for about the same price as a cab).

Other good trails near Waikiki are in the Makiki Valley, Tantalus Mountain, and Manoa Valley area. A hike through jungled vegetation will take you to **Manoa Falls**, a perfect spot for swimming and relaxing. Easily reached by bus, the **Kaneaole Trail** starts in Makiki Valley, turns west onto the **Makiki Valley Trail**, which cuts across the valley, then goes north on the Nahuina Trail, eventually coming to the Manoa Cliffs. From here you can take the **Puu Ohia Trail** northeast and go down into Manoa Valley via the **Aihualama Trail**.

Manoa Falls is less than a mile from here. The wind makes an eerie, musical sound as it blows through stands of bamboo. Bordering the trail, the leaves and branches of koa trees form a ceiling overhead. The roots of banyan trees drip to the ground like hair. Right before you reach Manoa Falls, you'll be yanked back into modern times with a view of Honolulu peeking through the woods. The trail out of the valley is just under a mile. You can catch a public bus back to Waikiki, or walk about three miles down Manoa Road to Waikiki.

Guava trees, red and pink mountain apples, and blood red Surinam cherries grow along the trails. Springs are hidden in the dense greenery off the paths. Job's tears are plentiful. Local people string this plant's white, black, and bluish-gray pellet-sized beans into rosaries and leis. Many birds hang out along the Manoa Cliffs Trail, including unusual native species such as the red and black *apapane* and the gray, black and white *elepaio*. You'll see plenty of eucalyptus, paperbark and bamboo trees on the **Puu Ohia Trail**. At the end of this trail, just beyond the turnoff for descending the Aihualama into Manoa Valley, you'll come to a dramatic sweeping view of Nuuanu Valley, the Pali Highway and a reservoir.

Kaena Point, the northwestern tip of Oahu, can be reached from either the North Shore or the leeward (Waianae) coast. From the leeward side, the two-hour, three-mile hike begins at Yokohama Beach (also known as Keawaula), a popular surfing spot. With the craggy cliffs to your right, you'll pass natural arches, caves, and places where the ocean spurts into the air like water from a whale's spout. At Barking Sands Beach (Kepuhi Point and Keaau Beach), the sand squeaks underfoot.

Approaching Kaena from Mokuleia on the wetter windward (North) coast, you'll pass cliffs (to the left) that are much greener than on the leeward side, and many more colorful flowers. Dramatic rock formations are interspersed with indigenous plants, salt pans, tide pools, sandy beaches and trails into mountain gulches. Look into the sky, and you might see hang gliders floating down from the cliffs.

Horseback Riding

With **Koko Crater Equestrian Center**, *Tel. 395-2628*, the trail cuts across Koko Head crater, not far from Waikiki.

At **Kualoa Ranch and Activity Center**, *Tel. 237-8515 or 237-7321*, in lush Kaaawa Valley on the windward coast (across from Kualoa Beach Park), you can take trail rides or participate in the deluxe action package that combines horseback riding with a helicopter whirl, a dune buggy (ATV) ride, snorkeling, scuba, and other fun. There's also a standard package, which doesn't include the scuba and helicopter ride. For all packages, the horses cost $10 extra.

If you've always wanted to trot along a beach, try the **Turtle Bay Hilton** resort, *Tel. 293-8811*, on the northern windward coast. You'll ride through 75 rolling green acres. Rates run about $32 per person for 45 minutes to an hour. **New Town and Country Stables**, *Tel. 259-9941*, in Waimanalo, is also worth checking out.

Jogging

A well-pounded 4.8-mile route circles **Diamond Head**, near Waikiki, passing the Diamond Head Lighthouse, and affording views of the ocean, as well as of ritzy residential neighborhoods. Enclosing Waikiki like parentheses, **Kapiolani and Ala Moana parks** also attract many joggers. On Sundays from March through November, you're welcome to join runners preparing the December **Honolulu Marathon**. Meet at the Kapiolani bandstand in the park at 7:30am. If you're up to the Marathon itself, join the crush, *Tel. 734-7200*. Running along the mile-and-a-half **Ala Wai Canal**, you might pass outrigger canoe teams preparing for competitions.

As far as the rest of Oahu goes, don't jog in remote areas, no matter how scenic. Call the **Running Room**, *Tel. 737-2422*, for tips on the safest and most appealing routes.

Kayaking

At **Twogood Kayaks**, *Tel. 262-5656*, in Kailua, you can rent a one-person kayak for $22 for a half day or $28 for a full day and two-person tandem kayaks for $29 for a half day or $39 for a full day, including free delivery and a lesson. Tandem kayaks can be rented for $145 for five days and $195 for seven days. Guided tours can also be arranged.

'Cuda Kayaks, *Tel. 261-8424*, charges only $20 for a single or $35 for a double for a full day. This company is based in Kailua as well.

Also see "Waimea Valley/Waimea Falls Park" in *Seeing the Sights*.

Parasailing

One of the most thrilling experiences I've ever had, parasailing is available on Oahu through **Waikiki Beach Services**, *Tel. 924-4941*, **Hawaii Kai Parasail**, *Tel. 396-9224*, **Aloha Parasail**, *Tel. 521-2446*, **Sea Breeze Parasailing**, *Tel. 396-0100*, and **Big Sky Parasail**, *Tel. 396-9224 or 396-0564*.

Rates run about $45 to $50 for 10 minutes in the air. What's parasailing? It's being strapped to a parachute that is tied to a boat by a long rope and floating high into the sky as the boat takes off. Coming back to earth is no problem. The boat slows down and you simply have to walk forward as your feet touch solid ground.

Sailing

On Waikiki Beach, you can arrange to sail on catamarans through concessions and "beach boys." Many sunset, moonlight, and dinner cruises leave from Kewalo Basin, not far from Waikiki. Sailing lessons are available through **Tradewind Charters**, *Tel. 973-0311*. To learn, plan to spend about $35 an hour for one person, plus $2 for each additional person, up to four. Transportation from Waikiki can be worked out. Tradewind also hosts a cozy three-hour sunset sail for up to six people for about $60 per person, including *pupus*, champagne, and non-alcoholic drinks.

Scuba Diving

You can learn to dive through **Dan's Dive Shop**, *Tel. 536-6181*, which offers a four-day certification course for about $300, as well as a $70 dive excursion on a catamaran.

The scuba course for beginners given by **South Seas Aquatics**, *Kapahulu Avenue, Tel. 735-0437*, runs about $100, including equipment; also at *Kalakaua Avenue, Tel. 922-0852.*

Tradewind Charters, Tel. 973-0311, also hosts scuba sails.

Other good scuba operations are Waikiki Diving Inc., Kalakaua Avenue, Tel. 955-5151 or 955-6766, and Aaron's Dive Shop, *Tel. 262-2333 or 261-1211, Fax 808/ 262-4158*, in Kailua. Aaron's also two other locations: *98-406 Kamehameha Highway, Tel. 487-5533*, and *Building 9, Camp Smith, Tel. 477-0514.*

Snorkeling

Many hotels have snorkeling equipment for rent or loan. While this water sport may seem intimidating to the uninitiated, it is actually very simple. Anyone can catch on in just a few minutes. If you've never tried it, ask someone who has snorkeled before to demonstrate. Or, if you take a snorkeling cruise or other snorkeling excursion, you'll get a lesson that prepares you to take the plunge.

Hanauma Bay ($6 admission) is Oahu's premier snorkeling site, which means it is always crowded (unless you arrive very early in the morning). This gorgeous, palm-studded crescent (its name means "curved bay") is cupped at the bottom of mountains. When you arrive, you'll be high above the water, but the plentiful coral, interspersed with smooth patches of sand, is clearly visible through the glasslike blue water. A tram can take you down to the beach, but most people choose to walk. Be sure to wear rubber-soled shoes or dive booties in the water, because the coral can give nasty cuts.

Many small pools between coral reefs are packed with fish, from longnose butterfly fish and moorish idols to potter's angelfish and iridescent parrotfish. Surviving on a diet of frozen peas, popcorn, and bread nibbled from human hands, they all stay happily plump. Walk around a slippery ledge to the left of the path down to the water, and you'll come to the **Toilet Bowl**, a pocket where water "flushes" in and out with the tides. But be careful, since the rush of water can be powerful.

There are various ways to get to Hanauma Bay, in addition to driving yourself. The city bus, *Tel. 848-5555*, will drop you off at the top of the hill for $1 or you can take the Red and Black Bus ($1), which will leave you right at the bay. Be sure to rent snorkel gear from your hotel or at Waikiki Beach before you get here. A trip with **Hanauma Bay Snorkeling Tours**, *Tel. 944-8828*, runs about $18. Transportation to and from the site and equipment are provided. It costs $12 if you use your own gear.

Dan's Dive Shop, *Tel. 536-6181*, organizes a half-day snorkeling excursion off shore near Ala Moana beach for about $28; **Tradewind Charters**, *Tel. 973-0311*, offers an upscale half-day snorkel and sail for about $70.

Spectator Sports

If you really want to feel like a local, join the sidelines for some of Oahu's most exciting sports:

On the North Shore during the winter, watch the **Triple Crown Hawaiian Pro Surfing Championships**. Lasting for two days, this spectacle takes place in November or December; the days chosen depend on how the waves are behaving. The locale is usually the Banzai Pipeline and Sunset Beach, which turns into a big party. Newspapers will keep you up to date.

Over two weekends every March, **Buffalo's Annual Big Board Surfing Classic**, *Tel. 696-3878*, takes place on Makaha Beach, on the Waianae coast. The atmosphere is also festive, with food galore and Hawaiian music.

In Hawaii, surfing is not limited to boards. Canoe surfing is also a big deal. Held on the first day after May 1 that the surf reaches at least 10 feet, the **Annual King Kamehameha Cup/Canoe Surfing Championship** takes place in Waikiki. Waikiki is also the site of the **Annual Ala Wai Canoe Challenge**, *Tel. 923-1802*, in January. After racing on the canal, paddlers take to land to compete in ancient Hawaiian games at the Ala Wai Field. In October, there's an outrigger canoe race from Molokai to Oahu.

Over Thanksgiving weekend, New Town and Country Stables, *Tel. 259-9941*, puts on a raucous **rodeo** that draws cowboys from the rest of the state and from the mainland.

At Makapuu Point, near Sea Life Park at the southeastern tip of the island, you can watch daring folks **hang gliding** off the cliffs.

If you ever thought Hawaii seemed too exotic to be part of the United States, just wait until football season and you'll have no doubts about Oahu's American heritage. The cream of the NFL crop plays the **Pro Bowl at Aloha Stadium** in Honolulu a week after the Super Bowl. College teams knock each other around here during the December Aloha Bowl. The January **Hula Bowl**, *Tel. 956-4852*, pits All-American college superstars against each other. Half-time erupts with hula and music, and tailgate parties flood the parking lot. During the season, the University of Hawaii Rainbows tear up the stadium, cheered by huge crowds. Express bus service is frequently offered from Kapiolani Park in Waikiki, *Tel. 848-5555.*

Volleyball is big in beach parks.

During the December **Honolulu Marathon**, *Tel. 734-7200*, spectators cheer runners at the Kapiolani Park finish line. The **Pan Am Hawaiian Windsurfing World Cup** is held in July at Kailua Beach on the windward coast. Check newspapers for periodic windsurfing competitions off Diamond Head Point.

Every February, the **PGA Hawaiian Open Golf Tournament** draws thick crowds to the upscale Waialae Country Club, *Tel. 734-2151*, not far from Waikiki.

The country's best basketball players are divided into four teams for the **Aloha Basketball Classic** at Honolulu's Neal Blaisdell Center, *Tel. 948-7523*, every April.

Surfing

On Waikiki Beach, "beach boys" working independently (with Parks Department approval), hang out to teach people to surf for about $12 an hour. From time to time, free lessons are sponsored by the Honolulu Department of Parks and Recreation, *Tel. 523-4523*.

Point Panic is a popular surfing spot near Kewalo Basin (also referred to as Fisherman's Wharf).

Most board-lovers agree that the best surfing in Hawaii is along Oahu's North Shore, from Hale'iwa to Kahuku. However, only experts should attempt to handle these monster curls. Each winter this area is pounded by some of the tallest, most shapely waves anywhere. The international surfing masters flock here each December and January for the **Triple Crown**. Each of these three contests takes five days.

The competitions kick off at the Banzai Pipeline, Sunset Beach, Waimea Bay and/or other prime surfing spots.

Yokohama and Makaha, on the northern Waianae coast, are other good locales for the sport.

Tennis

Hotels with tennis courts give guests first priority, but most are available for the use of non-guests as well. One of the seven courts at the **Ilikai Hotel Nikko Waikiki**, *Tel. 949-3811*, in Waikiki is lit for night play, and you can learn the game or improve your techniques at the frequent tennis clinics. Lessons are also available at the two courts of the **Pacific Beach Hotel**, *Tel. 922-1233*, in Waikiki, as well as at the one court at

Waikiki's **Hawaiian Regent Hotel**, *Tel. 922-6611*. Also in the Waikiki area, **Ala Moana Park**, *Tel. 594-7031*, has ten free public tennis courts; the **Diamond Head Tennis Center**, *Tel. 971-7150*, has 10; and **Kapiolani Park** is home to four.

Water Skiing

Try **Suyderhoud Water Ski Center**, *Tel. 395-3773*.

Windsurfing

One of the best places to rent equipment, take lessons, and go on group sails in **Naish Hawaii**, *Tel. 262-6068 or 261-6067*, based in Kailua, on the southeastern windward coast. This outfit is run by Robby Naish, a world champion windsurfer, and his family.

You might also try **Windsurfing Hawaii**, *Tel. 261-3539*, in Kailua as well; or **Surf 'n Sea**, *Tel. 637-9887*, in Hale'iwa, on the North Shore.

Working Out & Spas

If you want to keep up with your exercise program or visit a spa, consider staying at Hilton Hawaiian Village, the Halekulani Hotel, The Royal Hawaiian, Sheraton Moana Surfrider, Sheraton Waikiki, or Sheraton Princess Ka'iulani (all in Waikiki), or Ihilani Resort and Spa on the Leeward coast. All of these resorts have fitness centers for the use of guests. Programs and facilities include weight rooms, exercise bikes and aerobics classes. At Ihilani, and extensive roster of spa treatments is available, from massages to body wraps.

Another option is the gym in the **Pacific Beach Hotel** on Kapiolani Boulevard in Waikiki, *Tel. 973-4653*. You can work out for a daily rate of $10 if you show a hotel key. There is a full complement of body building equipment and machines. Classes include Step, Power Jam, Abs & Back, and Basic Yoga.

Or look into the **Clark Hatch Physical Fitness Center**, *Tel. 536-7205*, in Honolulu, which lures the health-conscious set with its indoor pool, racquetball court, treadmills, weight-training machines, and aerobics classes.

SHOPPING

Stores on Oahu are as varied as the island itself. Crowded, jumbled T-shirt shops share Waikiki streets with **Gucci** and **Tiffany**. Most of Oahu's stores are found in Waikiki, and these (whether in hotels or on the street) tend to be more expensive than elsewhere on the island.

Selling everything from food, juice, and liquor to suntan oil, beach towels, and *zoris* (rubber flip-flops), **ABC drug stores** are on practically every block; but beware: when items here are not on sale, they can be quite a bit more expensive than at other stores.

Many say that **Long's**, another drug store chain, often has the best buys in macadamia nuts and Kona coffee. Note that the majority of the goods at the International Marketplace in Waikiki are not made in Hawaii.

Locals frequent **Ala Moana Center**, **Pearl Ridge Shopping Center**, and **Kahala Mall**.

There are so many shops on Oahu that you'll certainly stumble onto your own favorites. Starting with malls, here are a few of the stores, outlets, and goods that have made the greatest impression on me.

ARTFUL SHOPPING

My favorite place to shop is Hale'iwa, the quiet North Shore former plantation town with weathered wooden buildings dating back to the 1920s and earlier. The clothing, jewelry and artwork in the many boutiques here are some of the most imaginative I've seen on Oahu.

Shopping Malls

Residents go to **Ala Moana Center**, *1450 Ala Moana Boulevard, Honolulu*, about five minutes from Waikiki by bus. Said to be the world's biggest open-air mall, this place is packed with nearly two hundred shops and almost two dozen restaurants. Liberty House, Hawaii's answer to Macy's, draws crowds here, and many enjoy browsing through **Shirokiya**, a Japanese department store filled with clothing, housewares, and food. The mall's ultra-snazzy **808 Palm Boulevard** section, the Rodeo Drive of Honolulu, attracts big spenders to its designer boutiques.

Appealing mainly to tourists, **Aloha Tower Market Place**, *101 Ala Moana, Honolulu*, has a variety of shops. A good bet in Waikiki is the **Royal Hawaiian Shopping Center**, where singers and other musicians provide free entertainment. From the ground floor flower stand, you can **mail a coconut** back to the mainland. Magic markers are provided for you to write the address and a message directly on the nut. Your friends back home are sure to get a kick out of this tropical postcard. Coconuts here range in price from about $1 to $2.50 and mailing will set you back another $4.50 or so (unless you take the coconut upstairs to the post office where you can mail it for a bit less).

For discounts, **Waikele Center**, an outlet mall, is popular with visitors and locals, even though it is away from the center of things.

The upscale **Ward Centre**, *1200 Ala Moana Boulevard, Honolulu*, is not to be confused with the older, plainer Ward Warehouse a block away. The sophisticated shops and restaurants of Ward Centre are trimmed in oak, with brass railings, and are set off by hand-carved wooden signs, brick walkways, wooden columns and stained-glass light fixtures and hanging lamps. On Fridays, once a month, you can shop to live jazz in the garden courtyard, with complimentary wine and pupus, from 5 to 7pm.

Down the street, **Ward Warehouse,** *1050 Ala Moana Boulevard, Honolulu,* at the corner of Ward Avenue, is across from Kewalo Basin. Here you'll find a worthwhile selection of shops selling everything from hand blocked batik clothing to Hawaiian coffee and tea. Monthly entertainment is offered in the 300-seat amphitheater. Annual events include a Japanese cultural festival in June and the Hawaiian Anthurium Society Show each Easter weekend.

Aloha Wear

While it's difficult to turn a corner without running into a store selling aloha shirts and muumuus, most stock the mass-produced polyester versions. Many locals love the muumuus with contemporary flair (more fitted than the usual billowy style) designed by **Mamo Howell.** Her creations are sold at Ward Warehouse, among other places. **Reyn's** (at the Kahala Mall) sells aloha wear in toned-down colors and less busy designs. For high quality apparel, try **Bailey's Antique Clothing Shop,** *517 Kapahulu Avenue,* where you'll find scores of tasteful designs by local shirt makers. Vintage shirts can run you anywhere from $30 to $500. Old rayon prints with buttons made of coconut shells are the most expensive.

Hilo Hattie's Fashion Center used to be known for snagging busloads of tourists to browse through its commercial-looking polyester aloha wear. However, this company has recently upgraded its product-line considerably, so I'd say its worth checking out.

Art Galleries

Many of Honolulu's best art galleries are in Chinatown. Some streets here are slowly being gentrified. Galleries began moving in during the 1980s, since rents were low and rental units were more spacious than in other parts of the city.

The Pegge Hopper Gallery, *1164 Nuuanu Avenue, Tel. 524-1160,* exhibits the work of one of Hawaii's most popular artists. Hopper's warm paintings of caramel-colored Hawaiian women dressed in mauve, oranges, purples and reds grace many a hotel wall, especially in the Neighbor Islands. Some works by other Island artists are clear examples that imitation is a synonym for flattery.

The Ramsay Galleries and Cafe, *1128 Smith Street, Tel. 537-2787,* with its tranquil garden, hosts group shows in a building that is a National Historic Landmark.

The Fine Art Associates at the Ad Loft, *1020 Auahi Street, Tel. 591-2489,* also showcases many local artists in solo and small group exhibitions. Whimsical handmade jewelry is sold here as well.

Wyland Galleries Hawaii, *66-150 Kamehameha Highway, Hale'iwa, Tel. 637-7498,* is a good example of all the creative juices that flow in Hale'iwa, the quiet, picturesque town on Oahu's less developed North Shore. With its beautifully landscaped garden and stone-paved pathway at the entrance, **Galerie Lassen,** *62-540 Kamehameha Highway, Hale'iwa, Tel. 637-8866,* seems a bit too glitzy for funky Hale'iwa. But you'll find a wide selection of sculpture and paintings inside.

Beach Wear & Water Sports Gear

Among the many boutiques vying for the attention of the beach-going crowd, **Local Motion,** *1714 Kapiolani Boulevard, Tel. 955-7873,* or *Koko Marina Shopping Center, Tel. 396-7873,* stands out with its brightly colored bathing suits, shorts, and tops guaranteed to bring smiles to many faces. For bathing suits, also visit **Tres Sea,** *Tel. 637-1241 in Hale'iwa and Tel. 263-3572 in Kailua,* which carries hand painted clothing as well, and **More or Less Beachwear,** *Tel. 637-6859,* and **Oogenesis Boutique,** *Tel. 637-4580,* all in Hale'iwa.

You can prepare for the lower depths at **South Seas Aquatics,** *1600 Ala Moana Boulevard, Tel. 949-5447 and 2155 Kalakaua Avenue, Tel. 922-0852.*

Crafts

In June, around July 4th, and in late November or early December, Honolulu's **Mission Houses Museum** hosts wonderful crafts fairs. You'll find everything from silk-screened and tie-dyed T-shirts and dresses, Hawaiian quilts, delicate hand washable silk scarves, and ethnic foods (such as German sausages) to koa wood necklaces (selling for $65 and $95) and Niihau shell necklaces ($3,000 to $5,000!). Check newspapers for the **Pacific Handcrafters Guild fairs,** held four times a year in Honolulu. Five days a week, there's a major **flea market** by Aloha Stadium. The Pearl City bus will take you there. Kam Drive-In, another popular flea market, is 20 minutes from Waikiki on the Pearl City bus.

If you've been searching high and low for knickknacks in the shape of food, try **Something Special,** *Kahala Mall or Windward Mall,* or various crafts fairs. You'll find ceramic sushi, manapua (Chinese rice pastry), and fortune cookies.

Magnets by Ruthie, *c/o Pacific Handcrafters Guild, P.O. Box 90663, Honolulu, HI. 96835, Tel. 254-6788,* creates sushi magnets, pseudo shave ice, and other realistic looking goods. Prices for these items range from about $4 to $15. For hand-painted, life-size wooden birds of paradise and other beautiful flowers, check out **Oceania** in Hale'iwa.

Hawaiian Art Deco

The bold colors and tropical flora and fauna designs of the 1920s and '30s live on in etched glasses, china vases, glass platters, decorated sheet music, jewelry, old travel posters, and worn newspaper ads sold in various Oahu stores. An appealing selection of art deco goods is on sale at **Corner Loft**, *Kahala Mall, Tel. 732-4149.*

For Hawaiiana, clothing, and jewelry, **Bailey's Antiques and Aloha Shirts**, *517 Kapahulu Avenue, Tel. 734-7628*, is worth a shot. Also try **Linda's Vintage Isle** in Waikiki, *373 Olohana Street, Honolulu, Tel. 942-9517*. If you're in the market for jewelry, **Mellows Antiques**, *841 Bishop Street, Honolulu, Tel. 533-6313*, is a good choice.

Hawaiian Quilts

Nineteenth-century Hawaiian women took what American missionaries taught them and added their unique Island stamp to quilt making. Antique quilts are collectors' items and museum pieces. New ones can cost thousands of dollars.

A good place to buy Hawaiian quilts and pillows is **Elizabeth's Fancy**, *767B Kailua Road, Kailua, Tel. 262-7513*. **Quilts Hawaii**, *2338 South King Street, Honolulu, Tel. 942-3195*, also has some quilts in stock. However, much of its business comes from commissioned bed covers and wall hangings. Queen-size quilts begin at about $3,800, while one for a king-size bed can run you $4,500 to $5,000. Expect to wait up to two years for completion. But once you've laid out the money and the time, you'll have a beautiful piece of usable artwork, something to be passed down for countless generations.

Hawaiiana

After roaming around the fascinating exhibits at the **Bishop Museum**, *Tel. 847-3511*, in Honolulu, be sure to spend some time in the gift shop. You'll find gorgeous bowls made of koa and monkeypod, books from the Bishop Museum press, riveting photos of old Hawaii that beg to be framed, attractive cards, tasteful T-shirts and preserves made from passion fruit, guava and mango. More wooden calabashes (carved bowls) are for sale at **Native Books & Beautiful Things**, *Merchant Street in downtown Honolulu, Tel. 599-5511*. This wonderful shop also sells woven baskets, quilts, and other crafts made by Hawaiian artists, along with books by and about Hawaiians.

Jewelry

In Hale'iwa, a good target for distinctive earrings and other jewelry is **Raising Cane**, *Tel. 637-3337.* (Also see Hawaiian Art Deco, Unusual Clothing, and Art Galleries in this section.)

Kites

With hundreds of different designs, **High Performance Kites**, *1400 Kapiolani Boulevard, Honolulu, Tel. 942-8799,* and *1450 Ala Moana Boulevard, Honolulu, Tel. 947-7097,* has kites that range in price from $5 to more than $200. On weekends, it is not uncommon to find the store owner or staff members giving demonstrations and kite repair assistance at Sandy Beach Park.

Just across the street from Kapiolani Park in Waikiki, **Kite Fantasy**, *2863 Kalakaua Avenue, Tel. 922-5483,* gives free kite-flying lessons, even to non-buying patrons. At the quiet Diamond Head end of Waikiki, this shop sells every thing from the simple to the elaborate. They even have the two-stringed variety that you can steer. This is a good place to get your kite for the annual festival in Kapiolani Park, held each March.

Koa Wood Products

Native koa is probably Hawaii's most prized wood. Its rich burnt-orange color and beautiful grain make it especially attractive for hand-crafted clocks, bowls, pencil jars, jewelry boxes, and, of course, furniture. Places to shop for koa goods include **Martin & MacArthur**, *841 Bishop Street, Honolulu, Tel. 524-4434;* **House of Kalai**, *1812 Auiki Street in Kalihi, Honolulu, Tel. 841-2623;* **Hawaiian Heritage**, *2870 Ualena Street, Honolulu, Tel. 839-6656;* and **Irene's Hawaiian Gifts**, *Ala Moana Center, Shop #1251, 1450 Ala Moana Boulevard, Honolulu, Tel. 946-6818.* (Also see Hawaiiana in this section.)

Kona Coffee

Long's and **ABC drug stores** frequently have good sales on a variety of blends, as well as pure Kona.

Leis

These fresh-flower garlands may seem corny or touristy to outsiders, but among residents of Hawaii these fragrant necklaces are worn and taken quite seriously. Some of the best and least expensive are found at the stands sprinkled throughout Chinatown, such as **Sweetheart's Lei Shop**, *69 North Beretania, Tel. 537-3011.* You'll also see lei shops all over Waikiki, but the selection isn't as good and the prices are higher.

Macadamia Nuts

Macadamia nuts are sold everywhere in Hawaii, from hotels to drug stores. The **Long's** and **ABC chains** keep their prices comparatively low. **The Hawaii Country Store**, *2201 Kalakaua Avenue, Waikiki, Tel. 922-6437*, also has good prices and stocks a wide variety of macadamia nuts, from candy-coated and chocolate-dipped to naked.

Natural Foods

Many people renting cottages or condos are drawn to **Celestial Natural Foods**, *66-443 Kamehameha Highway, Hale'iwa, Tel. 637-6729*, on the North Shore. There's a small cafe on the premises. In addition to sandwiches, salads, homemade cookies and Tofutti to go, you'll find shelves stocked with goodies including lehua blossom and macadamia honey; pregnancy, male vitality, and laxative tea; cranberry-apple or apple-apricot sauce; sea vegetable chips; and brown rice flakes cereal.

Pineapples

At **Fresh From Hawaii** kiosks, scattered around Waikiki, you can arrange to have freshly picked, boxed pineapple delivered to the airport upon your departure or sent straight to the mainland. To have three pineapples waiting for you at the airport, plan to pay about $9. It will cost you about $25 to have three sent to the mainland; they'll travel by air-courier and will arrive within two or three days.

Pottery

One of Oahu's most distinctive types of ceramics is *raku*, a 400-year-old Japanese art. The tradition is being carried on by **Gail Bakurtis, Potter**, *Pokai Bay Street in Waianae, Tel. 696-3878*, **Jeff Chang Pottery**, *550 Queen Street, Tel. 538-6447*; **Tropical Clay**, *470 North Nimitz Highway, Tel. 537-2492*; **Nohea Gallery**, *Ward Warehouse, 1050 Ala Moana Boulevard*; **Art a la Carte**, *the Ward Centre, 1200 Ala Moana Boulevard*; and the **Elephant Walk**, *Ala Moana Center, 1450 Ala Moana Boulevard, Honolulu*. Also check out **Guild Craft Fairs**, *Tel. 254-6788*.

T-Shirts

With half a dozen Waikiki outlets packed with amusing, imaginative, and colorful designs, Crazy Shirts gets lots of attention, even in T-shirt City (a.k.a. Waikiki). I find the cotton tees here of much higher quality than at many other shops. Another good place to consider stopping is the large **flea market** in the Aloha Stadium parking lot. It's open five days a week, and you can get there by the Pearl City bus. Various craft fairs, such as those held by the **Pacific Handcrafters Guild**, have wide selections too.

Unusual Clothing

At **Montsuki**, *1148 Koko Head Avenue, Tel. 734-3457,* Janet and Patty Yamasaki, mother and daughter, design and make women's and men's clothing incorporating traditional kimono fabric that is anywhere from 15 to 25 or even 100 years old. In a marriage of styles from the East and West, they use silk and satin, sometimes combining the material of two or three different kimonos in one outfit. Most of the cloth comes from Japan, but they also import fabrics from India and other countries, always keeping an eye out for unusual natural materials. At **Anne Namba Designs, Inc.**, *2964E Manoa Road, Honolulu, Tel. 988-9361* (in the Manoa section of Honolulu), browse among contemporary one-of-a-kind women's fashions created from Japanese kimonos as well.

In **Hale'iwa**, on the quiet North Shore, **Raising Cane**, *Tel. 637-3337,* sells colorful women's and children's sportswear and bathing suits hand painted by the owner. Also in this town, **Kaala Art**, *Tel. 637-7065,* carries gorgeous Tahitian pareos, Cambodian silk sarongs and Thai embroidered hats; and **Oogenesis Boutique**, *Tel. 637-4580,* sells great dresses, shirts, and bags for women. You'll find African clothing and jewelry at **Patali African Creations**, *44-171 Nanamoana Street, Kaneohe, Tel. 235-1077,* run by designer Beatrice Ainsworth, originally from Malawi, East Africa. Also check out the various crafts fairs held by the **Pacific Handcrafters Guild**, *Tel. 254-6788.*

PRACTICAL INFORMATION

Emergencies

If you have an emergency, call *Tel. 911.*

Medical Attention

You don't need an appointment to be seen by one of the physicians participating in the 24-hour **Doctors on Call** program, *Tel. 971-6000.* If necessary, doctors will come to your hotel or condo. Twenty-four hour clinics are set up at the **Outrigger Waikiki**, *Tel. 971-6000,* and some other hotels.

Hospitals are **Queen's Medical Center**, *1301 Punchbowl Street, Honolulu, emergency: Tel. 547-4311, main number: Tel. 538-9011;* **Staub Clinic**, *888 South King Street, Honolulu, Tel. 522-4000;* and **Kapiolani Medical Center for Women and Children**, *1319 Punahou Street, Honolulu, emergency: Tel. 947-8633, main number: Tel. 973-8511.*

Those who wish to try acupuncture, the highly successful ancient Chinese healing technique, should make an appointment at the **Waikiki Acupuncture Clinic**, *2255 Kuhio Avenue, Suite 742, Waikiki, Tel. 923-6939.*

For outpatient care, the **Honolulu Clinic**, *1010 Pensacola Street, Honolulu, Tel. 593-2950*, provides a range of ambulatory services including Urgent Care.

Post Offices

The branch closest to most hotels is the one in Waikiki's Fort DeRussy on Saratoga Avenue. Some shopping centers, such as the Royal Hawaiian on Kalakaua Avenue, and some hotels have post office branches as well. Most are open from 8am to 4:30pm. For the branch nearest you, call *Tel. 423-3990*.

Surf Report

To find out where the best waves are, call *Tel. 836-1952*.

Tourist Information

The state's main office of the **Hawaii Visitors & Convention Bureau** (HVCB), *2270 Kalakaua Avenue, 8th floor, Honolulu, HI 96815, Tel. 923-1811*, is located on Waikiki's thoroughfare. Hours are 8am to 4:30pm, Monday through Friday.

12. MAUI

The second-largest member of the Hawaiian archipelago, at roughly 729 square miles, Maui is also the second-most visited. It is named for the demi-god who stood on the rim of 10,023-foot **Haleakala volcano** and snared the sun with a long rope to slow its journey across the sky. This Maui did because the fiery yellow ball sped by too swiftly for anyone to put in a good day's work. For instance, night always fell before the *kapa* cloth that women pounded from water-soaked bark had had a chance to dry.

Maui, the most built-up of the Neighbor Islands, has quickly developed as a Pacific Rim Center. It is now home to more millionaires than almost anywhere else. Drawing quite a few affluent travelers, some of its most luxurious accommodations are attractions in themselves. Many vacationing mainlanders – from surfing bums to yuppies and middle-aged couples – have turned into residents over the years.

Once actually two separate islands, Maui consists of two volcanic peaks divided by lush valleys thick with sugar cane and pineapple fields. From the air, it looks as if a pair of mountainous cookies, one much smaller than the other, had been placed too close together when they went into the oven. Maui's shape is sometimes described as the head and torso of a short-haired woman in profile. Her head forms West Maui, dominated by the West Maui Mountains. Her neck is the six-mile isthmus that slopes gently toward Mount Haleakala, which commands larger East Maui – her bust, shoulder and side.

Along with prime **scuba** and **snorkeling** sites, buff-colored beaches ring the island. Many young, fitness-oriented travelers are lured by the **mountain bike excursion** down Haleakala volcano, **horseback riding** in the crater, scenic **hiking** trails, good **camp sites,** and excellent waves and **windsurfing** breezes. Health-food stores and fruit stands do big business in avocado/alfalfa sprout sandwiches and smoothies (those California shakes made from fresh fruit and yogurt).

During the winter, Maui is the **whale-watching** capital of the state. Year-round, the historic, picturesque port town of **Lahaina** offers a

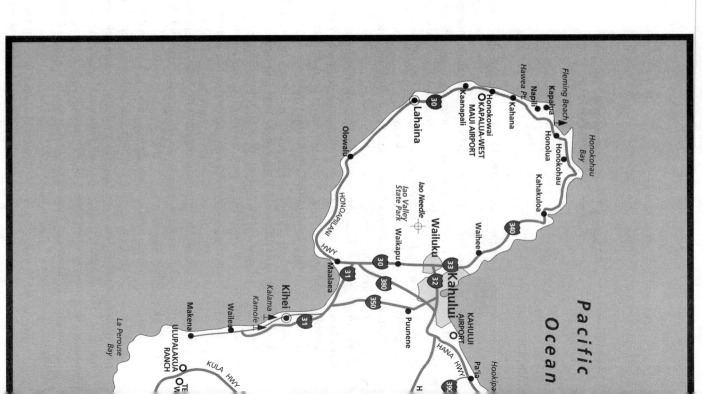

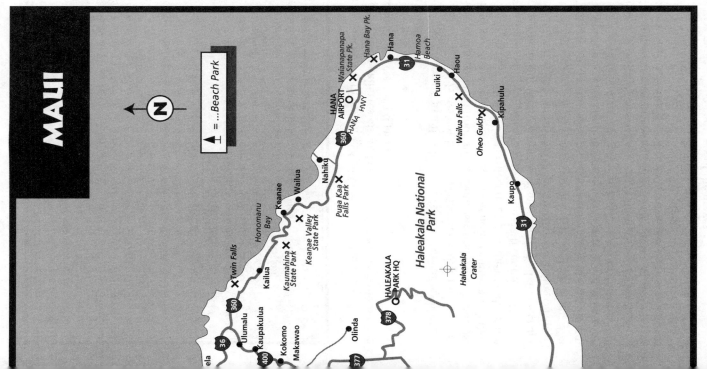

MAUI

N

⊥ = ...Beach Park

WHALE WATCHING

*From November through June, migrating **humpback whales** bound through Hawaiian waters. Maui provides the state's best vantage point, with hundreds coming to its waters. Growing as long as 45 feet and weighing as much as 40 tons, these are the fifth-largest of the great whales. Scientists believe that they travel the 3,000 miles from Alaska to breed in Hawaii's warmer climate, giving birth 12 months later. Baby whales weigh only about 2,000 pounds (!) and spend the winter fattening up off Maui's shores.*

*While whale-watching cruises depart several times a day from Lahaina and Ma'alaea harbors, conservationists encourage people to view these aquatic giants from land (and with a good pair of binoculars, you'll do just fine). The sound of so many people-packed boats can interfere with the whales' mating. If you're determined to view the whales by sea, try the two-and-a-half hour cruise run by the **Pacific Whale Foundation**, Tel. 879-8811, based in Kihei, on its research vessel. The money from your ticket will go toward the foundation's work.*

glimpse into Hawaii's 19th century whaling days. Maui also boasts quite a few worthwhile **art galleries**, as well as a vineyard where **wine tasting** takes place in an old converted jailhouse.

Hawaiian Roots

Despite the influx of mainlanders and other outsiders, pockets remain on Maui where Hawaiian is still the language of choice. Many Hawaiians live in and around flourishing **Hana**, isolated from the tourist centers. However, most remnants of the indigenous culture are found underground – literally. The earliest artifact dug up on the island, on the south side of East Maui, dates back to about the sixth century AD.

Here, as well as on other Hawaiian islands, periodic battles erupt among developers, archaeologists, and Hawaiians over building on and/or unearthing ancient burials and other sacred sites. A descendant of a missionary family, the late developer Colin Cameron was born on Maui. The chairman of the Maui Land & Pineapple Company, of which the Kapalua resort was a subsidiary, he had been known to contribute healthy sums of money to cultural causes and conservation projects. However, in 1986, he began making plans to build a beach front hotel, a Ritz-Carlton, at Honokahua, near Kapalua, on the northwest coast, at a well-known Hawaiian burial site. The Kapalua Land company started quietly conducting the archaeological study required before any building was done. The intent was to remove all the contents of the graves.

After a period of heated controversy, local Hawaiian activist groups finally gave in to the disinterment. Along with the Office of Hawaiian Affairs, they came to an agreement with the developers about the care and treatment of each artifact and set of bones. But once exhumations began, the remains of nearly 900 people were uncovered, some of whom had probably been buried as far back as 1,200 years ago. Also discovered were fish hooks, *ulu maika* (lawn bowling) stones, and rare shell jewelry. When the news of the number and antiquity of burials reached the Hawaiian community, outrage over the disturbance of the graves was refueled.

In late 1988, Hawaiians from all islands poured into Maui to participate in a 24-hour vigil at the site. The following week, a ceremony of mourning was held, highlighted by prayers and chants. It was not that other buildings hadn't been planted on sacred ground. But this project had become a symbol for what indigenous people would no longer tolerate. After another 24-hour vigil was held, this time in front of the Honolulu home of Governor John Waihee (Hawaii's first Hawaiian governor), the head of state called for a truce, and work on the project stopped.

Finally, in February 1989, Hannibal Tavares, Mayor of Maui County, reported that the activists and Colin Cameron had reached a new agreement. The site of the hotel would be moved inland, away from the burial mound, so that no more bones would be touched. The skeletons that had already been dug up would be reburied and the mound restored. This explains why the Ritz-Carlton Kapalua hotel is set back from the ocean.

ARRIVALS & DEPARTURES

Most travelers fly into **Kahului Airport**, just east of the neighboring towns of Kahului and Wailuku. Vans transport travelers between the Kahului Airport and Kaanapali. However, the smaller, newer **Kapalua-West Maui Airport** is convenient for many visitors since it is close to Kaanapali, Honokowai, Kahana, Napili, and Kapalua. Hana is reached by air from either airport or by car.

From Kahului, the ride to Lahaina is about 40 minutes; to Kaanapali, about 50 minutes; to Kihei, 20 minutes; to Wailea, 35 minutes; and to Makena, 45 minutes. Lahaina (about ten minutes south of Kaanapali) is some 45 to 50 minutes north of Kihei and Wailea and an hour from Makena. Small planes fly into **Hana Airport**, from both airports as well as from other Hawaiian islands.

Inter-island ferries connect Maui with Lanai. Call *Expeditions, Tel. 661-3756*, $25 each way, for schedules of the trips between Lahaina and Lanai.

ORIENTATION

The busiest sandy crescent, palm-studded **Kaanapali Beach**, is a younger, far less congested version of Oahu's Waikiki. Most of Maui's action – by day and by night – takes place here and in neighboring **Lahaina**, on the west coast. There's a wide array of restaurants, hotels and condominiums, along with excellent golf courses and tennis courts. The only problem with all these convenient diversions is that during the most popular seasons (the summer and Christmas through Easter), Kaanapali and Lahaina are jam-packed with tourists.

Those who find these vacation playgrounds too crowded can choose among several other quieter, less-developed resort areas. To the north are **Kapalua** and **Napili**, while **Kihei**, **Wailea**, and **Makena** lie to the south. Many of these resorts come complete with their own tennis courts and golf courses. And it's not difficult at all to find un-peopled strands along the miles of tranquil, beautiful beaches that stretch from Ma'alaea, on southern West Maui, to Makena, on southern East Maui. For the utmost in seclusion, head to remote **Hana**, on the far eastern coast of the island.

GETTING AROUND MAUI

By Shuttle Bus

Although Maui has no island-wide public transportation system, shuttle service is available to guests of various hotels. In Kaanapali, these buses run between accommodations, Whalers Village Shopping Center, and the town of Lahaina. Kapalua and Wailea also offer local bus service within each resort.

By Car

To see the rest of the island, you'll need to rent a car. Traffic along the roads connecting Lahaina, Kaanapali, and Kahului is particularly sluggish during rush hours. There is no road, at least not a driveable one, that will take you around the whole island of Maui. Therefore, you will find yourself doing a fair amount of back tracking if you plan to do extensive touring. Allow at least two hours from the Wailea area to the summit of Haleakala and about 2.5 hours from Lahaina.

A four-wheel-drive vehicle is best for getting to some of Maui's most scenic hideaways, such as Polipoli State Park, on the slopes of Haleakala volcano, the fishing village of Kahakuloa on West Maui, and La Perouse Bay, south of Makena resort. Although it is against rental agreements to take even four-wheel-drives onto unpaved roads, many visitors ignore these rules so as not to miss some of Maui's best sights.

Maui's car rental companies are quite competitive, so you can sometimes get away with paying under $30 a day for a compact car. Make your reservation as far ahead of your arrival as possible, especially if you're vacationing during the summer or between late December and the end of February.

By Guided Tour

If you'd rather leave the driving and guiding to someone else while you ramble around Maui, here are some tour operators who can accommodate you. Most transportation is air-conditioned.

The transportation offered by Maui's main tour companies ranges from hulking motor coaches to mini-vans and cozy limousines. Visitors are picked up either at their hotels or nearby. Be sure to ask about the size of the vehicle, the number of passengers, and the locations and number of stops so that there are no surprises once you climb aboard. The driver keeps up a constant commentary while you cruise along the road. Sometimes the jokes he or she must have told hundreds of times can wear on your nerves. On one bus tour, I thought I would scream if the driver asked us to repeat "Alo – HAH" one more time as we boarded and reboarded. However, visitors can usually cull intriguing and amusing bits of information from the drivers' good-natured chatter. Most people rip them about $1 per passenger.

There are four basic kinds of tours. Sometimes called the **Circle Island Tour** (even though none of these actually circles this expansive island), the first is a full-day excursion. It might include Iao Needle, the historic attractions in the town of Wailuku, and other parts of West and Central Maui. Other tours make stops at Haleakala volcano and upcountry, while still others throw in some good snorkeling. These tours cost about $40 to $70.

If you'd like to confine yourself to Haleakala and upcountry, these half-day tours – which usually include stops at Tedeschi Vineyards and Winery and a protea farm – cost about $50.

One of the most popular trips is the 6-hour **Haleakala Sunrise Tour**, which begins in the dark of night. By the time you reach the summit of the volcano, the sun will be ready to start coming up over the crater. A continental breakfast, sometimes with champagne, is served atop the mountain by some companies. The cost is about $60 to $75.

The van tours to **Hana**, the remote village at the end of a spectacular, jungled cliffside highway, can last nearly 12 hours. While these excursions call be exhausting, the scenery along the way is fabulous and you don't have to worry about dealing with the tricky twists and turns yourself. These tours cost about $55 to $86.

Maui's tour companies are based in Kahului. **No Ka Oi Scenic Tours**, *Tel. 871-9008*, conducts a popular Hana tour, including lunch. Other good outfits that run a variety of excursions are **Robert's Hawaii Tours**,

RENT A FRIEND

When you're away from home, what could be more fun than having friends take you to all their favorite places? If you don't know anyone on Maui, don't worry. When a couple I know recently vacationed here, they couldn't stop raving about Rent-A-Local. Tel. 877-4042, a personalized tour company based in Kahului. You can arrange to have a guide meet you at your hotel or condo and, in your rental car, drive you wherever you want to go. Guides are happy to share their favorite hideaways – secluded beaches, waterfalls, back roads, and other little-known scenic spots. If you like, they'll take you to meet residents (perhaps with similar interests, hobbies, or professions) at their homes. Begun by a part-Hawaiian woman, this behind-the-scenes manner of getting to know Maui has really caught on. Cost: $200 for the day for two people, $25 for each additional person.

Tel. 871 6226; Polynesian Adventure Tours, Tel. 877-4242 or 800/622-3011; and Trans Hawaiian, Tel. 877-7308 or 800/ 553-8765.

WHERE TO STAY

Some of Hawaii's most expensive accommodations can be found on Maui, where the majority of places to stay fall into the luxury category. However, before you turn to another island, note that there are also quite a few inexpensive-to-moderate sleeping quarters, including hotels, condominiums, B&Bs, and housekeeping cabins. In addition, even the more costly hotel rooms and condos can be quite economical if shared with friends.

Maui has more condos than anywhere else in Hawaii. These home-like units with kitchens are popular among many travelers, especially families. While most don't have restaurants or night spots, many condo complexes are on the beach and the majority come complete with pools and other hotel-style facilities and services. In most cases, these apartments are individually furnished by their owners, so units within a single complex may vary greatly in decor.

The island's tourism development began in earnest in the 1960s with the Kaanapali beach resort in West Maui. The 18-hole Kaanapali Golf Courses, the many tennis courts, and the profusion of water sports remain big draws. West Maui is the busiest visitor center today. Up north are the condos and hotels of upscale Kapalua and more down-to-earth Napili, Kahana, and Honokowai. Just south of Kaanapali, other accommodations are found in Lahaina, the picturesque old whaling port. Far quieter than Kaanapali and Lahaina, Wailea is a meticulously planned

MAUI'S BEST ROOMS

Cream of the Crop

Ritz-Carlton Kapalua, *Kapalua: Golf and serious pampering in a gorgeous, sprawling setting.*

Kapalua Bay Hotel, *Kapalua: This verdant, tranquil resort attracts golfers.*

Hyatt Regency Maui, *Kaanapali: The elaborate decor features Pacific and Asian art and artifacts.*

Westin Maui, *Kaanapali: An al fresco museum marries an aquatic playground.*

Grand Wailea Resort & Spa, *Wailea: Splashy and expansive, this one is packed with sculpture and other art.*

Four Seasons Resort Maui, *Wailea: This is quietly elegant.*

Kea Lani Hotel, Suites & Villas, *Wailea: Moorish architecture and upscale apartments make this one stand out.*

Hotel Hana Maui, *Hana: Expect rustic luxury in a lush, remote setting.*

Moderate or Inexpensive

One Napili Way, *Napili: This condo is bright and modern.*

Plantation Inn, *Lahaina: Victorian charm pervades this inn.*

Lahaina Inn, *Lahaina: Handsome antiques furnish this small hotel.*

Bloom Cottage B&B, *Kula: If you're looking for a cozy home away from home, this is it.*

Silver Cloud Upcountry Guest Ranch B&B, *Kula: This place puts a paniolo (cowboy) spin on a tropical vacation.*

resort area in East Maui. Though not nearly as pretty to look at, the accommodations in neighboring Kihei are less expensive than those elsewhere on the island. In arid, southern East Maui, posh Makena is the youngest resort. Apart from lush, isolated Hana, it is Maui's least developed tourist mecca.

Featured in Chapter 10, *Best Places to Stay.*

Kapalua

THE RITZ-CARLTON KAPALUA, *1 Ritz-Carlton Drive, Kapalua, HI 96761. Tel. 808/669-6200 or 800/262-8440, Fax 808/665-0026. 548 rooms. Double rooms begin at $285. Major credit cards.*

You'll find all kinds of extras - nightly turn down service; bathrobes; a marble bath with a separate shower and a telephone; mini bar and refrigerator; an in-room safe. On these fifty sprawling acres, you'll have several bars and excellent restaurants to choose from, along with tennis courts, and a three-level swimming pool. Sports include snorkeling, scuba diving, windsurfing, sailing, and hiking.

Set on a gentle slope above the white sand beach, the hotel borders one of Kapalua's three championship golf courses with views of the Pacific and the cloud-capped island of Molokai. Transportation between the airport and the hotel can be arranged.

KAPALUA BAY HOTEL, *1 Bay Drive, Kapalua, HI 96761. Tel. 808/669-5656 or 800/367-8000, Fax 808/669-4694. 196 rooms. Double rooms begin at $275. Major credit cards.*

Nestled at the shore in an area where tall pines stud grassy slopes, the Kapalua Bay Hotel has long been one of Maui's most tasteful resorts. With the renowned Halekulani corporation taking over its management, it is sure to maintain the highest standards of aesthetics, comfort, and service. The open-air lobby looks out to the pool and the ocean. Boutiques are found in a breezy arcade. The manicured grounds are set off by palms, bright flowers, a waterfall-fed stream, and a wooden footbridge over a pond. Parties are often held at the coconut grove by the beach. Guests enter their attractive, spacious rooms (with both air conditioners and ceiling fans) through wide double wooden doors. Baths are done in marble and (as is the trend with many of Hawaii's more expensive properties) are thoughtfully designed for simultaneous use by two people who don't want to get in each other's way: the twin sinks are opposite each other; there are bath a tub and a stall shower; and the toilet is in a separate room within the bath.

A couple of Maui's best restaurants are on the premises. The resort is also adjacent to three of the island's most challenging golf courses, and tennis courts and an exercise room are available. The year-round children's program gives parents a break. A shuttle bus provides transportation around the grounds.

THE KAPALUA VILLAS, *500 Office Road, Kapalua, HI 96761. Tel. 808/669-8088 or 800/545-0018, Fax 808/669-5235. 250 units. Rates begin at $185 per unit. Major credit cards.*

Looking like residential suburbia, various groups of villas are scattered across the sprawling grounds of this condominium complex. Some of the one- and two-bedroom units are elevated on verdant slopes, while others are closer to the water or the golf course. Handsome furnishings, modern kitchens, lofty ceilings with exposed beams, and spacious bathrooms make these apartments a pleasure to come home to. Guests are welcome to use all facilities of the Kapalua Resort, including the beaches, pools, golf courses, tennis courts, and shuttle bus. Hotel-style room service is even available in these villas.

LUXURIOUS ECO-TOURISM

If you're into saving the environment, but you also love living large and being pampered, consider one of the "Eco-Packages" offered by the three accommodations on the upscale Kapalua resort in West Maui. When you book a Golfer's Dream, Bed & Breakfast, Honeymoon, or other special package here, the hotel of your choice will donate a bit of your money to the **Nature Conservancy of Hawaii** for the preservation of Maui's plants, animals, and rainforests. Ask about the 2- to 5-mile guided hikes that include breakfast and lunch.

Contact the **Ritz-Carlton Kapalua**, Tel. 800/262-8440 or 808/669-6200; **Kapalua Villas**, Tel. 800/545-0018 or 808/669-8088; or **Kapalua Bay Hotel & Villas**, Tel. 800/367-8000 or 808/669-5656.

Napili

The boutiques, gourmet restaurants, golf, and tennis of the upscale Kapalua Resort are right next to more modest Napili.

NAPILI POINT, 5295 Honoapiilani Road, Lahaina, HI 96761. Tel. 808/669-9222 or 800/669-6252, Fax 808/669-7984. 115 units. Rates begin at $184 per condo. Major credit cards.

In each of these one- and two-bedroom condominium units, a private lanai affords a view of the ocean. While apartments aren't air conditioned, ceiling fans and tradewinds do the job just fine. Vanity areas and small bathrooms are adjacent to bedrooms, and irons and ironing boards are provided, along with washer-dryers. Kitchens contain microwaves, dishwashers, blenders, and coffee makers. Sports facilities include two freshwater swimming pools. Tennis and golf can be arranged in nearby Kapalua. Guests get to know each other at the manager's cocktail parties, nature walks and pineapple-cutting events. Inquire about car/condo packages.

NAPILI KAI BEACH CLUB, 5900 Honoapiilani Highway, Napili Bay, HI 96761. Tel. 808/669-6271 or 800/367-5030, Fax 808/669-0086. 162 rooms. Double rooms begin at $160. Major credit cards.

The extra touches in rooms are part of what makes this small, bay side hotel stand out in the crowd. Private lanais have views of the ocean. Located in low-rise buildings, rooms come with kitchenettes. Guests choose among four swimming pools, a jumbo whirlpool, two 18-hole putting greens, and golf and tennis at the nearby Kapalua resort. Ask about borrowing tennis racquets and snorkels and masks. Every week vacationers mingle at the manager's cocktail party and book ringside seats for the Hawaiian music and dance performance. The oceanfront (and economical) Sea House Restaurant and Whale Watcher's Bar are convenient to travelers.

During Easter, July, August, and Christmas time, the hotel offers free children's programs. Hawaiian games, hula lessons, Hawaiian storytelling, lei-making, nature/ecology walks, watermelon-eating contests, and parent/child putting contests are all part of the fun for the youngest editions.

ONE NAPILI WAY, 5355 *Lower Honoapiilani Road, #101, Napili, HI 96761. Tel. 808/669-2007 or 800/841-6284, Fax 808/669-5103. 14 units. Rates begin at $150 per condo. Four night minimum stay required.*

If you'd like to stay in one of Napili's newest and most attractive condos, book a vacation rental here. Arriving guests are greeted with small baskets of goodies. The bright, spacious apartments come with one, two, or three bedrooms, large screen TV and VCR, Jacuzzi in the master bath, roomy closets, and washer/dryer. Sparkling kitchens are equipped with everything from microwaves to blenders and ice cream scoops. Children are welcome at this family-run accommodation. The swimming pool, whirlpool, and barbecues are fenced in for the safety of little ones. Cribs, high chairs, and strollers are available for rent. A sandy beach, at Napili Bay, is a short walk away.

HONOKEANA COVE, 5255 *Lower Honoapiilani Road, Lahaina, HI 96761. Tel. 808/669-6441 or 800/237-4948, Fax 808/669-8777. 33 rooms. Double rooms begin at $105. Major credit cards.*

These two-story wooden buildings enjoy a dramatic waterfront setting. The swimming pool overlooks a sharply curving shore covered with smooth rocks. You don't have to swim far for excellent snorkeling. Near the pool, a towering, 150-year-old kamani tree shades the palm-studded lawn. Flowers greet guests in each condo. Apartments range from one- to three-bedroom, some with lofts. More than a few guests have been coming here for over a decade. You'll have to book at least three nights here, and maid service is only provided if you're staying for 12 nights or longer. Sea turtles live in the cove.

THE MAUIAN ON NAPILI BAY, 5441 *Lower Honoapiilani Road, Lahaina, HI 96761. Tel. 808/669-6205 or 800/367-5034, Fax 808/669-0129. 44 units. Rates begin at $100 per condo. Major credit cards.*

Many repeat guests wouldn't stay anywhere else, and they are loathe to let too many others know about their find. The two-story buildings at the edge of Napili Bay house comfortable studio apartments, cooled by ceiling fans. The absence of telephones and TVs makes this a good place for truly getting away. Each unit has a kitchen with a microwave. Every week, the general manager bakes for guests.

Near the quiet curving beach and shuffleboard courts, a small oval swimming pool is surrounded by a grassy tree-shaded lawn. Waterfront views from all lanais take in the West Maui Mountains, and humpback whales sometimes pass by during the winter. Restaurants are within walking distance.

NAPILI SUNSET, *46 Hui Drive, Lahaina, HI 96761. Tel. 808/669-8083 or 800/447-9229. 43 units. Rates begin at $95 per condo.*

Overlooking Napili Bay, this complex offers studios along with one- and two-bedroom condos with large, modern, full kitchens, TVs, phones, irons, and safes. For a view of the water, book one of the larger units. Guests amuse themselves in the heated pool and on the beach, where there is a gas barbecue. Snorkeling is quite good at the reef just offshore. Note that this property has excellent access for disabled travelers.

NAPILI VILLAGE, *5425 Lower Honoapiilani Road, Lahaina, HI 96761-9050. Tel. 808/669-6228 or 800/336-2185. 30 units. Rates begin at $90 per condo. Major credit cards.*

While a few of these modest condos have ocean views, many look out to gardens. Units come with small full kitchens. Facilities include a swimming pool, barbecue, and laundry. You'll also find a general store, a snorkel shop, and a beauty salon on the premises. From the grounds, there is convenient access to the beach, and brief strolls will take you to good restaurants, shops, and Kapalua Bay golf. Make reservations at least two months in advance.

HALE NAPILI, *65 Hui Road H, Lahaina, HI 96761. Tel. 808/669-6184 or 800/245-2266. 18 units. Rates begin at $90 per condo. Major credit cards.*

On Napili Bay, this economical condo is convenient to the beach and within walking distance of resort shopping at Kapalua Bay and restaurants. Perched above the shoreline, rooms have spectacular views. Expect to find king or queen-size beds, pull-out sofas, ample closets, full kitchens, and stall showers. This place books up quickly, so you'll need to make your reservation anywhere from six months to a year in advance.

Kahana

SANDS OF KAHANA, *c/o Sullivan Properties, Inc., P.O. Box 55, Lahaina, HI 96767-0055. Tel. 808/669-1199 or (888) 669-0400, Fax 808/669-8409. 196 units. Rates begin at $145 per condo.*

One-, two-, and three-bedroom apartments are available at this beachside condo looking out to the islands of Molokai and Lanai. Views from most private lanais are oceanfront or ocean view; the least expensive rooms have no view. Families like the large apartments, which come with cable TVs and VCRs, washer/dryers, and full kitchens. In addition to two swimming pools (one for children), there's also a hot tub, putting green, three lighted tennis courts, and a fitness room. Breakfast, lunch and dinner are served at the poolside restaurant. The Kapalua-West Maui Airport is less than a mile away.

MAHINA SURF CONDO HOTEL, 4057 Honoapiilani, Lahaina, HI 96761. Tel. 808/669-6068 or 800/367-6086, Fax 808/669-4534. 56 units. Rates begin at $115 per condo. Major credit cards.

During high season, you'll need to reserve one of these one- or two-bedroom comfortable condos at least six months in advance. All provide full ocean views, except for a handful with partial ocean views. Ceiling fans cool the air instead of air conditioning. Full kitchens are equipped with microwaves and dishwashers. All units come with radios and color televisions, and some also have VCRs. The two-story horseshoe-shaped building housing these apartments encloses a heated swimming pool. Also on the premises are barbecue grills, a Laundromat, and a lending library.

A sandy beach is about a five-minute stroll away. Golf courses and public tennis courts are about three miles from here. The front office remains open from 8:30am to 4pm, so be sure to make special arrangements in advance if you are checking in or out at other times.

Honokowai

EMBASSY SUITES RESORT – MAUI, 104 Kaanapali Shores Place, Lahaina, HI 96761. Tel. 808/661-2000 or 800/669-3155, Fax 808/667-5821. 413 suites. Rates begin at $260 for 1 to 4 adults in a suite. Major credit cards.

Each unit in this resort is a luxurious suite, with one or two bedrooms, a living room, two telephones, a lanai and a kitchenette. Culinary gadgets include a microwave oven and coffee maker (with complimentary coffee), and there's also a wet bar. The bedroom-sized baths are decked out with two marble vanities, a stall shower, and a tub. For indoor entertainment, suites are equipped with two remote control TVs (19" in bedrooms and 35" in living rooms), VCRs (the resort has a video library), stereos, and cassette decks. Room service is available until 11pm. Most suites have views of the ocean. On the lanais of the two presidential suites, telescopes allow visitors to zero in on whales as they glide by during the winter.

Guests are invited to indulge themselves in a complimentary full breakfast every morning and the manager's alfresco cocktail party every afternoon. Small bridges span streams filled with fish. Lilies, bird of paradise, and hibiscus flourish in gardens. A 24-foot waterslide ensures that giggles accompany the act of getting into the one-acre swimming pool. After a workout in the fitness center, sore muscles can be soothed by the whirlpool or a massage. All living rooms have full-size sofa beds. The year-round children's program make this a good choice for families. Although this is hardly a budget resort, two people can turn a one-bedroom terrace-view suite into an economical deal by sharing it with another couple (or a couple of kids), using a "Family Suite Package."

MAHANA, *110 Kaanapali Shores Place, Lahaina, HI 96761. Tel. 808/661-8751 or 800/922-7866, Fax 808/661-5510. 216 units. Rates begin at $200 per condo. Major credit cards.*

The best feature of this hotel is its location. Situated right on the ocean's edge, it offers some of the best views on western shores: rolling hills to the southeast, the Maui coastline directly south, the attractive Embassy Suites hotel and the northern coastline, and the ocean, which starts just beneath hotel lanais. If guests could dive from their balconies, they would end up right in the shallow crystal waters with the coral reefs that make snorkeling so good. The nicely furnished lobby opens to a view of the pool and ocean. A convenience store, selling liquor, souvenirs, and sundry items, is on the grounds. All guest rooms have ocean views. Those above the first floor have lanais. The double rooms also boast separate lanais off the master bedrooms, and the master baths come with bidets.

While the location of this hotel may be special, the studios and one- and two-bedroom units are decidedly unremarkable. Individually owned, they are clearly not governed by very demanding standards of decor.

MARC PAKI MAUI, *3615 Lower Honoapiilani Road, Lahaina, HI 96761-9398. Tel. 808/669-8235 or 800/535-0085, Fax 808/669-7987. 110 units. Rates begin at $175 per condo. Major credit cards.*

A circular driveway leads to the reception area of this condo, which opens to a courtyard with a waterfall, rock garden, and lily pond. Birds chirp loudly. The studios, one-bedroom, and two-bedroom/two-bath units are off al fresco hallways with views of the mountains. Some lanais look down into the flourishing courtyard. Most apartments, which vary in decor, are quite attractive. Number 324 has a large kitchen with a blue-tile counter, a commodious living/dining room, and sliding doors between the large bedroom and the living room. The lanai runs the length of the living room and the bedroom. Washers and dryers are found near the elevators (and in some units). Weekly Aloha Mai Tai parties and local telephone calls are complimentary.

Although Paki Maui is on the waterfront, the shore hasn't been sandy year-round since the early 1980s, when a severe storm washed the beach away. The sand returns periodically, so ask about its status when you make your reservation. However, an always-sandy beach is within walking distance. A small shopping center is right across the street.

ASTON KAANAPALI SHORES, *3445 Honoapiilani Highway, Lahaina, HI 96761. Tel. 808/667-2211 or 800/922-7866, Fax 808/661-0836. 463 units. Rates begin at $135 per condo. Major credit cards.*

This condominium is located just north of Kaanapali. The lobby opens to a lush, jungled courtyard with waterfalls, red ginger, crotons, and palm trees. A garden foot path winds along a fish-stocked pond. Lanais of first-floor rooms lead to the beachwalk. Ceilings are high and living rooms (in the one- and two-bedroom apartments) are spacious. Studios with kitchens and hotel rooms with refrigerators, wet bars, and microwave ovens are also for rent. Laundry facilities, storage closets, cable TV, and kitchens with dishwashers are features of one- and two-bedroom units. However, in the one-bedroom apartments, the only telephone is in the living room, along with the one television.

Furnishings include rattan couches with thick floral cushions, bamboo and glass coffee tables, and end tables. Non-smoking rooms (in which you don't have to worry about the stale odor from previous puffing guests) are available, along with rooms with wheelchair access. The two swimming pools make this resort especially appealing. Two whirlpools, a sauna, a putting green, and a restaurant and lounge are also on the grounds. Condo guests receive a discount at the fitness center. The three lighted tennis courts are open until 10pm and the closest golf course is only about three miles away. Parents in need of a break can send their children off to the condo's Camp Kaanapali.

PAPAKEA OCEANFRONT RESORT, *3543 Honoapiilani Highway, Lahaina, HI 96761. Tel. 808/669-4848 or 800/367-7052, Fax (510)939-6644. 364 units. Rates begin at $120 per condo. Major credit cards.*

There's plenty of elbow room between the low-rise buildings that house the condo units at this spacious resort just north of Kaanapali. The home-like studios and one- and two-bedroom apartments are cooled by ceiling fans instead of air conditioning. Ponds churning with fish, paths bordered by flowering bushes and bamboo, putting greens, and shuffle-board provide contrasts between nature and recreation. Facilities include two swimming pools, two whirlpools, and three tennis courts.

Kaanapali

All of Kaanapali's accommodations are convenient to the Royal Kaanapali Golf Courses, tennis courts, and the beach. Shuttle service is available within the resort as well as to Lahaina. Kapalua-West Maui is the closest airport.

On the Beach at Kaanapali

SHERATON MAUI, *2605 Kaanapali Parkway, Lahaina, HI 96761. Tel. 808/661-0031 or 800/782-9488, Fax 808/661-0458. 510 rooms. Double rooms begin at $270. Major credit cards.*

It's hard to believe that when Sheraton Maui opened in 1963, it was the only full-scale hotel on Kaanapali Beach, a stretch now lined with snazzy resort hotels and condos. The first guests paid just $15 a night for their rooms! After closing for two years during a $150 million renovation, the hotel reopened in late 1996. Once again, it is among Hawaii's premier resorts.

Various buildings, none taller than six stories, are spread over 23 beautifully landscaped acres. The impressive lobby welcomes vacationers with a panoramic view of the 80-foot-high black lava Pu'u Keka'a rock formation, the islands of Molokai and Lanai floating in the dark blue water, and gorgeous white sand. Koa wood, local artwork, bright floral arrangements, and Hawaiian kapa cloth decorate the lobby. All of the upscale guest rooms and suites come with lanais and most face the ocean. Not only are fifteen rooms accessible to visitors in wheelchairs, but 10 are designed for people with impaired hearing.

Along with a fresh water swimming lagoon, facilities include three tennis courts (lit for night play), and a fitness center. Scuba diving, sailing aboard a catamaran, and other diversions are easily arranged at the Beach Activities Desk. One of Maui's best snorkeling areas is right in front of the hotel, around Pu'u Keka'a (a.k.a. Black Rock). Kaanapali golf courses are within walking distance.

Each evening begins with the hotel's famous torch lighting and cliff-diving ceremony, which recreates the legend of Pu'u Keka'a. Travelers have three restaurants to choose from, and, at night, live Hawaiian music entertains people at the Reef's Edge Lounge. The seasonal Keiki Aloha program offers a slew of special activities for children.

MAUI MARRIOTT, *100 Nohea Kai Drive, Lahaina, HI 96761. Tel. 808/667-1200 or 800/763-1333, Fax 808/667-8192. 720 rooms. Double rooms begin at $270. Major credit cards.*

You won't go wrong booking a room here, but there are plenty of other Maui hotels (both in this price range and less expensive) with a lot more character. Toward the southern end of Kaanapali, this large hotel contains relatively standard rooms, though they are nicely decorated with light woods and ocean colors. Room service is available from 6am to 10pm. Very long open-air hallways form balconies enclosing a courtyard that sprouts tall palms. Depending on where your room is, you may be in for a long walk every time you get off the elevator on your floor. Most rooms gaze out to the ocean. Palm trees also grow up from the spacious lobby, with its unobtrusive shops.

At Nikko, a popular Japanese steak and seafood restaurant, chefs turn cooking into a humorous performance at the grills at tables where patrons are seated together, family style. The daily Hawaiiana arts and crafts program is complimentary. Three of the five tennis courts are lit at night and the hotel has a resident tennis pro. There are also two large swimming pools with waterfalls, a pair of whirlpools, and an open-air exercise area with a Nautilus weight-training system. Water sports are easily arranged. **THE WESTIN MAUI**, *2365 Kaanapali Parkway, Lahaina, HI 96761. Tel. 808/667-2525 or 800/WESTIN1. 761 rooms.*

Next door to Whalers Village shopping center, this flamboyant resort is an attraction in itself. Some consider it overdone and overwhelming, while others revel in its lavish touches. It was developed by Chris Hemmeter, Hawaii's version of Donald Trump. The hotel's motto seems to be, "Why have one waterfall when 16 will do?" The first splashes across from the entrance to the breezy lobby, which is dressed in muted beiges and pale pinks. Other waterfalls pour over rocky outcroppings into swan-filled ponds and the five swimming pools. Guests delight in swimming under the cascades and whizzing down water slides into the pool.

The multimillion-dollar international art collection turns the grounds into an al fresco museum. Mammoth Chinese statues, tremendous urns and columns not much smaller than redwood trees line corridors. Huge bronze horses and other animals seem to hulk around every corner. You won't be surprised to find that weddings often take place in the gazebo and elsewhere. After the grounds, most guest rooms are surprisingly small, though elegantly decorated. This is because the Westin Maui was another, more modest hotel in its earlier incarnation. Each room has a coffee maker, iron and board and a refrigerator. Accents include marble and glass-topped tables and heavy, wide chaise lounges.

Nine restaurants and lounges and 28 dramatically decorated suites add to the overall elegance. Guests are invited to take advantage of the fitness center (treat yourself to an outdoor massage) and a full range of beach activities. A daily resort fee of $5 includes complimentary valet parking, newspaper, Hawaiiana programs, local calls and long distance access, and resort tours. A children's camp attracts families to the resort.

HYATT REGENCY MAUI, *200 Nohea Kai Drive, Lahaina, HI 96761. Tel. 808/661-1234 or 800/233-1234, Fax 808/667-4499, 815 rooms and suites. Double rooms begin at $260. Major credit cards.*

Developer Chris Hemmeter created the Hyatt before trying to outdo himself with the Westin Maui. Many people prefer the Hyatt's more understated approach. The lobby is paneled in honey-brown wood. Parrots and macaws perch uncaged on brass rings. Buddha heads and other sculptures stand on pedestals. Near the Napili wing shops, a glass-covered coffee table serves as a showcase for New Guinea headdresses, headbands, and shell necklaces. Art and artifacts from Burma, Thailand and China, among other places, are displayed here and there. Rotund penguins waddle and huge koi dart around various pools. A swinging rope-and-wood-plank bridge spans a section of the sprawling-half-acre swimming pool.

Neighboring the Royal Kaanapali Golf Courses, the Hyatt offers snorkel and scuba lessons, a lava tube waterslide into the pool, boogie boards, kayaks, bikes, six tennis courts, and sails on a 55-foot catamaran. Camp Hyatt organizes a variety of activities for children. Stargazers should ask about the hotel's astronomy program. Vacationers are drawn to the health club and some begin their honeymoons by tying the knot in the wedding gazebo. Each night, there's a torch lighting ceremony. Guests have a choice of restaurants and, on weekend evenings, the nightclub entertains the party crowd.

Corridors outside guest rooms are decorated with glass-enclosed pieces of art. In rooms, the TV and refrigerator are hidden in handsome armoires, and dressing areas are spacious. Yukatas (Japanese robes) are provided for guests to use during their stay. Traditional island-style furniture has clearly inspired some pieces in rooms. Transportation can be arranged between the hotel and the Kapalua-West Maui airport, Lahaina Cannery (for shopping), and the town of Lahaina.

KAANAPALI ALII, *50 Nohea Kai Drive, Lahaina, HI 96761. Tel. 808/667-1400 or 800/642-6284, Fax 808/661-0147. 264 units. Rates begin at $230 per condo. Major credit cards.*

The waiting list for the Christmas holidays and other peak seasons can be nearly a year long for these upscale condos. Artfully landscaped grounds surround fresh water swimming pools. There are also a Jacuzzi, exercise room, and saunas. Unlike in many condos, the front desk is open 24 hours a day, and a special security key is necessary to enter buildings. A concierge is on hand to arrange sports, tours, and other activities. The four buildings have six one- and two-bedroom apartments on each floor. Rooms look out to the mountains, the garden, and/or the ocean. In some units, the master bathroom has a whirlpool. Baths come with separate vanity areas and are equipped with bidets. Other facilities include microwaves, dishwashers, trash compactors, blenders and coffee makers. All rooms have the use of washers and dryers. In Building #3, oceanfront two-bedroom apartment #3106 is fabulous. The full ocean view provides excellent whale watching from the lanai, especially at sunset. A special security key is necessary to enter buildings.

Although there is no food and beverage facility on the property, Kaanapali Alii guests may charge meals at the Royal Kaanapali Golf Course Clubhouse as well as at Maui Marriott and Westin Maui restaurants. A three-night minimum rental is required, except during Christmas time, when guests must book at least 10 nights.

THE WHALER ON KAANAPALI BEACH, *2481 Kaanapali Parkway, Lahaina, HI 96761. Tel. 808/661-4861 or 800/367-7052, Fax 808/661-8315. 360 units. Rates begin at $200 per condo. Major credit cards.*

Whalers Village shopping center and the two Royal Kaanapali championship golf courses across the street make convenient neighbors for the Whaler. The difference between this quietly elegant condominium and a full-service hotel is barely detectable. Sunlight streams into the open-air lobby, which has a granite floor. There's a beach front swimming pool, whirlpool, five tennis courts with a pro shop, a general store, an exercise room, and a sauna. A masseuse is available by appointment. The studio and one- and two-bedroom apartments are found in two 12-story towers. While waiting for the elevator, guests stand on sea blue tiles and gaze out at the mountains, ocean, and courtyard. Special touches in units include 10-foot-high ceilings, marble baths, full kitchens with parquet floors, and 12' x 2' closets. Guests have signing privileges at several nearby Whalers Village restaurants.

ROYAL LAHAINA, *2780 Kekaa Drive, Lahaina, HI 96761. Tel. 808/ 661-3611 or 800/447-6925, Fax 808/661-6150. 592 rooms. Double rooms begin at $195. Major credit cards.*

Reminiscent of totem poles, Polynesian tikis welcome guests to this lava rock complex, Kaanapali's second-oldest hotel. Shops lead the way to the lobby, paneled in dark wood, where more stores are found. Appealing to conventions and large groups, this hotel has a commercial, busy feel, balanced by its demonstration of Hawaiian quilt-making and other crafts, in addition to the usual lei making. Even the birds chirp loudly all over the property.

In the main wing are the medium-sized, individual rooms. The well-spaced low-rise cottages are attractive enough. Set on a grassy, tree-shaded lawn with a nearby gazebo, these shingle-roofed buildings have either one or two stories. Some ocean view rooms open to dramatic coastal vistas. Six deluxe Ali'i Suites are furnished with authentic reproductions of furnishings in the palaces of Hawaiian royalty. In the afternoon, hot and cold pupus accompany the live music in the indoor/outdoor lounge overlooking the flourishing main pool area and the picturesque sandy beach. Other swimming pools and the 11-court Royal Lahaina Tennis Ranch are among the facilities. The hotel's 27 acres include one of Kaanapali's golf courses, where the Del Mar Golf College provides high-tech video analysis.

KAANAPALI BEACH HOTEL, *2525 Kaanapali Parkway, Lahaina, HI 96761. Tel. 808/661-0011 or 800/262-8450, Fax 808/667-5978. 423 rooms. Double rooms begin at $150. Major credit cards.*

Centrally located, this hotel dates back to the 1960s. The crescent of low-rise buildings cups a palm-shaded patio that gives way to the broad beach. Live Hawaiian music hangs in the air by the Polynesian-style wooden roofs that resemble the bows of ships. A whale-shaped swimming pool is a short walk across the lawn. Rooms (which vary mainly in terms of their views) are quite spacious, with a dressing room, refrigerator, coffee maker, ironing board, and lanai. Hotel activities include lei-making, *ti* leaf skirt making, hula lessons, complimentary scuba lessons, and aqua-aerobics. For a small fee, guests may play tennis in Lahaina.

The coffee shop at Kaanapali Beach Hotel is known for its good prices for breakfast, lunch, and dinner. Along with a beauty shop and massage parlor, there is also a shop selling resort wear and moderately priced gifts. Each evening at sunset, guests can witness the lighting of the torches at nearby Black Rock (Pu'u Keka'a), just south of the hotel. This symbolic ritual honors the spirits who have come to the farthest point west on the island to dive off the rock from this world into the next. The hotel encourages its staff to become knowledgeable about Hawaiian culture by providing time to attend classes. This commitment allows staff to better respond to the queries of guests.

Near the Beach at Kaanapali

MAUI ELDORADO RESORT, *2661 Kekaa Drive, Lahaina, HI 96761. Tel. 808/661-0021, Fax 808/667-7039. 90 units. Rates begin at $160 per condo. Major credit cards.*

Some of these low-rise condominium units are separated from the beach by a palm-studded golf course while both a street and a golf course lie between the water and others. If you're not in the mood to walk to the beach, take the hourly shuttle. For those who forgo the Pacific, three swimming pools are on the premises. The 11-court Royal Lahaina Tennis Ranch is next door.

Each of the large studio, one- and two-bedroom apartments has a private lanai. Some of the one-bedrooms and all of the two-bedrooms have two baths. The tub and toilet are separated from the vanity and sink area. Kitchens have microwaves, toasters, and coffee makers. Groceries, wine, and other liquor are sold in the lobby.

KAANAPALI ROYAL, *2560 Kekaa Drive, Lahaina, HI 96761. Tel. 808/879-2205 or 800/367-7040, Fax 808/874-3497. 105 units. Rates begin at $160 per condo. Major credit cards.*

A golf course, ponds, and Kaanapali Parkway stand between this condominium and the beach. Whalers Village beach front shopping and dining complex is a short stroll away. On the grounds are a pool, Jacuzzi, sauna, and two tennis courts. Some of the baths in these two-bedroom, two-bath apartments have their own private lanai gardens. Each unit is equipped with a washer, dryer, and full kitchen.

MAUI KAANAPALI VILLAS, *45 Kai Ala Drive, Lahaina, HI 96761. Tel. 808/667-7791 or 800/922-7866, Fax 808/922-8785. 250 units. Rates begin at $130 per condo. Major credit cards.*

An Aston property, this hotel/condominium is within shouting distance of the sand. In addition to individual rooms, guests may stay in studios or one- and two-bedroom suites. Hotel-style rooms have refrigerators, while the large units come with full kitchens. Three swimming pools are found on the spacious, pleasantly landscaped grounds.

Lahaina

Shuttle service is available between here and Kaanapali.

PUNOA BEACH ESTATES, *45 Kai Pali Place, Lahaina, HI 96761. Tel. 808/667-5972 or 800/642-MAUI, Fax 808/661-1025. 10 units. Rates begin at $475 per 2-bedroom condo. Major credit cards.*

Each of these two- and three-bedroom condo apartments has a beach-front lanai, a party-sized whirlpool tub in the master bedroom, two color TVs, a cassette deck, video recorder, bar, refrigerator and ceiling fan. Individually furnished, these units are accented with koa wood and etched glass windows. Some have high-pitched natural wood ceilings. You might find sleep-inducing armchairs, Asian vases, Japanese screens, or reproductions of Chinese carpets. Facilities include a swimming pool, paddle tennis courts, a sauna, and washer and dryer. Every day, the newspaper appears at each suite. The heart of Lahaina is a brief stroll away.

PLANTATION INN, *174 Lahainaluna Road, Lahaina, HI 96761. Tel. 808/667-9225 or 800/433-6815, Fax 808/667-9293. 19 units. Double rooms begin at $120. Major credit cards.*

This cozy Victorian-style inn makes up for its non-beach location with a myriad of extra touches. Although this two-story building located in the historic whaling district of Lahaina was born in the 1980s, it draws travelers into the turn of the century. The individually decorated guest rooms feature stained-glass windows, Tiffany-esque lamps with fringed shades, floral wallpaper, brass and canopy beds with ruffled coverlets, wicker rockers, and hardwood floors. Remote-control TVs and refrigerators are discreetly tucked away in period oak armoires. While rooms are centrally air-conditioned, they also have ceiling fans. Most open to lanais. Baths are highlighted by brass fixtures and porcelain pedestal sinks. When combined, rooms turn into suites. (One suite has a full kitchen.)

Complimentary fax service, a historic guide, VCRs, and tapes are available. Lush plantings surround the artfully tiled swimming pool and Jacuzzi. Meals are served at indoor/outdoor Gerard's, the ground floor restaurant. (Guests of the inn receive discounts for meals.) Ask about room/car packages as well as honeymoon and dive packages.

LAHAINA SHORES BEACH RESORT, *475 Front Street, Lahaina, HI 96761. Tel. 808/661-4835 or 800/642-6284, Fax 808/661-4696. 199 units. Rates begin at $120 per condo. Major credit cards.*

Conveniently located at the end of Lahaina boardwalk, this six-story condominium is the only accommodation in town that is on the beach. While a medley of stores and restaurants are nearby, this is one of the least crowded parts of Lahaina. The large, white plantation-style building has tall columns and a beautiful arched porte cochere. Trimmed in oak, the attractive lobby is spacious and simply furnished. As in major hotels, someone is on duty at the front desk 24 hours a day. The swimming pool is just off the lobby. Public tennis courts and a basketball court are across the street, while a 10-minute drive will take you to the closest golf courses.

Although the studio and one-bedroom ocean view or mountain view apartments are not as eye-catching as the rest of the hotel, they are perfectly comfortable. Guests have a choice of restaurants next door at the 505 Front Street complex.

LAHAINA INN, 127 Lahainaluna Road (off Front Street), Lahaina, HI 96761-1502. Tel. 808/661-0577 or 800/669-3444, Fax 808/667-9480. 12 rooms. Double rooms begin at $89, including continental breakfast. Major credit cards.

In the thick of things in central Lahaina, this neo-Victorian inn (formerly the Lahaina Hotel) in a handsomely restored building is one of Hawaii's nicest places to stay. People keep an eye on street life as they relax in armchairs and rockers on the lanai that runs along the second story. Glossy wooden doors lead to rooms that are beautifully decorated with antiques. Complementing floral wallpaper, Oriental rugs dress up hardwood floors. Stained-glass lamps sit on night stands by tall armoires. Chandeliers and fans hang from ceilings. (Rooms are all air-conditioned.) Lace curtains flutter in the breeze.

With wrought iron, brass, or carved wooden headboards, beds are either doubles or kings. Views take in the harbor and the mountains. Although there are no TVs in rooms, European-American classical music is piped in 24 hours a day (you can turn it up, down, or off whenever you like). If this hotel reminds you of Manoa Valley Inn on Oahu, it's because they were both restored by Rick Ralston, the founder and president of Crazy Shirts, Inc. David Paul's Lahaina Grill, considered by many to be one of Hawaii's best restaurants, is adjacent to the lobby.

ALOHA LANI INN...A MAUI GUEST HOME, 13 Kauaula Road (off Front Street), Lahaina, HI 96761. Tel. 808/661-8040 or 800/572-5642, Fax 808/661-8045. 3 rooms. Double rooms begin at $69. Major credit cards.

The beach is across the road and Lahaina's harbor, restaurants, shops, and night spots are just a few blocks from this attractively decorated (and economical) guest house. Vacationers in the three rental rooms share the kitchen, living/dining room, stereo, TV, books, lanai, barbecue grill, and baths. Two of the units offer wonderful sunset views and the sound of the surf can lull guests to sleep. Twin beds are in one room while the others sport doubles. A two-night minimum stay is required.

Kula

KUAIHELANI ESTATES, *Rural Route 4, Box 43, Kula, HI 96790. Tel. 808/878-3534 or 800/441-2087, Fax 808/878-3933. 2 cottages. Rates are $125 per cottage. A two-night minimum stay is required.*

Kuaihelani is Hawaiian for "a special place in the high heavens." At a 3,000 foot elevation, this lovely Bed & Breakfast on six flourishing acres certainly is. It consists of two cottages in a grove of jacaranda trees that are bright with purple blossoms from May through October. You'll breathe cool upcountry air perfumed with eucalyptus and wake up to an orchestra of songbirds and cows. Views of Maui's south shore are particularly striking at sunrise.

Also dubbed the honeymoon suite, the one-bedroom Tudor Cottage can sleep four comfortably. Note the hand painted tiles of Franklin pheasants, which live in the area, the maplewood floors, the French doors, the claw foot bathtub with a dramatic ocean view, the wood burning fireplace, and the wrap-around lanai. You'll find a TV, VCR, and a walk-in closet as well. The equally attractive two-bedroom, two-bath Makai Cottage, overlooking the north shore, can accommodate six.

Guests are greeted upon check-in with a fresh protea floral arrangement, a bottle of wine, Kona coffee, and gourmet chocolates. Breakfast might consist of Canadian bacon, eggs, croissants, muffins, and orange juice. The friendly owners are happy to help arrange sailing charters and other diversions.

KULA LODGE, *Rural Route 1, Box 475, Kula, HI 96790. Tel. 808/878-1535 or 800/233-1535, Fax 808/878-2578. 5 rooms. Double rooms begin at $110. Major credit cards.*

Perched high on the upcountry slopes of Haleakala and with crackling fireplaces, this rustic mountain lodge isn't exactly what most travelers envision when they think of Hawaii. Two wooden cabins house the five units, two of which have fireplaces, four of which have lofts, and two of which have whirlpools. From this height, the views – stretching out to the Pacific – are spectacular. Note that even though cabins don't have kitchenettes, they each have coffee makers. Down comforters are an added attraction. The restaurant serves breakfast, lunch, and dinner.

BLOOM COTTAGE, *Rural Route 2, Box 229, Kula, HI 96790. Tel. 808/878-1425, Fax 808/878-1425. 700-square-foot cottage. Double occupancy rates: $105; $15 per extra guest. No smoking. No children under age 12.*

When you're ready to visit the summit of Haleakala (only 45 minutes away), consider spending a couple of nights here instead of driving all the way from the coast. On a cool upcountry slope of the volcano, this Bed & Breakfast is nestled amid herb and flower gardens. Kahului Airport and the closest beaches are about a half hour drive away. Here in the land of horse and cattle ranches, botanical gardens, and farms, you'll be away from the crowds of Maui's resort areas. Tedeschi Winery is just a ten minute drive from Bloom Cottage and good restaurants aren't far. The homey cottage has a fully equipped kitchen and a wood-burning fireplace in the living room, as well as a TV, hairdryer, and phone. One of the two bedrooms comes with a single bed, the other with a queen. Film classics are available for romantic viewing on the VCR. The hosts will be happy to provide warm jackets for crater viewing. Fresh fruit, bread and muffins, local jams, and freshly ground coffee are offered at breakfast.

SILVER CLOUD UPCOUNTRY GUEST RANCH B&B, *Rural Route 2, Box 201, Old Thompson Road, Kula, HI 96790. Tel. 808/878-6101 or 800/ 532-1111, Fax 808/878-2132. 13 rooms. Double rooms begin at $75. Major credit cards.*

On 500 acres, this peaceful Bed & Breakfast sits high in the cool, clear hills of Kula and has a sweeping view of the ocean and Lanai, Molokai, and Kahoolawe islands. It is only about an hour from the summit of Haleakala volcano, so you can drive up to see the sun rise over the crater and return in time for breakfast. A complete morning meal is included in the rates, by the way. Tedeschi Winery is just five miles away, as is the small town of Makawao, where you'll find a variety of shops and restaurants.

With views of the mountains and the ocean, rooms are nestled in three buildings and there are no telephones or TVs to shatter the tranquillity of the setting. Some come with kitchenettes. Two units, the Haleakala Suite and the very private Lanai cottage, have complete kitchens and either a fireplace or wood burning stove.

What would paniolo (cowboy) country be without horses? Watch them run in the corral or take a trail ride. Many guests can't resist spending some time parked in the hammock strung between two macadamia trees amid colorful flowers. Evenings can be on the chilly side at this 2,800 foot elevation, so be sure to bring a sweater. Since Silver Cloud is so popular, you may need to make a reservation as far as a year in advance!

Kihei

MAUI SCHOONER RESORT, *980 South Kihei Road, Kihei, HI 96753. Tel. 808/879-5247 or 800/877-7976, Fax 808/875-0259. 58 units. Double rooms begin at $180. Major credit cards.*

One of Kihei's newest condominiums, this is also among its most attractive places to stay. Separated from the beach by smooth, expansive lawns with tennis courts, the various red-roofed low-rise buildings surround the swimming pool and sauna. Microwaves make using the modern kitchens tempting, and each apartment is also equipped with two TVs, a VCR, and a washer/dryer. The living/dining areas and bedrooms are spacious. Lanais look out to the ocean. Overnight film development and video rentals are available.

THE MAUI COAST HOTEL, 2259 South Kihei Road, Kihei, HI 96753. Tel. 808/874-6284 or 800/426-0670, Fax 808/875-4731. 260 rooms. Double rooms begin at $130. Major credit cards.

This centrally located hotel, with two night-lit tennis courts, is across the street from the beach. Each room has its own lanai, mini-refrigerator, and in-wall room safe. Championship golf courses are nearby.

MAUI LU RESORT, 575 South Kihei Road, Kihei, HI 96753. Tel. 808/879-5881 or 800/922-7866, Fax 808/879-4627. 120 rooms. Double rooms begin at $120. Major credit cards.

Built in and around a former private home, this simple and comfortable Aston accommodation has buildings on both the inland and beach sides of the road. Guests will have to walk a bit to get to the sandiest part of the shore. The superior rooms are good choices and the one-bedroom cottages are quite spacious. Palms and other trees shade the 28-acre grounds. Along with a pool and tennis, there are shops, a restaurant, a lounge, and evening entertainment. Many guests comment on the friendliness of Maui Lu employees.

KIHEI BEACH RESORT, 36 South Kihei Road, Kihei, HI 96753. Tel. 808/879-2744 or 800/367-6034, Fax 808/875-0306. 37 units. Rates begin at $110 per condo. Major credit cards.

This six-story concrete building contains one- and two-bedroom apartments that are pleasant enough. Lanais look out to Ma'alaea Bay, frequented by whales during the winter, the West Maui Mountains, Haleakala volcano, the beach and uninhabited Kahoolawe island. In addition to the sandy shore, there's a swimming pool. Kitchens are outfitted with dishwashers, microwaves, and garbage disposals.

KAMAOLE SANDS, 2695 South Kihei Road, Kihei, HI 96753. Tel. 808/874-8700 or 800/367-5004, Fax 808/879-3273. 440 units. Rates begin at $105 per condo. Major credit cards.

Ten buildings on fifteen landscaped acres make this more like a miniature city than a condo. A swimming pool, two whirlpools, and four tennis courts are on the premises, along with a barbecue grill. Guests may arrange other diversions through two activities desks (the first in the lobby, the second pulsed). If your condo is in building #10, which is closest to the beach (and farthest from the main entrance), available parking spaces may be limited since most are used by the many permanent residents in this building.

Note that (in units larger than studios) while bedrooms have ceiling fans, only living rooms are air-conditioned. Some units look out to common walkways, so you'll need to keep your curtains closed for privacy. Rooms are decorated pleasantly enough, but maintenance could be better. During a recent visit, ants shared my living quarters and the refrigerator was leaking.

MAUI SUNSET, *1032 South Kihei Road, Kihei, HI 96753. Tel. 808/879-0674 or 800/854-8843, Fax 808/854-8843, 225 units. Rates begin at $100 per condo. Major credit cards.*

These one- and two-bedroom oceanfront condo units come with a swimming pool, a Jacuzzi, and tennis court. There are also a putting green, croquet lawn and exercise room. Guests are welcome to use the laundry facilities, and maid service is available upon request. Many guests find overnight film developing convenient bonus.

MAUI KAMAOLE, *362 Huku Lii Place #204, Kihei, HI 96753. Tel. 808/879-2778 or 800/367-5242, Fax 808/879-7825. 100 units. Rates begin at $95 per condo. Major credit cards.*

If you don't mind being on a gently sloping hillside overlooking the shore instead of on the beach, these modern one-bedroom/two-bath and two-bedroom/two-bath condo apartments are an excellent choice. Near the Kamaole Beach Parks, the spacious units, in two-story buildings, have full kitchens with built-in microwaves. They are decorated in rattan, with glass-topped tables. Each condo also contains a color cable TV, VCR, telephone, and washer/dryer. Sliding glass doors lead to lanais where rails are overhung with flowers. While apartments are air-conditioned, they also have ceiling fans. In the two-bedroom duplex units, the upstairs bedroom is in a loft above the living room and can be closed off with shutters. Units with ocean and garden views are the most popular (and most expensive). The swimming pool, whirlpool and barbecue grills provide diversions. A four-night minimum stay is required.

SUGAR BEACH RESORT, *362 Huku Lii Place #204, Kihei, HI 96753. Tel. 808/879-2778 or 800/367-5242, Fax 808/879-7825. 200 units. Rates begin at $90 per condo. Major credit cards.*

These concrete-block, balconied buildings may not look like anything special from the outside, but the one- and two-bedroom beach front condos are perfectly comfortable, especially for family vacations. On a good stretch of beach in north Kihei, all units have lanais with views of the water, color TVs, washer/dryers and full kitchens with microwaves. Facilities include two swimming pools, tennis courts, a sauna and a hot tub.

HALE KAMAOLE, *362 Huku Lii Place #204, Kihei, HI 96753. Tel. 808/879-2778 or 800/362-5242, Fax 808/879-7825. 65 units. Rates begin at $85 per condo. Major credit cards.*

Across the road from Kamaole Beach Park Three (a very nice stretch of sand), the grassy terraced grounds of this condominium are filled with flowers. Many repeat guests book the split-level two-bedroom apartments. One-bedroom units are also available. All units come with blossom-draped lanais and electric kitchens with dishwashers, as well as air conditioning and telephones. There's a tennis court in addition to two swimming pools and barbecue pits. Maid service is provided at an added cost and a laundry room is on the property. A minimum stay of four nights is required (or an extra cleaning fee is charged). Rates here are especially attractive during the summer.

NONA LANI COTTAGES, *455 South Kihei Road, Kihei, HI 96753, Tel. 808/879-2497 or 800/733-2688. 8 units. Double rooms begin at $80.*

These one-bedroom shingle-roofed cottages are set on an appealing grassy lawn across the road from the beach. Flowers and fruit trees flourish here. Guests relax on their lanais, which gaze out to the ocean. Each unit can sleep four. Kitchens are fully equipped. Barbecue grills and laundry facilities are available. Kihei's restaurants and stores are conveniently located nearby. Four nights' minimum stay is required.

MANA KAI MAUI, *2960 South Kihei Road, Kihei, HI 96753. Tel. 808/ 879-1561 or 800/367-5242, Fax 808/874-5042. 60 units. Rates begin at $75 per unit. Major credit cards.*

The location on a wonderful expansive beach makes up for the unexciting architecture and guest rooms of this modest eight-story hotel/ condominium. A swimming pool is on the premises along with a bar, restaurant, and a couple of stores. Water sports enthusiasts may arrange their schedules here at an office of the Ocean Activities Center. Lanais are open to the ocean. While some rooms are petite and have no kitchens, the price is certainly right. Others have complete kitchens. Consider reserving a rental car when you call for your room reservation.

KIHEI AKAHI, *362 Huku Lii Place #204, Kihei, HI 96753. Tel. 808/ 879-2778 or 800/367-5242, Fax 808/879-7825. 140 units. Rates begin at $65 per condo. Major credit cards.*

This centrally located condominium is affordably priced, an attraction for families and honeymooners. Guests can learn about local vegetation along the marked flower and plant trail.

LUANA KAI RESORT, *940 South Kihei, Kihei, HI 96753. Tel. 808/ 879-1268 or 800/669-1127, Fax 808/879-1455. 113 units. Rates begin at $65 per condo. Major credit cards.*

Most of these one- and two-bedroom carpeted apartments are nicely done with rattan furnishings. Each unit contains a TV, large full kitchen, dining/living room, and washer/dryer. Since pathways wind through the grounds in front of units, lanais on the upper floors of the three-story buildings are the most private. There's a swimming pool, and tennis courts sit on the wide, grassy lawn between rooms and the narrow beach.

Wailea

Shuttle service is available to area golf courses, tennis courts, a gym, and a shopping center. A 1.5 mile beach walk runs from the Renaissance Wailea to the Kea Lani.

GRAND WAILEA RESORT & SPA, *3850 Wailea Alanui Drive, Wailea, HI 96753. Tel. 808/875-1234 or 800/888-6100, Fax 808/874-2442. 761 rooms. Double rooms begin at $380. Major credit cards.*

With nearly 800 rooms (all of them ocean view), this addition to Hawaii's megaresort family opened in 1991 as a Hyatt. The hotel stands on a beach, but the ocean almost seems mundane next to the other bodies of water here. The main swimming pool, set off by a fountain that is lit after dark, takes up 15,000 square feet. A 2,000-foot-long river pool boasts the world's first water elevator; gushing water pushes a basket-like cubicle through a tube with rock on three sides and a glassed-in aquarium on the fourth. For those who would like to begin their honeymoons with nuptials in Hawaii, there's a wedding chapel on the grounds. A walk through the garden reveals small romantic hideaways, such as swinging benches for two.

Vacationers have a choice of restaurants, including an authentic Japanese inn and a thatched roof ohia wood seafood restaurant on a lagoon. The spacious, full-scale health spa tempts visitors to keep in shape and be pampered. Scuba lessons are available in a specially designed pool. Guest rooms – which each have a private lanai, three telephones, a remote-control TV, and a bathroom with a tub and separate shower – are quite large. Guests in the Napua Tower have a private lounge area with a pool table; a breakfast buffet is spread every morning, early afternoon tea is set, and hors d'oeuvres are available each evening. Note that this hotel books quite a few large conventions. If you'd rather not be bombarded by these often invasive groups, when you make your reservation, ask if any are scheduled for the time you'd like to vacation.

FOUR SEASONS RESORT MAUI AT WAILEA, *3900 Wailea Alanui Drive, Wailea, HI 96753. Tel. 808/874-8000 or 800/334-MAUI, Fax 808/874-2222. 380 rooms. Double rooms begin at $340. Major credit cards.*

Featured in Chapter 10, *Best Places to Stay.*

The elegant lobby sets the tone for this gracious beachfront hotel, which opened in the spring of 1990. The Four Seasons Resort Maui's reputation for exceptional cuisine has spread quickly, with Seasons restaurant its culinary showpiece. Even the smallest guest rooms are large, each complete with a TV and VCR. Comfortable teak furniture decorates lanais. The brightly lit bathrooms are fabulous, all with glass-enclosed, marble-tiled stall showers, bath tubs, double sinks, and endless counter space. Room service is available around the clock.

The two-level upper pool, complete with a waterfall, has a section for children designed so that parents can be in the deeper area while keeping an eye on the kids. With two Jacuzzis, the main pool has a fountain in the middle. At sunset, Hawaiian music wafts out from the poolside cafe.

Live dance music draws people to the Lobby Lounge at night. A pool table, large screen TV, and full bar are found in the game room. Along with an exercise room, massage rooms, and a steam room, the health club has a centrifugal dryer so you can work out or take a swim on your last day without having to pack a wet bathing suit. Parents should ask about the complimentary children's program for those aged five to 12.

KEA LANI HOTEL, SUITES & VILLAS, *4100 Wailea Alanui, Wailea, HI 96753. Tel. 808/875-4100 or 800/882-4100, Fax 808/875-1200. 413 suites; 37 villas. Rates begin at $295 per suite. Major credit cards.*

This luxury resort sits on Polo Beach. The white Mediterranean-style buildings are set against 22 acres of colorfully landscaped grounds. Each oceanfront villa has its own plunge pool. One-, two-, and three-bedroom villas are available along with one-bedroom suites. Huge, elegant marble baths come with tubs and separate showers. Guests may watch the large screen color TV in the living room, with a VCR, or the TV in the bedroom. There is an extensive video library. Units also come with CD laser discs and audio-cassette players as well as AM/FM radio stereos. Kitchenettes are equipped with refrigerators, microwave ovens, and coffee and tea. Two of the three swimming pools are joined by a water slide, and there is a fitness center.

RENAISSANCE WAILEA BEACH RESORT, *3550 Wailea Alanui Drive, Wailea, HI 96753. Tel. 808/879-4900 or 800/992-4532, Fax 808/874-9421. 345 rooms. Double rooms begin at $290. Major credit cards.*

Complimentary shuttle service is provided to Wailea shops, golf courses, and tennis courts from this pleasant beach resort. The attractive rooms, with spacious lanais, three telephones, refrigerators, computer dataports, safes, and sitting areas, all have cable TV with VCRs (the television set is secreted away in an attractive armoire). Plush suites - accented with rattan and louvered doors - are ocean view. Baths, with double sinks, are done in white marble. A torch lit path leads from hotel rooms and restaurants to the beach, twisting and turning through ponds and lush granary. Snorkeling is excellent by the lava rocks off the beach to the left. The main swimming pool (there are two) is free-form and guests may take the plunge in two whirlpools.

Vacationers dine at various restaurants; a luau is held every Monday evening. The fitness center contains a variety of exercise equipment. Camp Wailea keeps children aged 5 to 12 entertained. For extra pampering and to be closest to the water, book a room in the Mokapu Beach Club.

ASTON WAILEA RESORT, *3700 Wailea Alanui, Kihei, HI 96753. Tel. 808/879-1922 or 800/922-7866, Fax 808/874-8331. 516 rooms. Double rooms begin at $215. Major credit cards.*

The first hotel in the area, this is a group of low-rise units and a seven-story main building scattered across 22 acres. Sporting koa wood rocking chairs and Pacific art, the attractive ocean view lobby resembles a living room without walls. Most guest rooms face the ocean and contain commodious dressing rooms. All have lanais. Floor-to-ceiling mirrors serve as sliding closet doors. The L-shaped junior suites are especially nice.

Guests spend much of their time on the three Wailea golf courses and tennis courts, in the three hotel swimming pools, two whirlpools, restaurants, and lounge. Once a week in the lobby, you can buy handicrafts made by local artists. In addition to lei-making classes and other crafts demonstrations, a luau is held at the water's edge three times a week. Attend this Hawaiian feast, and chances are, you'll see a breathtaking sunset during the festivities. Many agree that the centerpiece of the action is the award-winning fire dancer. Aston Wailea's children's program (available several days a week) attracts families to the resort.

THE PALMS AT WAILEA, *3200 Wailea Alanui Drive, Wailea, HI 96753. Tel. 808/879-5800 or 800/688-7444, Fax (303)369-9403. 77 units. Rates begin at $200 per condo. Major credit cards.*

One of Wailea's nicest condos, the Palms offers contemporary apartments decorated in earth tones and pastels, with open, airy layouts. Life-like silk plants are among the furnishings. Lanais are large, with lots of seating as well as tables for dining al fresco. Kitchens are modern, complete with icemakers, blenders, toasters, and coffee makers. A washer/dryer comes with each unit and there is lots of closet space. You'll find a swimming pool and whirlpool on the grounds. Golf, tennis, shopping, and the beach are all nearby.

My only problem is that bedrooms are air-conditioned, but living rooms have ceiling fans instead and can get a bit warm.

WAILEA VILLAS – DESTINATION RESORTS, *3750 Wailea Alanui, Wailea, HI 96753. Tel. 808/879-1595 or 800/367-5246, Fax 808/874-3554. 782 units in 4 villages. Rates begin at $145 per condo. Major credit cards.*

Two of these condominium complexes are on the beach, but all are surrounded by flourishing, well-tended, sprawling grounds. Swimming pools are here for those not in the mood for the sand. The upscale apartments come with one, two, or three bedrooms, full kitchens, and private lanais. Guests receive discount golf rates.

Wailea Ekolu Village and Wailea Grand Champions Villas are right on Wailea's Blue Golf Course. The Wailea Tennis Club is nearby. Wailea Elua is where you'll find the most attractive – and most expensive – apartments. Wailea Ekahi is beach side, and families find it especially appealing. A concierge is on hand to see to guests' needs, such as making arrangements for children's programs.

WAILEA GRAND CHAMPIONS VILLAS, *3750 Wailea Alanui, Wailea, HI 96753. Tel. 808/879-1595 or 800/367-5246, Fax 808/874-3554. 188 units. Rates begin at $175 per condo. Major credit cards.*

At this condo you can literally tee off in your backyard. Appealing to golf lovers, the guest units, in two-story buildings, are right on the green of Wailea's Blue Golf course. There are also Laykold night-lit courts for tennis enthusiasts. Kitchens of these one- and two-bedroom units open onto lanais overlooking the golf course – but there are plenty of restaurants nearby for those who don't intend to put fire to any pans. Master bedrooms have their own lanais, and living/dining areas are spacious. On the attractive 11-acre grounds are two pools, two Jacuzzis, and barbecue areas. The closest beaches are a two-minute drive away and beach towels are provided for guests' use. Families with little ones may make arrangements through the concierge for participation in children's programs. Ask about golf and tennis packages.

Makena

MAKENA SURF, *3750 Wailea Alanui, Wailea, HI 96753. Tel. 808/879-1595 or 800/367-5246, Fax 808/874-3554. 107 units. Rates begin at $300 per condo. Major credit cards.*

With views of four islands (if you count Molokini), this attractive condo complex appears much smaller than it is. It sits at the foot of a hilly golf course. Guests are drawn to the sandy beach, two swimming pools, and four tennis courts. Use of tennis rackets and tennis clinics are complimentary. Guests get to know each other during the weekly poolside receptions. Grounds are meticulously manicured.

The one-, two- and three-bedroom units are found in three-story buildings, one right at the ocean's edge, the others on a grassy rise. These rooms are accented with oak cabinets, sliding glass doors that lead to lanais, large closets, and remote-control TV. Rooms in the newer two-story building are larger, with higher ceilings, and are quieter. All downstairs units have either marble floors or carpeting, while all upstairs units are carpeted. The ultra-modern dream kitchen includes a Sub Zero refrigerator, mirrored walls, and whitewashed oak cabinetry. Guest bathrooms have full soaking tubs and showers. Master bathrooms are huge, with a separate shower, Jacuzzi tub, double sinks, and walk-in closets. Ask the concierge about children's programs.

MAUI PRINCE, *5400 Makena Alanui, Makena, HI 96753. Tel. 808/874-1111 or 800/321-MAUI, Fax 808/879-8763. 310 rooms. Double rooms begin at $270. Major credit cards.*

The high standard of service, the unobtrusive staff, and the spare, stylish decor bring many repeat guests to this attractive beach front hotel. In the open-air lobby, tall wooden louvered doors are pushed back by day to expose the central octagonal courtyard below. Gaze down, and you'll see a garden with a waterfall, streams, and lush plantings. The Prince Court is the hotel's signature Hawaii regional restaurant. Complete with a sushi bar, Hakone is an excellent Japanese dining spot.

Al fresco corridors outside guest rooms overlook the garden courtyard and the volcano propping up clouds in the distance. Most rooms have views of the Pacific from their lanais. Special touches include remote-control TVs, video cassette players, refrigerators stocked with complimentary fruit juices and bottled water; slippers and robes for guests' use during their stay; and handheld shower nozzles. Room service is available from 6am to midnight.

The two round pools near the two golf courses are disappointingly small and shallow, but a landscaped pathway leads to the hotel's beach and other beaches are also nearby. Note that golfers can reserve their tee times when making their hotel reservations. Tennis (on six courts) and horseback riding can also be arranged. Ask about the sports and activities package. Children aged 5 to 12 are invited to participate in the Prince Kids Club, which includes activities such as painting coconuts, feeding fish, castle-building, arts and crafts, scavenger hunts, and lunch.

Hana

HOTEL HANA-MAUI, *P.O. Box 9, Hana, HI 96713. Tel. 808/248-7211 or 800/321-4262, Fax 808/248-7202. 93 rooms. Double rooms begin at $395. Major credit cards.*

In a remote part of Maui, this is the kind of place many people picture when they think of Hawaii. The post-WWII Hotel Hana-Maui is perfect for those with a taste for rustic elegance. Don't go looking for all the trimmings you'd expect at other equally expensive hotels: There are no TVs or radios in guest rooms and room service isn't available; ceiling fans stand in for air-conditioning. Yet pampering is no stranger. Travelers sleep in individual rooms, suites, cottages and a restored nineteenth-century plantation house that rests on a hilltop. All bathtubs have views of gloriously colorful patios or gardens. Hulking rattan furniture stands on bleached hardwood floors and counters are topped with stone. Replicas of traditional Hawaiian quilts cover beds, and walls are decorated with original local art. Rooms also have refrigerators, ice-machines, and wet bars.

Hot tubs are found on lanais at Sea Ranch Cottages, among the most luxurious of the hotel's accommodations. They were built to resemble old plantation houses. One swimming pool and the hot tub sit on a rise overlooking the cottages and the rocky shore. This is where you'll find the Wellness Center, where you can work out on exercise machines or take an aerobics class. Horses are fenced off in a neighboring field. Across the road, the garden swimming pool is near the original guest rooms, by the restaurant, bar, and shops. The more scenic beach is about 2.5 miles away, but there's also another one a brief stroll down the road. Horseback riding, guided hikes to secluded waterfalls, snorkeling excursions, and hula and ukulele lessons are among the activities open to guests. There are also free bicycles, two tennis courts, a three-hole putting green, and a jogging trail that follows the route of a famed ancient Hawaiian runner.

HEAVENLY HANA INN, *Box 790, Hana, Maui, HI 96713. Tel. and Fax 808/248-8442. 3 suites. Rates begin at $180 per suite.*

This is one of my favorite small places to stay because it exudes character. At the entrance, two stone lions stand as sentinels at an elaborate Japanese gate decorated with Japanese lanterns. The one- and two-bedroom suites are outfitted with shoji screens, fresh flower arrangements, queen-size or twin futon beds, and other Japanese-style furniture. Each of the tiled baths, which look out to gardens, sports a Japanese-style soaking tub and a separate shower.

HANA KAI-MAUI, *1533 Uakea Road, Hana, HI 96713. Tel. 808/248-8426 or 800/346-2772, Fax 808/248-7482. 18 units. Rates begin at $125 per condo.*

If you want to be on a beach in Hana, this condominium is the place to stay. Unfortunately, however, the picturesque shore here is rocky and thus better for sunbathing than swimming. A spring dribbles into a lava rock decorative pool. All with large lanais and kitchens, the commodious apartments face the water. Guests are welcome to play ping pong and horseshoe. Don't expect telephones or radios.

BED & BREAKFASTS & PRIVATE HOMES

One of the best ways to get to know the real side of Maui is to stay in a Bed & Breakfast or private home. Note that a minimum number of nights stay may be required. To find out about vacation homes or B&Bs in addition to those described in this chapter, contact the following:

Bed & Breakfast Honolulu, *3242 Kaohinani Drive, Honolulu, HI 96817. Tel. 595-7533 or 800/288-4666;*

Bed & Breakfast Hawaii, *P.O. Box 449, Kapaa, Kauai, HI 96746. Tel. 822-7771 or 800/675-7832.*

To rent a private home in Hana, contact **Hana Kai Holidays.** Tel. 248-7742 or 800/548-0478.

HANA PLANTATION HOUSES, *P.O. Box 249, Hana, HI 96713. Tel. 808/923-0772 or 800/228-4262, Fax 808/922-6068. 12 units. Rates begin at $80 per unit. Major credit cards.*

These former plantation cottages along the Hana coast have been transformed into exceptional vacation rentals with a quiet ambiance that offers relief from hectic mainland tensions. Most offer luxurious views of the ocean or the mountains. Some feature hot tubs and whirlpools. Some cottages are oceanfront or in botanical gardens.

Housekeeping Cabins

Some people book cabins in Maui's parks more than a year in advance, so make your reservations as far ahead of your trip as possible. This is an inexpensive way for outdoor-types to absorb Maui.

WAIANAPANAPA STATE PARK, *Division of Parks, 54 South High Street, Wailuku, HI 96793. Tel. 808/984-8109. Rate: $45 for up to four people per cabin; $5 for each additional person.*

Near Hana, this is a good choice for spending a few nights after the gorgeous 52-mile, twisting, turning drive from Kahului. The 12 cabins sit on a precipice above a striking black sand beach where the body surfing is often quite good. Only very strong swimmers should attempt to explore the freshwater caves. On the other hand, the four-mile trail to Hana isn't too rigorous a hike. As many as six people can sleep in each shelter. Cabins come complete with electricity, hot water, stoves, refrigerators, cooking and eating utensils, showers, beds, bedding and towels.

POLIPOLI STATE PARK, *Division of Parks, 54 South High Street, Wailuku, HI 96793. Tel. 808/984-8109. Rate: $45 for up to four people per cabin; $5 for each additional person.*

Six thousand feet above sea level on a slope of Haleakala volcano, Polipoli State Park offers a solitary three-bedroom cabin that accommodates up to ten people. There is no electricity or refrigeration, but cooking and eating utensils, beds, bedding, and towels are all provided, along with wood and gas lanterns. You may have to remind yourself that you're in the tropics when you enter the forest, dense with cedar, ash, Monterey cypress and a stand of California redwood trees. It also gets quite cold up here. Along the many hiking trails, you might come across such birds as quail or ring-necked pheasants. If you happen to be here in June, look for ripe Methley plums.

HALEAKALA NATIONAL PARK CABINS. *To secure one of these cabins, you'll have to enter a lottery by mailing your choice of dates (at least three months in advance) to Haleakala National Park, P.O. Box 369, Makawao, HI 96768. Tel. 808/572-9306, but no telephone or fax requests will be accepted. Note that weekends, holidays, and the summer months are the most popular - and thus busiest - times for camping here. Rates: $40 for 1 to 6 people; $80 for 7 to 12 people.*

Eerie and stark but rugged, Haleakala's volcanic crater offers three cabins for experienced campers. Kapaloa Cabin rests nearly six miles down from the trailhead at the volcano's summit. The hike down to Holua Cabin is almost 7.5 miles long. And you'll have to trek just under 10 miles to reach Paliku Cabin. Each shelter provides limited water, a wood-burning stove, firewood, and cooking and eating utensils. While cabins are furnished with beds, you'll have to provide your own blankets or sleeping bags and your own light.

Remember: at night and in the morning, it gets mighty chilly at the summit and in the crater; but the sun is surprisingly strong, so be sure to bring sunglasses and sunblock. Light rain gear will also come in handy. Keep an eye out for silversword, the rare and delicate endangered plant; wild goats; and the nene goose, Hawaii's state bird.

WHERE TO EAT

Maui's restaurants are concentrated in West Maui and northwestern East Maui. Kahului and Wailuku are home to a selection of good, casual eateries patronized mainly by locals. Some of them serve Hawaiian

---

BEST EATS ON MAUI

The Cream of the Crop

Chez Paul, *Olowalu, just south of Lahaina: The accent is French.*

Seasons, *the Four Seasons Wailea: The gourmet meals are almost too beautifully presented to eat.*

A Pacific Cafe, *Kihei: The blend of Pacific and continental cuisines is wonderfully creative.*

Hali'imaile General Store, *upcountry Maui: Colorful sophistication comes to the countryside.*

David Paul's Lahaina Grill, *Lahaina: The tequila shrimp with firecracker rice is truly hot!*

Joe's Bar & Grill, *Wailea: Celebrities love the imaginative comfort food.*

Hula Grill, *Kaanapali: The chef who runs this place helped create Hawaii's new regional cuisine.*

Inexpensive

Thai Chef, *Lahaina: Sample the ginger coconut soup and spring rolls.*

Komoda's, *Makawao: Maui's best bakery is known for its delicious cream puffs.*

Tasty Crust, *Wailuku: Join the crowds for a real local breakfast.*

Casanova's Deli and Restaurant, *Makawao: Expect delicious sandwiches, pasta, and pizza.*

cuisine. You'll notice that, unless you're at a luau, contemporary "Hawaiian food" usually includes items such as Spam and eggs, Portuguese sausage, and *saimin* (noodle soup with vegetables and meat) – a reflection of the islands' varied ethnic influences. Many restaurants serve one version or another of **hula pie**. What is it? Ice cream on a crunchy cookie crust with macadamia nuts and whipped cream – real low calorie!

Tedeschi Winery and Vineyards on Ulupalakua Ranch in upcountry Maui produces the state's only **local wines**, from a pineapple variety to bubbly.

Kapalua

THE BAY CLUB, *Kapalua Bay Hotel. Tel. 669-5656. Reservations required. Dinner entrees: $25 to $45. Credit cards accepted.*

One of Maui's most attractive (and most expensive) restaurants, the Bay Club sits in a wooden building with its own pool and deck, and a glorious view of Molokai and Lanai. Open to the palms and the ocean, the room is refreshed by tropical breezes. While it's a wonderful spot for lunch, the quiet tunes of a pianist also make it appealing in the evening. Large ceiling fans rotate above high-backed rattan chairs and handsome paneled walls. The menu features delicious seafood, prepared in a variety of delicious ways.

Kahana & Kaanapali

SWAN COURT, *Hyatt Regency Maui, Kaanapali Beach. Tel. 661-1234. Reservations recommended. Dressy at night (jackets optional for men). Dinner entrees: $26 to $39. Credit cards accepted.*

Swans float past tables near the lagoon in this elegant open-air dining room that has been dubbed "Most Romantic Restaurant" by the *Lifestyles of the Rich and Famous* TV show. Your feelings about the show notwithstanding, this truly is an exceptional (and expensive) place to dine, whether for dinner, lunch or the breakfast buffet. The chef has won awards for his veal chops and Baked Alaska. Other good selections include chicken cooked in bourbon and fish with mushrooms and capers.

NIKKO, *Maui Marriott, Kaanapali Beach. Tel. 667-1200. Reservations required. Dinner entrees: $19.95 to $39.95. Credit cards accepted.*

If you've ever been to Benihana of Tokyo, you'll know what to expect at this Japanese steak and seafood house. Diners sit at communal tables where the food is cooked by a chef who tells a stream of jokes while catching bowls of rice he has tossed behind his back, throwing shrimp over his shoulder onto the grill, and juggling huge razor-sharp knives.

SUNSET TERRACE, *Hyatt Regency Maui, Kaanapali Beach. Tel. 661-1234. Reservations required. Entrees: $15 to $30. Credit cards accepted.*

The luau buffet is accompanied by the Drums of the Pacific Polynesian

Revue. Mai Tais and other drinks flow from the open bar. Diners choose among teriyaki chicken, sautéed *ono*, sweet and sour pork, teriyaki steak and other traditional Hawaiian dishes. For dessert, try the macadamia nut pie. Arrive early to get a good seat.

ROY'S KAHANA BAR & GRILL, *Kahana Gateway Center, 4405 Honoapiilani Highway, Kahana. Tel. 669-6999. Reservations recommended. Dinner entrees: $14.95 to $26.95. Credit cards accepted.*

After making a name for himself with his Honolulu restaurant, Roy Yamaguchi opened another one on Maui. Look for imaginative creations such as blackened *ahi* (tuna) with spicy soy mustard. Desserts might include fresh peach creme brulee, dark chocolate soufflé, or apple cobblers with blueberries or peaches. Jazz plays in the background while talkative diners watch the chefs at work in the open kitchen.

ROY'S NICOLINA RESTAURANT, *Kahana Gateway Center, 4405 Honoapiilani Highway, Kahana. Tel. 669-5000. Dinner entrees: $14.95 to $26.95. Credit cards accepted.*

The menu is very similar to that of Roy's Kahana Bar & Grill, its sister restaurant right next door. But the ambiance in this dimly lit dining spot is much more quiet and romantic. The menu offers a few tempting vegetarian dishes in addition to seafood, poultry, and red meat. Along with duck with star anise cabernet sauce and crispy coconut shrimp sticks, you might find grilled vegetable and Thai chicken pizza.

HULA GRILL, *2435 Kaanapali Parkway, Building P, Whalers Village, Kaanapali Beach. Tel. 667-6636. Reservations recommended. Dinner entrees: $14.95 to $24.95. Credit cards accepted.*

Chef Peter Merriman first made a big splash with Hawaii's new regional cuisine on the Big Island, starting at the Mauna Lani Bay Hotel, then moving to his own restaurant, Merriman's. Now he brings to Maui this exciting melange of Pacific, Asian, and European cooking styles, emphasizing fresh local produce. Try to reserve an oceanside table and arrive before dark so you can watch the sun set.

I love the sweet, garlicky dipping sauce served with the foccacia bread (you can even buy a bottle to take home). Seafood is the focus of the menu. You might begin with Tahitian poisson cru (fish marinated in lime juice and coconut milk with Maui onions), sashimi, or macadamia nut and crab dim sum. Seared on the outside and raw in the middle, the wok-charred ahi resembles rare roast beef. The Kula vegetable primavera in a garlic cream sauce is a good choice for pasta, and the free range jerk chicken breast with tropical fruit chutney is also delicious. For dessert (but only if you promise to jog an extra mile or two the next day), consider the coconut creme brulee or the ice cream sandwich (vanilla ice cream, macadamia nut brownies, raspberry puree, and whipped cream!).

LEILANI'S ON THE BEACH, *Whalers Village, Kaanapali Parkway. Tel. 661-4495. Dinner entrees: $14.95 to 19.95. Credit cards accepted.*

You may have a long wait for a table on weekends, but most of the food is worth it. Decorated with local art, some walls are paneled in golden brown wood. Others are made of exposed rugged lava rock. Many enjoy dining on the curved terrace overlooking the water. Friends and I have had the best luck with the charbroiled teriyaki tuna; ginger chicken; deep-fried Malaysian shrimp; Cajun-style fish; and baby back pork ribs. Down-stairs at the beachside grill, tables are lit by the dancing flames of torches.

SOUND OF THE FALLS, *Westin Maui, 2365 Kaanapali Parkway, Kaanapali. Tel. 667-2525. Open 9am to 1pm only. Entrees: $10 to $25. Credit cards accepted.*

This al-fresco restaurant by the hotel's huge waterfall-fed swimming pool is a good choice for an elaborate Sunday buffet brunch, featuring everything from champagne and a sushi bar to waffles.

Lahaina

GERARD'S, *The Plantation Inn, 174 Lahainaluna Road. Tel. 661-8939. Reservations required. Dinner entrees: $24.50 to $32.50. Credit cards accepted.*

This casual restaurant began as a small bistro near Front Street. It is now ensconced in plusher digs in a wonderful turn-of-the-century-style inn. The inner dining room is graced with stained glass over French doors, brass, and oak. White wicker chairs are set off with floral cushions in pinks and greens. The lanai, filled with white garden furniture, is enclosed by Victorian pillars, an elegant balustrade, and delicate latticework. Pink umbrellas fringed in white shade outdoor tables while fluffy hanging plants rustle in the breeze. Try the roasted Hawaiian snapper with hot pepper, orange, and ginger, the venison with berry compote, or the lamb stew with spinach ravioli. The creme brulee and the macadamia nut chocolate cake are popular for dessert.

DAVID PAUL'S LAHAINA GRILL, *Lahaina Inn, 127 Lahainaluna Road. Tel. 667-5117. Reservations recommended. Dinner entrees: $20 to $30. Credit cards accepted.*

If you're dining in a group of six to eight, you could be in for a real treat at this bistro: you can arrange for David Paul Johnson himself to prepare a special dinner for you at the chef's table. The atmosphere is always cheery and elegant, with white table linen, delicate china, and small crystal vases with fresh flowers. Expect to find "new American cuisine" with Pacific Rim flair, such as Kalua duck with plum wine sauce, tequila shrimp with firecracker rice, or pan-seared ahi. The crab meat appetizer arrives looking like a sundae topped with avocado and caviar. Be sure to save room for dessert. You'll probably find yourself agreeing with those who call the orange basil ice cream "orgasmic."

KIMO'S, 845 Front Street. Tel. 661-4811. Dinner entrees: $15 to $30. Credit cards accepted.

A great place for drinks and sunset watching, Kimo's is a popular steak and seafood restaurant. Sit upstairs or downstairs on the lanai at the water's edge. Potted plants and flaming torches add to the pleasant atmosphere. The selection of local fish is broad, from *hapu* (Hawaiian sea bass) and *uhua* (deep-sea pompano) to *a'u* (broadbill swordfish) and *ahi* (Hawaiian big game yellowfin tuna). Preparation of the fish is your choice, from broiled in lemon butter to grilled spicy Cajun style. Also on the menu are teriyaki sirloin steak, hamburgers, and Koloa pork ribs glazed with plum sauce. Children's portions are available. If you leave room for dessert, try the macadamia nut ice cream, hula pie, or the lilikoi (passion fruit) sherbet.

LONGHI'S, 888 Front Street. Tel. 667-2288. Dinner entrees: $15 to $28. Credit cards (but not reservations) accepted.

The accent is on the Italian at this noisy waterfront dining spot that sells T-shirts emblazoned with its logo. Despite its long-standing popularity, some meals I've had here were disappointing. My bland pesto penne, for example, was totally devoid of zip. Instead of handing out written menus, the waiters sit down with diners or squat to eye level to present the mercurial choices orally. Most of the ingredients are Maui-grown. The pasta, breads, and pastries are all made on the premises. Although greasy, the pizza bread with jalapenos is delicious. The midday menu might feature lobster, shrimp, or Greek salad, crab and chicken cannelloni, or pasta marinara. Breakfast begins with freshly squeezed orange juice and freshly ground Kona coffee.

AVALON, 844 Front Street. Tel. 667-5559. Reservations recommended. Dinner entrees: $14 to $26. Credit cards accepted.

This colorfully decorated restaurant features Hawaiian regional cuisine with an Asian flair. Try the grilled chicken breast in a ginger sesame dressing served with crunchy rice noodles, macadamia nuts, and Hawaiian field greens; the seafood in black bean sauce; or the steamed Chinese dumplings. If you're into celebrity watching, this is a good choice.

SUNRISE CAFE, 693 Front Street, near the library and Baldwin Home Museum. Tel. 661-8558. Reservations recommended. Dinner entrees: $10.95 to $17.95. Credit cards accepted.

This tiny cafe emphasizes healthy eats, serving lightly stir-fried vegetables and brown rice with most of the fish, chicken, and shellfish entrees. Try the cappuccino prawns and the cheese cake – both have won culinary awards. No alcohol is served, but you are welcome to bring your own.

MOOSE McGILLYCUDDY'S, 844 Front Street. Tel. 667-7758. Dinner entrees: $9.95 to $22.95. Credit cards accepted.

Sit on the second-floor lanai, and you'll overlook Front Street action. For breakfast, you'll get a poster-sized menu offering pancakes, all kinds of omelets, and other delicious choices. Monday and Thursday nights, folks pack the house for the all-you-can-eat king crab dinners. Drawing a young crowd, this place gets pretty wild after dark, with entertainment until 2am.

THAI CHEF, *Lahaina Shopping Center. Tel. 667-2814. Closed for lunch Saturday and Sunday. Dinner entrees: $7.95 to $13.95. Credit cards accepted.*

This casual, low-profile restaurant is a good place to take a break from shopping in Lahaina. Tucked away in a very local shopping center, it serves ginger coconut soup; spring rolls; red, green, or yellow curry chicken; garlic vegetable shrimp; beef broccoli; pad Thai (a noodle dish); vegetarian selections; and other well-seasoned favorites. Try the Thai tapioca pudding for dessert. If you want alcohol with your meal, you'll have to bring your own.

Olowalu

CHEZ PAUL, *West Maui (Highway 30, about 4 miles south of Lahaina). Tel. 661-3843. Reservations required. Dinner served at either 6:30 or 8:30pm. Dinner entrees: $22 to $33. Credit cards accepted.*

With just over a dozen tables – each sparkling with china and crisp linen – this is one of Maui's finest restaurants. Mirrors enlarge the cozy dining room, lit by flickering candles. There are only two seatings, either 6:30pm or 8:30pm. The imaginative French menu is always changing. One day you might find veal cooked with green apples and Calvados while another you might run across local opakapaka fish poached in white wine, bathed in a creamy sauce with capers and shallots. Food is always artistically presented.

Wailuku & Kahului

THE CHART HOUSE, *500 North Puanene Avenue, Kahului. Tel. 877-2476. Reservation recommended. Dinner entrees: $16.50 to $26.95. Credit cards accepted.*

The food here has never knocked me out. However, this steak and seafood restaurant is quite popular, perhaps more for its pleasant harbor side location than its meals. I've had the best luck with the charbroiled yellowfin tuna in a lemon sauce. There's also a Chart House in Lahaina (*1450 Front Street, Tel. 661-0937*).

THE ICHIBAN RESTAURANT, *47 Kaahumanu Avenue, Kahului. Tel. 871-6977. Dinner entrees: $8.95 to $12.95. Credit cards accepted.*

You'll find many Japanese diners at this casual restaurant that serves delicious sashimi, tempura, sukiyaki, and teriyaki.

CHUMS RESTAURANT, *1900 Main Street, Wailuku. Tel. 244-1000.*

Entrees: $6 to $8.

Breakfast, lunch, and dinner are all busy times of day here. The wooden booths make for comfortable seating. Walls are decorated with old advertisements bearing slogans such as "Thompson's Bread for the Family" and "Guinness for Strength." If you try a *loco moco* (beef patty, egg, rice and lakes of gravy), you might be mistaken for a *kamaaina* (long-time resident). Also on the menu are Portuguese bean soup, *saimin*, won ton soup, curried beef stew, chili, oxtail soup, and other hearty homestyle selections.

TASTY CRUST, *1770 Mill Street, Wailuku. Tel. 244-0845. Inexpensive.*

Locals swear by the pancakes and saimin served at Tasty Crust, a.k.a. "T.C. Restaurant."

RAMON'S, *2102 Vineyard Street, Wailuku. Tel. 244-7243. Inexpensive.*

Credit cards accepted.

As one resident puts it, "This is where they cook local food the way it's supposed to be cooked." Don't come here unless you're *very* hungry. The portions of kalua pork, lau lau, hamburger steak, and other favorites are quite generous. The expanded menu includes Mexican specialties such as enchiladas, tacos, and chile rellenos.

MA-CHAN'S OKAZU-YA, *199 Dairy Road, Kahului (near the airport).*
Tel. 877-7818. Inexpensive.

If you'd like to sample a variety of ethnic foods of Hawaii, this cafeteria-style restaurant is the place. The shrimp tempura, pork tofu, teriyaki cod fish, salt cabbage, pork adobo, curry stew, and Spanish meat balls are all good selections.

Pa'ia Area

MAMA'S FISH HOUSE, *799 Poho Place. Tel. 579-8488. Reservations recommended for dinner. Dinner entrees: $10 to $20. Credit cards accepted.*

Just outside Pa'ia, popular Mama's Fish House is located along the Hana Highway. While it is something of an institution, some diners have thought it overpriced and touristy; and a few say it serves up more hype than good food. But you would probably do well to try the sweet potato fries, the fish filet stuffed with shrimp, or the smoked fish mousse. Some say lunch is the best meal here.

KIHATA RESTAURANT, *117 Lower Pa'ia, Pa'ia. Tel. 579-9035. Closed Monday and for lunch on Sunday. Inexpensive. Credit cards accepted.*

This eatery, complete with a sushi bar, serves good Japanese cuisine. Try the noodle dishes.

Makawao Area

HALI'IMAILE GENERAL STORE, *900 Hali'imaile Road, Hali'imaile. Tel. 572-2666. Reservations required. Dinner entrees: $16 to $28. Credit cards accepted.*

Located upcountry, this restaurant snags many residents as well as vacationers on their way to and from Haleakala Crater. (However, note that it closes between lunch and dinner.) This gourmet dining spot seems just a bit out of place in the middle of pineapple fields. Born as a plantation store back in 1925, it was turned into a restaurant in 1988 by a successful local caterer, Beverly Gannon, and her husband, Joe. Fresh flowers and artwork splash the bright, spacious dining room with color. The window above the bar is etched with a depiction of the building. You can also eat outside on the lanai.

For dinner, you might start with fish cakes with a ginger cilantro remoulade or crab dip on a pizza crust, then move on to Szechuan barbecued salmon with caramelized onion and orange peel or rack of lamb Hunan style with sesame and black beans. For dessert, don't miss the Kona coffee cheesecake and other freshly baked goods.

CASANOVA'S DELI AND RESTAURANT, *1188 Makawao Avenue, Makawao. Tel. 572-0220. Deli open for breakfast and lunch; restaurant open for lunch and dinner. Dinner entrees: $10 to $22. Credit cards accepted.*

A funky little Italian eatery, the deli is the place to find a variety of fresh breads and pastries along with pasta and pizza. Sandwiches range from smoked salmon, chicken breast with mozzarella and pesto sauce, and salami and cheese to marinated zucchini and goat cheese or veggie burgers. Soups, salads, and bagels are also on the menu. Dine on the lanai, where residents often relax behind newspapers.

For heavier fare, head into the restaurant. The ricotta and spinach dumplings and the tube pasta with chicken, broccoli, and sun-dried tomatoes in a cream sauce are both really good. Entertainment on weekends and Wednesday nights brings the party crowd.

POLLI'S, *1202 Makawao Avenue, Makawao. Tel. 572-7808. Dinner entrees: $7.95 to $11.95. Credit cards (but not reservations) accepted.*

The Buffalo chicken wings get good reports at this mostly Mexican restaurant. Sizzling fajitas and seafood enchiladas are house specialties. Few patrons pass up a chance to sample one of Polli's margaritas. Breakfast, lunch, and dinner are served daily.

CAFE MAKAWAO, *3682 Baldwin Avenue, Makawao. Tel. 572-1101. Inexpensive.*

If you're in the mood for something organic, healthy, and light, stop for breakfast, lunch, or dinner here. Salads and imaginative sandwiches highlight the afternoon and evening menus.

KITADA'S KAU KAU KORNER, 3617 Baldwin Avenue, Makawao.
Tel. 572-7241. Inexpensive.

This rustic diner lures many Portuguese cowboys. It serves an excellent plate lunch, and saimin is on the menu – even for breakfast. Portions are large and patrons refill their own coffee cups and soda glasses.

Kula

KULA LODGE, Haleakala Highway, Route 377. Tel. 878-1535. Dinner entrees: $14 to $23. Credit cards accepted.

Perched on the edge of a cliff upcountry, this rustic dining spot yields a fabulous view of the island. The mahi-mahi burger is a good choice and there is a selection of vegetarian dishes. If you're on your way back from watching the sun rise over Haleakala Crater, consider stopping here for breakfast. Try the Belgian waffles with fresh strawberries or mangoes (when in season), topped with coconut syrup.

GRANDMA'S MAUI COFFEE, Keokea. Tel. 878-2140. Entrees: $5 to $6.

A family-run bakery and restaurant, this eatery serves coffee that is grown on Maui and roasted by owner Al France himself. He uses a roaster that was passed down from his great-great grandmother and is more than a century old. The recipes for the delicious baked goods have also been around for generations. Consider stopping here for breakfast. Other crowd pleasers are the sandwiches, stews, barbecue chicken, and Portuguese red bean soup.

Kihei & Wailea

SEASONS, Four Seasons Resort Maui at Wailea. Tel. 874-8000. Dinner only. Jacket and tie recommended for men. Reservations encouraged. Dinner entrees: $30 to $40. Credit cards accepted.

The continental and Pacific Rim presentation of local fish, grilled meats, and vegetables is spectacular here. Meals look more like works of colorful abstract art than food, but they are so delicious, they couldn't be anything but. Instead of butter, bread is spread with purees such as a melange of smoked tomatoes, roasted eggplant, and cheese. Breezes blow in from the terrace while soft music plays in the background. Weathered teak and bamboo paneling and a working fireplace add to the memorable ambiance. Dessert is accompanied by a selection of gourmet coffees. For a special occasion, ask about the "Tasting Menu" to sample a variety of dishes.

PACIFIC GRILL, Four Seasons Resort Maui at Wailea. Tel. 874-8000. Dinner entrees: $20 to $30. Credit cards accepted.

The upscale hotel's "casual" restaurant surprises with choices such as

Vietnamese coconut lemon grass shrimp soup, Thai spring rolls, Korean beefsteak, and warm herb bread that can be slathered with a spicy concoction of *kim chee*, onions, and sour cream.

CARELLI'S ON THE BEACH, *Keawakapu. Tel. 875-0001. Dinner only. No reservations accepted. Dinner entrees: $21 to $34. Credit cards accepted.*

This very popular oceanside Italian restaurant is redolent with garlic and olive oil. The authentic food and music make you feel as though you are on the Italian Riviera instead of the Wailea coast. Seafood is excellently prepared. The special on the menu might be *cioppino* (fish stew) or an imaginative chicken dish. While the food is delicious, recent patrons report that the snooty service was not as polite as it could have been.

SEAWATCH, *Wailea Golf Club. Tel. 875-8080. Dinner entrees: $20 to $24. Credit cards accepted.*

The golf bag drop and valet parking outside is indicative of the mixed ambiance of casual and elegant dining inside. While the sports bar lounge with a big-screen TV and deep, comfortable cushioned chairs attracts jocks and other sports enthusiasts, the dining room seems ready for a wedding party. With an incredible view of Molokai, Lanai, the golf courses, and the mountains, Seawatch serves breakfast, lunch, and dinner. Miso-glazed tiger prawns and kiawe-grilled rack of lamb are good choices.

JOE'S BAR AND GRILL, *131 Wailea Ike Place, Wailea. Tel. 875-7767. Dinner entrees: $16 to $28. Reservations recommended. Credit cards accepted.*

The folks who have made such a big splash with Hali'imaile General Store, in upcountry Maui, have opened this restaurant to more raves. The casual, chatty, open-air atmosphere is friendly and inviting. Guests are usually greeted by the owners, who seem always at hand. Don't be surprised if Natalie Cole or some other celebrity is dining at the next table. You'll find comfort food (with a twist) on the menu, such as meatloaf with barbecue sauce and mashed potatoes and grilled pork chops with sweet potatoes and dried fruit compote. The lobster pot pie is delicious. Consider kicking off your meal with a smoked salmon quesadilla with goat cheese and avocado-corn salsa, pan-seared soft shell crab, or shrimp and sweet potato fritters with red pepper remoulade.

A PACIFIC CAFE, *1279 South Kihei Road, Suite B-201 (Azeka Shopping Center), Kihei. Tel. 879-0069. Dinner entrees: $16 to $25. Reservations recommended. Credit cards accepted.*

A shopping center seems an unlikely setting for what promises to be one of your best dining experiences on Maui. The beamed cathedral ceiling, Polynesian art, and lush plants around the windows let you forget you're in a mall. Your meal will come on gorgeous plates that are individually designed by the wife of owner Jean-Marie Josselin. Then there is the matter of the many ingredients that go into each dish. To begin, you might choose the salmon firecracker roll with hot and sour chili vinaigrette and green papaya salad, the kalua pork and cabbage potstickers, or the baked sizzling New Zealand mussels with cashew, lemon, garlic, and brown butter balsamic syrup. Not one but three different types of bread come with dinner, my favorites being the foccacia and the ginger curry muffins. Your entree might be yellowfin tuna (cooked on the kiawe-wood burning grill) with garlic mashed potatoes, or roast duck with a sun-dried cherry star anise sauce. If you still have room for dessert, you can't go wrong with the guava sorbet.

LOBSTER COVE AND HARRY'S SUSHI AND PUPU BAR, *100 Wailea Ike Drive. Tel. 879-7677. Dinner only. Dinner entrees: $16 to $25. Credit cards accepted.*

The skilled sushi chef gets high praise from locals, who say that this restaurant serves the best sushi around. The pupus (Hawaiian appetizers) ain't bad either. There are wonderful sunset ocean views from the patio.

RADIO CAIRO, *Rainbow Mall, 2439 South Kihei Road, Suite 201A, Kihei. Tel. 808/879-4404. Reservations suggested. Dinner entrees: $12.95 to $19.95. Credit cards accepted.*

Original art from central and western Africa decorates this lively restaurant. Some sweet, some spicy, some mild, dishes are influenced by the cuisines of a variety of African countries. Popular choices include South African sosaties (skewered and grilled chicken marinated in apricot sauce), Marrakesh Tik Dip (a Sudanese blend of beans, peas, and spices), Moroccan curried vegetables with coconut sauce, Tanzanian spiced cabbage, and prawns piri-piri (a hot and spicy specialty from Mozambique). Portions are large, so two people often share a single order.

THAI CHEF, *Rainbow Mall, 2439 South Kihei Road, Kihei. Tel. 874-5605. No lunch served Saturday or Sunday. Dinner entrees: $7.95 to $13.95. Credit cards accepted. Beer and wine available at this location.*

Like its sister restaurant in Lahaina, this is a casual, low-profile restaurant. It serves ginger coconut soup; spring rolls; red, green, or yellow curry chicken; garlic vegetable shrimp; beef broccoli; Pad Thai (a noodle dish); vegetarian selections; and other well-seasoned favorites. Try the Thai tapioca pudding for dessert. If you want alcohol with your meal, you'll have to bring your own.

ALEXANDER'S FISH, CHICKEN & RIBS, *1913 South Kihei Road, Kihei. Tel. 874-0788. Entrees: $5.95 to $10.95. Credit cards accepted.*

If the fish and chips weren't so greasy, they probably wouldn't taste so good. Despite the boast that Alexander's uses only 100% heart-smart canola oil for their fried foods, you wouldn't want to eat here every day. But this fast food restaurant, with some outdoor seating, is worth one stop. Calamari, oysters, and shrimp are on the menu along with local fish such as mahi-mahi, ono, and ahi. You can choose something fried, broiled, barbecued, Cajun or teriyaki style. Order a sandwich, a combination meal, or a 13-piece basket for a picnic. Sides include corn bread, beans, buffalo wings, mixed veggies, onion rings, and hush puppies.

Makena

PRINCE COURT, *Maui Prince Hotel. Tel. 874-1111. Reservations required. Dinner entrees: $18 to $30. Credit cards accepted.*

The delicious Hawaii regional cuisine is further enhanced by the setting – candlelight, windows with louvered shutters that open to a courtyard graced with a garden. Many of the vegetables and spices are locally grown. On the menu, you might find conch chowder with Molokai sweet bread, slipper lobster in caviar cream, or Pacific clam scampi. Dessert specialties include Hana apple banana custard and chocolate macadamia nut caramel flan.

HAKONE, *Maui Prince Hotel. Tel. 874-1111. Dinner entrees: $16 to $30. Credit cards accepted.*

At this restaurant with a sushi bar, more than gifted chefs were imported from Japan. Most of the materials used to build Hakone were also brought from the East, including the wooden floor boards and the wall hangings. The bright, spare decor is in keeping with Japanese tradition, as is the delicious food.

Hana

HANA RANCH RESTAURANT, *Tel. 248-8255. Dinner Wednesday (pizza night), Friday, and Saturday only. Dinner entrees: $7.95 to $18.95. Credit cards accepted.*

Everyone from ranch hands and hotel workers to vacationers dines here. Tour groups crowd the restaurant during the buffet lunch. The dinner menu includes lobster, ribs, pasta, prawns, and fish, and the wine list is surprisingly good for such a remote dining spot.

THE RIGHT CHIP

*Affectionately known as Maui Potato Chips, **The Original Maui Kitch'n Cook'd Potato Chips** fly off supermarket shelves, despite their hefty price tag (sometimes more than $4 a bag). These famous crunchy chips have many competitors (such as Maui Style Potato Chips and Hawaiian Potato Chips), but you should try to stick with the originals. Cut from unpeeled potatoes, they are surprisingly thick, delicately salted, pleasantly un-greasy and preservative-free. A Japanese American couple who had been interned on the mainland during WWII began making these chips on Maui during the 1950s. Not long after mainland companies got wind of this delicious, quiet revolution, they began imitating these snacks.*

SEEING THE SIGHTS

The Arts

While commercial, touristy art can certainly be found on Maui, the island is better known for its many accomplished artists producing quality work. Maui sports more than three dozen galleries, mostly in Lahaina. Art exhibits and other cultural events take place throughout the year. A few hotels are virtual museums, such as the Westin Maui (with all kinds of antiques and its oversized marble Asian and European replicas) and the Hyatt Regency Maui (where an 18th century Burmese Buddha is only one item in the hotel's multi-million dollar collection). Both of these resorts are on Kaanapali Beach.

Begun in 1934 by a group of women headed by socialite Ethel Baldwin, the **Hui Noeau Visual Arts Center**, *2841 Baldwin Avenue, Makawao. Tel. 572-6560. Free admission. Open Tuesday to Sunday, 10am to 4pm*, is Maui's original art collective. A nonprofit art institute, Hui Noeau was begun in 1934 by a group of 21 women, headed by Ethel Baldwin, a prominent member of one of Maui's leading families. Located upcountry, just outside the center of the paniolo (cowboy) town of Makawao, it is housed in Mediterranean-style Kaluanui, the old Baldwin estate built in 1917. This gracious, sunny two-story building, now a historic landmark, rests on the upper slopes of Haleakala volcano, providing a perfect vantage point for a panoramic vista of the island. Colorful flowers are everywhere.

Near the entrance to the driveway, you'll see the ruins of one of Maui's first sugar mills. The nine acres of grassy grounds are studded with tall Cook Island pines and camphor trees. A reflecting pool sets off a scrupulously trim garden. Its name meaning "Club of Skills," Hui Noeau was born as a casual gathering of women who painted, sketched, and made pottery in the gardens of various homes, including Kaluanui. One of the other meeting places was the Baldwin beach house at Spreckelsville, where Ethel Baldwin's grandson, Colin Cameron (former president of the multimillion-dollar Maui Land and Pineapple Company) lived.

Today, exhibits and classes are open to visitors. If you miss one of the periodic art exhibitions, don't worry. Artwork and crafts are always on sale in the **gift shop**, which carries baskets, local posters, ceramics, hand-painted clothing and other imaginatively rendered items. Lectures through-out the year might be offered on weaving; hand paper making with fibers; Japanese woodblock printing; or *raku* and the art of tea ceremony ceramics. The ceramics studio, by the way, is housed in the former stables and tack rooms out back.

Workshops might be held on lei-making, Chinese calligraphy, pho-tography, jewelry-making and sculpture. The Hui currently has more than

---

MAUI'S BEST ATTRACTIONS

Whale Watching, November through March
Sunrise Over Haleakala Crater
Oheo Gulch Swimming Holes, Haleakala National Park
Drive Along Hana "Highway"
Guided Trek with Hike Maui
Hui Noeau Visual Arts Center, Makawao

---

600 members, from Hawaii, Australia, the mainland, and Canada. An annual Christmas craft fair takes place on these grounds.

After two decades of planning, the Maui Arts and Cultural Center has opened in Kahului. Its two theaters – one seating more than 1,000 people, the other, 200 – draw national touring companies as well as local drama groups. Art exhibitions are held in the 3,500-square-foot gallery. In March, the celebrated **Art Maui**, the island's most acclaimed art show, takes place here and the Kapalua Festival of the Arts draws crowds to the otherwise quiet Kapalua resort in West Maui.

The Art School At Kapalua, *800 Office Road, Kapalua, Tel. 665-0007,* offers both adults and children individual classes in everything from ballet and photography to ceramics, landscape painting, and figure sculpture. Prices of classes vary.

WEST MAUI

Created before Mount Haleakala in the east, the rugged **West Maui Mountains** have had more time to become expertly sculpted by the elements: Their last volcanic eruption probably occurred some 5,000 to 10,000 years ago, while Haleakala crater is thought to have spewed lava as recently as 500 to 1,000 years ago. West Maui is the busiest section of the island. It is home to **Kaanapali**, the major resort area; jungled **Iao Valley** (great for hiking) with its prominent Iao Needle; and the adjoining towns of **Kahului** (the island's port) and **Wailuku** (its administrative center). From Kaanapali Beach, along the west coast, there are striking views of Molokai and Lanai.

The North and East: A winter surfing area just north of Kapalua, **Honolua Bay** played a pivotal role in recent Hawaiian history. In 1976, the *Hokulea,* a replica of a double-hulled ancient Polynesian sailing canoe, set off from here with a 17-person crew for a two-month journey to Tahiti and back. The point of the excursion was to prove that Hawaii's ancient Polynesian settlers not only could have sailed but did sail to Hawaii on purpose and without the benefit of modern navigational techniques. The day the *Hokule'a* reached Tahiti was declared a national holiday as a huge crowd of Tahitians welcomed their long-lost cousins.

Honolua Bay, which attracts snorkelers in addition to surfers, provides one of the many dramatic vistas you'll see from lookouts as you drive north along the pine-fringed coast. The island of Molokai snoozes across the water. With the winding **Honoapiilani "Highway"** high above the shore, this undeveloped area offers many vantage points for spotting whales. Sprawling pineapple fields give way to jagged cliffs. Blind curves open up to views of gaping valleys. Spiky succulents, vine-clothed bushy trees, and leaning palms border the road. Suddenly the trees and shrubs vanish and rolling, rocky hills replace the lush greenery. Cows graze in the low grass. After the road narrows to one lane, you'll pass over a slip of a bridge.

Near Mile Marker #16 on West Maui's east coast, you'll gaze down on a huge round boulder at the edge of a bay, a rocky beach, and a red-roofed church with a steeple. You've reached the picturesque fishing village of **Kahakuloa**, one of Maui's first settlements. When you descend into this remote town, you might hit a traffic jam: Asking, "Ice tea or fruit punch?" children at a roadside refreshment stand often wave down cars, not letting them pass until drivers have paid the toll of purchasing a beverage or a bag of chips. The cool drinks certainly hit the spot and many visitors enjoy spending some time chatting with these kids.

After crossing a bridge over a rocky riverbed, you'll be in ranch land, with fenced-in cattle. The mountainous terrain is studded with pines and the road winds upward, affording sweeping views of the oceanfront. Hikers and others in the mood for scenic, rugged hideaways will come upon quiet beaches and good snorkeling spots along this eastern coast. East Maui looms in the distance, with its cloud-ringed summit of Haleakala. To continue circling West Maui, you can pass through the town of Wailuku, perhaps making a slight detour to Kahului, then go south toward Ma'alaea and northwest to Lahaina, Kaanapali, Honokowai, Kahana, Napili, and back to Kapalua.

Near the Kapalua-West Maui Airport, **Kapalua** draws vacationers with truly upscale tastes – and pocketbooks. The smooth, bright green expanses between the volcanic peaks and the beige shore are peppered with dark green Norfolk pines. Plush hotels, the sprawling Kapalua Bay and the Ritz Carlton Kapalua, beachfront and inland condominiums, and comfortable villas are scattered across 750 artfully planned acres. The locale for celebrated chamber music festivals and wine symposia, serene Kapalua is also known for its gourmet restaurants and chic boutiques. There's no need to be a golfer to enjoy the stunning vistas of duck-filled ponds and rolling hills on the Arnold Palmer-designed fairways. And tennis buffs have a hard time staying off the courts.

At the **Hawaiian Pineapple Plantation**, *Maui Pineapple Company, Ltd., Kapalua, Tel. 669-8088 (Kapalua Resort Activity Desk); open Monday through Friday, 9:30am to 12pm and 1pm to 3:30pm; cost: $19, including one pineapple, no children under age 12*, long-time plantation workers will lead you through Hawaii's largest pineapple plantation and cannery. As you take in sweeping views along the slopes of the West Maui Mountains, you'll learn about the history of the fruit that has been such a major part of the state's economic backbone. During the 2 1/2 hour tours, yellow company vans carry visitors into fields where ananas (pineapples) are being harvested. Vacationers will even have a chance to pick their own fruit to take home.

Along with Kapalua, the area between here and Honokowai to the south is one of my favorite parts of Maui. I get such a peaceful feeling driving along the narrow coastal road (not the highway) that winds past colorful vegetation, private homes, and low-rise condominiums. The few high-rise buildings here and there seem out of place. It's hard to believe that quiet **Napili**, a small, laid-back residential community with beach front condos, is only about a 15-minute drive north of bustling Kaanapali. Many vacationers have been returning for years to the same Napili condos. They are quite happy that many visitors haven't even heard of this area, with its handful of stores and restaurants.

While this region is picturesque, some of the coastline is rocky and a few of the beaches aren't especially good for swimming. High-rises are more plentiful in **Kahana** and **Honokowai**, two more quiet condominium communities just north of the main tourist center. From 7:30am to 11:30am, Monday and Thursday, **Honokowai** hosts a **Farmer's Market**, packed with all kinds of freshly plucked fruit, vegetables, freshly baked muffins and bread, cheeses, fresh juices and tropical flowers.

Kaanapali

If you arrive in Maui during the winter and drive to Kaanapali (which means "rolling cliffs") from Kahului Airport, you might spot whales from the sea cliffs along northwest West Maui. Cars may be pulled over while people stand on the nearby bluffs to get good looks at the mammoth mammals. Once vacationers reach Kaanapali, many park themselves in the resort and never budge. After all, the palm-fringed beach is gorgeous. Kaanapali is also Maui's center for renting jet skis, water-skiing, and windsurfing (whether you want to take lessons or just rent equipment). In the morning, rainbows often shimmer above the Pacific.

Deluxe hotels and condominiums sit across the electric blue water from the islands of Molokai and Lanai. At the Hyatt Regency Maui, parrots flap around an atrium ablaze with elaborate flower arrangements in tall vases. At The Westin Maui, swans glide across carp-filled ponds;

larger-than-life Buddhas line walkways, and weathered South Pacific art decorates corridors. Kaanapali also boasts a good selection of restaurants, Polynesian revues, waterfront luaus, shops, and tennis courts. *Mauka* (inland) of the three-mile beach, the two rich green 18-hole Kaanapali Golf Courses and patchwork land slope up ever so gently toward the West Maui Mountains, crowned with plump white clouds.

Along with shuttle buses, the steam-driven **Lahaina-Kaanapali and Pacific Railroad** (also called the **Sugar Cane Train**), Tel. 661-0089, takes passengers on a 12-mile round-trip ride through thick sugarcane fields. It was inspired by the turn-of-the-century trains that carried cane to the mills. Six round-trip excursions run daily between Puukolii and Lahaina. Free transportation is provided to Lahaina Harbor and the historic section of Front Street in a double-decker bus. The train ride costs about $13 round trip and $9 one way.

A ROYAL PLAYGROUND

With Hawaii's original capital in neighboring Lahaina, the Kamehamehas – the islands' most celebrated royal family – used Kaanapali as their playground. In these waters they fished, maneuvered their immense koa wood surfboards, and raced their outrigger canoes. On land, they satiated themselves at banquets and entertained each other with hula performances. Along the lowlands now covered by the golf courses, these alii also played ancient games such as ulu maika (lawn bowling).

As resorts go, Kaanapali is still a pup, born in 1962. During the 1950s, the board of directors of AmFac, owners of Kaanapali and most of its adjacent sugar cane fields, came up with the idea of turning the area into a resort. To discuss their plans, they got together for a luau on the beach at **Puu Kekaa** (a.k.a. **Black Rock**), a peninsula used as a diving platform by Maui's King Kahekili. (Today, every evening as the sun slips into the ocean, a diver reenacts these skillful leaps over the craggy rocks.) According to ancient tales, Puu Kekaa was also the departure point for the volcano goddess, Pele, who left to seek a new home elsewhere in the islands.

At the time when the AmFac businessmen dreamed up the resort, many residents of drowsy Maui earned their living either picking pineapple or cutting cane. After the demise of the whaling business in the 1800s, seamen had virtually deserted Lahaina, where streets were now lined with many broken-down, weather-beaten, and boarded-up buildings. The seat of the Hawaiian monarchy had left here to relocate in Honolulu.

Today, the Royal Lahaina Resort stands where Kaanapali's first 31 vacation cottages were built in 1962. Sheraton Maui, erected at Puu Kekaa – the site of AmFac's brainstorming feast – held its grand opening in 1963. Rooms went for a mere $15 a night. Now transformed into the splashy Westin Maui, the Maui Surf followed. Other hotels and condominiums sprouted during the 1960s, 1970s, and 1980s. Until 1981, Kaanapali had a horse-racing track.

Whalers Village is an open-air, oceanfront shopping center with two worthwhile museums (on whales and whaling) and several good restaurants. The **Whalers Village Museum,** *Whalers Village, Kaanapali Parkway, Kaanapali, Tel. 661-5992; free admission; open 9:30am to 10pm daily,* displays 19th century whaling implements, photos, the skeleton of a 30-foot sperm whale, and an old whaling boat. Videos provide additional information about Maui's lucrative whaling years. Also stop by **Hale Kohola Museum** (House of the Whale), *2435 Kaanapali Parkway,* Tel. 661-9918, which is devoted to the humpback whale.

Whale Watching is possible November through March. Humpback whales – which can be 45 feet long and weigh 40 tons – also appear along the coasts of other Hawaiian islands. Maui, however, is recognized as the whale watching capital of the archipelago, since the bulk of these massive visitors come to its shores. You'll get the most out of your vigil if you've packed a pair of binoculars. **The Pacific Whale Foundation,** *Tel. 879-8811,* sponsors cruises, with a marine biologist on board, to raise money for research and preservation of the humpbacks. Many other whale watching cruises depart from Lahaina. In recent years, some ecologists have urged people to cut down on the large number of boats that go searching for whales. These crafts can be disruptive to breeding and the general comfort of the animals.

Instead of traveling by sea, they suggest you choose a vantage point on land, such as the top of the cinder cone at Big Beach in the Makena area. You'll still have a great view as these giant mammals fluke (lift their tails into the air), breach (jump partially out of the water), and spurt water from their blowholes. Check with the **Whale Report Center** on the dock next to the *Carthaginian II* in Lahaina for up-to-date information about the best places to spot whales.

Lahaina

Just south of Kaanapali, much of Lahaina (the first royal capital of the Hawaiian Islands) has now been declared a National Historic Landmark. It was a flourishing whaling port during the 19th century. **Herman Melville,** of *Moby Dick* fame, was among the hundreds of sailors who passed through. Kaahumanu, Hawaii's regent and the favorite wife of King Kamehameha I, worried that the transient, unruly seamen would have a bad effect on residents. Coming from Oahu and the mainland to assist the queen, American missionaries helped pass laws against such behavior as spitting in public, and wanton sex between foreigners and Hawaiians both on land and at sea.

Lahaina began to fall into decay around 1850, when Hawaii's whaling industry started to slip and the islands' capital was officially moved to Honolulu. Today, with tourism, sugar, and pineapple Maui's main industries, much of the old town's charm (but little of its bawdiness) has been restored. Drunken sailors no longer pug it out on the shore or join rowdy packs in search of willing or unwilling Hawaiian women. Sunlight glints off the windows of the refurbished or recreated wooden Front Street buildings that now house a jumble of restaurants, cafes, T-shirt shops, jewelry stores, and clothing boutiques. Take the time to wade through the touristy souvenirs and you'll find a welcome array of quality goods. Most of Maui's major **art galleries** are in Lahaina, many along the main street.

The town was named for the relentless sun (*la haina*) that can be especially merciless in the afternoon. However, afternoon is also the time when you're likely to see rainbows, if you look *mauka* (toward the mountains). The town is most crowded during the cooler, earlier part of the day. Don't even think about trying to find a parking space then. Opt for the **Sugar Cane Train** (which is particularly popular among Japanese tourists) or one of the shuttles that run between town and accommodations in neighboring Kaanapali.

Lahaina is composed of only about four mile-long streets, which run parallel to the waterfront. Most of the sights are found on or adjacent to a half-mile section of Front Street. Plan to spend a couple of hours poking around here. The **Baldwin House Museum**, *Front Street, near Dickenson, Lahaina (next door to the Master's Reading Room), Tel. 661-3262, admission: $3 per person, $2 seniors (or $5 per couple or family), including a 20-minute tour, open 10am to 4:15pm daily,* is a good place to stop as soon as you get to Lahaina, since members of the Lahaina Restoration Foundation supply free walking tour maps of the historic town. The name of a prominent local family with missionary roots, Baldwin crops up frequently in Hawaiian history and on contemporary places of interest. The Maui News is owned by this clan, which has built schools, parks, and other public institutions. The Baldwins are respected for giving generously to the islands that gave them their wealth.

This The 19th-century home of the Reverend Dwight Baldwin, M.D., this whitewashed stone building contains furnishings that once belonged to this missionary physician, his children, and grandchildren. From the mid-1830s through the late 1860s, Dr. Baldwin and his family welcomed countless patients, fellow missionaries, whaling captains, and members of the congregation who came to chat or to seek medicine or advice.

Today, visitors are invited to take a look at the 1859 Steinway piano; the imported china on display in the dining room; the gleaming four-poster *koa* wood bed and the monkeypod crib; and Maui's first toilet. The opium-smoking couch from China was a gift from a ship captain to the Baldwins. Outside the master bedroom is the grape arbor under which Mrs. Baldwin taught sewing and Bible classes for Hawaiian women and children. On Lei Day, the second and last Thursday of every month, local women string aromatic flower garlands in front of the house.

Next door to the museum is the **Masters' Reading Room**, which was constructed in 1833, making it Maui's oldest building. Now headquarters of the Lahaina Restoration Foundation, it was once a mission storeroom and place of relaxation for the crews of visiting ships.

The **Hawaii Experience Domed Theater**, *824 Front Street, by Lahainaluna Road, Lahaina, Tel. 661-7111; admission: $6.95 adults, $3.95 children*, near Longhi's and Kimo's restaurants, features a 45-minute film about Hawaii with a presentation similar to that of the multimedia New York Experience. Tucked among the old-style buildings along Front Street, it sports a 60-foot domed screen, which almost seems to surround the audience. With flashing lights and eight-channel sound, the movie is truly entertaining. The adjacent souvenir shop sells unusual T-shirts and beach bags, among other items.

All kinds of whaling artifacts are displayed at the **Lahaina Whaling Museum**, *865 Front Street, Lahaina, Tel. 661-4775; free admission; open 9am to 10pm, Monday to Saturday and 9am to 9pm Sunday*, which was started by T-shirt king Rick Ralston (owner of the Crazy Shirts chain). You'll see weathered harpoons, old photographs, and intricately carved ivory.

Docked at the harbor, the *Carthaginian II, a Lahaina Harbor in front of the Pioneer Inn, Tel. 661-8527; admission: $3 adults, $2 seniors, children accompanied by parents free, open 10am to 4pm daily*, a striking replica of a 19th century square-rigged ship, is a museum. The original *Carthaginian* (featured in *Hawaii*, the movie based on James Michener's novel) was anchored at the harbor here until 1972. Built in Germany during the 1920s and later transformed into the type of ship the missionaries sailed in from New England to Hawaii, the Carthaginian II underwent extensive renovations in 1989. A video presentation on whales and the sounds they make is a highlight of the small exhibit below deck.

Along the seawall near the ship, look for the Hawaii Visitors & Convention Bureau warrior marker that points to a cluster of rocks in the water. Ancient Hawaiians believed that the **Hauola Stone** here, roughly resembling a chair, had a curative effect on the infirm who sat in it and let the waves bathe them. Facing the harbor are the foundations of King

Kamehameha I's **Brick Palace** and the place where a royal *taro* patch once thrived. Missionaries built nearby **Spring House** above a freshwater spring. Now surrounded by the **Wharf Shopping Center**, the building shelters a large lighthouse lens that directed ships to safety in the old days.

Set back from the water, the **Pioneer Inn**, *at Hotel and Wharf Streets, Lahaina, Tel. 661-3636*, dates back to 1901. A red-roofed, multi-winged building – with its creaky porch and walls hung with whaling relics and turn-of-the-century signs – this hotel, bar, and restaurant is one of Lahaina's most distinctive landmarks. The forest green wooden structure is set off with white railings around the first-floor verandah and the second-floor balcony. The original wing has tiny, dim, airless guest rooms and the newer wing (1966) has more comfortable accommodations. The bar - which makes an intriguing stop for a cool drink - and restaurant are popular among non-guests.

OLD RULES

At the front desk of the Pioneer Inn, ask for a copy of the Inn's old rules:

"Women is not allow in you room. If you wet or burn you bed you going out.

You are not allow to gambel in you room. You are not allow to stears in the seating room or in the dinering room or in the down you are drunk. You must use a shirt when you come to the seating room.

You'll be happy to know that things have calmed down here consider-ably since the days when these rules were vigorously enforced.

Just across the way is the sprawling old **banyan tree**. It was planted in 1873 to celebrate the 50th anniversary of the arrival of Protestant missionaries in Hawaii. Thrown wide like many open arms, the branches drip vertical shoots that grow into additional trunks resembling elephant legs. Since it covers nearly an acre, it is difficult to believe this is only one tree. There are plenty of benches and plenty of shade. However, sit at your own risk, unless you have an umbrella to protect yourself from the droppings of the mynahs and other talkative birds.

The historic **Lahaina Courthouse**, *Wharf Street, Lahaina (by the banyan tree); open from 10am to 4pm daily*, is located in front of the banyan tree. King Kamehameha III never finished building the palace he began near this site. After a storm destroyed the partial structure (which had been serving as a courthouse), the stones, wood and other materials were used to create this new courthouse in 1859. Now the District Court is found here, along with the **Lahaina Art Society**, which displays some of its paintings in the cells of the old jail.

A portion of the **Old Fort**, built on these grounds in the 1980s, has been reconstructed near the courthouse. Walking south along Front Street, you'll come to **Holy Innocents Episcopal Church**, where a Hawaiian Madonna adorns the altar. Kamehameha III's palace and Princess Nahienaena's grass house were once near here.

Turning left on Shaw Street and left again onto Wainee, you'll find **Waiola Church and Cemetery**, *Wainee Street, near Shaw Street, Lahaina*. This small house of worship stands on the site of Wainee, the first stone church built in Hawaii (in 1832). It could accommodate as many as 3,000 parishioners. However, apparently the gods were not with Wainee. It was badly damaged in a storm in 1858. Then in 1894 it was set ablaze by Hawaiians furious at the overthrow of their monarchy and the US annexation of the islands. Not only did the church represent foreign influence in Hawaii, but Wainee's minister believed that the American takeover had been a good move.

Another church was built here, but it too suffered a fire and then was tousled in a storm. The church that stands here today was built in 1953. Poke around the graveyard, and you'll discover the tombstones of Hawaiian *alii* (royalty), commoners, and missionary families. Queen Keopuolani, a wife of King Kamehameha the Great, was laid to rest here. One of the earliest members of the *alii* to convert to Christianity, she played a major role in spreading missionary influence by convincing other Hawaiians to follow suit.

The **Seaman's Cemetery**, *Wainee and Dickinson Streets, Lahaina*, is located next to the cemetery of Maria Lanakila Church. Buried here are many sailors whose presence as a group in Hawaii helped shape the islands. One, for example, is Thomas Johnson, a black seaman who traveled on the whaler *Acushnet* with Herman Melville. Only a couple of tombstones are left in this 19th century graveyard.

Just north along Wainee Street from the Waiola Church and Cemetery, Lahaina's largest Buddhist congregation holds services at the **Hongwanji Temple**. On Prison Road, right off Wainee Street, **Hale Paahao** (Old Prison), open 9am to 4pm daily, was built in 1852 by convicts themselves to give rowdy, drunken whalers a place to spend the night while thinking about changing their disruptive ways. Seamen who found themselves confined to "Stuck-in-Irons House" were guilty of such crimes as not getting back to their ships by the curfew at sunset.

To learn about Maui's Chinese heritage, pay a visit to the **Wo Hing Society**, *858 Front Street, Lahaina, Tel. 661-3262, open 10am to 4pm daily*, which began as a temple back in 1912. Immigrant Chinese plantation laborers constructed this building as a temple home and recreational center for unmarried men who had fallen on hard times. The Lahaina Restoration Foundation has since turned it into a museum celebrating the contributions of the Chinese to the island. Films about Hawaii dating back to the late 1890s are shown here and Chinese artifacts are on display. You'll find Maui's only public Taoist altar upstairs.

During the 1830s, King Kamehameha III held royal bashes in the building that later became **Seamen's Hospital**, another block north. It now houses **Lahaina Printsellers**, where you can browse through antique maps and other nautical items.

A short drive north of the center of town, **Lahaina Jodo Mission**, *Ala Moana Street, close to Mala Wharf outside the main part of Lahaina*, is restful, blossom-filled Japanese cultural park that is definitely worth a stop. Its back to the mountains, an imposing statue of Buddha that commands this tranquil, flower-filled park was put here in 1968 to commemorate the centennial of the arrival of Hawaii's first Japanese immigrants. The pagoda, with its trio of roofs, serves as a sacred memorial to the dead. Both the pagoda and the small temple are closed to the public, but you're welcome to look inside.

To the south, about two miles up Mt. Ball *mauka* (inland) of Lahaina, the verdant campus of **Lahainaluna School**, *Tel. 662-3000*, treats visitors to a panoramic view of pineapple and cane fields, the harbor and the islands of Lanai and Molokai. Touted as the oldest secondary school west of the Rockies, Lahainaluna opened its doors as a mission school in 1931. The majority of the first students were Hawaiians. The missionaries had only recently turned the islands' language into a written one by developing a 12-letter alphabet, and printed material in Hawaiian was scarce. Within three years, the school was printing the island's first newspaper – in Hawaiian.

Classes were taught in Hawaiian until the 1870s. David Malo, the school's most celebrated graduate, was a member of the first class. He went on to become a teacher, minister, and author of highly respected scholarly works. Today when the school year draws to a close, the students take part in an annual performance of music and dance and they play ancient Hawaiian sports, all in Malo's honor.

On the grounds, visit **Hale Pa'i**, a restored printing house that is now a museum. Located in the oldest building on campus, it produced textbooks on grammar, history and a variety of other subjects.

A sign marks the time capsule that was buried on May 23, 1981, the school's 150th anniversary. It is open for visitors from 9am to 4pm, Monday through Friday. To get there, hike or drive toward the huge white L (for Lahainaluna, of course) near the mountain's summit. You'll enter the grounds between two stately rows of royal palms.

South of town, narrow Olowalu Beach is a great snorkeling spot just off the road.

Kahului & Wailuku

Maui's commercial and industrial center, **Kahului** is about 23 miles (or a 35-minute drive) from Lahaina. The island's main airport is just outside town. If you've packed a pair of binoculars, you might want to stop at **Kahana Pond Wildlife Sanctuary**, *Route 396 between Kahului and the airport*. Bird lovers won't want to miss this waterfowl preserve where migratory fowl and native birds mingle. They flutter around the serene pond peppered with tiny grassy islets.

Also not far from the airport, the **Alexander & Baldwin Sugar Museum**, *3957 Hansen Road, Pu-unene (just south of Kahului), Tel. 871-8058; admission: $4 adults, $2 children age 6 to 7; open 9:30am to 4:30pm daily during summer, Monday to Saturday after Labor Day*, illustrates the importance of sugar cane to Hawaii's economy and cultural history. One of Hawaii's "Big Five" companies, Alexander & Baldwin has its roots in the islands' early New England missionary families. The corporation, now one of Maui's main landowners, is responsible for planting thousands of acres of sugarcane.

Built in 1902 adjacent to the company's sugar mill, this museum originally served as the home of the plantation overseer. In addition to a working model of a sugar processing machine and a restored 1882 steam locomotive, you'll see old photographs, a field worker's uniform (protective hat, scarf, and gloves), and a reproduction of a labor contract, written in Hawaiian, that dates back to 1876.

Sugar and pineapple headed for the mainland depart from busy, crowded Kahului Harbor in town. On Kaahumanu Avenue, the Kaahumanu Center is Maui's largest shopping mall. The **Maui Arts and Cultural Center**, *Tel. 242-2787*, an impressive $28-million theater and visual arts complex, is worth a visit. If you're in town on a Wednesday between 8:30am and 2pm, stop at the **Kahului Farmers Market.**

To the west, the adjoining town of **Wailuku** is older, greener, hillier and generally more attractive than Kahului. Over a third of the island's population lives in these two towns, which are separated by Wailuku Gulch. Especially if you're staying in a condo or private home, consider taking care of your grocery shopping in Kahului or Wailuku, where prices are the lowest on the island. Sitting in the foothills of the West Maui Mountains, Wailuku is the administrative center of Maui County (which includes the islands of Molokai, Lanai, and uninhabited Kahoolawe). Houses in this town range from tin-roofed plantation-style cottages to suburban-style homes surrounded by lovingly landscaped grounds.

The art deco architecture draws a great deal of attention to **Iao Theater**, built in 1927, on North Market Street in Wailuku's historic district. On Sundays starting at 9am, the sound of hymns sung in Hawaiian floats out from the parishioners seated in the koa wood pews at nearby **Kaahumanu Church.** This house of worship is generally closed to the public at other times. A small stone building set against the mountains, it was named for the favorite wife of Kamehameha the Great.

Beside the church, two white, red-roofed buildings, their entrances decorated with lively tiles, make it difficult not to take photos of the whole scene. **Hale Hoikeike,** 2375-A Main Street (Route 32), Wailuku, Tel. 244-3326; admission: $4 adults, $3.50 seniors 60-plus, $1 children age 6 to 12; open 10am to 4pm, Monday to Saturday, also referred to as Bailey House and Maui Historical Society Museum, is a 19th century missionary house built of lava rock in 1833. It contains Maui's most extensive public collection of Hawaiian artifacts (some from before the arrival of Europeans). On display as well are furniture and clothing used by missionaries.

Stop for a quiet picnic in **Iao Valley's** pleasant **Kepaniwai Park and Heritage Gardens,** Iao Valley Road (Route 32), where typical houses of Hawaii's various ethnic groups stand in honor of the islands' diversity. You'll see a Hawaiian grass shelter, a Portuguese villa and a New England salt box, among buildings from other locales. The rocky stream here is backed by mountains. During the late 18th century, a vicious battle was waged in this area: Kahekili of Maui practically wiped out the whole army of Kalaniopuu, and bodies clogged Wailuku Stream. The translation of Kepaniwai is "damming of the waters," and Wailuku, downstream, means "bloody river." Along Iao Valley Road (Highway 32), banana trees and other lush plantings flourish in front yards. Here in the Black Gorge area, tour-bus drivers are fond of pointing out the mountainside rock formation that resembles John F. Kennedy's profile. While driving along this scenic road, you'll see the dramatic lime and forest green West Maui Mountains looming in the distance.

Traveling with the kids? Need a break from the beach? Next to Kepaniwai Park is the **Hawaii Nature Center.** This is a good place to bring children for a variety of enjoyable (but educational) activities based on the environment.

The highway dries up at **Iao Valley State Park.** The valley began as the crater of the West Maui volcano and was enlarged by wind and rain. Rising 1,200 feet from the ground, Iao Needle points to the sky like a giant green finger. There are about ten major botanical zones on Maui, ranging from desert to soggy, from the tropics at sea level to an alpine region at the summit of Mount Haleakala. Each area contains a different group of plants. In tropical Iao Valley, bathed by about 150 inches of rainfall a year, the variety of plant, animal, and insect life is greater than anywhere else on the island.

HOOFING IT & PICKING IT

Iao Valley is a wonderful area for hiking, especially if you enjoy picking fruit. Apple, banana, mango, guava, and coffee trees grow wild. This last plant produces red coffee berries in the fall. Remove the skin from the berry and suck on the two beans in each. The coating has a candy-like flavor. But don't try to eat the beans! If you happen to be hiking in July or August with dirty hair, look for the three-inch red bulbs of the shampoo ginger plant, which contain a clear liquid that can serve as a natural shampoo; there won't be any suds, but it will leave your hair soft and silky. (The Paul Mitchell hair care company has even marketed it commercially.)

Just south of Wailuku in Waikapu is the **Maui Tropical Plantation**, *Route 30 at Waikapu, Tel. 244-7643, open 9am to 5pm daily.* These 112 flourishing acres are a working plantation. Take a narrated tram tour and you'll learn about both agriculture and aquaculture on Maui. You'll also have a chance to taste freshly cut sugar cane and various tropical fruits. Protea, orchids, and anthuriums blossom in the flower nursery. Fresh fruit and gifts are on sale in the plantation's market. Stay for lunch or a barbecue dinner.

EAST MAUI

Maui's larger, eastern section attracts the active vacationer not content simply to lounge on a beach. The dormant Haleakala volcano begs to be explored inside and out, whether you hike or take a horseback or mule ride into its crater, or coast 38 miles on a bicycle down its outer slopes. You'll find everything in this part of Maui, from cowboys and rodeos to a vineyard, eucalyptus, and redwood trees, and even Charles Lindbergh's grave. Offshore Molokini crater captivates snorkelers and divers with its whirl of fish and other marine life. Getting to remote Hana – at the end of a winding, cliffside road way over on the isolated east coast – is an adventure in itself. This drowsy town has a greater concentration of Hawaiians than most other parts of Maui.

While there are all kinds of outdoor activities in East Maui, those who care to do nothing more than bask in the sun can choose among miles of little-used beaches, starting at Makena and continuing up along the western coast. Great for swimming, many of these beaches are also perfect for surfing and boardsailing. During the winter, this is the first part of Hawaii visited by migrating **whales**. Dotted with condos and hotels, Maui's quieter resorts have sprouted along this shore. It is also the driest section of Maui. Landlubbers entertain themselves with several golf courses and a host of tennis courts (many of which are free). While the islands of Lanai and Kahoolawe are anchored out in the Pacific, Haleakala, propping up the clouds, looms in the background off the side of the main road. This massive volcano slopes gradually upward, changing from pale green to black-green.

Kihei

About nine miles (a 20-minute drive) from Kahului, residential **Kihei** is far more laid back than Kaanapali up north. It stretches for about six miles along both sides of South Kihei Road. Stay at one of the many condos here, and you'll be right near one of the sunny **Kamaole waterfront parks** that attracts snorkelers, scuba divers, and big-game fishing enthusiasts. Oceanside baseball and soccer games in **Kalama Park** offer many opportunities to mingle with locals.

After Kaanapali, Kihei was the first of Maui's other vacation playgrounds to spring up. In sharp contrast to Kaanapali, Wailea, and Makena, it clearly was not a planned resort. There seems to be no question that each developer did as he or she pleased. Randomly scattered amid clumps of condos and hotels are a couple of shopping centers, a few restaurants (from Hawaiian plate lunch stands to Mexican or steak and seafood spots), and individual stores selling beachwear, souvenirs, and water sports equipment.

KIHEI'S CHARM

Despite the undistinguished look of some parts of the Kihei community, several of the comfortable condos here are quite attractive – and they are less expensive than in swankier parts of the island. There is also far more of a local feeling to this area. The person next to you on the beach or in a restaurant is more likely to live on Maui. It's easy to find residents happy to share directions to their favorite island eateries or hideaways. If you're staying in a condo, consider stopping at Kihei's farmer's market, from 1:30 - 4:30pm on Tuesdays and Fridays at Suda's Store.

Wailea

Just south of Kihei, **Wailea** is about a 50-minute drive from Lahaina and Kaanapali, and about 35 minutes from Kahului. If you're looking for a spacious, meticulously laid out resort, you'll find it here. With five separate beaches along a mile and a half of shore, Wailea is three times the size of Kaanapali, but less developed. The artfully designed hotels, condos, and Wailea Shopping Village complement each other and the beautiful sandy coastline. Wailea is much greener than Kihei, thanks not to Mother Nature, but to an extensive sprinkler system. Some of Maui's best golf courses spread themselves out here. The Wailea Tennis Center is near the Aston Wailea Hotel. Windsurfing, boogie boarding, and scuba diving are popular in this area, and lessons are available.

Wailea was built in the early 1970s by Alexander & Baldwin, one of Hawaii's Big Five companies whose wealth dates back to the islands' plantation and missionary days.

Makena

Just over an hour's drive from Kaanapali and 45 minutes from the Kahului airport, **Makena** is Maui's newest and most tranquil resort. This is the best place to stay if you want to be in a deluxe hotel or condo off the beaten path, but within striking distance of mainstream action. The sleek Maui Prince, the first of Makena's accommodations, opened its louvered sliding doors in 1986. Now there is also a plush condominium, two 18-hole golf courses, and tennis courts. Don't be surprised if you see cacti along the road in this arid region.

Hippie colonies once thrived at **Makena Beach**. Snorkeling is as good as it ever was off Makena Landing, where black pebbles are underfoot. In 1874, just a few days after becoming king, David Kalakaua arrived at Makena Landing with Queen Kapiolani aboard the S. S. *Kilauea*. They had come to pay a visit to Captain James Makee, the owner of a large ranch in neighboring Ulupalakua. Makee often entertained his guests in a big way: When the royal couple reached the shore, they were met by about 150 dancers, singers, and horsemen, and nearly 100 torchbearers who accompanied their carriage to the ranch.

Near the landing, you might pass a wedding in progress at small but popular **Keawalai Church**. Off the cactus-bordered road not far from here is wide, long, **Big Beach** (a.k.a. Oneloa). This long, broad strip of sand that seems to go on forever is backed by Puu O'Lai ("cinder cone"), a petite gumdrop-shaped hill. The beach is studded with kiawe trees, which have huge gnarled trunks bent to one side by the wind. Nude bathers gather on a small section of this shore. You'll find some **petroglyphs** (ancient rock carvings) at the far end of the beach (to the left if you're facing the water). Friends of mine who honeymooned in Kaanapali said, as gorgeous as their hotel beach was, they drove nearly an hour every day to this beautiful beach. They loved the tranquillity and found it easy to get into conversations with locals here. Offshore are uninhabited Kahoolawe and **Molokini Crater**, a wonderful snorkeling and scuba diving spot. (Make arrangements at your accommodation to take a cruise there.)

From November to April, you might even see humpback **whales** in these waters. It's best to rent a four-wheel-drive vehicle to get to **Ahihi-**

Kinau Natural Reserve (also called **Cape Kinau**), a Hawaiian archaeological site, and picturesque **La Perouse Bay**, a prime snorkeling spot, which takes its name from the first European to visit Maui (a French adventurer who arrived in 1786). The sprawling coffee-colored terrain in this area looks as if the earth has been dug up. It is actually crumbling lava from Haleakala's most recent eruption (back in 1790).

On your way here from Makena, you'll pass some spectacular private waterfront houses. This rugged coast is popular among fishermen.

Upcountry Maui

The region between about 3,000 and 7,000 feet up along the north, west, and southwest slopes of Haleakala is known as **upcountry Maui.** However, exploring this area and driving to the volcano's summit should be done on separate days. The land here is given over to cool breezes, agriculture, small towns, rodeos, and ranches for cattle, sheep, and horses. Although upcountry sits just above the beach resorts of Kihei, Wailea, and Makena, people coming from those areas must take the one paved route through Kahului. Makena even lies along the lower slopes of Ulupalakua, but this upcountry ranch must still be reached in the same roundabout (though scenic) way.

After leaving Kahului, Highway 37 wanders up through rippling sugarcane fields, past pineapple plantations, and by patches of cabbage, onions, tomatoes, cucumbers, and flowers sprouting from the burnt orange and rich, red earth. To the north, Kahului Bay glistens in the sun, while Ma'alaea Bay shimmers to the south. Guava bushes and avocado trees border roads. Winding Piiholo Road is overhung with old eucalyptus trees, which emit a soft, sweet fragrance. They are anchored on top of low, earthen roadside walls, with their roots peeking through the dark orange soil. East of Highway 37, suburban-looking **Haiimaile,** with its huge jacaranda trees and popular gourmet restaurant in an old general store, was once a pineapple plantation village.

Not far south of Haiimaile, rustic 19th-century **Makawao** is well known for its *paniolos* (Hawaiian cowboys), and its annual July 4th **rodeo** and parade. Any time of year, it is not unusual to see people riding horses through the pretty, residential streets, lined with low wooden buildings. Not only does Makawao have a public park with a horse ring, but hitching posts are planted by parking spaces in town. Hibiscus and bougainvillea splash color all over.

Until it was rejuvenated during the 1970s, Makawao was a depressed town of boarded-up storefronts. Now the main street is bordered by boutiques and other shops. Many people interested in holistic health and alternative healing seem to have settled here. The modern Buddhist temple and the Makawao Library make intriguing stops. Few people pass up a visit to **Komoda's Store and Bakery** (on Baldwin Avenue), famous for its cream puffs and other goodies. At the **Hui Noeau Visual Art Center** on Baldwin Avenue, visitors are welcome to take lessons in various disciplines, or attend exhibits and lectures.

Residential **Pukalani** ("hole in the heavens"), just southwest of Makawao, is filled with more pretty houses, flowers, horses, and fields. The only upcountry golf course, and a handful of eateries and stores, call this town home. The **Kula** district begins here. Kula itself is about a 45-minute drive from Kahului. Just after you pass Pukalani, along Highway 37, you'll see an octagonal church on a hillside, with impressive Haleakala at its back. Dating from 1897, the **Church of the Holy Ghost** was constructed especially for Portuguese immigrants who had come to Maui to work on its upcountry ranches and farms.

Kula, sprawling from 1,000 to 4,000 feet up the slopes of Haleakala, may be known for its patches of onions, cabbage, and lettuce, but its real fame comes from its flourishing **protea farms**. More than 200 acres here (more than 70 percent of Hawaii's total protea-growing land) are given over to this colorful blossom that is native to the southern regions of Africa and Australia. At the **University of Hawaii Kula Experimental Station**, visit the garden to see many different kinds of protea, varying in diameter from two to 12 inches.

Near where Route 37 becomes 377, **Kula Botanical Gardens**, *Route 37, upcountry, Tel. 878-1715; admission: $4 adults, $1 children age 6 to 12; open 9am to 4pm daily,* flourishes with streams that snake across attractively landscaped mountain slopes in a trim, verdant oasis. This land once belonged to Princess Kinoiki Kekaulike. Complete with picnic tables, the grounds also contain a picturesque pond, bridges, rare native *koa* trees, bamboo, stately Norfolk pines and an array of orchids and other colorful flowers.

At **Sunrise Protea Farm**, *Route 378, upcountry, three miles past the Haleakala National Park turnoff, Tel. 876-0200; open 8am to 4pm daily,* you can, after admiring exotic proteas at this farm 4,000 feet above the Pacific, arrange to have cut flowers sent to the mainland. You might also pay a visit to **Upcountry Protea Farm.**

Kula Lodge, *on Haleakala Highway (Route 37),* makes a pleasant choice for a filling lunch. It's also very popular for breakfast among those returning from watching the sun rise over Haleakala crater. The fabulous views from the restaurant are free. Also in the Lodge you'll find the **Curtis Wilson Coast Gallery** where paintings of pastoral Kula landscapes are on display. Even if the some of the $3,300 to $60,000 price tags are out of your range, this is worth some of your time.

Polipoli Spring State Recreation Area sprawls along the southwest slopes of Haleakala, just above Makena. However, not only will you have to get there from Makena by going north, then doubling back, but it's best to rent a four-wheel-drive. If you're into unspoiled natural beauty, hiking trails, and wouldn't mind seeing some **redwoods** and sweeping views of the island, you won't be disappointed. Since the park is so large and only four-wheel-drives can make the most scenic part of the trip, it is usually very quiet. When the weather cooperates, you can see as far as the Big Island of Hawaii. Polipoli ("mounds" or "breasts") is a good place for day trips as well as overnight hiking and camping jaunts.

This lofty park is part of the **Kula and Kahikinui Forest Reserve**. In the 1920s, during a reforestation and conservation project, the state planted a cluster of California redwoods and hundreds of cedar, ash, cypress, and sugi. Pines and cypress shade **Polipoli Campground**, where the free campsites have facilities including tables, water, flush toilets, and burners for cooking. Groups of up to 10 people can find inexpensive shelter in a state housekeeping cabin. Although there is no electricity or refrigeration here, the cabin does have gas lanterns, a gas stove, cooking and eating utensils, beds, bedding, and cold showers. The view from here is spectacular, especially at sunset.

To get to Polipoli from Kahului, take Route 37 past Kula, turn left on Route 377 for just under a half-mile, then turn right onto rugged, bouncy Waipoli Road and take it about 10.5 miles to its end. The narrow road snakes high up, affording views of grazing cattle, open land and the Pacific. Then you're abruptly surrounded by tall, fragrant eucalyptus. Some people hitchhike to the summit of Haleakala (even though hitchhiking is illegal in Hawaii) and then hike eight miles down the Skyline Trail (which begins on the south side of Science City) to Polipoli park.

Back on Route 37, if you continue south you'll come to **Sun Yat Sen Memorial Park**, where an arresting Chinese statue is set against the mountains. Sharing its slope with seaside Makena, **Ulupalakua** is a cattle and sheep ranch where the smell of eucalyptus wafts through the air. A wonderful site for a picnic, this area offers panoramic views encompassing the West Maui Mountains, the ocean, and tiny Molokini island. This is where you'll find Hawaii's only vineyard, **Tedeschi Vineyards and Winery**, *Ulupalakua Ranch, upcountry (off route 37), Tel. 878-6058; free admission; open 9am to 5pm daily*. The tasting is done in a former jail that was once also used as a ladies' card room. Try the pineapple wine or the Maui Blanc de Noirs brut champagne. For sale in the tasting room are wine corks that pour and store, wine glasses, wine cooling bags, cookies, salad dressing, macadamia nuts – oh, and wine.

The grounds are beautifully landscaped. Begun as a sugar plantation in 1850, this ranch once had a billiard hall, a bowling alley, and the only swimming pool in Hawaii. Both King Kalakaua and Robert Louis Stevenson visited often. The poet has written that he was stunned by the amount of champagne the monarch was able to consume while he relaxed in this upcountry getaway.

From here you can continue along the rugged road to **Kaupo**, with its general store, and even all the way to flourishing Hana. Although the trip from Ulupalakua Ranch to Hana is only some 37 miles, the rough condition of the road means that the trip will take hours, even in a jeep. You'll notice that the metal signs along the road are pock-marked with bullet holes; they're used for target practice out here in what appears to be the middle of nowhere. You'll overlook the lava fields caused by the last eruption of Haleakala (in 1790) which spread down to La Perouse Bay. Cows graze all around.

Corrugated tin-roof houses appear here and there, along with the **Shrine of St. Joseph Church** (built in 1862). Jagged cliffs rise on the *mauka* (mountain) side, and the ocean is always in sight down below. Just after mile marker #34, you'll come to **Kaupo General Store**, where you can stop for refreshments. Talk to the man who works there to find out how he came to be in such a remote spot. You may also see **Just Like Mom's**, a truck that has been transformed into a mobile hamburger stand that is usually parked nearby

The largest dormant volcano in the world, massive **Haleakala** ("House of the Sun") rises two miles into the sky in **Haleakala National Park**. It hasn't erupted since 1790. This mountain ensures that Maui's climate is schizophrenic: lush in the north and east, parched in the southwest. Pushed across Maui by northeasterly trade winds, rain clouds bump up against Haleakala. Moving up along the slopes into the cooler air, they let loose their water on northern and eastern Maui. By the time the clouds make it to the southwestern portion of the island, they have spent most of their rain.

IT'S COLD UP THERE!

Before making the trip to the summit of Haleakala, be sure to check weather conditions, visibility, and the exact times of sunrise or sunset, Tel. 572-7749. (Visibility is best early in the day, by the way.) Especially if you're heading up to watch the sunrise, don't forget to bring some very warm clothing; a jacket and/or thick sweater, gloves, a hat, long pants, heavy socks, etc. The high altitude often means the temperature at the top is as much as 30 degrees cooler than in coastal areas. Also, it is not uncommon for the weather to be dry and sunny at sea level while rain pours down at the summit.

Haleakala Highway (Route 37) winds through upcountry Maui. The 30-mile drive from Kahului to the crater should take about 1.5 hours. After going about a dozen miles through the picturesque rural landscape, make a left onto Route 378, the steep Haleakala Crater Road. At the entrance to the park, each car pays about $5 and each bicycle about $1.50. There is no charge for senior citizens. Right inside the entrance, a side road on the left will take you to Hosmer Grove, about a half-mile away. Picnic tables are found in this campground, along with a quiet trail that wends its way past non-native trees such as fir, juniper, cypress, and eucalyptus.

Open daily from 7:30am to 4pm, **Park Headquarters** are located about a mile from the entrance to the park. This is where visitors obtain camping permits and oral or written information about the volcano. Ask about guided walks along the crater rim (conducted sporadically in summer months). Outside the headquarters, toward the back of the building, you'll see some *nene geese*, Hawaii's state bird.

Kalahaku Overlook, at 9,325 feet, is one of few places where you can see rare **silversword**. Resembling a cone-shaped, gray or purple sea anemone, this delicate yet hearty plant thrives where few others can, at high altitudes with extreme temperature fluctuations. Even when the thermometer hits the 90s here during the day, snow can fall that night. Kalahaku's silverswords are protected from goats and humans by a stone wall. They take anywhere from 10 to 20 years to reach maturity and their full 8- or 10-foot height. These plants die after blooming only once and scattering their seeds. The best time to see them is from May, when the flowers begin to look like silver puffs, through August, when the stalk has grown and the blossoms have sprouted yellow and magenta. From this overlook, there are thrilling views of the stark, lumpy crater.

Ten miles from Park Headquarters, the glassed-in **Haleakala Visitor Center** is perched at 9,745 feet. It is generally open from 6:15am to 3:30pm. This is the place to be for the most spine-tingling views of the crater's lunar landscape. It's a prime spot for sunset watching. The ebony lava looks like petrified molasses and the cinder cones resemble licorice gumdrops. Rocky formations come in chocolate brown, reds, oranges, sooty black, golden, charcoal gray, and even some greens. Throughout the day, the sun alters the crater's hues. (The view is especially intense during the morning or late afternoon.)

Each hour from 9am to noon, the ranger conducts talks about the volcano. Among other interesting tidbits, you'll learn that the crater is so deep that even if the 110-story World Trade Center buildings were placed on the top of each other, they would still stand 300 feet below the crater rim! From the Visitor Center, you can hoof it a few hundred yards to the **White Hill Overlook**. Along the way, you'll pass stone shelters where ancient Hawaiians once bedded down while visiting Haleakala.

Unless you're in a plane or a helicopter, you can't get any higher than the **Puu Ulaula** observation point, at Haleakala's 10,023-foot summit. When the weather is clearest, the wrap-around view takes in the crater, the rest of the island, Lanai, Molokai, the Big Island of Hawaii, and Oahu. The nearby domes of Science City, which is not open to the public, house a research and communications center for scrutinizing the sun and moon, tracking satellites and missiles, and testing lasers.

YOU'RE NOT MARK TWAIN

During his 1866 visit, Mark Twain delighted in pushing boulders from the summit down the sides of the crater. He watched with glee as they hit the steep walls with explosions of dust, sometimes bouncing 300 feet into the air, shrinking in size until they vanished from view. However, that was then and this is now. Today Haleakala National Park prohibits visitors from moving any rocks, dirt, animals, or plants. And don't even think about touching silversword, since human contact can easily destroy these endangered plants.

Instead of tumbling boulders for kicks as Mark Twain once did, consider hiking or riding horses or mules into the crater or coasting down the outside of Haleakala on a mountain bike (see Biking under *Sports & Recreation* later in this chapter). The most exciting version of the bike ride begins with a view of the sunrise over the crater. You'll start down the mountain bundled up in jackets, sweaters, gloves, and long pants. By the time you reach the end of your ride, you will have peeled off layer by layer to T-shirt and shorts. You'll whiz along hairpin curves, through sweet-smelling eucalyptus forests that give way to plumeria trees, pineapple fields, and sugar cane plantations. The ride culminates in a hearty breakfast or lunch at a restaurant.

While riding horses or mules or hiking in the crater, you'll have close-up views of silversword and other plants as well as of goats, mongooses, boars, partridges, and the brown and beige Hawaiian *nene goose* (which grows to two feet in length). The heavy silence – punctured only by the swirling wind and the crunching of rocks and stones underfoot – has a presence of its own. You'll discover that many of those cinder cones that looked like small gumdrops from above are actually several hundred feet high. Ancient Hawaiians once worshipped their gods in sacred Haleakala.

Down in the crater, you'll stumble upon the crumbling altars and shelters they left behind. Along the **Halemau Trail**, you'll come to the 10-foot-wide, 65-foot-deep **Bottomless Pit**, where early Hawaiians tossed the umbilical cords of newborns to ensure that children would become worthy adults.

Hana Bound

Tucked away on the isolated east coast of East Maui, **Hana** is removed from the rest of the island by far more than geography. "Fight Smog. Buy a Horse," suggests one of the bumper stickers sold at the general store in the drowsy town. When the population is not swelled by itinerant tourists, it hovers around a mere 1,000. Many residents are Hawaiian and most people earn their living through fishing or ranching. The jagged mountains, green expanses, and explosion of flowers seem to have changed little since the ancient Polynesians called this area home. Today, verdant Hana has attracted celebrities such as Richard Pryor, Kris Kristofferson, George Harrison, and Jim Nabors, who all bought houses in the vicinity. This is also where Charles Lindbergh chose to be buried.

Surprisingly, the mention of Hana elicits contrasting opinions from veteran travelers. Some insist "You've just *got* to go," while others dismiss the trip as a waste of time, saying "All that driving – and then there's nothing much to see when you get there." True, the drive is long and not for the faint of heart, and the diminutive town is completely devoid of sights that scream "tourist attraction." But those who are disappointed have misunderstood the point of the journey. At least half the excitement is in the trip itself – along a dramatic, scenic "highway."

Most people pop in and out in a single day. However this flourishing region of Maui is best appreciated by those who stay at one of the handful of accommodations for a couple of days. This way, they get a taste of the intoxicatingly low-key ambiance that blankets Hana before and after the day-trippers swarm the town. They have time to go hiking, horseback riding, and swimming at the black sand beach. They are able to unwind, talk story with some of the people who live here, and absorb remnants of Hawaiian history.

Hana Highway came into being when the feet of ancient Hawaiians pounded out a path. Convicts broadened it during the 1920s, but it wasn't paved until 1962 and couldn't accommodate regular traffic until it was further improved in 1982. Washouts aren't uncommon and the damp weather is hard on the road. In some places, vehicles creep along at 10 miles an hour or less. Hundreds of precarious curves lead to dozens of one-lane bridges over rocky streams and past quiet settlements, thick rain forests, waterfalls, swimming holes, a riot of blossoms, and flourishing state parks where people pause for picnics.

The road hugs the edge of a precipice, high above dark sand beaches, pitch black boulders, and deep blue waters with vigorous white surf. Hit with about 100 inches of rainfall a year, this coast is extremely lush. The air is perfumed by wild ginger, plumeria, orchids, eucalyptus, and mangoes ripening on trees. Ferns, bamboo, and monkeypods decorate the roadside. Just off the highway, many trails are popular with hikers, some of whom spend three or four days camping in the area.

HANA "HIGHWAY"

While you can get to Hana by small plane or helicopter, the most thrilling way is to drive (or be driven along) the 52 twisting, turning, climbing, cliff-edge miles from Kahului on Route 36 (Hana Highway). The one-way trip can take anywhere from 2.5 hours to a leisurely 3.5 or 4, depending on your speed and number of stops. The earlier you leave, the less traffic you'll have to contend with.

Since the driver spends much more time concentrating on the narrow, snaking road than gazing at the magnificent scenery, many travel companions let one person take the wheel in one direction and another on the way back. Consider picking up a narrated tour of the trip on audio cassette tapes (sold in Kahului at the Shell gas station across from Dairy Center, Windrigger Maui on Dairy Road, and ABC stores, among other places. The tapes, which vary in length, cost about $15.) If you're tempted to stop to buy pakalolo (marijuana) from one of the guys who casually sell it along the road, don't forget that it's illegal and that you could end up with a side trip to a Hawaiian jail.

So that neither of you has to worry about negotiating the road, you might want to get to Hana with one of the 12-hour van tours. Even if you're just going for the day, carry your towel and bathing suit so you can take advantage of a mountain pool or one of Hana's beaches.

Near Kahului, **Pa'ia** is the last town you'll come to before reaching Hana, so it's your last chance to fill up on gas or any other necessary supplies. The historic main street in this former sugar plantation town is lined with a collection of old and new Western frontier-style buildings. Some of the original turn-of-the-century structures have been converted into boutiques, restaurants, bakeries, antiques stores, "self-discovery" bookstores, natural foods shops, and galleries, such as **Maui Crafts Guild.** Look for the tiny white courthouse/police station. Across the street from a Protestant church, the **Manto Kuji Soto Buddhist Temple** is backed by the water. Don't be surprised if you see some fruit and cans of 7-Up or beer in the graveyard. People customarily place the deceased's best-loved food or drink on tombstones.

In 1880, Samuel T. Alexander and Henry P. Baldwin opened the sugar mill in Pa'ia, boosting the town's economy by turning it into a plantation community. Residential camps sprang up around the mill. As with plantations throughout Hawaii, each of these settlements was populated by a different ethnic group made up of foreign immigrants. The twin sections of Upper Pa'ia and Lower Pa'ia developed a half-mile apart. During WW II, when thousands of US Marines and other service-men were stationed nearby, the town flourished further. After the war, faced with labor union demands for better wages and more humane working conditions, Alexander & Baldwin began closing down some of its camps.

In the 1950s and 1960s, hundreds of plantation families started leaving Pa'ia after buying new homes in Dream City, a Kahului housing community developed by Alexander & Baldwin. This left Pa'ia's plantation camps empty and its streets virtually deserted by the mid-1960s. Then, in the late 1960s and early 1970s, a new breed of folks began to fill the town – hippies from the mainland. Today, the flower children have given way to people attracted to nearby Hookipa and Spreckelsville beaches. **Hookipa Beach County Park** is one of Maui's premier surfing and windsurfing spots, with waves often reaching 15 feet.

After Hookipa, the road cuts through sugar cane and pineapple fields backed by bright swards of green. It then begins to meander roller-coaster style over hills and through valleys. At almost every turn, a new waterfall and swimming hole appears. **Maliko**, a particularly lush valley studded with palms, is the site of an old Hawaiian village. Wispy pines line one side of the road while banana plantations stand on the other. Along with the more familiar kind, you'll see the small, firm apple bananas (also called Chinese bananas).

From time to time, tiny depressions – miniature valleys – dip away from the edge of the road. Locals will tell you that the very tart fruit of the *liliko'i* vines and trees (a.k.a. passion fruit) will make you pucker up when you bite into it. The buttercup-like blossoms of *hau* plants open yellow in the morning and turn red as the day goes by. Thick ferns form roadside walls and the wind whistles through stands of bamboo. One of the most striking trees you'll see on the way to Hana is the rainbow eucalyptus, whose smooth bark is vertically striped with red, yellow, green, and brown, as if someone had sat in its branches and poured paint down the trunk.

Grazing beef cattle add clumps of brown and beige to the many shades of green. You'll pass a lone house or church here and there. Some of the homes in this area have windmills for generating power. An island resident told me that one house even has bicycle-generated power: the people who live there spend part of each day pedaling away. Rusty roadside mail boxes and flower-filled front yards mark residential neighborhoods, such as **Kailua**, an old plantation town. As the road climbs, panoramic views open up.

B.Y.O. H2O

While you'll come to a pipe at the edge of the highway that always spouts fresh spring water, I wouldn't recommend stopping for a drink. The water is wonderfully clear and refreshing, but it's near a tricky curve where traffic could be a problem if you stopped. So be sure to bring your own bottled water in case thirst hits during the trip.

The highway's first bridge is about 13 miles from Pa'ia, at Twin Falls, which is just what its name implies: a pair of waterfalls. To find them, park your car and walk along the right side of the stream until you reach the pool at the base of the cascades. Continue walking to the left for a bit and you'll discover a more impressive fall, also with a pool that is fine for swimming. You'll see many cars parked by **Puahokamoa Falls**, which thunders into a rocky stream, bordered by picnic tables. But you may want to resist the temptation to stop here since even more spectacular waterfalls await you farther along.

Kaumahina State Park is about 24 miles from Hana. The name means "the rising moon," and I'm told that if you stick around after dark, you'll see the lunar orb coming up over the ocean. In addition to picnic tables and shelters, you'll find drinking water and flush toilets here. The crunch of tourists usually thins out by 3pm or so. To camp here, you'll need to obtain a free permit. Like the bony, interlacing fingers of dozens of hands, roots cover the ground, so be careful when walking. Across the road from the park, a lookout point affords a sweeping view of the royal blue Pacific and Keanae Peninsula. A quilt of taro patches spreads across this flat jut of land, the site of a Hawaiian village.

After another mile, massive **Honomanu Valley** sprawls to the right, with its 3,000-foot cliffs and plummeting waterfall. Bright African tulips dapple the highway's greenery with reddish-orange blossoms. Dipping down to sea level, the road passes un-peopled **Honomanu Beach**, where the waves are excellent for **surfing**. Mountain apple trees are abundant along this stretch. The small, red pear-shaped fruit has a delicious white pulp inside.

Hana Highway then takes a steep climb before coming to Keanae Arboretum, where you can splash in **Piinaau Stream**. A hike into the arboretum, filled with many native as well as introduced plants, will give a glimpse of pre-modern, natural Hawaii. Various kinds of *taro* grow in patches and tropical trees provide shade. The **Keanae Overlook**, a favorite among shutterbugs, is near mile marker 17. You'll gaze down on smooth, rectangular *taro* patches and the ocean. Haleakala volcano is visible in the distance. Almost a mile after mile marker 20, **Wailua Lookout** provides a vista of Wailua Canyon and small Wailua Village, with its tiny church.

FRUIT TO GO

There are many fruit stands near Wailua Lookout. When the vendors are absent, it's not unusual for them to leave the fruit beside an honor box where customers are trusted to drop in their money.

Back along the craggy lava coast, you might see local fishermen casting nets into the ocean just as ancient Hawaiians did. Distinctive monkeypod trees, bright red hibiscus and yellow and white plumeria are plentiful in this area. If you hike or drive into **Keanae village**, you'll get a close-up view of the missionary church that was built in 1860, allowed to deteriorate, and then reconstructed by locals in 1969.

Uncle Harry's refreshment stand, in Keanae, makes a good stop along the road to Hana. It is owned by the son of the late Harry Kunihi Mitchell, one of the state's greatest composers of Hawaiian music and a prominent leader in the **Hawaiian Rights Movement** that blossomed in the 1970s. Mitchell founded La'au Lapa'au, a movement designed to save the knowledge of herbal medicine so that it could once again be passed down through the generations. Hawaiian traditional medicine had been banned by the government when Americans took over. Parents had stopped teaching it to their children for fear of reprisals.

The actions of members of Protect Kahoolawe 'Ohana, another organization founded by Mitchell, eventually led to an end to the military's bombing of the offshore island of Kahoolawe. Dotted with ancient religious sites, this arid, uninhabited chunk of land had been used for years by the navy for target practice.

The subject of the protests against the US Navy bombing of Kahoolawe is very controversial indeed, especially concerning one incident in particular. According to some people, protesters would sneak ashore and hide so that the military would have to stop the bombing until they were found. The story goes that two young men went over by boat one night and were never heard from again. The Navy claimed that they had been lost at sea. But these protesters were known to be strong swimmers, and besides, some say, remnants of their belongings had been recovered on Kahoolawe. The truth about what actually happened remains nebulous. In May, 1994, the state of Hawaii finally regained jurisdiction over the island. Now a sanctuary for nature and culture, it will be restored by the Navy by the year 2004 or so.

If the person working at the fruit stand is in a talkative mood, you might learn a bit more about the struggles Hawaiians have gone through since foreigners first arrived. I once got into a long conversation here with a woman who told me that the ban on speaking the Hawaiian language wasn't lifted until about 1977. Cared for by her grandparents while her parents worked, she learned to speak Hawaiian, even though her parents didn't. When they were growing up, it was illegal for parents to teach their children their native tongue. Those who did learn it had to do so secretly. Browse around the displays of Hawaiian woodcarvings and other crafts, and read the clippings on the wall about Uncle Harry and his legacy.

About a half-mile from Wailua Lookout, **Waikane Falls** are considered by many to be the most picturesque in the region. At **Puaakaa State Park**, the road passes two more waterfalls with inviting pools. White angel trumpet flowers dangle from branches like Christmas tree ornaments. Hawaiian strawberries, which turn white when they ripen, grow wild. You'll also see heliconia, also known as lobster claws because of their shape and orange color, and yellow poincianas, whose fluffy blossoms have inspired people to nickname them "scrambled egg trees."

Next you'll come to oceanside **Waianapanapa State Park**, where you can camp out on a rise overlooking a black sand beach or stay in a cabin. Pronounced *Why-ah-nah-pah-nah*-pah, the name means "glistening water." The swimming is good and there is an abundance of hiking trails and wild fruit waiting to be plucked. There are caves here you can hike to and swim in.

CAVE TALES

According to a legend about one aquatic Waianapanapa grotto, a Hawaiian princess fled from her jealous husband. She made the mistake of hiding on a ledge in a cave that was known to be used by lovers for secret rendezvous. Her frenzied husband ran everywhere searching for his wayward wife. While he was catching his breath by the cave, he caught something else as well: a glimpse of her reflection in the water at the grotto's entrance. Convinced that she must have gone there to meet another man, he flew into a rage, bashing her head against the wall and killing her.

Locals say that it is the princess's blood that, even today, turns the cave pool red every April. Some claim you can still hear the echoes of her terrified shrieks. However, according to others, the water turns crimson from the tiny red shrimp that multiply in the pool in the spring and the "shrieks" are the sound of the wind whooshing in and out of the grotto. Exploration of most of Waianapanapa's caves is best left to divers or extremely strong swimmers. Everyone else can swim off the striking black sand beach.

At the edge of Hana, 60-acre **Helani Gardens** is worth a stop, especially if someone is around to give a bit of commentary on some of the more unusual plants and flowers. Admission is a couple of dollars.

Hana

The coastal, agricultural town of **Hana** lies about three miles south of Waianapanapa State Park. Actually, it's a bit of an exaggeration to call it a town since it consists of a restaurant, a post office, a hotel, a ranch and a couple of stores and gas stations. It was from this area that King Kamehameha the Great first set out, in 1795, to conquer the rest of the Hawaiian Islands (a mission he didn't accomplish until 1810). Some of the first Polynesians to arrive in Hawaii settled in Hana.

Today it is home to a larger percentage of Hawaiians than most other parts of the island. You won't find any city lights here. The air is frequently filled with the squawks of mynah birds or hymns sung in the Hawaiian language wafting from a church. Petite corrugated roof houses are surrounded by bright flowers and expanses of ranchland. Mount Haleakala's lower slopes are given over to thick forests.

In its heyday, before Europeans came to Hawaii, Hana bustled with some 45,000 to 75,000 people. By the 1830s, the population had shrunk to about 11,000. Beginning in the 1860s, sugar plantation workers were hustled in from China, Japan, Portugal, and the Philippines. The mills kept the economy healthy, especially during the 1920s and 1930s. Then, after WWII, the plantations began to close down and massive unemployment swept through the area. To stave off disaster, Paul Fagan, a San Francisco entrepreneur, purchased sugar plantation land and turned it into a ranch for Herefords. In an equally daring move, he built a cluster of low-rise buildings and opened one of Hawaii's earliest non-Waikiki resorts.

Thanks to this visionary, both the ranch and the resort, now called **Hotel Hana-Maui**, remain Hana's economic backbone. As a matter of fact, they are virtually the only game in town as far as jobs go. If you wonder about the large **white stone cross** on a hill overlooking Hana, it was planted there by Fagan's wife to honor her husband after his death in 1960. For a sweeping view of Hana, go up to the cross. If you're staying at Hotel Hana-Maui, you can get a ride in a van. Some people don't mind the hike, even though they have to wade through herds of cows and sidestep cow dung.

Until it was sold in the late 1980s, Hotel Hana-Maui was caught in a steady decline. The new owners pumped goo-gobs of money into it, doing extensive renovations and also buying 4,500 acres of ranch land. Today it is one of Hawaii's most pleasant – and most isolated – resorts. Across from the two adjacent public tennis courts, **Wananalua Church** dates back to the 1830s. In an intertwining of heritage, much of the volcanic stone used to build this European-style church was taken from the remains of ancient Hawaiian *heiau* (temples). And the mortar was ground from coral that was collected by Hawaiians who dived from old-style Polynesian canoes.

Down the road from the hotel, **Hana Bay** is a good place to snorkel or stumble into conversations with locals. The beach here has grayish sand, a combination of pulverized coral and volcanic ash. The calm waters make swimming pleasant.

A short trek from Hana bay will take you to the **Lighthouse on Kauiki Head**. In the old days, people would stand on top of the hill and let the rest of the village know when they spotted schools of fish so they could cast their nets. A legend explains why clouds so often hover so close to the top of this cinder cone: The demi-god Maui united a pair of lovers here for eternity by turning one into the hill and the other into the mist above it. **Red Cinder Beach**, which has drawn nude bathers for quite some time, lies over Kauiki hill. Celebrated for having inspired so many Hawaiians to convert to Christianity, Queen Kaahumanu (a wife of King Kamehameha the Great) was born in one of the caves near Kauiki in 1768.

Few people pass through Hana without stopping at **Hasegawa's General Store**. Whether you're looking for a T-shirt, a whimsical bumper sticker, baby food, barbed wire or film, you're likely to find it here.

There's also the **Hana Cultural Center Museum**, *Tel. 248-8622; open 10am to 4pm daily; no admission fee.* The second name of this museum, Hale Waiwai, 'O Hana, means "House of Treasures of Hana." Among the relics of days gone by here are photographs of Hana's sugar mill era during the early 1900s and everyday Hawaiian implements such as *poi* pounders.

Beyond Hana

Several miles south of Hana, **Oheo Gulch**, *Route 31, Kipahulu district of Haleakala National Park*, lies near the coastal edge of Haleakala. Frequently referred to as "Seven Pools" or "Seven Sacred Pools," these volcanic swimming holes are actually closer to 30 in number and no one ever considered them sacred. As it heads for the ocean, the Oheo Stream flows down the valley, spilling into a series of volcanic holes in the rocks.

The best time to visit Oheo Gulch is early in the morning, before the van- and car-loads of tourists arrive. From a bridge, you'll look down on a handful of people cooling off, and depending on when you arrive, diving into the holes in the charcoal colored rock. I don't recommend your following the lead of locals and diving in, since hidden rocks can be deadly if you're not familiar with the holes.

The energetic can hike to upper pools and waterfalls. Makahiku Falls is about a half-mile from the parking lot, while Waimoku Falls is about a mile and a half farther.

A couple of miles farther along the narrow, bumpy road, **Kipahulu** is the site of **Charles Lindbergh's grave**. Extremely fond of Hana, this master aviator chose to be buried here, at difficult-to-find **Palapala Hoomau Congregational Church**. On your way here, you'll pass houses ranging from plush to small and weather-beaten, **St. Paul's Church**, and the tall chimney (partially obscured by vegetation) of a crumbling sugar mill. Just beyond the mill and a pasture, you'll come to a steel gate and a road that leads to the church. Inside, you might find a program from a recent service containing hymns written in Hawaiian. This plain, one-room house of worship was built in 1864 on a cliff high above the Pacific. You'll find Lindbergh's tombstone in the small graveyard. Of the many places he had been around the world, he is said to have found Hana the most beautiful. Against his doctor's advice, he left his sickbed in New York and returned to Hana to die in 1974.

Just past this church, the road from Hana gets quite rough. If you're traveling in a four-wheel-drive vehicle, consider continuing along **Kaupo Road**. This slim, rugged stretch is rocky and desolate in parts. But it offers breathtaking cliffside views of the ocean far below. Some five miles from Lindbergh's grave (about 15 miles from Hana), you'll come to the small **Kaupo general store**, which sells everything from groceries and cold sodas to fishing tackle. Also along this route, a weathered graveyard where many Hawaiians are buried surrounds **Hui Aloha Church**, a small wooden building.

If you keep going west, then follow the road north, you'll come to **Tedeschi Winery**. From here you can continue along Route 37 through upcountry Maui back to Kahului. Or you can turn off the highway just after **Waiohuli** onto Haleakala Highway to stop at **Kula Botanical Gardens**, then head up Haleakala Crater Road to the volcano's summit. However, because the driving is so draining, it's best to return from Hana and see the crater on separate days.

NIGHTLIFE & ENTERTAINMENT

When the stars come out, most of Maui's partying crowd heads for bars, dance spots, night clubs, lounges, luaus and dinner cruises in and around Kaanapali, Lahaina, and Wailea. Some restaurants turn into local hangouts, with music and heavy-duty socializing. Many hotels have some kind of entertainment, at least on weekends, perhaps a contemporary combo or a single Hawaiian singer strumming a ukulele and crooning haunting traditional melodies.

When you're in the mood to see a side of Maui most visitors miss, find out what's doing at the **Maui Arts and Cultural Center** in Kahului. In addition to two theaters, this complex has a spacious gallery.

Hawaiian Style

Most **luaus**, all with plentiful authentic Hawaiian (plus modified Hawaiian) foods, feature lively Polynesian revues. I've heard good things about the luaus at the **Aston Wailea Hotel** (the setting is a lawn at the edge of the Pacific) and the **Hyatt Regency Maui** in Kaanapali. However, I recommend checking newspapers for the occasional local luaus hosted by civic groups or other community organizations to raise money for various causes. Many people find these usually smaller-scale affairs more enjoyable than the crowded, commercial shebangs hosted by or near hotels.

For a comfortable balance between commercial and intimate, try the beachfront **Old Lahaina Luau**, 505 Front Street, Lahaina, Tel. 667-6671. Guests may choose between sitting at tables or on *tatami* mats. The cost is about $56 for adults and $28 for children age 2 to 12.

Local Hangouts & Happenings
MAUI TROPICAL PLANTATION'S HAWAIIAN COUNTRY BAR-BECUE, *Wailuku. Tel. 244-7643. Tuesday, Wednesday, and Thursday from 5pm to 7:30pm. Cost: $50 for adults. Children age 5 to 12, $20.*

When cowboys came to Hawaii from South America, Hawaiian tongues turned the word "Espanol" (Spanish) into "Paniolo." This *paniolo* (Hawaiian cowboy) party is kicked off with a narrated tram tour of acres of the state's most important agricultural crops. Then appetites are satisfied with a filling barbecue dinner, accompanied by an open bar, a Hawaiian-style country and western musical performance, and square dancing.

MAKAI BAR, *Maui Marriot Hotel, Kaanapali. Tel. 667-1200.*

Try this night spot for Hawaiian entertainment with an ocean view.

SPATS, *Hyatt Regency Maui, Kaanapali. Tel. 661-1234*

Serving dinner only the rest of the week (except Monday), this Italian restaurant turns into a night club on weekends.

MAUI COMMUNITY THEATER, *Iao Theater, 68 North Market, Wailuku. Tel. 242-6969. Tickets: $15 to $18 for adults; discounts for children and seniors.*

This local theater group presents productions at the **Maui Arts and Cultural Center** in Kahului, as well as being in residence at the Historic Iao Theater. Dating back to the turn of the century, it is one of Maui's earliest troops. The group puts on about half a dozen productions a year, from Broadway musicals to variety shows.

BALDWIN THEATRE GUILD, *1650 Kaahumanu Avenue, Kahului. Tel. 243-5673. Tickets: $8 for adults, $5 for students, and $6 for seniors.*

Various comedies, dramas and musicals are put on by this group.

CASANOVA'S, *1188 Makawao Avenue, Makawao. Tel. 572-0220.*

Bringing pizza and dance music together, this is the place to party on Wednesday nights (when there's a D.J.) and weekends (to live music). The periodic live bands range from local groups to name brand entertainment: Los Lobos and Richie Havens are among those who have performed here.

KAPALUA MUSIC FESTIVAL, *Kapalua Resort. Tel. 669-0244 or 800/ KAPALUA.*

Every summer since 1982, the soothing sounds of European classical music have floated through the air in northern Western Maui during this festival. Renowned musicians come from the New York and Chicago Philharmonic Orchestras, Juliard, and other parts of the mainland and the world. The glorious, verdant grounds of the Kapalua Resort make this a particularly appealing setting. Concerts take place at the **Maui Arts and Cultural Center's** Castle Theater in Kahului as well as at Kapalua hotels and Sacred Hearts Church in Kapalua.

MAUI SYMPHONY ORCHESTRA, *Tel. 244-5439. Tickets: $5 and up for adults and $3 and up for children under age 10.*

One of the symphony's most popular performances is the July 4th concert, which takes place on the picturesque Kaanapali Golf Course. Fireworks punctuate the music. In addition to a Christmas concert, the symphony sometimes also plays al fresco pop performances, European classical concerts, and opera music.

INTERNATIONAL FILM FESTIVAL, *Maui Arts and Cultural Center, Kahului. Tel. 800/752-8193.*

Films from the US, the Pacific, and Asia are screened from the end of November to the beginning of December.

Special Events

March brings **Whalefest Week,** highlighted by foot races, music, and crafts, to Kaanapali. On **King Kamehameha Day,** in June, the whole state honors the great warrior responsible for uniting the Hawaiian Islands. Also in June, European classical sounds come to this beautiful, tranquil resort area of Kapalua, with chamber music played by masters from all over the United States, during the **Kapalua Music Festival.** This is also the month for the **Kapalua Wine & Food Symposium.**

If you're vacationing around July 4th, be sure to catch the raucous annual **rodeo** at Makawao, in upcountry Maui, where *paniolos* (Hawaiian cowboys) do their thing. **Aloha Week,** in September and October, is the state's largest celebration of Hawaiian culture. For some local flavor, make a point of at tending the August **Maui County Fair.** In September, super athletes compete in the **Maui Triathlon.**

SPORTS & RECREATION

Maui offers a host of ways to keep in shape, most of them aquatic. At the **Ocean Activities Center,** *Tel. 879-4485,* you can rent Windsurfing boards, wave skis, outrigger canoes, Hobie cats, snorkel gear, and boogie boards. Lessons are also available. In addition, arrangements for sailing and fishing charters can be made at the Lahaina harbor, as well as for scuba and snorkeling excursions, parasailing, and cruises to watch whales or to visit neighboring Lanai and Molokini crater (for snorkeling). If you're interested in renting jet skis, surfing, or water-skiing, head to Kaanapali Beach, which also has excellent golf courses and tennis courts.

Beaches

Two of Maui's most beautiful beaches are at the island's extremes: Kaanapali in western West Maui and Oneloa (Big Beach) in southwestern

---

MAUI'S BEST SANDY STRANDS

Oneloa (a.k.a. Big Beach), Makena, East Maui
Black Sand Beach, *Waianapanapa State Park, near Hana, East Maui*

Hookipa, *near Pa'ia, East Maui*
Baldwin Beach Park, *near Pa'ia, East Maui*
Kaanapali, *West Maui*

East Maui. Spend some time driving around the island to see the variety of sandy (or sometimes rocky) shores.

Kaanapali, *West Maui*

This is where most of Maui's visitors congregate – and with good reason. A broad, 3-mile, palm-edged crescent, Kaanapali (Maui's premier resort area) is lined with attractive hotels and condominiums. All kinds of water sports facilities are available here. There's also a healthy selection of restaurants and shops, both in accommodations and in oceanfront Whalers Village Shopping Center.

Oneloa, *Makena, East Maui*

Often called **Big Beach**, this 100-foot-wide, 3,000-foot-long beige sandy strip faces the islands of Kahoolawe and Molokini. Even though a honeymooning couple I know was staying in gorgeous Kaanapali, they took the 70-minute drive to this beach every day. They explained that they loved the low density of fellow bathers, especially during the week. Most of the people who use this beach are locals, and my friends said they enjoyed getting into conversations with residents here. During the '60s, Oneloa was a favorite hangout for hippies, who lounged in and around the tents they pitched. People can still camp out here.

The area is full of cacti, jade plants, and *kiawe* (mesquite) trees, with huge gnarled trunks bent over by the wind. Like a giant thimble, **Puu O' Lai** (cinder cone) stands guard over the beach. On the other side of this volcanic hill is **Little Beach**. This isolated pocket lures nude bathers even though police periodically remind them that public nudity is illegal in Hawaii.

Honolua, *Route 30, north of Napili and Kapalua, West Maui*

Surfing and **windsurfing** are excellent at this picturesque beach. Part of a marine life conservation district, the bay here is a great place for spotting **whales**. All of the paths down to the beach are quite steep, rocky and slippery with pine needles. You'll need to grab onto trees as you descend. In 1976, a replica of an old sailing canoe set off from here to Tahiti and back, to retrace the route of the ancient Polynesians who sealed the Hawaiian Islands.

D.T. Fleming State Park, *northern West Maui, off Route 30, just north of Kapalua Resort*

Another beach that is quiet on weekdays, this one has picnic tables, grills, rest rooms, and showers. However, the tides can be quite powerful, so swimming is recommended only to the strongest of swimmers. The Ritz-Carlton Kapalua overlooks this white strand.

Napili Beach, *northern West Maui, just outside Napili Kai Beach Club*

This tranquil sandy crescent is a good choice for escape. An offshore reef ensures that the water remains calm and that snorkeling is rewarding. The facilities of the condominium, however, are for guests only.

Honokowai Beach, *just north of Kaanapali, West Maui*

Although some parts of this beach are rocky, you can splash around in the volcanic pool. Picnic tables and showers are provided.

Lahaina Beach, *West Maui*

This slim stretch of sand, ending at Lahaina's small boat harbor, borders waters calmed by an offshore reef.

Puunoa Beach, *just north of the Lahaina harbor, West Maui*

Another beach that is enclosed by reefs, this one extends to the old Mala Wharf.

Olowalu Beach, *off Route 30, south of Lahaina, West Maui*

There are no facilities here and you'll have to park at the edge of the road, but this sandy beach is one of the island's best **snorkeling** spots. Petroglyphs are found in the Olowalu area.

Papalua State Wayside Park, *south of Olowalu, West Maui*

The offshore reef makes for calm waters and good snorkeling at this sandy stretch bordered by *kiawe* trees.

Awalua Beach, *near Olowalu, West Maui*

Locals flock here for the swimming and **new surfers** try to hone their craft.

Kamaole Beaches, *Kihei, East Maui*

If you want to mingle with locals, these three beach parks are a good place to start. You might stumble upon a soccer game or see families flying kites.

Wailea Beaches, *west coast of East Maui*

In this peaceful region – a far cry from the bustle of Kaanapali – five appealing crescents claim nearly two coastal miles.

Hookipa, *near the town of Pa'ia, not far from Kahului, East Maui*

Many people stop here on their way to Hana, but most come for the **windsurfing** and **surfing**, which boardsailors swear by. You can rent sports equipment in shops in the town of Pa'ia. Championship international competitions in both sports are held here each year. If you plan to hike on the way to Hana, this is a good place to fill your water bottles.

Baldwin Beach Park, *near Pa'ia, East Maui*

With the West Maui mountains in the background, this gorgeous curve of sand is among the island's most beautiful beaches. It is named for one of Maui's oldest and wealthiest families. Camping is allowed with a permit from the county.

Spreckelsville Beach, *near Pa'ia, East Maui*

This beach is great for **windsurfing.**

Hamoa Beach, *just past Hana, toward Kaupo, East Maui*

An unspoiled stretch of salt-and-pepper sand backed by thick greenery and rolling hills, this beach is lapped by exceptionally clear blue water. The Hotel Hana-Maui uses this beach, and its facilities are reserved for guests. However, as with all of Hawaii's beaches, the sand and water are public property.

Black Sand Beach, *Waianapanapa State Park, near Hana, East Maui*

This ebony sand was created when hot lava hit cold ocean water. This cove sits at the bottom of a cliff edged by jagged black lava sculpture-like formations. The electric blue water, bursts of white surf, and bright green vegetation against the tar-black lava and sand is a fabulous sight. A path winds down to the crescent, which is often scattered with smooth black rocks and driftwood. To the right (if you're facing the water) is a small **cave.** You must squat to enter.

Once inside, you may be able to straighten up and walk all the way through to the surf crashing on the other side. Lava pebbles crunch underfoot. Bordered by greenery, a hole in the ceiling shows a piece of the sky.

Kaihalulu Beach, *Hana, East Maui*

Also called **Red Cinder Beach,** this is one of Maui's most remote coves. The rugged path that leads to it begins near the community center and a Japanese cemetery. However, it isn't marked, so you'd do well to ask a resident to point you in the right direction. You'll walk around Kauiki Hill, with meadows and hills in the distance. The coastline in this area is rocky and the ocean quite rough. When you arrive at the beach, you'll see that the cove is enclosed by 300-foot-tall rust-colored, iron-rich cliffs. As more visitors stumble upon this beach, the nudists that used to sunbathe here are dwindling in number.

Biking

One of the most enjoyable things to do on Maui is cycle 38 miles down Haleakala volcano, especially after watching the sun rise over the crater. The temperature, landscape, and aromas all change dramatically from top to bottom. Cold, rocky, and brown at the summit, the volcano gives way to expanses of wheat-colored grass and the air grows warmer. Views of the West Maui Mountains and patchwork farmland open up in the distance. With each hairpin turn, more tufts of green appear. Mail boxes stand in front of houses set back from the road. A wonderful fragrance envelopes bikers as they pass through a eucalyptus forest. The sweet perfume of plumeria blossoms wafts by. Suddenly everything is green and the steep mountain slopes have flattened out considerably. With heads bent to the ground, lethargic cows and horses stand in pastures behind fences made of branches and wire. By the time they reach the bottom, the bikers – who shivered in gloves, sweaters and windbreakers at the summit – have stripped down to shorts and T-shirts.

Companies that operate these mountain bike excursions offer two versions: the sunrise expedition and the later morning trip. You'll be picked up in the middle of the night (around 3am) if you plan to get to the summit before the sun does. Vans carry passengers and the mountain bikes you'll be given at the top. It's freezing up there, so even though the bike companies provide windbreakers and gloves, be sure to bring your own warm layers as well. A breakfast of pastries is served while the sun starts to bathe the crater in light. After riding down, you'll have a picnic or brunch at a restaurant. Those who don't want to drag themselves out of bed can take the later morning trip, which also ends with a picnic or meal in a restaurant.

Most of the riding is coasting so it's more fun than hard work. The leader keeps in touch by walkie-talkie with the driver of the van, who follows the train of bikers, watching to make sure everyone is okay. Through hand signals, the leader tells riders to slow down, stop, or pull over when necessary. If anyone gets tired, they are welcome to ride in the van.

The companies that lead these excursions are **Maui Downhill**, *Tel. 871-2155, 877- 8787, or 800/ 535-2453*, and **Maui Mountain Cruisers**, *Tel. 871-6014 or 800/ 232-MAUI.* For the sunrise trip, make sure the company you use will promise to notify you in a timely fashion if the ride is canceled due to bad weather at the summit. Rates average about $115-$120 per person, including brunch or lunch.

If you'd simply like to rent a bicycle, note that it is safest not to venture onto Maui's 2-lane highway or other narrow main roads. It's best just to ride in the immediate vicinity of your accommodation. **West Maui Cycles**, *Tel. 669-1169*, provides free delivery and pick up of rentals.

Biplane

For a blast from the past, take a spin in an old-fashioned bi-plane. Contact **Biplane Barnstormers**, *Tel. 878-2860*. One or two passengers ride in the open cockpit in the front while the pilot sits in the back. Prices for one or two people range from $150 for a half hour to $450 for 90 minutes.

Camping

On the road to Hana, **H.P. Baldwin Beach Park**, one of the county parks on Maui's east side, is especially popular among the outdoor set. Facilities at Hawaii's county campgrounds include water, toilets, cold-water outdoor showers, tables and grills. For information about various county sites, permits, and fees (which are minimal), contact the **Department of Parks and Recreation**, *Tel. 808/243-7389 or 808/572-8122 in East Maui; Tel. 808/879-4364 in southern Maui; or Tel. 808/661-4685 in West Maui*. Two county parks, at **Kanaha** and at **Papalaua Beach**, are also open to campers. All sites require permits.

Two pleasant state parks are found in eastern Maui as well: **Waianapanapa State Park** (near Hana) on a precipice high above a beach with striking ebony sand; and **Kaumahina State Wayside Park**, on a palisade above the coast.

Polipoli Springs, another state park, spreads along the lofty slopes of Haleakala volcano. It's a good choice for day trips as well as overnight adventures, but you'll need a four-wheel-drive. In addition to a stand of California redwoods, you'll find one cabin and campgrounds. The cabin is reserved far in advance, so make your plans early if you want ready-made shelter here. From many lookout points, you'll have wonderful panoramic views of Maui. All of Hawaii's state parks are free. For camping permits and cabin reservations, contact **State Parks Camping**, *Division of State Parks, 54 South High Street, Wailuku, HI 96793, Tel. 808/984-8109*.

About 10 miles south of Hana and 60 from Kahului Airport, **Haleakala National Park** is also free. In this moonscape of a park, the silence-broken only by the wind and the crunching of rocks and stones underfoot-is intense. There is no water or other facilities, except the three multibunk cabins on the crater floor. These dirt-cheap lodgings are always booked-months in advance, in fact. For permits and cabin reservations, contact **Haleakala National Park**, *P.O. Box 369, Makawao, HI 96768, Tel. 808/572-9306*. For guided hikes into Haleakala crater, contact **Crater Bound**, *Tel. 808/878-1743*, based in Kula.

Cruises

Cruises take vacationers to the island of **Lanai** (a 1.5-hour ride) for a day of snorkeling at a marine preserve, riding kayaks, taking a glass-bottom boat trip, or cooling out in hammocks strung between coconut palms in the $4 million beach park known as **Club Lanai**. There are good hiking trails and activities also include volleyball, biking, and treasure hunts. An open bar sits on a mini-island in the middle of a pond. A continental breakfast is served, as well as a barbecue lunch that might include goodies such as teriyaki chicken; Korean-style ribs, mahi-mahi, pasta salad, and garlic bread. This cruise, which costs about $158, leaves from Lahaina Harbor at 6:45am and returns at 4:30pm. No alcohol is served, but you may bring your own. **Club Lanai Cruise**, *Tel. 871-1144*, which charges $79 per person, also cruises this area.

Other ways of exploring the coral reefs if you are not a snorkler are through trips on glass-bottom boats. Try **Seven Seas Cruises**, *Tel. 667-6165*, or **Nautilus**, *Tel. 667-2133*.

Hordes of young people climb aboard catamarans and other boats for dinner and sunset cruises, many of which feature open bars and dancing. You'll sit down to dinner for about $69 on the 65-foot, 87-passenger *Spirit of Windjammer* schooner, *Tel. 661-8600*, accompanied by live entertainment. A sunset dinner cruise, *Tel. 661-8787*, leaves from Ma'alaea. The two-hour cruise provides a four-course meal and entertainment for $90 per person.

Fishing

Deep-sea fishing enthusiasts on Maui are rewarded with catches of mahi-mahi, Pacific blue marlin, tuna, and other game fish. No licenses are required. The harbors in Lahaina and Ma'alaea (southern West Maui) are the places to make arrangements for charters. Trips are usually four or eight hours and boats provide all gear, including bait and ice. Try **Ace Sportfishing**, *Tel. 667-7548*, or **Finest Kind Sportfishing**, *Tel. 661-0338*. For shore fishing, the most sheltered spots are along the southern coast.

Many locals enjoy fishing from piers at Kahului Harbor or off beaches and in ponds not far from Kahului Airport. Although people are no longer permitted to fish from Hamoa Beach (used by the Hotel Hana-Maui), the fishing off **Hana Beach State Park** is quite good. Many of Maui's best shore fishing spots are at the end of rugged roads that require four-wheel-drive vehicles and are difficult to find. The **Maui Visitors Bureau**, *Tel. 800/244-3530*, should be able to hook you up with a shore fishing guide who is familiar with the places where cliffs and the surf are safest.

Golf

Maui has quite a few top-rated championship courses, in both East and West Maui. Hugging the lower mountain slopes of West Maui, the **Royal Kaanapali North Golf Course** was designed by Robert Trent Jones,

Sr. Both this course and its sister, the **Royal Kaanapali South Golf Course**, *Tel. 661-3691* for either, are graced with wonderful ocean and mountain scenery. Green fees are about $100 for both resort guests and $120 for non-guests.

I'm not a golfer, but I could spend hours on the gorgeous championship courses at the **Kapalua Golf Club**, *Tel. 669-8044*. The fourth hole on the Bay Course here is in a stunning location atop a lofty peninsula enclosed by the ocean. Complete with duck-filled ponds and rolling hills, these courses are considered among the world's best by the pros. They play host to popular annual tournaments. At the championship Plantation course, which opened in 1991, green fees are $130 for Kapalua Bay Resort guests.

To make reservations at any one of the dramatically located **Wailea Golf Club Orange Courses**, *Tel. 875-5111*. The Blue Course is a popular relaxing course. The Emerald Course has a panoramic ocean view. The challenging Gold Course is set in a natural terrain of Hawaiian grasses, lava fields and *wili wili* trees. Guests at any Wailea resort may reserve a tee time up to five days in advance. $90 for the Blue and Emerald Courses; $100 for the Gold Course.

Maui's public courses are less expensive, but their views are no less expansive. The **Pukalani Country Club**, *Tel. 572-1336*, sprawls in Kula, upcountry Maui. Note that the high altitude may make you somewhat light-headed. Green fees are only $45 for groups and $30 otherwise. In an arid part of the island, **Silversword Golf Course**, *Tel. 874-0777*, sits in Kihei near Wailea. Fees are $60 (winter rates slightly higher). At **Waiehu Municipal**, *Tel. 243-7400*, by the beach at Wailuku, fees are a mere $30 or so for a round, plus a cart fee of $7.50 per person.

Opened in December, 1991, the 18-hole **Waikapu Sandalwood Golf Course**, *Tel. 242-4653*, overlooks East Maui and the ocean. It is 15 minutes from the Kahului airport, 13 miles from Wailea, and 23 miles from Kaanapali. The greens fee of $75 includes cart and locker room.

If you want to learn the strokes, you can take lessons at any of Maui's courses or contact **Del Mar Golf Course**, *Tel. 667-7111*, at the Royal Kaanapali or **Maui Parbusters**, *Tel. 871-8633*, at Pukalani. Call the **Wailea Golf and Tennis Clubs**, *Tel. 875-5111*, for information about clinics for adults as well as children.

Hang Gliding

Tandem hang gliding is available in Wailea, *Tel. 572-6557*, so if you're not quite daring enough to go it alone, you're in luck. During these 35-minute flights, an experienced hang-glider takes off with a passenger from a 10,000 foot elevation and they float down to the beach. A camera is mounted on the hang glider to record the descent for posterity. The price ($250) is as steep as the trip down, but worth every penny according to the initiated. Also consider a 45-minute sunset flight on a motorized hang glider.

Helicopter Rides

Since these whirls can be so expensive, you should choose your tour carefully. And if you're planning to visit the Big Island of Hawaii or Kauai, I recommend that you wait to take a helicopter tour over one of those islands. For my money, the most exciting tour on Maui is the flight over Hana and Haleakala volcano. **Blue Hawaiian Helicopters,** *Tel. 871-8844 or 800/745-BLUE,* offers a 45-minute version for $130 per person.

This company also has a 65-minute tour of the whole island for $180; you'll probably pass over inaccessible flourishing valleys and thundering waterfalls, as well as start Haleakala volcano. Another choice is the 65-minute West Maui and Molokai trip for $180. Ask about getting a videotape of your trip to take home. If you fly with **Sunshine Helicopters,** *Tel. 871-0722,* another reputable company, you can get 50% off a Sunshine sailing cruise. Flights leave from Kahului Airport.

Hiking

Maui offers countless scenic hiking trails, some near resort areas. Many people enjoy walking in the tropical rain forest of **Iao Valley** in West Maui, with its prominent green Iao Needle rock formation. At **Olowalu,** south of Kaanapali, you call take the 30-minute trek to the petroglyphs. After taking a road through the sugarcane fields into Olowalu Valley, you'll spot these ancient rock carvings on a promontory about 25 feet above the path.

On the far side of the cinder cone at **Oneloa Beach** (a.k.a. **Big Beach**) in Makena in southern East Maui, a trail leads from **Little Beach** 360 feet to the top of the cone. Any time of year, the views from this wooded site are exceptional. During the winter, this is a wonderful vantage point for whale watching.

The extremely hardy may want to hike into stark, eerie **Haleakala Crater,** with its three dozen miles of steep trails. Keep in mind that the high altitude will make you tire more quickly than usual and you may become light-headed. Periodically from June through August, national park rangers lead morning **nature walks** starting at the Visitor Center or Hosmer Grove, *Tel. 808/572-9306.* **Crater Bound,** *Tel. 808/878-1743,* based in Kula, leads hikes into Haleakala Crater.

Sliding Sands is one of the volcano's least rigorous trails. Beginning at the summit, it dips about four miles to the crater floor. Plan to spend twice as much time getting back up as going down. Even if you don't go all the way to the bottom, you'll still get more than a taste of Haleakala's

DOUBLE FALLS

Few avid hikers can resist the trails along the Hana Highway. You'll need at least three or four days of hiking and camping to truly appreciate this jungled region. Hookipa Beach County Park, a popular surfing and windsurfing hangout, is a good place to stop to fill water bottles.

First you'll come to Twin Falls, about 20 miles from Kahului Airport. The four-mile round-trip trail begins by the turnoff right before Hoolawa Bridge. Follow the jeep road through meadows and by Hoolawa Stream. Wild guava is plentiful, both the common yellow type and the smaller, red, strawberry variety. Various trails off the jeep road lead to small pools. At one pool, about a half mile along the trail, you might see locals diving off the rocky lava ledge over which a waterfall crashes into a pool. Residents also swing into the water from the rope tied to a branch of a banyan tree. This is a popular site for skinny dipping. Whenever you're swimming in natural pools, be careful of submerged rocks.

The jeep road roughly follows the river for another mile before you reach an irrigation ditch. After about 100 yards along the bank of the ditch, you'll see the first of the Twin Falls. Take the trail on the right around this fall to get to the second fall. Take a refreshing dip in the pool below either waterfall.

rugged appeal. Be sure to dress warmly and to bring lightweight rain gear. You'll also need sunglasses and sun block.

About six miles beyond **Twin Falls**, the **Waikamoi Ridge Trail Nature Walk** is some two miles round trip. You'll know you've come to the beginning of the trail when you see a parking area and a picnic table on a cliff overlooking the highway to the right. Passing through a bamboo forest, this trail also goes by mahogany, tree ferns, guavas and many other kinds of vegetation.

Kaumahina State Park provides flush toilets, drinking water, shelters and picnic tables. The crowd of tourists here usually disappears by 3pm or so. This park sits on a bluff with a dramatic view of the Keanae Peninsula.

If you hike into the **Keanae Arboretum**, beyond Kaumahina State Park and Honomanu Beach, you'll find all kinds of labeled native and imported plants, as well as many varieties of taro growing in patches.

Hiking about a quarter-mile to the caves at **Waianapanapa State Park**, near Hana, is a popular pursuit. Hotel Hana-Maui offers guided hikes through forests and to waterfalls in the area. At **Oheo Gulch** (a.k.a. Seven Pools or Seven Sacred Pools), beyond Hana, don't stop at the lower pools that are usually crowded with visitors. The first of the upper falls is only about a half-mile from the parking lot.

HIKE WITH A GUIDE

One of the best outfits for guided treks is **Hike Maui**, P.O. Box 330969, Kahului, Maui, HI 96733, Tel. 808/879-5270, run by Ken Schmitt, who leads half-day, full-day, and overnight rambles along coasts, through rain forests, or into the mountains. Swimming is often part of the trip. A naturalist, botanist, geologist, and anthropologist, Schmitt has also studied history, zoology, mythology, and classical languages.

Along the way, he identifies plants, flowers, birds and animals, plucking fruit for hikers to sample. A picnic lunch is always included, as well as roundtrip transportation from central Maui. Day hikes range from five to 10 hours, including driving time, and prices run from about $70 to $110.

Horseback & Mule Riding

To ride through lush scenery and a working cattle ranch in West Maui, contact **Mendes Ranch & Trail Rides**, Tel. 871-5222. You'll travel about six miles up and down a hillside, with fabulous views of waterfalls and the ocean. This adventure ($135 for 2 1/2 hours) ends with a paniolo-style open pit barbecue lunch. Feel like splurging? Call **Sunshine Helicopters**, Tel. 871-0722, about the combination horseback and helicopter tour.

In Hana, you can trot along the rugged coast with horses from **Hana Ranch**. Bring your camera – the guide will be happy to take shots of you against dramatic backgrounds. Arrangements should be made through **Hotel Hana-Maui**, Tel. 248-8211.

VOLCANIC TROT

Pony Express, Tel. 667-2200, based in Kula, specializes in horseback rides into Haleakala Crater. One of these trips runs from 9:30am to 3pm (about $120 per person) covering 7.5 miles to and from the crater floor, where riders unsaddle themselves for a picnic lunch. The other excursion lasts from 9:30am to 5:30pm (about $150 per person), and in addition to visiting the crater floor, riders are treated to many more natural wonders. Pony Express also offers a leisurely ride through the rolling hillside and through a eucalyptus forest about a mile below the entrance to Haleakala Crater. Pony Express keeps its groups small, so be sure to make reservations at least three days in advance.

Travelers no longer have to go to Molokai for dramatic mule rides. The **Maui Mule Ride**, Tel. 244-6853 or 878-1743, takes people 3,000 feet down into Haleakala crater with certified guides. You can choose the 2,

5, or 6 1/2 hour trip. The first time I mounted a mule, I was surprised at how much smoother the ride was on these sure-footed animals than on horseback.

Parasailing

To be gently lifted into the air by a parachute, contact **Parasail Kaanapali**, *Tel. 669-6555*, **UFO Parasailing**, *Tel. 661-7836*, or **Lahaina Para-Sail**, *Tel. 661-4887*. Note that parasailing is not available during whale-watching season.

Sailing

Many of the larger hotels run their own catamaran or glass-bottom boat cruises or sailing trips. I have heard some good reports about **First Class Charters**, *Tel. 667-7733 or 800/ 600-0959*, and **Captain Nemo's Trilogy** catamaran, *Tel. 661-5555*. Other reputable companies are **Island Marine Activities**, *Tel. 661-8397 or 800/ 833-5800*, in Lahaina; and **Sail Hawaii**, *Tel. 879-2201*.

Scuba Diving

In addition to Maui's coasts, there are some wonderful dive sites off neighboring Lanai and Molokai. Full certification (about $275 for the 4-day course) is available on Maui in PADI, NAUI, and SSCI training programs.

Among the most experienced dive operators are **Ed Robinson's Hawaiian Reef Divers**, *Tel. 879-3584 or 800/635-1273*, in Lahaina; **Captain Nemo's**, *Tel. 661-5555*; **Hawaiian Reef Divers**, *Tel. 667-7647*, in Lahaina; **Central Pacific Divers**, *Tel. 667-7647*, in Lahaina; **Lahaina Divers**, *Tel. 667-7496*; **Dive & Sea Center**, *Tel. 874-1952*, in Kihei; and **Maui Sun Divers**, *Tel. 879-3337*, also in Kihei.

Snorkeling

In addition to **Molokini Crater** and other nearby sites (see *Volcanic Plunge*, below), try snorkeling right off the beach. Among the best locations are **Black Rock** (also called Pu'u KeKa'a) in front of Sheraton Maui on Kaanapali Beach; **Honolua Bay**, **Kapalua Beach**, **Napili Bay**, **Honokeana Bay**, **Olowalu Beach**, **Makena Landing**, on the small bay (which is covered with black lava pebbles), **La Perouse Bay**, and **Hana Bay**. Snorkelers often congregate off mile markers #13 and #14 on West Maui at the narrow beaches right off the highway. However, locals will tell you that the underwater sights are better at the lesser known spot off mile marker #11, where diving is also particularly good. Also contact **Ocean Activities Center**, *Tel. 879-4485 or 800/798-0652, Fax 808/879-7427*.

VOLCANIC PLUNGE

Some of Maui's best (though often crowded) snorkeling and diving is at **Molokini**, a partially submerged volcano whose crater just breaks the surface of the ocean. Depths here range from 10 feet to more than 60 at the drop-off. A variety of companies offers snorkeling or scuba trips to this location as well as other sites, including the **Ocean Activities Center**, Tel. 879-8811, and 879-4485, the nonprofit **Pacific Whale Foundation**, Tel. 879-8811, and **Lahaina Divers**, Tel. 667-7496. The sail to the islet takes about 45 minutes. Schools of butterfly fish, triggerfish, yellow tang, bluespine, pinktail durgeon, unicorn fish, and even zebra moray eels swarm snorkelers and divers, who sometimes feed them bread crumbs. Porpoises often frolic in these waters. From November to April, there's a good chance you'll also spot humpback whales. Even if you don't see one of these gigantic mammals, you may hear them calling out to each other when you're under water.

The 3-and-a-half hour **Trilogy Snorkeling Cruise**, Tel. 661-4743 or 800/874-2666, is one of the most enjoyable ways for snorkelers to get here. Masks and fins are provided. Since the catamaran departs early (about 6:30am) when the water is calmest, you'll be treated to a breakfast of homemade cinnamon rolls with coffee or tea. Lunch might consist of pineapple-glazed chicken, tossed green salad, corn on the cob, and freshly baked bread.

One of the most enjoyable snorkeling excursions is hosted aboard **Navatek II**, Tel. 661-8787. You leave from Ma'alaea Harbor. First you'll be served a full breakfast, including Belgian waffles topped with fruit and syrup such as guava or blackberry. Then the chef prepares lunch right on the boat: grilled chicken, burgers, sausages, salad, and fresh vegetables. Wine, mixed drinks, and soft beverages flow freely. And all during the cruise, vacationers munch on chips and fresh tropical fruit. The six-hour trip includes an ecology lecture. Oh, and of course, snorkeling – at one or two locations. The trip lasts from 8:45am - 2:45pm; it takes place Monday to Saturday.

Up to 35 passengers can ride in the 48-foot inflatable **Maui Nui Explorer**, Tel. 661-3776. This is the one to choose if speed and snorkeling are your thing. The captain rides waves, hugs coastline curves, and gets daringly close to rocks jutting from the water. You'll stop at three snorkeling sites and there's a nature expert aboard to tell you all about marine life and local conservation efforts. The price ($116 for adults; $87 for children ages 5 to 12; no children under age 5) includes a continental breakfast, mid-morning snack, deli lunch, and mid-afternoon snack. The boat pushes off at 8am and returns at 2pm.

Trilogy, *Tel. 661-4743 or 800/874-2666*, based in Lahaina, runs a very good half-day snorkeling excursion to fish-filled Molokini islet, actually a partially submerged volcanic crater. To take advantage of the best (calmest) sea conditions, the tour departs at 6:45am. Delicious home-baked cinnamon rolls help wake up drowsy passengers. Costing about $80, this cruise also leaves from Ma'alaea Harbor.

A portion of the profits of **Lanai Snorkeling and Sailing** catamaran trips, *Tel. 667-0800 or 667-2299*, is donated to the preservation of Maui's marine environment. The six-hour excursion ($80 for adults, less for children) includes two or three snorkeling destinations, snorkeling instruction, breakfast, a deli lunch, snacks, and soft drinks. If you're lucky, you'll spot both turtles and dolphins in addition to all kinds of fish and coral.

Submarine Rides

To explore the lower depths (but only if you're not going scuba diving), board the 48-passenger **Atlantis Submarine**, *Tel. 667-2224 or 800/548-6262*, which takes the 100-foot plunge off Lahaina Harbor. Rates begin at $70 for adults and $40 for children, who must be at least 3 feet tall. (Note that although you'll be underwater for 45 minutes, this excursion includes a boat ride to the sub; so you should allow about two hours for the whole deal.) Ask about packages that include a helicopter ride, whale watching (from January through March), or a luau.

Surfing

Hookipa Beach, in northern East Maui, is probably the most popular surfing (and windsurfing) spot on Maui. Championship surfing competitions are held here every year. **Honolua Bay**, in northern West Maui, also has excellent waves, which can rise up to 15 feet during the winter. For an overview of the hot-dogging surfers, drive down the red dirt road at Lipoa Point. You'll cut through pineapple fields before reaching the 200-foot cliffs that serve as a perfect vantage point for the surfers' aquatic ballet. During the summer, Ma'alaea Harbor, in southern West Maui, and Big Beach (a.k.a. Oneloa), in southwestern East Maui, draw many surfers. To learn to surf, contact **Maui Surfing School**, *Tel. 875-0625*, $60 per person.

Tennis

There are tennis courts all over Maui, in hotels, condos, and elsewhere. The **Wailea Tennis Club**, *Tel. 879-1958*, has the greatest number: three grass courts, nearly a dozen hard surface courts, and a 1,000-seat tennis stadium; call the Club for details about clinics for both adults and children. The **Royal Lahaina Tennis Ranch**, *Tel. 661-3611*, at Kaanapali boasts 11 courts, six of which are lighted. **Kapalua Tennis Garden**, *Tel.*

669-5677, has 10 lighted courts on which tennis attire is required. The six-court **Makena Tennis Club**, *Tel. 879-8777*, is one of Maui's newest. Court time generally runs about $12 to $15 a day per person; resort guests receive discounts. Private lessons cost about $55 an hour and are widely available (as well as cheaper group lessons). You'll find six lighted public courts at **Lahaina's Civic Center**, *Tel. 661-4685*, and two in **Hana**.

Whale Watching

From December to April, **humpback whales** migrate to Hawaii's waters to give birth, especially around Maui. A variety of cruises operate out of Lahaina for close-up views of the majestic members of this endangered species. In addition to **Trilogy**, *Tel. 661-4743 or 800/874-2666*, whale watching excursions are run by the **Pacific Whale Foundation**, *Tel. 879-8811*, based in Kihei, **Sentinel Yachts**, *Tel. 661-8110*, in Lahaina and **Ocean Activities Center**, *Tel. 879-4485*, in Kihei. The cost is $30 for adults and $18 for children.

Windsurfing

Maui's best beach for boardsailing is Hookipa Beach, in northern East Maui, about 35 miles from Lahaina. International competitions take place here throughout the year. Windsurfing gear is sold at stores in nearby Pa'ia. Wind and wave conditions are also excellent at **Honolua Bay**, in northern West Maui. Most of the larger hotels give windsurfing lessons, and many won't charge you for the land demonstration on a simulator. Instruction begins at about $40. You'll pay from about $40 an hour to rent boards without taking lessons.

In addition to hotels, lessons are given by **Maui Surfing School**, *Tel. 875-0625*; **Ocean Activities Center**, *Tel. 879-4485*; **Kaanapali Windsurfing School**, *Tel. 667-1964*; **Maui Magic Windsurfing Schools**, *Tel. 877-4816*; **Windsurfing West Maui**, *Tel. 871-8733*; and **Hi-Tech Surf Equipment**, *Tel. 877-2111*.

Working Out & Spas

For weight machines, aerobics classes, and massage, try the **Valley Isle Fitness Centers**, *Tel. 667-7474*, in Lahaina; *Tel. 874-2844* in Kihei; or *Tel. 242-6851* in Wailuku), **Powerhouse Gym**, *Tel. 879-1326*, in Kihei, or **Lahaina Nautilus Center**, *Tel. 667-6100*.

You don't have to be a hotel guest to use the weight room or take aerobics classes at the **Maui Marriott**, *Tel. 667-1200*, in Kaanapali, but you will be charged a small fee. The **Grand Wailea**, *Tel. 875-1234*, sports a world-class health spa. Also among the island's best health clubs is the one at the **Westin Maui**, *Tel. 667-2525*, in Kaanapali, but, alas, its weights, aerobics classes, and massages are only for hotel guests. Ditto for the health spa in the **Hyatt Regency**, *Tel. 661-1234*, in Kaanapali. In Wailea, daily aerobics classes are conducted at the **Renaissance Wailea**, *Tel. 879-4900*, and the **Aston Wailea**, *Tel. 879-1922*, among other hotels.

Spa Luna, *Tel. 572-1300*, in Makawao is the place to go in upcountry Maui for serious pampering. Treatments include massage, reflexology, acupuncture, body wraps, and hydrotherapy, and there are classes in yoga and tai chi along with wellness workshops.

SHOPPING

While the larger hotels have clusters of boutiques on the premises, I find it more fun (and more economical) to wander in and out of the small stores along Front Street in Lahaina. If you're in the market for locally produced ceramics, jewelry, clothing, candies, and other items, keep an eye out for the **Made on Maui** logo. Shopping centers tend to stay open later, 9am to 9pm, than stores elsewhere which are usually open 9am to 5 or 6pm. Here are some of my favorite spots to part with money:

Shopping Centers

To go where the locals go, head for the **Kaahumanu Center**, *275 Kaahumanu Avenue, Tel. 877-3369*, in central Kahului. Here among some five dozen shops and restaurants are Hawaii's two main department stores: **Liberty House** and **Shirokiya**, a Japanese contribution to the islands. The indoor, air-conditioned **Lahaina Cannery**, *1221 Honoapiilani Highway, north end of Lahaina, Tel. 661-5304*, resembles the 1919 Baldwin Packers pineapple cannery that once stood on this site.

Toward the southern end of Lahaina are **The Wharf**, *658 Front Street, Tel. 661-8748*, and **505 Front Street**, *Tel. 667-2514*. **Whalers Village** is an open-air collection of boutiques (including Versace, Chanel, Coach, Prada, and Tiffany) and waterfront restaurants right on Kaanapali Beach. There are also two small whaling museums.

Aloha Wear

Over the years, the quality of clothing sold at commercial **Hilo Hattie's**, *1000 Limahana Place, Lahaina*, in West Maui, has improved. You might also find here some of the popular Banana Butter produced at the Maui Jelly Factory in Makawao. For more aloha shirts, poke around **Reyn's**, *Tel. 661-5356, at the Lahaina Cannery* Shopping Center and in Kapalua, *Tel. 669-5260*.

Liberty House, with a handful of branches in hotels and elsewhere on Maui, has a healthy choice of moderately priced floral print muumuus and shirts.

Art Galleries

There's something about Maui that gets creative juices flowing. Witness the large number of galleries, exhibits, and artists' cooperatives on the island. Held at the **Maui Arts & Cultural Center** every spring, **Art Maui**, *Tel. 572-2560*, is the island's most celebrated show, featuring the work of the most accomplished local artists.

The efforts of island marine artists are displayed for **The Ocean Arts Festival**, held from January through March at **Lahaina Galleries**, *Tel. 667-2152 or 800/228-2006*, to benefit the Pacific Whale Foundation, a non-profit research group. Perhaps the best known of these aquatic artists is Robert Lyn Nelson, whose surreal paintings and sculpture combine views from above and below the ocean's surface. Lahaina Galleries has four branches on Maui.

No art lover should pass up a chance to visit **Hui Noeau Visual Arts Center**, *2841 Baldwin Avenue, Makawao, Tel. 572-6560*, in an elegant old estate in *paniolo* (cowboy) country. (See *Seeing the Sights* in this chapter for details about exhibits and classes.)

Lahaina Printsellers, *Lahaina Cannery Mall, Tel. 667-7843*; the **Wharf**, *Lahaina, Tel. 661-3519*; and **Whaler's Village**, *Kaanapali, Tel. 667-7617*, stocks antique maps and engravings, some done as early as the 16th century (every item is certified). The old hospital that houses the main Front Street shop once nursed infirm and injured whalers back to health. Ask to see the 18th century engravings done from the sketches made during the voyages of British Captain James Cook, the first recorded European to visit Hawaii. The gallery can frame the work you buy in gleaming native Hawaiian *koa* wood. Also try **Grand Wailea Resort**, *Tel. 874-9310*, and **Kapalua Shops**, *Tel. 669-5549*.

A cooperative called the Lahaina Art Society runs the **Old Jail House Gallery**, *649 Wharf Street, Lahaina, Tel. 661-0111*, on the waterfront. More than a few misbehaving whalers were sentenced at this historic former court house and lock-up. The **Village Gallery**, *120 Dickenson Street, Lahaina, Tel. 661-4402*, sells much local artwork, from oil paintings to reasonably priced hand crafted jewelry.

In Pa'ia, a small frontier town on the road to Hana, an artists' community flourishes. **The Maui Crafts Guild**, *Tel. 579-9697*, is located in a handsome old wooden building with an upstairs lanai. Browse through the outstanding collection of basketry, lava rock sculpture, hand-painted silk scarves, ceramics, paintings, and beaded earrings, all by Maui residents. Although most of the artists are Caucasian, the themes are Pacific.

Local Woods and Crafts and the studio of **Eddie Flotte** are also located here. This Philadelphia transplant with a keen eye for everyday details has preserved many a Pa'ia street scene in watercolor renditions:

the town's weathered historic buildings, a group of old men playing cards and drinking soda. Also see Crafts in this section.

Books

Whalers Book Shoppe, *Wharf Shopping Center, 658 Front Street*, stocks a good selection of Hawaiiana titles.

Chocolate

Chocoholics should investigate the chocolate-covered roasted coffee beans at **Escape to Maui**, at the Kamaole as well as the Lahaina Cannery shopping centers; and more goodies at **Rocky Mountain Chocolate Factory**, *Lahaina Cannery*).

Coffee

For various blends of Hawaiian coffee, try **Sir Wildred's**, *the Lahaina Cannery, Lahaina, Tel. 667-1941*; **Maui Mall**, *Tel. 877-3711*; **Take Home Maui**, *Dickenson Street, Lahaina, Tel. 667-7056*; the **Coffee Store**, *Kaahumama Center; Tel. 871-6860*; and **Maui Coffee Roasters**, *Kahului, Tel. 877-2877*.

Crafts

The goods sold at **Maui's Best** are all made on the island by local artisans and crafts people. You'll find everything from sweatshirts and bamboo flutes to macadamia nut popcorn and tea. Also on sale are stuffed animals, candles, *koa* wood bowls, shell jewelry and silk-screened T-shirts. Maui's Best outlets reside at the *Kamaole Shopping Center, Tel. 875-8165*, and in *Kihei, Tel. 879-4734*.

Maui on My Mind, *Lahaina Cannery Shopping Center, Tel. 667-5597*, and *Whaler's Village, Kaanapali, Tel. 661-5643*, stocks stenciled Christmas ornaments, *koa* wood jewelry boxes, and pillow covers done in Hawaiian quilt designs.

At **Hemporium**, *Tel. 572-7876*, in Makawao, all of the locally produced jewelry, bags, and clothing are made of hemp.

Elephant Walk, *Tel. 874-0296, 661-6129, 667-2848, or 874-2555*, is a must for all those elephant collectors out there. This snazzy gift shop and gallery also carries pottery crafted by local Hawaiian artists, Niihau shell jewelry, custom *koa* products, Hawaiian rag dolls, Pele glass sculpture, hand-painted T-shirts, and an extraordinary collection of kaleidoscopes.

At the **Maui Crafts Guild**, *Tel. 579-9697*, in the small town of Pa'ia on the northern coast of East Maui, you might find intricately woven baskets, hand-painted raw silk bags, and sculpture created from handmade paper. For unusual crafts, shop at **Foreign Intrigue Imports**, *505 Front Street, Tel. 667-4004*.

See also Art Galleries, Koa Wood Products, and Distinctive Clothing.

Distinctive Clothing

Silks Kaanapali, *Tel. 667-7133*, has a great selection of hand-painted women's apparel, as well as kimonos, scarves, belts, and unusual jewelry. More hand-adorned clothing, scarves, jewelry, and handbags are found at **Cruise**, *Whaler's Village, Kaanapali, Tel. 667-1974*. All are original designs by local artists or crafts people from California. Also drop by **Lahaina Cannery Mall**, *Tel. 661-9007*, and **Grand Wailea Resort & Spa**, *Tel. 874-9021*, for striking clothing.

Maui Four Winds, *820 Front Street, Lahaina, Tel. 667-7117*, sells hand-painted shirts and other clothing. **Hurricane**, *Makawao, Tel. 572-5076*, is where you'll find attractive hats and women's clothing; it's brother store, **Tropo**, has an unusual collection of classic men's Hawaiian shirts.

Flowers

Check at **Kula Lodge** in *Upcountry Maui, Tel. 878-1535*, for the best way to send gift shipments of fresh and dried flowers to the mainland. And who ever said you can't give yourself a gift?

Fruit & Vegetables

Take Home Maui, *121 Dickenson, Street, Lahaina, Tel. 661-8067*, does not charge extra for delivering some of the island's natural treats to your hotel or to the airport upon your departure.

Hawaiian Instruments

For handmade traditional musical instruments, try **Na Kani O Hula**, *430 Hookahi Street, Wailuku, Tel. 243-9322*.

HAWAIIAN QUILTS

Introduced by 19th century New England missionaries, quilts took on a unique life of their own in Hawaii. Instead of the patchwork American style, local quilts have a large, symmetrical single-color design that is appliquéd onto a solid-color background. The cut out designs are reminiscent of the snowflake patterns snipped from folded paper by schoolchildren.

*Since stitches on Hawaiian quilts are minuscule, these bed covers and wall hangings are very time-consuming to create and thus quite costly. A quilt for a double bed could run you $2,200 to $7,000 or more. Wall hangings can cost between $300 and $1,000 and pillow shams, about $75 to $150. Not only do you need deep pockets to invest in these future family heirlooms, but you also need a lot of patience: A commissioned quilt can take from six months to two years to complete! Try **Quilters Corner**, Tel. 661-0944, or **Rhonda's Quilts**, Tel. 667-7660.*

Hawaiian Music

Bounty Music, *Kahului, Tel. 871-1141*, is the place to go for Hawaiian records and tapes.

Jewelry

Silks Kaanapali, Tel. 667-7133, has good selections of jewelry you won't find anywhere else. **Hawaiian Island Gems**, *Whalers Village, Tel. 667-7839*, is the place for top quality pearls, coral, emeralds, and other fine gems and stones at good prices. At **Weber Goldsmith Gallery**, *Wailea Shopping Village*, the resident artist specializes in unique custom goldsmithing, mostly 18k gold, some platinum, all precious gems. This gallery features local designers. All items are one-of-a-kind or limited production art.

Kites

Try **Kite Fantasy**, *Lahaina Cannery Shopping Center; Tel. 661-4766*, on the Honoapiilani Highway in Lahaina.

Koa Wood Products

In upcountry Maui, **Woods of the Land**, *810 Haiku Road, Unit 24, Haiku, Tel. 575-9422*, should have some *koa* wood items among its carved bowls, plates, boxes, and other crafts. Note that this lustrous native Hawaiian wood is becoming more scarce and thus more expensive than in years past.

See also Crafts.

Macadamia Nuts

These are grown on the Big Island of Hawaii, but you'll have no problem finding them at most grocery stores and many other shops.

Maui Potato Chips

You'll pay more than you might expect, but the thick, flavorful **Original Maui Kitch'n Cook'd Potato Chips** are worth every penny (and every calorie). Quite a few other brands with similar names vie for your dollars, but locals swear by the real McCoy. Bags of these crispy spuds are available in most grocery stores.

Maui Wine

Tedeschi Vineyards and Winery in upcountry Maui, *Tel. 878-6058*, produces the state's only local wine. You can taste-test Maui Blush, Maui Blanc (pineapple wine), or Maui Brut-Blanc de Noirs (homegrown bubbly) before buying at the winery or pluck a bottle from one of the grocery shelves around the island.

SCRIMSHAW

*More scrimshaw is sold in Maui than anywhere else in the world (even New England). This art form dates back to Maui's 19th century whaling days. These new or antique etched bones, teeth, and tusks are sold in many Lahaina shops. **Lahaina Scrimshaw,** 845 Front Street, Lahaina, Tel. 661 -8820, prices range from under $10 for key chains and pendants to thousands for antiques or carved elephant tusk sculptures.*

Perfume

If you'd like to take Hawaiian aromas home, stop at **Island Tan,** 360 Hoohana, Tel. 877-6882, and Whalers Village, Kaanapali, which sells locally produced fragrances in addition to cosmetics.

T-Shirts

While you'll encounter scores of stores selling T-shirts, **Crazy Shirts** – with its quality tailoring and wide variety of designs – is the king. This statewide chain store has several locations in Lahaina, including the Front Street and Lahaina Cannery branches. Also worth checking out is **Sun-Tees Hawaii,** Lahainaluna Road, Lahaina, Tel. 667-1995, which stocks silk-screened shirts with imaginative and unusual designs.

PRACTICAL INFORMATION

Alcoholics Anonymous

Call AA, Tel. 244-9673, about participating in local meetings.

Emergencies

Call Tel. 911.

Medical Attention

Maui Memorial Hospital, Wailuku, Tel. 244-9056.
Kula Hospital, Kula, Tel. 878-1221.
Hana Medical Center, Hana, Tel. 248-8294.
Doctors on Call, Hyatt Regency Maui, West Maui, Tel. 667-7676.
Kihei Clinic, Kihei, East Maui, Tel. 879-1440.
Wailea Medical Services, Wailea, Tel. 879-7447.
The Wailea-Kihei Center, Tel. 874-8100.

Post Offices

For information about the closest branch, call Tel. 667-6611 in Lahaina.

Time

Call *Tel. 242-0212.*

Tourist Information

The **Maui Visitors Bureau,** *1727 Wili Pa Loop, Wailuku, HI 96793, Tel. 244-3530, Fax 244-1337.*

Weather

Especially when you plan to be out exploring remote areas, you may want to call ahead, *Tel. 877-5111,* to find out about current weather conditions where you're going.

13. HAWAII - THE BIG ISLAND

Alternatively lush and stark, the island of Hawaii is one of the most unusual-looking and diverse places I've ever seen. Its striking appearance is due in part to the fact that it is still growing. **Kilauea**, the world's most active volcano, continues its periodic spurts of lava, which solidifies and adds to the island's land mass. From safe lookout points and helicopters, people watch the magnificent pyrotechnics. Called "vog" (volcanic fog), a haze hangs in the air for a few days after each of these intermittent eruptions. However, the sun shines through. Recent and ancient lava flows, ebony or chocolate in color, and moonscapes of volcanic craters stretch for miles in some regions.

In other areas, waterfalls plunge into jungled valleys and mist clings to rolling hills. Flower nurseries, macadamia nut orchards and coffee plantations thrive in the rich volcanic soil. With its paniolos (cowboys), rodeos, and herds of Herefords, **Parker Ranch** is the largest privately owned cattle ranch in the United States. **Mauna Kea**, a dormant volcano 13,796 feet above sea level, and active **Mauna Loa**, 13,677 feet above the ocean, are the world's tallest mountains (if measured from their aquatic bases). During winters when there is enough snow, experienced skiers can actually whiz down the slopes of Mauna Kea.

Hawaiian Roots

Some contemporary Hawaiians believe, as their ancestors did, that Pele, the volcano goddess, has lived in every volcano in the archipelago and now resides in the Big Island's Halema'uma'u Crater in Kilauea Caldera. She is said to have chosen Hawaii as her home after being run off Kauai by her sister, Na Maka, goddess of the sea, escaping to Oahu, and then fleeing to Maui. Ancient Hawaiians were known for their keen understanding of their environment. Thus it is not surprising that Pele's journey parallels the births of the Hawaiian islands, from the oldest to the youngest, according to present day geologists.

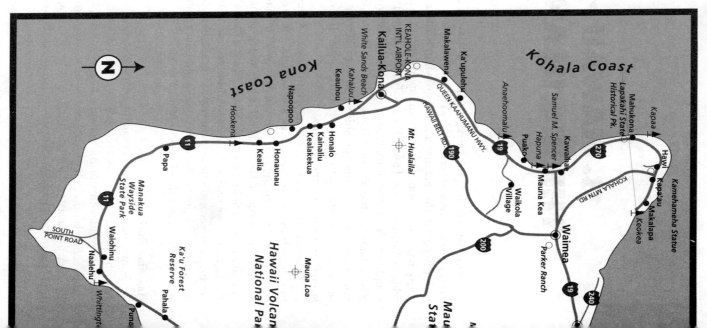

Kona Coast

Kohala Coast

White Sands Beach
Kailua-Kona
KEAHOLE-KONA
INT'L AIRPORT
Napopoo
Keauhou
Kahaluu
Makalawena
Ka'upulehu
Mahukona
Lapakahi State
Historical Pk.
Kapaa
Hawi
Kapa'au
Makalapa
Keokea
Kamehameha Statue
Samuel M. Spencer
Anaehoomalu
Hapuna
Puako
Mauna Kea
Kawaihae
KOHALA MTN RD
Hookena
Kealia
Honaunau
Honalo
Kainaliu
Kealakekua
Papa
Mt. Hualalai
QUEEN KAAHUMANU HWY.
HAWAII BELT RD.
190
19
270
240
19
Waikola
Village
Waimea
Parker Ranch
200
11
11
Manakua
Wayside
State Park
SOUTH
POINT ROAD
Waiohinu
Naalehu
Whittingt
Puna
Pahala
Ka'u Forest
Reserve
Mauna Loa
Hawaii Volcan
National Pa
Mau
Sta

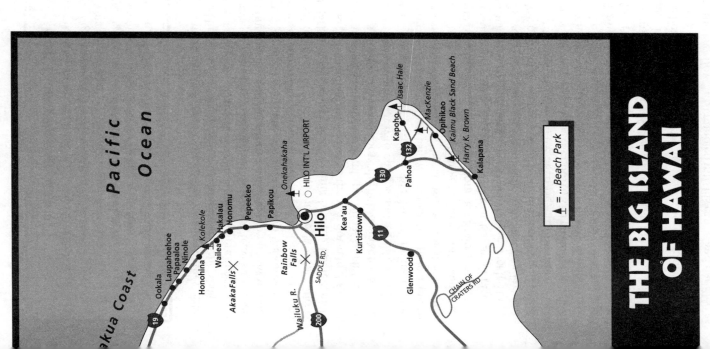

THE BIG ISLAND OF HAWAII

Ancient Hawaiians had their own version of sledding, but they didn't use snow. Called holua, this adult sport was the highlight of the Makahiki Festival, the annual season of peace. The holua runs were made from piled, packed lava rocks that were cushioned with grass, leaves and mats, then wet with hundreds of gallons of water. Clinging to narrow wooden sleds, called papa, competitors zoomed headfirst down the runways.

Remnants of several holua runs remain on the Big Island, in Kona. The one in Keauhou, just south of Kailua-Kona, was declared a National Historic Landmark in 1964. It was probably built by King Kamehameha around 1814. Like a steep highway, it went all the way down to the coast, about a mile from its start. The upper 3/4-mile portion is still intact. Fifty feet wide, it rises as high as eleven feet above the hillside in some sections. The lower quarter mile has given way to condos and a golf course.

According to one legend involving a Big Island holua contest, Kahawali, the chief of Puna, in the east, was about to enter a match. Dancers and musicians were keeping the crowd occupied while they waited for the competition to begin. Itching with curiosity about the reason for all the partying, Pele descended from her Kilauea home. She disguised herself as a local chief and demanded that Kahawali race her down the hill instead of the man he'd planned to challenge. Tickled by the boldness of this woman, the chief agreed. But the holua was far more difficult than Pele had expected, and she was soundly beaten by Kahawali.

Shouting that the contest must have been rigged, she insisted on a rematch. Someone must have damaged her borrowed papa, she told him. He agreed to another bout. But then she demanded that they switch papas so that all would be fair. He dismissed her request, climbed onto his papa, and began whizzing down the slope. An infuriated Pele jumped up and down, waving her fists in the air, sparking a volcanic eruption. Riding the red-hot river of lava, she pursued Kahawali down the hill.

It made no difference to her that the dancers, musicians, and onlookers were being swallowed up by the fiery cascade. Horror swept over the chief as he realized who his competitor really was. Leaving his entire family to the lava flow, he scrambled into his canoe and paddled as fast as his arms would move, fleeing to Maui, Lanai, Molokai, and finally hiding out at the home of his father on Oahu.

Perhaps because Pele, such a powerful female god, is at the helm, the Big Island is where women first won more equal footing with men. After the death of Kamehameha the Great in 1819, Kaahumanu, his favorite wife, convinced Liholiho (Kamehameha II) to end the kapu (taboos) against women dining with men and eating certain foods (such as coconuts, bananas, and pork). This led to an overthrow of the old, restrictive Hawaiian gods. However, soon the arrival of American missionaries brought a new form of restraint to the islands. Yet, despite the many changes Hawaii's spirituality has gone through, Pele has survived.

Pele is a vibrant and mysterious part of the lives of more than a few Hawaiians today. She is said to spend much of her time wandering near volcanoes. People frequently report seeing a long-haired woman who suddenly vanishes when observers get too close. In 1988, worshippers of Pele became embroiled in a legal battle with developers of a proposed geothermal energy plant. The Hawaiians believed that their religious rights would be violated if the plant were built as planned near Kilauea Volcano, on what they considered sacred land. They feared that its construction would lead to Pele's demise. The Hawaii Supreme Court ruled that the plant would not prevent people from having access to this sacred region and that it would not infringe on religious rights. The Court noted that the original development site had been moved several miles away from the area that has traditionally been considered Pele's home. However, this project remains controversial.

To see well-preserved ancient heiau, petroglyphs and royal fishponds once off-limits to commoners, visit the Kohala Coast in the northwest. The larger of the two rocks in front of Hilo's library, on the eastern side of the island, is known as the Naha Stone. As a teenager, Kamehameha the Great is said to have moved this 7,000 pound monolith. In doing so, he fulfilled the prophecy that the man who could budge it would someday unify the Hawaiian islands. Hilo is also known for its prestigious annual Merrie Monarch Festival, during which *hula halau* (hula groups) from all over the state take part in competitions (see Special Events in the *Nightlife & Entertainment* section in this chapter).

ARRIVALS & DEPARTURES

The Big Island's two main airports are **Hilo International Airport** (a.k.a. General Lyman Field) in the east and **Keahole-Kona International Airport** in Kona on the west coast. Hilo International is barely five minutes from most of Hilo's hotels and about 30 minutes from Volcano. From Keahole, the drive is about 35 to 50 minutes to Kona-Kohala hotels, 10 minutes to Kailua-Kona, and 20 to Keauhou. Some accommodations on the Kona-Kohala Coast and in Kailua-Kona and Keauhou provide transportation to and from Keahole Airport.

Many first-time visitors are struck by the landscape they see as they swoop down on Keahole Airport, which is built on top of a desert-like lava flow. The black runways cut through ebony and dark brown expanses punctuated by tufts of dry yellow grass. Along the roads to and from the airport, the green palms and purple, red, and orange bougainvillea provide a stunning contrast to the dark, barren terrain.

ORIENTATION

So as not to be confused with the whole state, Hawaii is commonly referred to as the Big Island. And, at about 4,000 square miles in size, big it is. Even if all the main islands in the chain were placed within its borders, they each would have plenty of elbow room. Some outsiders are under the mistaken impression that, because of its size and name, Hawaii is the main island in the chain and thus the home of the capital, Honolulu (which is actually on Oahu).

For such a huge place, the Big Island is sparsely populated and has a great deal of undeveloped land. It is nearly twice as large as the other main islands combined, yet only about ten percent of the state's residents call it home. Although it was the first part of the archipelago to be inhabited, it is the geological baby of the bunch. It's only been around for about a million years, as opposed to the first main island, Kauai, which was created more than five million years ago. Thus, the Big Island hasn't had time to develop as many beaches as its older siblings. However, sandy shores here come in a variety of colors: eggshell, pitch black, salt and pepper, and (believe it or not) even green (from olivine crystals).

The best beaches are along the 40-mile Kohala Coast, in the northwest. This side of the island is treated to the least amount of rainfall in all of the inhabited Hawaiian chain. The Big Island's most expensive resorts are found here. Following the lead of the Mauna Kea Beach Resort, some of these hotels are virtual museums of art and artifacts from the Far East, the South Pacific, and Hawaii. Many remnants of Hawaii's past remain in this area, which is peppered with heiau (temples), petroglyphs (ancient rock carvings), and royal fishponds. Hotels including the Mauna Lani Bay Hotel & Bungalows and Kona Village Resort have incorporated some of these fishponds and petroglyphs into their grounds.

To the south, the town of Kailua-Kona is a jumping off point for excellent marlin fishing and the headquarters for international fishing tournaments. There are few beaches here along the Kona Coast, where the dramatic shore is trimmed in craggy black lava set off by green lawns and palms. However, some of the island's best snorkeling sites can be found along here. The many hotels and condominiums in this area are

ROYAL LAND

Northern Kohala is the birthplace of Kamehameha the Great, the ambitious Big Island king who brought the whole archipelago under his rule. The kingdom's seat of government was moved from the Big Island to Lahaina, Maui, in 1820, and finally to Honolulu in 1845.

close to a wide selection of shops and restaurants. On the other side of the island, not far from partly flourishing, mostly desolate Volcanoes National Park, Hilo is the island's capital and largest town. While this residential community does have some hotels, agriculture and shipping contribute far more heavily to its economy than tourism does. This is because the few nearby beaches are rocky and Hilo receives a great deal of rain. Even when the weather is dry, the sky is often gray. However, this eastern side of the island is wonderfully lush, sprouting papayas, sugar cane, and thousands of varieties of orchids.

GETTING AROUND THE BIG ISLAND

To really appreciate the Big Island of Hawaii, you'll need to stay at least a week. You may want to divide your time among a hotel on the Kona-Kohala Coast (if you can afford it), one in Kona, and one in Hilo.

It's certainly true that at 93 miles at its longest and 76 miles at its widest, the Big Island lives up to its name. It takes some seven hours to drive the nearly 250 miles of road that ring the island. Mainly 2-lane, the roads are slim and curvaceous with no shoulders in some sections.

By Bus

There is no island-wide bus system on the Big Island. But Hele-On Buses travel between Kailua-Kona and Hilo daily (except Sunday when there is no service) for about $8 each way. In Keauhou and Kailua-Kona, complimentary shuttle buses take guests of hotels and condos to the Kona Country Club golf course and shopping centers.

By Car

Rental cars provide the most flexibility. It's best to reserve autos well in advance of your arrival, especially if you plan to travel between November and March, during August, the week before Easter (when the Merrie Monarch Festival takes place in Hilo), or in October (during the annual Ironman Triathlon). Remember, sights, attractions, and gas stations can be far apart on the Big Island. Used to the long distances, many residents have no problem with driving 50 miles just to visit a friend for an evening or to eat at a particular restaurant.

One main road goes around the southern portion of the island. Two roads cut across the northern segment: Saddle Road (Highway 200) runs between Mauna Kea and Mauna Loa volcanoes from Hilo to South Kohala. Here it joins Highway 190 to head north to Waimea or south to Kailua Kona; and after following the Hamakua Coast in the east, Highway 19 heads inland, then meets Highways 250 and 270 for the journey to North Kohala, or follows the western coast (on Queen Kaahumanu Highway) down to Kailua-Kona.

The drive from Kailua-Kona to Hilo should take about 2-1/4 hours via the northernmost route and 3-1/4 hours via the southern route. Driving from Kona to Hilo on Saddle Road (the middle route) will take roughly 2-1/4 hours. Some vacationers choose to spend a night or two in Hilo when they're ready to visit Volcanoes National Park and the Hamakua Coast. Volcanoes National Park is only a 45-minute drive from Hilo, while it is about two hours from Kailua-Kona. Waimea is approximately 1-1/4 hours from Hilo and 50 minutes from Kailua-Kona.

By Guided Tour

Several bus companies offer **circle-island tours** ($45 to $75) that include the Kona-Kohala Coast, Kamuela/Waimea, Hawaii Volcanoes National Park, Hilo, and the Hamakua Coast. However, these trips can last anywhere from nine to twelve hours and are extremely tiring. A more rewarding way to see the island is in segments. Bus companies offer tours to specific areas in addition to their more extensive excursions.

A good company to try is **Roberts Hawaii Tours**, *Tel. 966-5483*, in Hilo or *Tel. 329-1688*, in Kona) which takes vacationers to Kohala, Waipio Valley, the green sand beach at Ka Lae (where people can usually see turtles offshore), and the summit of Mauna Kea volcano. If you like traveling in small groups, **Paradise Safaris**, *Tel. 322-2366*, is a fine choice.

It limits its van tours to Mauna Kea to seven or fourteen people at a cost of $130 per person. Hot soup, a sandwich, a hot beverage, gloves, and a hooded parka make this dramatic trek more comfortable.

WHERE TO STAY

On the sunny western shore of the Big Island, the **Kona-Kohala Coast** has some of the world's most sumptuous resorts. Scattered along the prime beaches, these hotels reflect the diversity of the rest of the island. Guests are accommodated in high style, whether they're in multi-story complexes or thatched-roof Polynesian-style hales. While there are many tennis courts, championship golf courses, and endless water sports facilities, the resorts' special touches are what really make them stand out. Some hotels are decorated with dazzling Pacific and Eastern folk art. The lush grounds of others are interlaced with fish ponds once reserved for Hawaiian royalty and fields of petroglyphs (ancient carvings in the lava flows). Guests can arrange to be picked up from and delivered to the airport in limousines.

More moderately priced hotels are found along the rocky shore of **Kailua-Kona** and **Keauhou**, where beaches are few. However, many travelers don't mind cooling off in swimming pools overlooking the waves thrashing the craggy lava coast. Cruises for snorkeling, diving and sightseeing are easily arranged, and golf and tennis are also excellent in this area. Most of the island's stores and restaurants are in the waterfront town of Kailua-Kona.

The majority of people staying in hotels in **Hilo**, on the wet east coast, are either tourists visiting the volcanoes, older couples, or business travelers. If you'd like to get away from the tourist meccas, consider staying in the paniolo (cowboy) village of **Kamuela/Waimea**, with its upscale boutiques and gourmet restaurants; the macadamia-producing town of **Honokaa** on the northern Hamakua Coast; remote, gorgeous **Waipio Valley** in the northeast; isolated **Ka'u**, way down in the south; or **Hawaii Volcanoes National Park.**

Note that even very expensive one-bedroom condominiums can be quite economical when shared with another couple (living rooms usually have sofa beds). For Bed & Breakfasts other than those described, and rental cottages, see the sidebar at the end of this section.

Kamuela/Waimea
WAIMEA GARDENS COTTAGES B & B, *P.O. Box 563, Kamuela, HI 96743. Tel. 808/885-4550 or 800/262-9912, Fax 808/885-0559. Three rooms.*
Rate: $115. Three night minimum stay. Major credit cards.

At the foot of the Kohala Mountains and two miles from the center of Kamuela/Waimea town, this cozy Bed & Breakfast opened in 1982. It has received a three-star "excellent" rating from the American Bed and Breakfast Association. A stream runs through the backyard. The entrance to the building, which houses two units, is a renovated turn-of-the-century wash house that was part of an old Hawaiian homestead. Each unit sleeps three and one has a fireplace. Ruffled, country-style pillows and floral bedspreads are part of the cheerful decor. Not only are rooms equipped with stereos, remote-control TV, books and beach towels, but they also have flannel robes in the winter or Japanese cotton yukatas during the summer. French doors open to brick patios.

While the older unit contains a small full kitchen and a bath with a stall shower, the newer studio has a kitchenette and a bath with double sinks and a full tub. When guests arrive, they find that their refrigerators have been stocked with breakfast goodies including island juices and whatever they requested beforehand. Local Hawaiian honey, jams, fresh fruit, and Kona coffee are also on hand. Visitors, who prepare their own breakfasts, are welcome to gather fresh eggs from the chickens or pluck herbs from the garden on the property. The home of the owners is right next door to the B & B. Some of the island's best restaurants are only two miles away and Mauna Kea hotel's beautiful beach is eight miles away.

PUU MANU COTTAGE B & B, *P.O. Box 563, Kamuela, HI 96743. Tel. 808/885-4550 or 800/262-9912. One room. Rate $105.5 night minimum stay required. Major credit cards.*

Early American-style wooden furniture and handsome antiques decorate this two-bedroom cottage that began life as a barn. Still marked "Lady" and "Pal," the old swinging doors to the kitchen and second bedroom belonged to two of the horses' stalls. The large sunny kitchen, done in oak, is stocked with breakfast goodies. Between the master bedroom, with a double bed, and the second bedroom, with twins, is the huge bathroom. Sunshine streams through skylights into the cozy living room, with a fireplace, built-in couches, potted plants, and shelves filled with books. A TV, radio and audio-cassette player are also provided. Lounge chairs on the wide front lanai offer a perfect vantage point for gazing at the hills and grazing horses.

KOA LANE COTTAGE B & B, *P.O. Box 563, Kamuela, HI 96743. Tel. 808/885-4550 or 800/262-9912. One room. Rate $95.*

Colorful artwork adorns the walls of the dining/sitting room, which has a stereo and TV. The adjoining full kitchen is spacious, and the sleeping alcove holds a queen-sized bed. There's also a separate bedroom, decorated with floral wallpaper, with twin beds. The large bath has a stall shower. French doors lead to the lanai. This pretty cottage offers wonderful views of Mauna Kea and the Kohala Mountains. Guests will find the refrigerator stocked with delicious breakfast provisions.

PARKER RANCH LODGE, *P.O. Box 458, Kamuela, HI 96743. 21 rooms. Tel. 808/885-4100, Fax 808/ 885-6711. Double rooms begin at $80. Major credit cards.*

The decor of this modest accommodation makes it clear that paniolo (cowboy) country is all around. Some units come with kitchenettes and are decorated with heavy country-style wooden furniture. TVs are hidden in cabinets. Many guests begin their days with Kona coffee served in the lounge. This inn is conveniently located near the center of town.

KAMUELA INN, *P.O. Box 1994, Kamuela, HI 96743. Tel. 808/885-4243 or 800/555-8968, Fax 808/885-8857. 31 rooms. Double rooms begin at $54. Major credit cards.*

Travelers wanting to get away from the crowds yet be within shouting distance of boutiques, gourmet restaurants and a theater should book a room at this appealing inn. Everyone raves about the large penthouse suite, which has great views from its lanai and a full kitchen. Guests are treated to a light breakfast on the common lanai. Out front, a bench swings from a huge tree. In the newly decorated lobby, discussion of news items in the complimentary daily newspapers adds to the friendly atmosphere.

Hamakua Coast

KALOPA HOMESTEAD GUEST HOUSE, *P.O. Box 1614, Honoka'a, HI 96727. In Kalopa. Tel. and Fax 808/775-7167. One cottage. Rates begin at $85 for two people. No smoking.*

Neighboring Kalopa State Park, this homey pine mountainside cottage (1,700 feet in the sky) is surrounded by eucalyptus trees. Nights are cool and lit by more stars than I thought existed. With two bedrooms, a double-sized futon in the living room, a large kitchen, and a bath and half, the cottage can accommodate six people. There's a Jacuzzi in the larger bathroom. (If you're lucky, you'll find goats milk and macadamia nut soap handmade by the owner.) The living room bay window overlooks a small tropical fish pond. Chilly nights are warmed by the wood-burning stove. Amenities include a TV, VCR, private telephone, washer, and dryer. Note that mosquitoes can be a problem here during the summer, so bring insect repellent (or Avon's Skin So Soft oil) and keep the doors closed. If you'll need a crib or high chair, make arrangements when you call or write for your reservation.

LUANA OLA B & B COTTAGES, *P.O. Box 430, Honoka'a, HI 96727. Tel. 808/775-7727 or 800/357-7727. Two cottages. Rate: $90. Credit cards accepted.*

Amid a jungle of tropical flowers, these two private cottages have wonderful views of the ocean. Great for whale watching, they sleep four and contain all the comforts of home, including TV, private telephone, microwave, refrigerator, burner, toaster, coffee maker, iron and board. You'll probably spend a lot of time on your lanai (star-gazing is excellent from these cottages). Don't forget to remove your shoes before entering! Use of laundry facilities is included in the rate.

PAAUHAU PLANTATION HOUSE B & B, *P.O. Box 1375, Honoka'a, HI 96727. On Highway 19, north of Hilo, Waipio area. Tel. 808/775-7222, 808/775-7382, or (in California) Tel. 310/542-2239. Three cottages, plus the main house. Rates for two people begin at $75. No smoking permitted indoors or on lanais.*

Just outside Honoka'a, this Bed & Breakfast is nine miles from luscious Waipio Valley. The main house, which you can rent with a group of friends or where you can book individual rooms, is listed on the National Register of Historic Places. It was built in 1921 and beautifully restored in 1985. Highlighted with rich redwood, this grand home features huge cool rooms with high ceilings, handsome antiques, and attractive paintings. From the master bedroom balcony, you'll gaze out to the ocean beyond a bougainvillea garden. An oval tub in the master bath is large enough for two and is surrounded by mirrors and candles. There are also two sinks, three eight-foot well-lit mirrors, and a separate shower. With comfortable window seats, the spacious living room sports a grand piano.

In the dining room, the formal Queen Anne table and chairs seat twelve. Each of the home-like cottages sleeps four and has a kitchen. Landscaped gardens decorate the five-acre grounds, where you'll find regulation night-lit tennis courts (racquets and balls are available) and a basketball court. There's a pool table in the recreation room. Families with children should note that high chairs and cribs are available as well. Parker Ranch is nearby and the Kona Coast is a 30-minute drive away.

HAMAKUA HIDEAWAY, *P.O. Box 5104, Kuihaele, HI 96727. Tel. 808/775-7425. Two units. Rate: $75 (Cliff House) & $85 (Tree House).*

This rustic hideaway near Waipio Valley is perfect if you crave solitude and fabulous natural scenery. The views are spectacular. You look out on the far wall of Waipio Valley and down the coast for thirty miles. With a king-sized bed and a complete kitchen, the Treehouse Suite makes you feel as though you're sleeping in the huge mango tree whose branches seem to grasp it. Yet, the TV, microwave, complete kitchen and bath tubs with jets are up-to-date technology. The more rustic Cliff House affords an equally breathtaking view.

From both apartments, you'll hear the nearby waterfall and stream and overlook the rugged cliffs above Waipio Valley and the ocean. Honoka'a, the closest town, is a 10-minute drive away. Both Hawaii Volcanoes National Park and the Kona Coast are about 90 minutes from here. You can see Maui in the distance.

WAIPIO WAYSIDE BED & BREAKFAST, *P.O. Box 840, Honoka'a, HI 96727. Tel. 808/775-0275 or 800/833-8849, Fax 808/ 775-0275. Smoking outside only. Five rooms. Rate: $65. Major credit cards.*

A renovated sugar plantation manager's home dating back to 1938, this two-story, corrugated tin roof wooden house sits in the midst of sprawling sugarcane fields two miles from Honoka'a. (Watch for the Honoka'a-Oceanside sign.) Enclosed by a white picket fence, it is set off by beautiful gardens of bougainvillea and other flowers. Tangerines, pears, avocados, mangoes, mountain cherries, and five kinds of bananas grow on the property. There's a tiny gazebo out back.

Two of the five guest rooms share baths. The baths have a lot of character: a large, old-fashioned, six-foot tub with various aroma-therapy products in the main bath and a skylight over a shower. All rooms are warmly decorated, with bright reading lights, ceiling fans, and antiques such as the 19th century barber's chair and the old Chinese chairs. (They all work!) One room has twin beds, while others have doubles. Expect a full breakfast of waffles, smoothies, homemade bread, island fruit and local organic Honoka'a coffee. Guests gather in the inviting common areas to plan their day.

Kona-Kohala Coast

FOUR SEASONS HUALALAI, *100 Ka'upulehu Drive, Kailua-Kona, HI 96740. Tel. 808/325-8000 or 800/332-3442, Fax 808/325-8100. 243 rooms. Double rooms begin at $450. Major credit cards.*

The Hawaiian art and artifacts that decorate this resort span the years from 1775 to the present. Huge picture windows behind the front desk bring views of Mt. Hualalai into the lobby, where the three-tiered chandelier is made of kapa (Hawaiian bark cloth). Along with a half-mile stretch of beach, the lush grounds are graced with distinct bodies of water. For instance, one pool, its bottom imprinted with seashells, has an infinity edge; another, ocean-fed and made of lava, is filled with tropical fish and thus is great for snorkeling and scuba instruction; a third, the quietest, is a natural pond. At night, hundreds of torches light the property.

Spacious guest rooms, with lanais or patios, overlook the beach or golf course. You may have a hard time leaving your marble bathroom; the tubs are some of the deepest I've ever seen, stall showers are large enough for a menage a trois, and windows look out to private gardens. The spa and sports club, complete with indoor/outdoor aerobics, a 25-meter lap pool, outdoor massage huts (treat yourself to time in these!), and lighted tennis courts, is perfect for working out or being pampered.

The Kids for All Seasons program makes this a good choice for families. Parents can drop off little ones aged 5 to 12 for supervised activities, including lava tube climbs and splashes in the children's pool, with its sandy bottom.

KONA VILLAGE RESORT, *P.O. Box 1299, Kaihua Kona, HI 96745. In Ka'upulehu, six miles north of airport. Follow sign to Kona Village 1.5 miles to gate house. Tel. 808/325-5555 or 800/367-5290, Fax 808/325-5124. 125 rooms. Double room rates begin at $425, including three meals a day. Major credit cards.*

Featured in Chapter 10, *Best Places to Stay.*

This has to be the most unusual resort on the island. Guest cottages are built in the architectural styles of a variety of Polynesian peoples. Some with thatched roofs, they stand on stilts above rugged lava flows, at the edges of beaches, or overlooking a lagoon. There are no telephones, radios, TVs, or air conditioners. Tradewinds and ceiling fans keep visitors comfortable in rooms attractive with their Polynesian decor.

Fresh Kona coffee, a coffee maker, and a mini bar are provided. Colorful batiks and other textiles decorate the walls and furnishings. There are no room keys but in-room safes are provided. Use of the fitness center and all sports, from tennis to snorkeling, are complimentary, as are children's programs, transportation to golf, and sports equipment. All meals, including weekly luaus and steak cookouts, are included in the rates. Pacific rim cuisine includes an emphasis on fish, accented by tropical fruits.

Sandy shores here come in black, salt and pepper, and white. There are also two swimming pools, two whirlpools, and three night-lit tennis courts. Tours can be arranged of the petroglyph fields and fish ponds, near where the hotel's famed luau is held.

HAPUNA BEACH PRINCE HOTEL, *62-100 Kauna'oa Drive, Kohala Coast, HI 96743. Mauna Kea Resort. Tel. 808/880-1111 or 800/882-6060, Fax 808/880-3112. 350 rooms. Double rooms begin at $345. Major credit cards.*

The Hapuna Beach Prince Hotel opened in 1994. Its somewhat stark contemporary design is a counterpoint to the natural setting of the ocean and the manicured gardens. All the guest rooms and suites, some quite spacious, have private lanais and views of gorgeous Hapuna Beach and the ocean. The elegant Hawaiian decor - highlighted by art and artifacts - is understated, with light wood and subtle colors in the rooms and imported marble and tiles in the baths.

Here on the grounds of the Mauna Kea Resort, you'll find a handful of restaurants, various boutiques, and all kinds of water sports, along with the Hapuna Golf course (which opened to rave reviews in late 1992), a fitness center, and a swimming pool. Guests can play on the 13 tennis courts. They can also sign for meals at the neighboring Mauna Kea Beach

HAWAII – THE BIG ISLAND 353

Hotel restaurants (and vice-versa). Hapuna Beach Prince Hotel is a half-hour from the airport, about 40 minutes from the village of Kailua-Kona, and a 15-minute drive from the pleasant town of Kamuela/Waimea.

MAUNA KEA BEACH HOTEL, *62-100 Mauna Kea Beach Drive, Kohala Coast, HI 96743. Mauna Kea Resort. Tel. 808/882-7222 or 800/882-6060, Fax 808/882-7007. 310 rooms. Double rooms begin at $325. Major credit cards.*

Built in 1965 as the first of Laurance Rockefeller's Big Island dreams, the Mauna Kea Beach Hotel reopened in 1995 after closing for extensive renovations. Fortunately, the grand elegance of its earlier incarnation has not only been maintained but enhanced. Classical details are blended with beautifully crafted woods and varied textures of natural fibers that reflect elements of Hawaiian culture, including hundreds of pieces of Pacific and Asian art. This blending of cultures is carried out in the very large rooms, each with a private lanai, and in the public spaces, with their soaring open-air design.

The Mauna Kea Beach offers all its guests dramatic views, from mountain to ocean to the natural white sand beach. All the amenities that you might expect are here, along with a few extras. There are reciprocal restaurant privileges with the neighboring Hapuna Beach Prince Hotel. The Mauna Kea is a half-hour's drive from the airport, 40 minutes from Kailua-Kona, and a 15 minute drive from the charming town of Kamuela/Waimea.

THE ORCHID AT MAUNA LANI, *One North Kaniku Drive, Kohala Coast, HI 96743. Mauna Lani Resort. Tel. 808/885-2000 or 800/845-9905, Fax 808/885-5778. 539 rooms. Double rooms begin at $310. Major credit cards.*

On a pleasant sandy cove, this beach resort sprawls across 32 acres. Waterfalls spill into beautifully landscaped ponds. Guests have use of two neighboring golf courses. Facilities include a swimming pool, tennis courts, several restaurants, and a health spa. The large guest rooms are elegant but comfortable, with hardwood furniture, potted plants, and lanais (most with ocean views). Twin closets and dressing areas lead to baths (tiled in marble, floor to ceiling), which have double sinks, and a separate tub and shower. Extras come in the form of robes for guests' use during their stay, a third telephone in the bathroom, remote-control TV and honor bars. Among the many amenities are use of equipment at the fitness center, valet parking in the day, and golf bag storage.

MAUNA LANI BAY HOTEL AND BUNGALOWS, *68-1400 Mauna Lani Drive, Kohala Coast, HI 96743. Mauna Lani Resort. Tel. 808/885-6622 or 800/367-232, Fax 808/885-1483. 350 rooms. Double rooms begin at $290. Major credit cards.*

The personal touches are part of what makes this hotel so special. Arriving guests are greeted with a kiss and a lei, then seated individually at a small check-in desk before being escorted to their rooms. The airy lobby is set off with white columns and a blue-tiled staircase (bordered by waterfalls) that leads down to a palm-rimmed pool. Ivy spills over balustrades and fragrant flowers are everywhere. A Hawaiian trio performs by the gardens in the afternoon and early evening while at night a combo plays jazz by the lobby bar. Walking tours are conducted of the historic fish ponds, some with baby sharks, that meander throughout the grounds.

Named for one of Hawaii's best known golfers, the Francis I'i Brown Golf Courses are two of the most attractive and challenging in the state. In addition to a large swimming pool, the active set is drawn to the ten tennis courts, the complete lineup of water sports at the beach, and the extensive fitness center. Couples enjoy spending evenings in the Jacuzzi.

The stark architecture and sparse decor of guest rooms and public areas are in dramatic contrast with the hotel's lush outdoors. All with lanais, guest rooms sport teak furniture and louvered doors, and ceiling fans as well as air conditioning. For the ultimate splurge, book one of the two-bedroom oceanside bungalows, each with its own swimming pool and Jacuzzi. The $3,000-plus a night price tag includes a chauffeured limousine, a butler around the clock, and a maid who unpacks, irons and repacks guests' clothes. Double koa wood entry doors open to a huge living room with a pink polished granite bar, potted plants, and koa wood or marble tile floors. Meals are catered to guests' tastes. Scenic lagoons encircle the bungalows in this five-acre complex.

MAUNA LANI TERRACE, *P.O. Box 384900, Waikoloa, HI 96738. Mauna Lani Resort. Tel. 808/883-8500 or 800/822-4252, Fax 808/883-9818. 30 units. Rates: $260 per unit. Major credit cards.*

Done in rattan, wicker, or contemporary styles, these luxurious and spacious bright one-, two-, and three-bedroom condominiums all have lanais and laundry facilities. Even the smallest units come with two baths, and kitchens are equipped with Sub-Zero refrigerators, trash compactors, microwaves and dishwashers. Guests take advantage of the large swimming pool, the children's pool, the Jacuzzi, the sauna and the picnic area with gas grills. There's a small fee to use the tennis courts, exercise room, and lap pool at the Racquet Club. This complex is conveniently located next to the Mauna Lani Bay Hotel and beaches are a brief stroll away. Golf at the adjacent fairway can be arranged at a reduced rate.

MAUNA LANI POINT, *68-1310 Mauna Lani Drive, Kohala Coast, HI 96743. Mauna Lani Resort. Tel. 808/885-5022 or 800/642-6284, Fax 808/885-5015. 60 units. Rates begin at $250 per unit. Major credit cards.*

Located on a peaceful corner of the resort, this plush condominium is run somewhat like a hotel. All desk clerks act as concierges. With a few days' notice, guests may arrange to be served breakfast in bed or on their lanai, with ferns and flowers part of the culinary presentation. They can also charge meals at Knicker's Bar & Lounge, The Gallery Restaurant, and The Beach Club, and for activities at the Francis H. I'i Brown Golf Course, the Racquet Club, and The Boathouse. Complimentary shuttle service is provided around the resort. Many of the individually decorated one, two- and three-bedroom apartments have features such as sunken living rooms; baths with sunken tubs, double sinks and rosewood trim; kitchens with ash wood cabinets, built-in cutting boards and wine racks, and microwave/convection ovens. Some units and the adjacent golf course have wonderful views of whales during the winter (especially February and March). The swimming pool, Jacuzzi, and dry sauna are tranquil even when the property is full. A barbecue pit and an open-air kitchen adjoin the pool.

HILTON WAIKOLOA VILLAGE, *69-425 Waikoloa Beach Drive, Kamuela, HI 96743. Waikoloa Resort. Tel. 808/885-1234 or 800/HILTONS, Fax 808/885-2900. 1240 rooms. Double rooms begin at $240. Major credit cards.*

This spectacular playground will put you in mind of Disneyland. Some call it "tastefully overdone," but most veteran vacationers do nothing but rave. Some areas – such as the Palace Wing, with its oversized columns, huge chandeliers, and sky-high mirrors – look like sets for *Land of the Giants.* The trio of hotel towers is connected by the aptly named mile-long Museum Walkway. It is decked out with everything from six-foot tall urns and antique marionettes to weathered spears from Papua New Guinea. You can be transported to and from your room in space-age monorails or boats along the lagoon. Note, however, that if you happen to forget something, it can take ages to retrieve it, whether you walk or ride. If the boat comes while you're waiting for the tram or vice versa, you'll have to run across a bridge to attempt to catch the other mode of transportation.

In this 62-acre resort, tropical gardens are aflutter with cockatoos, macaws, and parrots. The restaurants are top notch. Among the wide selection, Donatoni's for Italian food and Imari for Japanese cuisine have built excellent reputations. Guests spend much of their time at the two golf courses, eight tennis courts, two racquetball/squash courts, spacious health spa, and three swimming pools. They can even win a chance, by lottery, to encounter a group of Atlantic bottlenose **dolphins.** There's no real beach here, just a slip of sand at the edge of a lagoon - but a beautiful beach is a brief walk or a shuttle ride away. An astronomy seminar, introductory scuba lessons, and power walks are all complimentary. There is valet parking and the hotel's circular driveway is small, so be sure to call ahead when you're ready for your wheels so your car will be waiting for you by the time you get to the front door.

VISTA WAIKOLOA, *South Kohala Management, P.O. Box 384900, Waikoloa, HI 96738. Mauna Lani Resort. Tel. 808/883-8500 or 800/822-4252, Fax 808/883-9818. 30 units. Rates: $225 per two-bedroom unit. Major credit cards.*

Like its sister condominiums run by South Kohala Management, the newest of luxury condos boasts similar amenities: washer/dryers in the units, daily maid service, high-end refrigerators and microwaves, along with cable TV, a swimming pool, and whirlpool. Mostly large two-bedroom units, attractively fitted out with tropical furnishings, these condos have either an ocean or garden/fairway view. Vista Waliokoa also has a three-bedroom penthouse, if you want to splurge.

When you're in the mood to leave the resort, the white sand Anaeho'omalu Bay beach is nearby. Condo rentals can be tied into a golf package.

SHORES AT WAIKOLOA, *South Kohala Management, P.O. Box 384900, Waikoloa HI 96738. Tel. 808/883-8500 or 800/822-4252, Fax 808/883-9818. 17 units. Rates begin at $185 per unit. Major credit cards.*

Between Hilton Waikoloa Village and the Royal Waikoloan, this condominium is adjacent to the Waikoloa Beach Golf Course. It is not on a beach, but sandy shores aren't far. The decor of the one- and two-bedroom units is pleasantly upscale. Kitchens feature microwaves and dishwashers and are fully furnished. Apartments also come with air conditioning, wet bars, and laundry facilities. Tennis courts are on the premises and there is a pool, a Jacuzzi and a picnic area with grills and a kitchen. Ask about golf packages.

MARC WAIKOLOA VILLAS, *P.O. Box 385134, Waikoloa, HI 96738. Tel. 808/883-9144 or 800/535-0085, Fax 808/883-8740. 104 rooms. Rates begin at $185 per unit. Major credit cards.*

For golfers these villas are ideally situated, facing the Waikoloa Village Golf Club. Besides the usual trappings of condominium living, the units include wet-bars, in-suite washer/dryer, and ceiling fans to make your stay more relaxing.

THE ROYAL WAIKOLOAN (Outrigger), *69-275 Waikoloa Beach Drive, Kamuela, HI 96743. 546 rooms. Tel. 808/885-6789 or 800/688-7444, Fax 808/885-7280. Double rooms begin at $150. Major credit cards.*

The Royal Waikoloan has a far nicer beach than its splashy but nearly beachless neighbor, Hilton Waikoloa Village. Many travelers prefer this more subdued hotel. The architecture of the six-story towers may be standard, but the rooms are nicely done and perfectly comfortable. Overlooking the gorgeous bay, the open-air lobby is filled with greenery and unobtrusive boutiques. Hawaiian history lives on here. Visitors may hike along the King's Trail (a.k.a. the Ala Mamalohoa) and come upon ancient petroglyphs carved in the lava. Guests also amuse themselves with the circular freshwater pool, all kinds of water sports, six tennis courts, and two 18-hole golf courses.

Kailua-Kona & Keauhou Area

KONA BY THE SEA, *75-6106 Alii Drive, Kailua-Kona, HI 96740. Tel. 808/327-2300 or 800/922-7866, Fax 808/327-2333. 86 rooms. Rates begin at $210 per unit. Major credit cards.*

On a rocky shore, this pleasant condominium boasts spacious upscale one- and two-bedroom units. For those who tire of cooking, there is a grocery shopping service. They'll even have your refrigerator stocked with your choices when you arrive. Well-manicured vegetation thrives around the freshwater oceanfront pool and Jacuzzi. In the second pool, also overlooking the sea, guests splash around in water from the Pacific.

KONA COAST RESORT, *78-6842 Alii Drive, Kailua-Kona, HI 96740. Tel. 808/322-8213 or 800/359-2566, Fax 808/322-8217. 263 units. Rates begin at $200 per unit. Major credit cards.*

Adjacent to the Kona Golf Club and across from Keauhou Shopping Center, this condominium rents very attractive one-, two- and three-bedroom apartments. All units have lanais and the modern kitchens come with microwaves. TVs, VCRs, and laundry facilities all contribute to the home-like surroundings of each unit. Two swimming pools are set amid 25 acres of landscaped gardens.

ASTON ROYAL SEA-CLIFF RESORT, *75-6040 Alii Drive, Kailua-Kona. Tel. 808/329-8021 or 800/922-7866, Fax 808/326-1887. 154 rooms. Rate: $165. Major credit cards.*

The entrance to this stark white terraced condominium is on the fifth floor. Balconies outside rooms overlook the sunny lobby that is lush with greenery and scattered with wicker sitting areas. Gardens, a waterfall and fish ponds add to the tropical ambiance. The waterfront here is rocky, but there are two swimming pools to choose from (one salt, one fresh) and a tennis court. A golf package is available. Units are available as studios and one- or two-bedrooms.

KANALOA AT KONA, *78-262 Manukai Street, Keauhou-Kona. Tel. 808/322-2271 or 800/657-7872, Fax 808/526-2017. 116 rooms. Double rooms begin at $150. Major credit cards.*

If you'd like a room with your own Jacuzzi, book an oceanfront suite at this plush condo. Apartments have one, two, or three bedrooms. Special touches include koa wood cabinets and marble. The modern kitchens come with microwave ovens and there's a restaurant on the premises, along with a cocktail lounge. Guests can keep in shape at the two tennis courts and three swimming pools.

KAILUA PLANTATION HOUSE, 75-5948 Alii Drive, Kailua-Kona. Tel. 808/329-3727, Fax 808/329-7323. Five rooms. Rates: $145 per room. Major credit cards.

Featured in Chapter 10, *Best Places to Stay.*

This beautifully designed Bed & Breakfast is among Hawaii's nicest accommodations. On two stories, the five spacious guest rooms are individually decorated. Three rooms are oceanfront, one is ocean view, and the other looks out at the mountains. All have private lanais, refrigerators, ceiling fans, TV, books and magazines.

Breakfast, featuring home-baked muffins, island fruit, and freshly ground Kona coffee, is served in the living/dining room, with its overstuffed couches. The plentiful windows and high ceilings give the house a bright, airy feeling. The surf crashes against the rocks. Sandy beaches are close at hand and the restaurants and shops in Kailua-Kona are within walking distance.

HOLUALOA INN, P.O. Box 831, Holualoa, HI 96725. Tel. 808/324-1121 or 800/392-1812, Fax 808/322-2472. Four rooms. Rate: $135.

One of the nicest small accommodations on the island - in the state, for that matter - this Bed & Breakfast sits high on a hillside with a fabulous view of Kailua-Kona and the Pacific. For the full effect, climb up to the rooftop gazebo. Modern in architecture, this handsome inn is built entirely of cedar and koa wood, accented with gorgeous stained-glass windows. Lanais surround the three-story building, and the huge front porch is wide enough for a party. A pool table is the centerpiece of the beautifully decorated lounge, where a fireplace, piano, paintings, book-shelves and taller-than-human abstract sculpture create a feast for the eyes.

All four of the individually decorated guest rooms have private baths, ceiling fans, potted plants, and clock radios. Because of its large size, tremendous view through bay windows, and whirlpool bathtub, the Hibiscus Room is the first choice of many repeat guests. This was once the master bedroom of this former private home. The sitting room of the Bali Room looks out to the ocean while the Oriental Room offers views of a verdant slope.

Breakfast is served in the dining room, which has a stunning view of the coast. Coffee and papayas - both grown on the inn's 40 acres - are offered, along with pastries, pancakes, French toast, or eggs. By the swimming pool, which has its own sweeping view, there is a TV room and kitchenette where the refrigerator is stocked with complimentary wine and cheese. Surrounded by pastures, coffee orchards, private homes, and art galleries, Holualoa Inn is a short drive from both Kailua-Kona restaurants and Magic Sands Beach. You'll need to book a room here at least two months in advance.

ROYAL KONA RESORT, 75-5852 Alii Drive, Kailua-Kona, HI 96740. Tel. 808/329-9532 or 800/774-KONA, Fax 808/329-9532. 452 rooms. Double rooms begin at $130. Major credit cards.

Ideally located, this hotel sits at the edge of Kailua-Kona, away from the hustle and bustle but close enough to many good restaurants and shops. While the ocean isn't safe for swimming here, there's a tiny sandy beach lagoon. A pool is also on the premises, along with tennis courts. The three six-story towers command 11 acres of lush coastline. The open-air lobby is always filled as guests shop or make plans at the activities desk. Rooms all have lanais, safes, and refrigerators. Coffee makers and Kona coffee are provided.

KING KAMEHAMEHA'S KONA BEACH HOTEL, 75-5990 Palani Road, Kailua-Kona, HI 96740. Tel. 808/329-2911 or 800/367-2111, Fax 808/329-4602. 457 rooms. Double rooms begin at $125. Major credit cards.

With its corridors lined with souvenir shops, the public areas are far too busy and commercial for me. But if you want to be in the heart of town and in a hotel with a beach (albeit small), this is a good choice. Kailua Pier is just across the way. This is the jumping-off point for fishing boats (especially during the annual Hawaiian International Billfish Tournament in late July or early August), glass-bottom boat and dinner cruises, and the boat to the Atlantis submarine (for which you sign up in the hotel). Free guided tours are conducted of the section of the grounds that was once the home of King Kamehameha and his court. In addition to a host of water sports, there are a pool and four tennis courts (two of them nightlit). Guest rooms, which all have lanais and refrigerators, are plain but comfortable.

KONA SURF RESORT & COUNTRY CLUB, 78-128 Ehukai Street, Keauhou, HI 96740. Tel. 808/322-3411 or 800/367-8011, Fax 808/322-3245. 530 rooms. Double rooms begin at $119. Major credit cards.

This resort has one of the most successful and popular Polynesian dance troupes on the Big Island. The Kona Surf is a favorite among honeymooners and other tourists who enjoy the American and Japanese cuisine. Trim, colorful gardens and bright green lawns provide a wonderful contrast with the black lava of the spectacular, craggy coast that is constantly pounded by the rough surf. At night, lights reveal the manta rays that swim up to the rocks at shore. All of the guest rooms are equipped with refrigerators and complimentary Kona coffee. Poke around the expansive grounds, and you'll stumble onto archaeological ruins of canoe sheds, stone altars, and fishing shrines.

A shuttle bus takes guests to town for two dollars. Kahaluu Beach Park, the closest sandy shore, is about one mile away. Ask for directions to the row of lava rock swimming holes that are about half mile from the hotel. There are two pools (fresh and saltwater). Scuba diving and snorkeling off shore at Keauhou Bay are rated among the topnotch sites in the world. If your sporting tastes are based on more solid ground, there are three tennis courts, volleyball, and shuffleboard on the property, as well as preferred tee times and in-house golf rates for guests.

MARC KONA ISLANDER INN, *75-5776 Kuakini Drive, Kailua-Kona, HI 96740. Tel. 808/329-3181 or 800/ 535-0085, Fax 808/326-9339. 147 rooms. Double rooms begin at $119. Major credit cards.*

Kailua Bay is across the street from this hotel. The style of the complex is reminiscent of old Hawaiian plantations. Bordered by torches and bushy palms, paths wind through the property. The pool patio is especially attractive. Amenities include free local telephone calls, air conditioning in all garden and ocean view hotel rooms, a small variety store, and laundry facilities.

WHITE SANDS VILLAGE, *Kailua-Kona, HI 96740. Tel. 808/329-5158 or 800/367-5168, Fax 808/329-5480. 108 rooms. Double rooms begin at $115. Major credit cards.*

The two-bedroom, two-bath apartments in these four-story shingle-roofed buildings vary quite a bit in decor, but many are perfectly comfortable. You might find rattan chairs and glass-topped tables in yours. All contain TVs and dishwashers. Kitchens are large, with breakfast counters with stools. Sliding glass doors open to lanais. Facilities include two tennis courts and a swimming pool. Magic Sands beach is just across the road.

KEAUHOU BEACH HOTEL, *78-6740 Alii Drive, Kailua-Kona, HI 96740. Tel. 808/322-3441 or 800/367-6025, Fax 808/322-6586. 310 rooms. Doubles begin at $100. Major credit cards.*

Rocky Kahaluu Beach, known for its excellent snorkeling, is a brief stroll from this resort that was built on royal land. The oceanfront side of the six-story building overhangs a lagoon, affording an aquarium-like view of the water below. At low tide, take a walk to see the petroglyphs. The pool patio is the first place you'll want to stop even before you check into your room. The view of the ocean, the beach, the Royal Kuakini Grove all in one sweep is nothing less than breathtaking. There's also a small pool for children. The upbeat music of a live band and the convenience of a full-service bar may make it difficult for you to tear yourself away.

The most recently renovated guest rooms are pleasantly done, with rattan furnishings, lanais, and ceiling fans in addition to air conditioning. Amid the lush gardens, you'll find the reconstructed summer cottage and royal bathing pool of King Kalakaua. Shuttle buses are provided to Keauhou Shopping Village.

KONA SEASIDE HOTEL, *75-5646 Palani Road, Kailua-Kona, HI 96740. Tel. 808/329-2455 or 800/367-7000, Fax 808/922-0052. 225 rooms. Double rooms begin at $95. Major credit cards.*

This family owned and operated hotel in the center of Kailua-Kona is a convenient place to stay at modest rates. The attractively but simply decorated rooms all have air conditioning, ceiling fans, cable TV, and kitchenettes. Among the services is a restaurant serving breakfast and dinner. After a swim in one of its two freshwater pools, you can easily stroll to the nearby shops "in town."

UNCLE BILLY'S KONA BAY HOTEL, *75-5739 Alii Drive, Kailua-Kona. Tel. 808/961-935-7903 or 800/367-5102, Fax 808/935-7903. 143 rooms. Double rooms begin at $77. Major credit cards.*

Across from sandy Kailua Bay, this is a centrally located hotel. In the shape of a half moon with an island in its center, its layout ties in perfectly with its Polynesian decor of thatched roofs, bamboo, and tropical flowers. There is an atmosphere of fun and friendliness in this very informal, homey, colorful family inn. The circular pool is only five feet deep, but all kinds of other activities can be easily arranged. The simply decorated bedrooms have lanais. If you're looking for something to do after dark, catch one of the nightly hula shows in the bar and restaurant.

Kealakekua

MERRYMAN'S BED & BREAKFAST, *P.O. Box 474, Kealakekua, HI 96750. Tel. 808/323-2276, Fax 808/323-3749. Four rooms. Rates: $75 per room. Major credit cards.*

Away from the bustle of Kailua-Kona, but close enough to its attractions, this charming Bed & Breakfast sits on a hillside in a country estate on over an acre of park-like grounds. Kealakekua Bay, all the rage for snorkeling, is nearby. Snorkel gear and beach towels are provided. Also in the area is the fascinating ancient historical park known as the Place of Refuge. Two of the four bedrooms share baths. With wood-paneled walls, they are decorated with wicker, lacy curtains, and colorful bedspreads. You might find a four-poster bed in yours. Fresh flowers in each room and the hot tub outside add to your pleasure. Sitting on the lanai, you can gaze at the ocean. The spacious living/dining room is bright and sunny, with a high ceiling.

Honaunau

THE DRAGONFLY RANCH: TROPICAL FANTASY LODGING, *P.O. Box 675, Honaunau, HI 96726. South Kona. Tel. 808/328-2159 or 800/487-2159, Fax 808/328-9570. Five rooms. Rate: $85. Major credit cards.*

If you are a nature lover, this Bed & Breakfast can be a romantic, though busy, hideaway. Here where people and dogs are always buzzing about, lush trees frame the spectacular view of the ocean. Each morning, you'll awake to an orchestra of birds. A walk through a "jungle" will take you to the honeymoon suite, which is open to the elements. Mirrors are on the ceiling above a king-sized canopy water-bed draped with mosquito netting. A shoji screen opens to a redwood room with queen-sized bed and indoor bath. An outdoor shower is in the garden. Privacy is furnished by plants. You'll sleep on two double beds in the Dolphin Room, and the Madame Pele room has a king-size bed and a private deck. Ask about guided swimming and dive excursions as well as Hawaiian lomi-lomi massages.

Ka'u

THE HOBBIT HOUSE, *P.O. Box 269, Naalehu, HI 96772. Tel. 808/929-9755, Fax 808/929-8045. One room. Rate: $105 including tax.*

Built by the owners in 1993, the rental wing of this beautiful, fanciful Bed & Breakfast is powered by solar and wind energy. You'll know you've arrived when you see the windmill, which serves as a beacon for the helicopters that swoop down with more adventurous guests. Most visitors arrive in a less dramatic way; they are picked up by the hosts in a 4x4 runner for the drive to the 1,800-foot perch. Ohia trees hold up the lanai, and free-form picture windows cast a vast view of South Point, where ancient Hawaiians first landed, and the ocean.

The windows of the vacation bungalow are stained glass framed in light oak. The full kitchen is also done in white oak. In the bath, a two-person hot tub sits beneath a window with that same expansive view. Comfortable robes are provided for guests' use during their stay. Visitors should feel free to strum the guitars. The continental morning meal — perhaps cereal, homemade banana bread, and fruit smoothies — is served on a picnic bench on the lanai (with that view again of the Hawaiian islands' southernmost point).

COLONY ONE AT SEA MOUNTAIN, *P.O. Box 70, Pahala, HI 96777. Tel. 808/928-8301 or 800/488-8301, Fax 808/928-8008. 76 units. Rates begin at $75 per condo. Major credit cards.*

Far off the tourist beat in Punalu'u, this condominium complex lures guests with its golf course, back sand beach, swimming pool, and tennis courts. The entry road curls through the flourishing, sprawling grounds, past palm groves and other lush vegetation. Outside the restaurant, there is a pond, known as Old Hawaiian Wishing Waters. The two-story shingle-roofed buildings house studio, one-, and two-bedroom apartments with lanais facing smooth, palm-studded lawns. Yours might be decorated Polynesian style, with lava rock walls inside. Maid service is once a week. The swimming pool and Jacuzzi overlook the rocky coast. People who choose to stay here like feeling as if they're in the middle of nowhere.

SOUTH POINT BED & BREAKFAST, *P.O. Box 6589, Ocean View, HI 96737. Tel. 808/939-7466. Three rooms. Rate: $55; discounts for longer stays. Major credit cards.*

A lane of flowering bushes leads to this Bed & Breakfast, perched on a hill with a fabulous view of South Point. The simply furnished units are quite comfortable. The large one is like a studio apartment, complete with a VCR and skylit kitchen. Breakfast is usually served on the lanai, with its sweeping view. Expect fresh fruit and homemade muffins, bread, or granola.

The host, an artist, paints and does pen and ink sketches. Guests are welcome to purchase her work, even commission a special piece. It is a short distance to good, inexpensive local fare. Extras include a babysitter for hire and incentives such as a discount coupon for the local pizzeria.

Hawaii Volcanoes National Park Area

CHALET KILAUEA – THE INN AT VOLCANO, *P.O. Box 998, Volcano, HI 96785. Tel. 808/967-7786 or 800/937-7786, Fax 967-8660. Six rooms. Double rooms: $125 to $395. Major credit cards.*

Six artfully decorated guest rooms and suites are in the main house of this wooded inn. The owners, a well-traveled young couple who met in Switzerland, pamper guests with extras generally found only in Hawaii's most expensive resorts. Thirsty terry-cloth and silk robes have been placed in rooms for guests to use during their stay. Vacationers are welcomed with chocolates and afternoon tea served by the fireplace in the spacious Gathering Room (a.k.a. the living room). Here floor-to-ceiling windows offer views of lush vegetation. Many of the masks, statues, wall hangings and other art pieces were collected by the owners during their travels through Zimbabwe, China, Thailand, Hong Kong, and elsewhere. With a bold black-and-white tile floor and a glossy black table, the art-deco dining room is the site of a full gourmet breakfast.

The Continental Lace suite has both a queen bed and a daybed, and a bath with a double whirlpool tub. Ballet slippers hang with a wedding dress on the wall. Baskets, paintings, rugs, and a batik bedspread and pillow cases from various African countries make a showplace of the Out of Africa Room. Antique Chinese screens and oriental rugs decorate the Oriental Jade Room. The shingled main building adjoins the more private cedar-paneled Tree House Suite. On the upper level, reached by a spiral staircase, the bedroom holds a king-size bed from which you look out to thick hapu ferns and ohia. Downstairs is a wet bar and a marble master bath with fireplace and double whirlpool tub. All rooms have phones, color cable TV, VCRs, private baths, electric blankets and private entrances. An outside Jacuzzi and the services of an on-site masseuse are available to sooth you.

The Inn also has six vacation homes, in a more isolated area about 1.5 miles away, but the main house is my choice for its charm and decor.

KILAUEA LODGE, *P.O. Box 116, Volcano, HI 96785. Tel. 808/967-7366, Fax 808/967-7367. 12 rooms. Double rooms $105. Major credit cards.*

Highly recommended by honeymooners, this is a good place for being alone together. Thick woods, tall cone-shaped pines, and giant ferns enclose the mountain lodge. The popular restaurant in the main house serves continental food nightly. The cozy rooms are accented with Hawaiian or Asian touches, wicker armchairs, and lacy curtains. Some have fireplaces or wood-burning stoves, high-pitched ceilings, and sky-lights. A complete breakfast is included in the room rates. Kilauea General Store and Volcano Golf Course are both nearby.

VOLCANO HOUSE, *P.O. Box 53, Hawaii National Parks, HI 96718. 42 rooms. Doubles begin at $90. Major credit cards.*

Play a round of golf on the Volcano Golf Course, then relax at this lodge perched at the rim of Kilauea Crater, 4,000 feet above sea level. The original Volcano House was a thatched-roof grass structure built during the 1840s that had room for 40 guests. In 1877, it was replaced by a Western-style inn with only four bedrooms in addition to its dining room and parlor. Queen Liliuokalani, Robert Louis Stevenson, and Mark Twain were among its guests.

The rustic inn that stands here today was built in 1941, and boasts 42 guest rooms. Visitors gather around the stone fireplace in the main building, which is usually crowded with sightseers. Anyone so inclined may pick out a tune on the koa piano here. Hearty meals, including some vegetarian selections, are served in the dining room. Uncle George's Cocktail lounge offers a magnificent view of the crater. Guest rooms are decorated with koa rocking chairs and other furniture and Hawaiian quilt designs. Some have private lanais and full baths while others have stall showers. Make reservations six months in advance if you're planning to vacation in the winter and three months ahead for other times of year.

CARSON'S VOLCANO COTTAGE BED & BREAKFAST, *P.O. Box 503, Volcano, HI 96785. Tel. 808/967-7683 or 800/845-LAVA. Three rooms and six cottages. Double room rate: $85. Major credit cards.*

A rose garden, peach and plum trees, bromeliads, and tall ferns all flourish amid these alternately jungled and manicured grounds. Attrac-tively decorated, some with antiques, each of the guest units is distinct. All have refrigerators, heaters, electric blankets and private baths. Two cottages have full kitchens. Built in the 1940s, the original cottages is nicely done with frilly curtains and floral soft furnishings. The one large room contains one queen-sized and one double bed as well as a woodburning stove. The Kau Room, with a queen sized bed, has a very high ceiling. Lace curtains and pictures of old Hawaii adorn the Kahaualea Room, which sports both a queen and a single bed. An added bonus of staying at

Carson's is being able to lounge in the hot tub in the open-air pavilion in the midst of the forest. For pet lovers, there are friendly dogs and a cat. A delicious full breakfast is delivered to your room.

HALE OHIA COTTAGES B & B, *P.O. Box 758, Volcano, HI 96785. Tel. 808/967-7986 or 800/455-3803, Fax 808/967-8610. Seven rooms. Double room rate: $85. Major credit cards.*

Built in 1931, a main house, guest cottage, and gardener's cottage have been transformed into this attractive Bed & Breakfast on the Dillingham Estate. Surrounded by Japanese sugi trees and beautifully sculpted flowering gardens, the property was once used as a retreat by an old Hawaiian family. The architecture of the cottages is an appealing blend of Victorian and California bungalow-style. All units have private entries and private baths. The two-room Dillingham Suite in the main house sports its own lanai. Honeymooners enjoy the quiet, secluded Hale Lehua Cottage. It contains a fireplace, microwave, refrigerator, and coffee maker. The two-story Ohia Cottage sleeps five comfortably and has a full kitchen. The newest cottage, the Ihilani, has a fireplace, kitchenette, octagonal sleeping area with a skylight, and a charming enclosed garden area with a fountain.

LOKAHI LODGE BED & BREAKFAST, *P.O. Box 7, Volcano, HI 96785. Tel. 808/985-8647 or 800/457-6924. Four rooms. Rate: $80. Major credit cards.*

The lanai of this cheerful house wraps around the whole building. Guests are greeted by friendly dogs and a cat also lives on the premises. Framed prize-winning leis (handmade by one of the owners) line hallway walls. Each of the four brightly furnished guest rooms has two double beds and its own private entrance. Soft background music plays in the house, which is filled with antiques. In the living room, guests are welcome to show off on the piano, antique pump organ, tenor harp, and other instruments. Vacationers get a kick out of using the working antique crank phone. They may also sit by the wood-burning fireplace and play konane, the Hawaiian board game (similar to checkers) or read a book from the library. The full breakfast buffet includes the chef's special homemade no-guilt, no-fat bread. Make reservations at least three weeks in advance.

VOLCANO BED & BREAKFAST, *P.O Box 998, Volcano, HI 96785. In Volcano Village, one mile from park entrance. Tel. 808/967-7244 or 800/736-7140, Fax 808/967-8660. Six rooms. Rates begin at $45. Major credit cards.*

Built during the 1930s, this refurbished three-story home offers six double rooms and shared baths. Views take in ginger, tree ferns, and an ohia forest. Visitors may get to know each other by the crackling fireplace or while using the common TV and VCR. The owners can provide tips on sights and activities. Breakfast features a buffet of local Hawaiian fruit, various breads, homemade preserves, and freshly roasted 100 percent Kona coffee.

BAMBOO HOUSE, *P.O. Box 1546, Pahoa, HI 96778. Tel. 808/965-8322, Fax 808/965-9340. One room. Double room rate: $45; discount to $35 on stays of three nights or more. Major credit cards.*

If you're looking for an inexpensive place to stay in the Volcanoes National Park area, follow the lead of young people, students, and other bargain hunters. You register for the accommodation by stopping at Pahoa Natural Groceries in Pahoa Village to see if a vacancy is available or phone ahead to the store (at the phone number above) and give your desired dates. A 25% deposit must be mailed ahead to the address above. The store is also where you pay the balance of the payment, register, and pick up the key.

Hilo Area

HAWAII NANILOA HOTEL, *93 Banyan Drive, Hilo, HI 96720. Tel. 808/969-3333 or 800/367-5360, Fax 808/969-6622. 325 rooms. Double rooms begin at $110. Major Credit Cards.*

Across the street from the nine-hole Naniloa Country Club Golf Course, Hilo's largest hotel sports two freshwater swimming pools and Hilo's sole health spa/fitness center. Four Mile Beach, considered to be the town's best sandy stretch, is about two miles away. The nicest rooms are those that gaze out to the harbor. Arriving guests are greeted with a homemade tropical non-alcoholic beverage. On Friday and Saturday nights, there's dancing in the night club. The pleasantly decorated rooms are air-conditioned and comfortable. Most have private lanais and views are of the bay, gardens, or mountains. When you're feeling lazy, room service is available. Ask about the hotel shuttle to and from the airport.

HILO HAWAIIAN HOTEL, *71 Banyan Drive, Hilo, HI 96720. Tel. 808/935-9361 or 800/367-5004, Fax 808/367-5004. 285 rooms. Double rooms begin at $110.*

In the modern open-air lobby, rattan lounge chairs and sprays of anthuriums are about the only touches of Polynesia. Walk out the back, however, and you'll have a wonderful view of Hilo Bay. Guest rooms look out to the water and Coconut Island or Banyan Drive. The majority of rooms have lanais, and one-bedroom units come with kitchenettes. In the evenings, a live band performs in the lounge. There's a swimming pool on the grounds.

HALEKAI BJORNEN, *111 Honolii Pali, Hilo, HI 96720. Tel. 808/935-8439, Fax 808/935-8439. Five rooms. Double rooms begin at $90.*

Two miles from downtown Hilo, this modern house is perched on a bluff overlooking the ocean and Hilo Bay. In this Bed & Breakfast, the comfortable guest rooms, with TV and large windows, have direct views of the swimming pool, hot tub, and the Pacific. Yours might have a glass shower, sitting room, atrium, and private deck. Palms rustle outside the bay windows by the breakfast table in the kitchen. For the morning meal, you might be treated to poi pancakes or macadamia nut waffles, with a choice of coconut, berry, or maple syrup, Kona coffee, and Portuguese sausage. Note that the owners also manage condo units in Hilo and Kona. The Hilo penthouse condo is two miles from downtown; the Kona condos are close to shopping.

HILO SEASIDE HOTEL, 126 Banyan Drive, Hilo, HI 96720. Tel. 808/935-0821 or 800/367-7000, Fax 808/922-0052. 135 rooms. Double rooms begin at $85. Major credit cards.

With an attractive fish pond out front and a gleaming koa wood lobby, this hotel, a short drive from Hilo, is not a bad deal. But it's not for travelers who mind walking up stairs, since many rooms are on the second and third floors of the low-rise buildings. Some rooms have views of the pond while others overlook the swimming pool, surrounded by ferns. All rooms have TVs and refrigerators. Not all have lanais, so be sure to ask if you want one. Ceiling fans cool the air. The adjacent restaurant and cocktail lounge provide guests with a bit of nightlife, even if it's just talking story with locals. Golf is across the street; Volcanoes National Park is 45 minutes away.

UNCLE BILLY'S HILO BAY HOTEL, 87 Banyan Drive, Hilo, HI 96720. Tel. 808/961-5818 or 800/367-5102. 143 rooms. Double rooms begin at $77. Major credit cards.

Similar to its sister hotel on the Kona Coast (Uncle Billy's Kona Bay Hotel), Hilo Bay is a low-rise Polynesian-style resort. In the lobby, Hawaiian flora, native artifacts, wood carvings, and kapa prints create a colorful, homey, informal environment. During the 1960s, Uncle Billy himself landscaped the glorious gardens that still slope down to Hilo Bay out back. Near the fish pond, steps lead to the lava rock coast that appears too barren to be sprouting so many palms. There's a swimming pool in addition to the lounge, as well as stores. Many locals enjoy the nightly happy hour and nightly hula show at Uncle Billy's restaurant (there's no cover charge). Friends and relatives of the owner sing and dance modern as well as ancient hula. Most of the guest rooms have kitchenettes and all come with private lanais, TVs, and air conditioning. Some have stall showers. When you make your reservations, ask about special discounts. This hotel, like Hilo in general, seems to attract many seniors.

DOLPHIN BAY HOTEL, 333 Iliahi Street, Hilo, HI 96720. Tel. 808/935-1466, Fax 808/935-1523. 24 rooms. Double rooms begin at $59. Major credit cards.

In quiet, residential Pueo, this hotel is about a five-minute walk from downtown Hilo and you'll need to drive to the closest swimming beach.

Guests enjoy congregating in the hotel lobby and exchanging recommendations for the restaurants that are within walking distance. This comfortable, cozy hotel is complete with a library of donated reading material, a basket of fruit for the taking, a pay phone (there are no telephones in rooms), and an engaging desk clerk who lends out coolers, umbrellas, an iron and ironing board, local and some national newspapers (which you'll be asked to return for other guests), and a lot of good advice.

All 24 studios (with full kitchens) have views of the lush gardens. There is no air conditioning, but wall fans are provided. This hotel draws quite a few repeat guests, many of them older travelers, and lots of families. Coffee and tropical fruit are complimentary.

BED & BREAKFASTS & PRIVATE HOMES

On Hawaii, many travelers enjoy staying at Bed & Breakfasts or in private homes because they see a side of the island that most vacationers miss. Bed & Breakfast owners and managers are as happy to help guests plan excursions, make dinner reservations, and rent cars as they are to allow them complete privacy. Totally independent travelers thrive in private rental cottages, where they are on their own. If you'd like to explore the idea of staying in a Bed & Breakfast besides one of those described above, or of renting a private cottage, contact the following companies. Note that a minimum number of nights may be required and that weekly rates can be less expensive than daily rates.

Hawaii's Best Bed & Breakfasts, P.O. Box 563, Kamuela, HI 96743. Tel. 800/BNB-9912 (reservations) or Tel. 808/885-0550 (information). This highly selective company specializes in upscale Bed & Breakfasts. The vast majority of rooms have private baths. Double room rates range from about $85 to $130 per night.

All Islands Bed & Breakfast, 823 Kainui Drive, Kailua, HI 96734. Tel. 800/542-0344 or 808/263-2342. This outfit handles private homes, cottages, and condominium apartments as well as Bed & Breakfasts. Rates average $75 to $100 per night.

Bed & Breakfast Hawaii, P.O. Box 449, Kapaa, Kauai, HI 96746. Tel. 800/657-7832 or 808/822-7771. This company also handles private homes and cottages. Rates run from $70 to $100 per night.

Bed & Breakfast Honolulu, 3242 Kaohinani Drive, Honolulu, HI 96817. Tel. 800/288-4666 or 808/595-7533. Prices range from $60 to $150. Kitchens are available in some units.

South Kohala Management, P.O. Box 3301, Waikoloa, HI 96743. Tel. 800/822-4252 or 808/883-8500. South Kohala represents private homes and estates, along with condos. Rates for houses range from $200 to $800 per night. House/car packages are available.

ARNOTT'S LODGE, *98 Apapane Road, Hilo, HI 96720. Tel. 808/969-7097. Rates: $17 for a bunk; $100 for a "suite" that sleeps five.*

A clean hostel run by Aussie Doug Arnott, this lodge attracts young travelers (many of them Australian) who are backpacking and hiking around the globe. You'll have a choice of female, male, or co-ed dorms. A tree house adjoins the lodge. The entertainment center is the gazebo, with a TV and an extremely comprehensive visitor information center. Two nights a week Arnott's hosts a barbecue mixer. A shuttle takes vacationers into Hilo three times a day. You can also rent bicycles for getting around.

But the main mode of transport is the feet. This is the place to arrange personalized **guided hikes** into lava valleys, along mountainsides, around Volcanoes National Park, to black and green sand beaches, hidden waterfalls, and other special places. Hikers reach trailheads in air-conditioned vans.

Housekeeping Cabins

The Big Island's state and national parks provide shelters for travelers who feel that being able to explore the outdoors is more important than sleeping in plush quarters. Some people book these housekeeping cabins more than a year in advance, so make your reservations as early as possible.

VOLCANOES NATIONAL PARK CABINS, *Contact Hawaii Volcanoes National Park, HI 96718, Tel. 808/967-7311, where units are $24; or Volcano House, P.O. Box 53, Hawaii National Park, HI 96718, Tel. 808/967-7321 or Fax 808/967-8424, where cabins start at $35.*

At 4,000 feet, Namakani Paio Cabins are three miles from Volcano House in Hawaii Volcanoes National Park. Extremely rustic, they are truly for folks who want to get up close and personal with nature. Units provide only the basics: twin-size bunk beds and one full-size bed with thin mattresses, one indoor light and one outdoor light. If you are claustrophobic, these cabins are not for you. Picnic tables and grills are available for meals. The community bath, with hot and cold water, has one shower, two toilet stalls and two sinks. A pay telephone is in the campground.

Two other cabins, located on Mauna Loa volcano in the park, are free. However, one is at the 10,000 foot elevation, a seven-mile hike from the beginning of the trail, and the second is an additional 11 miles away, at Mauna Loa's 13,679-foot summit! You'll have to bring a sleeping bag, but beds and water are provided at these shelters.

POHAKULOA CABINS, *Contact the Division of State Parks, P.O. Box 936, Hilo, HI 96721, Tel. 808/974-6200.*

While you're hiking around these cabins, 6,500 feet up the grassy ranching slopes of Mauna Kea, be careful of the hunters who sometimes use these shelters. You'll find the seven state park cabins just off Saddle Road, 33 miles from Hilo. Some sleeping up to six people, these units have electricity, hot showers, cooking and eating utensils, beds, linens and towels. Some also come with fireplaces.

HAPUNA STATE PARK CABINS, *Contact the Division of State Parks, P.O. Box 936, Hilo, HI 96721, Tel. 808/974-6200.*

If you'd prefer to be down on one of the Big Island's most beautiful white sand beaches, consider these A-frame cabins. Beds are built-in wooden benches, so be sure to bring a sleeping pad to put under your sleeping bag. Facilities include shared showers and a common dining area, with a refrigerator and electric stove. Cooking and eating utensils are provided. Note that Hapuna Beach can be too rough for swimming during the winter. If you feel like treating yourself to some gourmet food or luxurious surroundings, two of the Big Island's most upscale hotels are nearby.

KALOPA CABINS, *Contact the Division of State Parks, P.O. Box 936, Hilo, HI 96721, Tel. 808/974-6200.*

In a region that is far lusher than arid Hapuna, these cabins are found in the northeast, two miles south of Honokaa and just inland from the scenic Hamakua Coast. The hiking trails in this flourishing state park are well-marked and some of the vegetation has been identified. Cabins sleep up to eight people each on bunk beds. Bedding is provided, along with a common dining and recreation hall with a gas stove and cooking and eating utensils.

WHERE TO EAT

The dinner hour is relished on the Big Island, not simply because there are so many good restaurants to choose from, but also because eating out is the primary entertainment at night. The most expensive places are found in the hotels along the Kona-Kohala Coast. Luckily, there are also plenty of good moderate and inexpensive restaurants to choose from, in the town of Kailua-Kona and around the island.

Those who can't live without that first cup of coffee will want to take home a bag or two of those famous Kona beans. Some of the fancier hotels stock guest rooms with fresh Kona coffee beans, grinders, and coffee makers. Another Big Island specialty is macadamia nuts, sold all over the island. Among the many sweet treats at the **Kailua Candy Company** are macadamia nuts in a variety of incarnations. At the roadside **Tex Drive Inn** stand in Honokaa, hot, sweet *malasadas* (Portuguese balls of fried dough) are popped into many a mouth. For a cool sweet, try the **Shave Ice Company** on Alii Drive and Palani Street in Kailua-Kona.

You'll find some of the island's best ice cream at **Hilo Homemade Ice Cream**, next to Tropical Gardens and Gallery in Hilo. You might sample flavors such as ginger, lilikoi (passion fruit), mud pie, rocky road, and green tea. Particularly popular among Asians, **mochi ice cream**, sold at KTA supermarkets, is a dough made of rice flour and sugar that is filled with ice cream, sort of like a dumpling. Uncooked and served frozen, it is as much a part of many island New Year's celebrations as apple pie is to an American Thanksgiving.

BEST EATS ON THE BIG ISLAND

Cream of the Crop

Merriman's, *Kamuela/Waimea: The tropical atmosphere and the creative Pacific rim cuisine are wonderful here.*

Sam Choy's Restaurant, *Kona: The seafood laulau moves quickly at this popular upscale local spot.*

Palm Café, *Kailua-Kona: Save this one for a special night, if you like romantic settings and delicious food.*

Seaside Restaurant, *Hilo: Offering an unusual dining experience, this family-run restaurant serves fish just plucked from the surrounding ponds.*

Inexpensive or Moderate

Kona Ranch House, *Kailua-Kona: This is one of my favorite breakfast haunts.*

Tex Drive Inn, *Honokaa: Stop here for a plate lunch while you're exploring this scenic area.*

Ocean View Inn, *Kailua-Kona: For a truly local experience, try some of this Hawaiian, Chinese, Japanese, or American food.*

Restaurant Miwa, *Hilo: You'll find some of the island's best Japanese dishes here.*

Kona-Kohala Coast

THE CANOE HOUSE, *Mauna Lani Resort. Tel. 885-6622. Reservations recommended. Dinner entrees: $27 to $35. Credit cards accepted.*

The dining tables, bar top, and fishing canoe hanging from the ceiling are all made of lustrous native koa wood at this oceanfront, open-air restaurant where meals are served in the courtyard or in the gazebo. An antique canoe paddle, a bowpiece, and other nautical items that were found on the resort property are on display. The water is flood-lit at night. Good choices are tempura ahi, hibachi chicken on crunchy noodles, and bamboo-steamed mahi-mahi with Chinese cabbage. The grilled garlic-infused lamb chops will tempt meat eaters.

THE ORCHID COURT, *The Orchid at Mauna Lani, Mauna Lani Resort. Tel. 885-2000. Reservations recommended for dinner. Dinner entrees: $25 to $40. Credit cards accepted.*

Open for breakfast and dinner, this restaurant serves creative dishes with many ingredients and preparation techniques borrowed from various countries of the Pacific Rim. For dinner openers, try the Waimea tomato and Kula onion salad, or vegetable samosas. Extra-special entrees include seared Pacific snapper, sesame crusted mahi-mahi, and, my favorite, seared sake marinated prawns. At the Sunday brunch, the theme of Pacific Rim cuisine is complemented by many other dishes in an extensive - and delicious - buffet.

DONATON'S RESTAURANT, *Hilton Waikoloa Village, Waikoloa Resort. Tel. 885-1234. Reservations recommended. Dinner only. Entrees: $18 to $30. Credit cards accepted.*

Vacationers, residents, and food critics alike rave about the Northern Italian cuisine here. In addition to pasta and gourmet pizza, seafood and meat are on the menu. Try the chicken breast with wild mushrooms and marsala sauce, the spaghetti a la vongole (with red or white clam sauce), or the veal topped with prosciutto and mozzarella. The cheesecake with amaretto or the fresh cannoli bring any meal to a sweet end. Reserve early if you'd like a table by the window or on the large lanai. The sunsets are fabulous from here and you can watch the boats along the canal.

THE GALLERY, *The Golf Clubhouse, Mauna Lani Resort. Tel. 885-6699. Reservations recommended. Dinner entrees: $16 to $36. Credit cards accepted.*

Panelled in warm, dark woods, this restaurant specializes in both continental cuisine and local seafood. Steak is also on the menu. You might find chicken with crab meat and roasted macadamia nuts, Cajun pasta Alfredo with sausage, and grilled pork chops with fresh apple dressing. Windows all around offer great views of the golf course and the Pacific. The comfortable, spacious bar, separated by Western-style swinging doors, adjoins the dining room.

TRES HOMBRES BEACH GRILL, *Kawaihae Center. Tel. 882-1031. Dinner entrees: $15 to $20. Credit cards accepted.*

I've gotten lukewarm reports about the Mexican food at this non-smoking restaurant. However, it does have a pleasant atmosphere for drinks and an unusual entrance, where walls are paneled with carved driftwood.

THE CAFÉ TIARE, *The Royal Waikoloan Hotel, Waikoloa. Tel. 885-6789. Reservations recommended. Dinner only. Closed Wednesday and Sunday. Dinner entrees: $10 to $30. Credit cards accepted.*

Crystal, etched glass, warm wood, and accents reminiscent of the era of the Hawaiian monarchy complement the strong menu in this attractive dining room. The menu has changed to have less emphasis on continental and more on Pacific Rim cuisine. The salmon baked in pastry and the local fish dishes are especially good.

CAFE PESTO, *Kawaihae Center. Tel. 882-1071. Open daily, Sunday-Thursday 11am - 9pm, Friday and Saturday until 10pm. Dinner entrees: $7 to $19. Credit cards accepted. Note that this is a non-smoking restaurant.*

The portions of pasta and designer pizza (in an array of varieties, from smoked ham and pineapple to shrimp and garlic) are generous here. For pasta, try the crab primavera with artichokes, roasted garlic, peppers, wild mushrooms and pesto; or the Cajun shrimp with sausage. Maybe you'll decide to begin with soup or Caesar salad and end with cornbread shortcake with blueberry topping or pecan pie. The artwork on the walls of this attractively decorated cafe is for sale.

North Kohala

BAMBOO RESTAURANT AND GALLERY, *Akoni Pule Highway, downtown Hawi. Tel. 889-5555. Closed Mondays. Dinner entrees: $11 to $18.*

Some folks come here just for the lilikoi (passion fruit) margaritas, but I also love the Asian-influenced fresh fish and other seafood. Both lunch and dinner are served.

MATTHEW'S PLACE, *Hawi. Tel. 889-5500. Open 10am to 8pm Monday to Thursday, 10am to 9pm Friday and Saturday, 10am to 7pm Sunday; closed Wednesdays. Hours subject to change. Inexpensive.*

Along Hawaii's main road, this tiny, mainly take-out restaurant is a good place to pick up plate lunches if you're headed for one of the remote beaches or other scenic spots in the north. The ahi sandwich is a good choice for lunch. Local fish and seafood such as garlic shrimp with linguini are specialties on its full-service menu. The saimin, steak, burgers, cheesecake and pies are also delicious.

KOHALA VILLAGE INN RESTAURANT, *55-514 Hawi Road, Hawi. Tel. 889-0105. Closed Tuesdays. Inexpensive.*

Monday is family night, which means that dinner will cost even less than during the rest of the week. Any time, try to baby back ribs, which might be marinated in a sauce of black beans and chili paste, or the fish special, which comes with produce recently harvested from nearby farms. Breakfast and lunch are also served.

Kamuela/Waimea

EDELWEISS, *Highway 19. Tel. 885-6800. No reservations taken. Closed Sunday and Monday. Dinner entrees average $22. Credit cards accepted.*

Opened in 1983 by Hans-Peter Hager, this Bavarian-accented restaurant is the oldest of Kamuela/Waimea's upscale dining places. Before settling here, Hager made the rounds as a chef at some of the state's best hotels: the Kapalua Bay on Maui and the Mauna Lani Bay, on the Big Island. The roast duck in orange sauce and the rack of lamb with mustard and garlic are good choices. Be prepared for a long wait for a table at dinner time. Some patrons have complained that the food is too salty and too heavy, but Edelweiss remains popular.

MERRIMAN'S, *Opelo Plaza II (Route 19 and Opelo Road). Tel. 885-6822. Reservations required, you might have to call a day in advance. Dinner entrees: $13 to $25. Credit cards accepted.*

Peter Merriman opened this dining spot with his wife in 1988, after drawing raves at the Mauna Lani Resort's Gallery restaurant (where he became executive chef when he was only 28). He is known for immersing himself totally in his work, often diving for some of the shellfish served. He has joined forces with farmers so that his produce can be as exotic and fresh as possible.

You might begin with chicken satay, shrimp summer rolls, or poisson cru (a Tahitian dish made with raw fish marinated in coconut milk, lime and onions). Entrees might be grilled chicken with mango glaze and watercress kim chee, boneless duck breast roasted in a banana leaf with won ton cabbage and pineapple relish, fish with coconut sauce, or stir-fried curried vegetables on brown rice. The wok-charred ahi, Merriman's signature dish, is delicious (singed around the edges, and raw in the center, it resembles a slice of roast beef). Entrees come garnished with flower blossoms. You can't miss with the coconut creme brulee for dessert. Helpful waiters take the time to explain the ingredients and preparation of each item on the menu. Tall potted plants, floral designs on the walls, and framed paintings make this a colorful, tropical setting. Parents take note: A special children's menu is available.

NORI'S SAIMIN TOO, *64-1035 Mamalahoa Highway. Tel. 885-9133. Open 9am to 9pm. Entrees: $3 to $10. Cash or checks only.*

Hawaiian beef stew, saimin noodles, and the chicken steak plate are popular here.

Honokaa

HOTEL HONOKAA CLUB, *Manane Street. Tel. 775-0678. Dinner entrees: $7 to $30. Credit cards accepted.*

The Western-style facade of the building, which has been a hotel and restaurant since 1908, may have seen better days and the inside may look as if it never left the fifties. But if you have a taste for homestyle local food, this is the place. The booths in the bar and the old cigarette machine convince you that you've entered another era. The CD juke box seems to be the only anachronism. You might stumble upon a lively discussion about the ballgame on the TV in the bar, separated from the large dining room with shoji screens. Huge picture windows overlook corrugated tin roofs, trees, and the ocean. Dinner might be chicken cutlet, shrimp tempura, teriyaki steak, shrimp curry, or lobster. A children's menu is available for the young crowd.

TEX DRIVE INN, *Highway 19. Tel. 775-0598. Dinner entrees: $6 to $8.*

Famous for its malasadas (Portuguese hole-less donuts) and plate lunches, this casual local spot serves up delicious Hawaiian curries, teriyaki beef, Portuguese bean soup, and some of the best hamburgers around. Stop here for breakfast, lunch, or dinner while you're exploring the area.

Kailua-Kona & Keauhou Areas

JAMESON'S BY THE SEA, *77-6452 Alii Drive, Kailua-Kona. Tel. 329-3195. Reservations recommended. Open nightly for dinner; closed for lunch on Saturday and Sunday. Dinner entrees average $22. Credit cards accepted.*

If you'd like a dramatic view of the crashing surf of Magic Sands Beach with your lunch, this restaurant is the place. Most people ask to be seated on the patio high above the ocean. On the menu you might find crab-stuffed mushrooms, salmon pate, seafood diablo (in a spicy red sauce), sesame chicken, or filet mignon. There are usually choices among three fish specials.

SAM CHOY'S RESTAURANT, *73-5576 Kauhola Street, Kaloko Light Industrial Park. Tel. 326-1545. Reservations recommended. Dinner entrees: $17.95 to $29.95. Credit cards accepted.*

Located in a complex of warehouses between the airport and the harbor, this restaurant is off the beaten path and prices ain't cheap. But Sam Choy's is very popular among both visitors and residents, in part because of the generous portions of delicious regional food. For breakfast, you might have Sam's Ultimate Stew Omelette (filled with beef stew), fried rice and eggs, banana hotcakes, or a Belgian waffle sandwich. Fried poke (fish flash-cooked on the outside), available only here, is a lunch favorite. The seafood laulau, with a blend of scallops, shrimp, and shiitake mushrooms steamed in ti leaves with soy sauce and butter is excellent. Also consider the Chinese duck with honey sauce or the macadamia nut chicken with mahi-mahi. For dessert, the poha berry white pineapple ice cream is great. The children's menu for those under age ten makes this a good place for families.

PALM CAFÉ, *75-5819 Alii Drive. Tel. 329-7765. Reservations recommended. Dinner entrees: $16 to $34. Credit cards accepted.*

This atmospheric restaurant has built quite a name for itself. On the second story of a handsome building, the open air dining room has a romantic view of the ocean and rustling palm trees. Its eclectic menu with southwestern and Pacific Rim touches includes a delicious smoked duck spring roll appetizer. For an entree try the wok chicken, free range chicken breast, soft shell crab, or Cajun-style ahi. Downstairs, breakfast, lunch, and dinner are served in the more casual and less expensive **Under the Palms** sister restaurant.

SEAFOOD PASTA PALACE RESTAURANT, *Waterfront Row, 75-5770 Alii Drive, Kailua-Kona. Tel. 329-4436. Dinner entrees average $16. Credit cards accepted.*

The two-for-one lunch specials draw many patrons to this pleasant spot overlooking the Pacific. For lunch, the personal pan pizza is a good choice as is pasta with frutti di mare. At dinnertime, the fresh catch of the day comes with a salad, and pasta topped with marinara sauce.

THE CHART HOUSE, *Waterfront Row, 75-5170 Alii Drive, Kailua-Kona. Tel. 329-2451. Reservations recommended. Dinner only. Entrees: $14 to $33. Credit cards accepted.*

Views of the Pacific come free with meals at this steak and seafood restaurant that takes up two floors. Koa wood, fresh flowers, and a waterfall are part of the attractive decor. The garlic cheese bread, Alaskan king crab, and prime ribs move quickly and the salad bar has a variety of nutritious and tasty items.

KONA INN RESTAURANT, *75-5744 Alii Drive, Kailua-Kona. Tel. 329-4455. Dinner entrees: $14 to $21. Credit cards accepted.*

Open to the ocean breezes, this waterfront restaurant is decked out in gorgeous, carved koa wood (walls, partitions, tables, and ceilings). Peacock chairs, oriental rugs, and slow-moving ceiling fans further enhance the atmosphere. Small birds alight on the tops of chairs and the edges of tables. The perky young waitresses are happy to make suggestions about their many local fish dishes. The overstuffed avocado and shrimp salad sandwich or the tuna on a croissant are good choices for lunch. Their version of mud pie is quite good. Sunset watching is a popular activity here.

QUINN'S, *75-5655A Pahni Road, Kailua-Kona. Tel. 329-3822. Dinner entrees average $12. Credit cards accepted.*

This restaurant is just across the street from the Hotel King Kamehameha parking lot. After walking through the bar (where a few people will probably be watching TV), guests come to the garden lanai where they dine al fresco with greenery spilling over rough lava rock walls. The teriyaki shrimp and the seafood brochette are popular, as well as the pepper steak with brandy. Quinn's does a landslide business in fish and chips. Burgers and sandwiches are also served (such as the vegetarian number with avocado, sprouts, tomato and onions).

FISHERMAN'S LANDING, *Kona Inn Shopping Village, Kailua-Kona. Tel. 326-2555. Dinner entrees average $10. Credit cards accepted.*

Many people make a habit of dining at this al fresco, oceanfront restaurant. As patrons enter, they are greeted by rows of glistening fresh fish on ice. Live fish dart around ponds inside, where waterfalls and lush planes add to the appealing atmosphere. Paths separate the various dining areas. Although all fish dishes are popular, they also serve steak along with shellfish prepared in a variety of styles.

KONA RANCH HOUSE, 75-5653 Ololi Street, Kailua-Kona. Tel. 329-7061. Reservations required at dinner. Dinner entrees: $8 to $22. Credit cards accepted.

In a gingerbread-trimmed house on a steep hill, this popular restaurant is bursting with atmosphere. Don't let the term "ranch house" fool you. In a formal dining room with linen, plants hang from the lattice-work ceiling. Spacious, comfortable booths hug walls. If you only eat here once, make it for breakfast. The wonderfully varied menu includes buttermilk pancakes, Belgian waffles, chicken crepes, biscuits and gravy, tropical granola, as well as burritos and Huevos a la Mexicana (eggs, ground beef, refried beans, and cheddar cheese in a flour tortilla). The cornbread is addictive. Lunch might consist of seafood salad, a turkey club with avocado, burgers or tacos. For dinner, the lemon chicken with capers moves quickly. Bring a serious appetite – portions are generous.

THE JOLLY ROGER, Waterfront Row, 75-5776 Alii Drive, Kailua-Kona. Tel. 329-1344. No reservations accepted. Dinner entrees: $6 to $25. Credit cards accepted.

This restaurant gazes out onto the ocean. Some people say that breakfast is better than the other meals served here. Fresh fruit, eggs and steak are among the offerings for the first meal of the day. At dinner, prime ribs and steak are in demand. The live music and dancing draw a young crowd every night after 10pm.

HUGGO'S, 75-5828 Kahakai, Kailua-Kona. Tel. 329-1493. Inexpensive. Credit cards accepted.

A popular local hangout for sunset watching and after-dinner drinks, Huggo's looks out onto the rocky shore. The water is clear enough to see the fish that seem to beg for diners to toss them crumbs. Steak and seafood are the main attractions here.

BANANA BAY, Uncle Billy's Kona Bay Hotel, 75-5739 Alii Drive, Kailua-Kona. Tel. 329-1393. Inexpensive. Credit cards accepted.

You can watch a hula show Saturday and Sunday evenings at 6pm while you dine al fresco by the pool. There's a large selection of fish on the menu.

OCEAN VIEW INN, Alii Drive, Kailua-Kona. Tel. 329-9998. Inexpensive.

With the atmosphere of an old-fashioned diner, this no-frills restaurant is almost always packed. People stream in for three meals a day. Owned and run by a family, it serves Hawaiian, Chinese, Japanese, and American food. If you want a plate lunch to go, this is the place.

TESHIMA'S RESTAURANT, *Highway 11, Honalo, Kona Coast. Inexpensive. Tel. 322-9140.*

Ask anyone along the Kona Coast to direct you to a good Japanese restaurant, and chances are you'll end up here. Nine miles south of Kailua-Kona, this family-run restaurant serves three homestyle meals a day. Drawing a very local crowd, Teshima is known for its shrimp tempura and homemade tofu. The fried rice omelet is also delicious. If you have a taste for sushi, you'll have to order it a day in advance. For dessert, try the apple pie.

MANAGO RESTAURANT, *Manago Hotel, Captain Cook. Inexpensive. Tel. 323-2642.*

There's nothing fancy about the dining room of this dilapidated hotel. But the food is well worth the trip — witness the number of locals always eating breakfast, lunch, and dinner here. Specializing in fish, Manago also serves pork chops and hamburgers.

Ka'u

KA'U DRIVE-INN, *Highway #11, Hawaiian Ocean View Estates. Inexpensive. Tel. 929-9291.*

Seemingly in the middle of nowhere, this local eatery is surrounded by lava fields. It may be a welcome sight on your way to Hawaii Volcanoes National Park or to South Point. The **South Point Bar** is nearby.

Naalehu

PUNALU'U SWEETBREAD BAKESHOP AND VISITOR CENTER. *Tel. 929-7343. Inexpensive. Credit cards accepted.*

The aroma of baking bread will snag you on your way to or from Hawaii Volcanoes National Park, about 40 minutes away. You can even watch the bakers at work and learn about the various stages from flour to loaf. Stop to relax in the colorful gardens while snacking on malasadas, doughnuts, anpan (sweetbread filled with beans or coconut) or sandwiches made with fresh bread. The newest sweetbreads include taro, guava, and cinnamon raisin with macadamia nuts. Also on sale are loaves of bread, pies, cookies, brownies, coffee, and ice cream; jams and jellies made from guava, pineapple, and papaya; and T-shirts and sweatshirts. Since this bakery is owned by Mauna Loa, macadamia nuts in all their incarnations are also in stock. A snack bar attracts many tourists.

Hawaii Volcanoes National Park

KILAUEA LODGE AND RESTAURANT, *Volcano Village, Old Volcano Road (near the entrance to the park). Tel. 967-7366. Open nightly 5:30pm to 9pm. Reservations recommended. Dinner entrees average $22. Credit cards accepted.*

People who've dined at this cozy mountain lodge surrounded by trees and other greenery rave about the food. Duck Provencale is its signature dish. On the menu you will also find fettuccine primavera, duck l'orange, broiled New York steak, chicken stuffed with mushrooms, and other continental dishes. Venison is also featured. There's an extensive, excellent wine list. Brass chandeliers hang from a wood-paneled ceiling and oriental rugs cover the floor. If it's nippy enough outside, a fire flickers in the hearth during meals.

VOLCANO GOLF AND COUNTRY CLUB RESTAURANT. *Tel. 967-8228. Lunch only (10:30am to 2pm), except holidays and weekends, when breakfast is served. Inexpensive. Credit cards accepted.* .

This pleasant restaurant is known for its award-winning desserts. It is also popular for its fish burgers. Honey chicken and saimin are on the menu as well. Sports fans often gather in front of the large screen television in the lounge area.

Hilo Area

NIHON RESTAURANT AND CULTURAL CENTER, *123 Lihiwai Street, Hilo. Tel. 969-1133. Reservations recommended. Dinner entrees average $25. Credit cards accepted.*

Traditional Japanese food is served here, with combination plates at lunch and dinner. The views of Liliuokalani Gardens and Hilo Bay add to the pleasure of the good food.

QUEEN'S COURT, *Hilo Hawaiian Hotel, 71 Banyan Drive. Tel. 935-9361. Reservations recommended. Dinner entrees average $24. Credit cards accepted.*

Locals pour into this restaurant, which serves standard American fare. With nightly buffets (including a special children's buffet), it is most crowded on Friday nights for the seafood buffet. Sweet potato cream pie with haupia topping is delicious. Another good time to dine here is at breakfast. Windows look out to Hilo Bay.

SEASIDE RESTAURANT, *across from James Kealoha Park, 1/4 mile from Onekahakaha. Tel. 935-8825. Dinner only. Entrees: up to $22. Reservations recommended.*

Started in the early 1900s, this family-run restaurant was washed away by the 1946 tidal wave that devastated Hilo. The grand re-opening was in 1947. Dishes retrieved from the ocean floor by a scuba diver are preserved behind glass at the entrance. Both a dining spot and an old-style Hawaiian fish farm, the restaurant is surrounded by pine trees and a natural pond stocked with rainbow trout, catfish, koi (carp), mullet, and others. Guests may tour the pond while waiting for their individually prepared meals.

Seaside claims to be the only restaurant in Hawaii that serves aholehole, a rare local fish that is raised in the pond here. Demand is so great for this sweet white fish that if you'd like to try it, you'd better call a day or two ahead to reserve yours. Other choices include mullet steamed in ti leaves, steak, and lobster. Dessert, which comes with each meal, might be warm apple pie or sherbet.

HARRINGTON'S, *Reeds Bay, 135 Kalanianaole. Tel. 961-4966. Reservations recommended. Dinner entrees average $20. Credit cards accepted.*

In a dramatic water's edge location, across from the Hilo Seaside Hotel, Harrington's is housed in a sprawling wooden building. Windows surround the dining room. Specials might be the catch of the day, such as Cajun-style prawns or seafood brochette. Harrington's also features prime ribs, New York pepper steak, and chicken Parmesan.

RESTAURANT MIWA, *Hilo Shopping Center, 1261 Kilauea Avenue, Suite 230. Tel. 961-4454. Reservations recommended. Dinner entrees: $8 to $22. Credit cards accepted.*

More than a few residents call this the best Japanese restaurant on the island. Served in a brightly lit, unassuming dining room, the food is indeed delicious. In addition to sushi, the menu includes sake-flavored steamed clam, hiyayakko (chilled tofu), charbroiled salmon, ahi (tuna) and unagi (eel). Tempura is its most popular dish.

SCRUFFLES, *1438 Kilauea Street. Tel. 935-6664 or 935-6678. Inexpensive.*

If you have gourmet taste but shallow pockets, try this place for local, Mexican, barbecued, and smoked foods. Favorites are the Hawaiian curries, including shrimp, chicken, and vegetable. Scruffles also makes a mean clam chowder. The freshly baked goods are hard to resist, as is the chocolate mousse.

KEN'S HOUSE OF PANCAKES, *1730 Kamehameha Avenue. Tel. 935-8711. Inexpensive.*

Open 24 hours a day, this popular eatery serves breakfast, lunch, and dinner. The huge menu for the morning meal includes the macadamia nut, banana, and coconut pancakes that made Ken famous; fluffy waffles; hearty omelettes; and Ken's corned beef hash. Lunch could be a sandwich, a burger, a bowl of saimin or a local Hawaiian favorite: a beef patty, mahi-mahi filet or slab of Spam topped with a fried egg and thick brown gravy on a bed of rice. Note that there's also a menu for dieters. At dinner time, the teriyaki chicken moves quickly. For dessert, try the macadamia nut or lemon coconut custard pie.

UNCLE BILLY'S, *Uncle Billy's Hilo Bay Hotel, 87 Banyan Drive. Tel. 935-0861. Inexpensive. Credit cards accepted.*

Only breakfast and dinner are served at this popular steak and seafood restaurant. For breakfast, try the Wiki Wiki special: ham, home fries, and scrambled eggs.

SEEING THE SIGHTS

The Kohala Coast & Kamuela (Waimea)

From royal fishponds and burial caves to heiau and petroglyphs, intriguing remnants of Hawaii's past are well-preserved along the sunny, beach-rimmed **Kona-Kohala Coast.** Some of the ponds and rock carvings have been incorporated into the grounds of luxury hotels. Kohala is the birthplace of Kamehameha the Great, the celebrated unifier of the Hawaiian islands. The beaches along this coast were once frequented by Hawaiian monarchs at play.

ROYAL FEET

Also called the King's Trail, Mamalahoa is a path that has been pounded by generations of royal feet into a gleaming black line through the rough lava. Some hotels lead jogging jaunts along this ancient trail, part of which was later broadened for travel on horseback.

Heading north from Kailua-Kona or Keahole Airport on **Queen Kaahumanu Highway** (named for Kamehameha I's feisty, favorite bride), you may think you're driving through a vast wasteland. No buildings or even gas stations border the road. As far as you can see, stark lava flows sprawl on both sides of the highway. Here and there the barren charcoal landscape is interrupted by hay-like pill grass, kiawe trees and cascades of colorful bougainvillea, which create a brilliant contrast. The Big Island version of graffiti also decorates the roadsides. Kids use white coral rocks to spell out phrases such as "Fred loves Noelani" on the black lava expanses, most of which resulted from the last eruption of Mt. Hualalai in 1801.

What could Laurance Rockefeller possibly have been thinking when he decided to build the **Mauna Kea Beach Hotel** in this desolate area in 1965? Well, his idea caught on, and other developers have followed suit. From most of the road, there's no sign of these plush resorts. They are tucked neatly out of sight at the water's edge, beyond the lava flows that stretch between the highway and the Pacific. Despite the ruggedness of the region, the grounds of these well-spaced hotels are startlingly green, with flowers in every hue and smooth lawns and golf courses. While the expensive Kona-Kohala coast has a (very) long way to go before it even begins to resemble Oahu's Waikiki or Maui's Kaanapali, some residents and loyal vacationers are dismayed by the recent increase in splashy hotels along this coast.

The South Kohala district begins at Anaeho'omalu, where a curving white sand beach gives way to a shallow bay. Commoners weren't allowed to fish at the royal ponds by the adjacent beachfront **Royal Waikoloan** hotel, but contemporary commoners are welcome to tour these picturesque bodies of water. The meandering fishponds at the **Mauna Lani Bay Hotel & Bungalows** at the Mauna Lani Resort, farther north, are also quite impressive. Here shuttle vans link hotels and condominiums with restaurants and golf courses.

Visits to the **Eva Parker Woods Cottage**, *Mauna Lani Bay Hotel, Kohala Coast, Tel. 885-6622*, can be arranged upon request. Mauna Lani's renowned Francis I'i Brown Golf Course is named after the high-living kamaaina who used this beach cottage for vacationing and entertaining. His many guests arrived by boat from various parts of the world. Built in the 1930s, the cottage sits at the edge of fishponds once reserved for alii. Today it is a museum of Hawaiian artifacts and local treasures.

At **Hilton Waikoloa Village**, the human-made sights are so lavish that guests may not notice that there is only a rocky shore and a small, artificial lagoon beach. Sleek boats cruise canals and long, columned corridors are lined with museum-like displays of Asian and Polynesian art and artifacts. At the this Hilton, you can **Swim with Dolphins**, *Tel. 885-2875*. If you're looking forward to getting in the water with these gentle, playful mammals, you'll have to win the lottery—literally. This is how participants are chosen, since this fabulous activity is so popular. Guests may enter the lottery to swim with the dolphins when they check in; non-guests must enter the lottery by 3:30pm on the day prior to the encounter. The cost is $95 per person; $150 per couple at 11am only, otherwise, individual rates apply. There is something wonderfully exhilarating about swimming with such large, warm, smooth-skinned creatures and not having to be afraid. Underwater, you can hear their conversations, which sound like clicks and laughter.

Further north in the **Pauko** area, the craggy shore is riddled with tidal pools that make perfect swimming holes for kids (even the adult variety). You'll also find petroglyphs here. Between Mauna Lani Resort and Mauna Kea Resort, **Hapuna State Recreation Area** has a beautiful strip of white sand and camping cabins set back from the water. Many consider this and neighboring **Kauna'oa Beach**, where the **Hapuna Beach Prince Hotel** and the **Mauna Kea Beach Hotel** are located, the most attractive shores on the Big Island.

Also near the Mauna Kea Beach Resort, about a mile southeast of Kawaihae, is **Puukohola Heiau National Historic Site**, *Kohala, Tel. 882-7218*. Kamehameha the Great built this hilltop temple to honor his family war god, Ku, in 1791. He invited his cousin (who also happened to be an arch rival) to attend the dedication, then killed him as soon as he arrived, sacrificing his body to Ku. Kamehameha was then prepared to begin his bloody attempts to bring all of the Hawaiian Islands under his control.

Where once there stood thatched roof shelters and carved wooden statues, a huge stone platform is all that remains of this heiau today. In an ironic juxtaposition, Puukohola overlooks 13th century **Mailekini**, a heiau constructed to celebrate four centuries of peace between the Big Island of Hawaii and Maui.

One way to get to the upscale ranching town of **Kamuela** (a.k.a. **Waimea**) is to turn mauka (inland) onto Kawaihae Road (Highway 19). This route will also take you across to the east side of the island, down the lush Hamakua Coast and to Hilo, the Big Island's largest town, where pleasant rainfall is abundant, especially in the evening.

Back on the Kohala Coast, **Samuel M. Spencer Beach Park,** just north of the Mauna Kea hotel, draws many local families for picnicking and camping out. From Samuel M. Spencer Beach Park, you'll have a good view of Puukohola and Mailekini heiau (see above), both within walking distance.

The snorkeling is good off **Lapakahi State Historical Park,** *North Kohala, Tel. 889-5566, open 8am to 4pm.* Dating back to the late 1300s, this fishing village was established on a rugged, isolated segment of the coast. As you enter, pick up a map at the guide station. Wear sturdy shoes to wander along the rocky, red dirt trails through the remains. The longer of the two marked routes is a mile. Identification signs and directions are carved into logs and rough tree trunks, so they blend into the natural landscape. You'll pass a palm-fringed beach scattered with black lava rocks and white chunks of coral. Most of the ruins are lava stone walls, dramatically set against pandanus trees, palms, and the choppy white surf.

You'll also come to a konane board (the Hawaiian answer to Chinese checkers), an old fish trap, nets, ancient tools and utensils, canoe sheds and other thatched roof shelters. Although there are benches here and there, you'll find little shade, and the sun can be quite strong. If you haven't brought your own water, drink some from the cooler at the guide station.

At the island's extreme northern tip, near Upolu Airport (which serves private planes), **Mookini Heiau,** *Hawi, North Kohala,* has stood since about A.D. 400. Perhaps comparatively few vacationers visit this ancient temple for fear that its past will catch up with them. Built for human sacrifices (among other uses), Mookini was the first site in the state to be listed with the National Register of Historic Places. This was probably where the birth rituals befitting a high-born child were performed for Kamehameha I, who began life nearby, during the late 1750s. People are said to have known early on that he would be a powerful and influential man. When his mother was nearly at the end of her pregnancy she was overtaken by a constant craving for tiger shark eyes. That same month, Halley's comet crossed the sky. The child became the first of the

Kamehameha line of rulers. As a young man, he prepared for his life as a warrior by dodging spears hurled at his chest. A rugged unpaved road not far from Upolu Airfield leads to the timeworn remains of the 20-foot stone walls on a hill. This large heiau is believed to have been constructed from rocks passed from worker to worker from a valley 14 miles away!

In green North Kohala, pastures speckled with Holstein cows are now far more prevalent than the sugarcane fields that once blanketed the area. At one point, five sugar plantations flourished in Kohala. The quiet streets of **Hawi**, the northernmost town on the Big Island, are lined with low Western front buildings. To get a real feel for this old plantation community, chat with patrons or the merchant at **M. Nakahara General Store**, where you'll find everything from rubber sandals and hardware to fabric and children's clothing.

The shelves of neighboring **Nakahara Grocery Store** are piled with foods that reflect the tastes of Hawaii's many nationalities: salted duck eggs, fresh poi, spicy dried squid, imported Japanese crackers and cookies, seaweed salad, shrimp chips, octopus *poki*, and *laulau* (leaves wrapped around pieces of pork or fish). If you're feeling adventurous, you might find some fixin's for a picnic here.

East of Hawi, **Kapaau** is the site of the imposing 1878 King Kamehameha Statue, which stands in front of the North Kohala Civic Center. On King Kamehameha Day in June, residents drape the monarch with scores of brightly colored leis. The statue bears a striking resemblance to the one in front of the Judiciary Building in Honolulu. This is because that statue was copied from this one. Intended for Honolulu, the original was modeled by an American sculptor in Italy, cast in Paris, and lost during a shipwreck off the Falkland Islands. So the replica, which now stands in Honolulu, was made. Then the original turned up. It seemed appropriate to erect it near the birthplace of the first ruler of the Hawaiian Kingdom.

Just east of here, a winding scenic drive through meadows and a residential neighborhood will take you to **Keokea Beach Park**. At the end of a rust-colored dirt road, you'll have a panoramic view of the frothy surf thrashing the shores of a rocky cove. On this eastern side of the North Kohala peninsula, the main road grinds to a halt at **Pololu Valley Lookout**. Awe-inspiring cliffs drop into deep valleys where wild boars, goats, pheasants, and horses roam freely. A rugged hiking trail dips three miles into Pololu and eventually makes its way to distant Waipio Valley, where Kamehameha I (Kamehameha the Great) was raised.

The 21-mile drive from Hawi south along the **Kohala Mountain Road** (Highway 250) to Waimea/Kamuela is one of the island's most scenic routes. An eerie mist often hangs over the towering ironwoods, open fields and country lanes. Just outside Hawi, the feathery branches of casuarina pines create a shady tunnel over the road. Cattle graze in lime green meadows and on the lower slopes of forest green hills. You'll pass **Kahua Ranch**, which sports windmills. The *paniolo* here are as likely to round up cattle on motorcycles as on horseback and as adept at growing produce as they are at raising sheep. Before you reach the town of Kamuela, you'll come to a lookout point from which you'll have an extensive view of the Kohala Coast.

When John Palmer Parker jumped ship in Hawaii in 1809, he found a job cleaning fish ponds for Kamehameha I. In 1816, Parker married Princess Keliikipikaneokaloahaka, Kamehameha I's granddaughter. The princess was called Kipikane for short. Thus, the New England haole became a member of the Hawaiian royal family.

Back in 1788, Captain George Vancouver had come to the islands with Captain James Cook, the man who let Europe know that Hawaii existed. When Vancouver returned in 1793, he brought Mexican long-horn cattle as a gift for Kamehameha. The king put a kapu on killing cows, decreeing that anyone who disobeyed the law would be put to death. But the cows reproduced so rapidly, trampling and eating such great quanti-ties of vegetation on Mauna Kea's slopes, that they soon threatened nearby communities. Kamehameha hired his American grandson-in-law to control and shrink the herd. In exchange, he gave Parker two acres of land. In 1847, the ex-sailor and his wife established **Parker Ranch**.

Today, at 250,000 rolling acres, this is the largest privately owned cattle ranch on US soil. Cowboys from Mexico and South America were brought in as ranch hands, and the word *paniolo* (a corruption of Espanoles) entered the Hawaiian vocabulary. Wild rodeos are periodi-cally hosted by the ranch. After Parker's death, ownership of these lands fell into the hands of a 14-year-old descendant, Thelma Parker. She grew up to be the mother of the late Richard Smart, the great-great-great-grandson of the founder and the most recent owner of the ranch before it was taken over by a trust.

If you'd like to visit, head for the **Parker Ranch Visitor Center and Museum**, *Kamuela/Waimea, Tel. 885-7655; admission to museum (open daily 9am to 5pm): $5; last admission to museum 4:45pm; admission to historic homes only (open weekdays 9am to 5pm, weekends 10am to 5pm): $7.50, dual admission: $10 per person, available 9am to 3pm.* The Museum at the Parker Ranch Visitor Center was started by Thelma Parker Smart. On display are her jewelry, her well-used Bible, and the blue gown she wore to the opera at Covent Garden in England when George V was crowned king in 1911. Exhibits also include old saddles, bridles and bits, branding irons, iron pots, brass plates, and an old wind-up telephone mounted on the wall. Portraits, photographs, and a short video tell the history of the ranch and the Kamehamehas, as well as of other relatives and family friends. One part of the museum is dedicated to Duke Kahanamoku, an Olympic swimming champion who introduced surfing to Australia in 1912 and served as sheriff of Oahu for 25 years.

Drive out to visit the two Parker family historic homes. The living room of opulent **Puuopelu**, the former home of Richard Smart, glitters with chandeliers hanging from skylights that flood the room with sunshine. Among the many original paintings are works by Degas, Renoir, and Chagall. Chests and tables are topped with stone camels and horses from China's Tang and Ming dynasties, Japanese vases, brass gondola ornaments from Venice, jade ranging in color from rose to bright green, Venetian glass, and Marie Antoinette and Louis XVI plates. In contrast, **Mana**, the older family home that was relocated next door, is a small, rustic affair, built in 1847. Its glossy walls, floors, and ceilings are made of rich brown koa. This gleaming wood was also used for the calabashes on display and the amazingly high headboard on the bed.

WHAT'S IN A NAME?

Waimea was the ancient Hawaiian name for the area, but it was dubbed **Kamuela** *(the Hawaiian version of Samuel) after Colonel Sam Parker, the son of John Palmer Parker. However, many people continued to call it Waimea and since there are Waimeas on both Oahu and Kauai, the US Post Office requested that the name be officially changed. So much for officialdom: This town is still commonly known by both names.*

At the crossroads of the island's main highways (routes 250, 19 and 190), **Kamuela/Waimea** rests in the Kohala Mountains. Nearly 3,000 feet above the dry, sunny Kohala Coast (a 45-minute drive away), it is about an hour's drive from Hilo (along Saddle Road). Rainbows often span its verdant fields where horses graze, enclosed by fences made of stones or roughlogs. Horseback riding past cattle in open fields or into forests thick with ferns and aromatic ginger is a popular pastime. Houses with gingerbread trim are complemented by neat, colorful gardens. Small churches coexist peacefully with modern mini-malls.

Kamuela/Waimea was born as a shopping and services area for ranch employees. As drowsy as this village is, development is happening too quickly for many long-time residents. They complain about the new homes and shopping centers that keep cropping up. Others are pleased with the changes. More than a few people from Honolulu and other busy parts of Hawaii have relocated to Waimea. They've been lured by the prospect of living in the country, yet being able to take advantage of

Waimea's chic boutiques, smattering of gourmet restaurants (several of which are owned by former chefs at some of Hawaii's most upscale resorts) and art galleries. Over the years, another draw for affluent families has been private **Hawaii Preparatory Academy**, which is one of the best schools in the state. It was founded in 1949 by an Episcopal bishop. Two of its four campuses — an elementary school and a middle school — are in central Waimea, and one (the high school) sprawls across more than 80 acres of Parker Ranch land.

At the **Kahilu Theater**, you might catch a classical concert, a hula performance, or a Broadway play. The late Richard Smart, the sixth generation owner of Parker Ranch, was largely responsible for the existence of the theater. He even appeared in some of the local productions. He was also the person who began the tours of Parker Ranch. You can see another impressive koa interior at **Imiola Congregational Church**, where wooden calabashes are suspended from the ceiling.

Most of the varied displays at **Kamuela Museum**, *at the intersection of Routes 19 and 250, Kamuela/Waimea, Tel. 885-4724; open 8am to 5pm daily; cost: Adults $5, seniors $4, children $2*, consist of a mishmash of haphazardly grouped items from Hawaii, other Pacific islands, the mainland, and China. You'll see everything from Hawaiian stone weapons, kapa cloth, fish hooks made from human bones, and a portrait of Queen Liliuokalani to a Nazi flag and a stuffed iguana. Albert Solomon runs the museum with his wife, Harriet (a descendant of John Palmer Parker), and tells some good stories about old Hawaii.

Moonwalking — Well, Almost!

More than 1,600 years ago, Polynesians used their knowledge of astronomy to guide them over thousands of miles of open ocean to Hawaii, first landing on the Big Island. Today, some 12 observatories on the 13,796 foot summit of **Mauna Kea** help contemporary scientists learn more about the heavens. The dry, generally cloud-free weather here on Hawaii's loftiest peak creates such prime conditions that scientists from Great Britain, the Netherlands, France, and Canada, as well as NASA, have built their country's major telescopes here. More than 90 percent of all the stars visible from anywhere on the planet can be seen from this perch.

Since the telescopic observation is done after dark, you'll have to go at night to see the stars. You can make reservations (at least two weeks in advance) for a free visit through the **University of Hawaii's Institute for Astronomy**, *Tel. 974-4205*. How much you see will depend on the weather. You can also take a free day-time excursion through the **Onizuka Center for International Astronomy**, *Tel. 961-2180*, or on your own to the bleak (sometimes snow covered) lunar-like summit to view the massive and complex equipment. Note that whether you take a tour or go on your own, you'll need to provide your own four-wheel-drive transportation. (Before you set out, check with your rental company about roads off-limits to their cars.)

Temperatures can dip into the 30s, so be sure to bundle up! On your way to the summit, don't be surprised if your bags of potato chips or other snacks burst from the pressure of the altitude, as ours did. And be forewarned that some people (like me) experience altitude sickness (dizziness, headache, fatigue, nausea). If these symptoms are relatively mild, ask for a few inhalations of pure oxygen through a tube at the summit. Otherwise, turn around and go back down. *Pregnant women and children under age sixteen are not allowed to make the trip at all.* People with heart disease or chronic respiratory problems should consult their doctors before heading out.

After climbing through Parker Ranch lands along Saddle Road (Highway 200), you'll turn onto Summit Road, with about 15 more miles to go until you reach the top. Some of the scattered *mamane* trees you'll see began growing 300 years ago. With the introduction of cows and sheep, the trees are dying out, since these animals eat the seeds, buds, and flowers. At these high elevations, you might catch a glimpse of native birds such as the *nene goose* (the state bird) and the small, bright yellow *palila.*

At 9,300 feet, you'll see a building resembling a Swiss chalet, where Mauna Kea scientists live. It sits on a mountainside near the **Onizuka Center for International Astronomy Visitor Information Center on Mauna Kea**, *Tel. 961-2180; hours vary, so call ahead; restrooms are always open; no four-wheel drive is required if you plan to come only this far, but you'll need one to continue climbing the mountain; pregnant women and children under age 16 are permitted only up to this elevation.* It's from here that the Center's tours to the summit begin. The center is dedicated to Ellison Onizuka, the astronaut from Hawaii who was killed in the *Challenger* explosion. Exhibits illustrate the work of the scientists who use the massive telescopes atop Mauna Kea.

Once the vegetation disappears, you'll come to the desert-like **Valley of the Moon**, where Apollo astronauts trained to get the feel of lunar life. In the distance, you may be able to spot piles of rocks jutting up from a flat area. Dating back to around A.D. 300, these are shrines constructed by ancient Hawaiian stone workers. Finally, you'll come to the telescopes, housed in domed white buildings that resemble huge igloos. The **W.M. Keck Observatory**, *Tel. 885-7887, open Monday to Friday, 10am to 4pm; no admission charge*, houses two ten-meter telescopes - the world's largest - and the only visitors gallery. (This is also where you'll find the summit's only public restrooms.) Watch the 12-minute video, then examine the displays, and telescopic equipment.

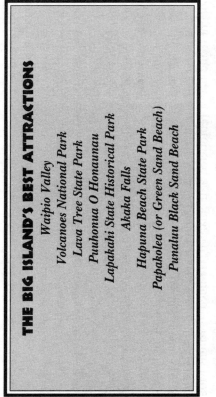

THE BIG ISLAND'S BEST ATTRACTIONS

Waipio Valley
Volcanoes National Park
Lava Tree State Park
Puuhonua O Honaunau
Lapakahi State Historical Park
Akaka Falls
Hapuna Beach State Park
Papakolea (or Green Sand Beach)
Punaluu Black Sand Beach

From the stone age to the space age, Mauna Kea spans the development of humankind.

Kailua-Kona & the Kona Coast

Although it caters primarily to tourists, the lively town of **Kailua-Kona** is a pleasant place to spend some time. Most of its low buildings are found along the mile or so segment of oceanfront Alii Drive between Hotel King Kamehameha Kona Beach in the north and the Royal Kona Resort in the south. Many of its boutiques and restaurants are housed in a variety of shopping arcades (some rather atmospheric). Visitors wander in and out of stores selling island specialties such as macadamia nuts, jewelry made from coral and shells, billowy color-splashed muumuus, guava jelly and lilikoi (passion fruit) jam, ceramic chimes and, of course, gourmet Kona coffee grown in surrounding plantations.

IF YOU'VE GOT THE TIME...

As in other tourist areas in the state, beware of the Kailua-Kona booths disguised as information and activities centers that are actually time-share sales counters. They'll offer free excursions or discounted luaus in exchange for sitting through a two-hour-plus hard-sell presentation at the time-share resort.

A prime al fresco perch for lunch or evening sunset watching is the waterfront Kona Inn, with its peacock chairs, Oriental rugs, ceiling fans and rich wood paneling. In August, Kailua-Kona is mobbed by anglers taking part in the Hawaiian Billfish Tournament and the Hawaiian International Billfish Tournament. October lures hundreds of muscled bodies to compete in the Ironman World Triathlon Championship, which begins in town. However, Kailua-Kona also offers several attractions that played important roles in Hawaii's history.

Alii Drive is shaded by immense gnarled banyan trees with dripping shoots, and branches that reach all the way across the street. This area was once the summer haunt of Hawaiian royalty. For a trip into the regal past, visit ocean-front **Hulihee Palace**, *75-5718 Alii Drive, Kailua-Kona, Tel. 329-1877; open 9am to 4pm daily; admission: $5 for adults, $4 for seniors, $1 for children.* Made of coral and lava, this two-story palace stands in a beautiful setting at the edge of Kailua Bay.

It was built in 1838 for Johan Adams Kuakini, governor of the island. Over the decades, many members of Hawaiian royalty spent several months a year relaxing at this vacation home. King David Kalakaua later bought it and had it remodeled and enlarged. He filled its rooms with Victorian furniture, imported rugs, and delicate china. After its new owner died in 1914, the palace fell into ruin. The Daughters of Hawaii, a group of women whose foreparents had been Hawaii's first American missionaries, convinced the territorial government to buy the building. In 1927, the Daughters themselves took over its restoration and turned it into the museum it is today.

Along with feather work and kapa cloth, much of Hulihee's original furniture is on display. Its prize pieces include a table inlaid with nearly two dozen different kinds of native wood and an artfully carved four-poster bed whose posts once resided in Kamehameha's grass palace. It is clear from the size of some of the chairs how large Hawaiians were. Kamehameha I is thought to have been nearly seven feet tall. Both Queen Kamamalu and rotund Princess Ruth Keelikolani were said to have been a towering six feet. The missionary influence is apparent in the architecture and furnishings.

Just across the street, **Mokuaikaua Church**, *Kailua-Kona, Tel. 329-0655*, built by missionaries, is the oldest Christian church in Hawaii. This house of worship symbolizes the merging of two cultures: The lava stones in its walls came from an old heiau that was no longer in use. Founded during the 1820s, it was completed in 1837 by the original group of New England missionaries. Inside, be sure to take a look at the model of the Thaddeus, the ship on which these Americans arrived, and the copy of the writings of one of the missionary wives explaining how she felt about her new life.

With its commercial lobby shops, Hotel King Kamehameha stands on the site of **Kamakahonu**, the king's royal compound. Nearby **Kailua Pier** is the departure point for yacht charters, glass-bottom-boat cruises, sunset sails, submarine sightseeing rides, parasailing and fishing charters. The catch is sometimes weighed here at the end of the day, most often during fishing tournaments. Local fishermen still cast their lines or nets from the seawall along Alii Drive, where vendors often sell hats, bags, mats and other lauhala weavings.

At the entrance to **Kailua Bay**, look for the totem pole-like tiki of restored **Ahuena Heiau**, *adjacent to King Kamehameha Beach Hotel, Kailua-Kona; arrange tours through the hotel, Tel. 329-2911.* From 1813 until his death in 1819, Kamehameha I ruled the Hawaiian kingdom from this restored thatched-roof structure. The surrounding area was reserved for the residences of his wives and close relatives. Ahuena Heiau was constructed to honor the god Lono. Whether it was used for human sacrifice is open to debate. However, there is no question that Liholiho, Kamehameha's son and the person who would become Kamehameha II, studied here, learning all about politics, navigation, fishing, sailing, and farming.

When Kamehameha the Great died at this heiau, his body received the traditional rites of passing: it was placed in a pit where the flesh was cooked off the bones and buried. So that no one could steal the great leader's *mana* (spiritual power), the bones were hidden (somewhere in North Kona). When the first missionaries arrived aboard the *Thaddeus* in 1820, they found the heiau in shambles. After the king's demise, it had been trashed by jubilant crowds when Liholiho, who had become Kamehameha II, had declared the ancient Hawaiian gods and their restrictive *kapu* (taboo) system null and void. The missionaries were more than happy to step in with their own brand of religion.

If you're staying at a hotel or condo with cooking facilities, locals say you'll find the best grocery prices at the supermarkets on Palani Road.

Scenic, flourishing **Holualoa**, 2,000 feet above Kailua-Kona on a mountain slope, is known for its art galleries. The road winds back and forth past beautiful vegetation up to this peaceful town, with its small

BIG ISLAND WALKING TOURS

Leaving stories about their lives for posterity, ancient Hawaiians carved stick figures in the lava flows throughout the islands. Hawaii's most extensive petroglyph fields *are found in South Kohala and North Kona, some on the grounds of resorts. Tours can be arranged through Kona Village Resort, Tel. 325-5555, Mauna Lani Resort, Tel. 885-6622, and the Royal Waikoloan Hotel, Tel. 885-6789, among others.*

You can also take the free **Walking Tour of King's Trail,** *a historical ramble that begins in front of the Pavilion at King's Shops, Waikoloa Beach Resort, on Saturdays at 8am. Wear sturdy shoes with heavy soles. To get to know Downtown Hilo, purchase a walking tour map (about $2) from the* **Lyman House Memorial Museum, Tel. 935-5021.**

wooden churches and flower-bedecked homes. In addition to other buildings, an old house has been converted into an art showplace. Although many of the artists are from the mainland, there is also a great deal of Hawaiian art on display, from calabashes to pick boards (large serving trays used at luaus). You'll also find block prints and oil paintings depicting old legends, carved ivory silver and brass jewelry, and fabrics tie-dyed with island-style designs.

The artists' workshop in **Holualoa Coffee Mill** is closed on Mondays, but other galleries are open then. In its earlier incarnation, the flourishing art workshop here was a dilapidated coffee plantation. Today classes are offered inside. Old wooden buildings in this plantation town have been given new life as galleries, such as the **Kona Art Center**, *Tel. 322-2307, Tuesday to Saturday, 10am to 4pm*, **Studio Seven**, and **Kimura's Lauhala Shop**. About 1,300 feet above sea level and resting on the slopes of Hualalai volcano, Holualoa now vibrates with creativity.

About a mile south of Kailua-Kona, you'll come to **Magic Sands Beach** (also called **Disappearing Sands** and **White Sands**), next to tiny St. Peter's Catholic Church. The beach is so named because, during the winter, the tides wash it away. The swimming and snorkeling are okay here in the summer, but a better beach for these pursuits — except when the surf is high — is **Kahaluu Beach Park**, farther on. Throngs of people pack the sand and pavilion on weekends.

As Alii Drive continues south, the profusion of flowers is spectacular, with peach, fuchsia, yellow, white, and orange blossoms bordering the road. This is where you'll see some of the area's more upscale hotels and condominiums. Beaches remain scarce, but swimming pools and green lawns artfully landscaped into the craggy black lava coast make up for the lack. In **Keauhou** ("kay-OW-hoe-oo," meaning "New Beginning"), transportation is available from area accommodations to **Keauhou Shopping Village** and **Keauhou-Kona Country Club Golf Course**.

In Honalo, the **Kona Daifukuji Mission**, a picturesque Buddhist temple, reminds visitors of Hawaii's multi-cultural heritage. The **Kona Historical Society Museum**, in nearby Kealakekua, gives some background on this rural village that has turned to business and banking. At **Kealakekua Bay**, a monument honors Captain James Cook, the first European to arrive in these islands. This fish-packed cove is a popular snorkeling site for catamarans and other pleasure boats.

Inland, the road winds through coffee country, along the lower slope of Mauna Loa volcano. Hawaii is the only part of the US where coffee is grown commercially. Stop at the **Royal Kona Coffee Mill Museum** and have a steaming cup. Highway 11 cuts through fertile land, with many different kinds of trees along the road: macadamia nut, wide-leafed breadfruit, mango, and tall skinny papaya.

BLACK GOLD

It was 1825 when coffee – soon to be Hawaii's black gold – first found its way to the islands, along with a sad cargo. The coffee plants, picked up during a stop in Brazil, arrived at Kona on the British warship that was carrying the bodies of King Kamehameha II and Queen Kamamalu. The royal couple had been visiting London when they both caught measles and died. First the coffee was planted in Manoa Valley on Oahu. Then, in 1828, farmers tried it on the Big Island. Kona's dry climate provided perfect conditions and it flourished as never before. Large-scale coffee growing eventually fell victim to rising labor costs, droughts, and dropping world coffee prices. Then in the late 1970s, people around the globe began developing a voracious taste for gourmet coffee, and the market began to soar once again.

At Kahikolu Church overlooking Kealakekua Bay are the remains of Henry Opukahaia, who convinced the first missionaries to come to Hawaii from New England. At the Hikiau Heiau place of worship, Captain Cook was honored as a god, which Hawaiians believed he was when he turned up in 1778. Also in the area is **St. Benedict's Painted Church**, a small gothic building on a hill with a view of the South Kona coast. At the turn of the century, a Belgian priest painted all the Biblical scenes that adorn the walls and ceilings to teach Christianity to Hawaiians, some of whom did not know how to read.

On the waterfront, **Puuhonua O Honaunau,** *Honaunau, Kona Coast, south of Kailua-Kona, Tel. 328-9877; admission: $2; Visitor Center open 7:30am to 5:30pm daily; popular with picnickers and fishing enthusiasts, the park remains open until midnight,* provided religious and political asylum for 12th century Hawaiians.

For ancient Hawaiians, kapu governed everything from dietary habits and sexual relations to land ownership. These taboos were believed to be divine will, and going against the gods could have far-reaching consequences for all Hawaiians. Therefore, the punishment for transgressors could be severe – often death. However, people who broke these sacred laws could be spared if they reached Puuhonua O Honaunau before being caught. Refugees were protected here by the *mana* (spiritual power) that remained in the bones of the dead chiefs who were buried in nearby *heiau* (temples). Through a ceremony performed by a *kahuna* (priest), the lawbreaker would be absolved of all guilt.

This refuge is adjacent to the ancestral home of the Kamehameha line. After a fight with Kamehameha I, Kaahumanu, his number one wife, is said to have hidden from him at Puuhonua O Honaunau, only to be given away by the barking of her pet dog. As usual in their tempestuous relationship, the loving couple finally made up. The land remained in the hands of Hawaii's royal family until the late 19th century, when it was bought by Charles R Bishop. Also called Place (or City) of Refuge, this 180-acre site — the most revered of Hawaii's religious sanctuaries — was restored and turned into a national historic park in 1961.

Sights include the Kaahumanu stone (where the regent hid during her tiff with Kamehameha), a reconstructed heiau, old-style thatched roof *hale* (houses), burial caves, a stone for playing *konane* (a royal game something like checkers), a royal fishpond, and a royal canoe landing. Be sure to wear sturdy shoes if you plan to walk through the lava fields to see the petroglyphs. Exhibits cover various aspects of ancient life, and traditional skills and crafts are demonstrated by staff members. Over the weekend closest to July 1, a three-day cultural festival is held in the park. Transformed into royalty, the staff is decked out in elaborate feather capes and helmets. Vacationers are invited to try their hands at lei making, lauhala weaving, poi pounding, and tying fishing nets. They can even help pull in a load of fish. Young folks particularly enjoy the La Paani festival, held the first Friday in February and November, during which local school children compete in Hawaiian games such as spear throwing, dart sliding, and arm wrestling.

Ka'u & Ka Lae (South Point)

Much of the land is desert in the **Ka'u** region, the southern portion of the Big Island. However, **Manuka State Park**, near the lower end of the Kona Coast, flourishes with an arboretum and its trails wind through greenery. Picnic pavilions make this a relaxing stop. **Ka Lae** (South Point), with its unusual green sand beach, is the southernmost tip of the United States. (It's about 1-3/4 hours drive from Kailua-Kona.) As Hawaiians have always believed, historians have concluded that this is the part of the archipelago where the ancient Polynesian settlers first stepped ashore. Some experts say that these original inhabitants arrived between A.D. 700 and 750, while others point to evidence that indicates they were here as early as A.D. 300 or even A.D. 150.

The Kamehamehas were frequent visitors to Ka Lae. Kamehameha I spent a great deal of time fishing for ahi here, while Kamehameha II enjoyed surfing off the point. When Kamehameha I fought (and won) a vicious battle with Keoua, the high chief of Ka'u, warriors and civilians alike hid in the lava tubes that ran between their village and the ocean. Now Ka'u is sparsely populated, but in its heyday, more people lived here than anywhere else in the island chain. Just 30 miles offshore, by the way, a new volcanic island, Loihi, should break the ocean's surface in a few thousand years.

For exploring the area, you'll fare best in a four wheel drive, but a regular car will do. About six miles west of Naalehu, a narrow road branches off Highway 11. This road heads south for 12 bumpy miles to Ka Lae. Along the way, you'll pass herds of cattle, horses, and a wind farm that generates electricity by taking advantage of the air's constant motion. Trees grow at right angles, bent by the wind.

Papakolea (or **Green Sands Beach**) is about a 60-minute hike from where the road ends by the boat yard at the water's edge. While four-wheel-drive trails will take you closer than the road, you'll still have to walk the last part. But if you've never seen olivine crystals before, it's worth the trek. At the bottom of a cliff, these green grains were created when the fiery lava from an 1886 eruption of Mauna Loa surged into the chilly ocean.

The green sand, the multi-hued blue of the Pacific, and the orange earth create a vibrant collage. Unfortunately, strong currents generally make the water dangerous for swimming. Fishing for tuna, on the other hand, is almost as popular here as it was in the old days. Ancient fishermen knew how to prevent their canoes from being carried away by the rough tides. They tied the boats to ropes that were secured in holes in the rocks on shore. Some contemporary anglers continue this practice.

Ka'u was used by the US Army during WWII. Along with environmentalists and archaeologists, residents of Ka'u are overwhelmingly against the proposed building of a space center in this historic area. They believe it would be dangerous to their health and safety and that it would interfere with a prime fishing site. Proponents of the spaceport say it could bring hundreds of jobs to this economically depressed region, but residents are convinced that these highly technical positions would be filled by outsiders anyway. Whether or not the space center is given the go-ahead, there will be some industrial development in Ka'u, such as a facility that makes organic fertilizer from algae. There are also plans in the works for constructing two large resort hotels in the area.

If you fancy the idea of being in the boonies, book a room at the **Shirakawa Motel** in Waiohinu. Look for **Mark Twain's monkeypod tree.** The original, planted by Twain in 1866, lost a battle with a 1957 storm. However, a new tree grew from its roots. Colonial-style **Kauahaao** Church dates back to the 19th century. Flat, pretty **Naalehu**, a former sugar plantation town nearby, is backed by scenic hills. Several handsome churches are clustered in this tiny town. Stop at a food stand here for *malasadas*, Portuguese hole-less doughnuts. Or watch bakers at work at **Punalu'u Sweetbread Bakeshop and Visitor Center,** then sit in the garden to eat a sandwich made with the bread. Although Naalehu is known as the most southern town in the US, you won't hear any drawls, but you'll sense the hospitality.

A thrill for many visitors is stretching out under a palm on the coal black sands of **Punalu'u Beach**, just northeast. If you'd like to spend some time in this area, try the **Seamountain at Punalu'u** condominiums. On a hill overlooking the village here, a small church honors Henry Opukahaia (the same man commemorated in Napoopoo), who urged the missionaries to bring Christianity to Hawaii. In the early days, the *kauwa* (enslaved class) were kept in an area near Punalu'u. To distinguish them from everyone else, they were forced to wear tattoos around their eyes or on their foreheads. From Punalu'u to Hawaii Volcanoes National Park Visitor Center, the drive is about 30 minutes.

Hawaii Volcanoes National Park & the Hilo Area

Whether you're coming from Hilo or the Kona-Kohala Coast, plan at least a full day for a trip to **Hawaii Volcanoes National Park**, *Volcano (the southeast)*, Tel. 985-6000 (general information, updates on eruption activity, camping, and weather from recorded messages); admission: $10 per car, $5 for bikers and hikers - keep your receipt, it is good for re-admission for one week; Visitor Center open 7:45am to 5pm daily; Park open 24 hours a day, year round, maps are available at the gate. Many vacationers camp out or spend a night or two in nearby inns or Bed & Breakfasts. The park is interlaced with 150 miles of hiking trails and scenic drives. You'll be more comfortable during the short hikes and walks if you've brought bottled water along, especially in the summer.

A national park since 1916, the island's most visited attraction takes up over 344 square miles, encompassing Kilauea and Mauna Loa volcanoes. More than two million people pour into the park each year, the majority arriving when eruptions are in progress. The terrain ranges from moonlike craters, steaming fire pits, and hissing fumaroles to thick rain forest. Picnic grounds, camping cabins, and 150 miles of hiking trails and scenic drives lure vacationers to this otherworldly landscape, about 4,000 feet above sea level. Note that at night temperatures can dip into the 40s.

Kilauea's caldera alone is two and a half miles long, two miles wide, and 400 feet deep. If you only have a day or several hours to spend in the park, take the 11-mile **Crater Rim Drive**, the park's main attraction. You'll

---

VOLCANIC HOTEL & GOLF COURSE

Volcanos National Park even boasts a golf course and a hotel. During a visit here, Mark Twain quipped, "The surprise of finding a good hotel in such an outlandish spot startled me considerably more than the volcano did."

see Halemaumau (the 300-foot-deep fire pit inside Kilauea), where Pele, the hot-tempered volcano goddess, is believed to live. Kamehameha II abolished the islands' restrictive religion in 1819. However, many Hawaiians continued to worship the old gods, even after American missionaries arrived the following year and began converting people to Christianity. In 1824, Queen Kapiolani, who had readily converted, decided to prove to those who had not yet embraced Christianity that Pele did not exist. She stood at the rim of Halemaumau and ate some red *ohelo* berries, known to be sacred to the goddess, without offering any to Pele first. When the queen was not struck down on the spot, she told her people that this showed that there was no such thing as Pele, or any other Hawaiian god.

Yet some contemporary Hawaiians maintain that Pele continues her wandering, sometimes in the form of a wizened old woman, other times as a beautiful girl with flowing hair. From politicians and business people to educators and reporters, residents have told of sightings of a mysterious woman just before eruptions. Thus, many people take very seriously the warning not to remove any rocks or volcanic sand from Hawaii, lest they anger the powerful goddess.

Kilauea's longest recorded series of eruptions began on New Year's Day of 1983. In early April, lava swept away the first house to be destroyed by the volcano in a quarter century. By the end of that year, more than a dozen homes and hundreds of housing lots had been smothered by the flow. After witnessing an eruption of the 4,090-foot Kilauea, Mark Twain remarked, "I have seen Vesuvius since, but it was a mere toy, a child's volcano, a soup-kettle, compared to this." Mauna Loa got in on the act in 1984, the first time it had erupted in nine years, and the first time both volcanoes had performed together in 65 years. Lava oozed onto the highway in 1986. Early the following year, just two months after the highway had been rebuilt, the road was swallowed by lava once again – to the delight of tourists with cameras. Highway 11 cuts through the park, and has been aptly named **Chain of Craters Road**, where you'll see old sections of the highway that were partially covered with lava.

During a fiery 1989 eruption, the former visitor center went up in smoke and a new one had to be built. By July of 1990, the lava flow had destroyed most of the town of Kalapana and eventually swallowed up famed Kaimu Black Sand Beach. A trucking company volunteered to move the historic Star of the Sea Painted Church, whose walls and ceilings are covered with colorful religious murals done in 1931. Luckily, town residents were safely evacuated.

Along **Devastation Trail**, you'll see the serious damage hot volcanic ash did to a dense rain forest. The trail along the boardwalk (15 minutes each way) takes you through a vast expanse of what looks like charcoal dust strewn with sun-bleached branches that were stripped of their bark by bursts of volcanic debris. Ohia trees and other new vegetation have begun to sprout up from the ashes. The trail ends at the edge of **Kilauea Iki Crater.** If you wish to walk only one way, have a companion drive here to meet you. Then he or she can walk back and be met by you at the other end. On the rim of Kilauea Crater, the **Thomas A. Jagger Museum,** *Hawaii Volcanoes National Park (three miles past entrance), Tel. 967-7643; no admission charge; open daily from 8:30am to 5pm,* displays the highly accurate seismographs used to pick up volcanic activity, even far below the earth's surface. You'll also see videos of Kilauea's eruptions and lava rocks that visitors are welcome to touch. **Halema'uma'u Overlook** is about a ten-minute walk away.

All this talk of destruction may make you hesitate to visit the park – or even the island for that matter. But bear in mind that, with a highly sensitive warning system, volcanic eruptions and the path of lava flows can be predicted. This means that sightseers are kept far away from any dangerous areas and homeowners are advised if they need to evacuate. Although a haze called vog (volcanic fog) hangs over the island during and after an eruption, this volcanic dust helps create some of the state's most dramatic sunsets (along the Kona-Kohala Coast).

CRATER POWER

It surprises many to learn that fatalities from Hawaii's volcanic eruptions have been few. Some of the last in recent history occurred in 1790, when a group of warriors battling Kamehameha I was wiped out by flying boulders, poisonous gases and fire. A hiking trail from the highway by the western edge of the park leads to an area where footprints of members of the retreating army can still be seen in the petrified lava.

Across the street from Volcano House (the current hotel) is **Volcano Art Center,** in a building that began life in 1877 as the park's lodge. The work of local artists sold here includes wood carvings, photographs, and paintings done on T-shirts, silk, and canvases. Within walking distance of Volcano House, you'll find **steam vents** and the yellow, sour smelling **sulphur banks.** About four miles from the hotel, take a brief stroll through a bird-filled rain forest thick with cushiony mosses and huge *hapua* ferns, their long stems tightly curled into spirals at the top. Then you'll come to gigantic **Thurston Lava Tube** and into a dense, ginger-scented fern forest. This cool, damp walk-through tunnel was created when hot lava continued to pour through an outer shell of cooled lava. Watch out for puddles.

A couple of miles west of the hotel, Kipuka Puaulu is a lush oasis that was spared by the surrounding lava. Also visit Tree Molds, which were formed when lava covered trees, burned them to ash, then cooled and hardened.

Volcano Winery, *35 Piimauna Drive, near the Visitor Center, Volcano, Tel. 967-7479 or 967-7772; open 10am to 5pm daily*, specializes in wines made from Hawaii's tropical crops. The tasting room is located in the gift shop. Fruity but dry Passion Chablis is blended from lilikoi (passion fruit) fermented with Chablis grape juice. While Lehua Blossom Honey Wine and Guava Chablis are both semi-sweet, Symphony is a light dry white.

With its small towns and coastal regions, **Puna**, in the east, is bright with anthuriums, orchids, ginger, and yellow *mamani*. While it also sprouts macadamia nuts, the district is best known for its delicious papayas. Here on the east rift of Kilauea volcano, **Wao Kele O Puna** ("Green Forest of Puna") is the last large tropical rain forest in the United States. One of the world's biggest geothermal power plants is under construction on forest land. The plant will use steam from below the erupting volcano to generate electricity. Worshippers of Pele – the goddess who Hawaiian tradition says resides in Kilauea's caldera – aren't the only people disturbed by the plan. Environmentalists believe it is ecologically dangerous (and unnecessary) to destroy any part of one of the world's scarce rain forests.

Ask a resident to direct you to **Kapoho**, where you can swim with green sea turtles in fish ponds. The brackish water is geothermally heated by fresh water being pushed up through the hot vents into the ocean. Some of the enclosures are natural, while others were constructed by human hands years ago.

Just over two miles from Pahoa, **Lava Tree State Park** is an eerie reminder of the power of Pele. In a 1790 volcanic eruption, lava surged through an ohia forest, leaving mounds, swirls, and rolls of lava that sparkle like iridescent crystal. Once lush with green leaves, trees trapped and ensnarled by molten lava are now bone dry and ghostly white. Branches stick out as if they tried to free themselves. Be careful of cracks and indentations while walking.

At **Cape Kumukahi**, the island's easternmost tip, you'll see the lighthouse that was miraculously spared by a 1960 flow. Now looking like rushing water that was suddenly frozen, the lava passed on both sides of the lighthouse without knocking it down. Directly south of Pahoa, palm-shaded Kaimu Black Sand Beach was once the island's most picturesque stretch of dark sand. However, this shore found itself in the direct path of a fiery lava flow in the early 1990s. Most of the town of Kalapana went up in flames. Fortunately, though, all residents were evacuated and the beloved **Star of the Sea Painted Church** was relocated.

The verdant rolling hills, flamboyant blossoms, carpet-like lawns, and grassy plains tell you that rain is no stranger to this side of the island. At the **Mauna Loa Macadamia Nut Orchard**, on the outskirts of Hilo, macadamia trees line one side of the long entry road and stately pines border the other. While touring the grounds, visitors learn how these fattening nuts are processed. Then they are invited to taste-test the different varieties before buying a can or two. When the sun cooperates, a colorful shimmering arc is caught in the mist at **Rainbow Falls,** *just off Waimeanue Avenue on Rainbow Drive, Wailuku River State Park, outside Hilo.* The best time to come is early in the morning. Just up the road, near Hilo Hospital, you'll come to **Boiling Pots**. These churning pools and series of cascades are created by the water rushing into large pits in the lava of the riverbed. The park here is a scenic spot for a picnic.

Thirty miles from Volcanoes National Park, **Hilo** is a quiet waterfront town with a handful of modest hotels. If you're driving along the highway from Volcanoes National Park between June and December, you'll be treated to a fragrant explosion of white and yellow ginger growing wild. Although most of Hilo's shores are rocky and its skies are more often gray than blue, its proximity to east coast attractions makes spending some time here worthwhile. The town does receive a lot of rain, but most of it falls either at night or in brief showers during the day.

HALTING FIRE

Had it not been for the bravery of Princess Ruth Keelikolani in 1880, Hilo might not exist today. Once when it seemed certain that the town would be overrun by lava from an eruption of Mauna Loa, the princess traveled all the way from Honolulu. Standing at the edge of the red-hot flow, she gave offerings to Pele and recited chants that had been passed down through the generations. In just a few hours, the liquid rock stopped moving.

Many of Hilo's easygoing residents are descendants of the Filipino, Japanese, and Chinese laborers who immigrated to work on the surrounding sugar plantations, once the foundation of Hilo's economy. In some of the cluttered, tin roof stores, merchants use abacuses instead of – or to double check – vintage cash registers. While cane fields remain, some have been replaced by macadamia nut farms and the omnipresent flower nurseries that bloom with orchids, anthuriums, and ginger. Visitors are welcome to tour the grounds of some of the nurseries and to buy inspected plants, cuttings, or seeds to mail to the mainland.

The cultural heart of the Big Island, Hilo is the site of the annual Merrie Monarch Festival, held each March or April at the Edith Kanakaole Tennis Stadium. Plays, concerts, and other local performances take place at the **University of Hawaii-Hilo** campus. The college, which has an art gallery, also sponsors periodic lectures and demonstrations on kapa making, lauhala weaving, and other Hawaiian traditions. Inquire about the annual courses in the school's Elder Hostel Program designed for senior citizens visiting from the mainland.

Most of Hilo's hotels are clustered along Banyan **Drive**, where the old Chinese trees, dripping hairy shoots, were planted by notables such as Amelia Earhart and Cecil B. de Mille during the 1930s. With huge leaves, all kinds of plants grow up the water tank-sized trunks of the banyans. Hilo draws many older vacationers, many of whom are often seen strolling along this scenic walkway. Although planes can be heard from the grounds of the hotels here, the noise isn't frequent or loud enough to be much of a nuisance.

A thick wall of coconut palms stands across from the stores along **Hilo Bay**, which is bordered by parks and gardens. In 1946, an Alaskan earthquake set off a *tsunami* (tidal wave) that quickly moved toward Hawaii. Traveling across the open ocean at perhaps more than 600 miles an hour, the series of waves slowed down — but grew in height — as the ocean floor rose toward shore. Gathering steam, the first wave suddenly sucked the water out of Hilo Bay. Some people ran into the dry seabed, delightedly scooping up the fish that had been stranded. Then, in a flash, the monster wall of water hit the shore. One hundred and fifty-nine people lost their lives and 163 were hurt. The *tsunami* also caused more than 25 million dollars in property damage. Another tidal wave struck Hilo in 1960. Today however, a very sensitive scientific warning system has been devised and is used throughout the state.

A small footbridge from Banyan Drive will take you across to tiny **Coconut Island** in Hilo Bay. Studded with palm trees, it's a popular setting for picnics and plain relaxation. Tranquil **Liliuokalani Gardens,** *on Hilo Bay, off Banyan Drive, Hilo,* is filled with Japanese-style pagodas, bridges, and ponds. Spend some time in the shade of a flat-topped monkeypod tree.

I love this tranquil park, especially early in the morning when the light is intense and shadows are long. In addition to a friendly lunch time bunch, the park attracts children who fish in the ponds with bamboo poles and local fishermen who catch *opae* (Hawaiian shrimp) with nets to use as live bait, as well as local wedding parties who come to have their pictures taken here. Although the park is named after Hawaii's last monarch, it was actually designed as a tribute to Hilo's first Japanese immigrants, who arrived as laborers in the sugar cane fields. A visit to Kyoto, Japan, inspired the haole plantation managers to build this artfully landscaped Japanese garden.

The many-tiered stone lanterns, one of them 10 feet high, were given to the park by Japanese officials in the early 1900s. In Asia, they were first used to illuminate evening religious services, then later found their way into private homes. A symbol of wealth, they were carved from granite or marble. These sturdy treasures were about the only part of the pond and bridge-filled park that was not washed away in the 1946 tsunami. The park was rebuilt, only to be swept away again in the 1960 tidal wave. Still, some of the stone lanterns remained intact, if mud-covered. In 1968, to commemorate the 100th anniversary of the Japanese presence in Hawaii, the government of Japan donated a wooden *torii* gate, two stone lion gates, and 13 more lanterns to the park.

FISHING ON DRY LAND

Early risers should check out Suisan Fish Market, at the edge of the Wailoa River near the Banyan Drive hotels. Every morning (except Sundays) between 7 and 8am, returning fishermen lay out glistening 50- to 100-pound ahi (yellow fin tuna) in neat rows along with other tropical fish. In Pidgin and at least a couple of other languages, they auction off their catch.

At **Wailoa State Park**, adjoining Suisan Fish Market, fishermen take to Waiakea Fish Pond in rowboats. Picnic tables and a shelter make this park a popular local hangout. At the octagonal **Wailoa Center**, on the grounds, you can see exhibits of the work of area artists. Visitor information is also available here. If you'd like to hear what the Hawaiian language sounds like, attend a service at **Haili Church** on Haili Street (sermons are also given in English). Built by Protestant missionaries from New England, it dates back to 1859.

Stop by the **Lyman Mission House and Museum**, 276 Haili Street, Hilo, Tel. 935-5021; admission (including guided tours): $5 adults, $2.50 children and seniors 60+; open 9am to 5pm Monday to Saturday, Sundays 1-4pm. Built in 1839, restored Lyman House was once the home of Hilo's first Christian missionaries, the Reverend David and Sarah Lyman. The museum next door, which opened in 1973, displays antiques from the days of Hawai'i's monarchy and items from the early 1900s. Some pieces date back to the time before Westerners arrived. In addition to Hawaiiana, exhibits also spotlight missionary life and the various ethnic groups that populated the islands.

The immense **Naha Stone**, which Kamehameha the Great is said to have moved as a teenager, stands in front of the Hawaii Public Library on Waianuenue Avenue. Beside it is the smaller **Pinao Stone**, which once guarded the entrance of a heiau. When the weather is right, locals head for **Onekahakaha Beach**, about three miles outside town, toward the eastern end of Hilo Bay. This is one of the area's few sandy shores.

Not many visitors know about the small **Panaewa Rain Forest Zoo**, *just south of Hilo, Tel. 959-7224; open daily from 9am to 4pm; no admission charge*, where a few animals native to the rain forest live in relatively natural settings. Peacocks have the run of the grounds. You'll also see the nene goose, Hawaii's rare state bird, and parrots, monkeys, African pygmy hippopotamuses, and a tapir. Neighboring the zoo is the **Panaewa Equestrian Center**, with its rodeo/racetrack and horse stables.

TWO SCENIC DRIVES

*The **Hamakua Coast**, between Hilo and the Waipio Valley Lookout, and the inland route along the **Kohala Mountain Road**, Highway 250, between Waimea/Kamuela and Hawi, including the Pololu Valley Lookout.*

The Hamakua Coast & Waipio Valley

The lush, rural **Hamakua Coast** is one of the island's most stunning regions. If you'd like to explore it at a leisurely pace, consider staying at one of its small accommodations near **Honokaa**. Several good curio and antiques shops have cropped up in this sleepy town. You can approach Hamakua from the Kohala Coast or from Hilo. About six miles north of Hilo, you'll come to **Old Mamalahoa Highway Scenic Drive** (off Highway 19), after passing through endless fields that melt into the verdant mountains. This four-mile stretch is bordered by royal palms, poincianas, breadfruit and African tulip trees. Flourishing ravines come into view and bridges span rocky streams. The road passes weathered sugar plantation towns, with old-fashioned movie theaters, tin-roofed houses, and wooden-frame churches. Stop at the bluff that gazes down on **Onomea Bay**, with its distinctive rocky formations.

If you'd like to visit **Hawaii Tropical Botanical Garden**, *Onomea Bay, off the Four-mile Scenic Drive, Hamakua Coast just north of Hilo, Tel. 964-5233; open 8:30am to 5pm; admission: $15 adults (tax deductible), children under 16 free (no credit cards for admission)*, get your ticket (or any visitor information you might need) at the little yellow church. From here, you'll ride down in a van. Formerly privately owned, this non-profit nature preserve in a tropical rain forest is filled with birds, marine life, jungled vegetation, streams, and waterfalls. The bright heliconias, bromeliads, and ginger are particularly striking. The garden sprawls along a craggy ocean coast. The flat trails are easy walking; insect repellent and umbrellas are provided.

At the Honomu Plantation Store, old photographs will give you a glimpse of what Hamakua once looked like. This is a good place to pick up fresh pineapples, Kona coffee, or macadamia nuts. You can even have your loot mailed to the mainland. At nearby **Akaka Falls State Park,** *ten miles north of Hilo, near Honomu Village,* water plummets more than 400 feet over a volcanic cliff. If it's a choice between Rainbow Falls and these cascades, make this 66-acre park your destination. A long (sometimes steep) trail winds up and down through a thick rain forest, with towering bright yellow bamboo stalks, banyan trees and flowers. Before you reach the main falls, you'll pass mini-cascades that flow under bridges. Benches are placed at strategic locations for rest stops.

Especially in the late-afternoon sun, **Laupahoehoe Point** is a beautiful spot. Its name means "leaf of lava," and indeed this is a narrow lava peninsula that is lapped by the Pacific. Local families enjoy barbecues in the stone pits here. Picnic tables and shelters are also provided. At the edge of the water is a monument to the 20 schoolchildren and their teachers who were killed here by the 1946 tidal wave.

Just beyond Paauilo, you'll come to flourishing **Kalopa State Park,** another good picnic locale. On the slopes of Mauna Kea, this 600-acre recreation area is filled with sweet-smelling eucalyptus, ohia trees, and koa forests. Camping facilities and cabins are on the premises. The drowsy town of **Honokaa,** with its Western-front buildings, is the king of macadamia nut production. Hawai'i's first macadamias were planted here back in 1881. More nuts come from this town than from anywhere else in the world. If you haven't yet seen how they're prepared for your palate, visit the **Hawaiian Holiday Macadamia Nut Co.** and munch on the free samples.

One of my favorite places in all of Hawaii is **Waipio Valley,** cupped by 2,000-foot cliffs. Kamehameha the Great (Kamehameha I) spent his formative years here. Located just northwest of Honokaa, it can be reached from both the Hamakua and Kona-Kohala Coasts (a 90-minute drive from either Hilo or Kona). At six miles long and a mile wide at the shore, this is the island's largest valley. In its heyday, 40,000 people called it home. Now, barely a few dozen live here, most of them taro farmers. A visit here makes an invigorating day trip.

Rental cars or private vehicles are not allowed beyond **Waipio Lookout.** Therefore, unless you head into the deep valley on foot, you'll have to pay someone to take you down the bumpy, nearly vertical entry road. Jeeps are the most popular mode of transport. Contact the **Waipio Valley Shuttle,** *Tel. 775-7121.* Your driver will tell you all about the passing sights, including old legends, ancient uses for plants and flowers, and the formation of the gorgeous black sand beach. Other enjoyable ways to see the valley are on a mule-drawn wagon with **Waipio Valley Wagon Tours**, *Tel. 775-9518*, $40 for adults, children half-price; and on horseback through **Waipi'o Na'alapa Trail Rides**, *Tel. 775-0419*, $78 for adults, $68 for children aged 8 to 14.

Down below, the roads are rocky riverbeds, bordered by aromatic jasmine and ginger, mango and guava trees, taro fields and edible fern shoots. You might catch a glimpse of wild horses. By the **black sand beach**, look for the white naupaka flowers that also grow in the mountains. Half the petals of each blossom seem to be missing. Legend has it that these flowers were once lovers whose families forbade them to marry, banishing one to the seashore and the other to the mountains.

While the ocean is too rough for swimming here, it's fine to take a dip in the fresh-water stream that bisects the ebony beach. (However, don't take a drink without first boiling the water for at least five minutes.) A narrow waterfall pours down one of the cliffs. The beach, scattered with driftwood, is backed by pines. Arrive early enough and you might see local surfers in action. If you'd like to absorb the valley's beauty slowly, camp out overnight.

NIGHTLIFE & ENTERTAINMENT

Days on the Big Island are far more active than nights. What little after-dark frivolity there exists mainly in Kailua-Kona, at bars and restaurants. Some hotel lounges in Kailua-Kona, Keauhou, and Kohala have Hawaiian singers and musicians or recorded entertainment, but it is generally on the low-key side. Most visitors follow the lead of locals and either *holo-holo* (move from place to place, bar hop) or turn in early.

Hula

If you're planning to vacation in early April, consider attending the **Merrie Monarch Festival**, *Tel. 935-9168*, the state's most important hula competition, which takes place over several evenings in Hilo. Both modern and traditional hula and chanting are performed. This event is named for King David Kalakaua, called the Merrie Monarch for his efforts in resuscitating the hula and other Hawaiian traditional arts that had been prohibited by New England missionaries. You'll need to order tickets months in advance. See also *Special Events*, below.

At **Banana Bay Restaurant**, *Tel. 329-1393*, in Uncle Billy's Kona Bay Hotel in Kailua-Kona, one free hula show is presented Saturday and Sunday at 6pm. At **Uncle Billy's Hilo Bay Hotel**, *Tel. 961-5818*, you can stop in for a hula show any night of the week.

Luaus

For the island's most authentic luau, make reservations (as many days in advance as possible) at **Kona Village Resort**, *Tel. 325-5555*, on the Kona Coast, just north of Keahole Airport. The plentiful food, musical show, and surroundings sweep visitors into the past. Some topped with thatched roofs, Polynesian *hale* (cottages housing guest rooms) stand on stilts above black lava flows or at the edges of beaches or lagoons. This special event takes place on Friday nights.

On Fridays, there's more action at **Hilton Waikoloa Village**, *Tel. 885-1234*, north of Kailua-Kona. More than 700 people are invited to this feast and Polynesian show. Next door, the **Royal Waikoloan**, *Tel. 885-6784*, hosts Sunday and Wednesday night dinner shows featuring a local hula *halau* (hula group). Guests even have an opportunity to purchase local crafts from artists who demonstrate their skills.

If you'd prefer a luau in Kailua-Kona, try the Monday, Friday, or Saturday affair at the **Royal Kona Resort**, *Tel. 329-3111*, or the feast at **King Kamehameha's Kona Beach Hotel**, *Tel. 329-2911*, Sunday, Tuesday, Wednesday, and Thursday.

Local Hangouts & Happenings

KONA INN, *Kona Inn Shopping Village, Kailua-Kona, Tel. 329-4455*.

This open-air waterfront restaurant is almost as popular for nightcaps as it is for meals. Ceiling fans, rich wood paneling, and peacock chairs enhance the pleasant atmosphere.

HUGO'S, *75-5828 Kahakai Street, Kailua-Kona, Tel. 329-1493*.

Overlooking a rocky shore, this restaurant is popular for drinks, especially around sunset.

KAHILU THEATRE, *Kamuela/Waimea, Tel. 885-6017*.

Entertainment ranges from local plays and Broadway musicals to hula groups, European classical dance troupes, performances of the Honolulu symphony, and jazz musicians and singers from Hawaii and the mainland. Check local newspapers to see what's doing when.

UNIVERSITY OF HAWAII-HILO, *Hilo, Tel. 933-3310*.

Check local newspapers for shows at the school theater, which sometimes feature international performers.

ECLIPSE RESTAURANT, *75-5711 Kuakini Highway, Kailua-Kona, Tel. 329-4686*.

Stick around after dinner and you can work off those calories on the dance floor (beginning at 10pm). The tunes are big-band on Sunday evenings and pop the rest of the week.

Special Events

One of Hawaii's most popular annual events is the **Merrie Monarch Festival**, a week-long celebration culminating with a three-day hula competition. It is held in Hilo during the week before Easter. Those who don't purchase their tickets far enough in advance (usually several months ahead) must be content to watch the graceful evening performances on television. The festival also includes free activities such as midday hula shows; a parade with floats and marching bands; a Hawaiian cultural fair with crafts, music and food booths; and displays of Hawaiian quilts, artifacts, historic photographs, and antique furniture.

The program is named for Hawaii's last king, David Kalakaua, dubbed the Merrie Monarch for his love of the arts and of having an all-out good time. During his 1874 to 1891 reign, he was largely responsible for bringing back the hula and other Hawaiian traditions that had been banned by American missionaries. They believed that the expressive body and hand movements were too sexually suggestive.

When this festival began during the 1960s, only women's *halau* (hula groups) competed. The event soared in popularity after a men's hula division was added in 1976. (Men, by the way, were the original dancers of hula in ancient Hawaii.) Today, it features both *kahiko hula* (ancient) and *auana hula* (modern) styles, accompanied by *mele* (ritual chants). Some halau spend years on the waiting list to participate.

While most groups are from the various Hawaiian islands, some come all the way from the mainland. Throughout the year, visitors on all islands should keep an eye out for any fundraising luaus hosted by hula halau to cover the cost of the costumes, leis, food, and transportation they'll need to take part in the festival. These luaus tend to be more down to earth than the more commercial affairs hosted by hotels and other tourist-oriented groups.

Vacationers can immerse themselves in more Hawaiiana at the **Puuhonua O Honaunau National Historical Park Annual Cultural Festival**, held in June and July. In June, in addition to the **Kamehameha Day Parade** in Kailua-Kona, there is also a celebration in Hawi (North Kohala) during which the statue of King Kamehameha I is draped with a multitude of long, colorful leis. Other festivals that highlight hula, lei-making, music, and Hawaiian games include the August happening at **Puukohola Heiau** on the Kohala Coast; **Aloha Week**, a major island-wide celebration in late September or early October; and the Annual **West Hawaii Makahiki Festival**, based on an ancient peace and harvest-time event, in Keauhou-Kona in October.

Famous for its beautiful blossoms and other vegetation, Hilo hosts **Annual Orchid Shows** in June and July, the annual **Big Island Bonsai Show** in July, and the **Annual Hawaii Horticulture Association Show** in late June. In November, the annual **Kona Coffee Festival**, held in Kailua-Kona, honors the harvest of these famous beans.

There are many Big Island events for those who like watching or participating in sports. In July, Mauna Kea Beach Hotel is the place to be for the Annual **Pro-Am Golf Tournament**, held on one of the world's top courses according to Golf Digest and other golf magazines. Complete with paniolos, Parker Ranch is the site of the **Rodeo and Horse Races** on July 4th and a **Round-Up Rodeo** in September.

More than 200 people race a mile through churning waves in the **Hapuna Rough Water Swim** held on the Kohala Coast in July. At Honokohau Harbor, just outside Kailua-Kona, men and women begin a three-mile outrigger race during the Annual **Kai E Hitu Long Distance Canoe Race** in August. More than 1,200 athletes from all 50 states and dozens of other countries compete in the rigorous 2.4-mile swim, 112-mile bike ride, and 26.2-mile marathon during the annual **Ironman World Triathlon**, which begins in Kailua-Kona in October.

Many competitions revolve around one of the Big Island's most cherished sports: fishing. The July **Kona Ahi Jackpot Fishing Tournament** and the **Light Tackle Tournament** take place in Kailua-Kona. In Kailua-Kona in August, during the annual **Hawaiian Billfish Tournament**, American teams are chosen for the annual week-long **International Billfish Tournament**, the island's most celebrated angler's competition, held later that month. In both events, fishing enthusiasts race to spots where they think they'll find the greatest number of marlin and yellowfin tuna.

ANGLING FOR LUCK

For good luck, some anglers still carry on the ancient traditions of bringing Hawaiian salt tucked securely in a ti leaf and ensuring that no bananas have found their way on board.

Every afternoon (around 4 or 5pm), the catch is weighed before a crowd of spectators at the pier by the King Kamehameha Hotel or at the Fuel Dock. Parades and parties are part of the festivities. Toward the end of August, children can get in on the act during the **Annual Keiki Fishing Tournament**, also in Kailua-Kona.

Celebrating Hawaiian Regional Cuisine, the annual summer **food and wine festival** at the Orchid Mauna Lani is a big hit. Cuisines of the Sun at the Mauna Lani Bay Hotel and Bungalows are popular winter culinary events.

SPORTS & RECREATION

Like everything else on the Big Island, sports come in a wide variety. Hawaii is renowned for its excellent deep-sea fishing, particularly for marlin and tuna, along the Kona Coast. Anglers come from all over to attend the annual **Hawaiian International Billfish Tournament**. Kailua-Kona is the mecca for water sports enthusiasts.

On land, hiking, camping, and biking are popular pastimes among both visitors and residents. Spectator sports are also plentiful. In October, the island plays host to the **Ironman World Triathlon Championship**. Periodically, and rodeos take place on Parker Ranch.

Beaches

From the black sand beaches of the southeast coast to the green sand of Ka Lae (South Point), the shores of the Big Island are true wonders of nature. These coasts also have their share of white sand beaches. Hapuna, on the Kohala Coast, is one of the most attractive on the island, perhaps even in the whole state. While Hawaii has many beaches, not all of them are easy to get to, and some are not calm enough for swimming. To step on Papakolea (or Green Sand Beach), for instance, you'll need a four-wheel-drive and some sturdy shoes for a three-mile hike. The water here is better for fishing than for cooling off. However, there are more than enough accessible (and swimmable) sandy stretches for any vacationer.

Although many hotels and condominiums are clustered in Kailua-Kona and Keauhou, most beaches are along the Kohala Coast, where resorts are plusher and far more spread out. In geographical order (starting in the north and moving counter-clockwise), here are my picks for the island's nicest beaches:

Waipio Valley Black Sand Beach, *Hamakua Coast*

Bisected by a stream, this beach is one of Hawaii's ebony strips that were created when hot lava hit the cold Pacific. Because the waves can be strong here, the safest swimming is in the pond where the stream joins the sea. Small, smooth rocks are scattered near the water's edge and driftwood lies bleaching on the black sand. A **waterfall** pours down a steep oceanfront cliff. You are likely to have this spot to yourself. The few people who do come here are mainly locals and, early in the morning, surfers. You can hike the nearly vertical road into the lush valley, take the Waipio Shuttle, which departs not far from the Waipio Valley Overlook, or arrange to visit through a tour company.

Keokea Beach Park, *North Kohala*

The pleasant drive along a winding road takes you past private homes, a graveyard, and a bright green pasture. When you reach the park, you'll see red cliffs set off by verdant vegetation and electric blue water with frothy, white surf. One covered picnic area is elevated, affording a panoramic view of the rocky cove. During the summer, the water is calm enough for snorkeling and fishing. Locals often gravitate here on weekends. In addition to a campsite at the water's edge, the park has restrooms and showers.

Mahukona, Northern Kohala

Don't look for sand here. Instead, you'll have a grassy expanse that is great for picnics and a good view of the island of Maui from the rocky shore. I met a man here who had been camping his way around the Big Island and said that this was one of his favorite spots. (Restrooms and fresh water are provided.) Scramble over the rocks and you'll find some good swimming, snorkeling, and scuba diving in these waters (during the summer only, though).

Lapakahi Park, Northern Kohala

After wandering around the partially restored remains of an ancient fishing village, strong swimmers, snorkelers and scuba divers will enjoy cooling off in the often rough water here. The shore is rocky. Restrooms and fresh water are on the premises.

Spencer Beach Park, Kohala Coast

Overlooked by Puukohola and Mailekini, the remains of two of the island's most important **heiau** (temples), this white sand beach is just north of the Mauna Kea Resort. Since it is protected by reefs, its waters are good for swimming. Camping is permitted and there are restrooms, fresh water, a paved volleyball court, tennis courts and a red-roofed pavilion for parties and picnics.

Kauanoa Beach, Kohala Coast

The presence of the Mauna Kea Beach Hotel does not detract from the beauty of this ivory curve. Like all of Hawaii's beaches, this one is open to the public. However, the hotel has its own beach facilities. During the winter when the surf is high, stick to the sand for sunbathing and other dry pursuits.

Hapuna Beach State Park, Kohala Coast

Some people consider this Hawaii's most gorgeous beach. Although its white sands certainly draw a fair number of swimmers, snorkelers, scuba divers, and sun worshipers, it is rarely crowded. The water is calmest during the summer. Rocky outcroppings enclose the half-mile stretch. At the northern end, where it looks as if the beach stops, find the shallow hidden cove. Children enjoy splashing in the tidal pools here.

Puako, *Kohala Coast*

Take a dirt road down to this white sand beach where kiawe trees provide shade. In the northern section, you'll find rewarding **snorkeling** around the tidal pools. A 20-minute walk leads to the petroglyphs off Puako Road.

Anaehoomalu, *Kohala Coast*

The nearby Hilton Waikoloa Village may have all the glitz, but the older, more sedate Royal Waikoloan hotel has the best beach. Picturesque Anaehoomalu is bordered by ancient fishponds that were reserved for the *alii*. Commoners had to fish in the ocean. Bathers are welcome to rent equipment here for windsurfing, sailing, scuba diving, snorkeling and surfing.

Honokohau, *just north of Kailua-Kona*

Adventurers will enjoy following the dirt path north of the harbor and beyond the dock that leads to this secluded beach. Lava rock covers much of the shore, but there are sandy patches here and there. Wander around the crumbling remains of ancient fishponds. You'll find an inland freshwater pool at the end of a trail that begins in the northern part of the beach.

Magic Sands (a.k.a. *Disappearing Sands or White Sands*) *Alii Drive, between Kailua-Kona and Keauhou*

Called by whatever name, the white sands of this beach come and go with the tides, often vanishing completely in the winter. Near petite St. Peter's Catholic Church, this is one of the island's best offshore **snorkeling** sites. To be caught in a swarm of fish, snorkelers bring frozen peas to feed them. Don't wear jewelry while swimming or leave it on your towel. Even when it appears calm, the water can be rough enough to separate you from your rings and chains. And waves can suddenly wash across your sunbathing spot. Local young men consider this a prime place for diving for tourists' jewelry. One resident told me he found a gold ring that brought him $5,000! When not in the water, people stretch out on the smooth black lava rocks or play volleyball.

Kahaluu, *Alii Drive, between Kailua-Kona and Keauhou*

These rocky salt and pepper sands draw many locals on weekends. The swimming and snorkeling (in only three to six foot depths) are fine during the summer, but the surf is high in the winter. **Green sea turtles,** an endangered species, are sometimes spotted here. Restrooms and fresh water are provided. This beach is next door to Keauhou Beach hotel.

Old Kona Airport Beach, *Kailua-Kona area*

Just offshore, intriguing coral configurations can be seen at depths of 40 to 60 feet. Snorkelers and scuba divers enjoy this beach, but plain swimming is better elsewhere. There is, however, a small sandy cove with placid tidal pools that are good for entertaining children. Restrooms and fresh water are on the premises.

Kealekekua Bay, *just south of Kailua-Kona*

This is the target for most of the Big Island's snorkeling cruises and glass-bottom boat trips. Indeed, the marine life is varied and plentiful. Bring some frozen peas or dog biscuits, and you'll have schools of fish nibbling from your hands. Scuba diving is also popular in this area. Now a marine preserve, this is the place where Captain James Cook, the first known European to arrive in Hawaii, was killed on February 14, 1779. A monument stands in his memory. There really isn't a beach here, just a rocky coast and vegetation. The best way to approach this site is from the water.

Ke'ei, *just south of Kealakekua Bay, Kona Coast*

Beside the village of Ke'ei, this salt and pepper strand gives way to shallow waters. The swimming is fine here and the **snorkeling** is even better. After taking the road that leads to Kealakekua Bay, turn left at the bottom of the hill. Drive another half-mile, then make a right onto a road through a lava flow and continue another half-mile to the shore.

Puuohonua O Honaunau, *south of Kailua-Kona, Kona Coast*

Climb into the bay at the Place of Refuge from the boat ramp near the park complex. Both the scuba diving and snorkeling are good here. Many people combine a swim with a visit to the exhibits at this fascinating historic park that once provided sanctuary for ancient Hawaiians who broke *kapu* (taboos).

Hookena, *South Kona*

The sand is steel-colored at this beach that is good for swimming during most of the year. The two-mile road to the shore is steep and slim, so drive with caution. Near the end of this street, the gas lampposts have been standing since the early 1900s. When Mark Twain visited the island during the 1860s, more than 2,000 people lived in the settlement here. Today the village could hardly be more quiet. Restrooms and fresh water are provided at the beach.

Papakolea or Green Sand Beach, Ka Lae (South Point)

The unusual color of the sand comes from the olivine crystals created in volcanic eruptions. This beach is one of the most difficult to get to on the island. After driving about an hour and 45 minutes from Kailua-Kona, you'll turn off the highway for 12 more miles to the boat yard where people leave their non-four-wheel-drive vehicles. Cupped at the bottom of steep cliffs, the petite cove is about an hour's hike from here. A four-wheel-drive will get you closer, but you'll still have a good walk.

The kelly green sands make an especially dramatic sight from above. However, your first thought will probably be, "How will I ever get down there?" Some people find the steplike section of rough, black lava boulders on the side or the smooth terraced rock at the back of the beach and climb down. Others slide down the nearly vertical sandy wall at the back. Whichever route you take, be careful! Even when there are others around, people often strip down to their skin in this beautiful, secluded spot.

Note that there's no shade here and the inviting waters can be dangerous for swimming.

Punaluu Black Sand Beach, Ka'u, southeast coast

These picturesque pitch-black shores are overlooked by the Sea Mountain condominiums, which have tennis courts and a golf course. In the adjacent beach park, you'll find picnic and camping facilities. **Turtles,** which you'll see swimming off-shore, lay their eggs in the dark sand. The currents are often too strong for swimming. Walk *mauka* (inland) and you'll come to fish ponds and remnants of a heiau.

Kamoamoa Black Sand Beach, southeast coast

One of the world's newest beaches, this half-mile black beauty was born during volcanic eruptions that took place between January and April of 1988. Here you'll see a recent example of how flaming lava explodes into tiny fragments when it meets the cold water.

Kalapana/Kaimu Black Sand Beach, Kalapana, Puna area, southeast coast

Before Kalapana/Kaimu was covered by a lava flow, this beach was popular among locals for fishing and surfing. Now it is an example of the power of a volcano. **Kamoamoa** (see above), a new black sand beach, was created by the eruption that obscured Kaimu. You win some, you lose some!

Onekahakaha Beach Park, Hilo

About three miles from Hilo, this calm white sand beach draws many picnicking families. It's probably Hilo's most popular scenic swimming beach. The shallow depth (only one to four feet), sandy ocean bottom, and calm water protected by a breakwater make it a great spot for children. Lifeguards are on duty and facilities include pavilions, showers and restrooms.

James Kealoha Beach Park, Hilo

This park borders a rocky bay that opens directly to deep waters. While this can be a great spot for snorkeling, fishing, and surfing, the water can be very rough and there's a powerful rip tide. People enjoy stretching out on the smooth, flat lava rocks. The calmest area, where you'll see a few pockets of white sand, is near Scout Island, close to the lifeguard station.

Richardson Beach Park, Hilo

Packed with coral, sponges, reef fish, eels, and octopi and visited by dolphins, this marine reserve is an excellent **snorkeling** site. The shallow bay area at the center of the shoreline is where you'll see the most colorful underwater scenery. Lifeguards are on duty every day.

Reeds Bay Beach Park, Hilo

Lapped by tranquil waters, this beach is known for its Ice Pond, fed by chilly **freshwater springs**. Restrooms and showers are on the premises.

Coconut Island, Hilo

Overlooking Hilo Bay, with Mauna Kea in the background, these palm-shaded shores are frequented by picnickers. A small bridge from Banyan Drive will take you to this isle.

Biking

Many people who really like to keep in shape hit the roads on two wheels. *Wearing helmets is highly recommended.* Guided excursions range from a week to 10 days. A company specializing in biking and hiking tours is **Chris' Adventures,** *Tel. 326-4600.* For rentals, try **Dave's Bike & Triathlon Shop,** Tel. 329-4522; **B & L Bike and Sports,** *Tel. 329-3309;* and **Hawaiian Pedals,** *Tel. 329-2294,* all in Kona.

Also try **Mauna Kea Mountain Bikes,** *Tel. 885-2091,* which offers rentals and guided tours (mainly downhill) that include a visit with llamas ($70 per person for a group of four; $65 for groups of five to 13).

Camping

Camping on the Big Island is best from June to October. The state and county parks have some beautiful beachfront and mountainside campsites. One of my favorites is lush **Waipio Valley,** with its black sand beach backed by cliffs. People can also camp in alternately stark and flourishing **Hawaii Volcanoes National Park**. In remote **Mauna Kea State Park**, you can rent wooden cabins with flush toilets and showers. There's an incongruous telephone booth sitting in front of one of the buildings. Outside, you'll also see nene geese (Hawaii's state bird) in barbed-wire pens along with Layson ducks, one of the world's rarest ducks. Also on the slopes of Mauna Kea, **Kalopa State Park** is filled with nearly extinct koa trees, eucalyptus, and ohia. These 600 acres of camping and hiking grounds are located two miles south of Honokaa on the Hamakua Coast.

Although the shore is covered with lava rocks and boulders instead of sand at **Mahukona State Park** in Kohala, this campsite makes a peaceful setting. Another good place to spend the night surrounded by nature is **Punaluu Beach Park**, known for its glistening black sand beach.

For permits and further details, contact the **Division of State Parks**, *75 Aupuni Street, Hilo, HI 96720, Tel. 808/974-6200*, or the **County of Hawaii Department of Parks and Recreation**, *25 Aupuni Street, Hilo, HI 96720, Tel. 808/961-8311*.

Cruises

Many adults enjoy the dinner/moonlight sails run by **Captain Beans' Cruises**, *Tel. 329-2955*. Vacationers depart from Kailua-Kona on a 142-foot Polynesian-style sailing canoe, complete with a live band, dancing, and open bar.

Another good company to try for dinner cruises is Fair Wind Sail, *Tel. 322-2788*, based in Keauhou-Kona, which uses a 50-foot catamaran.

Fishing

The Kona Coast is famous for its deep-sea fishing. While tournaments are held on the Big Island throughout the year, the August Hawaiian International Billfish Tournament, centered in Kailua-Kona, is the star attraction.

Some of the Big Island's best fishing spots are off the beach at Samuel M. Spencer Beach County Park; off Kailua Pier in Kailua-Kona; in Kealakekua Bay; offshore at Napoopoo Beach County Park; and at Punaluu Beach County Park.

For fishing charters, try **Blue Hawaii Sportfishing**, *Tel. 322-3210*, **Kona Charter Skippers Association**, *Tel. 329-3600*, **Medusa Sport Fishing**, *Tel. 329-1328*, all based in Kailua-Kona, **Kona Marlin Center**, *Tel. 326-1177*, in Honokohau, or **Cheers Sportfishing**, *Tel. 329-6484*.

Boats are available year-round for marlin fishing. Most depart from Honokohau Harbor, not far north of Kailua-Kona. Prices begin at about $140 per person sharing with up to six people, for a full day. More luxurious craft can set you back anywhere from $500 to $750. Half-day charters are also available. For further information about half- and full-day fishing charters, contact **Kona Activities Center**, *Tel. 329-3171 or 800/367-5288 from the mainland*, or **The Charter Locker**, *Tel. 326-2553*.

Golf

Particularly along the Kona-Kohala Coast, where black lava flows provide a wonderful contrast with the green swards, this island has some of the state's most appealing courses. *Golf Digest* rates the **Mauna Kea Beach Golf Course**, *Tel. 882-7222*, on the Kohala Coast, among the world's best. All with ocean or dramatic mountain views — sometimes both — the Big Island's other courses aren't far behind. The **Hapuna Golf Course**, on the Mauna Kea Resort, was named "The Most Environmentally Sensitive" in the state by the US Golf Association. The 18-hole Jack Nicklaus course at the **Hualalai Golf Club**, *Tel. 325-8000*, is one of the Big Island's newest. The Francis I'i Brown Golf Course at the **Mauna Lani Resort**, *Tel. 885-6655*, also in Kohala, is another award-winner.

Waikoloa sports three beautiful courses. The first two were designed by Robert Trent Jones, Jr.: the **Waikoloa Village Golf Course**, *Tel. 883-9621*, on the mauka (mountain) side of the road, and the **Waikoloa Beach Golf Course**, *Tel. 885-6060*, adjoining the Hilton Waikoloa Village and the Royal Waikoloan hotels. The third course, the **King's Course**, *Tel. 885-4647*, is also at the Hilton Waikoloa Village.

In the Keauhou-Kona area, there's the **Kona Country Club**, *Tel. 322-2545*. It comes as a surprise to many visitors that there is even a course in Hawaii Volcanoes National Park: **Volcano Golf and Country Club**, *Tel. 967-7332*. In Punaluu, known for its black sand beach, you'll find the **Sea Mountain Golf Club**, *Tel. 928-6222*, on the grounds of a condominium development.

Greens fees are lowest at Hilo's **Naniloa Country Club Golf Course**, *Tel. 935-3000*, and **Hamakua Country Club**, *Tel. 775-7244*, a nine-hole course in Honokaa. There is also **Waimea County Club**, *Mamalahoa Highway*, *Tel. 885-8053*, an 18-hole course.

Helicopter Rides

If Kilauea (the most active of Hawaii's two active volcanoes) is erupting and you can afford it, take a helicopter tour above Hawaii Volcanoes National Park. You'll hear the bubbling, crackling, and hissing, and see red hot fountains of lava and ribbons of the fiery molten rock flowing from the crater. Actually, with its steaming pits, lunar terrain, and pockets of rainforest, this park is pretty spectacular even when the volcanoes are quiet.

All helicopter companies offer variations on the following routes: Kilauea or Mauna Loa (the island's second active volcano); the Kona-

Kohala coastline, the town of Kamuela/Waimea, Parker Ranch, the Hamakua Coast, Waipio and Waimanu Valleys, black sand beaches, and remote white-sand coves. In the north, you might hover near sheer cliffs pocked with an ancient burial cave that still contains skulls and bones.

Some flights combine the Kona Coast with a whirl above Puuhonua O Honaunau (Place of Refuge), Captain Cook Monument and Kealakekua Bay, and Hawaii Volcanoes National Park. Prices range from about $100 for a 30-minute ride to $300 for two hours. Shop around for the best deals. Some companies add a $5 per person National Park surcharge for volcano flights.

Volcano Heli-Tours, *Tel. 967-7578,* is based right at the volcano. This company includes a brief video on the latest eruption. **Kenai,** *Tel. 882-1851 or 969-3131,* departs from both Kailua-Kona and Hilo. If you're staying on the Kohala Coast, consider **Mauna Kea Helicopters,** *Tel. 885-6400,* which lifts off from Waikoloa.

Hiking

Hiking trails lead through virgin valleys, lava fields, and dense wilderness. Routes range from the rugged to the relaxing. Many footpaths cut through **Hawaii Volcanoes National Park.** Since lava can be thin, brittle, and wickedly sharp in places, you should be sure to stick to marked trails. The four-mile hike across the floor of Kilauea Iki, a dormant crater, isn't difficult. The lava beneath your feet will feel warm, even though it's rock hard. Trail maps and other information are available at the Hawaii Volcanoes Visitor Center.

I love hiking in green **Waipio Valley.** Try the six-mile trail that leads from the black sand beach to the back of the valley. If you're in really good shape, you might attempt the trail over the hill to the next valley, where hunters kill wild boar. The trails in **Pololu Valley** should also be reserved for the extremely fit. Beginning at Pololu Valley Lookout, one walk lasts about 10 hours and will take you through several neighboring valleys. With its colorful botanical garden, **Manuka State Park,** in south Kona, is good for more easygoing hiking.

Horseback Riding

Arrange to horseback ride on expansive **Parker Ranch,** in Waimea/Kamuela, by calling the **Mauna Kea Stables,** *Tel. 885-4288.* This is the *only* way you can ride on Parker Ranch. You'll go through wooded trails bordered by wild flowers, pass herds of cattle in pastures, and see cinder cones that seem to have fallen out of the sky onto the flat land. Rainbows aren't uncommon in this misty region. The distant hills come in endless shades of green.

Kohala Na'alapa Trail Rides, *Tel. 889-0022*, leads scenic trail rides in the Kohala Mountains for $75 per person. For a 2.5-hour ride through the Kohala Mountains, contact **Paniolo Riding Adventures**, *Tel. 889-5354*, at Ponoholo Ranch, on Kohala Mountain Road in Kamuela/Waimea; this trip will run you $85 per person.

WAIPIO VALLEY ON HORSEBACK

An unforgettable Big Island experience is seeing remote Waipio Valley with **Waipi'o Na'alapa Trail Rides**, *Tel. 775-0419; $78 for adults, $68 for children ages 8 to 14. Don't forget your camera. During the scenic ride, your guide will tell you all about the history, legends, facts, and folklore of the Big Island in general and the valley in particular. In a van, you'll descend the steep, winding dirt road and pass through the river to reach the valley floor where your horse will be waiting for you.*

You'll clippity-clop through waist-deep irrigation canals and past rushing streams. Waterfalls tumble hundreds of feet from mountainsides. Since the majority of the (few) people who live in the valley are taro farmers, you'll see plenty of plots where this root (used to make poi) is grown. Your guide will point out all kinds of vegetation, including jabon trees, which bear a fruit that's a cross between an orange and a grapefruit. Be sure to have a taste. You might also spot wild horses and rare birds such as the koloa. Mid-way through the ride, you'll come to the black sand beach that gleams like satin in the sun.

Parasailing

To float in the air while suspended from a parachute that is tied to a moving boat, contact **Kona Charter Skippers Association**, *Tel. 329-3600.*

Plane Rides

For a flight-seeing trip in a modern plane, try **Big Island Air**, *Tel. 329-4868* or, from Neighbor Islands and the mainland, *Tel. 800/303-8868.* Some tours concentrate on the Big Island, while others give bird's eye views of the rest of the chain.

If you'd rather get a feel for the early days of flight, book a seat on a reproduction of a 1935 WACO bi-plane through **Classic Aviation**, *Tel. 329-TOUR*, or, from inter-island and the mainland, *Tel. 800/695-8100.* Before taking off, each passenger is dressed in a white scarf, cloth helmet, and goggles. Be sure to bring your camera so you can have your portrait shot in front of the plane. Sitting cozily side-by-side in the open cockpit, passengers wear headphones so that they can speak to and hear the pilot as he provides a running commentary on the sights below. Flying seven days a week, Classic Aviation conducts tours of the volcano beginning in Hilo and tours of the Kona-Kohala Coast from Kona. Note that because of Hilo's mercurial weather, tours in that area are often rescheduled. Those along the Kona-Kohala Coast are a great way to pick your next hotel or beach. Lasting from about 40 to 80 minutes, flights range in price from $100 per person for a 40-minute trip to $175 for an 80-minute aerobatic tour.

Sailing

Most of the time when people are on boats around the Big Island, they are there to snorkel, scuba dive, or fish. The majority of pleasure boats that depart Kailua-Kona are headed to Kealakekua Bay for snorkeling excursions. If you're interested in half- or full-day sailing charters, contact **Kona Charter Shippers Association**, *Tel. 329-3600*, or **Pacific Blue Charters**, *Tel. 329-9468*.

Scuba Diving

Diving is most rewarding for those who are certified. Various operators offer three- to five-day PADI courses for about $125 a day for group lessons. Underwater exploration is concentrated along the Kona Coast. Try **Mauna Kea Divers**, *Tel. 883-9298*; **Big Island Divers**, *Tel. 329-6068*; **King Kamehameha Divers**, *Tel. 329-5662*; **Kona Coast Divers**, *Tel. 329-8802 or 800-KOA-DIVE from the mainland, Fax 808-329-5741*; or **Fair Wind Sailing and Diving Adventures**, *Tel. 322-2788*.

Snorkeling

Big Island fish are especially friendly when you come bearing gifts of bread or frozen peas. The Kona-Kohala Coast is great for snorkeling. **Kapaa Beach Park** in northern Kohala is one of the best places for swimming among multi-colored coral and other marine life. The waters of Kona's **White Sands Beach** (a.k.a. Magic Sands or Disappearing sands), which vanishes in the winter, are always teeming with many different kinds of tropical fish.

Several outfits, such as the fun-filled **Fair Wind catamaran**, *Tel. 322-2788*, and **Captain Cook Cruise**, *Tel. 326-2999*, take snorkelers to the crystal waters near the Captain Cook Monument at Kealakekua Bay. If you're lucky, a playful school of porpoises will swim along as you sail. Winter vacationers are sometimes treated to the sight of whales.

Other good sail/snorkel operations include **Snorkel Bob's**, *Tel. 329-0770*, **King Kamehameha Divers**, *Tel. 324-5662*, and **Kona Charter Skippers Association**, *Tel. 329-3600*. Sea adventures and ecosystem talks at the Marine Preserve are offered by **Captain Zodiac Raft Expeditions**,

Tel. 329-3199, along with snorkeling at Kealakekua Bay, where Captain Cook was killed in 1779. Whale watching is part of winter excursions.

If a bouncy ride in a rubber raft that zips in and out of sea caves is more your style, contact **Captain Zodiac Batting Expeditions** or **SeaQuest Rafting Adventures**, Tel. 322-3669.

Snow Skiing

Some winters (when there's enough snow) experienced skiers can whoosh down the slopes of Mauna Kea volcano. Although conditions are best in February and March, **Ski Guides Hawaii**, Tel. 885-4188, is open from around December through April, depending on Mother Nature. This company provides four-wheel-drive transportation, skis, warm clothing, and other gear. The cost begins at about $150 per person, including lunch.

Spectator Sports

One of Hawaii's biggest spectacles is the **Ironman World Triathlon Championship**, held each October. When it began in 1978, only 15 people (all men) entered the biking/swimming/running competition and only 12 of them finished. Now based in Kailua-Kona, this event draws nearly 2,000 male and female athletes each year.

Thousands of people also watch the **Hawaiian Canoe Races** that take place during the spring through fall season, when various clubs compete for the championship. Call Parker Ranch, Tel. 885-7655, to find out about the periodic **rodeos** hosted here.

Submarine Rides

I'd only recommend a dip with **Atlantis Submarine**, Tel. 329-3175 or 800/548-6262, if you're not planning to snorkel or scuba dive during your vacation, or if you take it during the winter when you might spot whales. These trips are expensive: $70 to $100 for adults; $40 for children; luau and sub or bi-plane and sub packages run $100 to $160 for adults and $50 to $120 for children. A slew of colorful fish — zebra-striped Hawaiian sergeants, monogamous butterfly fish, yellow tangs, balloon-like puffer fish, blue-striped snapper — swim right up to the portholes.

However, the fish swarm around not because of plant-life (which is scarce) but because they are drawn to feeding stations (net bags) anchored to coral reefs (or to the scuba divers you can watch feeding them during some trips). In other words, beyond the fish, there isn't much marine life to see along the path of the sub. The Atlantis descends from 40 to 60 feet. It's capable of going down to 150, but the scenery isn't particularly exciting at that depth. The boat that takes passengers to the sub leaves from Kailua Pier, by King Kamehameha Hotel Kona Beach (which is where people sign up for the trip).

Surfing

Mainly a local sport on the Big Island, surfing is popular off shores including **Kalapana Black Sand Beach**, where there's an area called Drainpipes that has huge waves; **Leleiwi Beach; Old Airport Beach; Punaluu Beach Park;** and **White Sands** (a.k.a. Magic Sands or Disappearing Sands). The waves at both Leleiwi Beach and **Hookena Beach Park** are great for bodysurfing.

Tennis

Tennis buffs may choose among scores of courts, especially along the Kona-Kohala Coast. Players aren't charged a fee at **Kailua Playground,** convenient to the Kailua-Kona area. Both guests and non-guests may play at no cost on the courts of the **Royal Kona Resort** and the **Racquet Club at the Kona Surf** hotel. A small fee is required to play at the **Royal Waikoloan, Waikoloa Village, King Kamehameha's Kona Beach and Sea Mountain Resort.**

In Hilo, there's a minimal charge to play at **Hilo Tennis Stadium** and **Waiakea Racket Club.** Free courts are found at Lincoln Park.

Note that while many of the larger hotels have tennis courts, some allow only their guests to use them.

Whale Watching

Especially between December and April, you can catch glimpses of these massive creatures that migrate to Hawaii from cooler climes. Some tour companies take sightseers on jeep excursions to elevated vantage points while others take people out on the sea. Try **Kona Charter Skippers Association,** *Tel. 329-3600,* $36 for 3 hours, or **Whale Watching with Captain McSweeney,** *Tel. 322-0028,* $46 for 3 1/2 hours. You can book other ocean or land whale watching tours through hotel activity desks.

If you'd like to strike out on your own, two good places for sightings are the Francis I'i Brown Golf Course on the grounds of the Mauna Lani Resort on the Kohala Coast and the tip of North Kohala. While humpbacks are seen from December to April; other whale-watching trips are year-round.

Windsurfing

Anaehoomalu Bay, where the Royal Waikoloan and Hilton Waikoloa Village hotels are located, is loved by board sailors for its perfect winds and waves.

Working Out & Spas

All on the Kona-Kohala Coast, the Orchid at Mauna Lani, Hilton Waikoloa Village, Mauna Kea Beach Hotel, Hapuna Beach Prince Hotel, Mauna Lani Resort, Kona Village, and Four Seasons Hualalai have good exercise rooms and/or health spas.

SHOPPING

Stores on the Big Island are concentrated along Alii Drive in **Kailua-Kona** and most of these are geared toward tourists. Although you won't be rubbing elbows with many locals, some poking around will introduce you to intriguing boutiques with distinctive wares. Many stores in town stay open until 7pm or even 9pm to catch the dinner crowd. The Kings shopping center of restaurants and boutiques is quite popular.

Resorts along the **Kona-Kohala Coast** boast some wonderful (and expensive) boutiques and art galleries. I've tried to resist, but I've ended up with gorgeous hand-painted silk dresses and scarves, funky handmade earrings, and colorful bathing suits with matching shorts and tops from stores at these hotels.

Other upscale shops snag passersby in **Kamuela/Waimea**, selling everything from gourmet cheeses to bowls and sculpture made of rare native woods. In recent years, some worthwhile curio and antiques shops have sprung up in the quiet town of **Honokaa**, on the Hamakua Coast.

The Big Island, by the way, is one of the best places in the state to find crafts made of island wood. The omnipresent **ABC Drug Stores** offer excellent prices for a variety of items, while being very overpriced for others. So shop carefully, keeping your eyes peeled for sales.

Here are some of the places that have made the greatest impression on me:

Shopping Malls

The **Parker Ranch Shopping Center** in Kamuela/Waimea, *Tel. 885-7178*, is where you'll find the Parker Ranch Visitor Center and nearly three dozen stores (selling everything from clothing and gifts to groceries and magazines). Stop by the **Parker Ranch Store**, *Tel. 885-5669*. This complex, patronized by locals, is not to be confused with the smaller, newer **Parker Square**, *Tel. 885-7178*, which has a fine collection of boutiques. Stop in at **Waimea General Store**, *Tel. 885-4479*, which sports an eclectic mix of Japanese *yukata* bathrobes, cookbooks and yarn, among other items. Another good place to wander around in the neighborhood is **Opelo Plaza.**

Since tourism does not have a major presence in residential Hilo, prices here are lower than in resort communities. The multi-million dollar **Prince Kuhio Shopping Plaza**, *Tel. 959-3555*, which remains open until

9pm on Monday to Friday, is one of the largest malls in the state. This is where you'll find **Liberty House**, Hawaii's answer to Macy's; and many smaller stores. **Kaiko's Mall**, *Tel. 935-3233*, counts J.C. Penney among its stores. **Hilo Shopping Center**, *Tel. 935-6499*, also has a wide selection of places to spend money.

Aloha Wear

Before you head to more commercial **Hilo Hattie's** (with branches in both Kailua-Kona and Hilo), and try **Cottage Crafted in Hawaii**, at Kailua-Kona's Kona Inn Shopping Village, which sells handpainted muumuus, shorts, and shirts; **Liberty House** department store in Hilo's Prince Kuhio Shopping Plaza, *Tel. 959-3555*; the lobby of **King Kamehameha's Kona Beach Hotel**, on the main drag in Kailua-Kona; or **Sig Zane's**, *Tel. 935-7077*, in Hilo, which specializes in fabrics and aloha shirts in original patterns and hula costumes for the town's annual Merrie Monarch Festival. Hilo's **Hana Hou**, *Kalahaua Street*, *Tel. 935-4555*, stocks a good selection of men's and women's vintage Hawaiian shirts, along with dresses in washable silk, in addition to distinctive crafts.

Art Galleries

Some of the island's most imaginative artwork is found in the galleries in **Holualoa**, a lush mountain town high above Kailua-Kona. The main workshop is housed in a renovated coffee plantation. **Holualoa Gallery** and **Studio 7**, *76-5920 Mamalahoa Highway, Tel. 324-1335*, are good places to find Big Island artistic works.

At the **Gallery of Great Things**, *Tel. 885-7706*, in Kamuela/Waimea, goods come from Hawaii, Asia, and the Pacific, including baskets imported from the Philippines and Japanese antiques. Another place worth a visit for art and antiques is **Upcountry Connection Gallery**, *Tel. 885-0623*, in Kamuela. Also see *Crafts* and *Koa Wood Products*.

Beach Wear

Some of the most attractive sportswear can be found at shops in the snazzy hotels along the Kohala Coast, but be prepared for hefty prices. Stores in Kailua-Kona are a bit easier on the wallet. Stop at **Island Life**, in the Kona Inn Shopping Mall, for T-shirts, and nearby **At The Beach** for better quality swimsuits and sportswear with unique designs, plus ethnic pottery, and lots of fish collectibles.

See also *Distinctive Clothing*.

Crafts

One of my favorite haunts for all kinds of Hawaiian-made goods is **Cooks Discoveries**, *Tel. 885-3633*, in Kamuela/Waimea. This shop is housed in the distinctive two-story Spencer Hotel building, where both Princess Ka'iulani and Robert Louis Stevenson stayed.

To find locally-made jewelry as well as items made on other islands, paintings, and knickknacks, some made by senior citizens, visit **Kona Arts and Crafts,** *Kailua Bay Inn Shopping Plaza, Kailua-Kona, Tel. 329-5590.* Try **Kohala Kollection,** *Kawaihae Center, Kohala Coast, Tel. 882-1510,* for jewelry, sculpture, paintings, pillows, woodcarvings and ceramics. In rooms next door, browse among the antique furniture and antique Hawaiian etchings, rare prints, and lithographs, some from the 18th and 19th centuries.

For hats, bags, and other items woven from pandanus fronds, stop at **Kimura Lauhala Shop,** *Tel. 324-0053,* in Holualoa, an upcountry town just *mauka* (inland) of Kailua-Kona. **Alapaki's Hawaiian Things,** *Tel. 322-2007,* in the Keauhou Shopping Village, carries woodwork and jewelry. **Originals by Oscar,** *Tel. 322-6767,* in the same mall, sells Niihau shell necklaces, made of the tiny rare shells found mainly on the remote island of Niihau.

In Hawaii Volcanoes National Park, **Volcano Art Center,** *Tel. 967-7511,* has an extensive display of koa wood bowls and cutting boards, hand-painted cotton T-shirts, unusual hand-made jewelry, paintings, ceramic wind chimes, books for children and adults, chopsticks made from various kinds of wood, and color-splashed *pareus* (a.k.a. sarongs).

The unique Hawaiian floral patterns on the clothing, cushions, bedding and other items sold at Hilo's **Sig Zane Designs,** *122 Kamehameha Avenue, Tel. 935-7077,* are handscreened by a husband and wife team. Worthwhile crafts are also sold in Hilo on Mamo Street across from the Saturday and Wednesday morning **farmer's market** on Kamehameha Avenue; Saturday is the best day to go, since you'll find more merchandise. For a variety of unusual knickknacks and other items, stop by **Peavian Logic,** *Tel. 961-6885,* on Keawe Street.

See also *Art Galleries, Koa Wood Products,* and *Beach Wear.*

Distinctive Clothing

For everything from the latest fashions in bathing suits and sportswear to evening wear, browse through the many shops at the hotels along the Kona-Kohala Coast - that is, if you're heavy on cash! You'll find more affordable prices at **Noa Noa,** *73-4776 B Kanalani, Alii Drive;* or at *King's Shops, Tel. 329-2337;* at the *Kona Inn Shopping Village, Tel. 885-5449,* which specializes in hand-painted cotton clothing and bags for women. All imported from Bali, the dresses, pants, blouses and satchels here come in a variety of eye-catching prints.

In Hilo, **Kristina Lilleeng,** *Tel. 961-0838,* sells beautiful yet functional women's clothing made from natural fibers and unusual fabrics. Each item is one-of-a-kind and custom alterations can be made on the day of purchase.

Flowers

The Hilo area is the flower capital of the island — perhaps of the state. Visitors are welcome to browse through several flower nurseries, where they can arrange to have inspected blossoms sent to the mainland. Among them are **Akatsuka Orchid Gardens**, *Tel. 967-7660 or 967-8234*, off Highway 11, 22 miles outside Hilo; and **Nani Mau Gardens**, *Tel. 959-3541*, within the town. Children love feeding the fish in the natural tide pools at Hilo's **Big Island Tropical Gardens**, *Tel. 961-6621 or 800/278-8005*, $4 entry fee, where the gift shop sells leis and other blossoms.

Hawaiian Quilts

Inspired by nineteenth-century American missionaries, Hawaiian women began making distinctive quilts of their own. The contemporary versions may be expensive (anywhere from several hundred to several thousand dollars), but these time-consuming artistic bed covers and wall hangings are extremely attractive and durable.

At **Waimea Design Center and Art Gallery**, *Tel. 885-6171*, in Kamuela/Waimea, wall hangings and baby quilts run about $675, while you'll pay from about $2,500 to $3,500 for a queen- or king-sized quilt. Because the work is so intricate, commissioned quilts can take from six to 24 months. With the help of her brother, **Kathy Puanani Nishida**, *Tel. 885-7754*, also in Kamuela/Waimea, incorporates many colors into her quilts instead of the usual white with one contrasting shade. Her comforters run from about $2,500 to $3,000 for twin size, $3,600 to $4,000 for a double, and $5,000 to $8,000 for a queen or king. In Hilo, check out the quilts at **Handmade Treasures**, *Tel. 961-0045*, which also sells attractive dolls and other handicrafts.

Jewelry

Many shops selling jewelry made from shells, kukui nuts, coral, silver, and gold are found along Alii Drive in Kailua-Kona. In Hilo, the **Jeweler's Gallery**, *54 Waianuenue Avenue, Tel. 969-9191*, specializes in custom design jewelry by local goldsmiths, and fine jewelry from Thailand and Bali. This shop also sells watercolors by local artists. **Black Pearl Gallery**, *Tel. 935-8556*, in Hilo, is renowned for it collection of Tahitian black pearls as well as white cultured and freshwater pearls. This shop has a second location in Kawaihae Harbor on the Kona-Kohala Coast.

Also see *Crafts, Art Galleries* and *Pottery*.

Koa Wood Products

Beautifully grained koa wood was once far more prevalent throughout Hawaii. In the old days, it was turned into everything from eating plates and pots for boiling water to royal surfboards and canoes. You'll find koa carvings (bowls, platters, trays, boxes, jewelry, konane boards—a game similar to checkers) at stores including the following: **Kamaaina Woods**, *Tel. 775-7722*, in Honokaa, which also sells work done in other woods, such as milo; **Dan DeLuz Woods**, *Tel. 935-5587*, in Hilo, which uses mango, monkeypod, and Hawaiian ash as well as koa; and **Woods of Hawaii**, *Tel. 929-7630*, in Naalehu.

See also *Art Galleries.*

Kona Coffee

Hilo is the best place to buy coffee, since it can be as much as $2 cheaper than in Kailua-Kona. Stop here at **Long's Drugs** at the Prince Kuhio Shopping Plaza, *Tel. 959-5881*. However, if Hilo isn't on your itinerary, try **Kona Kai Farms**, *Tel. 328-9015*, in Kailua-Kona, across the street from the World Square Shopping Center; or **Long's Drugs** Kailua-Kona, *Tel. 329-1380*.

Macadamia Nuts

You'll find the best prices at **Long's Drugs**, *Prince Kuhio Shopping Plaza, Hilo, Tel. 959-5881*, and in *Kailua Kona, Tel. 329-1380*; and Payless **Drug Store** in Hilo. If you'd like a free factory tour, a complimentary sample and the opportunity to make a purchase, the Big Island offers a choice between the **Mauna Loa Macadamia Nut Factory**, *Tel. 966-8612*, the most popular, just south of Hilo, and **Hawaiian Macadamia**, *Tel. 775-7201*, in Honokaa on the Hamakua Coast.

Natural Foods

Along Route 130 on your way to Lava Tree State Park, **Pahoa Natural Groceries**, *Tel. 965-8322*, is a good place to stop for a picnic lunch. Time seems to have stopped somewhere in the 1960s at this little market in the little town of Pahoa. The store is stocked with healthful sandwiches, fresh fruits, juices, and snack foods. (This is also the place where you can register for a stay at nearby Bamboo House guest house, popular among young people, students and bargain hunters.)

Pottery

Decorative and functional ceramics, including unique Japanese *raku* ceramics, are on sale at **BT Pottery**, *Kona Marketplace, Tel. 326-4989*, and **Holualoa Gallery**, *Tel. 332-8484*, in Holualoa, near Kailua-Kona.

T-Shirts

You'll have endless choices at the shops on and near Alii Drive in Kailua-Kona. **Crazy Shirts**, *at Kona Shopping Arcade*, has a state-wide reputation for good buys in high-quality T-shirts. Most hotels — such as **King Kamehameha's Kona Beach Hotel** in Kailua-Kona — also have a fair share of shirts with appealing logos. In Hilo, try **Creative Hawaii Arts T-shirt Factory**, *Kalanianaole Avenue, Tel. 935-7393.*

PRACTICAL INFORMATION

Emergencies

Dial *Tel. 911* or call the closest police station.

Medical Attention

In the Kailua-Kona area, contact **Kona Hospital**, *Highway 11, Kealekekua, Tel. 322-9311.* On the east coast, call **Hilo Hospital**, *1190 Waianuenue Avenue, Tel. 969-4111.*

Post Office

To find out the location of the branch closest to you, call *Tel. 329-1927* in Kailua-Kona and *Tel. 935-2821* in Hilo.

Time

Not that you should worry about this while you're on vacation, but, just in case, call *Tel. 961-0212.*

Visitor Information

Detailed maps and other information are available for Hawaii, the Kona-Kohala coast and Keauhou. Contact the **Hawaii Visitors & Convention Bureau**, *75-5719 West Alii Drive, Kailua-Kona, HI 96740, Tel. 808/329-7787 or 250 Keawe Street, Hilo, HI 96720, Tel. 808/961-5797.*

Volcano Action

For the latest on eruptions, call *Tel. 967-7977.*

Weather

So that you can best plan your touring and activities, call *Tel. 961-5582.*

14. KAUAI

If I had to choose my favorite Hawaiian island, Kauai would probably win.

My opinion certainly wouldn't be in the minority. Even many Oahu residents are quick to name Kauai as their most loved Neighbor Island. Therefore, one afternoon while I was relaxing in a hot tub at the island's most sumptuous hotel, I was startled out of my serenity by a conversation I overheard between a pair of fellow soakers. Draining her mai tai with a slurp, one woman told another, "I went driving up north yesterday and there was nothing to see. I should have just stayed here." I was flabbergasted. Nothing to see?

In my book, jagged mountains, smooth green cow-studded meadows, craggy cliffs, waterfalls, rainbows spanning bays, and deserted sandy crescents hardly constitute "nothing." Perhaps this woman was so dazzled by the elaborate human-made pleasures of the island's first megaresort that, as far as she was concerned, nature's handiwork paled by comparison. It's good that this vacationer didn't do the location scouting for *Jurassic Park, South Pacific*, Michener's *Hawaii* and *The Hawaiians*, Elvis's *Blue Hawaii, Raiders of the Lost Ark, The Thorn Birds*, or *Fantasy Island*. These and other well-known film and television productions would have looked mighty different without the scenes that were shot on Kauai.

The island has recovered nicely from its 1992 visit from Iniki, the most powerful hurricane to hit Hawaii this century. A few structures are still being rebuilt, but Kauai remains as beautiful as ever. The oldest of the main Hawaiian Islands, it has had plenty of time to be sculpted by the elements. Its 553 square miles are embellished by some of the state's most stunning scenery, from meandering rivers and streams to the breathtaking, 4,000-foot cliffs of **Na Pali Coast** and 10-mile-long, two-mile-wide, 3,600-foot-deep **Waimea Canyon** (dubbed the "Grand Canyon of the Pacific," by Mark Twain).

Rising more than 5,000 feet, **Mt. Waialeale** (why-ollie-ollie) stands at the center of the nearly round island. This extinct volcano is considered the wettest spot on earth. Almost 500 inches of rain (about 40 feet!) fall on this misty mountain each year, and its dark green slopes are striped with white cascades. No wonder its name means "overflowing water." But this precipitation is surprisingly localized. Just a few miles west, there's an arid region that receives a mere six inches of rain a year.

On the mountain, lava tubes spew miniature rivers. The water pouring down the slopes has carved out Na Pali Coast and other cliffs. At the summit, strong winds prevent ohia trees from growing more than *six inches* off the soggy ground! Consider taking a helicopter tour over this mountain. Elsewhere on Kauai, human hands have further enhanced the island's striking vistas with taro patches, sugar cane fields, and somnolent rural towns.

The northernmost of Hawaii's inhabited islands, Kauai and tiny neighboring **Niihau** are the only major members of the archipelago that can't be seen from any of the other islands. Eighty miles of rough, churning ocean lie between Kauai and Oahu.

THE LAST HOLD-OUT

Kamehameha the Great found Kauai so difficult to reach that he was unable to conquer it in battle as he had the other islands. He finally managed to bring it under his rule, thus uniting the Hawaiian Islands - but only after tricking Kauai's chief into handing it over. Kauai King Ka'umu'ali'i agreed in order to prevent bloodshed and loss of lives.

After Hurricane Iwa hit Kauai in 1982, new luxury hotels, condos, and upscale restaurants opened. Sightseeing companies increased rubber raft excursions, whale-watching cruises, and helicopter tours. Yet tourism does not seem to predominate on Kauai today. This island is not for people who thrive on crowds or nightlife. While it does have its share of resort hotels, shopping centers, and good restaurants along with a smattering of museums, art galleries, and night spots, its main draws lie outdoors. Hiking, camping, and scuba diving are all excellent here.

Hawaiian Roots

Kauai is famous for its tales of **Menehune,** the race of miniature people who were the Hawaiian version of European leprechauns or trolls. The difference is that the Menehune may have truly existed. According to a census taken toward the end of the 1700s, 65 Menehune living in Wainiha Valley were under the domain of Kauai's King Ka-umu-ali'i. These hirsute, dark-skinned people were said to be a mere two or three feet tall, with red faces, wide noses, overhanging foreheads, and scraggly

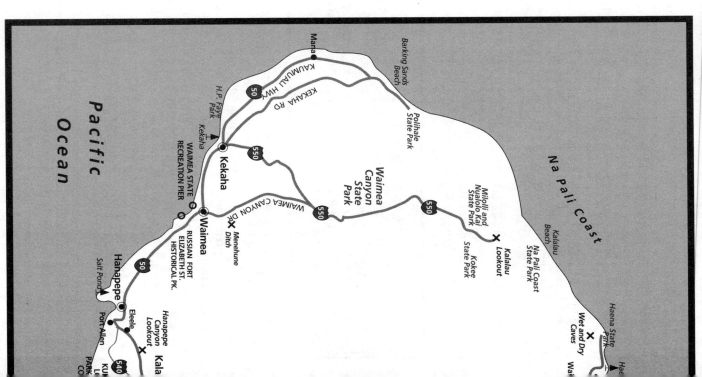

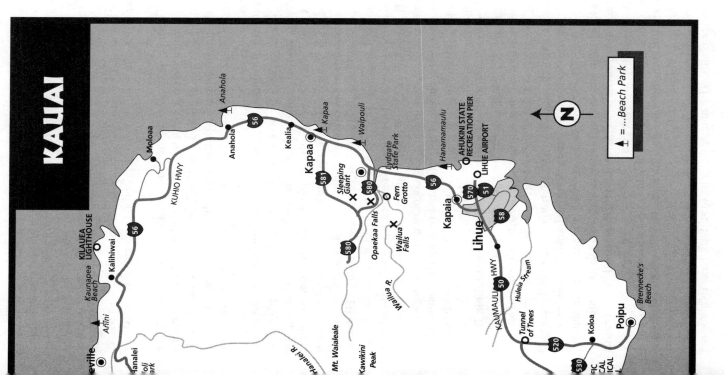

straight hair. Fond of dining on taro and shrimp, the Menehune weren't big on conversation - but when they did speak, their deep gravely voices sounded like rolling down hillsides into the ocean. They got a real kick out of playful activities such as rolling down dogs growling. With their compact, muscular bodies, they were well suited for their celebrated stone masonry. For instance, impressive Menehune Ditch, in southwestern Kauai, is believed to have been built by members of this nocturnal race in just one night.

The Tahitian word for "Menehune" means "commoner." Some historians theorize that the Menehune were inhabiting Tahiti when the Polynesians first arrived there and that these little people eventually made their way to Hawaii. Legend says that when their chiefs began to worry that too much interbreeding with Hawaiians would dilute their race, the Menehune sailed away on a floating island.

In residential Waimea, west of Poipu, you're likely to hear the Hawaiian language spoken and Hawaiian music that isn't played in exchange for tourists' dollars. More Hawaiiana is found along the Coconut Coast, from Lihue north. At the **Kauai Museum** in Lihue, displays include ancient Hawaiian featherwork, *umeke laau* (carved wooden bowls), and elaborate necklaces made of tiny shells or braided human hair and whalebone. In Wailua, Highway 580 is also known as **King's Highway,** since in the old days Hawaiian regents were carried along this road so that their royal feet were not sullied by touching the ground. Off this highway, **Pohaku Ho'ohanau** is a sacred *heiau* (temple) where ancient Hawaiians used to make sacrifices to the gods. The coconut grove at **Lydgate State Park** once served as a place of refuge for law-breaking Hawaiians. They could escape punishment - often death - if they reached this beach before being caught.

Farther north along the east coast, you'll come to **Anahola Beach Park.** During the late 1980s, Hawaiians and other sympathetic residents camped out in tents to demonstrate the need for decent, affordable housing. They protested the taking of land from Hawaiians, specifically this 1.5-acre beach park, which, along with ten adjoining acres, is managed by Kauai County. They pushed for native Hawaiian businesses to be developed at the park. Although the government had set aside land for native Hawaiians, these Kauaian Homelands have poor or nonexistent roads, water and drainage systems, and utility lines. In addition, waiting lists for parcels of this land are years long.

At Ke'e Point on Na Pali Coast, just after the road ends on the north shore, an ancient stone **hula shrine** still stands. This altar honors Laka, the goddess of hula. Before each dance, performers would decorate the shrine with lama wood wrapped in yellow kapa cloth and strands of maile vine and other plants. The dancers' chants would ask Laka to allow her spirit to slip into their bodies so their movements could be as artful as hers. After each performance, they would remove their colorful leis and some of their costumes, leaving them in back of the altar. Today some hikers are lucky enough to pass the shrine when offerings have been placed here or even when a hula *halau* (school or group) is dancing at this time-honored site.

ARRIVALS & DEPARTURES

Your plane will land in **Lihue**, Kauai's capital, where the island's main airport is located. Find out if your accommodation provides complimentary transportation to and from the airport. If not, you can get where you're going by bus, van, taxi, limousine, or rental car. The major auto rental agencies have desks at **Lihue Airport.** Guests are transported in vans to and from the cars.

The town of Lihue is a five-minute drive from the airport. Wailua and Kapaa hotels and condos are about 15 minutes away. The drive to Hanalei and Princeville, in the north, will take just over an hour from Lihue. From Lihue Airport to Poipu in the south, the ride should last about 30 minutes. Plan to spend at least two hours on the road to get to the lodge and cabins in wooded, mountainous Kokee.

ORIENTATION

The sandy shores in the north are absolutely gorgeous, but during the winter their waves are much too rough for swimming, snorkeling, or diving. At this time of year, head south to Poipu - the island's most popular resort area - or to the east side of the island, where the water remains much calmer throughout the year.

Known as the Coconut Coast, the beach-rimmed eastern strip north of Lihue, the capital, is studded with hotels and condominiums. Encompassing Wailua and Kapaa, this area is rich in Hawaiian history. Golfers are drawn to Princeville in the north, Kauai Lagoons and Wailua in the east, and Poipu in the south. If you choose to stay in quiet Waimea, west of Poipu, you'll get a taste of day-to-day life for residents. You can even sleep in a lodge in the forest of lofty Kokee State Park, where the temperature gets surprisingly cool at night.

Thanks to the fact that Kauai receives more rain than the rest of Hawaii, it is covered with a multitude of flowers and other flourishing vegetation. Shrouded in mist, lopsided mountain peaks and verdant expanses take on a mystical beauty when showers hit. The sunniest regions are along the southern coast, where the Poipu resort area is located, and the western shore, where 15-mile Polihale (the island's longest beach) is found. Hanalei and Princeville, in the north, are the resorts where rain is most frequent. Thus the north is wonderfully green.

GETTING AROUND KAUAI

Allow at least three days for leisurely exploring - one for Poipu up the east coast to Kapaa; another for Kapaa up along the north shore through Hanalei and Princeville to Haena, where Kuhio Highway (Route 56) ends; and the third for the southern coast west of Poipu, up to Waimea Canyon, Kokee State Park and Kalalau Lookout.

You may want to spend another day or an afternoon on Polihale beach on the west coast. You'll need a four-wheel drive for the backroads of Kokee State Park. For the many travelers based in Poipu, driving time to Waimea and Kekaha is about an hour; to Kapaa, about 45 minutes; to Hanalei, about an hour and 40 minutes.

By Bus

There is no public bus system on Kauai.

By Car

Just one main road goes around most of Kauai. Since it doesn't encircle the island completely and since no roads cut all the way across the interior, you'll have a second chance to see whatever you missed the first time you passed it. I never mind backtracking, since Kauai's scenery is spectacular coming and going. But if you'd rather not cover the same territory twice, consider moving from a hotel in one part of the island to an accommodation in another.

DRIVING TIPS

During morning and afternoon rush hours, avoid Lihue and the road between Lihue and Kapaa, unless you don't mind moving at a crawl. When you're going on sightseeing drives (such as to Waimea Canyon), it's best to leave as early as possible so that you don't end up stuck behind exhaust-spewing tour buses.

By Guided Tour

If you'd rather not drive yourself, **tour buses** visit all of Kauai's major sights. You'll cover a lot of territory by taking the full-day Wailua River/Fern Grotto/Waimea Canyon tour offered by most companies. Part of the day will be spent cruising up the river to the fern-covered cave. Other sightseeing highlights on this trip include Opaekaa Falls, Menehune Fishpond, and Fort Elizabeth (a.k.a. the Old Russian Fort).

Those who like riding in style should check out **Kauai Island Tours,** Tel. 245-4777, which carries sightseers in stretch limos, and **Roberts**

Hawaii Tours, *Tel. 245-9558.* **Trans Hawaiian Services,** *Tel. 245-5108 or 800/533-8765,* and **Polynesian Adventure Tours,** *Tel. 246-0122 or 800/622-3011,* are other reputable companies.

If you're interested in an excursion that zeroes in on sights involving Kauai's myths, legends, and history, consider the 5-hour van tour offered by **North Shore Cab Tours,** *Tel. 826-6189,* based in Hanalei. You'll hear how various dramatic natural formations came to be, according to ancient Hawaiians, as well as tales about Kauai's New England missionaries, the hula goddess, and the Menehune (the legendary race of miniature people). You'll see where scenes from several movies were shot. Tours, with pick-ups at north shore hotels, cost about $50 per person.

For an in-depth look at wooded Kokee State Park and spectacular Waimea Canyon, **Kauai Mountain Tours,** *Tel. 245-7224 or 800/452-1113,* uses small four-wheel-drive vans to travel the back roads of Kauai's western region. As you see Waimea Canyon from striking vantage points and drive across rocky streams, you might pass through forests of redwood, koa, and eucalyptus. You'll take short walks along trails flourishing with wildflowers, ferns growing some fifteen feet high, and a variety of mosses. Your guide will point out medicinal plants and rare birds. You may even spot wild goats, black-tailed deer, and wild boars.

If you take the full-day tour, you'll stop for lunch at one of several scenic picnic areas, perhaps by a creek. (Vegetarians are happily accommodated as long as they let the tour company know when they make reservations.) Since these are truly mountain tours, the ride can be very bumpy and jerky, especially after a rain. A full-day trip (about seven hours) with lunch will run about $86 for adults, and $58 for children under 12.

By Taxi

Taxis are available, but they are practical only for short rides or for travelers with money to burn.

WHERE TO STAY

Where you stay on Kauai may depend on what you plan to do. Poipu, along the southeast coast, is the island's driest resort area. The beaches are excellent here, especially during the winter when those along the north coast are too rough for swimming. During the summer, Poipu's shores are great for surfing, both body and board. This area is close to Lihue, the capital, and attractions such as Kilohana Plantation, Grove Farm Homestead, Waimea Canyon, and botanical gardens.

Because of rocky shores or strong currents, some east coast beaches are not as good for swimming as others. Many are sandy and all are fine for sun worshipping, picnicking, and strolling. Along this shore, hotels and condos in Wailua and Kapaa are near the 18-hole Wailua Golf Course

KAUAI'S BEST HOTELS

Cream of the Crop

Princeville Hotel, Princeville: This luxury resort is in one of Hawaii's most beautiful - and peaceful - regions.

Secret Beach Hideaway, Kilauea: If you'd like a tranquil cottage all to yourselves, this place couldn't be more romantic.

Hyatt Regency Kauai Resort & Spa, Poipu: For serious pampering in a wonderful beachfront setting, this is an excellent choice.

Moderate or Inexpensive

Waimea Plantation Cottages, Waimea: Set in an expansive palm grove, these home-like beachfront cottages are a great way to experience Kauai.

Gloria's Spouting Horn B&B, Poipu: If you're looking for the peace and intimacy of a bed & breakfast, but you also want to be on the water, book a room here.

and Coconut Market Place shopping center. Also nearby are sights including ancient heiau, both Opaekaa and Wailua waterfalls, Wailua River, and Fern Grotto.

In the north, where refreshing showers aren't unusual, Hanalei and Princeville attract serious golfers to various courses. Lovers of verdant tranquility are also drawn to this region. As gorgeous as they are to look at, the waters off many of the beaches along this coast should be avoided during the winter. Sights in this area include impressive Na Pali cliffs, stunning valleys covered with taro patches, the distinctive peaks known as "Bali Hai," a couple of small museums, and wet and dry caves.

Kauai offers a healthy selection of hotels, condominiums, and Bed & Breakfasts. Even after the arrival of the opulent Westin Kauai (now the Marriott) in Lihue during the late 1980s, most remain comfortably low-key. Families or couples traveling together are drawn to Kauai's many apartment-like condominiums. Rooms in most are individually furnished by owners, so decor may vary from unit to unit within a complex.

Poipu

HYATT REGENCY KAUAI RESORT & SPA, *1571 Poipu Road, Koloa, HI 96756. Tel. 808/742-1234 or 800/233-1234, Fax 808/742-6229. 600 rooms. Double rooms begin at $300. Major credit cards.*

Featured in Chapter 10, *Best Places to Stay.*

In memory of the sugar cane fields that once blanketed the land where the Hyatt now stands, a brass sugar-cane leaf motif is used in everything from wall decorations to railings and door handles. The ocean here can be dangerous for swimming, but it remains a prime local surfing spot. Heated saltwater lagoons have been built at the edge of the Pacific, and elaborate swimming pools are terraced down the hillside. Complete with waterfalls, the main pool winds under bridges, past flourishing greenery and boulders draped with bougainvillea. Both children and adults climb the steps over and over again to the top of the 150-foot water slide for the splashy ride to the bottom.

At the extensive health spa, the lap pool is in a sunny courtyard, and whirlpools are open-air. Each massage or wrap room has a private courtyard. Four tennis courts and an 18-hole Robert Trent Jones, Jr. golf course also keep guests occupied. Tennis racquets can be borrowed.

WHALER'S COVE, *2640 Puuholo Road, Koloa, HI 96756. Tel. 808/742-7571 or 800/225-2683, Fax 808/742-1185. 25 units. Rates begin at $225 per unit. Major credit cards.*

Although this attractive condo complex is on a rocky shore, it's a great place for winter whale watching and the beach is only a five-minute drive away. It is close to a fine snorkeling/scuba diving cove. Facilities include a heated oceanfront swimming pool. All suites have two bedrooms and two baths, but some units are larger than others. Some units have whirlpool baths. Cooled by ceiling fans instead of air conditioning, these modern apartments have TVs, high ceilings, huge walk-in closets, cushiony carpets, and rich brown koa molding and doors. In most master baths, there's a whirlpool tub, some with a view of the Pacific, along with two free-standing sinks. Patios are large and shaded by palms. Kitchens are decked out with microwave ovens, dishwashers, and washers/dryers. The 18-hole Poipu Bay and Kiahuna golf courses are nearby, as are tennis courts and other Poipu attractions. The hosts are always happy to direct vacationers to special sights and attractions on the island.

POIPU KAPILI, *2221 Kapili Road, Koloa, HI 96756. Tel. 808/742-6449 or 800/443-7714, Fax 808/742-9162. 60 units. Units begin at $155 a night.*

Across the road from the water, these sprawling low-rise balconied buildings are set amid artfully landscaped grounds. Some of the greenery has a practical use. There is an herb garden from which guests are encouraged to pick their favorite seasonings for the dishes they cook. All of the one- and two-bedroom apartments and penthouse units have high ceilings, ceiling fans, and louvered wooden sliding doors leading to lanais. In the one- and two-bedroom apartments, modern microwave and dishwasher-equipped kitchens with stools at their counters open onto tremendous living/dining rooms. A tub is in one bath while the other has a stall shower.

The units are quite spacious. A pool and tennis courts are on the premises and good swimming beaches are not far. Complimentary coffee and pastries are served by the pool every Friday morning.

KIAHUNA PLANTATION, 2253 Poipu Road, Koloa, HI 96756. Tel. 808/742-6411 or 800/688-7444, Fax 808/742-9015. 224 units. Rates: $175 to $350. Major credit cards.

Set amid 35 acres of landscaped grounds, beachfront cottages and low-rise buildings contain one- and two-bedroom apartments. With lanais and high ceilings, these cozy condos are decorated with tropical furniture and white ceramic tile floors. The small kitchenettes are equipped with microwaves, stoves, refrigerators with icemakers, dishwashers, and even wine glasses. There is no pool but a variety of water sports may be arranged at the beach; tennis courts and a pool are across the street.

Ask about seasonal children's activities. Every Tuesday and Thursday, garden tours are offered of Moir Gardens, with over 100 varieties of cacti from all over the world, and of the Hawaiian Garden. In the original plantation manager's house, the Piatti Restaurant, one of the three restaurants on the premises, is known for its delicious seafood and Italian fare. Its wraparound lanai and garden view make it especially inviting.

SHERATON KAUAI RESORT, 2440 Hoonani Road, Poipu Beach, HI 96756. Tel. 800/782-9488. 413 rooms. Double rooms begin at $175. Major credit cards.

Closed since it lost a battle with Hurricane Iniki in 1992, the Sheraton is scheduled to reopen as a rebuilt deluxe beachfront resort, so check its status. Three- and four-story buildings are being added to the concrete beachfront units and garden wing buildings. The porte cochere and check-in area in the oceanfront section of the resort will have wonderful views of the water. Guests will be able to hit the health spa and the pool surrounded by tropical foliage. Parents can drop little ones off at the children's center.

GLORIA'S SPOUTING HORN B&B, 4464 Lawai Beach Road, Koloa, HI 96756. Tel. 808/742-6995, Fax 808/742-6995. Three rooms. Rates: $160 per room. No children under age 14. No smoking inside the house.

Featured in Chapter 10, Best Places to Stay.

For those who would like to stay in a Bed & Breakfast and want to be on the ocean, this is the place. Although the shore is rocky here, it's wonderfully scenic, with a small sandy beach and dramatic crashing surf. Popular Poipu Beach is a mile away. A romantic outdoor lava rock beach shower is shaded by a mango tree - but don't worry, it's enclosed and perfectly private!

Gloria's sports a striking willow-branch canopy bed in one room. Each of its three guest rooms has a Japanese-style soaking tub in its private bath. All rooms have TVs, VCR's, microwaves, bar sinks, telephones, refrigerators and ceiling fans.

The lobby/dining area is decorated in American farmhouse pine. Breakfast is served on the oceanfront lanai or at the dining table inside. Guests (including my husband and me on our own honeymoon) have raved about the generous helpings of peach French toast with peach syrup, well-seasoned quiche, and fluffy pancakes that Gloria whips up. In addition to complimentary coffee, tea and cocoa, guests can choose from various liqueurs, wines and soft drinks, also complimentary.

POIPU BED AND BREAKFAST INN, *2720 Hoonani Road, Kolo, HI 96756. Tel. 808/742-1146 or 800/552-0095, Fax 808/742-6843. Nine rooms. Rate: $85. Major credit cards.*

Four guest rooms are found in the main building, a restored former home dating back to 1933. Lanterns light the walkway to the front lanai, which is shielded from the road by a tall hedge. White Victorian wicker with floral cushions, glass-topped cables, and potted plants adorn the common sitting room. Ceilings and walls are paneled in bleached wood. Well-stocked bookshelves invite browsing for a good read. With all the antiques, colorful carousel horses, and other knickknacks around, it is not surprising that the owner is an artist.

Each attractive room has a remote control TV, clock radio, and a VCR. There is a guest refrigerator on the rear lanai and a barbecue at both buildings. Many units have whirlpools (some for two); many have kitchenettes. Air conditioning or ceiling fans cool the house. Continental breakfast can be served in bed upon request. Afternoon tea is set up daily on the lanai or in the sitting room. Guests also get to know each other while playing backgammon or Monopoly in the common room. Beaches aren't far. Smoking is not permitted inside the house.

Rooms are also in another building, the Oceanview Inn, plus Kalaheo Garden Cottage, a budget vacation rental, and in Oceanfront Beach Cottage at Spouting Horn. In addition, Poipu B&B Inn owns a two-bedroom, two-bath condo at nearby Whaler's Cove.

PRINCE KUHIO CONDOMINIUMS, *P.O. Box 1060, Koloa, HI 96756. Tel. 808/742-6120 or 800/325-6423, Fax 808/325-6423. 70 units. Rates begin at $75 per unit. A seven-night minimum stay is requested.*

The location and the price make this a favorite among repeat visitors. Studios, one-bedroom, and two-bedroom apartments are rented to vacationers here, all with lanais and TVs. Greenery surrounds the swimming pool. The two beaches across the road are best for sunbathing and snorkeling. Good swimming beaches are within a 1.5 mile walk or drive along the ocean. The Kiahuna Plantation golf course is about a 10-minute walk from here. Inquire about rental car packages.

VICTORIA PLACE, *P.O. Box 930, Lawai, HI 96765, Tel. 808/332-9300, Fax 808/332-9465. Four rooms. Rate: $80 per room. No smoking in the house.*

With only three guest rooms and a studio apartment, this hillside Bed & Breakfast gazes down on lush foliage, undulating sugarcane and coffee fields, and the ocean. Guest rooms look out to the pool deck, enlivened by gardenia, bougainvillea, ginger, and hibiscus. One room is set up for wheelchair access. Families or friends can rent connecting rooms. With a private entrance, king-sized bed, living room and kitchenette, the downstairs studio is called Victoria's Other Secret. Guests share the living room, with a TV and a breezy lanai. Books are found in all rooms. All the necessities are provided: mats, coolers, towels, chairs, boogie boards, and the like.

The hearty continental breakfast includes homemade breads and four or five tropical fruits. Vacationers receive personal attention from the gregarious proprietor, Edee Seymour, who steers them to little-known restaurants, beaches, and scenic hideaways. Her personal attention suggests why she was the recipient of the Aloha Spirit Award. She is also happy to make dining reservations and arrangements for rental cars, helicopter tours, and horseback riding. (Guests receive Edee's discount.) Poipu beaches are only about a 10-minute drive away. Twenty minutes behind the wheel will take you to Lihue. Kukuiolono Golf Course and the boutiques and restaurants of Koloa Town are each about five minutes away.

GARDEN ISLE COTTAGES, *266 Puuholo Road, Koloa, HI 96756, Tel. 808/742-6717 or 800/742-6711. Thirteen units. Rates begin at $72 per unit.*

In a quiet section of Poipu, these studios and one- and two-bedroom apartments are located in various cottages. Some are closer to the water than others; the Sea Cliff Cottages sit on an ocean cliff overlooking an inlet. There is a pool and the nearest sunning and snorkeling beach is one block away. Restaurants are not far. Sections of the grounds are pleasantly overgrown with banana trees, bougainvillea, and hibiscus. Weekly housekeeping service is provided for some units, while others have washers and dryers.

KOLOA LANDING COTTAGES, *2704-B Hoonani Road, Koloa, HI 96756, Tel. 808/742-1470 or 800/779-6773, Fax 808/332-9584. Five units. Rate: $60 per unit.*

This small accommodation appeals to vacationers looking to escape the crowds. It offers a mere studio along with a one-bedroom and two two-bedroom cottages, with full kitchens, exposed beam ceilings, and cable TV. Accommodations in the main house include two bedrooms and two baths. Fruit trees on the grounds provide guests with delicious snacks. Beaches are a stroll away, and a variety of restaurants are also nearby. The owners give guests as much - or as little - personal attention as they need. Rates don't include the onetime cleaning fee (about $20). A laundry room is on the premises.

Kalaheo

CLASSIC VACATION COTTAGES, *2687 Onu Place, P.O. Box 901, Kalaheo, HI 96741. Tel. 808/332-9201 or 800/685-719, Fax 808/332-7645. Four units. Rate: $70 per unit. Additional charge for one-night stays.*

Just west of Poipu and near Kukuiolono Golf Course, this Bed & Breakfast is designed for travelers who want a clean, comfortable place to stay, but don't want to spend a lot. Repeat guests are no strangers to the four pleasantly decorated units surrounded by attractive landscaping. With complete kitchens, these cottages are graced with antique stained glass windows. Each contains snorkel gear, boogie boards, beach towels, and mats.

The hosts are happy to make arrangements for kayak rides, sailing trips, fishing charters, or any other diversions. Poipu beaches are about a 10-minute drive away and a five-minute ride will take you to the closest golf course. Honeymooners receive a bottle of wine in addition to the macadamia nuts and chocolates all arriving guests are given.

Waimea

WAIMEA PLANTATION COTTAGES, *9700 Kaumualii Highway, Waimea, HI 96796. Tel. 808/338-1625 or 800/9-WAIMEA, Fax 808/338-2338. 48 units. Rates: $160 to $310 per unit. Major credit cards.*

Away from south shore crowds, this secluded accommodation is an excellent place to unwind. It feels exactly like the kind of environment people come to Kauai for. Dating from 1910 to 1930, these homey cottages, some of which are on the beach, were once the homes of sugar plantation workers. Set amid a beautiful palm grove, they now have one to five bedrooms, full kitchens, cable TV, telephones, and AM/FM stereo cassettes. Not all units have air conditioning, but ceiling fans and ocean breezes cool things off just fine.

All cottages are on the ocean side of the road, but some are closer to the water than others. The sand is dark on this tranquil beach and the water is murky due to silt from the river that runs into the ocean. However, there's a pool on the grounds, and a swimming beach is about a mile west of here, in Kekaha. Check the status of the hotel restaurant, which is scheduled to reopen. Otherwise, local restaurants are not far. Shopping is nearby in the town of Waimea. Horseback riding and other types of recreation can be easily arranged.

KOKEE LODGE, Waimea Canyon Drive, Kokee State Park, Box 819, Waimea, HI 96796. 12 cabins. Tel. 808/335-6061. Rates begin at $40 per cabin. Major credit cards.

See Housekeeping Cabins at the end of this section.

Lihue Area

KAUAI MARRIOTT RESORT & BEACH CLUB, Kalapaki Beach, Lihue, HI 96766. Tel. 808/245-5050 or 800/220-2925, Fax 808/245-2993. 588 rooms. Double rooms begin at $260. Major credit cards.

Part hotel, part time-share, this splashy, sprawling resort was created as a Westin in the late '80s. It was one of the state's first megaresorts. In 1992, Hurricane Iniki left it in shambles. Extensive rebuilding has resulted in a handsome vacation playground with 51 acres of bright gardens. The attractive guest rooms differ in size and view. Vacationers splash in the huge swimming pool, rimmed by waterfalls and five whirlpools, or relax at the beach. They can also go kayaking, windsurfing, snorkeling, scuba diving, sailing, and fishing. There is a fitness center, as well as a children's program, and four restaurants, from casual to elegant. Two 18-hole championship golf courses, both designed by Jack Nicklaus, and tennis courts are within walking distance at 800-acre Kauai Lagoons.

THE BANYAN HARBOR RESORT, 3411 Wilcox Road, Lihue, HI 96766. Tel. 808/245-7333 or 800/422-6926, Fax 808/246-4776. 148 units. Rates begin at $140 per unit. Major credit cards.

A reader from Ventura, California, wrote to me with high praise for this condominium on Kalapaki Bay (across from the Kauai Marriott Resort & Beach Club). The individually decorated ocean- or garden view two-bedroom apartments are a serious bargain when rented by one couple. When shared by four people, the price is truly rock bottom - especially if you factor in the pool, barbecue area, tennis court, shuffleboard courts, washer/dryer in each unit, and the proximity of the beach. Golf at a nearby course is easily arranged. The grounds may be rather undistinguished, but the economical rate may be a deciding factor. Weekly hula and lei-making classes introduce travelers to Hawaiiana.

Kapaa & Wailua

While the beaches along this coast are aesthetically pleasing, not all are swimmer-friendly.

KAUAI COCONUT BEACH RESORT, P.O. Box 830, Kapaa, HI 96746. Tel. 808/822-3455 or 800/222-5642, Fax 808/822-1830. 311 rooms. Double rooms begin at $175. Major credit cards.

At Coconut Plantation and on Waipouli Beach, this hotel has a commercial but fresh, pleasant look. Palms, breadfruit trees, ironwoods, and flowers thrive around the grounds. There's a hot tub by the pool and sundeck as well as nearby tennis courts. River kayaking excursions may also be arranged. A four-story waterfall is the centerpiece of the bright lobby, which is decorated with stained glass. Pupus are served in the lounge in the afternoon. All with cable TV, sitting areas and lanais, the moderately sized guest rooms differ mainly by location and view. Many look out to the ocean. In-room safes are available for a minimal daily fee. This hotel hosts a popular **luau** that received the Hawaii Visitors Bureau Kahili Award for Authenticity.

LAE NANI, *410 Papaloa Road, Kapaa, HI 96746. Tel. 808/822-4938 or 800/367-7052, Fax 510/939-6644. 84 units. Rates begin at $160 per condo. Major credit cards.*

On the beach adjacent to Coconut Plantation Market Place shopping complex, this pleasant condominium makes a great homebase for convenient trips to some of Kauai's most popular attractions. Each of the one- and two-bedroom apartments is individually decorated, with a fully-equipped kitchen and ceiling fans. In addition to the oceanfront swimming pool, there's a lava rock saltwater pool that is perfect for children, a tennis court, and a barbecue area. The 18-hole Wailua golf course is just a mile away. Don't be surprised if staff members invite you to join them in a game of croquet or volleyball. You won't even have to leave the grounds to see the remains of an old Hawaiian heiau (temple). Ask about economical condo/car and family packages.

OUTRIGGER KAUAI BEACH HOTEL, *4331 Kauai Beach Drive, Lihue, HI 96766. Tel. 808/245-1955 or 800/688-7444, Fax 808/246-9085. 341 rooms. Doubles begin at $140. Major credit cards.*

This beach resort is located in Hanamaulu, between Wailua and Lihue. Rose-colored tiles and potted plants decorate the spacious lobby which is sprinkled with pleasant sitting areas. Featuring a cave and waterfalls, the sprawling main pool is divided into sections. Multicolored flowers surround the water. At sunset each day, torches are lighted around the pool. Whether vacationers are diving novices or certified, they should check out the excellent **scuba program** here. Found in red-roofed white buildings, the comfortable guest rooms, tastefully decorated, all have lanais that look out to the ocean, the gardens, or the mountains. Guests have a choice of restaurants and lounges. A concierge floor and lounge provide extra amenities. The nightclub is a popular hangout among the younger crowd. Tennis courts are also on the premises.

WAILUA BAY RESORT, *3-5920 Kuhio Highway, Kapaa, HI 96746. Tel. 808/245-3931 or 800/367-5004, Fax 808/822-7339. 234 rooms. Doubles begin at $136. Major credit cards.*

The spacious reception area with its high-pitched beamed ceiling leads to a Japanese garden out back. Peacocks roam the grounds while carp add orange and white to ponds. A footbridge takes guests to one of the two swimming pools, and facilities also include tennis courts. A rough but attractive beach is a five-minute-walk away. All of the chicly decorated guest rooms have cable TV, refrigerators and safes. The studios with kitchenettes and one-bedroom cottages appeal to families. Vacationers may take part in the Hawaiian crafts demonstrations. Every weekend, there's live island entertainment in the lounge.

PLANTATION HALE CONDOMINIUMS, 484 Kuhio Highway, Lihue, HI 96746. Tel. 808/822-4941 or 800/688-7444, Fax 808/456-4329. 145 units. Rate: $130. Major credit cards.

Managed by Outrigger, this all-suite condominium offers three swimming pools, a putting green, and a shuffleboard court. Situated at Coconut Plantation in Kapaa, it is near all kinds of shops and restaurants. Waipouli Beach is within walking distance. Done in mauve and peach, each one-bedroom suite is pleasantly furnished with white rattan and glass-topped tables. They all have lanais, rather small living rooms, full kitchens, TVs, ceiling fans, closet safes, and baths with dressing areas.

ASTON KAUAI BEACHBOY HOTEL, 4-484 Kuhio Highway, Kapaa, HI 96746. Tel. 808/822-3441 or 800/922-7866, Fax 808/822-0843. 243 rooms. Double rooms begin at $120.

This group of three-story buildings is near the Coconut Plantation Market Place. All rooms in the hotel have lanais and TVs. In addition to a restaurant, lounge and shops, there's a beachfront courtyard with a swimming pool, tennis courts, and shuffleboard. This Aston property is a good choice for budget-conscious travelers who want to be on the water. To learn more about local culture, guests can take advantage of the many library books, watch hula groups practicing weekly on the grounds, and play Hawaiian games on the lawn.

PONO KAI RESORT, 4-1250 Kuhio Highway, Kapaa, HI 96746. Tel. 808/822-9831, Fax 808/822-9054. 143 units. Rates begin at $120 per unit. Major credit cards.

After the unassuming front desk, actually a small open-air counter, the manicured, pine-studded grounds come as a surprise. Two- and three-story wooden buildings stand along the beach, which is good for swimming. Lanais face the water, with its continual breakers. Some of these one- and two-bedroom condos have shag rugs and other furnishings reminiscent of the 1970s, while more modern apartments come with rattan tables and chairs and tiled patios. The master bedrooms are quite large. Units are equipped with up-to-date full kitchens, two TVs, VCR, and ceiling fans. Not all are air-conditioned. Facilities include a swimming pool, tennis courts, bicycles, cribs, highchairs, playpens, and video rentals are all available through the 24-hour front desk. Coconut Plantation Market Place and the Wailua Golf Course are nearby.

ISLANDER ON THE BEACH, *484 Kuhio Highway, Kapaa, HI 96746. Tel. 808/822-7417 or 800/847-7417, Fax 808/822-1947. 196 rooms. Double rooms begin at $100. Major credit cards.*

Another Coconut Plantation accommodation, these three-story shingle-roofed buildings are surrounded by attractively planted grounds. There's a pleasant, spread-out feel to the property. The ocean is visible through the back entrance of the lobby, which is decked out with potted palms, a glossy round koa table, and wooden stairway railings. Guest rooms are somewhat small but come with wet bars, refrigerators, safes, coffee makers, dressing areas, TVs, and lanais. The oceanfront units have microwaves.

KAUAI SANDS HOTEL, *Wailua, HI 96746. Tel. 808/822-4951 or 800/367-7000, Fax 808/922-0052. 201 rooms. Double rooms begin at $100. Major credit cards.*

This modest hotel sits right on the water. The plain rooms are perfectly comfortable, with air conditioning, ceiling fans, and double or king-size beds. Some have kitchenettes. Many overlook the two swimming pools. All come with lanais, TVs, and refrigerators. While a restaurant and lounge are on the premises, a wide selection of shops and restaurants is nearby. An exercise room is a recent addition. And if you like karaoke singing, this is the place.

KAPAA SHORES RESORT CONDOMINIUMS, *4-0900 Kuhio Highway, Kapaa, HI 96746. Tel. 808/822-3055 or 800/827-3922, Fax 808/822-1457. 81 units. Double rooms begin at $95. Major credit cards.*

These modest condos across from Kauai Village shopping center all have private lanais. One- and two-bedroom suites come with cable TV and complete kitchens. The beach in front of the property is good for sunbathing, but swimming is not recommended since the water is rough and the shore is rocky. The Wailua Golf Course is just over three miles away. Guests may arrange other activities at the front desk, which is open from 7am to 7pm. After hours, they can contact the staff. The pool and Jacuzzi are open from 8am to 10pm, and there are two gas barbecue grills, with grassy areas for sunbathing.

THE ORCHID HUT BED & BREAKFAST, *6402 Kaahele St., Kapaa, HI 96746. Tel. 808/822-7201. One room. Rate: $85. Two adults, maximum. No smoking.*

Overlooking the Wailua River and Valley, this three-room cottage in Kapaa is not far from restaurants and supermarkets. Your hosts leave breakfast fixings in the kitchenette with a refrigerator, microwave, and hot plate. An iron, ironing board and hair dryer are also provided. Bird watchers have a field day in this pastoral setting. The tea house, with a view of the river, is a relaxing place to pass time. A five-minute drive will take you to the beach.

ALOHA COUNTRY VACATION RENTALS, *9700 Kaumualii High-way, Waimea, HI 96796. Tel. 808/822-0166, Fax 808/822-2708. Three rooms. Rates: $50 per room.*

If you'd like to be in a country setting, but close to shopping, restaurants, the beach, and the airport, consider this Bed & Breakfast. The Sleeping Giant mountain gazes down on a broad valley, a running stream, and the sprawling backyard, flourishing with grapefruit, lichee, tangerine, banana, avocado, and guava trees. Birds are in deep conversation all around, and a tempting hammock is strung in the shade of a tree.

The 14-room Spanish-style private house sits on two acres. All guest units were rebuilt after their tangle with hurricane Iniki in 1992. Guests sleep in two of the upstairs suites with private baths. Decorated with antiques (as is the rest of the house), both suites have queen size beds. Visitors may also stay in one of the three brightly furnished cottages out back with a kitchenette and separate driveway. All units have fans. Homebaked bread or rolls, fresh local fruit, juice, coffee and tea are served for breakfast. The owners, a couple from Kauai (she) and Oahu (he), live in the main house.

Princeville, Hanalei, & Kilauea

The beaches along this coast can be too rough for swimming during the winter.

PRINCEVILLE HOTEL, *P.O. Box 3069, Princeville, HI 96722. Tel. 808/826-9644 or 800/826-4400, Fax 808/826-1166. 252 rooms. Double rooms begin at $360. Major credit cards.*

Featured in Chapter 10, *Best Places to Stay.*

As you drive into the porte cochere, you'll feel as though you're driving right into the huge lobby, which is behind a tall wall of glass sliding doors. Inside, the two- or three-story windows dazzle with fabulous views of Hanalei Bay and the jagged Bali Hai mountains. Antiques catch the eye, such as the 18th century Flemish tapestry of children playing.

The swimming pool area sports a swim-up bar, three half-moon-shaped Jacuzzis, a children's pool, and one of the hotel's three restaurants. A fitness center is nearby. Some guestrooms are graced with imported antiques, whirlpool bathtubs, VCRs and lanais. Rooms feature papered walls and overstuffed couches with throw pillows. Guests get a kick out of the magic windows in all rooms; a flip of a switch turns them from opaque to transparent, revealing the ocean and the Bali Hai mountains.

All rooms also have snazzy marble baths with double sinks accented with gold-plated fixtures. If you're on your honeymoon, or simply in love, ask about the romantic beachside dinners for two. The gourmet meal served by your private waiter isn't cheap, but some couples can't resist.

Transportation to the Princeville golf courses, extensive health spa, tennis courts, and shops is complimentary.

SECRET BEACH HIDEAWAY, *P.O. Box 781, Kilauea, HI 96754. Tel. 808/828-2862 or 800/820-2862, Fax 808/828-286. One cottage. Rate: $275 per night. One-week minimum.*

Dramatically set on a bluff high above a beach known for its crashing surf, this beautifully decorated guest house is a fabulous place for a honeymoon or other romantic tryst. The ocean is seen through floor to ceiling windows in the bedroom, the living room/dining room/kitchen, or from the patio, at the edge of the great sloping lawn. Sunsets are particularly stunning from here. Couples at this cozy, isolated accommodation will feel completely at home with the TV/VCR, cassette deck and tapes, CD player, washer/dryer, and fully equipped high-tech kitchen. Guests may find themselves spending more time in the bathroom than usual; the spacious shower boasts two heads and glass doors that slide open to an enclosed garden where bathers can let Mother Nature dry them off.

The outdoor Jacuzzi hot tub is placed so that you have a view of the ocean. The walk down to the beach (which can be too rough for winter swimming but perfect for sunning) will take you past artfully manicured flowering plants and bushes. The eleven acres are fully gated.

MARC PRINCEVILLE PU'U PO'A, *5454 Ka Haku Road, Princeville, HI 96714-0899. Tel. 808/826-9602 or 800/535-0085, Fax 808/826-4159. 56 units. Rates begin at $262 per unit. Major credit cards.*

All of these upscale Princeville condo units situated on a beautiful ocean bluff have extensive ocean views. Done in whites and beiges, rooms are bright and sunny, each with an atrium and a lanai. The two-bedroom, two-bathroom apartments come with a deep soaking tub, washer/dryer, cable TV, and fully equipped kitchen. On the grounds are a swimming pool and a tennis court. A path leads to the hideaway beach, which is excellent for snorkeling. Housekeepers tidy up apartments about every three days.

MARC PALI KE KUA, *5300 Ka Haku Road, Princeville, HI 96714-0899. Tel. 808/826-9066 or 800/535-0085, Fax 808/826-4159. 98 units. Rates begin at $185 per unit. Major credit cards.*

These condos sit high on the cliffs above the sea on the north shore. Some have views of the dramatic mountains while others face the water. The attractive tropically decorated suites are cooled by ceiling fans, although the breezes off Hanalei Bay provide natural cooling. Facilities include a washer/dryer, cable TV, and fully equipped kitchen. The location makes this accommodation accessible to golf at the nearby Makai and Princeville Prince courses.

HANALEI BAY RESORT & EMBASSY SUITES KAUAI, *P.O. Box 220, Hanalei, HI 96714. Tel. 808/826-6522 or 800/827-4427, Fax 808/826-6680. 280 rooms. Rates begin at $160. Major credit cards.*

Banana trees, palms and other tropical foliage flourish throughout the extensive grounds of this clifftop Princeville resort. It's both a condominium complex and a hotel. In addition to a restaurant serving Pacific Rim cuisine, there are eight tennis courts, two swimming pools, and a huge whirlpool on the premises. Transportation is provided around the property, to or from the beach (about a five-minute walk away), and around Princeville. You'll also get free rides to and from the golf course. Guest quarters are quite spacious. Hotel rooms (without kitchens) are available as well as studios and one-, two- and three-bedroom suites. Lanais come with absorbing views. The top-floor units of these low-rise buildings have lofts. Hotel rooms share coin-operated laundry facilities while suites have their own laundry and ice machines.

THE CLIFFS AT PRINCEVILLE, *P.O. Box 1109, Hanalei, HI 96714. Tel. 808/826-6585 or 800/367-7052, Fax 808/826-6478. 202 units. Rates begin at $155 per unit. Major credit cards.*

Gazing down on the ocean from its lofty perch, this Princeville condominium accommodates guests in one- to four-bedroom apartments. Oak and rattan furniture decorates the spacious units, some of which have two-story living rooms and sleeping lofts. While apartments come with cable TV, they don't have telephones. Balconies off the master bedroom and living room look out to gardens or the Pacific. For a game of pool or Ping-Pong, head to the recreation center, which also sports a whirlpool and fireplace. Both a swimming pool and tennis courts are on the grounds and other activities may be arranged through the front desk.

HANALEI COLONY RESORT, *P.O. Box 828, Hanalei, HI 96741. Tel. 808/826-6235 or 800/628-3004, Fax 808/826-9893. 52 units. Rates begin at $110 per unit. Major credit cards.*

Near Haena and next to Charo's restaurant and gift shop, these two-story wooden buildings sit along the beach very close to the water in a remote part of the island. Palms and other vegetation border golf course-smooth lawns. Facilities include a swimming pool and whirlpool hot tub. Each decorated differently, the homelike condo apartments have full kitchens, spacious lanais, and ceiling fans. In yours, you might find wicker bar stools at the kitchen counter and straw mats and baskets decorating the walls. Bedrooms are defined by partitions, so they aren't soundproof. Units aren't equipped with air conditioning, TVs, telephones, or dishwashers, but alarm clocks are available from the office. Here guests can book boat, raft, helicopter, scuba, and snorkeling excursions. Linens and towels are exchanged daily at the housekeeping window, and guests may use the coin-operated washer and dryer.

HALE 'AHA BED & BREAKFAST, P.O. Box 3370. Princeville, HI 96722. Tel. 808/826-6733 or 800/826-6733, Fax 808/826-9052. Four rooms. Rates range from $85 per unit to $210 for the penthouse. Major credit cards. Three-night minimum stay.

On a Princeville golf course, here's a pleasant alternative to the area's pricier accommodations. Guests receive golf discounts and are close to all the restaurants and diversions of the surrounding upscale resort. There's a small fee for use of the nearby fitness center, pool, and tennis courts. With twin, queen, or king-sized beds, the modern, brightly furnished guest rooms come with refrigerators and TVs. The penthouse sports a separate bedroom, dining area, washer/dryer, and cathedral windows in the living room. It can sleep up to four. Both this and the honeymoon suite have whirlpool baths. Views from lanais take in the fairways, ocean, and mountains.

BED & BAY HANALEI, P.O. Box 508, Hanalei, HI 96714. Tel. 808/826-9844 or 800/437-3507, Fax 808/822-0577. One cottage. Rates begin at $75.

Just a block from Hanalei Bay, this small, rustic 1930s-style cottage is within walking distance of the pleasant town of Hanalei. The grounds flourish with fragrant plumeria, banana trees, and palms. You'll have views of a waterfall from the landscaped outdoor shower, but there is also an indoor shower lined with alpine slate. The kitchen comes complete with dishes, utensils, pots and pans, a refrigerator, gas burners, and a toaster oven. A queen size bed is in the main room. You'll probably spend a lot of time in a hammock on the lanai. To make sure you truly feel at home, there's even a washer and dryer.

BED & BREAKFASTS & PRIVATE HOMES

Staying in a Bed & Breakfast or renting a private home can give you more than a glimpse of Kauai beneath the surface. Many of these accommodations, all run and decorated with a personal touch, are in residential communities. Daily prices for double rooms run from about $60 to $170. Most are in the $60 to $100 range. A minimum number of nights may be required. If you'd like to find out about Bed & Breakfasts in addition to those described above, or about renting private homes and cottages, contact the following companies:

• **Bed & Breakfast Hawaii**, P.O. Box 449, Kapaa, Kauai, HI 96746. Tel. 808/822-7171 or 800/733-1612.

• **Bed & Breakfast Honolulu**, 3242 Kaohinani Drive, Honolulu, HI 96817. Tel. 808/595-7533 or 800/ 288-4666.

Housekeeping Cabins

KOKEE LODGE, *Waimea Canyon Drive, Kokee State Park, Box 819, Waimea, HI 96796. 12 cabins. Tel. 808/335-6061. Rates begin at $40 per cabin. Major credit cards.*

High in the mountains of Kokee State Park, 3,600 feet above sea level, these simple cabins are halfway between spectacular Waimea Canyon and Kalalau Lookout. Wild fowl roam the grounds. The cool misty air in these thick woods is sweet with the smell of eucalyptus and pine. Here on a tropical island, blankets and wood-burning stoves get much use (wood is available at an additional cost). Each of the studio and two-bedroom cabins (sleeping from three to seven people) contains a refrigerator, gas or electric stove, cooking and eating utensils, beds, blankets, pillows, linens and a hot shower. The newer cabins, paneled in aromatic cedar, are far nicer than the older units.

In season, hikers enjoy picking wild plums and fishing for rainbow trout in streams (freshwater fishing licenses are required). In the main building, the restaurant serves light breakfasts and lunches daily. There is also a gift shop. The petite Kokee Natural History Museum is next door. The Lodge is 40 miles from Lihue Airport, at least a 90-minute drive. The last 15 miles are along a steep, curvaceous, narrow road.

WHERE TO EAT

Kauai may not be famous for its culinary expertise, but it has enough good restaurants to keep most vacationers - and residents - satisfied. They run the gamut from roadside to gourmet settings. Note that some serve dinner only. Dress is casual at all but a couple of places.

Created by Walter Lappert to combat the idleness he found in retirement, **Lappert's Ice Cream** is manufactured near Hanapepe. You can buy some at the stand there, or at restaurants and stores around the island. Fresh local fruits are incorporated into this smooth, rich treat, such as *lilikoi* (passion fruit), guava, coconut, papaya, mango, pineapple, and lichee.

Sold at **Taro Ko Chips**, a tiny Mom-and-Pop factory in a former home in Hanapepe, crisp sliced and fried taro is a refreshing alternative to potato chips. Tiny purple threads decorate each delicious chip, sprinkled with garlic salt. This snack is made from the same root that when mashed and fermented becomes poi. But unlike the ancient Hawaiian staple, these chips win over the uninitiated with one bite.

Another winner is locally produced **Kukui Nut Guava Jam**. Hanapepe's **Kauai Kookie** is also a good stop. For mouth-watering pastries and breads, try **Kilauea Bakery** in Kilauea.

KAUAI'S BEST EATS

Cream of the Crop

Dondero's, Poipu: Try this attractive setting for delicious Italian food.

Tidepools, Poipu: Excellent seafood is served at this restaurant where cozy seating areas hang over the water.

A Pacific Cafe, Kapaa: Since so many of the Pacific Rim dishes here look and smell so good, you'll have a hard time choosing.

Roy's Poipu Bar & Grill, Poipu: More than a dozen daily specials are offered at this popular spot where the menu is always changing.

Moderate or Inexpensive

Hanamaulu Cafe, Tea House, and Sushi Bar, Hanamaulu: Both excellent Japanese and Chinese selections are on this menu.

The King and I, Waipouli: If you like spicy Thai food, this is a great choice.

Hamura Saimin, Lihue: Consider stopping at this Japanese restaurant when you're in town.

The West & South

TIDEPOOLS, Hyatt Regency Kauai, Poipu. Tel. 742-1234. Dinner only. Reservations recommended. Dinner entrees: $25 to $30. Credit cards accepted.

Live music entertains guests who stop in the large circular bar before dinner. Plants spill over the rafters. Various dining areas are scattered in this series of thatched roof hales (shelters) at the edge of a lagoon. Some tables have the open-air nooks overhanging the water all to themselves. The contemporary Hawaiian cuisine adapts traditional regional cooking to today's palates; some of the dishes use ingredients indigenous to the Hawaiian islands. The specialties of the house include fish, which comes blackened, sautéed, grilled, or baked. You might try pepper crusted ahi with a champagne sauce or charred ahi sashimi with three lentil salad, along with Tidepools' special papaya relish. Other imaginative creations include a vegetarian sampler that includes bok choy, sautéed mixed vegetables, and ramen noodles. Meat eaters can choose between filet mignon and prime rib. If you can't decide between land and sea, try one of the combination meat and seafood entrees.

DONDERO'S, Hyatt Regency Kauai, Poipu. Tel. 742-1234. Dinner only. Reservations recommended. Dinner entrees: $17.50 to $29. Credit cards accepted.

At this excellent Italian restaurant, green tiles and wine bottles decorate walls, and colorful jars of antipasto are on display. The soft fresh bread that accompanies meals is dipped in a wonderfully seasoned tomato and onion sauce. The wine list is outstanding. Among the pasta, my favorites are the roasted red bell pepper gnocchi with sautéed lobster and the spaghettini alla pescatora. The midwest lamb chops with warm potato salad, marinated chicken breast with a spicy diablo sauce, and the delicately seasoned veal scaloppini are beautifully prepared and presented. Come before dark for a view of the palms, gardens, and the sea.

KEOKI'S PARADISE, *Poipu Shopping Village, 2360 Kiahuna Plantation Drive, Poipu. Tel. 742-7534 Reservations recommended. Dinner entrees $10 to $20. Credit cards accepted.*

A lagoon, fringed with lush vegetation and complete with lava rocks and waterfalls, meanders between the tables in this very popular open-air restaurant. Dishes on the menu include several different types of fish prepared in a choice of ways (from teriyaki to baked with orange-ginger sauce), pork ribs glazed with plum sauce, and shrimp with macadamia nut pesto. Whet your appetite with a tangy lilikoi (passion fruit) margarita, a frozen mai tai, or a frothy pina colada. While the dining room is often filled with families, the thatched roof bar, which serves pupus and other snacks, draws a friendly crowd of young singles.

For dessert, few pass up the hula pie (macadamia nut ice cream on an Oreo cookie crust, topped with chocolate sauce, whipped cream, and macadamia nuts). The live music several nights a week adds to the pleasant atmosphere.

HOUSE OF SEAFOOD, *1941 Poipu Road, Poipu Kai Resort, Poipu. Tel. 742-6433. Dinner only. Reservations recommended. Dinner entrees $10 to $20. Credit cards accepted.*

Every night, the menu changes at this popular restaurant decorated with wicker and potted plants. Whether you order fish, shrimp, lobster or scallops, your meal will include chowder or salad, rice pilaf, vegetables, and rolls that are straight from the oven.

TAISHO, *5470 Koloa Road, Old Koloa Town. Tel. 742-1838. Dinner entrees $10 to $18.*

Begin dinner at this mostly Japanese restaurant with sashimi, hamachi, spring rolls, or fried chicken wings. For entrees, preceded by soup, good choices are the jumbo shrimp tempura, unagi kabeyaki (eel), ginger pork, and teriyaki beef. A full sushi bar is on hand.

BRENNECKE'S BEACH BROILER, *Poipu. Tel. 742-7588. Reservations recommended. Dinner entrees: $7.50 to $30. Credit cards accepted.*

Diners may watch the chef in action at this popular restaurant overlooking the water. Tables on the second floor have the best view of the shore. Distinctively flavored kiawe-grilled ahi and seafood, such as Alaskan King Crab, are house specialties but they also do a fine job with prime ribs and steak, as well as the more mundane burgers and pizza.

ROY'S POIPU BAR & GRILL, *Poipu Shopping Village, 2360 Kiahuna Plantation Drive, Poipu. Tel. 742-5000. Dinner entrees: $7 to $18. Credit cards accepted.*

After making a name for himself on Oahu and Maui, Roy Yamaguchi opened this dining spot in 1994. With a hefty selection of daily specials, the creative European-Asian-Pacific menu is always changing. Expect to find dishes such as seared opakapaka (snapper) with black bean sauce, dumplings stuffed with smoked duck, crispy lemongrass chicken with Thai red curry, ravioli of summer vegetables with green peppercorn sauce, and grilled shrimp with mushrooms and risotto.

KOKEE LODGE, *Kokee State Park. Tel. 335-6061. Breakfast and lunch served every day. Inexpensive. Credit cards accepted.*

Nestled in thick wilderness 3,600 feet above Kauai's tropical coast, this rustic mountain lodge serves salads, sandwiches, and other light selections.

HANAPEPE BOOKSTORE CAFE & ESPRESSO BAR, *3830 Hanapepe Road, Hanapepe. Tel. 335-5011. Open Tuesday through Saturday for breakfast and lunch, Thursday, Friday, and Saturday for dinner. Inexpensive. Credit cards accepted.*

This colorful restaurant/boutique could have been plucked straight from New York's artsy Greenwich Village. The vegetarian selections are quite varied. Good choices include the fritatta with zucchini, onions, red peppers, mushrooms, and parmesan; pasta with sun dried tomatoes, corn, onions, cilantro, peppers, and cheese; the grilled vegetable sandwich; the gorgonzola/brie ravioli with Italian white beans; and the garden burger. Sit at the counter or a table and admire the original artwork adorning the walls. On Thursday afternoons, you can also stop off at the farmer's market across the street. Live music will accompany your meal on nights when dinner is served.

GREEN GARDEN, *Hanapepe. Tel. 335-5422. Dinner reservations recommended. Closed Tuesday nights. Inexpensive. Credit cards accepted.*

Many locals recommend this family-oriented dining spot for its steak, fish, and shrimp. The emphasis is on homestyle Chinese and American cooking. However, I suggest you avoid Green Garden at lunch time, when busloads of tourists pour in on their way to and from Waimea Canyon. The name is a perfect description of the restaurant - all the potted and hanging orchids and other plants and flowers give diners the feeling that they are outdoors.

LAWAI RESTAURANT, *2-3687 Kaumualii Highway, Lawai. Tel. 332-9550. Inexpensive. Credit cards accepted.*

While enjoying homestyle Hawaiian, Chinese, Japanese, and American food, talk story with the folks at the next table. This casual eatery is known for its sweet and sour spare ribs, shrimp tempura, and saimin. All three meals are served daily.

OMOIDE BAKERY & DELICATESSEN, *Hanapepe. Tel. 335-5291.*

Lunch only. Inexpensive.

A very local crowd gathers at this deli every day for generous portions of homestyle Japanese, Chinese, and American food kept hot on steam tables.

TOI'S THAI KITCHEN, *Eleele. Tel. 335-3111. Inexpensive.*

In this casual restaurant, popular selections include shrimp chips, Pad Thai noodles, chicken satay, and green, red, and yellow curries.

BRICK OVEN PIZZA, *2-2555 Kaumualii Highway, Kalaheo. Tel. 332-8561. Open 11am to 10pm. Closed Mondays. Inexpensive. Credit cards accepted.*

Many residents consider this the best place to come for pizza on Kauai.

Lihue Area

GAYLORD'S, *Kilohana Plantation, Puhi (outside Lihue) Tel. 245-9593. Reservations required. Dinner entrees: $16 to $30. Credit cards accepted.*

In a flower-filled courtyard at the back of a 19th century plantation main house, this restaurant has a wonderful view of smooth lawns and Mt. Waialeale in the distance. While lunch is served, some patrons have found the food better at dinner. If you arrive before the sun goes down, you can take advantage of the scenery and wander around Kilohana's boutiques. You might even take a spin in the carriage drawn by a Clydesdale horse. But the food is the attraction in this somewhat formal setting. Meat lovers might favor the herb crusted rack of lamb, seasoned with Dijon mustard and served with pasta or the New Zealand venison whose sauce varies nightly. My favorite is the chicken Kauai, a boneless, skinless breast pan-sauteed with pineapple, papaya, and port wine sauce (the sweetness is subtle). End the meal with a cup of espresso from the restaurant's old Italian coffee machine.

DUKE'S CANOE CLUB, *Kauai Marriott (near Lihue), Tel. 246-9599. Dinner entrees: $13.95 to $23.95. Credit cards accepted.*

Duke's, like its Waikiki counterpart, is dedicated to the great surfer Duke Kahanamoku. Expect to find creatively prepared seafood, prime ribs, steaks, and poultry. Be careful not to fill up on the delicious salad bar; leave room for the daily catch. Some nights, Duke's features strolling musicians who will take your requests.

BARBECUE INN, *2982 Kress, off Rice Street, Lihue. Tel. 245-2921. Dinner entrees: $7.95 to $20.*

For many of its nearly sixty years, this restaurant has won the praise of locals who have recommended it highly for its varied plate lunches and other homestyle dishes. A new chef has added Pacific Rim gourmet dishes to the menu. The family owners (now the third generation) pride themselves on baking their own breads and pies daily. Even the gourmet fish and lobster dishes have homestyle touches, and at moderate prices. **HANAMAULU CAFE, TEAHOUSE, AND SUSHI BAR,** *Highway 56, Hanamaulu, just north of Lihue. Tel. 245-3225. Closed Mondays. The main dining room opens early for dinner (4:30pm to 9pm). Reservations recommended. Entrees: $6 to $12. Credit cards accepted.*

You can choose between Japanese and Chinese food at this attractive indoor/outdoor teahouse set off with a pond and landscaped gardens. While there's a sushi bar, some Japanese selections are cooked on an open grill. Cantonese entrees include sweet and sour spareribs, crab claws, and chop suey. The restaurant is known for its Chinese fried chicken plate lunches and its Japanese plate lunches with teriyaki beef, chicken, or fish, and miso soup. For dessert, try the deep-fried custard rolled in powdered sugar and sesame seeds. The Tea House section of the restaurant is open for special occasions only.

HAMURA SAIMIN, *2956 Kress, off Rice Street, Lihue. Tel. 245-3271. Open Monday to Saturday 10am to midnight; Sunday 10am to 9pm. Inexpensive.*

After visiting the Kauai Museum, consider stopping at this restaurant around the corner for lunch. The heaping bowls of delicious saimin are filled with homemade noodles. Other popular items are barbecued beef or chicken, udon, wonton, and fried noodles. For dessert, treat yourself to a slice of *lilikoi* chiffon pie or buy a whole pie. Watch the chefs in action in the open kitchen. The stools and counters are reminiscent of a 1960s coffee shop.

This is the kind of place where the owners feel compelled to add a note to the wall menu (with its black and red moveable letters) saying, "Please do not stick gum under counter." There's a gumball machine in the corner, and kids seem to ignore this request. However, what the restaurant lacks in decor, it certainly makes up for in generous portions of excellent food.

KIIBO RESTAURANT, *2991 Umi Street, off Rice Street, Lihue. Tel. 245-2650. Inexpensive. Credit cards accepted.*

In addition to bento lunches and sushi, you'll find teriyaki, tempura, sukiyaki, and other Japanese specialties.

YOKOZUNA RAMEN, *3100 Kuhio Highway, Lihue. Tel. 246-1008. Lunch: 10:30am to 2:30pm, dinner: 5pm to 10:30pm, Sunday: dinner only. Inexpensive. Credit cards accepted.*

This friendly restaurant serves excellent saimin, tempura, and other Japanese food, as well as Chinese, Korean, and local food.

MA'S FAMILY RESTAURANT, *Lihue. Tel. 245-3142. Inexpensive.*

Pancakes made with bananas or papaya are a specialty for breakfast at this modest place that is popular with locals. The Kauai Museum is nearby.

KAUAI CHOP SUEY, *Lihue. Tel. 245-8790. Open for dinner Tuesday through Sunday; lunch and dinner on Saturday. Inexpensive.*

Many residents give high marks to the Cantonese food served at this local spot.

The East Coast

A PACIFIC CAFE, *4-831 Kuhio Highway, Kauai Village, Kapaa. Tel. 822-0013. Dinner only. Reservations recommended. Dinner entrees: $16 to $30. Credit cards accepted.*

Woks and a wood-burning grill add a special flavor to the Pacific Rim dishes served at this chic restaurant. Framed photos and paintings (for sale) adorn the walls of the bright, cheerful dining room. The grill is in full view, and chefs' hats constantly bob up and down behind the pick-up counter. To help you decide what to have, take a peek at other people's orders before waiters whisk them away. This restaurant won an award from *GQ* for its signature dish of wok charred mahi-mahi.

Each day, there's a new array of selections, all prepared and presented with an artistic eye for color, texture, and surprise. To start, you might find Thai Caesar salad with wonton chips, sautéed crab cakes with papaya basil sauce, or sizzling squid salad with sesame lime dressing. Then perhaps you'll choose among seared Australian salmon with orange ginger sauce, sirloin steak with lemon grass peanut crust and citrus sauce, and potato and tofu lasagna with ginger scallion pesto. If you've left room for one of their delicious desserts, indulge yourself with the Toasted Hawaiian, white chocolate cake, and haupia topped with macadamia nut mousse.

THE BULL SHED, *796 Kuhio Highway, Waipouli. Tel. 822-3791. Dinner only. Reservations recommended. Dinner entrees: $10.95 to $23.95. Credit cards accepted.*

The portions are generous at this often crowded oceanfront steak and seafood restaurant. Patrons dine family style at large tables. The huge slabs of teriyaki sirloin and prime rib move quickly. Rack of lamb is another popular choice. Meals include an unspectacular salad bar.

MARGARITAS, *4-733 Kuhio Highway, Kapaa. Tel. 822-1808. Open 4pm to 9:30pm. Happy Hour: 4pm to 6pm.*

This Mexican restaurant serves above-average burritos, enchiladas, tacos, and - of course - margaritas (lime, peach, strawberry, or *lilikoi*). You'll dine at the edge of an open field: if you sit outside, friendly mules may come over to your table looking to share your taco chips. Try the belt-buster super burrito, stuffed with sirloin steak, refried beans, and cheese, topped with lettuce, tomatoes, guacamole, and sour cream; the vegetarian quesadilla extravaganza, with cheese, green chilies, olives, scallions, and tomatoes smothered in sour cream and guacamole; the tacos filled with grilled ahi (tuna); or the boneless chicken breast marinated in barbecue sauce, broiled, and served with Spanish rice and salad.

KAPAA FISH & CHOWDER HOUSE, *1639 Kuhio Highway, Kapaa. Tel. 822-7488. Dinner only. Reservations recommended. Dinner entrees: $8.50 to $15.95. Credit cards accepted.*

Spicy Cajun-style fish and shrimp are served at this attractive restaurant, along with seafood fettuccini and Alaskan crab legs cooked in beer. Entrees for landlubbers are also well prepared.

THE KING AND I, *4-901 Kuhio Highway Waipouli Plaza, Waipouli. Tel. 822-1642. Dinner entrees: $5.25 to $10.95. Credit cards accepted.*

I love this Thai restaurant. The spicy meat and seafood dishes are well seasoned with hot peppers, peanuts, and coconut. Porcupine shrimp gets its look from crispy noodles, and it's delicious.

PAPAYA'S, *Village Shopping Center, Wailua. Tel. 823-0191. Open Monday to Saturday 9am to 8pm, closed Sundays. Inexpensive. Credit cards accepted.*

I tried this restaurant, espresso bar, and bakery after several readers had written to me raving about it, and I found it as good as they said. Food here is prepared with all natural ingredients, without preservatives. Most of it is locally grown and raised. For breakfast, consider the tofu scramble, banana pancakes, the quiche, or the granola with fruit. For lunch or dinner, you might try the ginger udon noodles, the tempeh, tofu, or chicken burgers, the chili with cornbread, or the basmati rice with eggplant. The curries and vegetable lasagna also get high marks, as do the salads, pizza, and homemade chocolate cake. The garden burgers are just as delicious. If you're staying somewhere with cooking facilities or a refrigerator, you may want to stop at the natural foods grocery section.

MEMA, *361 Kuhio Highway, Wailua. Tel. 823-0899. Inexpensive.*

The well-seasoned Thai and Chinese food is delicious at this cozy restaurant. Try the shrimp rolls or the broccoli soup, chicken in coconut milk with red chili, sweet and sour pork, and red, yellow, or green Thai curries. You'll have a choice of brown, white, or sticky rice.

NORBERTO'S EL CAFE, *4-1373 Kuhio Highway, Kapaa. Tel. 822-3362. Dinner only. Inexpensive. Credit cards accepted.*

Probably the best place on Kauai for Mexican food, Norberto's serves a wide variety of fajitas, burritos, tacos, tostadas, and enchiladas. Chips, salsa picante, soup and rice and beans accompany entrees.

ALOHA DINER, *971F Kuhio Highway, Kapaa. Tel. 822-3851. Inexpensive.*

When you're ready for some authentic Hawaiian food, come to this no-frills diner. In addition to *poi* (made from mashed, fermented taro root), you'll be able to sample lomi-lomi salmon (chunks of the salted fish mixed with chopped onions and tomatoes), kalua pig, fried *akule* (a dried fish) and *poke ahi* (raw yellowtail tuna and seaweed in sesame oil), among other dishes. There might be some haupia (coconut jellied pudding) for dessert.

KOUNTRY KITCHEN, *1485 Kuhio Highway, Kapaa. Tel. 822-3511. Inexpensive.*

Locals pile in for breakfast, which is the best of the three meals served here daily. Friendly waiters serve large portions, such as the Polynesian omelette, stuffed with kim chee, Portuguese sausage, onions and cheese; or the Kountry Kitchen omelette, with hamburger or tuna, onions, peppers, tomatoes and cheese; both with cornbread. The lunch menu features burgers, from bleu cheese to mushroom, club sandwiches, grilled mahi-mahi, and blueberry cobbler for dessert.

DUANE'S ONO-CHAR BURGER, *Anahola. Tel. 822-9181. Inexpensive.*

Not to be confused with Ono Family Restaurant in Kapaa, this is a roadside stand. "Ono" means delicious in Hawaiian, and these burgers are just that, according to many residents who rarely pass by without stopping to munch. This is a good lunch spot along the way to the north shore. If you'd prefer not to eat on the run, take a seat at one of the round tables in the shade of the royal poinciana trees. The house specialty is the avocado burger, which also comes piled with alfalfa sprouts, cheddar cheese and lettuce, and is smothered in teriyaki sauce.

DRAGON INN, *4901 Kuhio Highway, Kapaa. Tel. 822-3788. Inexpensive.*

Some residents consider this Kauai's best Chinese restaurant. Try the shrimp and black bean sauce.

ONO FAMILY RESTAURANT, *4-1292 Kuhio Highway, Kapaa. Tel. 822-1710. Inexpensive.*

I've never understood the popularity of this roadside restaurant. The casual, pleasant decor - wooden booths and tables with cane-back chairs - is nice enough. However, french fries, grilled cheese, and other dishes seem greasier than necessary. The outdoor dining area looks inviting, but it's filled with the sound of cars whizzing along the main road. Perhaps if I liked buffalo, I'd change my tune. Yes, burgers made from ground buffalo meat are prepared here in ten different ways, such as with pineapple and teriyaki sauce, or mushrooms and cheese. If you're not adventurous enough for this, regular beef burgers also come with a variety of toppings. Otherwise, try the chili or sandwiches. For breakfast, consider omelets, hash and eggs, or French toast.

The North

THE BALI HAI RESTAURANT, *Hanalei Bay Resort, Princeville. Tel. 826-6522. Dinner entrees: $10.95 to $22.95.*

Come before dark and you'll take in the clifftop view of Hanalei Bay. The cuisine is Pacific Rim and specialties include Black Angus beef and creatively prepared fresh fish. In the evening, live musicians range from guitarists singing original Hawaiian songs to an accomplished church choir.

CASA DI AMICI, *2484 Keneke Street, Kilauea. Tel. 828-1555. Reservations required. Dinner entrees: $10.95 to $22. Credit cards accepted.*

In a quiet part of Kauai, this al fresco restaurant serves some delicious Italian food. Fluffy plants hang from the high open-beam ceiling. Lattice-work dividers define dining areas. Italian music plays softly in the background.

Try the pasta with walnuts in a Romano cheese cream sauce. The pesto and Alfredo sauces are also good, as are the veal, beef, and chicken dishes.

CHARO'S, *Hanalei Colony Resort, Haena. Tel. 826-6422. Reservations recommended. Dinner entrees $10.95 to $25. Credit cards accepted.*

This oceanfront restaurant, with a limited menu of Spanish, Italian, and French food is often crowded. Its most popular dish is Chicken Barcelona, but the food is not the main attraction. Walls are decorated with large photos of the scantily-dressed owner Charo, the Latin "coochie coochie girl," who drops by from time to time. If you miss her in person, you can visit the adjacent gift shop, where pictures of Charo are on everything from posters to T-shirts.

ZELO'S BEACH HOUSE, *Hanalei. Tel. 826-9700. Dinner entrees: $7 to $20. Credit cards accepted.*

This restaurant and grill is a good place to stop while you're touring the north shore. For a light snack, consider the soup and salad - or maybe a bowl of French onion and a pesto pasta salad - or a burger (beef or veggie). Full meals come with a green salad, garlic bread, vegetable, and rice pilaf or baked potato; entrees include lemon herb shrimp scampi, smothered steak with mushrooms and onions topped with melted provolone, and Hawaiian chicken (marinated in teriyaki sauce and grilled with pineapple). There is also a variety of delicious pastas, from fettuccini alfredo and ravioli to chicken parmesan and linguini with clam sauce and toasted pine nuts. If you feel more like Mexican food, try a chicken, steak or tofu fajita or burrito, or a seafood taco.

Room for dessert? The grasshopper pie (mint ice cream on an Oreo cookie crust, topped with fudge, whipped cream, and macadamia nuts) and the *lilikoi* (passion fruit) chiffon pie both move quickly.

PAU HANA PIZZA & KILAUEA BAKERY, *Kong Lung Center Garden Courtyard, Kilauea Road and Keneke Street, Kilauea. Tel. 828-2020. Closed Sundays. Bakery hours: 6:30am to 9pm. Pizza hours: 11am to 9pm. Inexpensive.*

Try this cafe for soup, salad, pizza, and fresh baked goods. The olive oil used for the pizza is organically grown (as are the salad greens) and you'll have a choice of whole wheat or traditional crust. While cheese and tomato pies are certainly available, these pizzas can also be far from ordinary. Toppings include anchovies, tiger prawns, house smoked ono (wahoo), barbecue chicken, smoked ham, roasted onions and red peppers, seasoned eggplant, sun-dried tomato pesto, and pineapple. Among the assorted cheeses are goat, feta, gorgonzola, and grated parmesan. At the bakery, the sourdough breads are popular, along with the cinnamon buns, croissants, and sesame, garlic, and chili pepper breadsticks.

SEEING THE SIGHTS
The South

Heading west on Highway 50 toward Poipu on your way from Lihue Airport, don't be discouraged if you can't make out **Queen Victoria's Profile** near the top of the Hoary Head Mountains to the left. Not everyone agrees that this rocky configuration looks like Her Majesty. To the right, Mt. Waialeale slopes upward. When you turn south onto Highway 520, a.k.a. Maluhia Road, you'll cut through the **Tunnel of Trees,** a dramatic passageway lined with stately eucalyptus whose branches reach out to each other overhead.

Established in the 1830s, Kauai's first sugar plantation once thrived where **Koloa Town** now stands. You'll see the timeworn smokestack and other remnants of the mill. Attractively refurbished or re-created 19th century wooden buildings give the town a Western frontier look. Some of the boutiques and galleries housed inside are better for browsing than for buying, since the upscale jewelry, clothing, and other goods come with (very) upscale price tags. Collectively, these stores are known as Old Koloa Town. Plaques outside the old plantation buildings tell their history and original use. One was a barber shop, another the site of a taro processing factory, and still others an ice cream and soda fountain, a music store, a fish market, a bar.

Across the street from the mammoth monkeypod tree, sugarcane has been planted to illustrate the variety of strains. Nearby you'll see a monument with bronze bas-reliefs of members of the different races and nationalities whose back-breaking work made Hawaii's sugarcane fields so prosperous. There's also the **Sugar History Museum,** located in the back of the central courtyard. In this small museum, you'll get a glimpse of life on early sugar plantations and sugar farming. Additionally, the

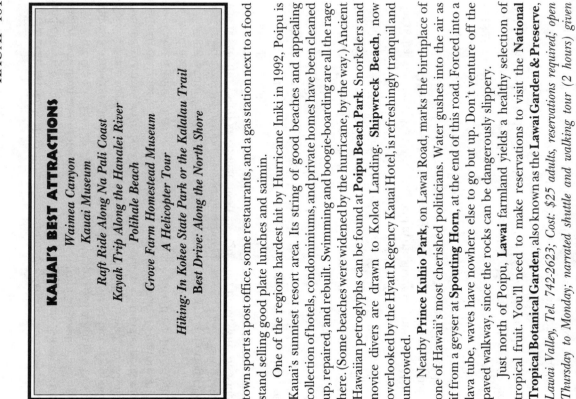

KAUAI'S BEST ATTRACTIONS

Waimea Canyon
Kauai Museum
Raft Ride Along Na Pali Coast
Kayak Trip Along the Hanalei River
Polihale Beach
Grove Farm Homestead Museum
A Helicopter Tour
Hiking: In Kokee State Park or the Kalalau Trail
Best Drive: Along the North Shore

town sports a post office, some restaurants, and a gas station next to a food stand selling good plate lunches and saimin.

One of the regions hardest hit by Hurricane Iniki in 1992, Poipu is Kauai's sunniest resort area. Its string of good beaches and appealing collection of hotels, condominiums, and private homes have been cleaned up, repaired, and rebuilt. Swimming and boogie-boarding are all the rage here. (Some beaches were widened by the hurricane, by the way.) Ancient Hawaiian petroglyphs can be found at **Poipu Beach Park**. Snorkelers and novice divers are drawn to Koloa Landing. **Shipwreck Beach**, now overlooked by the Hyatt Regency Kauai Hotel, is refreshingly tranquil and uncrowded.

Nearby **Prince Kuhio Park**, on Lawai Road, marks the birthplace of one of Hawaii's most cherished politicians. Water gushes into the air as if from a geyser at **Spouting Horn**, at the end of this road. Forced into a lava tube, waves have nowhere else to go but up. Don't venture off the paved walkway, since the rocks can be dangerously slippery.

Just north of Poipu, **Lawai** farmland yields a healthy selection of tropical fruit. You'll need to make reservations to visit the **National Tropical Botanical Garden**, also known as the **Lawai Garden & Preserve,** *Lawai Valley, Tel. 742-2623; Cost: $25 adults, reservations required; open Thursday to Monday; narrated shuttle and walking tour (2 hours) given Thursday to Monday 9am, 11:30am, and 2pm, by the National Tropical Botanical Garden, a non-profit organization.*

Little known by people who aren't botanists or conservationists, this flourishing 186-acre garden is a good place for anyone who appreciates the beauty (and the importance) of natural splendor. Some experts predict that no tropical rain forest will survive the year 2,000 in Central and South America, having fallen victim to the economic promise of the lumber and cattle business. In addition to killing off many resident species of plants and animals, this will have a devastating effect on the ozone layer and on oxygen production worldwide. This garden serves as a center for the preservation and protection of the world's tropical plants.

Visitors take a van ride along a curving, bumpy road down into Lawai Valley. Giant green lily pads cover practically the whole surface of a pond. They are said to be strong enough for a human being to walk on. Along Lawai Stream are strands of bamboo, kukui nut trees, monkeypods and palm trees. Double-coconut trees take more than 70 years to mature, and then seven more before their unusual nuts reach their full weight (sometimes 50 pounds).

Tours of the flourishing grounds include a visit to a neighboring 100-acre garden estate that boasts a commanding view of Lawai Bay. Here you'll see the vacation cottage used by Queen Emma, wife of King Kamehameha IV, during the 1880s. Ancient Hawaiian taro terraces and stone walls remain.

Back on Highway 50, you'll come to the picturesque village of **Kalaheo**. Most of the people who live in the attractive homes of this settlement are Portuguese immigrants who came to Hawaii to fish and work on the plantations. If you're carrying picnic fixings, consider stopping at **Kukuiolono Park**, with its Hawaiian display, Japanese gardens, and golf course. The view from this lofty height is wonderful.

More beautiful blossoms await visitors at 12-acre **Olu Pua Gardens**, about a half mile up a private road just past Kalaheo. This plantation estate dating back to the 1930s features a pond in the shape of a hibiscus. Along Highway 50, **Hanapepe Overlook** brings cars and tour buses to a halt. Lush vegetation and bright green geometric plots of farmland cover deep Hanapepe Valley. Smooth hills roll gently in the distance. In stark contrast, the dramatic canyon cliffs are a vivid orange. Here in this chasm in 1824, the son of Kauai's King Ka-umu-ali'i was the leader of the island's final military maneuver. Most of the land in this area belongs to the Robinson family, the haoles who own Niihau, the offshore island where the population, language, and lifestyle are Hawaiian. The Robinsons, who speak fluent Hawaiian, also claim about a third of the land on Kauai itself. Their sugar mill is the only non-union mill in the state, but their wages are comparable with unionized companies and their benefits are said to be pretty good.

Weathered wooden buildings border the streets of Hanapepe, which is reminiscent of an old Western town on the mainland. Chickens do their jerky dash back and forth across the road. A few upscale shops struggle to keep afloat on the often deserted streets. This agricultural town once bustled with energy. Then came a highway that bypassed it, and a shopping center was built nearby. Along the *makai* (ocean) side of the main highway **Kauai Soto Zen Temple** makes an eye-catching landmark.

At the end of Lele Road, you'll come to **Salt Pond Beach Park**, where salt is still dried in the sun as it has been for generations. From nearby **Burns Fields**, arrange to take off in a glider plane or a helicopter.

The West

A few miles west of Hanapepe, the overgrown ruins of 19th century **Fort Elizabeth**, more commonly called the **Russian Fort**, sit on a rise above the Waimea River. You might say that the remains of this fort stand as a reminder of the tricks that could be pulled in the days before airplanes, telephones, Fax machines, and e-mail. Commonly called the Old Russian Fort, it was built around 1816. While in the employ of Baranov's Russian American Trading Company of Alaska, Georg Anton Scheffer arrived in Hawaii. Pretending to be a heart specialist, he cared for the infirm King Kamehameha I. In exchange, the grateful monarch gave him some prime oceanfront land. Scheffer began building a fort there. When the king saw that he had put up the Russian flag over the foundation, he promptly took the land back and continued building the fort for himself.

Then Scheffer heard that the king of the island of Kauai was tired of being ruled by King Kamehameha. He sailed to Kauai and convinced King Ka-umu-ali'i that the czar would help him regain Kauai's independence. In addition, he promised Russia's help in ousting Kamehameha so that Ka-umu-ali'i and the czar could split the rule of the other Hawaiian islands. After receiving more waterfront land and a royal gift of 30 Hawaiian commoners, Scheffer began building Fort Elizabeth, again flying the Russian flag. The charlatan's downfall finally came when the commander of a Russian naval ship arrived in Hawaii. Word reached King Ka-umu-ali'i that Scheffer was nothing but an impostor and that the czar had absolutely no desire to control or do battle with Hawaii. The Kauaian king quickly threw Scheffer off the island and sent a message to King Kamehameha asking him to disregard anything he might have heard about Ka-umu-ali'i being disloyal to the kingdom. If only the king of Kauai could have checked Scheffer's references!

Across the Waimea River Bridge and about 2.5 miles up Menehune Road, **Menehune Ditch** is an aqueduct said to have been constructed by Kauai's legendary race of little people. Archaeologists have lent credence to this theory by pointing out that the stones were cut and put together in a manner that bears no resemblance to any other construction done by Hawaiians. They also note that markings have been found here that seem to have no connection with early Hawaiian drawings, symbols, or designs.

Not far from the Russian Fort is the site where British Captain James Cook first landed in Hawaii in 1778, at Waimea Bay. The unassuming **Captain Cook Monument** stands on the roadside in the rural town of

Waimea. Cows laze in the shade of trees. Some houses are flanked by the bushy, dwarfed variety of palms; no need to climb them for coconuts -just reach up. If you're headed to Waimea Canyon, Kokee State Park, or Kalalau Lookout, turn *mauka* (inland) up **Waimea Canyon Drive.** For another route, continue west on Highway 50 to Kekaha, then turn *mauka* onto wider **Kokee Road** (Highway 550).

Sugarcane, cornfields, and rows of other crops stretch for miles along much of Highway 50. Outside the mill in the plantation town of **Kekaha,** a sign reads, "Sorry, absolutely no factory tours." However, during harvest season (mid-February through mid-December) anyone is welcome to watch the machinery heaving the stalks onto trucks that seem about to buckle under the weight of all the cane. The smell of molasses mingles with the perfume of the plumeria and other flowers that border the area's handsome wooden homes. West of Kekaha, dune buggies often roar down the sand of **Kekaha Beach Park,** off Highway 50. Overlooked by commanding sea cliffs, **Polihale** is Kauai's longest beach. On weekends, this broad stretch of sand also draws the dune buggy crowd, but it is practically deserted at other times. You'll reach the beach after driving to the end of Highway 50, then turning *makai* (left) onto a rutted, rocky dirt road that snakes through sugarcane fields toward the Pacific. Between Kekaha and Polihale, you'll find a string of other pretty beaches, some with dark sand.

Waimea Canyon Drive and Kokee Road meet each other near **Waimea Canyon Lookout.** Especially during winter months, be sure to take a sweater when you visit what Mark Twain called "The Grand Canyon of the Pacific." This 10-mile-long, two-mile-wide, 3,600-foot-deep chasm is a study in pinks, reds, oranges, greens, browns, and golds. The intensity of color changes with the moving sun. In one of Mother Nature's amusing coincidences, these hues are repeated in the bright plumage of the wild chickens that greet visitors in the parking lot. Goats move effortlessly along the rocky, nearly vertical edges of the cliffs. You can see this vast natural wonder by helicopter, by driving to the Waimea Canyon or Puu Hinahina Lookouts, or by hiking to other vantage points in and around Kokee State Park.

Along the road up to the lookout, cacti are scattered across the dry hills. Yellow tufts of grass sprout from the prairielike terrain. After some hairpin curves, the ocean and the island of Niihau reveal themselves in the distance. The road continues to snake uphill, past silky oak trees with their bright red-and-yellow blossoms, the pink flowers of banana poka vines, pines, and koa trees (once used to make canoes). Consider stopping at rustic Kokee Lodge, farther up, for a meal.

Some 45 miles of Hawaii's most rewarding and extensive hiking trails crisscross 4,435-acre **Kokee State Park,** beginning at around 3,000 feet.

Allow at least a full day if you're planning to hike. Trails range from comfortable strolls to challenging treks. For instance, the trail to scenic Waipoo Falls is not long, while more extensive, more rugged routes will take you through dense eucalyptus-studded forest to a cluster of California redwoods. If only easygoing sightseeing is on your agenda, half a day will suffice. All kinds of rare birds and plants flourish in this region. Goats perch precariously at the nearly vertical edges of Waimea Canyon. Delicious *lilikoi* (passion fruit), blackberries, and local Methley plums grow wild. Vistas take in the imposing cliffs of Na Pali Coast, beaches, jungled valleys, and even a swamp.

OLD WOOD & FEATHERS

Kokee State Park's misty forests were once a prime source of lustrous koa wood, which was cut into surfboards, canoes, paddles, and weapons. Ancient Hawaiians also came here armed with nets and poles smeared with a gluelike substance. They caught the most brilliantly colored birds, plucked their feathers, then released the animals. The plumes were fashioned into ceremonial helmets, robes, and leis to be worn by the alii.

You may hear Kokee's moa (wild fowl) conversing loudly with each other. The ancestors of these chickens arrived in Hawaii by canoe with the early Polynesian settlers. Kauai is one of the only parts of the state where these birds still thrive. The ancient Polynesians also carried the ancestors of Kokee's *pua'a* (wild pigs) when they sailed across thousands of ocean miles from Tahiti. Early Hawaiians often killed and buried pigs to appease the gods. These animals were almost as weighty a sacrifice as human beings. Pigs served other purposes as well: Their meat was eaten, but only by men, and boar tusks were transformed into jewelry. Unfortunately, hunting of wild boar, deer, and some game birds is permitted in Kokee at various times of year, so be *careful*. Rainbow trout fishing is allowed in eight streams and a 15-acre artificial lake in Kokee. However, this sport is limited to August and September, and anglers need to obtain freshwater fishing licenses, which are sold at **Kokee Lodge.**

The first of the lodge's 12 rustic cabins were built during the 1950s and the last in 1970. The weather can be downright chilly up there, so the wood-burning stoves in the cabins get lots of action. In addition to having a restaurant and gift shop, the lodge is next door to the **Kokee Natural History Museum,** *Tel. 335-9975, open daily 10am to 4pm, no admission charge, but they do ask for a $1 donation,* a small museum containing Kokee memorabilia that is worth a few moments.

NO PLACE TO HIDE

An old legend explains how the meadow facing Kokee Lodge came into being. This verdant open expanse once sprouted as many trees as the rest of the area. A trans-island trail to Kalalau Valley cuts through these dense woods. Residing in this forest was a terrifying akua (spirit), who got his kicks hiding behind trees and then roughing up, even sometimes killing unsuspecting travelers. The people of Kauai begged one of their gods to do away with this cruel spirit. The evil akua paid no attention to the god's orders to cease and desist. The deity became so infuriated at the spirit's disrespect that the god swooped down and tore up all the trees by their roots. He piled them up, set them ablaze, and decreed that trees would never again grow here and thus akua would have no place to hide.

When the weather cooperates, the Kalalau Lookout, at about 4,000 feet, affords views of serrated mountains, waterfalls, treetops in the sprawling valley, and the beach-rimmed ocean. A rewarding hiking trail starts here. In ancient times, Kalalau was one of Kauai's major settlements. The crumbling heiau where religious sacrifices were made and the agricultural terraces where taro and other crops once grew are virtually all that remain of the villages today.

The East

After driving north of Poipu through the **Tunnel of Trees** and heading east, you'll come to **Kilohana**, not far from Lihue. Since 1986, this Wilcox family sugar plantation estate has welcomed the public to its 35 landscaped acres. Art galleries, jewelry stores, crafts shops, and other boutiques fill the rooms of the handsome old house. A flower-lined courtyard has been transformed into an attractive restaurant. Agricultural displays and rides in a carriage drawn by Clydesdales also entertain visitors. Across the road, Kukui Grove Shopping Center is one of Hawaii's many malls.

About five minutes outside Lihue, 19th century **Grove Farm Homestead** is still a working farm. Its 80 acres also serve as a living museum, giving travelers a glimpse of old Hawaii. Every week, cruise ships sidle up to shore at **Nawiliwili Harbor**, Kauai's main port. This commercial dock is also the place to board boats for sightseeing, fishing, and snorkeling excursions. Not far from here is **Kalapaki Beach**, fronting the Kauai Marriott Resort and Beach Club. Adjacent to the Kauai Marriott Resort & Beach Club is **Kauai Lagoons Tours**, *Tel. 245-2222 or 800/367-2914* (South Sea Tours). Instead of cages, the animals in this human-made but natural-looking wildlife preserve are kept in check by moats. Actually, the monkeys, llamas, nene geese, pink flamingoes, pheasants, wallabies, and other creatures live on small, tree-shaded islands. Visitors glide by on mahogany launches.

Huleia Stream spills into Nawiliwili Harbor. Although it is fed by rain-drenched Mt. Waialeale, its average depth is only four feet and it is no more than ten feet at its deepest. It meanders through densely jungled Huleia National Wildlife Refuge, where the opening scenes of *Raiders of the Lost Ark* were filmed. Mynah birds screech and egrets perch amid the tangle of mangroves along the shore. Fiery red ginger, monkeypod, and mango trees, hibiscus, and elephant ear plants also border this 18-mile waterway, only three miles of which are navigable. Some parts of the stream swirl around boulders. While the wildlife sanctuary is closed to the public, you can see it from a kayak (a wonderful experience) or by small boat. Another place to catch a glimpse of the refuge is from the **Menehune Fishpond Overlook** on Niumalu Road, a quiet, mountainous thruway.

Also called **Alakoko** ("rippling blood"), this fishpond was believed by ancient Hawaiians to have been built by the Menehune, Kauai's legendary elflike race. The aqueduct stretches 900 feet along Huleia Stream. Watched over by the craggy Hoary Head Mountains, this pond is still used for raising mullet, as it has been for centuries.

DON'T PEEK!

According to early Hawaiians, the elf-like Menehune agreed to construct stone-enclosed Alakoko fishpond for a young prince and princess. However, they made it clear to all that absolutely no one would be allowed to watch them at work. In just one night, they built the pond. The heavy stones were transported to the stream by passing them from person to person in a line that stretched for 25 miles. When the job was almost done, the royal pair could no longer resist taking a look at the industrious little people. Catching them on their hillside perch, the Menehune turned the two into the twin stone pillars that you can see today on the ridge above the pond.

In Lihue, the county seat for both Kauai and Niihau, all kinds of Hawaiiana is on display at the **Kauai Museum**, *4428 Rice Street, Lihue, Tel. 245-6931; open Monday to Friday 9am to 4:30pm, and Saturday from 9am to 1pm; admission: $5.*

Cultural, artistic, and geological exhibits highlight the pasts of Kauai, Niihau, and the rest of Hawaii. Feather helmets and cloaks here are particularly striking. Polynesian sailors got the idea for the intricate craft of fashioning clothing from feathers during their travels in South America. Once worn by the alii during battles, these centuries-old garments remain bright in color. Ancient Hawaiians could tell a person's rank by the length and design of his cloak - the longer the cape, the more lofty his social position. Warriors carefully guarded their helmets, which they believed contained their *mana* (power) and that of their ancestors. They proudly passed their helmets down to their sons, unless, of course, these prized possessions had been taken from them during wars.

The museum also contains an intriguing display of calabashes, both wooden (*umeke laau*) and gourd (*umeke pohue*). The shape of a plate or bowl indicated the kind of food that would be served in it. Dog meat and pork were presented on long shallow platters, while poi was put into round bowls. Water was boiled by putting hot rocks into water contained in high calabashes with thick bottoms. Beautifully grained though it was, native koa wood was not used for cooking or dining dishes since it poisoned food. Instead, containers made of this prized wood were reserved for storing shells, kapa cloth, feathers, and other dry household goods. Woods that floated, such as wiliwili and hau, were carved into storage containers for fishing gear on canoes.

The neighboring island of Niihau was known for its elaborately decorated gourds. Decaying leaves and dark mud were mixed into ink, which was used to paint the hollowed-out and dried containers. Niihau is also famous for its shell leis, examples of which you'll see at this museum. The tiny, intricately patterned shells are found on the beach only during certain months, so it can take years to gather enough to make a necklace. Thus these leis, sold today in stores throughout Hawaii, are very expensive. Another necklace exhibited is the *lei niho palaoa*. Only alii of the highest status were allowed to wear these leis made of tiny strands of braided human hair, usually adorned with an ivory pendant. On May 1 (Lei Day), a lei-making contest is held at the museum - for garlands made of flowers, not hair. Be sure to check out the Hawaiian quilts that were inspired by New England missionary women.

Lihue Airport is just outside town. The shore from Lihue north is known as the Coconut Coast, for its many palms. As you drive along Kuhio Highway (Highway 56), you'll be treated to great views of Kauai's trademark open land. As you travel north, the color green seems to come in an increasing number of shades, from lime to forest. You might see a few horses, their heads bent to the grass, then pass a huge pasture with a single cow.

Whether or not you're in the mood for upscale shopping, **Kilohana**, *Highway 50, Lihue, Tel. 245-5608; shops open daily 9:30am to 9pm*, a boutique-filled former plantation estate, is worth some time. A carriage drawn by Clydesdale horses and a wagon take people for spills around the spacious grounds. Opened to the public in 1986, the main house has been carefully restored, gleaming with Douglas fir and Northern California pine. In the entryway stand two huge, highly polished calabashes made of beautifully grained monkeypod wood. These cask-shaped containers were used for storage.

Receptions and weddings are held in the long, wide living room. The handsome koa wood bench here is more than a century old, and exposed beams cross the high ceiling. The war clubs were imported from New Guinea. Shops selling paintings, ceramics, Japanese antiques, clocks, jewelry, Hawaiian artifacts and clothing now occupy the nine bedrooms, some of the nine bathrooms, and many of the closets. Oriental rugs decorate wooden floors. The guest cottage out back has been converted into a boutique as well. From Gaylord's, the restaurant in the flower-lined courtyard, you'll have a view of Mt. Waialeale.

Established in 1854, **Grove Farm Homestead Museum**, *Highway 58, a mile southeast of Lihue, Tel. 245-3202; admission: $5 adults, $2 for children 12 and under; tours conducted at 10am and 1pm on Monday, Wednesday, and Thursday; reservations required,* formerly a sugar plantation, was in operation until 1978. Still a working farm, the homestead and grounds are now an 80-acre living museum.

Visitors learn about the plantation life of the Wilcox family, one of Kauai's wealthiest clans. The plantation was started by George Wilcox, one of the sons of missionary teachers Abner and Lucy Wilcox, who had moved to Hawaii from Connecticut during the 1840s. Armed with a Yale University degree, Wilcox was among those who revolutionized agriculture in the islands. In the days when it took a ton of water to produce a pound of sugar, he was one of the first people who began using irrigation ditches, railcars instead of oxcarts, and plows that were powered by steam instead of oxen.

From Highway 583 or from Maalo Road (off Highway 56), gaze down on **Wailua Falls.** These dramatic 80-foot cascades were used in the opening of the old *Fantasy Island* television series. The cliff over which the water tumbles into a pool served as a diving platform for daring alii. A nearly vertical hiking trail leads down to the falls. In **Wailua** ("sacred water"), remnants of the Hawaiian past have made their way into the present. Nothing much remains of **Holo Holo Ku Heiau** beyond a flower garden marking the small grassy area. However, human sacrifices were once made at this site. In more recent history, hippie types were living here, unbeknownst to the authorities, until there was a fire in the stone structure and pots and pans were discovered inside. Hawaiian women once went to the neighboring heiau, **Pohaku Ho-Ohauau,** to give birth to ensure that their children would become kings or chiefs. Fronted by a small lawn, these rocky ruins sit by the side of the road.

Left in shambles by Hurricane Iniki and closed since then, nearby **Coco Palms Resort** was the kind of hotel most people envision when they think of Hawaii. Thatched-roof bungalows sat at the edge of a lagoon near a thick palm grove. The lagoons were built for Queen Deborah Kapule, Kauai's last reigning monarch, who once lived on the grounds. The coconut grove was originally planted during the mid-19th century by a German physician. Unfortunately, the future of the hotel is uncertain.

Off Highway 580 is the lookout for **Opaekaa Falls** ("rolling shrimp falls"). The namesake crustaceans once lived at the bottom of these mammoth cascades. Across the road and far below, the **Wailua River** wends its way between the mountains. At the end of Highway 580, **Keahua Arboretum** is a good place for a picnic or a hike to a private swimming hole.

Boats leave from Wailua Marina, off Highway 56, for **Fern Grotto**, three miles up the Wailua River. The only way to see this gaping cave dripping with ferns and other vegetation is to take a commercial cruise from Wailua Marina. Packed with people on long rows of seats, the flat-bottomed boats ease along the river. The leisurely ride, between jagged mountains and cliffs with orange earth showing through the greenery and past hau trees and other vegetation, is almost as picturesque as the fern-covered cave. Along the way, a band plays and passengers are coaxed into ensemble hula lessons. The ridge known as the Sleeping Giant gazes down on the water. Lining the banks are "scrambled egg trees," with their fluffy, butter-colored flowers, and blossoming hau trees, with their tangle of low-growing, crisscrossed branches. As passengers walk along the path to the cave, wild chickens parade by. Their long red and orange feathers look too bright to be real. Other fowl rustle through the bushes of this extremely lush forest.

When sightseers reach the cave, musicians from the boats perform "The Hawaiian Wedding Song" to show off the acoustics of the grotto. The song is quite appropriate, since dozens of weddings take place here each year. For evening ceremonies, torches are lit along the path. Couples are transported to and from the grotto in a special wedding boat. Hundreds of ferns grow from the cave walls and water trickles from above. Even on sunny days, the light is dim here, so be sure to bring fast film if you plan to take photos. While this is a wonderfully primordial setting, it would be much more pleasant if you didn't have to see it in the company of so many other people. The companies that take tourists there have the river sewn up.

Also next to Wailua Marina, luaus are held at **Smith's Tropical Paradise**, *Tel. 822-4654; costs – for botanical gardens: $5 adults, $2.50 children 3 to 12; for luau and show: $47 adults, $27 children 7 to 13, $18 children 3 to 6; for show alone: $12 adults, $6 children 3 to 12.* Freckles Smith began his career as a busboy at Coco Palms Resort, the hotel that stood nearby until Hurricane Iniki destroyed it in 1992. Today he's the president of Smith's Motorboat Service which runs tours to Fern Grotto and operates this 30-acre botanical park. Paths wind past many-hued tropical planes and scenic lagoons. You can see the grounds by foot or take a guided tour. Guided tram tours are available for groups of 15 or more at $10 per person. An optional tram tour is available for luau guests only for an additional $1. Luaus followed by international musical revues are held Monday through Friday evenings. A highlight of the feast is watching the steaming imu pig being removed from its earthen oven (a hole in the ground filled with redhot lava rocks).

From **Wailua Bridge**, the view of the river, palms, jagged mountains, and beach is spectacular. **Lydgate State Park**, at the mouth of the Wailua River, attracts strong swimmers and snorkelers with its lava pools. Ancient Hawaiians found refuge at this beachfront coconut grove when they had committed crimes against the gods.

You'll find some good boutiques and restaurants at the **Coconut Plantation Market Place**. This attractive open-air mall in **Waipouli** (whose border blurs with Kapaa's) is part of a development that includes a group of hotels on a rocky beach.

THE BIG SLEEP

*The mountain ridge known as the **Sleeping Giant** is visible from Waipouli and the town of Kapaa. Hawaiian legend has it that the overgrown Puni fell into his slumber after a hard-fought battle. Another story explains that the giant simply gorged himself at a luau and never woke up from his nap. From Kapaa, it will take about an hour to hike to Puni's chin. A picnic table invites trekkers to relax a spell. Between June and October, the guavas are ripe for plucking off their trees. If you take the left-hand path just before the trail ends, you'll come to an overlook with a sweeping view of Kauai's eastern shore.*

Tourists are far outnumbered by residents in Kapaa. Along the main street, stores and restaurants reside in handsome restored buildings that date back to the 19th century. The shops and eateries of **Waipouli Town Center** draw a local crowd. Across from a Catholic cemetery, **Kealia Beach** is better for sun-bathing than swimming, since the undertow can be dangerous. Calmer waters are found at **Anahola Beach Park**. This tranquil, shady strip has been the site of demonstrations protesting the poor condition of Hawaiian Homestead Lands in the area. The roadside

Duane's Ono-Char Burger, in Anahola, is a favorite place for a snack among locals.

Kauai's countryside is especially dramatic in this northern region. The many shades of green are set off by the iron-rich rust-colored earth, the orange blossoms of African tulip trees, aromatic white and yellow plumeria petals, and the spidery red and yellow flowers of Australian silky oaks. Open expanses give way to papaya and banana groves. The distinctive, narrow peaks of Anahola Mountain loom in the distance.

The North

The northern coast is my favorite part of Kauai, perhaps even of the whole state. Because of the amount of rain this region receives, it is stunning in its lushness. (December and January are rainiest.) Towering above all the wild greenery, farm plots, secluded beaches, mountaintops form abstract sculpture against the sky. If you are staying elsewhere on Kauai, plan to spend a full day in and around Hanalei and Princeville, about an hour's drive from Wailua and an hour and 40 minutes from Poipu. Allow more time if you want to include hiking along the dramatic cliffs of Na Pali or viewing these promontories from a helicopter or boat.

North of Anahola, Kilauea Bridge will take you into the town of **Kilauea.** Unusual in shape, round **St. Sylvester's Catholic Church** is nestled amid red lobster claw plants, crotons, and mango and avocado trees. At one point, a group of hippies turned themselves into squatters in this modern house of worship. The stained-glass windows of **Christ Memorial Church,** built of lava rock in the 1940s, were imported all the way from England.

Kilauea Point Wildlife Refuge, *Tel. 828-1413, open 10am to 4pm, except holidays,* a bird sanctuary by the Kilauea Lighthouse is a nesting place for frigates, boobies, and other seabirds. Bring your binoculars or a telephoto lens for eyeball-to-eyeball views of red-footed boobies, frigates, laysan albatross, and red-tailed tropic-birds. More seabirds nest along the rugged cliffs of this promontory than anywhere else in the main Hawaiian islands. Called *a* in Hawaiian, red-footed boobies usually build their homes in shrubs or small trees. These birds are two feet long and white in color. *Iwa,* or frigates, like to swoop down on boobies and other birds in flight to steal the fish they're carrying.

Big black-and-white *moli,* or laysan albatross, pass most of their time hunting for squid and fish. They only step on dry land when they're ready to court or breed. Until these birds mature, they can spend as many as *six years* on and above the open ocean without touching terra firma. Thus, they are less than graceful on land. Their slow, goofy-looking waddle makes them an easy catch for wild dogs and other predators.

Kilauea Point, a promontory with wraparound views high above the crashing ocean, is also a great place for spotting dolphins, monk seals, green sea turtles and – from December to May – humpback whales. If you're very lucky you'll see one of these 45-foot mammals jump completely out of the water. The lighthouse here was erected in 1913. Its beam could be seen for 20 ocean miles and planes could spot 90 miles away.

The view from **Kalihiwai Valley Overlook** takes in the flourishing dale and a waterfall. Kalihiwai Road leads to Anini Road, which runs into **Anini Beach.** Novice windsurfers and snorkelers cut their teeth on these waves. **Kalihiwai Bay,** a tranquil curve of sand, is also part of the quiet, residential community. Back on Highway 56, you'll pass tiny **Princeville Airport.** Area helicopter tours take off from here. Horseback riding can be arranged at nearby **Pooku/Princeville Ranch Stables.**

Developed as a vacation resort, the community of **Princeville** is one of Kauai's most scenic regions. Sprawling across the tops of cliffs, the 11,000 acres overlooking valleys are sprinkled with upscale condominiums, private homes, and the beautiful **Princeville Hotel.** Made up of three 9-hole greens designed by Robert Trent Jones, Jr., the **Princeville Makai Golf Course** is considered one of the best in the world. The 18-hole **Prince Golf Course** is another top place for teeing off. From many parts of town, the striking Makana mountain peaks can be seen. Immortalized in *South Pacific,* they are still commonly known as **Bali Hai.** In Princeville Center, a post office is conveniently located just inside the grocery store.

THE LITTLE PRINCE

The Princeville area was once a sugar plantation belonging to Robert Crichton Wyllie. Originally from Scotland, he became minister of Foreign Affairs for the Hawaiian kingdom in 1798, holding the position for nearly seven decades. He chose the name Princeville for his plantation in honor of young Prince Albert, the child of Kamehameha IV and Queen Emma. Wyllie was known for his no-holds-barred entertaining. In 1862, he threw the four-year-old prince a royal birthday party, highlighted by a grand parade of 200 costumed Hawaiian men and women on horseback.

Sadly, the prince died of an illness before his fifth birthday. Following Wyllie's death, Princeville passed into the hands of the Scotsman's nephew. But the plantation was beset by so many financial problems that the new owner committed suicide. In 1895, Albert Wilcox, a member of a missionary family originally from Connecticut, bought the land. He rescued it from total ruin by curtailing the failing sugar crops, turning the highlands over to cattle ranching, and renting the low-lands to Chinese rice farmers.

The breathtaking view from **Hanalei Valley Overlook** encompasses many taro patches. A river cuts through the tapestry of farm plots, which carpet the valley against a background of irregular mountain ridges. Also down below, the Hanalei National Wildlife Refuge offers 900 acres of protection for endangered waterfowl. On its way into the valley, Highway 56 passes along a creaky, arched, one-lane bridge that was built in 1912. Despite its elderly appearance, residents are too attached to it to replace it. Kayaking is common on the river here and cows graze in a pasture along the bank.

Hanalei was one of the earliest areas settled by the ancient Pacific voyagers who first came to Hawaii. When they arrived, the region was covered with marshes. After they were through with it, the mushy terrain had been turned into thriving farmland, complete with dams and irrigation ditches. According to ancient Hawaiians, Kauai's last Menehune resided here. Some present-day locals say that *mo'o* (giant lizard gods) still live in Hanalei's mountain pools. Many rainbows decorate this lush part of Kauai. An old story explains how these colorful arcs came to be: A stranger arrived with sheets of kapa dyed in various hues. He threw the bark cloth into a pool at the base of a waterfall and the colors were forever reflected in the mist.

Hanalei ("crescent bay") aptly describes the namesake sandy cove cupped by mountains. This narrow roadside beach is good for swimming and snorkeling near the pier, where the water is calmest. Across the road from the water, vacation rentals are scattered here and there. Look for the signs with telephone numbers outside these private homes that are rented to travelers. This verdant part of the north shore couldn't possibly be as beautiful as it is without a healthy dose of rain. In fact, the slim, winding, dipping road to Hanalei is sometimes closed for hours (even days on rare occasions) when the river rises in a heavy deluge. Schools have been known to close and people have had to sleep in their cars until they could get home.

In the small, pretty town, what is now the **Waioli Mission House Museum**. *Highway 56, Hanalei, Tel. 245-3202; donations appreciated; open 9am to 3pm Tuesday, Thursday, and Saturday*, is where one of Kauai's wealthiest and most influential haole families got its start. The plain koa wood furniture on display reflects the life style of Abner and Lucy Wilcox, Connecticut missionaries who moved to this home during the 1840s. This husband-and-wife team spent more than two decades teaching at a school for Hawaiian boys from Kauai and Niihau. Abner had a reputation for being extremely strict with his students, while Lucy was known for her softer, gentler touch. They raised seven sons, and their children and grandchildren went on to become prosperous, leading citizens. George Wilcox, for example, built a vast fortune from his Grove Farm sugarcane plantation near Lihue (now a living museum). Albert became wealthy by buying and selling Princeville Plantation. The Wilcox mansion on Hanalei Bay, still the family home, was built by him.

A dearth of workers for Kauai's plantations brought contract laborers from China, then from Japan. As the Asian community grew, rice paddies gave way to taro. The building that now houses the **Hanalei Museum** was originally the home of some of the area's first Chinese immigrants, the Ho family. Displays bring to life old Hanalei in particular and old Hawaii in general. The Chings are another early Chinese family whose legacy lives on, in **Ching Young Village** shopping center. In 1896, Ching Young and his wife, Man Sing, immigrated to Hawaii. Here they had eight children, bought a rice mill, and opened a general store. Today this general store is where you'll find arts and crafts and flower shops.

Artists, poets, and other creative types are drawn to these and other boutiques and galleries in Hanalei. Perhaps the town's artistic leanings are a holdover from the early 1970s, when Hanalei was flooded with hippies, mostly from the mainland. The area's serene atmosphere changed drastically when some 60 of these transients began camping out in nearby Haena, on land owned by Howard Taylor, brother of actress Elizabeth Taylor. They fancied themselves "getting back to nature." "Shelters thrown together with old lumber and sheets of plastic went up both on the ground and in trees.

Some of these flower children earned their living by doing odd jobs in and around town. Others went on welfare or grew and sold marijuana. Local residents were disgusted and angered by the lifestyle of these young people. Finally, after years of fighting through the legal system, the state purchased the land, turning it into Haena State Park, and the hippies were sent packing.

Before you reach Haena from Hanalei, you'll cross some more scenic one-lane bridges and come to **Lumahai Beach**. It was on this lovely mile-long cliff-enclosed stretch that Mitzi Gaynor sang about washing that man right out of her hair in *South Pacific*. Travelers can gaze down on this cove from the road or carefully pick their way down the steep trail to the sand. Boats and rubber rafts leave for cruises along dramatic Na Pali coast from nearby **Makua Beach**. This broad stretch of sand, where the water is relatively calm, affords wonderful views of the cliffs.

Limahuli Garden, *Ha'ena, North Shore, Tel. 826-1053; tours on Tuesday, Wednesday, Thursday, and Saturday; cost: $15 guided, $10 self-guided, run by the National Tropical Botanical Garden, a non-profit organization,* set in a lush valley surrounded by mountain peaks, attracts serious botanists and herbalists. Ancient Hawaiian agricultural terraces and old vegetation remain in this historic region. You'll learn about past uses for a wide variety of fruits and plants, such as how taro root, which became the lifeblood of early Hawaii, and the bark that was used to make kapa cloth. Among other vegetation is the octopus tree, autograph tree, breadfruit, jackfruit, bananas, mangos, and mountain apples. Be sure to bring your mosquito repellent! And be prepared to do a lot of walking, some of it on slippery ground.

Farther along Highway 56, **Maniniholo Dry Cave** gapes at the side of the road. You can walk deep inside this high-ceilinged grotto that is nearly as large as a football field. Lunch wagons wait to serve people at **Haena State Park**, across the road from the cave. **Haena Beach**, great for shelling, is also good for strong swimmers when the water is calm. Local children and adults swim in the rocky stream by the Haena State Park sign on the roadside. A waterfall trickles into the natural pool here. By the old houses in this area, you might see goat and pig skins hung out to dry like laundry, with birds perched on the lines. Some people believe that **Waiakapalae** and **Waiakanaloa Wet Caves** were scooped out by Pele, the fiery volcano goddess. Although the stagnant water is no longer safe for swimming, the caves are impressive sights.

Highway 56 dries up at **Ke'e Beach State Park**, where the 11-mile **Kalalau Trail** along Na Pali Coast begins. From the beach, you'll have a fabulous view of the cliffs. The climactic scene in *The Thorn Birds* TV miniseries in which a young woman and a priest give in to their love for each other was filmed on this shore. Even Pele, the volcano goddess, could not resist Ke'e's romantic charms. She transformed herself into a beautiful mortal so she could join a hula festival here. Human desires suddenly overcame her, and before she knew it, she had fallen deeply in love with the island's dashing Chief Lohiau. A trail from the beach leads to **Lohiau's Dance Pavilion**. This stone shrine honors Laka, the hula goddess. Present-day hikers sometimes come across offerings left at the altar by contemporary dancers and worshippers.

Meaning "the cliffs" in Hawaiian, **Na Pali Coast** is accessible only by foot. However, you can enjoy spectacular views of it from both the air and the sea. Whether this ruggedly beautiful coastline is seen from a boat or raft, through a helicopter window, or while hiking along it on the Kalalau Trail, no traveler should miss an opportunity to visit the region. About two strenuous uphill miles along the hiking trail, picturesque **Hanakapiai Beach** is a favorite stopping-off point for trekkers. Although the beach is at its widest and the waves at their calmest during the summer, the water here can be dangerous for swimming year-round.

When the water is calm enough (in the spring and summer), sightseeing boats cruise by 4,000-foot precipices and past old valleys. (Some cruises include lunch and snorkeling.) Zodiac rubber rafts skirt waterfalls and zip into the caves behind the cascades. Towering over small sandy coves, the striated mountains and cliffs are a melange of greens, oranges, and browns. Huge patches of red earth are visible where chunks of the cliffs have broken off and tumbled into the sea over the centuries. The tiny moving figures boaters see in valleys and along the trail are goats and hikers. Sometimes following boats, pairs of dolphins show off by spiraling out of the water in unison or rolling on their backs and slapping their tails on the ocean's surface. Huge sea turtles poke their heads out of the Pacific.

Old superstitions remain about the region. Fishermen will tell you that if the mood hits, the fickle Na Pali spirits can make it difficult for certain travelers on particular days. Stories are passed around about mysterious happenings that tell adventurers to come another day instead. People have arrived at the trailhead minus that backpack of food and supplies they were positive they put in the trunk of their car. Others have set out in a boat in prime condition only to have it break down out of the blue. But visitors need not worry - all you have to do is heed the warning signs.

DID FATHER KNOW BEST?

A triplet of peaks known as the **Three Sisters** *watches over Kalalau Valley. According to legend, a storm ripped through a coastal village in Kalalau, sweeping away homes and taro fields. Three goddesses who lived in mountain caves behind the valley felt sorry for the poor mortals below. They turned themselves into human beings and went down to help the villagers. With this divine aid, the results of the storm's vicious handiwork were repaired in just one day. While the villagers rejoiced, grateful for this superhuman assistance, the father of the sisters fumed. How dare his daughters lower themselves by fraternizing with mere mortals! To punish the wayward goddesses, he transformed them into the pillars of stone that still stand.*

Historians believe that Na Pali was the first part of Kauai to be settled, probably around 989 A.D. The fertile land was well-suited for all the agricultural terraces the early Hawaiians built, and fresh water streamed down mountainsides. Villages were peppered with *heiau* (temples). Since each valley was surrounded by virtually impenetrable cliffs, it was difficult for hostile outsiders to reach this isolated region. Thus Na Pali was far more peaceful than the rest of the island. The Reverend Hiram Bingham, the head of the original group of missionaries in Hawaii, was the first Westerner to visit Na Pali, where he settled in 1822.

Especially in **Kalalau Valley**, hikers can stumble upon ancient, crumbling heiau, house sites, food pits, and taro terraces. When horses were brought here by boat in 1864, children were terrified by the strange, massive beasts. Taro farmers and their families lived in this valley until around 1919. Coffee and *ti* plants (for making *okolehao* - Hawaiian whiskey) were grown commercially in nearby valleys until the 1920s. During the latter part of that decade, two men were said to have moved all the way from Honolulu to one of Na Pali's secluded nooks so that they could distill bootleg liquor.

Locals will tell you about "the Hermit of Kalalau," a doctor who moved into one of the caves by the beach during the late 1950s. In the late 1960s and early 1970s, mainland hippies joined him in the valley. Kauaians were scandalized to discover that these young people were living on and around sacred, historic heiau, house sites, and taro terraces. Although locals complained about this lack of respect, most of the hippies remained in Kalalau until the late 1970s, when they were finally evicted by the state at the same time as those living in Haena.

NIGHTLIFE & ENTERTAINMENT

On Kauai, life after dark is far quieter than on either Oahu or Maui. The island does have a couple of dance spots. However, most evening entertainment is centered around restaurant bars and hotel lounges, where live music often accompanies pupus and conversation. Those who don't mind being part of a crowd of fellow tourists should consider taking an evening cruise or attending a luau. While some of the larger hotels host luaus, many visitors prefer to attend the feasts held outside the resorts. Check local papers to see what's happening at Kauai Community College.

Hawaiian Style

SMITH'S TROPICAL PARADISE, *Waihua Marina, Waihua. Tel. 822-4654 or 822-9599. Luaus held here from Monday through Friday, beginning with the 6pm imu ceremony. (To tour the gardens as well, arrive by 5pm.)*

The 30 tropical acres of flowers, plants, and trees make visitors feel as though they have stepped into old Hawaii when they attend the **luau** given here. While riding in the tram or walking through the grounds, you'll pass several lily ponds. The first is huge, with a large rocky fountain. Royal palms, banana trees, crotons, and bougainvillea surround the water. Hundreds of birds flutter around the rain forest garden, filled with stalks of bamboo, red ginger, scarlet lobster claws, pineapples, and papaya trees.

Before the feast, everyone observes the outdoor imu ceremony: The boned kalua pig, the centerpiece of the meal, is removed from its oven - a hole in the ground that has been heated by red-hot rocks. Featuring Hawaiian, Maori, Samoan, Tongan, Japanese, and Chinese music and dances, the performance takes place on a stage across a lily pond from the audience. The Samoan fire dancers are a big hit. While the bleachers are covered, the stage is open to the sky.

TAHITI NUI, *Kuhio Highway, Hanalei. Tel. 826-6277 or 826-7320. Cost: $40 adults, $17 children 5 to 11 (including fruit punch; cocktails are extra).*

Up on the quiet north shore, this **luau** hosted by a convivial group of folks is much more intimate than most. The singing, dancing, and telling of anecdotes is done in a truly down-to-earth manner - sans glitz. The proprietor, who usually sings during the show, is from Tahiti. She begins the evening with a Tahitian prayer. At the end, visitors are plucked from the audience to join the children and adult dancers and singers on stage. The casual atmosphere and Polynesian decor of this restaurant capture Hawaii as it once was. Of course the menu includes the usual filling luau fare: kalua pig, chicken long rice, lomilomi salmon, taro, poi, white sweet potatoes, and haupia (a jiggly coconut pudding). Luaus are hosted here several nights a week.

Local Hangouts & Happenings
THE KAUAI COMMUNITY PLAYERS, *Tel. 245-3408.*

Call or check newspapers to find out when and where this local theater group is performing. They generally produce five or six plays a year.

KUHIO'S, *Hyatt Regency Kauai, Poipu. Tel. 742-1234.*

This flashy dance club is one of the island's most popular night spots. It's the place to be Fridays and Saturdays, from 9pm to 2am.

LEGENDS NIGHTCLUB, *Pacific Ocean Plaza, 3501 Rice Street, 2nd floor, Nawiliwili. Tel. 245-5775.*

Open from 9:30am to 4am, this spacious dance club draws people mostly under age 30. Music is usually American pop and there's an extended happy hour on Wednesdays.

Special Events

On **Lei Day** (May 1), everyone decks themselves out with floral garlands, and a fierce lei-making competition is held at the Kauai Museum in Lihue. The museum also hosts a holiday festival in December. The **Aloha Festival**, the state-wide celebration of Hawaiian culture, featuring street fairs, hula performances, and crafts demonstrations and sales, occurs in September or October. Similar activities highlight the annual **Captain Cook celebration** in Waimea (January), along with canoe and foot races and all kinds of food.

FESTIVAL FOR THE AFTERLIFE

Perhaps Kauai's most colorful annual event is the Japanese O-Bon Festival, which runs from mid-June through August. Rooted in Buddhism, this series of weekend ceremonies and dances pays homage to the ancestors. After a brief religious service, live drums accompany taped Asian music. Inside a roped-off circle, people of different races dressed in colorful kimonos and happi coats dance gracefully. The cho-chin (Japanese paper lanterns) hanging above their heads are believed to light the path of the souls of the deceased, who are thought to come home every summer.

Waiting to buy local specialties - such as yakitori (skewered chicken cooked over charcoals), mochi (steamed squares of sweetened, pounded rice), shave ice (snow cones), pronto pups (corn dogs), and flying saucers (a hamburger between two slices of bread) - spectators cluster around food stands. There is usually a "ball throw" booth as well as "dime toss" and "ring the bottle" concessions and dart games. Each O-bon dance ends promptly at midnight.

Hosted by Kauai's Koloa Jodo Mission, a special tradition takes place following sunset on the Sunday after the Saturday night O-Bon dance. Residents and tourists crowd Kukuiula Small Boat Harbor, while members of the temple launch a boat stocked with food. Trailing behind it are rafts carrying cho-chin. Each paper lantern has been bought from the temple by a different family so that each clan will be represented. In this way, participants symbolically send the souls of the departed back to the Buddha Land of Peace. The food ensures that the souls won't grow hungry).

SPORTS & RECREATION

Hiking, camping, scuba diving, kayaking, and fishing are all excellent on Kauai. Snorkeling excursions and other water sports are easily arranged through hotels.

Beaches

Generally speaking, in the winter beaches along the south shore are calm and thus good for swimming, while north shore beaches are too rough for swimming but fine for expert surfers. Summer months bring good surfing and bodysurfing waves to the south shore and flatten most northern waters enough for safe swimming. The waters along the eastern shore are often not good for swimming since they can have high waves and strong currents. Some of the quietest beaches are along the western shore, past Kekaha. These strands are frequented by locals more than visitors.

Polihale, west coast

Mid-summer is the safest time to swim in these waters. During the rest of the year, the long, broad, white sand beach watched over by soaring Na Pali sea cliffs is best used as a sunbathing and picnic spot. Dune buggies kick up the sand on weekends, but the beach is refreshingly empty and quiet at other times. Since there are no trees, there is no natural shade - just a few picnic shelters by the base of the cliffs. You may want to bring an umbrella. Restrooms and showers are provided. Camping is permitted here in tents. When you turn left at the end of Highway 50, you'll be on a bumpy dirt road that winds through seemingly endless sugar cane fields. Looming ahead, the horizontally striped cliffs bear a strong resemblance to Mount Rushmore. Note that some car rental agencies prohibit drivers from taking vehicles onto dirt roads.

Kekaha Beach, southwest shore

The sound of dune buggies often slices the air along this long, narrow, sandy stretch off Highway 50. The undertow is strong and there are usually many breakers. But when the water is calm enough, this is a popular spot for teaching local children to surf. Picnic tables are provided. Camping is permitted.

Waimea Beach, southwest coast

This strip is popular among locals and vacationers who want to get away from the crowds.

Salt Pond Beach Park, Hanapepe, south shore

Families gravitate to this spot, since the relatively flat waters are fine for swimming. Take advantage of the picnic tables. Unlike some darker beaches in the area, the sand along this beautiful curve is white.

Brenneke's Beach, Poipu, south shore

Bodysurfing and boogie-boarding are once again all the rage here, after recovery from Hurricane Iniki, which struck in 1992. This shore has reclaimed its place as one of Kauai's most popular beaches.

Prince Kuhio Park, Poipu, south shore

Although this beach is on the rocky side, it's a pleasant place to spend some time.

Piopu Beach Park, south shore

Very busy on weekends, Poipu Beach is excellent for surfing. Snorkeling is also rewarding here, and waves are usually manageable for bodysurfing. The shallow natural pool off to one side of the bay seems to have been designed for toddlers and other young children. There are also a playground and a grassy lawn. Lifeguards scan the water. Showers and restrooms are available. Be sure to take a spin in this neighborhood, you'll see some beautiful homes.

Kalapaki Beach, *Nawiliwili Park, southeast coast*

The swimming is excellent at this sandy curve fronting the lavish Kauai Marriott Resort. Windsurfing is popular among locals here.

Ahukini, *east coast*

Stop here if you're in the mood for some good snorkeling.

Hanamaulu Beach Park, *east coast*

Campers enjoy this waterfront park where nice shells can often be found. However, in the past, this beach has had problems with polluted water.

Lydgate State Park, *Wailua, east coast*

In the old days, Hawaiians who had broken kapu (taboos) fled to the Place of Refuge here, thus avoiding punishments that could include death. Swimmers and snorkelers enjoy splashing around in the rock-enclosed natural pool that's about the size of a football field.

Wailua Beach, *east coast*

When the waves are small enough, this is a good spot for swimming or for novice surfers to get the hang of hanging ten.

Kapaa Beach Park, *east coast*

The swimming and fishing are generally good here. This is mainly a local hangout. Picnic tables and barbecue pits are provided.

Anahola Bay, *northeastern shore*

With mountains in the background, this curving sandy strip is fine for swimming. Waters are calmest at the southern end and by Anahola Stream at the northern extreme. Restrooms and showers are provided. The adjacent state park is popular with campers.

Anini Beach, *north shore*

This protected beach is one of the best north shore strands for swimming during the summer. Windsurfers enjoy this spot. During the winter, waves should be left to master surfboarders.

Hanalei Beach Park, *north shore*

Taking a dip here is safest by the old landing. The surfing is particularly good during the winter.

Lumahai Beach, *north shore*

Famous for its role in South Pacific, this beautiful beach is not safe for swimming. However, it's a great place to spend some quiet time sunbathing, picnicking, or searching for olivine crystals in the sand.

Makua Beach, *north shore*

If you plan to cruise along Na Pali Coast, you'll board your boat or Zodiac raft here. The view of the cliffs is wonderful, especially in the late afternoon. Since the waters are protected, swimming and snorkeling are fine here during the summer.

Ke'e, *north shore*

You'll know you've found this beach when Highway 56 grinds to a halt. This pristine crescent near the beginning of the Kalalau Trail was the setting for the seduction of a young woman by a priest in "The Thorn Birds," the television mini-series. Be careful of the slabs of rock at the water's edge.

HULA GODDESS HIKE

A jungled path from Ke'e Beach leads to an ancient hula platform, where the blessings of Laka, the hula goddess, are still sometimes invoked. You might see offerings left by recent dancers. The walk is about 10 minutes each way, but only attempt it if the sea is calm. To find the rocky oceanside path, go left (facing the water) around the point. You'll pass some homes and turn inland toward the mountains. Bordered by lush palms, feathery pines, and spikey succulents, the trail begins to climb. When you see the hillside where huge boulders are arranged in lines and in clusters, you've arrived. Above a wall of rocks, cliffs rise in the background, and the land abruptly drops off to the water. Pandanus trees and casuarinas rustle in the breeze while yellow and red flowers splatter the greenery. The view of the turquoise ocean, set off by white surf, is truly spectacular from here.

Haena State Park, *north shore*

Swimming is recommended here only for the strongest of swimmers and only when the water is very calm. However, the shelling and fishing are good. Picnic tables and barbecue pits are provided.

Hanakapiai, Na Pali Coast, northwest shore

Hikers reach this picturesque strand after trekking about two miles along the Kalalau Trail. While it's a scenic place to relax, the currents can be treacherous, so swimming is not advised. A freshwater stream adds to the beauty of the setting. However, sometimes during the winter, the beach vanishes beneath the high tide.

Biking

Cycling is particularly rewarding on this largely rural island. Mountain bikes can be rented at **Outfitters Kauai**, *Tel. 742-9667*, in Poipu and the company will provide maps, helmets, water bottles, and other gear and information if you prefer to do it on your own. You can also join a mountain bike tour through the backroads of Kokee State Park or elsewhere. In addition, two-wheelers are available at **Pedal and Paddle**, *Tel. 826-9069*, in Hanalei, and **Kayak Kauai Outfitters**, *Tel. 826-9844 or 800/437-3507*, in Hanalei, and *Tel. 822-9179* in Kapaa. Plan to spend $16 to $22 a day. Four-day and weekly rates are also available.

> ## ADVENTURES IN KAUAI
>
> *Through Kayak Kauai Outfitters, Tel. 826-9844, 822-9179, or 800/437-3507, you can arrange everything from hikes through Kokee State Park and Waimea Canyon to six-day guided kayaking, camping, and hiking excursions along Na Pali Coast.*

Boat & Raft Rides

When north shore waves are at their calmest, during the summer, many sightseers cruise in rubber rafts along stunning Na Pali Coast. Most trips include **snorkeling**. Call **Captain Zodiac**, *Tel. 826-9371 or 800/422-7824* (from the mainland), sometimes also called Na Pali Zodiac. Don't let the word "raft" put you off. These motor-powered craft are actually just small boats. Your Zodiac might slip into a roofless cave, past a waterfall at its mouth. You might spot dolphins or huge sea turtles. Both the 3.5 and 5-hour trips include snorkeling. Passengers on the longer excursion are also taken to a secluded beach and given lunch.

During the winter, these excursions are offered if the weather and ocean conditions are good. However, at this time of year, the trip can be especially bumpy, something like riding on a trotting horse, and the water may be too rough for the raft to enter sea caves. One advantage of a winter cruise, though, is that you may spot whales, which come to Kauai around mid-November and leave in mid-May.

Smith's Motor Boat Service, *Tel. 822-4111,* and **Waialeale Boat Tours,** *Tel. 822-4908,* conduct cruises up the Wailua River to **Fern Grotto** (about $16 for adults; $8 for children under age 12). The ride is beautiful, as are the cave and its flourishing surroundings. Unfortunately, though, each flat-bottomed boat is packed with more than 100 tourists. Such an appealing setting would be best viewed with fewer people around. The outside of the fern-covered cave is dim, even on sunny days, so be sure to bring a flash or fast film. As you glide along the river, you'll be told about the passing sights, serenaded with live guitar and ukulele music, and coaxed into taking group hula lessons. Since Fern Grotto is frequently the site of weddings, you might see a bride and groom in their own special boat. Note: Waialeale Boat Tours also offers guided kayak tours to Fern Grotto. $25 single or $50 double. Lunch is additional. All excursions depart from Wailua Marina.

Camping

Tent camping is permitted at various state and county parks and other scenic beachfront and inland locales, including the following: **Anahola State Park** on the northeast coast, **Anini Beach** on the north shore, **Haena State Park** on the north shore, **Hanalei Beach Park** on the north shore, **Hanamaulu Beach Park** on the southeast coast, **Kapaa Beach Park** on the eastern shore, **Kekaha Beach Park** in the southwest, **Kokee State Park** in the mountains in the west, **Polihale State Park** on the west coast, and **Salt Pond Beach Park** on the southern coast.

Campers must obtain permits for state parks from the **Division of State Parks,** *3060 Eiwa Street, Room 306, Lihue, HI 96766, Tel. 808/274-3445,* or, for county parks, from **Parks and Recreation,** *4444 Rice Street, Suite 150, Lihue, HI 96766, Tel. 808/241-6660.* These offices can also supply maps and further details. However, note that **Sugi Grove Picnic Area,** at the edge of a stream, is one of the few places in Kokee State Park where you can camp overnight without a permit.

Fishing

Arrange ocean charters through **Sportfishing Kauai,** *Koloa, Tel. 742-7013;* **Gent-Lee Fishing,** *Lihue, Tel. 245-7504;* **True Blue Charters & Ocean Sports,** *Lihue, Tel. 246-6333;* or **Anini Fishing Charters,** *Kilauea, Tel. 828-1285.*

A full day of shared charter fishing runs from $120 to $160, while a half-day goes for about $90. If you'd prefer to charter a boat for your own group, a full day will cost from about $600 to $800, while a half day will run $400 to $500.

For freshwater fishing, you'll need to obtain a license through **Aquatic Resources,** *3060 Eiwa Street, Room 306, Lihue, Kauai, HI 96766,*

Tel. 274-3344. **Cast and Catch Freshwater Bass Guides,** Tel. 332-9707, can show you the best fishing spots on the south shore. Black and peacock bass are found in Kauai's streams and ponds. In Kokee streams and an artificial lake, a rainbow trout season runs on certain days in August and September; you can buy the required license at Kokee Lodge.

For small jacks and reef fish, try the reefs near Hanalei Bay. Be extremely careful, however, since the tide can be quite strong here. There's also good fishing for barracuda, small ula, and jacks off the end of the breakwater at Nawiliwili. At night, locals wade out at Anini Beach on the north shore to spear lobsters and fish. Other fishing can be set up through **JJ's Big Bass Tours,** Tel. 332-9219. If you'd like to join a group of local fishermen, you may be able to make arrangements through the **Chamber of Commerce,** Tel. 245-7363, or **Lihue Fishing Supply,** Tel. 245-4930.

You should plan to spend $100 for five hours of freshwater fishing and $150 per eight hours per person.

Golf

Serious golfers stay in Princeville on the verdant north shore. Made up of three 9-hole courses, the renowned **Princeville Makai Golf Course,** Tel. 826-3580 or 800/826-4400, was designed by Robert Trent Jones, Jr. Fees, including carts, are about $95 for resort guests and $115 for non-guests.

The 18-hole **Princeville Prince Golf Course,** Tel. 826-5000, is another good place to tee off in the area. Fees are about $120 for people staying in the resort and $150 for outsiders.

Down south in Kalaheo, the 9-hole **Kukuiolono Golf Course,** Tel. 332-9151, charges only $7 for greens fees and $6 for carts for those playing nine holes and $12 for those playing 18.

To play on the 18-hole **Wailua Municipal Golf Course,** Tel. 241-6666, in Wailua, plan to spend $25 during the week and $35 on weekends, plus $14 for a cart for 18 holes.

You can also tee off at the 18-hole **Poipu Bay Resort Golf Course,** Tel. 742-9489, by the Hyatt (guests: $90; non-guests: $135). Both this and the 18-hole **Kiahuna Golf Course,** Tel. 742-4595, in Poipu were designed by Robert Trent Jones. Jr., and encompass Hawaiian archaeological sites. Fees are $55 for 18 holes, $28 for 9 holes. The **Kiele Golf Course** and the **Lagoons Course** are other options.

Helicopter Rides

If your wallet is amenable, don't miss an opportunity to take a helicopter tour on Kauai. Prices range from about $60 per person for a 20-minute flight to $200 for a 90-minute whirl. Trips including drop-offs are more expensive. While Waimea Canyon, Hanalei Valley, and Kalalau Valley can all be seen from lookout points on land and the cliffs of Na Pali Coast can be seen by boat, there's nothing like getting an aerial view of these spectacles. And unless you're a bird or in a low-flying plane, the only way to see lush Mt. Waialeale Crater is by helicopter. Most flights take off from Princeville, but a few depart from Lihue Airport. Some companies provide complimentary ground transportation from hotels to take-off points.

Do be aware, however, that there is a raging controversy on Kauai and in Hawaii in general about helicopter tours and the growing number of tour companies. Some feel that the number of trips should be cut dramatically because of the noise. As one hiker put it, "It's terrible to hike for hours into a remote area only to have the silence shattered by such a loud, unnatural sound." She told me of the time she and a friend were almost startled off the ledge of a cliff by a copter that suddenly rounded a bend.

The 20-minute ride from Princeville on **Hawaii Helicopter,** *Tel. 826-6591,* covers Na Pali Coast, Bali Hai Beach, and Hanalei Valley and costs about $65. Other companies to consider are **Island Helicopters,** *Tel. 245-8588,* **South Sea Tours and Helicopters,** *Tel. 245-2222,* and **Ohana Helicopter Tours,** *Tel. 245-3996.*

Until the late 1980s, only people with Hawaiian blood were allowed on neighboring Niihau. **Niihau Helicopter,** *Tel. 335-3500,* takes sightseers to this "Forbidden Island." These flights don't go anywhere near where people live, but occasionally people from the village have come to the beach where the helicopter lands to meet visitors. See *Day Trips & Excursions* in this chapter for more information on Niihau.

Hiking

Some 45 miles of hiking trails cut through mountainous, forested **Kokee State Park,** at the edge of Na Pali Coast. Before setting out, call for a weather update, *Tel. 808/335-9975,* after 8am. Be sure to stop at the **Kokee Natural History Museum** for trail maps and information about current trail conditions. To get the most out of the park, consider spending at least three days, camping or staying in one of the cabins at Kokee Lodge.

You'll find trails that lead to exhilarating cliff-edge views of vast Waimea Canyon. Appearing to defy gravity, goats perch along the sheer edges of the chasm. **The Kukui Trail** is the only hiking path that goes into **Waimea Canyon.** Some three miles long, it is well marked and well maintained. Of course, it's all downhill (about 90 minutes), then all uphill (about three hours), so you'll have to pace yourself carefully. The trailhead is along the road up to Waimea Canyon Lookout, after the western and eastern roads have met. Other trails lead to waterfalls, swimming holes, or deep into the forest, where you can find a stand of California redwood trees. Nude bathers are not an uncommon sight in the pool below Waipoo Falls No. 1. A favorite spot for relaxation and a picnic is stunning Waipoo Falls No. 2, which overlooks the canyon.

Families should consider trying the two mile hike along the **Pu Ka Ohelo-Berry Flat Trails.** In addition to California redwoods, they'll pass Australian eucalyptus, Japanese Sugi pines, and other striking trees. Hikers should look out for Methley plums and vines laden with ripe *lilikoi* (passion fruit). Banana poka is a favorite snack for Kokee's wild pigs.

The **Na Pali region** is also best appreciated in a leisurely three days or so. Be very careful of the sheer cliff edges. Erosion can cause them to be quite dangerous. The 11 mile **Kalalau Trail,** which runs from Haena Beach Park to Kalalau Valley, can be especially hazardous between October and May, and during June rains. Note that even if it has rained only slightly, the trail can be very slippery and muddy. Some hikers say you'll pass the most impressive scenery in the first mile. Hanakapiai, with its flourishing foliage and small beach, is about an hour's (mainly uphill) hike (two miles) from Haena Point. You'll see one of Na Pali's many waterfalls in the valley here. When you reach Kalalau Stream, you can play Tarzan - just grab the hanging ropes and swing across the water. Kalalau is Na Pali's largest valley, and perhaps its most beautiful. The beach here has lovely ivory sand. Listen for Kamapuaa, the hog man, who is said to live in several of Na Pali's valleys. He frequently changes form - one moment he might be rain and the next he might turn himself into an ocean wave.

For maps and details about guided hikes, call **Outfitters Kauai**, *Tel. 808/742-9667*, in Poipu.

Horseback Riding

In the Princeville area, **Princeville Ranch Stables** (a.k.a. **Pooku Stables**), *Tel. 826-6777 or 826-7473*, conducts trail rides along sea cliffs high above the churning Pacific, through wide open fields, and in Hanalei Valley, with its patchwork of farm plots. The 4-hour **Waterfall Picnic Ride** ($105 per person, including a gourmet lunch) features a short but steep hike (you'll have to use a rope to get down and up a 10 foot drop) to the 70-foot Kalahiwa Falls, where you'll swim. The ride is about an hour each way, with the rest of the time for picnicking and swimming.

For the less adventurous or those with slimmer wallets, the 1.5-hour **Hanalei Valley Country Ride** ($55) is also wonderful. During the ride along the ridge line through fields of ginger, hip-high ferns, and purple-blue wildflowers, you'll have gorgeous, sweeping views of Hanalei Valley, far below. The entire ridge line is a conservation area. At the beginning and end of the trail, you might spot your dream house among the luxurious homes on the other side of the road. Also consider the **Cattle Drive Ride** ($125 for 2 hours) and the **Anini Bluff & Beach Ride** ($95 for 3 hours). During the summer, make reservations at least a week in advance, especially for the picnic ride. The size of groups is anywhere from two to eight people year-round.

Another good company is **Silver Falls Ranch**, *Tel. 828-6718*, near Kilauea; the two-hour waterfall picnic ride runs $95 - you'll even have a chance to swim in a secluded pool. **CJM Country Stables**, *Tel. 742-6096*, near the Hyatt Regency Kauai in Poipu, leads 2 hour beach rides for $56 and 2 1/2 hour beach and breakfast rides for $72. If you're staying at the Kauai Marriott, try **South Sea Tours**, *Tel. 245-5050, ext. 5919*. **Espirit de Corps Riding Academy**, *Tel. 822-4688*, just outside Kapaa, is worth checking out as well.

Kayaking

One of the most exhilarating activities in Kauai is paddling a kayak along the tranquil Hanalei River, through a wildlife refuge. With hulking mountains in the distance, you'll glide beneath canopies of trees and past taro fields and all kinds of birds, including rare red-headed boobies. Bright yellow hau blossoms float on the water. Being chased by bass, tiny white fish suddenly jump out of the water from time to time. The river is extremely peaceful, since no motorized craft are allowed. The paddling is easy, with plenty of time to simply float and enjoy the scenery. Contact **Kayak Kauai Outfitters**, *Hanalei, Tel. 826-9844, and Kapaa, Tel. 822-9179 or 800/437-3507*, which runs a 3-hour guided kayak and snorkel trip through the Hanalei River National Wildlife Refuge ($55 per person).

Another kayak trip goes along Huleia Stream through the jungled Huleia National Wildlife Refuge. **Island Adventure**, *Tel. 245-9662 or 800/1331-8044*, leads daily three-hour morning or afternoon tours (about $45/person). Each person gets his or her own kayak. The group might consist of anywhere from 10 to three dozen people. At the end of the scenic excursion, paddlers are shuttled overland back to their cars.

If you want to go it alone, rent one- or two-person kayaks for ocean or river paddling from **Peddle and Paddle**, *Tel. 826-9069*, or **Kayak Kauai Outfitters**, *Hanalei, Tel. 826-9844 and Kapaa, Tel. 822-9179*. Expect to spend from $25 to $75.

Sailing

For sunset dinner cruises, moonlight sails, winter **whale watching** trips, Na Pali Coast tours, and other group excursions, try **Kayak Kauai Outfitters**, *Hanalei, Tel. 826-9844 and in Kapaa, Tel. 822-9179* or **South**

Sea Tours, *Tel. 245-5050, ext. 5919,* near Lihue. Charters can be arranged through **Bluewater Sailing,** *Tel. 822-0525,* in Kapaa.

Catamaran Kahanu, Tel. 826-4596, boasts that people sailing along Na Pali in its 36-foot catamaran are not packed like sardines the way folks are on the rubber rafts of some companies. Their cat is small enough to back under a few waterfalls, yet spacious enough to allow dry storage and elbow room. The cost of the four-hour trip, including a snack and 90 minutes of snorkeling, is $85 for adults and $65 for children. Other outfits to consider for Na Pali boat trips are **Blue Water Sailing** (above) and **Captain Andy's Sailing Adventures,** *Tel. 822-0525 or 828-1142,* in Poipu. See also Snorkeling in this section.

Scuba Diving

Since Kauai is the oldest of Hawaii's main islands, the coral below its waters has had more time to build colonies on top of colonies. Thus, its reefs are some of the state's most complex and scenic. Most of Kauai's best diving is along the southern, protected coast. Many good south shore dive sites are just 10 to 30 minutes away from Port Allen and Kukuiula Harbor. One of Kauai's best cave dives, called Sheraton Caverns, is just off-shore from the Sheraton Kauai Hotel in Poipu. Lobster and sea turtles hide out in the various underwater grottos that range from 35 to 60 feet in depth. The 65- to 80-foot-deep **General Store** is a U-shaped reef filled with an unusual variety of marine life. Shrimp, lobster, and red squirrel fish reside in its two caves. This site also boasts a wrecked 19th century steamship.

Koloa Landing is a good place for new divers to test the waters. The reef here at this old boat landing slowly descends to 25 feet. Old bottles and fittings from 18th and 19th century whaling ships and trading vessels can occasionally be found on the ocean floor. Underwater explorers will also see parts of the old train track that once ran between Koloa Landing and the area's sugar mill. All kinds of fish swarm around, including butterfly fish and blue-striped snapper. Divers get a kick out of feeding the moray eels here.

Diving along Kauai's north shore is excellent, but the waters are calm enough only during the summer. There are some striking underwater lava tubes and archways in this region. Along the eastern shore, divers can explore the Wreck of the *Lakenbach,* a German freighter that sank in a storm in 1951. Some of the ship's plates, dishes, silverware, and bottles remain in the galley.

To arrange dives or to take scuba classes or lessons in underwater photography, inquire at **Kauai Sea Sports,** *Tel. 742-9303,* in the Poipu area; **Fathom Five Adventures,** *Tel. 742-6991,* in Koloa Town; **Dive Kauai,** *Tel. 822-0452,* between Wailea and Kapaa; and **Ocean Odyssey,** *Tel. 245-8681* at the Outrigger hotel.

Snorkeling

Most of the Na Pali cruises include snorkeling. Sea turtles and dolphins are often spotted in this area. During most of the winter, when the water is rough along the north shore, the majority of cruises are conducted along other coasts. Try **Captain Zodiac Raft Expeditions,** *Hanalei, Tel. 826-9371;* **Kauai Kayak Outfitters,** *Hanalei, Tel. 826-9844 or Kapaa, Tel. 822-9179;* **Snorkel Bob's Kauai,** *Lihue, Tel. 245-9433 or Poipu, Tel. 742-8327;* **Fathom Five Adventures,** *Koloa Town, Tel. 742-6991;* **Hanalei Surf Company,** *Tel. 826-9000,* for snorkel rentals only; and **Captain Andy's Sailing Adventures,** *Koloa, Tel. 822-7833.* You can also rent gear or arrange boat trips through you accommodation.

Surfing

The best surfing is along the north shore during the winter and in the Poipu area in the summer. To rent boards or for lessons, try **Nuku Moi Surfing School,** *Tel. 742-8019,* or **Hanalei Surf Company,** *Tel. 826-9000.*

Tennis

Kauai has no shortage of tennis courts. In addition to some 70 hotel courts, there are nearly two dozen public courts lit for night play. Some resorts charge guests from $4 to $10 to play, while others offer free tennis. Non-guest charges range from $5 to $12.

Water Skiing

Contact **Kauai Water Ski & Sports,** *Kapaa, Tel. 822-3574,* or make arrangements through your hotel.

Windsurfing

Also called board sailing, this sport can be arranged through **Sea Star Kauai,** *Tel. 332-8189,* or **Windsurf Kauai,** *Tel. 828-6838.* Both lessons and equipment rental are available. Many hotels can also arrange windsurfing lessons or board rental.

Working Out & Spas

If you're staying in the Princeville area, you'll find it convenient to use the extensive spa and fitness center at the entrance to the **Prince Golf Course** for about $15 per day. The exercise room and class studio have one of the world's most spectacular views. You'll be so dazzled by the rolling green swards of the golf course and the verdant mountains that you won't even realize you're breaking a sweat. This is also the place for exceptional toe-to-earlobe massages among other delicious body treatments. The **Hyatt Regency Kauai** has another snazzy exercise room and a health spa, where the facials and massages are fabulous. Consider scheduling a private exercise session with a personal trainer.

SHOPPING

Like the other major islands, Kauai has a variety of shopping centers, some with a good selection of worthwhile stores. A few of these malls stay open until about 9pm, to catch the dinner crowd, while others close at 5pm. Shops are also found in hotels, but prices are quite high. While Old Koloa Town (in Koloa, near Poipu) has some tempting shops, prices are hotel-steep. Outside of resort areas, Kauai offers some moderately priced family-run stores, where patrons can spend some time talking story with the owners. If you want to rub elbows with locals, head to Kapaa, Waimea, Eleele, or Lihue. Here are some of Kauai's most memorable shops:

Shopping Centers

One of Kauai's most attractive places to spend time and money is **Kilohana**, *3-2087 Kaumualii Highway, Puhi*, a converted plantation estate. Bedrooms, bathrooms, and closets in the gracious main house have been transformed into upscale showcases for Japanese antiques, Hawaiian and South Pacific crafts and artifacts, clothing, jewelry, paintings, and ceramics. Shoppers are invited to take horse-and-carriage tours around the grounds. (See also *Seeing the Sights*.)

Across the road is **Kukui Grove Center**, *3-2600 Kaumualii Highway, Tel. 245-7784, the island's largest mall*. Complimentary shuttle service is provided from some areas. Locals are the main patrons of the **Rice Shopping Center**, *4303 Rice Street, Lihue*. Those with wallets to match their expensive taste should wander around **Kiahuna Shopping Village**, *2360 Kiahuna Plantation Drive, Poipu*. Locals prefer **Waimea Canyon Plaza**, *Highway 50, Waimea*, and modest **Eleele Shopping Center**, *Highway 50, near Hanapepe*. There's more local flavor at **Waipouli Town Center**, *4-901 Kuhio Highway*, at the southern end of Kapaa.

Shoppers are entertained with hula dancing and music during the afternoon at flower-filled **Kinipopo Shopping Village**, *356 Kuhio Highway, Kapaa*. North of here, beachfront **Coconut Plantation Market Place**, *4-484 Kuhio Highway, Kapaa*, is set in a stunning coconut grove. The weathered shingle-roofed buildings enclose a courtyard with fountains and plants. Pipes, pumps, wheels, cranks, and other plantation machinery are painted bright red, yellow, and green. The restaurants and shops (selling handmade jewelry, Niihau shell necklaces, scrimshaw, T-shirts, resort wear, and other goods) are open late.

Also in Kapaa, newer **Kauai Village**, *4-831 Kuhio Highway*, was built to resemble a 19th century Hawaiian plantation town. Waterfalls and colorful indigenous plants add to the pleasant atmosphere for shopping.

On the north shore, **Princeville Center**, *5-4280 Kuhio Highway, Princeville*, has a healthy selection of boutiques and restaurants. More down-to-earth, **Ching Young Village** in nearby Hanalei offers crafts shops, clothing stores, and restaurants.

Art Galleries

Photographer Diane Ferry hand tints her photos, which she sells at **Kauai Images Gallery**, *937 Kuhio Highway, Kapaa, Tel. 822-1950*, along with original works by other notable local artists. At **Montage Galleries**, *Kapaa, Tel. 823-0030*, paintings, limited edition prints and posters by some of the state's best-known artists are displayed. Niihau shell jewelry and handmade gold pieces are also sold here.

Evolvelove Artist Gallery, *Hanalei, Tel. 826-6441*, sells everything from basketry, ceramics, and woodwork to batiks, hand-painted clothing, and Hawaiian art.

Beachwear & T-Shirts

Hot Rocket, *Ching Young Village, Hanalei, Tel. 826-7776*, carries some great T-shirts in bold designs. Many people like the lively sportswear and bathing suits at **M. Miura Store**, *4-1419 Kuhio Highway, Kapaa, Tel. 822-4401.*

Crafts

Up north, be sure to visit **On the Road to Hanalei**, *Tel. 826-7360.* **Hanapepe Bookstore Cafe & Espresso Bar**, *3830 Hanapepe Road, Tel. 335-5011*, in artsy Hanapepe down south is far more than a bookstore and cafe. You can also browse through jewelry, original paintings, perfumes made from Hawaiian blossoms, herbal soaps and lotions, straw hats in bold colors, candles, greeting cards, painted boxes, decorative ceramic tiles - the list goes on. When you visit the **Kauai Museum**, *Tel. 245-6931*, in Lihue, the gift shop is worth some time.

Distinctive Clothing

For more hand-painted clothing and jewelry as well as Bali imports, try **Tropical Tantrum**, *Kapaa, Tel. 822-7302 or Hanalei Center, 826-6944.* **Tropical Shirts**, *Coconut Plantation Market Place, Kapaa, Tel. 822-0203*, and Kiahuna Shopping Village, *Poipu, Tel. 742-6691*, sell hand-embroidered or silk-screened shirts, dresses, and other fashions for women, men, and children.

Fruit, Vegetables, & Flowers

Sunny Side Farmer's Market, *4-1345 Kuhio Highway, Kapaa, Tel. 822-0494 or 822-1154*, sells local fruit, vegetables, and flowers, which you can have delivered to your hotel, or mailed (inspected) to the mainland. In addition to pineapples, you'll also find papayas, apple bananas (the little sweet ones), mangos, coconuts, and sugar cane (which some folks like to chew on). Major credit cards are accepted. Boxed, inspected pineapples are also sold at the airport, but prices may be a bit higher for the convenience.

Hawaiian Quilts

Inspired by New England missionaries, Hawaiian women put their own spin on the American quilting tradition. You'll find examples of this distinctive island art form at **Kapaia Stitchery**, *Kuhio Highway, near Lihue, Tel. 245-2281*. This shop also sells other kinds of original needlework as well as muumuus and aloha shirts made to order from tropical fabrics.

Jewelry

Kauai is the best part of the state to buy Niihau shell leis, since they are somewhat cheaper here than elsewhere. These necklaces are sold, among other places, at **Kilohana Plantation** near Lihue; and **Kauai Gold Limited**, *Coconut Plantation Market Place, Kapaa, Tel. 822-9361*, which also carries scrimshaw and gold jewelry.

Jim Saylor Jewelers, *1318 Kuhio Highway, Kapaa, Tel. 822-3591*, stocks an unusual collection of designs (handmade on the premises), along with rare gems from a variety of countries. At the **Goldsmith's Gallery**, *Kinipopo Shopping Village, 356E Kuhio Highway, Kapaa, Tel. 822-4653*, some of the handcrafted gold jewelry is quite imaginative. **Spouting Horn** in Poipu, may offer some good buys in jewelry among the displays of vendors. See also *Art Galleries and Crafts*.

HARD LEIS

Before you invest in a rare Niihau necklace, do some research to make sure it's authentic. Some fakes have been passed off as the real thing. Niihau is the only island where these minuscule shells, decorated with delicately detailed natural designs, wash ashore in significant quantities. Each lei takes anywhere from 20 to 200 hours to complete, since the tiny shells must be picked out of the sand, sorted by size, shape, and color; then cleaned, drilled with holes, and strung into intricate patterns. This painstaking work, the scarcity of the shells, and the beauty of the necklaces account for the hefty price tags (they may cost hundreds, sometimes thousands of dollars each). The rarest colors are red and deep pink.

Macadamia Nuts

Prices tend to be the lowest at **Star Market,** *Tel. 245-7777,* and **Long's Drugs,** *Tel. 245-7771,* both in the Kukui Grove Center just outside Lihue.

Natural Foods

Try **Papaya's Natural Foods,** *Kauai Village Shopping Center, Kapaa, Tel. 523-0190.*

EXCURSIONS & DAY TRIPS

Niihau

Seventeen miles off Kauai's southwestern coast, Niihau is often referred to as "the Forbidden Island." Until the late 1980s, only people with Hawaiian blood were welcome here (with the exception of the haole family that owns the island). It was 1864 when Elizabeth Sinclair, a wealthy widow from Scotland, bought the narrow 19-mile-long land mass from King Kamehameha for $10,000. Over the years, her descendants, the Robinson family, have made sure that old Hawaiian traditions are maintained here. Niihau is the only place in Hawaii where Hawaiian is the primary language. Plumbing, cigarettes, alcohol, and guns are all alien to its 200 or so residents.

Most people work on the Robinson's cattle and sheep ranch or sell honey or charcoal. Another lucrative though time-consuming industry is the making of leis comprised of tiny, rare Niihau shells. These intricate necklaces, sold throughout Hawaii, can cost hundreds or even thousands of dollars each. Some residents of the state commend the Robinsons for their success in keeping a piece of old Hawaii alive in the present. In 1987, using the whirlybird for medical emergencies on Niihau, so the money you spend on this trip will go to a worthy cause. **Niihau Helicopter,** *Tel. 335-3500,* leaves from Burns Air Field, a mile and a half from Hanapepe and costs $250 per person. These flights don't go anywhere near the town of Puuwai, but occasionally people from the village have come to the beach where the helicopter lands to meet visitors.

Helicopter tours were begun from Kauai to supplement the cost of

If you're lucky, you'll find some intact Niihau shells in the sand and see some dolphins, seals, and perhaps green turtles. The adventurous can eat some raw (in other words, live) *opihi,* a local seafood delicacy. It lives in a quarter-sized shell whose shape resembles a mini volcano or an umbrella. Found on rocks, it tastes something like salty, chewier abalone.

If you'd like to learn a little about Niihau before you take this tour, go to the Kauai Museum (see *Seeing the Sights*).

PRACTICAL INFORMATION

Emergencies

Call 911.

Medical Attention

If you need medical care, contact on of the following:
Wilcox Memorial Hospital, *Lihue, Tel. 245-1100*
Kauai Veterans Memorial Hospital, *Waimea, Tel. 338-9431.*
Kauai Medical Group, *Lihue, Tel. 245-1500; Kukui Grove, Tel. 245-5651; Koloa, Tel. 742-1621; Kapaa, Tel. 822-3431; or Kilauea, Tel. 828-1418.*

Post Offices

To find the location of the branch closest to you, call *Tel. 245-4994.*

Tourist Information

Hawaii Visitors & Convention Bureau, *3016 Umi Street, Suite 207, Lihue, HI 96766, Tel. 245-3971.*

Weather

Especially when hiking or traveling to distant parts of the island where the weather may be quite different from where you are, consider calling *Tel. 245-6001.*

15. MOLOKAI

Although Molokai is the closest neighbor island to Oahu, it couldn't possibly be more different. Lying about 25 miles across Kaiwi Channel, it is considered by many to be the most Hawaiian member of the archipelago, in part, because more than half of its nearly 7,000 residents are descendants of the original inhabitants of the island chain. But this perception is also due to Molokai's sleepy pace, the friendliness of its people and its historic sights, such as ancient fishponds, crumbling *heiau* (temples) and legend-laden valleys.

Hula is said to have been born on the slopes of Maunaloa, in the west, where the goddess Laka learned to dance. Held in May, the **Annual Molokai Ka Hula Piko Festival** commemorates this birth, with demonstrations of woodworking, quilting, and deer-horn scrimshaw in addition to music and dance. Almost a third of the local population turns out for the revival of the ancient **Makahiki Festival** each January, when competitions are held in traditional Hawaiian games.

Although Molokai has a smattering of hotels and condominiums, residents have little use for the concept of tourism. No buildings rise higher than three stories, and fast food chains, traffic lights, and shopping malls are nonexistent. **Kaunakakai,** the only real town, consists of one main street lined with weathered, single-story shops. Instead of Molokai molding itself to suit outsiders, visitors are happily absorbed into the gentle life of the island.

Molokai draws the adventurous traveler, the person who thrives on hiking and camping, or vacationers looking simply to relax. A popular activity among visitors is the hike or mule ride along a narrow cliffside trail down to Kalaupapa Peninsula, the site of Molokai's famed **"leper colony."** Another excursion is the safari through **Molokai Ranch Wildlife Park,** where all kinds of East African and Asian animals roam freely across terrain that resembles Kenya and Tanzania. Many people also enjoy the bouncy horse-drawn wagon ride with stops at the island's largest heiau and a mango grove, plus demonstrations of throwing Hawaiian fishing nets, husking coconuts, and creating traditional arts and crafts. In addition to swimming at some gorgeous west coast beaches, water sports include surfing, snorkeling, kayaking, sport fishing, sailing, and whale watching. Most restaurants are small and unpretentious, and few and far between. Nightlife on this island means talking story with locals over a few beers or taking a drive to see the lights of Honolulu or Maui.

The Way It Was

Perhaps Molokai's refreshing lack of development has its roots in history. For the most part, foreign explorers left the island alone. Captain Cook, who brought Hawaii to the attention of the Western world in 1778, bypassed the island altogether. It wasn't until 1786 that British captain **George Dixon** became the first foreigner island residents ever met. After that, Molokai was again left undisturbed by outsiders, until 1832, when a group of American Protestants established a mission.

Then in 1848, **King Kamehameha III** ordered the Great Mahele land division. In a break with tradition, land could now be owned by individuals as private property. German immigrant **Rudolph Meyer** got busy, buying large tracts that the turned into grazing areas for cattle and sheep. By the 1870s, **King Kamehameha V** had purchased much of this property, which became known as Molokai Ranch. In 1898, a group of Honolulu businessmen bought the ranch and tried to change it into a sugar plantation. They might have been successful had it not been for the salty irrigation water.

In the early 1900s, **Charles M. Cooke**, a member of one of Hawaii's leading haole families, turned the land back into the cattle ranch it is today. For a time, **Molokai Ranch** also processed honey, and the island became one of its leading producers in the world. During the 1920s, Libby and Del Monte leased sections of the land, and pineapple plantations flourished at the hands of Japanese and Filipino immigrant workers. The plantation towns of Maunaloa and Kualapuu were born.

Then in the 1970s, the pineapple industry began to die on Molokai, ironically, because owners had found that doing business in places such as the Philippines was far more profitable than having Filipinos and others work in Hawaii. Tourism and diversified agriculture have replaced pineapple as the island's economic base.

Hawaiian Roots

There is a strong dedication to preservation of traditional Hawaiian culture on Molokai. Many heiau dot the landscape. One is among the largest in the state. Called **Ili'ili'opa'e**, it is included in the Molokai Wagon Ride tour.

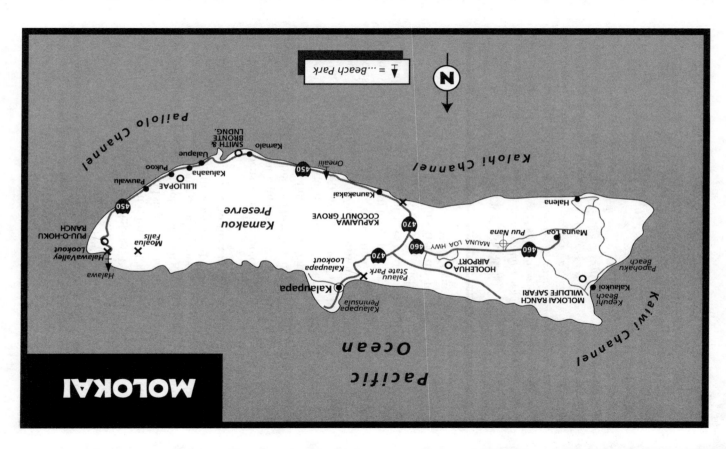

Although Polynesian settlers imported the friendly aloha spirit to Hawaii when they arrived over a millennium ago, warfare was common-place among ancient Hawaiians. Thus, every year, the four-month **Makahiki festival** marked a merry cease-fire. This time of peace honoring the god of fertility, Lono, was celebrated with unbridled feasting and battles of a good-natured sort. Today on Molokai, the two-day revival of this festival takes place every January in Kaunakakai Park. While the event draws a couple of thousand residents, it is not well known among outsiders. The best of Hawaii's musicians and singers are brought over to perform along with top *hula halau* (hula schools). Church groups prepare kalua pig, raw and stewed fish, and all kinds of other food. Everyone is invited to help themselves. Mixed among the shorts and T-shirts in the crowd are men wearing *malo* (loin cloths) and women in *pa'u* (wraparound skirts or dresses).

The celebration opens when schoolchildren march into the park displaying the traditional banners of various island districts. The star banner, draped with feather and fern leis, honors Lono. As the chanting and hula begin, youngsters fidget in anticipation of the highlight of the day: competitions in Hawaiian games. Several hundred children and adults form teams to compete in *ulu maika* (lawn bowling), *'o'o ihe* (spear hurling), *kukini* (foot races), *pohaku* (throwing a weighty rock), and *haka moa* (wrestling in a circle with one foot tied). From 9 to 11am on the first full day, visiting adults may sign up to participate.

Another time to see performances of traditional dance is during the annual **Molokai Ka Hula Piko festival**, each third Saturday in May. Celebrating the birth of hula, this free day-long event takes place at Papokahu Beach Park at Kaluakoi. More than 3,000 onlookers fill the

---

HOLY LAND

Toward the end of the 1500s, Lanikaula, a renowned kahuna (priest,) was so revered that people came to Molokai from all over Hawaii to ask his help in solving their problems. Kawelo, a jealous colleague from Lanai, decided to do away with Lanikaula by using sorcery. Molokai's kahuna discovered the plot, but only in time to make arrangements with his sons to hide his bones, so no one would be able to steal his powers. A kukui grove was planted near the place by Halawa Valley where the bones were thought to be buried. Even though the trees are now dying, the land is still considered extremely sacred by contemporary Hawaiians. On several occasions during the 1980s, protests forced condominium developers who wanted to build at other sacred sites to give up their plans.

park. You'll see both *kahiko* (kah-HEE-ko), the stern, ancient style of hula, and *auana* (ow-WAH-nah), the lighter, more sensual contemporary version. Handheld *uli uli* gourds, filled with beans and elaborately decorated with feathers, sound like maracas. *Ipu* gourds, once worn as helmets with cut-out eyes, are sometimes used as well.

Wearing long hair is part of the hula tradition. Women and girls braid their waist-length tresses the night before, then unbraid it so that it is full and wavy the day of hula. Men wear malo (loin cloths) with one flap or two flaps. Each *halau* (hula group) is led by a *kumu hula* (master instructor). The audience always manages to work up a huge appetite, which is fine because food is in abundance. You'll find everything from fresh fish and shrimp to Korean ribs and Hawaiian shave ice. Be sure to arrive early to claim the scarce shade available under the few kiawe trees. (The program runs from 9am to sundown.)

ARRIVALS & DEPARTURES

Most visitors land at Hoolehua Airport, near the center of the island. Shuttle vans operate between the airport and hotels and condos at the Kaluakoi Resort in the northwest, and Kaunakakai on the southern coast. Taxis are also available. If you're renting wheels, it's best to make arrangements before you arrive and pick up your car at the airport, from **Budget or Dollar.**

With **Molokai Off Road Tours and Taxi**, *Tel. 553-3369*, you'll pay about $16 from Hoolehua Airport to Kaunakakai, about a 10-minute drive, and $26 to the Kaluakoi Resort, about a half hour away. (This company also conducts four-wheel-drive tours to sights that can only be reached by dirt roads, such as Moomomi Beach, Waikoulu Lookout and the Sandalwood Pit.) **Kukui Tours & Limousines**, *Tel. 553-5133*, is another reliable company.

Through various tour companies, travelers may fly from Honolulu directly to Kalaupapa Peninsula, but only to join a ground tour of the historic area.

ORIENTATION

Just eight miles across the Pacific, the high rises of Maui's Kaanapali Beach resort seem to be in another world. Part of Maui County, Molokai is Hawaii's fifth largest island. Only Lanai, eight miles to the south, is less developed. A long, narrow strip of land some 261 square miles in size, Molokai was formed by two main volcanoes. **Maunualoa** stands 1,381 feet tall in the parched and prairie-like west while 4,970-foot **Kamakou** soars in the jungled east.

Also lush, the north shore is treated to some 245 inches of annual rainfall, which has created magnificent ravines. Clouds cling to multi-hued mountainsides. Where the elements have cracked the earth apart, gashes of red dirt peer through the green. At the bottom of a 1,600-foot cliff, huge, pancake-flat Kalaupapa Peninsula seems to be a geologic afterthought. At the eastern tip of the island is gorgeous **Halawa Valley and Beach Park**. The fire hydrants along the country road seem an intrusion in such pristine surroundings.

GETTING AROUND MOLOKAI

By Car

Ranging from seven to 10 miles wide and about 38 miles long, Molokai is best explored in a rental car, which you can pick up at the airport if you've made prior arrangements. Driving is pure pleasure in Molokai, not only because the scenery is so spectacular (particularly in the east), but because you'll run into little traffic. Just watch out for mongooses, fond of dashing across the road in front of moving vehicles. It's difficult to get lost on this island, since main roads aren't plentiful.

By Guided Tour

Several van tour companies will be happy to show you the sights when you don't feel like driving.

Half- and full-day tours are arranged through **Molokai Off-Road Tours & Taxi**, *Tel. 553-3369*. On the shorter excursion, stops include Kalaupapa Lookout, the Meyer Sugar Mill at Kalae, and Purdy's macadamia nut farm. The longer trip also introduces visitors to Kaluakoi Resort; the artsy crafts shops of Maunaloa town; Kaunakakai, with a lunch stop - for an additional charge - at oceanfront Hotel Molokai; and the gorgeous east coast up to Halawa Valley Overlook. You can be picked up at your hotel, or at the airport if you're flying in for the day.

Whether you ride a mule down a cliff, fly, or hike into historic **Kalaupapa Peninsula**, you are required to join an organized ground tour (about $30 if you walk both ways or fly in). Visitors must be on an escorted tour or obtain a permit to walk in; otherwise, there is a fine of $500. Contact **Damien Molokai Tours**, *Tel. 567-6171*. Inquire about hiking down and flying out. Bring your own lunch. Call **Molokai Ranch Outfitters Center**, *Tel. 552-2791 or 800/254-8871*, for horseback trail rides and wildlife conservation park tours.

WHERE TO STAY

Casual is the word that best describes both the accommodations and the friendly service at the few hotels and condominiums on Molokai. Spread along a beautiful beach in the west, the low-rise **Kaluakoi Hotel & Golf Club** is the only large hotel on the island. Crowds on Molokai just don't exist, so the whole island is a good place for escape. But if absolute seclusion is what you have in mind, eastern Molokai offers a handful of condos, Bed & Breakfasts, and private cottages. Note that these accommodations may require that you stay a minimum number of nights, usually two. With limited stock, grocery stores on Molokai are few and far between, so you would do well to bring at least some food with you if you plan to do any cooking.

MOLOKAI'S BEST HOTELS

Kamalo Plantation Bed & Breakfast, East Molokai: This home-like accommodation in a lush, tropical setting.

Paniolo Hale Resort and Condominium, West Molokai: You can't go wrong in one of these spacious, comfortable apartments.

West Molokai

MARC KE NANI KAI RESORT, *Kaluakoi Resort, P.O. Box 289, Maunaloa, HI 96770. Tel. 808/552-2761 or 800/535-0085, Fax 808/552-0045. 120 rooms. Rates begin at $148 per unit. Major credit cards.*

This condominium has a pleasant residential feel. The one- and two-bedroom units each have a full kitchen and washer/dryer. Furnished in rattan and wicker, the pleasant rooms open onto lanais. The two-story townhouses overlook the golf course and colorful gardens. Tennis courts, a swimming pool, and a Jacuzzi are among the other facilities. The beach, which can be seen from some rooms, is about a five-minute walk away. Housekeeping service is provided every three days. Ceiling fans and natural breezes cool apartments instead of air-conditioning.

The office is open from 8am to 5pm, so if you'll be checking in or out before or after hours, be sure to make arrangements beforehand to pick up your key or finalize your departure.

KALUAKOI VILLAS, *1131 Kaluakoi Road, Maunaloa, HI 96770. Tel. 808/591-2235 or 800/367-5004, Fax 808/596-0158. 78 units. Rates: $125 to $200 per unit. Major credit cards.*

Here's a pleasant condominium next to the Kaluakoi Golf Course. Choose where you want to stay from an array of oceanside villas, suites, and studios. Some have wonderful full ocean views while others have partial water views. They all come with lanais, TV/VCRs, kitchenettes with microwaves, daily housekeeping service, and other home-style conveniences. Ceiling fans stand in for air-conditioning. You won't find telephones in units, but messages are relayed to guests from the office or manager. Unlike many condos, where the decor varies from unit to unit according to the owners, these are standardized, furnished with attractive island-style rattan. Guests are free to use the pool, convenience store, restaurant, and other facilities of the Kaluakoi Resort. Travelers often get to know each other around the communal gas barbecue grill.

PANIOLO HALE RESORT AND CONDOMINIUM, *Maunaloa, Molokai, HI 96770. Tel. 808/552-2731 or 800/367-2984, Fax 808/552-2288. 32 units. Rates begin at $100 per unit. Two-night minimum stay required.*

The golf course runs between these one- and two-story condominium buildings and the beach. (The only problem is, for those ground-floor oceanfront rooms facing the fairway, passing golf carts can interfere with privacy.) All of the spacious, brightly furnished studios, one-, and two-bedroom apartments have full kitchens and lanais. Some are duplexes. A couple even come with private hot tubs (guests are charged extra for heating, though). Views take in the ocean and lush gardens in this plantation-style setting. In addition to a swimming pool and paddle tennis court, the gas barbecues give guests a chance to mingle. Housekeeping service is provided once a week. Videos and books can be borrowed from the office. The bar and restaurant of the Kaluakoi Hotel are right next door.

KALUAKOI HOTEL & GOLF CLUB, *Kaluakoi Resort, P.O. Box 1977, Maunaloa, Molokai, HI 96770. Tel. 808/552-2550 or 800/365-6944, Fax 808/552-2821. 126 units. Double rooms begin at $95. Major credit cards.*

The two-story buildings and beachfront 18-hole championship golf course are spread across 130 acres. Palm-edged Kepuhi Beach, with low lava cliffs at one end, borders the fairway. Unfortunately, the water is usually too rough for swimming, but there is a pool on the premises and calmer beaches are not far. The hotel also has a Jacuzzi and four Laykold tennis courts. Wild turkeys and deer roam around the fringes of the property. Since the grounds, sprouting palms and bougainvillea, are so wonderfully spacious, visitors sometimes get the feeling that they have the place to themselves.

However, don't expect swanky decor in the guest rooms- the best way to describe furnishing is "nondescript." TVs are provided and rooms come with kitchenettes (guests are asked to wash dishes upon departure). Lanais are a good size for pleasant relaxation.

Kaunakakai Area

MARC MOLOKAI SHORES SUITES, *P.O. Box 1037, South shore. Tel. 808/553-5954 or 800/535-0085, Fax 808/553-5954. 100 units. Rates per unit: $141. Major credit cards.*

Skyscrapers by Molokai standards, these three-story wooden buildings house modest one-bedroom/one-bath and two-bedroom/two-bath condominium apartments. Overlooking the ocean, each unit comes with a full kitchen, lanai, cable TV, and ceiling fan. There are no phones in the units, so your messages will come through the office. The beach is not good for swimming, but guests amuse themselves at the pool, nine-hole putting green, shuffleboard, and picnic area with barbecue grills. The lawns are landscaped with all kinds of gardens. At night, flaming torches add to the pleasant atmosphere.

HOTEL MOLOKAI, *P.O. Box 546, Kaunakakai, HI 96748, South shore. Tel. 808/553-5347 or 800/423-6656, Fax 808/553-5047. 51 rooms. Double rooms begin at $65. Major credit cards.*

Architecturally speaking, this is the hotel with the most character on Molokai. A long dug-out canoe hangs in the open-air lobby, which leads to the lush grounds. Black columns, dramatically carved like Hawaiian tikis, decorate the open-air dining room that sits at the edge of the ocean. The beach is disappointing, so guests gravitate to the small swimming pool (which is sometimes used for dips after dark). Two-story wooden cottages are topped with shingled, Polynesian-style concave roofs. The rustic guest rooms open to lanais with swinging chairs large enough for two. Inside, some have twin beds, while others sport queens or kings. Rooms vary greatly, from tiny to family-sized. Some have kitchenettes. In others you'll make do with refrigerators only. Many units are dark and somewhat stuffy. For one of the few with air conditioning, be sure to ask when you make your reservation. All are equipped with fans.

PAU HANA INN, *P.O. Box 860, Kaunakakai, HI 96748, South shore. Tel. 808/553-5342 or 800/922-7866. 40 units. Doubles begin at $65. Major credit cards.*

Here at Molokai's oldest hotel, the lively atmosphere makes up for the uninspired decor of the modest rooms, which are found in various cottages. Unless you're on a *very* tight budget, opt for an oceanfront unit instead of a rather claustrophobic standard room.

Pau Hana is a great place to meet island residents. On weekends (which begin Thursday night), the inn throbs with the sounds of a live band, and it may seem as if most of Molokai has come to party. The beach isn't attractive enough to lure people into the water, but the grassy shore is fine for sunbathing. Most guests hang out at the swimming pool with its tree-shaded patio, or at the popular restaurant (where many enjoy sinking their teeth into the prime rib). The sprawling banyan tree by the popular waterside bar is more than a century old.

East Molokai

MARC WAVECREST RESORT, *HC-01 Box 541, Kaunakakai, HI 96748, between Kamalo and Pukoo. Tel. 808/558-8103 or 800/535-0085, Fax 808/558-8206. 126 units. Rates begin at $120 per unit. Major credit cards.*

On the dramatic eastern coast, these remote one-bedroom condominium apartments, in three-story wooden buildings, attract travelers staying on Molokai for extended periods. Although TVs are provided, there are no telephones in the neat rooms, which vary in size and decor. Shaded with tall trees, the fertile grounds burst with bird-of-paradise, both pink and white ginger, hibiscus, ti plants, and croton.

Lanais afford wonderful views of the landscape, the rugged, unspoiled coast, and the islands of Lanai and Maui. The rocky beach gets very muddy at times, so swimming is usually out, but fishing and whale watching are fine here. The swimming pool and lighted tennis courts also keep vacationers occupied.

HALE KAWAIKAPU, *Leimoku Ltd, 532 Elepaio Street, Honolulu, HI 96816, 17.6 miles east of Kaunakakai. Tel. 808/521-9202. Two units. Rates: $85 to $125.*

The name means "House of Sacred Waters," and there certainly is something spiritual about this retreat with its many Polynesian touches. A house and a cottage sit between the palm-lined beach and a deep valley backed by hulking mountains. The house sleeps six and the cottage sleeps four. Ensuring privacy, a grassy expanse accented with bright flowers and clusters of bushy coconut trees separate these rental units. With its tall Polynesian-style shingled roof, the smaller cottage screams "Hawaii." The lanai faces the gardens and ocean, visible through the curving trunks of palms. The other unit, somewhat more Western in style, has two bedrooms, two baths, an oceanfront lanai and a dishwasher. Kitchens in each building are fully equipped and washing machines are in both. You'll also find snorkel gear and barbecue grills.

HONOMUNI HOUSE, *Star Route 306, Kaunakakai, HI 96748, Honomuni Valley, 17.4 miles east of Kaunakakai. Tel. 808/558-8383. One unit. Rate is $85 per day; discount to $510 plus tax for stay of one week.*

Up to four people can stay in this cedar cottage surrounded by smooth lawns, a tropical garden, and towering trees draped in morning glory vines. It sports a living/dining room with a convertible sofa, an enclosed sleeping area, a color TV, an outdoor shower (hot water) in addition to the complete indoor bathroom, a covered lanai, and a full kitchen. Picture windows seem to bring the lush greenery inside. Guests receive complimentary eggs as well as papayas, bananas, and other fruit fresh from the garden.

The closest beach is a brief stroll away (but you might have to climb a locked gate to get to it) and a rocky stream teeming with freshwater fish and prawns is also nearby. Visitors enjoy hiking to waterfalls, natural swimming pools, and the remains of ancient Hawaiian house foundations and taro terraces. Mangoes, bananas, plums, breadfruit, and ginger grow wild in the forest. Tall monkeypod trees and palms shade the grounds. Guests are welcome to borrow from the library of Hawaiiana and Pacific literature. This area is an important historic region since Kamehameha I set off from here to conquer Oahu. The manager and her daughters can guide you on hikes in the beautiful area and describe the vegetation and the uses made of plants by native Hawaiian people. They encourage children and, besides volleyball and croquet, have toys and a swing for the younger set.

VACATION RENTAL, *P.O. Box 1507, Kaunakakai, HI 96748, Pukoo, south shore. Tel. 808/553-3648 or 800/553-3648, Fax 808/553-3783. One unit. Rate: $75. Minimum stay of two nights required.*

Set in a waterfront coconut grove, this rental (formerly called Swenson's Vacation Rental) is perfect for total tranquillity. The nearby sandy beach is fine for swimming. The home-like cottage has a large living room with a stereo and TV, a separate bedroom with a queen-size bed, and a full kitchen. When you don't feel like cooking, the Wavecrest store is close by. Make reservations as far in advance as possible.

KAMALO PLANTATION BED & BREAKFAST, *HC01, Box 300, Kaunakakai, HI 96748, 10 miles east of Kaunakakai. Tel. 808/558-8236, Fax 808/558-8236. Two units. Rates begin at $70 per unit. Minimum 2-night stay at the Cottage, no minimum stay for the suite. No children.*

This Bed & Breakfast is set in a tropical garden at the foot of Molokai's highest mountain. Rainbows, waterfalls, flowering trees, and the remains of an ancient Hawaiian temple add to the mood of serenity. In season, guests may have their fill of freshly plucked fruit from the surrounding trees. The hosts live on the five-acre grounds, but vacationers have complete privacy. (Note, though, that they do have several lively dogs that have the run of the property.) The owners are always happy to point vacationers toward their favorite hiking trails, beaches, and hidden spots.

Accommodations are provided in two settings. An island-style cottage, Planter's Cottage, sleeps two to four (with an added charge for third and fourth persons). It has a fully equipped kitchen, radio/tape deck, and indoor/outdoor showers. For bird watching or sunning, it also has a small deck overlooking a garden and the remains of a Hawaiian temple. The Kukui Suite is my personal favorite. In the guest wing of the main house, it consists of an cheerfully decorated room with a separate sitting area, full bath, and private entrance. It has a refrigerator, radio/color TV, and microwave. The lanai, visited by a variety of birds, is a pleasant place to relax. There's a game of Scrabble on hand for evenings or rainy days.

A healthful Aloha breakfast, including fresh tropical fruit and freshly baked bread, starts your day off in the main dining room of this attractive B&B. Good swimming beaches are a short drive away.

WHERE TO EAT

If you're into unpretentious restaurants that serve as local social centers, and enjoy homestyle food from a variety of ethnic backgrounds, then Molokai is your island. Hawaiian saimin, poi and plate lunches, Filipino stews, Chinese chicken with cashew nuts, Korean ribs, New York strip steak - it's all here. The smallest and least expensive places line Ala Malama Street in Kaunakakai. The food at the Kaluakoi Hotel's **Ohia Lodge** and Hotel Molokai's **Holo Holo Kai** might not win any awards, but it's perfectly satisfying. Be sure to try some **Molokai bread**, which you can buy fresh from the oven at **Kanemitsu Bakery** in Kaunakakai.

West Molokai

OHIA LODGE, *Kaluakoi Hotel. Tel. 552-2555. Reservations recommended. Dinner entrees: $18 to $20. Credit cards accepted.*

Ask to be seated by the tall, wood-framed glass doors or large windows that are open to the patio overlooking the ocean. Serving continental cuisine, this is Molokai's most upscale restaurant - actually it's the island's only upscale restaurant. Don't eat too much at the salad bar, or you won't have room for the rack of lamb crusted with macadamia nuts and sesame seeds, filet mignon, or one of the other dinner entrees. The desserts, including pies, cakes, and ice cream, are also worth a corner of your stomach. I love the key lime tart. In the adjoining Ohia Room, an musician provides soothing background sounds.

Central Molokai

KUALAPUU COOKHOUSE, *Kualapuu, near the airport. Tel. 567-6185. Closed Sundays. Inexpensive.*

A handsome weathered wooden building trimmed with lush vegetation houses this popular restaurant. With its long counter, soda fountain, and swivel stools, it has an old-fashioned feel. A large antique wok is suspended above the stove and pandanus frond baskets hang above the counter. An old red, green, and gold Del Monte sign decorates a wall, along with aged farming tools and photographs of the island. Patrons, who also dine at tables, gravitate toward the mahi-mahi sandwiches, teriyaki chicken, stir-fried beef, and saimin. Burgers, nachos, salads, stir-fried or teriyaki beef or chicken, and chili are also made. For many, the highlight of a meal here is a slice of homemade pie: lime, banana, coconut, or chocolate macadamia nut, to name a few. Whole pies are sold as well. Emblazoned across waiters' aprons are the words "Slow Food Chain" - and they aren't kidding. Be patient. Since the food is prepared to order, it can take a while. Arrive early for dinner. The menu sometimes shrinks near closing time.

Kaunakakai Area

OVIEDO'S, *Ala Malama Street, Kaunakakai. Tel. 553-5014. Dinner entrees average $7.50.*

The Filipino food served at this cafeteria-style restaurant for lunch and dinner is cooked with homegrown herbs and spices. Adobos (stews), the main attraction, are made with turkey tail, beef, pig's feet, or mongo beans. Order a mixed plate and your entree will come with rice and vegetables. Oviedo's has Molokai's best selection of ice cream, often including butter brickle, rocky road, and mint chocolate chip.

BANYAN TREE TERRACE RESTAURANT, *Pau Hana Inn, south shore. Tel. 553-5342. Inexpensive. Credit cards accepted.*

A short walk from Kaunakakai, the restaurant at the island's oldest hotel draws a very local crowd. There's a little-used fireplace in this al fresco dining room with a water view. Teriyaki steak and Hawaiian dishes are on the menu along with mainland favorites such as barbecued ribs, broiled fish, prime rib, and honey-dipped chicken.

KANEMITSU BAKERY AND COFFEE SHOP, *Ala Malama Street, Kaunakakai. Tel. 553-5855. Inexpensive.*

The only bakery in town, Kanemitsu is famous for its unusual breads. Choose among raisin nut, cheese, onion cheese, brown wheat, and French Molokai. Be sure to put your order in early. Hundreds of loaves are baked here each day, but they are often sold out within an hour and a half of the bakery's 5:30am opening! The delicious Mexican butternut, sesame, and macadamia nut cookies are also baked fresh daily. The diner-style restaurant is open from 5:30am through lunch. Try the banana hotcakes, the cheese omelette served with rice or toast, or the hamburger deluxe.

MOLOKAI PIZZA CAFE, *15 Kaunakakai Place, Kaunakakai. Tel. 553-3288. Inexpensive.*

Besides pizza and pasta, this restaurant serves fresh fish and salads.

OUTPOST NATURAL FOODS, *across from the State building, Kaunakakai. Tel. 553-3377. Close Saturdays. Inexpensive.*

This is the place to go for buying organic food in bulk or for eating a nutritious, healthful meal. The vegetarian lunch bar features low fat specials.

MOLOKAI DRIVE INN, *next to Molokai Visitors Association, Kaunakakai. Tel. 553-5655. Open Sunday through Thursday 6am to 10pm, Friday and Saturday 6am to 10:30pm. Inexpensive.*

If you're in a hurry to get to the beach or to explore the island, you might want to stop here for take-out. The mahi-mahi is a good choice.

East Molokai

NEIGHBORHOOD STORE 'N COUNTER, *Kamehameha Highway. Tel. 558-8498. Inexpensive.*

In addition to being a convenience store, this friendly place serves homestyle breakfast and lunch.

SEEING THE SIGHTS

Kaunakakai, Central Molokai, & the North

Watched over by mountains, rustic Kaunakakai (*cow-nah-cock-eye*) is where you'll find what little action there is on the island. Studded with parked pickup trucks, Ala Malama, the main drag, is barely two blocks long. You won't see traffic lights here or anywhere else on the island, but you will see bushy palms whose fronds rustle over telephone wires. Also bordering the street are low wooden general stores, a couple of restaurants, a post office, a library, and a courthouse in a former Catholic church.

The **Molokai Museum and Cultural Center,** *Lanai, Tel. 567-6436,* in the restored R.W. Meyer Sugar Mill, is on the National Register of Historic Places. Besides containing artifacts and memorabilia, it is the site of the Annual Molokai Museum Festival. If you're passing by from Monday to Saturday between 10am and 2pm, take a guided tour.

Few people leave town without stopping at **Kanemitsu Bakery,** a Molokai institution. Get there early before the best goodies are snapped up. Deep-sea fishing boats leave from nearby **Kaunakakai Wharf,** which is often piled with watermelons, honey and other goods ready for export. Just west of town along the main road, you'll come to **Kapuaiwa Grove.** These neat rows of coconut palms were planted (and nicknamed) for Prince Lot, a Molokai resident who went on to become King Kamehameha V. Planted during the mid-1800s, this is one of Hawaii's few remaining royal coconut groves. Across the street, a handful of late 19th century houses of worship stand along picturesque **Church Row.** Their simple architecture reflects the plain lifestyles of Hawaii's early missionaries.

Curving north toward central Molokai, Maunaloa Highway leads to Kalae Road, which will take you to the plantation town of **Kualapuu** ("sweet potato hill"). Prosperous during the heyday of pineapple, this quiet town hit a serious slump when Del Monte pulled out in the early 1980s after nearly 50 years. The huge rubber-lined reservoir you can see from the road was built to irrigate the pineapple fields that have been replaced by a coffee plantation. North of town, the tiny A-frame shelters are used to raise fighting cocks. Although this bloody sport is illegal throughout the state, it is a popular leisure activity among some residents.

Filled with rare birds and other native wildlife, indigenous trees, unusual plants, and thriving ohia forests, **Kamakou Preserve** is a must for lovers of the outdoors. Arrange an escorted day-long hike by contacting the **Nature Conservancy of Hawaii Molokai Field Office**, *P.O. Box 220, Kualapuu, Molokai, HI 96757, Tel. 553-5236*. Bring your own picnic lunch and drinking water. Reservations must be made several months in advance for these monthly events.

The town of **Hoolehua** and neighboring Palaau were declared Hawaiian Homestead land in the 1920s. This means that people of Hawaiian ancestry are entitled to lease agricultural lots at little cost. However, the dry terrain and scarce water for irrigation forced farmers to lease their land to large pineapple companies, until this practice was declared illegal. After the reservoir was built during the 1960s, conditions improved.

Near the airport, **Purdy's Nuts**, *Tel. 567-6601, open 9am to 1pm most days*, specializes in macadamias grown in a family-run grove. A tour of the macadamia nut farm includes cracking and tasting the roasted nuts as well as sampling fresh local fruit and honey. Since 1980, Tuddie Purdy has run this grove with his mother. The processing of nuts is completely natural.

North of Hoolehua, near Palaau State Park, residential **Kalae** was once the homestead land of King Kamehameha V. No one could set foot on the premises without royal permission. The one-story homes are gaily painted light blue, turquoise, pale green, and yellow. You may see a striking cluster of tall trees in the area. This is the cemetery of **Rudolph Meyer**, the 19th century German immigrant who bought so much Molokai Ranch land. He married a Hawaiian chief, Dorcas Kalama Waha, with whom he raised eleven children. Until his death in 1897, he served as manager of the ranch under the ownership of Kamehameha V, Bernice Pauahi Bishop, Charles Reed Bishop, and the Bishop Estate.

Palaau State Park is ideal for camping. I love walking barefoot through the ironwood forest on a carpet of pine needles along a trail that leads to **Kauleonanahoa**. Also known as **Phallic Rock**, this huge stone points skyward. It has been shaped by the elements - and with a little help from human hands, no doubt. In the old days, women who hadn't been successful in becoming pregnant would sit on the rock in an attempt to awaken their fertility.

Another trail leads to **Kalaupapa Lookout**, backed by thick pines. **Kalaupapa National Historic Park**, *on the north coast*, is officially called Makanalua Peninsula, but it is more commonly called Kalaupapa. The tragedy and human triumph that made this peninsula famous began after the arrival of foreigners in Hawaii. Since the indigenous population had been without contact with outsiders for so many centuries, they had no natural immunities to the communicable diseases of other peoples. When Westerners arrived, bringing their new illnesses, Hawaiians were unable to combat these alien germs. Within a century after the arrival of haoles in 1778, the population had shrunk from some 300,000 to a mere 50,000. Hawaii's first known case of Hansen's Disease (leprosy) occurred during the 1840s. The frightfully disfiguring affliction was so contagious that King Kamehameha V, thinking first and foremost of protecting the larger general population, began banishing the victims to Molokai's isolated Makanalua Peninsula.

Like the walls of a fortress, the 2,000-foot cliffs that rise up from this large flat tongue of land quashed any notion of escape. So did the rough water that hurls itself against the glossy black lava rocks on all three sides of the peninsula. At over 3,000 feet, some of the sea cliffs on the north shore are the tallest in the world. Treated like criminals, the exiles were not even provided with building materials or other supplies. They were forced to live out in the blazing sun by day or in the chilly air at night. Some found shelter under trees or in caves. Others fashioned makeshift driftwood huts. These houses were always in danger of being torn apart by a stronger person who decided to steal the wood for himself - unless of course the bully simply chose to evict the occupant. The small quantities of food sent from Honolulu caused many a vicious fight among the hungry, ailing, and embittered residents.

Consider taking the **Molokai Mule Ride**, *Tel. 567-6088 or 800/567-7550*, along the narrow zig-zag trail down a 1,600-foot cliff to Kalaupapa Peninsula. Completed in 1887 and just over three miles long, the trail begins in Palau State Park on the north shore. For additional information, see Mule Ride in the *Sports & Recreation* section of this chapter.

In the beginning, there wasn't even a dock at the peninsula. As boats neared the coast, ill passengers were thrust overboard and forced to swim ashore, clutching whatever belongings they could. Many didn't make it through the treacherous water. Ancient Hawaiians had farmed taro and sweet potatoes on this fertile land. However, because of the lawlessness and physical discomfort of the angry population, these victims of Hansen's Disease were not able to make even a half-decent life for themselves here. Many Hawaiians outside the peninsula tried in vain to hide the first signs of leprosy they noticed in themselves or in loved ones. Sometimes, so that they would not be forever separated from family members, healthy people exiled themselves along with their sick relatives.

When **Father Damien de Veuster,** a Catholic priest from Belgium, arrived in Kalaupapa in 1873, he planned to stay only a few months. But within two days he decided to remain indefinitely. He turned St. Philomena, a chapel that had been built by a visiting priest the year before, into a hospital until a permanent one could be built. He himself slept under a tree until every other resident had shelter. This tireless self-sacrificing man built another church and served as a doctor, farmer, and gravedigger.

In 1889, Father Damien died of Hansen's Disease. In April 1989, on the 100th anniversary of his death, a week-long tribute to this revered priest took place in Hawaii. He has been beatified, is in the process toward canonization and is now Blessed Father Damien. The reliquary containing his right hand was taken throughout the state in 1995 before being returned to his original resting place, Kalawao, Molokai. (His body had been moved in the 1930s to Belgium by the Belgian government.)

Today, leprosy can be treated with sulfone drugs and thus is far less feared. Victims of the ailment are no longer forced to live here and almost all have gone elsewhere. Those who remain do so by choice, having known no other lifestyle since they were either born here or brought as young children. Residents give tours of the settlement to visitors who hike or take the twisting, turning mule ride down the 1,600-foot cliff or who arrive by plane or hike down.

MOLOKAI'S BEST ATTRACTIONS

Cliffside Mule Ride
Giraffe Picnic
Papohaku Beach
Best Drive: East to Halawa Valley Lookout

Western Molokai

West of Kaunakakai, past Kapuaiwa Grove and Church Row, the road climbs, then descends to the isolated town of **Maunaloa.** The brief main street of this former plantation settlement sports a few worthwhile artsy stores, including the amusing Big Wind Kite Factory and the Plantation Gallery. Past the turnoff for Kaluakoi Resort and at the end of the highway, this town was built in 1923 by the Libby corporation to house its pineapple plantation workers and management. Libby pulled up stakes in 1975. Today most of the residents are the last of the Filipino and Japanese laborers, some of whom have turned to tourism for work.

The town is now the headquarters of **Molokai Ranch**, *Molokai Ranch Outfitters Center, Kaluakoi, West Molokai, Tel. 552-2791 or 800/254-8871; cost: $35 adults, $18 youths 13 to 17, $10 children 3 to 12; tours are conducted daily at 8am, 10:30am, and 1pm*, a working cattle ranch and, with 50,000 acres, the island's largest landholder. Resembling the plains of Kenya and Tanzania, this arid, flat, red-dirt expanse is home to hundreds of animals from East Africa and Asia. They were originally imported to control (by consumption) the scrub and brushes that were interfering with the ranch's cattle pasture land. In 1975, this region was opened to the public as a wildlife park. Bouncing along in a van, travelers can come eyeball-to-eyeball with quite a few exotic beasts, including eland, oryx, Indian black buck, axis deer, Barbary sheep, crowned cranes, peacocks, zebra, and giraffe. Some of the animals are fed by the park's caretakers while others are left completely wild.

The **giraffe picnic** is a real highlight. If your group is small enough, you'll each get a turn holding a long bean between your teeth while a giraffe leans down and extends its long tongue to retrieve it. (Don't forget your camera!) You may also want to volunteer for the special honor of serving as the giraffes' picnic table; you'll be given an apron, then have feed poured all over you. The animals will then gently eat their meal from your chest, your neck, and other body parts. This intimate encounter is wonderfully ticklish! Less adventurous visitors can simply feed the animals from the palms of their hands.

These 2-hour tours, in a van or an open wagon depending on the size of the group, are sometimes canceled after a rain because of washed out or muddy roads. So even if you have reservations and it hasn't rained on your part of the island, be sure to call ahead to Molokai Ranch Outfitters Center, the ranch activities department, before showing up. Call them also for information about camping, horseback riding, and participating in the **Paniolo Roundup** (cattle herding). If you're vacationing around Thanksgiving, check out the **Stew Cookoff**, an annual rodeo-food-games-and-musical event that attracts some 3,000 people.

After the death of Kamehameha V in 1873, Molokai Ranch lands passed on to Princess Bernice Pauahi Bishop, whose husband built Honolulu's Bishop Museum in her honor.

In days gone by, the forests of Maunaloa volcano were filled with ohia trees. When the bright red blossoms were strung into a lei, it was believed that love was sure to follow. Kaana, on the slopes of the mountain, is where tradition says the goddess Laka learned the hula. The only reason it is performed anywhere outside of Molokai today is that Laka traveled throughout the archipelago and taught the special meaning-laden dance to as many people as she could. Perched atop a hill, **Maunaloa Piko Stone** is where the umbilical cords (piko) of babies born nearby were placed to guarantee a prosperous, happy life.

KEEP AWAY

While many ancient Hawaiians saw Molokai as a religious sanctuary, others were kept away by frightening tales of island sorcery. The poisonwood gods it was known for first presented themselves at an ulu maika (stone bowling) course at Maunaloa. Among the men betting on the stone discs as they rolled them, Kaneiakama was losing badly. A god appeared to him, advising him to increase his wagers. Grateful when he won, he gave a large portion of his winnings to the god. In a flash, a grove of trees appeared. Becoming their caretaker, Kaneiakama discovered that when the wood was whittled into images, it could have devastating effects on enemies. Molokai was thus able to keep hostile outsiders at bay.

Along beautiful, white Kepuhi Beach, the Kaluakoi Resort has just one hotel (the island's largest, the Kaluakoi Hotel and Golf Club), and three condominiums. The golf course borders the stretch of sand, which is watched over by impressive Kaiaka Rock at its southern end. Just north is lovely, historic **Kawakiu Beach**. Long before the arrival of Europeans, people made fishhooks and adzes and fished in a settlement here. However, once Kamehameha V got hold of the land for ranching, commoners could no longer freely use the area. Now part of a beach park, the archaeological sites are being preserved, including house platforms and other ruins. To the south, three-mile **Papohaku Beach** is the largest white sand beach in the state and one of the most attractive.

Eastern Molokai

East of Kaunakakai, a few small hotels sit along the coast. Kalokoeli Fishpond is among a mere handful of ponds that remain out of more than 60 that once bordered the southern shore. Many of them were constructed during the 13th century. These rocky walls enclosed fish so that they could be fattened up while protected from all but human predators. When they were plump enough, they were netted for the alii. Impromptu concerts, beach parties, and other frivolity often takes place at **Onealii Beach Park**. There are some beautiful homes in this area. If you drive up to Kawela Plantation, a residential development, you'll have a great view of the fish pond down below.

On the *makai* (ocean) side of the road at Kamalo, watch for the **Smith and Bronte Monument** that honors Ernest Smith and Emory Bronte. On their way from California to Honolulu, the pair survived the crash landing of the world's first transpacific flight in 1927. Nearby is **St. Joseph's Catholic Church**, built in 1876 by Damien Joseph De Veuster, famous for his selfless work with victims of Hansen's Disease who had been banished to Kalaupapa Peninsula. Father Damien, as he was better known, also served as pastor to the rest of the island. A few miles farther down the road, he also built **Our Lady of Seven Sorrows**, which stands behind a tall wooden cross planted in the spacious lawn. In the background looms majestic Mt. Kamakou, Molokai's tallest mountain. From the waterfront, you can gaze across to Maui and Lanai.

Just east of Kamalo on the *mauka* side of the road, **Ili'ili'opa'e Heiau**, *off Highway 450*, constructed during the sixteenth century, is the second largest heiau in the state. It once sprawled over more than five acres. Honoring Hawaii's highest gods, its four terraces were 150 feet wide and 50 feet tall. The rocks used to build it were lugged all the way from the Wailau Valley, separated from this shore by a mountain. Human sacrifices were performed at this heiau.

An old story tells of the cruel high chief who killed nine sons of a local resident in the name of the gods. The bereft father prayed to the powerful shark god that inhabited the island's north shore waters. Suddenly, the area was hit with a terrible storm accompanied by floods. The chief and his wicked followers were washed into the Pacific, where the sharks had a feast. Today people still leave stones wrapped in ti leaves as offerings after praying here.

Behind the heiau trail, you can hike straight up to a scenic lookout point and take in the islands of Lanai, Maui, and Kahoolawe. Since the heiau is extremely sacred and on private property, you must visit it either along with other sights during the **Molokai Horse and Wagon Ride** or by requesting permission from Ms. Pearl Petro, *P.O. Box 125, Kaunakakai, Molokai, HI 96748*, and enclose a stamped, self-addressed envelope.

Between Kamalo and Pukoo, you'll pass **Wavecrest** condominium. The surrounding vegetation is extremely lush in this area, and craggy mountains soar on the left. The road narrows and the greenery becomes increasingly thick, with banana trees and palms along the coast in the Pukoo area. You'll pass a modern house in the shape of a geodesic dome. More trees appear, each one taller than the last, with vines clothing the entire length of their trunks.

Keep an eye out for Chevy and Nova, two old cars that have become flourishing planters in the front yard of a home. Locals will tell you that the parents of the family named two of their children after the autos because they are where the youngsters got their start in life! There is good swimming as well as camping at sandy **Waialua Beach**. Nearby you might come to a self-service stand piled with fresh fruit - simply leave your money in a box. In little tent-like shelters, fighting cocks are raised in this area.

Once you see **Murphy's Beach**, you'll begin climbing uphill on a narrow, winding road through **Pu'u O Hoku Ranch**. From here you'll have spectacular views of the rocky shoreline, crashing waves, and endless greenery, including tall stands of bamboo. At **Rock Point**, a fishing and surfing area, rugged outcroppings stand like huge anthills along the coast. Soon the eye takes in rolling hills and verdant open land.

Finally, you reach dramatic **Halawa Valley Overlook**. Historians believe the **Halawa Valley** is Molokai's oldest settlement, dating back to about A.D. 650. Few people have lived here since the massive tidal wave swept through in 1946, destroying both homes and crops. Just before the road begins to dip into the valley, the grove of kukui nut trees stands in memory of Lanikaula, the beloved kahuna. This is the most sacred part of the whole island. The wide stream that once fed the valley's farms meanders through the lush greenery before pouring into the ocean. This shore was once a favorite surfing spot among alii. Unfortunately, hiking is no longer allowed into the valley beyond the limits of the Beach Park.

NIGHTLIFE & ENTERTAINMENT

Action after dark centers around the hotels, where dinner conversation and talking story over drinks is about all there is to do. On Thursday, Friday, and Saturday nights, island action is at **Pau Hana Inn**, in Kaunakakai, where a crowd parties and dances to live music. Loosely translated, "pau hana" means "quittin' time," and this hotel is exactly where many locals go for happy hour when they are done with work. Between the bar and the restaurant at the **Kaluakoi Hotel**, you can hear more subdued live music in the evenings.

The local newspaper will announce any community dances, church fundraisers, or shows that might be taking place. Perhaps your trip will coincide with a free Balinese dance performance or other event at the Molokai Public Library.

SPORTS & RECREATION

Various activities can be arranged through your accommodation, the **Kaluakoi Hotel & Golf Club**, *Tel. 552-2550*, and the **Molokai Visitors Association**, *Tel. 553-3867 or 800/800-6367*.

Beaches

Molokai's best beaches lie along the west coast, with views of Oahu in the distance. This is where you'll find Papohaku, the largest white sand beach in the state. However, during the winter, when waves grow their tallest, on this coast it's best to stick to dry land. The narrow south shore beaches that run past hotels and condos in the Kaunakakai area aren't especially attractive, but their waters remain more placid year round. Here are Moloka'i's most appealing sandy stretches:

Kawakiu Beach Park, *northern part of Kaluakoi Resort*

Good swimming conditions and intriguing archaeological ruins make this handsome beach worth visiting. In ancient times, a Hawaiian settlement was built at this site. The outdoor showers come in handy. You'll need to hike to the beach or take a four-wheel drive.

Kepuhi Beach, *Kaluakoi Resort*

There's a constant breeze at this half-mile stretch of white sand that individual Kaluakoi Hotel guests often have to themselves. Be careful during the winter when waves are the roughest.

Papohaku Beach, *Kaluakoi Resort*

Enclosed by rugged lava flows, this broad, three-mile strip is Hawaii's most expansive white sand beach. Wells were once dug for the fresh water that gets trapped in the rocky outcroppings in back of the sand. A small fishing village once stood at this site, and old stones used to grind adzes have been discovered nearby. You may not notice that anything is missing, but during the 1950s sand was taken from here and shipped to O'ahu to be used in construction. Picnic facilities, barbecues, showers, and rest rooms are provided. Tent **camping** is permitted amid the palms and kiawe trees on the spacious lawn that backs the sand.

Pohakuloa Beach, *about 1.5 miles past Papohaku Beach, West Molokai*

This tranquil cove is especially popular on weekends, particularly among families. However, on Molokai, there is no such thing as a crowded beach. Swimming is excellent most of the year. An outdoor shower is on the grounds.

Po'olau Beach, *about a half-mile past the Kaluakoi Resort*

Locals sometimes fish from surfboards off this inviting white shore. The waves are often good for **surfing**. A pleasant setting for **camping** out, this beach has a view that reaches all the way to Kaneohe, 35 miles away on O'ahu, when the sky is clear.

Onealii Beach Park, *off Highway 450 on the south shore, near Hotel Molokai*

While cooling off in calm waters, you'll gaze across to the islands of Lanai and Maui. Although the shore is narrow here, this is the most appealing of the south shore beaches, where nature has been stingy with the sand. Tree-shaded picnic tables, outdoor showers, and restrooms make this a good choice if you're staying in the area.

Halawa Beach Park, at the eastern end of Highway 450

At the far eastern end of the island, this dark sand beach is a bonus after the spectacular snaking drive through this lush region. This crescent was once favored by Hawaiian royalty for surfing. Don't go near the water during the winter, when currents are extremely dangerous. However, during the summer, swimming is usually fine. Even when you're not swimming, the setting is wonderful, so take advantage of the picnic facilities. Outdoor showers mean you don't have to feel gritty during the return drive.

Biking

For mountain biking, contact **Molokai Ranch Outfitters Center,** *Tel. 552-2791 or 800/254-8871.* **Molokai Bicycle,** *Tel. 553-5740 or 800/709-BIKE,* has a pick-up and drop-off service for bike rentals and tours.

Boating

Fishing boats and pleasure cruises take off from Kaunakakai Wharf. For day trips to the island of Lanai, sunset sails, and winter whale-watching excursions, try **Molokai Charters,** *Tel. 553-5852.*

Camping

Molokai's county-operated campgrounds are at **Po'olau Beach,** about a half-mile from Kaluakoi Resort in the northwest, and **One Alii.** Both sites have restrooms with showers and drinking water, and barbecue pits. Camping permits must be obtained from **Department of Parks and Recreation,** *Kaunakakai, HI 96748, Tel.808/553-3204.* For tent camping in state-run **Palaau State Park,** contact the **Division of Parks,** *P.O. Box 153, Kaunakanai, HI 96748, Tel. 808/984-8109.*

For more upscale camping in one- and two-bedroom solar-paneled canvas units built on platforms, each with a deck and bathroom facilities, consider **Paniolo Camp** on Molokai Ranch. For details, contact the **Molokai Ranch Outfitters Center,** *Tel. 808/552-2791 or 800/254-8871.*

Fishing

Locals often cast lines from Kaunakakai Wharf, in the evening after the boats have stopped loading. Fall and winter are the peak fishing seasons at Halawa Beach County Park. There's some great fishing along Molokai's cliff-edged north shore. Call **Molokai Fish and Dive,** *Tel. 553-5926,* about setting up charters for deep-sea excursions. Sometimes visitors can arrange to share trips with locals.

Golf

At the Kaluakoi Resort, the **Kaluakoi Golf Club,** *Tel. 552-2550,* has an 18-hole championship, Ted Robinson-designed course that runs along the beach in West Molokai. You'll also find the nine-hole **Ironwood Hills Golf Course** at Kalae, in central Molokai.

Hiking

For cultural trail hikes of petroglyphs and heiau, including legend-telling and botany lessons, contact **Molokai Action Adventures,** *Tel. 808/558-8184.* This company can also take you on a waterfall hike.

By contacting the **Nature Conservancy of Hawaii-Molokai Field Office,** *P.O. Box 220, Kualapuu, Molokai, HI 9675, Tel. 808/553-5236,* at least two months in advance, you can arrange other exciting escorted hikes. For instance, a guided hike through **Kamakou Preserve** will surround you with some of Molokai's most unhampered beauty. So as not to disturb nature at its most natural, you'll move through the rainforest along a groaning wooden boardwalk. Rare and indigenous flora and fauna thrive here. You might spot birds such as an *olomao* (Molokai thrush) or a *kakawahie* (Molokai creeper), which survives nowhere in the world except in this preserve. The topography spans the spectrum from rain forest to alpine bog. At the top of the mountain, red-blossomed ohia trees grow a mere four inches off the ground.

Before you arrive, the jeep will pass the **Sandlewood Pit,** a deep hole in the ground. It was dug to equal the size of a ship's hull. As soon as it was full, workers could hug the sweet-smelling wood down from the mountains to the next ship in line to carry this cargo to China. Unfortunately, since this business was so lucrative, Hawaii's sandlewood forests were com-pletely denuded. In addition, this work was so arduous and laborers were forced to leave their families for such long periods, that many of them tore up seedlings to diminish the growth of new trees. The entrance to Kamakou Preserve is at the **Waikolu Valley Lookout,** which opens up views of waterfalls, jungled vegetation, and the ocean in the distance.

Horseback Riding

Arrange to jump in the saddle by contacting **Molokai Ranch Outfit-ters Center,** *Tel. 552-2791 or 800/254-8871,* or the folks who organize the **Molokai Horse and Wagon Ride,** *Tel. 558-8132 or 800/670-6965.*

Kayaking

To take a picturesque kayak trip, contact **Molokai Action Adven-tures,** *Tel. 558-8184,* or **Fun Hogs,** *Tel. 552-2555 or 800/989-3284.*

Mule Ride

For many vacationers, the most memorable part of their stay is the **Molokai Mule Ride,** *Tel. 567-6088 or 800/567-7550,* along the narrow zig-zag trail down a 1,600-foot cliff to Kalaupapa Peninsula. Completed in 1887 and just over three miles long, the trail begins in Palaau State Park on the north shore. Participants are asked to bring rain gear since the clouds are often dripping up here. As riders descend, the weather usually dries up quickly, so the trip isn't called off unless a downpour at the top is extremely heavy.

On automatic pilot, the sure-footed mules get riders safely down the 3.5 mile trail with 26 switchbacks. Some veterans say it's best to walk down (about an hour to 90 minutes) and ride a mule back up, so you can stop along the way to appreciate the dramatic cliff-edge scenery and take photos. But this is discouraged by the mule ride folks, so even if you hike one way, you'll have to pay the same amount as riding down and up.

With sheer drop-offs on one side, the cliff walls are festooned with clinging ferns and unusual flowers on the other. Look for clusters of air plants, whose tubular sprouts resemble the intact, empty skins of grapes. Tree branches form umbrellas. When you reach the pancake flat penin-sula that seemed miles down from above, you'll come out along a shore covered with charcoal rocks and boulders that give way to a black sand beach. If it's the right time of year (winter), you might spot whales. With the mountains in the distance, you'll look back at the cliff and be amazed that you were "topside," as residents say, not long before.

After tying up the mules, you'll climb into a van for a tour conducted by one of the last remaining residents of the community where people with Hansen's Disease (leprosy) were exiled before drugs were discovered to treat the illness. Sights include St. Philomena Church, which once served as a hospital; medical facilities; houses; graveyards; a bookstore in a former Buddhist temple; and the memorial to Blessed Father Damien, the 19th century Belgian priest who made such a difference in the lives of ailing residents until he himself contracted the disease and died. Cameras are welcome, but photos of residents are not allowed. Sightseers have a picnic lunch before returning on mule-back (or leaving by plane or on foot, if they have arranged to do so); however, the meal is very light, so you may want to bring your own munchies to supplement it.

Participants must be at least 16 years old and must weigh no more than 225 pounds. Day trips from other islands are popular. Reservations should be made through **Molokai Mule Ride** at the numbers above or through **Damien Tours,** *Tel. 567-6171,* at least two weeks in advance, especially during the summer. This all-day activity costs $120 per person, including airport pickup and return, if needed.

Plane Rides

For a forty-minute aerial tour of Molokai's dramatic north shore, make arrangements through **Molokai Air Shuttle/Kalaupapa Air Shuttle,** *Tel. 567-6847 or 545-4988.* Plan to spend about $50 per person; a minimum of two is required. You can also book flights between Molokai Airport and historic Kalaupapa. Round trip flights run around $50 per person; a ground tour of Kalaupapa settlement, the former "leper colony," will cost $30 per person.

Sailing

For sightseeing day-sails, snorkeling or whale watching excursions, and overnight cruises, contact **Molokai Charters,** *Tel. 553-5852.* Sailing lessons are also available. You can find out about other boats at Kaumakakai Wharf.

Scuba Diving & Snorkeling

The **Kaluakoi Hotel,** *Tel. 552-2550,* and **Molokai Fish and Dive,** *Tel. 553-5926,* rent gear. Bill Kapuni's **Snorkel & Dive Adventure,** *Tel. 553-9867,* is another good choice. **Molokai Action Adventures,** *Tel. 558-8184,* will take you to a special snorkeling spot where you can play with octopi, see the endangered green sea turtles, and commune with lots of beautiful tropical fish.

Spectator Sports

During the international **Kayak Challenge** each May, one-person kayaks race 32 miles from Molokai to Oahu across the treacherous Kaiwi Channel. This championship competition is the only open ocean kayak race in the world. Both male and female paddlers test their skill and endurance. Spectators can watch the start of the race at the beach by the Kaluakoi Hotel. In September, women race canoes in the **Bankoh Na Wahine O Ke Kai race,** and in October the men take their turn paddling from Molokai to Oahu in the **Bankoh Molokai Hoe.**

Tennis

You'll find courts at the **Kaluakoi Hotel and Golf Club,** *Tel. 552-2550,* the **Ke Nani Kai Resort,** *Tel. 552-2761 or 800/535-0085,* and **Marc Wavecrest Resort,** *Tel. 558-8103 or 800/535-0085.*

Wagon Ride

During the **Molokai Horse and Wagon Ride,** *Tel. 558-8132 or 800/670-6965,* vacationers step into the past at sacred Ili'ili'opa'e heiau (see *Seeing the Sights*) and visit Mapulehu, site of the world's largest mango grove. Its original trees, which came from Vietnam, Laos, and Cambodia, were planted around the 1930s by the Hawaii Sugar Planters Association. The company intended to market the mangoes. Unfortunately, in those days, not enough people had a taste for the sweet, juicy fruit. Now the demand is soaring in the US as well as other parts of the world, such as Japan.

Daily Coffees of Hawaii, *Tel. 567-9241 or 800/709-BEAN; adults $14; children (4 to 12) $7*, mule-drawn wagon tours (for 90 minutes to 2 hours, between 10am and 3pm) provide a view of a working coffee plantation.

SHOPPING

Although stores are certainly scarce on the island, there are some imaginative shops in the small, red dirt town of Maunaloa, about seven miles from the Kaluakoi Resort in West Molokai. Here are some of my favorite places to spend money:

Crafts & Coconuts

Adjoining the famed Big Wind Kite Factory in Maunaloa, the **Plantation Gallery**, *Tel. 552-2364*, is an absolute must. It's easy to spend hours here browsing through all the colorful clothing, masks, woodcarvings, and jewelry from Indonesia, Papua New Guinea, Thailand, Nepal, Malaysia, China, and other countries. Bathing suits for both children and adults, books, cards, wind chimes, and tribal musical instruments are also on sale. If you don't want to carry your loot on the plane, you can have it shipped.

Head to **Dolly Hale**, near the Kite Factory, for hand-painted coconuts to mail to friends back home. Hand-crafted dolls are also sold here.

On the main drag in Kaunakakai, be sure to visit **Dudoit Imports**, *Tel. 553-5011*. Among the locally produced crafts and the imports, you're likely to find things you didn't even know you were looking for. One of the sisters who owns the store makes fish, shrimp, and roses from palm fronds. You'll also see watercolors, ceramics, mats, blankets, and plants along with earrings created from wiliwili seeds, old books, koa wood bracelets, and antique jewelry.

Artists of Molokai, *Tel. 553-3461*, is a network of local professionals in the arts who create contemporary and traditional works with a Hawaiian flavor. Their creations include quilts, wearable art, wood carvings, and jewelry, as well as paintings and sculpture. Call to learn who's exhibiting where and to make appointments for studio visits.

Another store I like for the beauty and artistry of its offerings is **H/ S Pali & Sons of Molokai**, *Tel. 567-6769*. They sell lovely haku headbands, akulikuli leis, and a variety of floral works.

Fruit & Spices

The **Spice Farm** and **Bill's Farm** are both located in Molokai Agricultural Park, in Hoolehua, near the airport. These huge red dirt plantations are great places to shop for Hawaiian bananas (which are sweeter and more flavorful than the mainland variety), Hawaiian watermelon, other fruits, vegetables, and freshly prepared spices.

Hawaiian Quilts

Erline McGuire, *Tel. 558-8347,* charges about $2,000 to $4,000 for a commissioned king- or queen-sized quilt. These missionary-inspired Hawaiian bedcovers are intricately and expertly produced and will last for countless generations.

He Ki'i Kapa (The Picture Quilt), *Tel. 553-5408 or 553-9989,* is another place for quilts and for items made from them. Call for an appointment to see the Hawaiian quilt pillow kits and the hand-made quilts, some mounted in frames for display.

Kites

The **Big Wind Kite Factory,** *Maunaloa town, Tel. 552-2364,* is worth some time whether or not you're in the market for something to fly. Run by former comedy writer Jonathan Socher, this shop sells kites handmade on the premises, as well as Indonesian imports. Visitors are welcome to watch the crafts people in action in the factory. Socher's Wife, Daphne, does the graphic designs. Edges are welded so that they don't fray and all are quality controlled. There are signed and limited edition kites, minikites, windsocks, endangered animal species kites, hula girl kites, teddy bear kites, two-string controllable kites, and exotic kites from Bali made with carved styrofoam. No two are exactly alike. Prices run from about $15.95 to $500. Custom-designed kites are also available. Don't worry if you've never flown a kite - you can get free lessons here too.

Macadamia Nuts

For some truly fresh-roasted nuts, stop by **Purdy's Natural Macadamia Nut Farm,** *Tel. 567-6601,* a family-run business (since the 1920s) on Hawaiian Homestead land in Hoolehua. No preservatives are used in the preparation of the nuts. Take a tour of the island's only working macadamia farm.

T-Shirts, Water Sports Gear, & Other Miscellany

In Maunaloa, **The Plantation Gallery** is the place to go for T-shirts and beach cover-ups in winning, original designs. Another extensive T-shirt collection resides in an unlikely locale: **Molokai Fish & Dive,** Kaunakakai, *Tel. 553-5926,* which sells an eclectic mix of merchandise. It is owned by Jim Brocker, a bird enthusiast who boasts his own aviary of over 100 exotic birds and shares his store with more than a few of his favorites. Besides parrots and T-shirts, you'll find unusual souvenirs and water sports equipment. He stocks books on Molokai as well, including the best selling *A Portrait of Molokai*.

Look for more T-shirts at attractive prices at **Imports Gift Shop**, *Tel. 553-5734*, also in Kaunakakai. This is a place for one-stop shopping from clothing to Hawaiiana to food and from fishing lines to quilts.

For your varied needs, try **Misaki's**, *Tel. 553-5505*, and **Friendly Market Center, Ltd.**, *Tel. 553-5595*, both grocery stores in Kaunakakai; **Molokai Sight & Sound**, *Tel. 553-3600*, for video rentals and one-hour photo processing; and Molokai Drugs, **Inc.**, *Tel. 553-5313*, for pharmacy items.

PRACTICAL INFORMATION

Emergencies
Call *Tel. 911*.

Medical Attention
Any time of day or night, you can receive medical assistance at **Molokai General Hospital**, *Kaunakakai, Tel. 553-5311*.

Post Offices
Branches are located in **Kaunakakai**, *Tel. 553-5845*; **Maunaloa**, *Tel. 552-2852*; **Hoolehua**, *Tel. 567-6144*; **Kalaupapa**, *Tel. 567-6479*; and **Kualapuu**, *Tel. 567-6638*.

Tourist Information
Contact the **Molokai Visitors Association**, *P.O. Box 960, Kaunakakai, Molokai, HI 96748, Tel. 553-3876 or 800/800-6367*.

Weather
The scenic eastern region can be wet, so before you head out, check the weather, *Tel. 552-2477*.

16. LANAI

"Now I guess I'll have to start locking my door," a resident of Lanai told me when we talked about the tripling of hotels on the island - from one to three. The Lodge at Koele, the second hotel, opened in the spring of 1990 and the Manele Bay welcomed its first guests in 1991. But, although more islanders may lock their doors today, many still leave their keys in their cars.

During a visit when rustic, 11-room Hotel Lanai was the only game in town, I got into another conversation with a man while I was wandering around the village known as Lanai City. When I told him I would be leaving the next day, he insisted on driving me to the airport. And sure enough, there he was the following afternoon, jumping out of his pickup truck to help me with my bags. Now with far more visitors on the island, residents can't be expected to keep up that kind of hospitality toward every stranger. However, so much of the openness and generosity that has been Lanai's trademark remains.

Until the appearance of the first resort hotel, almost everyone visiting Lanai came to see friends or family, hunt deer, fish, hike, or camp. While the island remains laid-back, there is now a variety of vacation diversions. Since long before the Lodge at Koele made its debut next door, the complimentary nine-hole Cavendish Golf Course has satisfied those with an urge to tee off. A challenging 18-hole Greg Norman/Ted Robinson course was added nearby, and another championship 18-holer, designed by Jack Nicklaus, was built at the oceanfront Manele Bay Hotel. Swimming, snorkeling, and fishing are good off Hulopoe Beach, with its broad stretch of white sand and rugged chocolate-colored cliffs.

Apart from the upscale dining rooms at the Lodge at Koele and those at Manele Bay, eating out is a real low-key affair. In town, there are a couple of unassuming breakfast and lunch spots and Hotel Lanai continues to serve delicious, filling meals. For decades, this hotel's front porch has been the local hangout in the afternoon and evening for drinking and talking story over snacks such as warm popcorn (jokingly referred to as "haole pupus"). Another cherished island pastime is attending church.

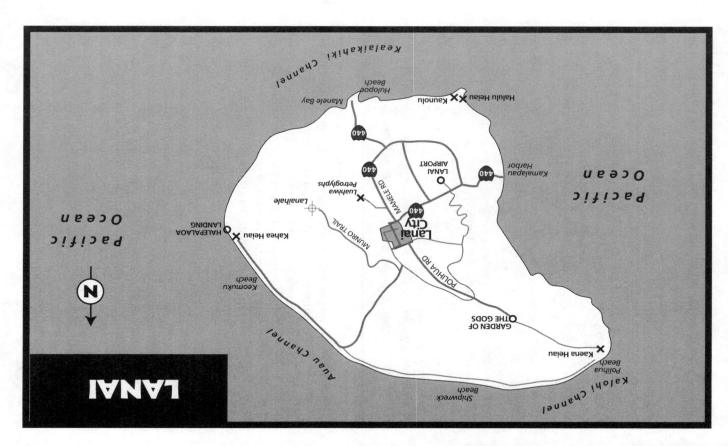

Lanai's 2,800 or so residents are of Filipino, Hawaiian, Japanese, Korean, Chinese, and European-American ancestry, as well as various mixtures of these and other nationalities. Almost everyone lives in Lanai City. Hardly a city, this is a trim plantation town of symmetrical cross-hatch streets. It was built to house the people who worked the island's pineapple fields. Neat gardens ablaze with electric-green banana trees and purple, orange, and red bougainvillea adjoin the small wooden homes. A tranquil park sprawls near the collection of small shops. The town is so informal that the first Hawaiian Bank is located in a private house! Since this upland village is nowhere near the beach and tall triangular Cook Island pines pierce cool, misty air, it's easy to forget that it's on a tropical island.

Lanai City is hemmed in the center of the island by vast fields that were once devoted exclusively to raising pineapple. In 1995 Dole Food Company, Inc., which had long owned much of Lanai, turned over most of its interests in the island to Castle & Cooke Properties, Honolulu. In recent years a trend has begun to diversify crops instead of relying solely on pineapple. Some of those lands now sprout other agricultural products while others lie fallow. Today there are fewer than 100 acres growing pineapple for local consumption.

WHEN PINEAPPLE WAS KING

In the days when pineapple was king of Lanai, the screaming plantation siren awakened workers each morning. (I guess I would have quickly lost my job because I often managed to sleep through it.) Amid the omnipresent rows of pineapple, you could see scores of pickers with their floppy wide-brimmed hats above months and noses covered with brightly colored bandanas for protection against bugs and dust. When they removed their goggles and just their eyes were showing they resembled surgeons or Muslim women. Even in the sweltering heat, they also had to use thick gloves to prevent cuts from the serrated leaves. If you waved as you passed, they sometimes raised pineapples into the air in greeting.

"Who's gonna pick pineapple now? No one," one laborer told me wistfully on the eve of the island's mini-boom in tourism. But then she went on to say how pleased she was that her children would have more than the choice of hitting the fields or leaving the island to find work.

Hawaiian Roots

Bits and pieces of old Hawaii are scattered throughout Lanai. Just south of Lanai City, a dirt road leads to **Luahiwa Petroglyphs**, extensive hillside rock carvings of stick figure people, animals, and boats etched sometime between 1500 and 1700. Near the southern coast, temple sites and more petroglyphs can be seen at Kaunolu, while Kaleina a Kaheekili, an awesome cliff, was once used as a testing ground of prowess among men who leaped off the edge. Crumbling fishing shrines and foundations of old canoe houses remain in the Manele Bay area. Kaunolu, just west of Hulopoe Beach, is the site of Kamehameha's old fishing grounds. A little farther west, part of sacred Halulu Heiau is still visible.

Not far from Kaiolohia Bay Beach, in the north, among other places, red boulders are piled with towers of increasingly smaller rocks. Although they have been described as imitation shrines, they have no cultural or historical significance. They were once used as trail markers. Today efforts are made to discourage people from stacking more rocks. Near Keomoku, an abandoned sugar plantation community on the east coast, the remnants of Kahea Heiau are overgrown and an old Hawaiian village called Naha stands in ruins.

The Way It Was

Habitation came hard to Lanai. The early Polynesian settlers believed that demons lived on the island. For five centuries after they had first colonized other parts of Hawaii, they left this island alone. The staple breadfruit figures in the history of Lanai. According to an old legend, the prankster son of the king of Maui decided to dig up some of the prized breadfruit trees, simply to irk his father. This extremely bold act earned the young man the shameful nickname Ka-ulu-la'au, ("the one who uproots breadfruit trees.") The king punished the rebellious youth by sending him to uninhabited Lanai. The evil spirits had seen to it that no one ever survived a night there. "You think you're so clever!" the father said to his son. "Let's see if you can make it until dawn."

Ka-ulu-la'au was told that if he could escape Lanai's wicked forces, he should let the people of Maui know by building a fire that they could see from across the water. An expert in his craft of trickery, the young man fooled the demons into thinking he was in one place when he was really in another, hiding from them throughout the night. To top it off, he sneaked up on a group of these spirits, who had had too much to drink during one of their dances on Mt. Lanaihale, and set them afire. The rest he killed by drowning. When the king and his entourage saw the fire and came to collect the son, they were amazed by what he had managed to do. They even decided to return with Ka-ulu-la'au in the future to settle Lanai.

A later king of Maui found this new acquisition attacked by a rival Big Island chief. Almost everyone on Lanai, which had been a peaceful island up until then, was slaughtered. A youthful Kamehameha - who would eventually fall in love with fishing on Lanai and later rule the entire archipelago - was among the Big Island warriors. It took more than two decades after the rest of Hawaii had been introduced to foreigners for the first outsider to settle on Lanai. In 1802, Wu Tsin arrived from China with plans to grow sugarcane. But he found the island's dry climate uncooperative.

During the 1830s, New England missionaries convinced the rulers of the Hawaiian kingdom to do something about the adultery that was rampant among Hawaiians. Until these Americans arrived, having more than one spouse had been perfectly respectable. Two penal colonies were set up to keep people in line. One was on Kahoolawe, for men convicted of theft, adultery, or murder, and the other on Lanai, for women who had committed these crimes. But the men swam the six miles from Kahoolawe to Maui, stole canoes and food, and sailed to Lanai. They then took the women back to Kahoolawe with them.

In 1917, the Baldwins, a wealthy *haole* family from Maui, bought the island of Lanai. No one could get off the ground with sugarcane crops. Some explained that this failure was divine payback since Kahea Heiau had been desecrated in order to build a railroad for transporting the cane. Then, in 1922, Jim Dole had other sweet thoughts. What about a major pineapple plantation? The Baldwins sold the island to him for $1.1 million, and the rest is history. Today, Castle & Cook, Inc. owns 98 percent of Lanai.

ARRIVALS & DEPARTURES

Lanai City, where the Lodge at Koele and Hotel Lanai are located, is about a 10-minute drive from Lanai Airport. Complimentary shuttles transport registered guests between the airport and both the Lodge at Koele and the oceanfront Manele Bay Hotel. A shuttle also connects these hotels with Hotel Lanai.

One way to sample a small part of the island is to sail ashore from Maui on one of **Trilogy Excursions Cruises**, *Tel. 661-7221*, full-day excursions. Another way is to sail from Maui to spend the day at remote Club Lanai. Ground tours are offered as well as an opportunity to swim, snorkel, and relax at a Tahitian-style beachfront village.

If you'd like to travel between Lahaina (Maui) and Lanai by ferry, contact **Expeditions**, *Tel. 661-3756*, about $50 per person round trip for the 45- to 50-minute ride each way. However, note that the trip can be rough.

ORIENTATION

At 141 square miles, Lanai is Hawaii's sixth-largest island. Beautiful Hulopoe Beach, the site of the Manele Bay Hotel, can be reached by the main road. But to see the island's other attractions - most of which are natural, ancient or both, and all of which are outdoors - you'll need to rent a four-wheel drive jeep. Outside of town, only a few paved roads cut through the rich, burnt-orange earth that blankets Lanai. So, if you do much exploring, be prepared to be covered with a gritty layer of dust by trip's end.

There are **petroglyphs, heiau,** a **ghost town** called Keomoku, the empty sands of Kaiolohia (also known as Shipwreck) and Polihua **beaches,** jagged red gulches, and an eerie jumble of boulders in the middle of nowhere known as the **Garden of the Gods.** From **Lanaihale,** at the end of the Munro Trail and the highest point on the island (3,370 feet), you'll be able to see almost all of the Hawaiian archipelago when the weather permits.

GETTING AROUND LANAI

There is no public transportation on the island.

By Car

The island's only national car rental agency is **Dollar Rent a Car,** *Tel. 565-7227,* run in conjunction with Lanai City Service.

If you want to see anything beyond town, Hulopoe Beach, and the hotels, you'll need to rent a four-wheel drive jeep. Before you set out, make sure you have very clear directions or are accompanied by an island resident. Although the island is a mere 13 miles wide and 18 miles long, it is easy to get lost driving through the endless fields and the desert-like expanses strewn with rocks and tufts of hearty brush. While searching for one sight or another, you might suddenly discover that you've been going in circles.

By Guided Tour

Lanai City Service, *Tel. 565-7227,* conducts guided tours of island sights.

By Taxi

For taxis, try **Lanai City Service,** *Tel. 565-7227,* which has a non-metered cab service.

WHERE TO STAY

Any of Lanai's three hotels is an excellent choice.

LODGE AT KOELE, *P.O. Box 310, Lanai City, HI 96763. Tel. 808/564-4000 or 800/321-4666, Fax 808/565-3868. 102 rooms. Double rooms begin at $330. Major credit cards.*

This elegant lodge was built around the sprawling banyans and tall pines that were already on the property. Eucalyptus, jacarandas, and gardens enhance the natural surroundings. Two massive fireplaces of stone from North Carolina are the focal points of the Great Hall. Overwhelming at first, this huge room is brightened by etched-glass skylights that cast fish designs on the floor. From wicker to wing chairs, each of the many sitting areas is done in different patterns, textures, and earthy hues. The exquisitely manicured, very English gardens out back are visible through windows and glass-paned doors.

With heavy leather armchairs, chess boards, and a Chinese weaponry set, the Trophy Room is filled with "masculine" touches. One chair is made of animal horns. This looks like the kind of place where a group of back-slapping cigar smokers would suddenly grow quiet if a woman walked in.

The irregular shape of some guest rooms reflects the octagonal corners of the wings. The decor is French country style, with fine linens with ruffles, floral designs, and four-poster beds with hand painted headboards. (For privacy, second-floor rooms are best.)

While sitting in a rocking chair on the main lanai, guests gaze across the fields and hills or watch the sun set. Afternoon tea is served in the music room off the lanai. The renovated chapel on the grounds is more than a century old. By day, guests swim in the heated pool, or play tennis, golf at the Experience at Koele, the neighboring course, or croquet. There's also lawn bowling and an 18-hole putting green on the grounds. At night, there's musical entertainment. Transportation is provided to the Manele Bay Hotel, Hotel Lanai, and the airport.

MANELE BAY HOTEL, *P.O. Box 310, Lanai City, HI 96763. Hulopoe Beach, south shore. Tel. 808/565-7000 or 800/321-4666, Fax 808/565-2483. 250 rooms. Double rooms begin at $265. Major credit cards.*

Featured in Chapter 10, *Best Places to Stay.*

At Lanai's first luxury beach resort, arriving guests are escorted to their elegant rooms to check in. Some guest rooms overlook the ocean while others gaze out to the flower-filled courtyards and pool. All have lanais and can be cooled by either ceiling fans or air conditioning. The dazzling marble baths come with double sinks and glass-enclosed stall showers in addition to tubs.

Guests relax in the bar; game room; library, with its old globe, chess and backgammon sets; and the Hale Aheahe, where they can hear contemporary Hawaiian and European classical music.

Two whirlpools sit at the edge of the swimming pool on the broad patio off the lower lobby lounge. Tennis courts, a spacious exercise room, steam room, Swedish shower and beauty center keep vacationers in good shape. Jack Nicklaus has designed the island's third golf course for the resort, a challenging oceanfront 18-holer. Water sports include scuba diving, snorkeling, and sailing.

HOTEL LANAI, *P.O. Box 120, Lanai City, HI 96763. Tel. 808/565-7211 or 800/795-7211, Fax 808/565-6450. 11 rooms. Doubles begin at $95. Major credit cards.*

Featured in Chapter 10, Best Places to Stay.

Built in the 1920s for guests of the Dole Company, this wooden country lodge has lots of character. The small rooms are found in two wings connected by the glassed-in lanai and include hardwood floors, ceiling fans, and quilts. Tiled baths come with pedestal sinks.

From the lanai, there's a great view of the sun setting between the pine trees. Some guests at this hotel come to hunt deer while others simply want to get away. I've met several couples from Oahu who use this as a weekend haunt.

WHERE TO EAT

Beyond the few hotels, there isn't much choice of dining spots on Lanai. However, the restaurants in Lanai City are all good places to mingle with residents. The Lodge at Koele and Manele Bay Hotel offer a meal plan, either FAP (three meals a day) or MAP (breakfast and dinner), so that guests may dine at restaurants at either accommodation.

THE LODGE AT KOELE, *outskirts of town. Tel. 565-4000. Reservations required. Dinner entrees: $22 to $30. Credit cards accepted.*

Diners have a choice of two restaurants at this elegant resort with a pronounced British feel. In the **formal dining room**, the Lodge's fine dining takes place. Guests enter through beveled glass French doors, china decorates walls, and a pineapple motif has been carved into the tall backs of the wooden chairs. Silver salt-and-pepper shakers catch the candlelight. Soothing piano music floats in from the Great Hall. Food is presented with an understated flourish. The menu might include Lanai venison carpaccio, Lanai's Farm collard field greens with a vegetable vinaigrette, pan-roasted duck with lemon, tomato soup with herb croutons and basil oil, grilled Hawaiian mahi-mahi with artichokes and pancetta and sundried tomato oil. Among the desserts might be a chocolate soufflé with praline sauce or a pineapple upsidedown cake with vanilla bean ice cream.

The more casual **Terrace**, which serves all three meals, sits along the back windows of the Great Hall, overlooking the glorious gardens. Dinner here could consist of braised lamb shank, grilled steak with spiced chili sauce and creamed corn, or pressed skillet chicken on field greens.

MANELE BAY HOTEL, *Lanai City, Hulopoe Beach. Tel. 565-7700. Dinner entrees $20 to $29. Reservations recommended. Credit cards accepted.*

Looking out to the water, the **Hulopo'e Court** puts a Pacific twist on French, Spanish, Portuguese, Italian, and Greek food. Among the creative entrees, you might find tiger prawns in tangerine olive oil with garlic, buckwheat pasta with vegetable vermicelli, fennel cured salmon, and roast rabbit with mushrooms and olives.

The days of the 19th century Hawaiian monarchy return in the decor of **Ihilani**, the hotel's fine dining room. Local artists hand-painted the ceiling design. Sit inside beneath chandeliers or outside overlooking the Pacific and the pool. Sparked by his travels around the world, King David Kalakaua imported many European and Asian culinary traditions to Hawaii.

HENRY CLAY'S ROTISSERIE, *Hotel Lanai, Lanai City. Tel. 565-7211. Dinner entrees average $15. Credit cards accepted.*

The fireplace at one end of the room takes the chill off cool winter evenings. Expect to find hearty Cajun-inspired dishes, such as Louisiana-style pork ribs, corn pone, crawfish pie, gumbo, and creamy clam chowder with oysters.

CHALLENGE AT MANELE CLUBHOUSE, *Tel. 565-2230. Entrees average $14. Credit cards accepted.*

Well prepared simple fare is served for lunch only, except from December to April when you can have dinner here as well.

EXPERIENCE AT KOELE CLUBHOUSE, *Tel. 565-4605. Entrees average $14. Credit cards accepted.*

This restaurant serves lunch only, in a pleasant setting.

BLUE GINGER CAFE, *7th Avenue, Lanai City. Tel. 564-6363. Inexpensive.*

Try this local alternative when you're ready for a break from hotel dining.

TANIGAWA'S, *7th Avenue, Lanai City. Tel. 565-6537. Inexpensive.*

Next door to Blue Ginger Cafe, this 1950s-style soda fountain, complete with swivel stools, is in a general store. It serves breakfast, lunch, and dinner; locals come for the burgers and grilled cheese sandwiches.

SEEING THE SIGHTS

Kaupe Cultural & Historical Musuem, *Lanai City*. Called the Pineapple Museum by locals, the old Dole building now contains a history of Lanai, from its earliest days through the ranching and pineapple industry. Exhibits incorporate the cultural influences of island residents. Browse among the artifacts from decades of pineapple farming.

Northern Petroglyphs, *near Kaiolohia Bay (more commonly known as Shipwreck Beach)*. These ancient stick figures have been carved into a pile of large rocks near the beach. Be very careful when you're climbing the rocks. It's best to wear rubber-soled shoes. When you reach the shore and come to a rock painted "Do Not Deface," head mauka (inland) toward the field of brown boulders. You'll come to the petroglyphs before you reach the boulder field.

LANAI'S BEST ATTRACTIONS

Hulopoe Beach
Garden of the Gods
The Island's Hotels

Garden of the Gods, *Kanepu'u, Northern Lanai*. The wind can be amazingly strong by this jumble of golden brown boulders with the ocean gleaming in the distance. As the light changes, so do the various hues of the strangely shaped rocks, which cast even stranger shadows. The most dramatic time of day to come is the early morning or late afternoon. On your way to the Garden of the Gods, you'll ride through the pumpkin colored, desert-like landscape. The red canyons that open to the Pacific are gorgeous.

Luahiwa Petroglyphs, *just south of Lanai City*. These early 19th century rock carvings aren't easy to find, so enlist the aid of a resident. Dramatically terraced on a hillside, these boulders are etched with some of the best preserved of the state's petroglyphs.

The **Munro Trail and Lanaihale**, *near Lanai City*. Hike or take a four-wheel-drive vehicle up the 8.8 mile Munro Trail. Most of the Cook pines that grow here and all over Lanai were planted by George Munro, whose family was from New Zealand, around 1910. These trees help prevent soil erosion. During the course of Munro's work as manager of a ranch, he planted seedlings as he traveled by horse or mule along the Munro Trail and on Lanaihale summit. From this 3,370-foot peak, you'll have fabulous views of 2,000-foot-deep Haola Gulch and, on a clear day, all the Hawaiian islands except Kauai and Niihau.

Keomuku Village, *east coast*. Now covered with scraggly vegetation, these ruins of homes and other buildings were once part of a booming sugar mill town. But in 1901, when the Maunalei Sugar Company died, so did these streets. The partially restored church is Lanai's oldest.

Kanauolu Bay, *west of Hulopoe Beach, south shore*. During the early 1800s, Kamehameha the Great spent his summers fishing at the village that once stood here. Today all that remain are its weathered stone foundations. A marked trail leads past each stone structure and cave. Signs and maps explain what visitors are seeing and provide historical information. Adjacent to this archaeological site, you'll find Kahekili's Leap, where warriors proved themselves by jumping more than 60 feet into the rough waters below. You'll need a four-wheel-drive vehicle to visit.

Arts Program

At the **Lanai Art Studio**, visitors are invited to take free art classes to learn things such as silk scarf making and pareo tying. Once a month, the **Lanai Visiting Artists Program** brings performing, culinary, and literary artists to the Lodge at Koele or Manele Bay hotels. You might be treated to jazz or European classical music, or Japanese dance. All events are free and open to the public.

NIGHTLIFE & ENTERTAINMENT

With some visitors sprinkled in, a local crowd is always drinking and talking story on the enclosed front porch of the Hotel Lanai. For more upscale entertainment after dark, try the Lodge at Koele and the Manele Bay Hotel. See what's on the screen or stage at the **Lanai Theatre/Playhouse**, *Lanai City, Tel. 565-7500. What else? Let's see . . . how about taking a drive to see the lights of Maui?*

SPORTS & RECREATION

Beaches

Although there aren't many beaches on Lanai, those that exist are extremely picturesque. The swimming is best at Hulopoe, overlooked by the Manele Bay Hotel. This is the only beach that you can get to on a paved road. You'll need to rent a four-wheel-drive vehicle to visit the others.

Hulopoe, south shore

Since the opening of the Manele Bay Hotel, on a bluff overlooking the sand, schools of Hawaiian spinner **dolphins** don't come as close to shore as they once did, but they still visit. The first time I came, when there was only a single 11-room hotel on the island, there was one other person here. This was a weekday, and when I returned on a weekend, the beach was "packed" - with two local families having a barbecue and playing ukuleles. However, despite the added tourism, this is still a wonderful beach and the island's most attractive. Walk or drive up a rocky road (to the left if you're facing the water), and you may see people fishing off the coffee-colored lava cliffs.

Around the point, the striking **monolith**, Pu'upehe, just offshore, is also known as Sweetheart Rock. In front of this huge chocolate chunk, you'll see a cozy cove with even whiter sand than Hulopoe.

Kaiolohia Bay, north shore

With its rust-colored sand and dramatic churning waves, this beach - more commonly called Shipwreck Beach - is best for very strong swimmers. When the water is at its calmest, snorkeling can be fun here.

You might see some people fishing for lobster. The shore faces Molokai and Maui, whose cloud-ringed heights make for some awesome scenery. Out in the water, you'll see a large rusted ship that was salvaged, later towed, and then became mired here. This coast is very windy, resulting in some interestingly shaped boulders along the coast. You'll reach this beach after twisting and turning down a long paved road with wonderful views of pine trees against a background of the Pacific and Molokai and Maui. Then you'll turn left onto a tree-shaded dirt road, with branches forming a roof overhead. A few private houses line the road.

Polihua, *north shore*

If, and only if, two beaches aren't enough for you, take a groomed dirt road that leads you to this usually empty white sand beach. It's often windy here and the water can be rough, but it's a peaceful setting. Molokai is the island across the water. Rental jeeps are allowed here.

Camping

Lanai offers six campsites to choose from. Contact the **Koele Company,** *P.O. Box L, Lanai City, HI 96763, Tel. 808/565-6661.*

Croquet

You can play both British and American style on the smooth lawn at the Lodge at Koele.

Fishing

Follow in King Kamehameha's royal footsteps and try angling from his favorite spot on Lanai: Kaunolu, on the south coast. After the barges leave, the less adventurous can try Kaumalapau Harbor, on the west coast. The fishing from Manele Bay, Hulopoe Bay, and Shipwreck Beach is okay for the casual sports person. Local fishing excursions can be set up through the Lodge at Koele and the Manele Bay Hotel.

Golf

Although people have described the nine-hole Cavendish Golf Course, adjacent to the Lodge at Koele, as "very average," there's also the Experience at Koele, an 18-hole Greg Norman/Ted Robinson course near the Lodge, and an 18-hole oceanfront Jack Nicklaus beauty at the Manele Bay Hotel on the south shore.

Helicopter Rides

Contact the Manele Bay Hotel or the Lodge at Koele to arrange helicopter tours.

Hiking

Hikers should try the Norfolk and Cook Island pine-lined 8.8 mile Munro Trail, which winds up to Lanaihale. From this spot, you'll have a sweeping view of the island, including a dramatic canyon, as well as much of the rest of the state. This difficult hike can take a full day. Some people also enjoy hiking part of the eight miles that connect Shipwreck and Polihua beaches on the windy north shore.

Horseback Riding & Carriage Rides

Make arrangements through the Lodge at Koele.

Nature Tour

Contact the Manele Bay Hotel or the Lodge at Koele to arrange a worthwhile **nature tour** of the island from a historical/cultural perspective.

Sailing

The Manele Bay Hotel and the Lodge at Koele offer sightseeing, whale watching, and snorkeling cruises.

If you're planning to be on Maui and would like to come to Lanai just for the day, consider one of the **Trilogy Excursions Cruises**, *Tel. 661-7221*, or sail from Lahaina to **Club Lanai**, *Kahului, Maui, Tel. 871-1144*, a beach playground on one of Lanai's remote coasts. Snorkeling, glass bottom boat trips, and wave skiing are available. During the winter, vacationers often spot whales. A continental breakfast is served on board the boat and passengers are treated to a picnic lunch after they arrive. The cruise itself takes just over a half hour each way. Full day and half day trips can be arranged.

Scuba Diving

Skindiver magazine has called Lanai one of the top 10 dive locations in the world. **Trilogy Excursions**, *Tel. 661-7221*, takes people down under. You can also arrange to dive through your hotel.

Snorkeling

This sport is convenient right at Hulopoe Beach, where the Manele Bay Hotel is located. Along with all the colorful fish, coral, and lava formations, perhaps you'll even spot one of the dolphins that sometimes swim close to shore. Snorkeling is even better at Kaunolu Bay, where visibility can be as much as 100 feet.

Tennis

Check out the courts at the Lodge at Koele and the Manele Bay Hotel.

Working Out & Spas

For relaxing massages, facials, and other pampering, or to sweat your way to a better body, visit the fitness center at the Lodge at Koele or the Manele Bay Hotel.

SHOPPING

In addition to hotel shops, there's **Marie M.'s Boutique** in Lanai City. This store stocks the island's most up-to-date fashions for men, women, and children. In town on Saturdays, the **flea market** sells local arts and crafts as well as Filipino and Japanese food.

Richard's Shopping Center, right across the street, carries everything from groceries and liquor to island T-shirts. **Maunalei Gifts** is also worth some time. Other good bets are the Pine Isle Market, and Akamai and International shopping centers.

PRACTICAL INFORMATION

Emergencies

Call *Tel. 911.*

Medical Attention

Lanai Community Hospital, *Lanai City, Tel. 565-6411.*

Post Office

The island's Lanai City branch can be reached at *Tel. 565-6517.*

Tourist Information

Destination Lanai, *P.O. Box 700, Lanai City, HI 96763, Tel. 808/565-7600 or Fax 808/565-9316*

Hawaii Visitors & Convention Bureau, *2270 Kalakaua Avenue, Honolulu, HI 96815, Tel. 923-1811*

Maui Visitors Bureau, *1727 Wili Pa Loop, Wailuku, HI 96793, Tel. 244-3530*

Weather

To plan ahead for touring various parts of the island, call *Tel. 565-6033.*

INDEX

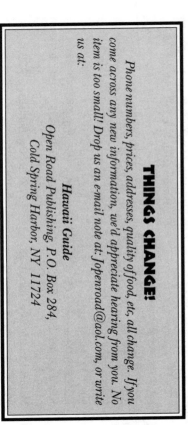

THINGS CHANGE!

Phone numbers, prices, addresses, quality of food, etc, all change. If you come across any new information, we'd appreciate hearing from you. No item is too small! Drop us an e-mail note at: Jopenroad@aol.com, or write us at:

Hawaii Guide
Open Road Publishing, P.O. Box 284,
Cold Spring Harbor, NY 11724

TRAVEL NOTES

TRAVEL NOTES

TRAVEL NOTES

TRAVEL NOTES

TRAVEL NOTES